ANSELM: Aosta, Bec and Canterbury

ANSELM

Aosta

Anselm Aosta, Bec and Canterbury

Canterbury

Papers in Commemoration of
the Nine Hundredth
Anniversary of Anselm's
Enthronement as Archbishop
25 September 1093

Edited by

D. E. Luscombe & G. R. Evans

Sheffield
Academic Press

ANSELM
Aosta, Bec and Canterbury

Papers in Commemoration of
the Nine-Hundredth
Anniversary of Anselm's
Enthronement as Archbishop,
25 September 1093

Edited by
D.E. Luscombe & G.R. Evans

Sheffield
Academic Press

Copyright © 1996 Sheffield Academic Press

Published by
Sheffield Academic Press Ltd
Mansion House
19 Kingfield Road
Sheffield S11 9AS
England

Typeset by Sheffield Academic Press
and
Printed on acid-free paper in Great Britain
by Bookcraft Ltd
Midsomer Norton, Bath

British Library Cataloguing in Publication Data

A catalogue record for this book is available
from the British Library

ISBN 1-85075-591-4

CONTENTS

Preface   9
Abbreviations   11
List of Contributors   13

RICHARD SOUTHERN
St Anselm at Canterbury:
His Mission of Reconciliation   17

Part I
ANSELM AND HIS ANTECEDENTS

KLAUS KIENZLER
Proslogion 1: Form und Gestalt   38

FREDERICK VAN FLETEREN
Augustine's Influence on Anselm's *Proslogion*   56

PAUL GILBERT, SJ
Veritas orationis selon le *De veritate*   70

Part II
ANSELM AND HIS CONTEMPORARIES

INOS BIFFI
Ragioni e non-Ragioni di un Esilio   84

MARK PHILPOTT
'In primis...omnis humanae prudentiae inscius et expers putaretur':
St Anselm's Knowledge of Canon Law   94

C.J. MEWS
St Anselm, Roscelin and the See of Beauvais   106

IWAKUMA YUKIO
The Realism of Anselm and his Contemporaries 120

M.B. PRANGER
The Mirror of Dialectics:
Naked Images in Anselm of Canterbury and Bernard of Clairvaux 136

WALTER FRÖHLICH
Saint Anselm's *Imago episcopi* 148

COSTANTE MARABELLI
Ecclesia Mater—Ecclesia Mater Cantuariensis:
Concezione della maternità ecclesiale di Canterbury 162

Part III
PHILOSOPHY AND THEOLOGY

COLOMAN ETIENNE VIOLA
Authority and Reason in St Anselm's Life and Thought 172

ALAIN GALONNIER
Sur quelques aspects annonciateurs de la littérature sophismatique
dans le *De grammatico* 209

A.J. VANDERJAGT
The Performative Heart of Anselm's *Proslogion* 229

T. LOSONCY
The *Proslogion* Argument and the Anselmian *Cogito* 238

JEANNINE QUILLET
Volonté et liberté dans le *De libertate arbitrii*
de S. Anselme de Cantorbéry 247

RICHARD CAMPBELL
The Conceptual Roots of Anselm's Soteriology 256

ADOLF SCHURR
Philosophische Überlegungen zu Anselm von Canterbury:
Cur deus homo 264

Part IV
ANSELM'S INFLUENCE

J.F. COTTIER
Le recueil apocryphe des *Orationes sive meditationes*
de Saint Anselme: sa formation et sa réception en Angleterre
et en France au XIIe siècle   282

JAY RUBINSTEIN
St Anselm's Influence on Guibert of Nogent   296

MICHAEL STAUNTON
Trial and Inspiration in the *Lives* of Anselm and Thomas Becket   310

YOKO HIRATA
St Anselm and Two Clerks of Thomas Becket   323

MICHAEL ROBSON
The Impact of the *Cur deus homo* on the Early Franciscan School   334

ROBERT B. STRIMPLE
St Anselm's *Cur deus homo* and John Calvin's Doctrine
of the Atonement   348

J. VUILLEMIN
Justice anselmienne et bonne volonté kantienne:
essai de comparaison   361

HELMUT KOHLENBERGER
Anselm spricht zu (post)modernen Denkern   376

Index of Authors   392

PREFACE

With a very few exceptions the papers that we have the pleasure to present here were all read by their authors at a conference held in Eliot College in the University of Kent at Canterbury on 22-24 September 1993. This gathering of scholars from many parts of the world was a memorable contribution to the celebration and commemoration of the ninth centenary of the enthronement of Anselm as archbishop in the cathedral of Canterbury on 25 September 1093. The conference vividly demonstrated the continuing appeal of Anselm as a religious figure and as a thinker.

That the conference took place is due to the work of many friends and colleagues. The academic planning was undertaken by Sister Benedicta Ward, SLG, Dr Peter Cramer and Dr Lesley Smith who were encouraged at every stage by Dr Helmut Kohlenberger and Sir Richard Southern. The University of Kent throughout provided invaluable help and hospitality, and our thanks go especially to Professor Alf Smyth and Jenny Schunmann and Dr Bruce Webster for their tireless work and unfailing support in countless ways, to Mrs Margaret Sparks, and to Paul Bennet, Director of the Cathedral Excavations and of the Canterbury Archaeological Trust, for—very much appreciated—guided visits and talks in the cathedral and at Patrixborne, Barfeston and Sandwich. We offer grateful thanks too to the British Academy, the Royal Historical Society, the Dean of the Faculty of Arts at Canterbury and the Department of History of the University of Sheffield for financial assistance. In addition we warmly thank Mrs Pat Holland of the same department for patient assistance from the moment that the conference was conceived to the publication of this volume. We are particularly grateful to the Dean and Chapter of Canterbury Cathedral for allowing us to reproduce the lecture that Sir Richard Southern gave in the cathedral on Sunday 25 September 1993. Finally, our thanks are due to Sheffield Academic Press for their efficient and helpful production of the book.

There is now a considerable record of scholarly publication of the proceedings of conferences in the past thirty-five years or so devoted to the life and works of Anselm. For this the International Anselm Committee, under the chairmanship of Professor Raymond Klibansky, has in no small measure been responsible, although each gathering has, of course, also owed much to the work of local committees. Since a list of the volumes published so far deserves to be available for convenient consultation, we give it here together with the names of the places at which the meetings occurred and their dates.

Spicilegium Beccense I. Congrès International du IXème centenaire de l'arrivée d'Anselme au Bec (Paris, 1959). Bec, 1959.

Die Wirkungsgeschichte Anselms von Canterbury, in *Analecta Anselmiana* 4.1-2 (1975). Bad Wimpfen, 1970.

Saint Anselme: ses précurseurs et ses contemporains, in *Analecta Anselmiana* 5 (1976). Aosta, 1973.

Anselm at Canterbury, in *Anselm Studies* 1 (1983). Canterbury, 1979.

Les Mutations socio-culturelles au tournant des XIe–XIIe siècles, in *Spicilegium Beccense*, II (Paris, 1984). Bec, 1982.

Episcopi ad saecula—St Anselm and St Augustine, in *Anselm Studies* 2 (1988). Villanova, Pennsylvania, 1985.

Anselmo d'Aosta, figura europea. Atti del Convegno di studi, Aosta 1° e 2 marzo 1988, ed. Inos Bibbi and Costante Marabelli (Biblioteca di Cultura Medievale; Milano, 1989). Aosta, 1988.

Anselmo d'Aosta: logica e dottrina, in *Rivista di storia della filosofia*, ns 48.3 (1993). Milan, 1989.

The European Dimension of St Anselm's Thinking (ed. J. Zumr and V. Herold; Prague, 1993). Prague, 1992.

A further volume entitled *Saint Anselme, penseur d'hier et d'aujourd'hui: La pensée de saint Anselme vue par nos contemporains*, to appear in the *Anselm Studies* series, is in press. Colloque international du CNRS, Paris, 1990.

Gillian Evans
David Luscombe
July 1996

ABBREVIATIONS

ABMA	Auctores Britannici Medii Aevi
CCCM	Corpus Christianorum. Continuatio Mediaevalis
CCSL	Corpus Christianorum. Series Latina
CSEL	Corpus Scriptorum Ecclesiasticorum Latinorum
FS	*Franciscan Studies*
JL	P. Jaffe, S. Lowenfield *et al.* (eds.), *Regesta Pontificum Romanorum... ad annum 1198*
MARS	R.W. Hunt and R. Klibansky (eds.), *Mediaeval and Renaissance Studies*
MGH SS	Monumenta Germaniae Historica. Scriptores in Folio
PL	J. Migne (ed.), *Patrologia latina*
RTAM	*Recherches de théologie ancienne et médiévale*
Schmitt, I–VI	F.S. Schmitt (ed.), *S. Anselmi Opera Omnia*

LIST OF CONTRIBUTORS

I. BIFFI
Milano, Italy

R. CAMPBELL
Department of Philosophy, The Australian National University,
Canberra, Australia

J.F. COTTIER
Université du Maine (Le Mans), France

W. FRÖHLICH
Oberstudiendirektor, Gymnasium Puchheim, Germany

A. GALONNIER
Centre d'histoire des sciences et des philosophies arabes et médiévales,
CNRS, Paris, France

P. GILBERT, S.J.
Pontificia Università Gregoriana, Rome, Italy

YOKO HIRATA
University of Takachiho, Tokyo, Japan

K. KIENZLER
Universität Augsburg, Augsburg, Germany

HELMUT KOHLENBERGER
University of Salzburg, Salzburg, Austria

T. LOSONCY
Department of Philosophy, Villanova University, Villanova, PA, USA

C. MARABELLI
Facoltà Teologica dell'Italia Settentrionale and Facoltà di Teologia di Lugano, Italy

C. MEWS
Department of History, Monash University, Clayton, Victoria, Australia

MARK PHILPOTT
St John's College, Oxford

M.B. PRANGER
Faculteit der Godgeleerdheid, Delenus Instituut, Universiteit van Amsterdam, Amsterdam, The Netherlands

J. QUILLET
Département de Philosophie, l'Université de Paris-XII, Paris, France

MICHAEL ROBSON, O.F.M. Conv.
St Edmund's College, Cambridge

JAY RUBINSTEIN
University of California, Berkeley, CA, USA

A. SCHURR
Universität Regensburg, Regensburg, Germany

SIR RICHARD SOUTHERN
St John's College, Oxford

MICHAEL STAUNTON
Faculty of History, University of Cambridge

R.B. STRIMPLE
Westminster Theological Seminary in California, Escondido, CA, USA

F. VAN FLETEREN
Augustinian Historical Institute, Villanova University, Villanova, PA, USA

A.J. VANDERJAGT
Faculteit der Wijsbegeerte, Rijksuniversiteit Groningen, Groningen, The Netherlands

C. VIOLA
CNRS, Paris, France

J. VUILLEMIN
Collège de France, Paris, France

I. YUKIO
Fukui Prefectural University, Fukui, Japan

ST ANSELM AT CANTERBURY:
HIS MISSION OF RECONCILIATION

Richard Southern*

When I sat down to write this lecture in commemoration of Anselm's arrival in Canterbury and his enthronement as archbishop on this day nine hundred years ago, I intended to deal with the subject in a thoroughly orderly fashion, describing first the general scene of European development during his lifetime and his attitude towards this development, and then the local scene which he had encountered first at Bec and then here in Canterbury. But one of the extraordinary things about Anselm is that he never allows you to deal with him in the way you want. In the gentlest possible way he turns your attention to details that seem relatively trivial, but turn out to be important—provided that you are willing to look at them through his eyes. And when you do this you discover why they were important, even though their importance has little to do with the common valuation of events. In this way he escapes every kind of classification, particularly any classification of 'general' or 'local', 'Hildebrandine' or 'anti-Hildebrandine', even (I would venture to say) Protestant or Catholic. Really it comes to this in the end: he is always and only concerned with the nature and activity of God and the response of human beings to this activity. This and this alone is the subject that he is concerned with, and in dealing with him you must follow him, for he is always intensely individual and personal, and yet equally intensely universal. And if you follow him, you will gradually see everything in a similar way, however crude our own formulations may be. So you must forgive me if my theme gets a bit muddled. Please put the blame on Anselm: I'm sure he will accept it charmingly.

*   This lecture was given by Sir Richard Southern in Canterbury Cathedral on 25 September 1993 to mark the 900th anniversary of the enthronement of St Anselm.

1. *Anselm in Canterbury*

So I find myself starting with Canterbury. And, for today's celebration, this is clearly right. But even here, at the very beginning, there is a problem.

The reason we are here is that we think of his coming here as a moment of great importance in the history of this cathedral and arch-bishopric, and even perhaps in our own lives; and his contemporaries would have agreed, whether or not they approved his coming. Yet if we ask how it was important, or what he did that made it important, we (like his contemporaries) really find it very difficult to say. Nothing that he aimed at doing on a grand scale, strictly in his role as archbishop, survived long. His claims for Canterbury—which he inherited from his predecessor Lanfranc, but to which he gave a much sharper edge and certainly a more deeply felt expression—came to nothing. He believed that the archbishop of Canterbury should have primacy over the whole of the British Isles. Further, he believed that he was ex officio the only legitimate papal legate capable of operating in this vast area. But these claims scarcely survived his lifetime. Moreover, nothing of his ambitious legislative programme had much effect, and his long negotiations with successive popes and kings might just as well never have taken place for all the practical effect they had. Only the wonderful choir of this cathedral, the outline of which still shows the influence of his visits to Cluny during his long absences from his archiepiscopal duties, is present with us today, but it too has developed in ways that were quite unforeseen when it was planned.

But surely he did not come to Canterbury with the idea of building a more magnificent choir than Lanfranc had thought necessary. So what was it that brought him here?

We cannot answer this question without first recognizing that, on a strict view of ecclesiastical law, he ought not to have come at all. He had been nominated as archbishop by the king (generally reckoned as one of the two worst kings England has ever had, though Anselm seems to have rather liked and respected him) in an outrageously uncanonical fashion which had been explicitly forbidden by Pope Gregory VII fifteen years earlier. According to this ruling, it was illegal for an archbishop to be nominated by a lay ruler, and worse still for him to receive from the king's hands the pastoral staff which was the symbol of his spiritual office. But Anselm had received both his office and his staff from the king, and he had then gone on to do homage—also forbidden by papal decree—to the king in the old style. And, not only that, he had received his pastoral staff and performed his homage in the presence and with the assent of bishops who were still, four years after Urban II's election, undecided between Urban and his imperially nominated rival Clement III.

These were really grave breaches of recent canon law, and it did not make things any better that Anselm took no active steps to hasten the recognition of Urban II or to get from the pope his pallium, without which—strictly speaking—he could not carry out his archiepiscopal functions. And when the papal legate eventually brought his pallium, Anselm told him he was too busy guarding the coast in the absence of the king (who was campaigning in Scotland) to come to meet him. Then, when the legate urged that he and the archbishops should jointly hold a Council, Anselm said it would be useless without the king's approval. All these little incidents convey an important truth: Anselm was very submissive in some ways, but extraordinarily independent when it came to dealing with the world, whether secular or ecclesiastical, and his way fitted into no common mould.

But then you may ask (as plenty of people at the time asked) if, by all the rules, his coming to Canterbury on this day as archbishop was quite out of order, why did he come? He claimed—but many then did not believe him, and some still do not—that he had no desire at all to become archbishop, and he wept for the happiness he had lost in leaving Bec. But he came nevertheless. According to this account—and (in my view) he was incapable of even the slightest deviation from what he believed to be the truth—he came because, if he had not come, the long vacancy at Canterbury, which had already lasted four years, would have gone on indefinitely, to the detriment of the spiritual life of the community at Canterbury and of the people of England generally. Like everything that Anselm said or wrote, his explanation is simple—too simple to be true, some people think—but the fact that the vacancy might have continued indefinitely is obviously true. The king was in very great need of money and the revenues of the vacant see of Canterbury had for four years been making a splendid contribution to his income, and would have gone on doing so while the vacancy lasted. It was only a temporary expectation of imminent death that had induced the king to nominate an archbishop. But the king had recovered, and if Anselm had refused, the vacancy could have lasted till the king's death. So—quite apart from any conviction that Anselm's words and actions are drawn from a deep well of holiness which excludes deceit—it is quite clear that a prolonged vacancy would have been the consequence of Anselm's refusal.

What hurt him most about the criticism that he should not have accepted the archbishopric was that the chief people who said this, and felt betrayed by his move, were the monks of Bec who thought he had meant—even perhaps had promised—never to leave them. It took several years for him to overcome their resentment. By contrast, the chief people who were delighted by his coming were the monks of Canterbury, who were divided on almost everything else.

It is tempting indeed to linger over this aspect of today's celebration, for though it may seem trivial, it goes right to the centre of Anselm's whole life: people wanted his presence because their religious lives and their communal lives were richer and deeper and more peaceful when he was there. Even those with different traditions of worship—and the cathedral community was sharply divided on this very point—felt the quality of their religious lives immensely enhanced by his presence. This was especially true at Canterbury, where the situation requires a little explanation.

The cathedral community which turned out to welcome Anselm on his arrival nine hundred years ago today was a deeply divided body— not for the first, nor (I imagine) last, time in its history. But the division then went very deep indeed. In 1093, nearly thirty years after the Norman Conquest, there was still a great chasm between the older English monks who had belonged to the cathedral before the arrival of Anselm's predecessor Archbishop Lanfranc twenty-three years earlier, and the more recent recruits, chiefly from either Bec or Caen, whom Lanfranc had imported and to whom he had given all the chief offices in the community. Lanfranc's reason for this brutal treatment of the English monks was simple. He wanted to have a nucleus of sympathetic helpers capable of carrying out the sweeping changes in monastic life, in daily services, in the ecclesiastical calendar, and in religious studies, which he had started introducing immediately after his arrival as archbishop in 1070. It may seem that, after this lapse of time, it was a bit too late in 1093 to do anything about it, but this is to underestimate the tenacity of those who have the duty of serving the church of Canterbury. Although in some ways the divisions had become less acute, in others—and especially during the long vacancy in the archbishopric before Anselm's arrival—they had got worse. So the community was still bitterly divided when he arrived, and Anselm was quite simply the only person who could heal the division, and he knew it.

How he knew this is a long story, and it may seem that we have more important matters awaiting our attention. But since a cathedral community, whether monastic or not, is concerned primarily with worship, and since divisions about the best way of fulfilling this duty threaten the whole foundation of life in a cathedral, we cannot proceed without understanding how Anselm viewed this issue.

To do this, we must go back to the time fifteen or sixteen years before 1093 when the hostility between the two groups in the community at Canterbury was at its most intense. How these two groups had come into existence can be very easily explained. Lanfranc, in the efficient way that was habitual with him, had started at once to bring the daily round of the religious life of the Canterbury community into line with the habits, disciplines and studies of the greater part of western Europe. The changes needed to bring this about involved almost every detail of daily life and worship, and Lanfranc had set to work on his task with great energy, rebuilding the cathedral and monastic buildings, restocking the library and throwing out a good deal of unintelligible stuff in Old English, writing and bringing into use a new monastic Rule of his own devising. Curiously enough, in his up-to-date way, he had chosen Cluny rather than Bec as his model, and he had reorganized the calendar and liturgy, and cleared out the bodies of long venerated pre-Conquest archbishops and others who were in his view quite ignorantly regarded as saints by the old monks.

In order to do all this, he had introduced into the community about half a dozen monks from Bec or Caen to whom he gave all the main offices in the church, and he had sent the ringleader of the dissident Anglo-Saxon monks to Bec to be disciplined by Anselm. But then a strange thing happened—at least it would have been strange if it had been anyone but Anselm. From this dissident, whom he was expected to discipline, Anselm heard about the Anglo-Saxon saints, and about the Rule of St Dunstan which had regulated the lives of the Canterbury monks before Lanfranc's arrival. Above all he got to know the dissident himself (his name was Osbern) and he wrote glowing accounts of him to Lanfranc: their souls (he wrote) had become so intertwined that he would find it hard to part from him.

We do not know what Lanfranc thought of this eulogy, but he seems to have been willing to take quite a lot from his old pupil Anselm, whom he had long ago saved from a very feckless existence and introduced to the monastic life. So, at the end of Osbern's penal exile at Bec, Anselm sent him back with strong letters of commendation, both to Lanfranc and to the former monks of Bec whom Lanfranc had installed at Canterbury. Rather vexingly, Anselm also asked to be sent a copy of the old monastic Rule of St Dunstan which Lanfranc had scrapped.

And this was not the end of the matter. A few years later, in 1079, when Anselm had just become abbot of Bec, he had to visit his monastery's English estates. Having arrived at Dover, he came straight to Canterbury to see his old friends. Here he followed his usual habit of having long discussions with groups of monks, and he especially singled out the English members of the community to talk to. Naturally they wanted chiefly to talk about the old saints whose bodies Lanfranc had thrown out of the cathedral. Among these, the one whose ejection they most resented was one of Lanfranc's predecessors, Archbishop Ælfeah. Lanfranc's reason for throwing him out was that almost nothing was known about him except that he had been killed by the Danes in 1012 for refusing to pay Danegeld. Lanfranc had judged this to be an insufficient ground for treating him as a martyr, and the English monks anxiously consulted Anselm on this point. Anselm spoke thus: a martyr (he said) is one who has died for the truth. But it appears that Ælfeah died for justice. Yet, if you think about it, where is the difference? Justice and truth are simply different aspects of the same thing: what we call 'truth' is justice in thought; and what we call 'justice' is truth in action. So, in dying for justice, Ælfeah died for 'truth in action', and in so doing he exhibited that quality which we require in a martyr.

I don't honestly know whether a canon lawyer would accept this interpretation, but the English monks of course were easily persuaded. More surprisingly, so was Lanfranc. It turns out that he had himself defined truth and justice in a similar way in commenting on St Paul's epistles some years earlier, so perhaps Anselm knew that he would be easily persuaded. At all events he at once ordered Archbishop Ælfeah's body to be brought back into the cathedral, re-instituted the liturgical observance of his feast day, and set the rebellious monk Osbern to work writing a life of the saint for use in the liturgy on his day.

This triumph of their point of view of course helped to soften the breach between the two parties among the monks, but it did not heal it, and the two parties in the Canterbury community continued to look on each other with varying degrees of contempt, resentment and hostility.

Especially during the long vacancy after Lanfranc's death in 1089, the English monks took the opportunity of searching among the debris of the old buildings for further evidences of lost relics of the old English saints, which of course they were not slow in finding, for the rubble of great cathedrals—as those who have recently been investigating the foundations of the nave have once more discovered—is filled with hidden treasures from the past.

One could say very much about the light that this little incident throws on the remarkable way in which Anselm's words, thoughts and mere presence broke down barriers and caused hostilities to wither away. For our present purpose, it may seem that enough has been said to show why Anselm's becoming archbishop helped to bring unity to a still divided community. But it did not end there. When Anselm was still hesitating whether to accept the archbishopric, still writing to the monks of Bec and to the duke of Normandy about the question of his accepting the archbishopric, Osbern, the old warrior for ancient usages, twice wrote to Anselm in despair at his delay. And, besides, the 'foreigners' in the community whom Lanfranc had brought from Bec, and who were Anselm's closest and oldest friends in the monastic life, also wanted him to come. So it would be an understatement to say that he stood *between* the two parties: rather he personified both. On any practical assessment of the position, therefore, apart from legal forms about which Anselm seems to have been either ignorant or indifferent, he had little choice in the matter.

Everything in the actual situation spoke in favour of his coming, and from the moment of his arrival at Canterbury we may date the beginning of a new age of peace and corporate activity embracing both the old English traditions and Lanfranc's Continental innovations in religious and intellectual life. And this beneficent influence spread from the Canterbury community to other communities in the great cathedrals and monastic churches of England.

The history of this process of religious and intellectual—as contrasted with political and social—integration still remains to be written, but as witness to its results I may simply mention the recent and splendid publication of one of the great monuments of this amalgamation of traditions. It consists of a magnificent Psalter of about 1140, written or directed by an English monk of Canterbury, in which the two traditions of Anglo-Saxon piety and what we may broadly call Lanfrancian learning are amalgamated in a single volume. Here we have visual evidence of the wealth of pre-Conquest literary, liturgical and artistic tradition which had survived at Canterbury largely as a result of the beneficent effect of Anselm's association with the community. How far Anselm's influence also stimulated a similar integration in the other great old English monasteries and cathedrals of Worcester, Durham, Evesham and Rochester, of course, we cannot precisely say. But some at least of this urge towards comprehension seems to have stemmed from Canterbury. On this ground alone, therefore, even if there were no others, Anselm's arrival at Canterbury on this day nine hundred years ago would deserve commemoration.

But there are other reasons too for celebrating his arrival. To understand them, we must look beyond the local scene to Christendom as a whole.

2. *The General European Scene*

There have, of course, been many attempts to place Anselm in his wide historical setting, and the conclusions reached in these attempts have been summarized in various ways. One of the most widely circulated of these summaries is to call him, 'the last of the Fathers, and the first of the Scholastics', and it is easy to see why this has had a wide appeal. It encapsulates one important fact about his lifetime from 1033 to 1109: these years span one of the most important changes in the intellectual history of western Europe and in the history of the western church. Broadly speaking, they marked a change from a period when the most articulate Christian witnesses were Benedictine monks dedicated to a very elaborate liturgical life in an impoverished and much threatened countryside, to a period of rapidly growing wealth and population in which the ideal of systematic knowledge applied to the organization of every aspect of life and thought was rigorously pursued. The earlier of these two periods can broadly be looked on as a time when the newly converted peoples of western Europe expressed their understanding of their new religion by founding great religious communities committed to an increasingly elaborate daily programme of worship. By contrast, the later period was one in which systematic thought was applied to the whole range of problems of Christian theology and organization with the aim of achieving a final and world-wide stability under the general direction of papal authority.

The monastic communities of the earlier period—among which this cathedral had an important but scarcely distinguished place—had been founded and richly endowed by semi-sacerdotal kings and emperors with vast potential resources of underpopulated and underdeveloped land. In a scene of great confusion and intermittent destruction these communities formed small kingdoms of supernatural order. The enemies of earthly prosperity were very conspicuous: Muslim invaders along the whole extent of the Mediterranean; Vikings threatening all the exposed coasts of western Europe; Slavonic invaders in the intermediate area from the Balkans to the Baltic Sea. As for Rome, the capital of the ancient world, it was for most people a distant place of pilgrimage, whence the successors of St Peter made infrequent interventions in the affairs of an impoverished and heavily burdened population.

This was the world into which Anselm had been born in 1033, and in which he grew up as a young man. But by the time of his arrival at Canterbury, the European situation had changed dramatically. Most of the extra-European invading peoples had reached the limits of their expansive energy and were everywhere being driven back; and a new distinctively and exclusively *western* Christendom was coming into existence, rapidly growing in wealth and population, expanding into the Viking north and into the Slavonic northeast, demolishing the Byzantine east, re-absorbing Muslim Spain and the whole area of Islam along the Mediterranean coast. The main directing forces of government and intellectual expansion, which were emerging in this new western Latin Christendom, were the papacy and the great schools—especially those of Paris and Bologna. Under the influence of these two great forces, and on the crest of an unparalleled growth in population and wealth, an intellectual and organizational transformation was taking place.

To speak only of the intellectual side of this transformation, an extremely ambitious programme of theological expansion was emerging in the last years of Anselm's life. In principle it was nothing less than the reconquest, to the utmost possible extent, of that knowledge of God, the divine purpose of the world, and the wonderful complexity of the natural world, which humankind had lost as a result of the fall. The expectation was that, on the foundations that had been rediscovered by ancient sages and scholars, a body of knowledge could be put together which would make systematic knowledge of the nature of God and the created universe available for human needs, and create an ordered community on earth with the means of preparing all individuals for eternal life.

Naturally this whole programme took a long time to develop into the great compendia of knowledge which emerged from the schools of the late thirteenth century. But—even by the time of Anselm's death in 1109—the masters of the schools of Paris, Laon, Reims, Orleans and Tours in the first place, with others emerging behind them, were beginning to feel their way towards this great culmination of human knowledge and organized life under the central directing influence of the papacy. It took a century and a half at least for this new movement of thought and organized life to reach its climax in the works of St Thomas Aquinas and his immediate successors, but the beginnings were there by the first decade of the twelfth century. By the time of Anselm's death in 1109, the ambition of gathering up the whole intellectual deposit of the ancient past, and moulding its various parts into a coherent body of ascertained truth and rules of behaviour, was already beginning to be seen as a practical possibility.

Now if we place Anselm's life in this context, we see at once that he stands at the junction of these two ages. He was born and spent his youth in the last years of the old biblical, monastic, liturgically oriented, poverty-stricken and embattled Christendom, and his maturity and old age coincide with the beginnings of the age which displays the abounding energy, optimism and intellectual comprehensiveness of the new masters of the western schools. And when we look at the freedom and boldness of Anselm's intellectual life, it is tempting to say that, though he was born into and lived throughout his life in the monastic setting of pre-scholastic Europe, his thoughts foreshadow the bold systematic creations of the scholastic age.

If we could think this, we could celebrate him as the link between the two contiguous but contrasting ages of Christian history, helping to bring them both together into a single harmonious whole. It is a tempting picture, and those who have been fascinated by it have recalled his association with the earlier age by calling him the 'last of the Fathers', and his association with the new age by calling him 'the first of the Scholastics'. The two phrases have the great attraction of giving him a connecting role in this great transformation, which is worthy of the marks of genius which are everywhere to be found in all that he said and wrote.

The only trouble about it is that his works neither foreshadow what was to follow, nor sum up (or even bear any obvious relationship to) the scholarship of the immediate past. On the contrary, they stand out as something quite distinct both from what had gone before and from what was to come. They recall one side of St Augustine's penetrating insight, and they foreshadow (if we must look for foreshadowings) the period *beyond* the scholastic centuries, when in the fourteenth and fifteenth centuries mystics and hermits and solitaries began to despair of the grandiose intellectual structures of the twelfth- and thirteenth-century scholastic masters, and to find new inspiration and models in Anselm's prayers, meditations and monastic dialogues.

This link between Anselm and the mystics of the late Middle Ages is too vast a theme for more than the briefest mention this afternoon, but if you read his prayers and meditations, then his letters, and then go on to read his treatises (they are all available in excellent editions and translations), you will see that they have characteristics which distinguish them sharply both from the compilations of the earlier period and from the highly organized scholastic works of the next two hundred years.

I may simply mention some of their distinctive features: first, whereas the most prominent feature of all scholastic works was their array of carefully selected and interpreted 'authorities' which underpin all their conclusions, Anselm's works never mention (except once under duress) 'authorities' to support his conclusions. One consequence of this is that none of his works sets about constructing a *system* by reconciling apparent contradictions in these authorities, which is the method of the scholastic age. Further, none of his works aims at systematic completeness, but only at illuminating dark or difficult areas of faith or practice. And further still, although he is never in doubt about the truth of what he is saying, there is always (except once) an element of the provisional in what he writes. The exception is his argument for the necessary existence of God, which of all his arguments has met with most dissent.

Most conspicuously of all, everything he writes is lucidly clear. The difficulty of his words never lies in their complexity of argument or language, but only in the need to sit back and think more deeply than, I suspect, any of us here today can ever do: what do these apparently simple statements mean: 'Faith seeking understanding... God is that than which nothing greater can be thought... The necessity of God's actions is nothing but the immutability of His perfect being?'

Anselm's works need much thought if they are to be understood, and they can probably never be finally and completely understood. But they never, or almost never, involve his reader in mind-stretching complex arguments as the scholastic writers do. He uses only simple words to say profoundly difficult things, which need reflection if they are to be understood. But he never says or aims at saying the last word on any subject. He only says what will get everyone some distance along the road to understanding.

These characteristics reflect the difference in aim and environment between Anselm and his scholastic successors. His thoughts spring, not from systematic classroom lectures, but from solitary meditation and intimate conversations with like-minded individuals in the monastic community. He is profoundly imbued with the idea that anyone who truly seeks will 'find', but what they find will be only a beginning of what still remains to be found, only an illumination of what must still remain an object of faith.

Anselm is no optimist. 'Many are called but few are chosen' was an often repeated biblical quotation of his. It was an expression of the pessimistic side of his nature, intensified for him by his recognition that he himself had been saved only by a divine intervention which had brought him—a castaway wanderer from his native land—to Bec in 1059 at the age of 26. The salvation brought by his conversion to the monastic life at Bec had been the whole story of his life from that date until 1093 when he came to Canterbury. During these years, he had spent many hours every day in the routine of daily services laid down in St Benedict's Rule, which had been greatly prolonged by the liturgical developments of the tenth and eleventh centuries. But he had also—and this was quite unprovided for in the Rule—spent many hours also in anguished private prayer and in spiritual conversation with his friends among the monks.

His prayers and meditations, which are the earliest of his surviving writings, are works comparable in one mood to the poems of George Herbert, and in another darker mood to those of Gerard Manley Hopkins. Indeed one could scarcely find a better introduction to the mixture of simplicity of aim and extravagant verbal complexity which are the characteristics of Anselm's prayers than this poem of George Herbert on *Prayer*:

> Prayer the Churches banquet, Angels age,
>   God's breath in man returning to his birth,
>   The soul in paraphrase, heart in pilgrimage,
> The Christian plummet sounding heaven and earth;
> Engine against th'Almighty, sinner's tower,
>   Reversed thunder, Christ-side-piercing spear;
>   The six-days' world transposing in an hour;

A kind of tune which all things hear and fear;
Softness and peace and joy and love and bliss,
    Exalted manna, gladness of the best,
    Heaven in ordinary, man well dresst;
The milky way, the bird of Paradise,
    Church-bells beyond the stars heard, the soul's blood,
    The land of spices; something understood.

Of course, the style of this poem is not that of Anselm, but the strange antitheses, the tensions of the individual soul in the presence of God mirrored in the contrasting images and rhymes and assonances, and at the end the 'something understood', are all to be found in the intimate and infinite world of Anselmian prayer and meditation, which inspired an ever-expanding literature of private, non-liturgical prayer. This whole movement was not created by Anselm but it was he more than anyone who opened the way, not into the scholastic modes of theological thought, but into the expanding world of individual prayer and meditation in the later medieval and modern worlds.

In his prayers, and in his meditations or dialogues on God, truth, free will, the fall of Satan, and the incarnation, which grew out of them, Anselm also opened the way to a new freedom of treatment of the divine economy of the universe. His treatises are remarkable for the sense of freedom of individual enquiry which they initiate without his having any desire to be an innovator. When Lanfranc expostulated with him on the absence of any quotation of authorities in his first important theological treatise, Anselm replied that everything he had written could be found in Augustine. Lanfranc, who knew Augustine as well or better than Anselm, said no more, but he knew that Anselm was breaking away from the example of his master. Everything that Lanfranc said is abundantly documented; but all that Anselm said or did is free of all constraints except those of fidelity to the great definitive formulae of the Christian faith.

This was the man who came to Canterbury nine hundred years ago today: a man wholly dedicated to the spiritual life, ignorant of politics, hopeless as an administrator, a man whose talk charmed everyone— even perhaps that ogre among medieval kings, William Rufus. Certainly a strange sympathy existed between them, and Anselm long defended the king. Ultimately the king's demands drove Anselm into exile, but even this and his later exile were voluntary, and his friends had some reason to think that he felt much happier in the hills near Capua finishing his great work, *Cur deus homo*, than he had ever felt in doing his work as archbishop. Equally, in the next reign, he seems to have been happier in exile at Lyons, preaching to the monks of Cluny and making a collection of his prayers for the Countess Matilda of Tuscany.

So, cutting through all the details which are vividly related by his biographer, we may ask: how did he look on his work as archbishop? I think we must say that he did not look on himself—as archbishops and bishops were increasingly coming to look on themselves—as an administrator. He saw himself as essentially charged with responsibilities, first, for the religious community at Canterbury; second, for defending rights and privileges that—having been given to the church of Canterbury as a perpetual possession—belonged to the heavenly kingdom; third, for defining, expounding and defending the doctrines and morals of the church, and legislating for their enforcement throughout the whole area of the British Isles.

These were the external duties that came to him as archbishop. They interrupted, but did not replace his continuing search for understanding the faith that he had seriously embraced in coming to the religious life: in investigating the necessary existence of God; the necessity for the incarnation; the nature of truth, of free will, of sin, of beatitude; and the constant prayer alone with God and in association with others at every level from two or three to the corporate acts of the whole community.

The man who asks these questions, and engages in these—and willingly *only* in these—activities, surely belongs to a new age. But he does not belong to the new age which was coming into existence in his later years. He belongs above all to the present.

3. *Anselm for Today*

My time is nearly up, and I am conscious that I have not fulfilled what might have been reasonably expected of a lecture purporting to deal with Anselm in his historical setting. The truth is that, however much he wished to fit into his background, he stood apart from his contemporaries, and he did not belong in method or spirit either to the heavily and magnificently articulated monastic past or to the vastly ambitious and impressive scholastic future.

Nothing is more astonishing than the contrast between the great age of western Christian development that was beginning during the last twenty years of Anselm's life and the tenor of his own work right to the end. The idea that his work forms a bridge between the period of western Christian development which was ending in his youth, and the new period that was producing its first fruits when he died, breaks down the moment it is put to the test. The simplest test is the utter absence of quotations from any authorities apart from the very numerous but seldom specifically identified words of the Bible. These, together with a single mention of the Nicene and Athanasian Creeds, and his one reluctant mention of Augustine as a general authority for all that he had written in his *Monologion*, are his sole acknowledged authorities. Indeed he looks on all elaborations, however valuable they might be in developing a sense of the immensity of the divine plan, as tentative explanations of an absolutely assured faith in the biblical revelation of God's purposes as reiterated throughout the liturgical year in the worship of the church. As for God's *Being*, he thought he had provided an absolutely assured basis for asserting its intellectual necessity—that is to say its necessity if any thinking at all was to be valid. And even his 'proof' of God's existence did not make superfluous the necessity of faith; the proof itself was after all the first and greatest achievement of 'faith seeking understanding'.

On this subject, and perhaps on this subject alone, he thought that reason and faith were entirely co-extensive. Beyond this point, although the statements of the Creeds were absolutely fixed and immutable, the elaborations of doctrine were in varying degrees tentative.

This is the hallmark of all that Anselm wrote and all that is reported of his spoken words. We cannot tell what he would have thought of the programme of the two centuries after his death. But we can say that, if he had himself used the scholastic methods of building up an assured body of truth, his work would have had a quite different character. His method is reflective rather than dialectical; it is an act of prayer rather than of debate. And it takes place among a group of like-minded monastic friends, rather than as a response to the clamour of questioners in the schools.

In fact, his works were treated with great respect by scholastic theologians, but they made no substantial impact upon their work; and it was only with the decay of systematic scholastic thought in the fourteenth century that his works, and especially his prayers and meditations, began to have admirers who did more than loosely imitate his manner: they, like his earliest disciples, adopted it and produced elaborations which have a life and value of their own.

The monastic environment was indeed essential to his work, but the routine of daily offices was a relaxation from, rather than a stimulus to, his own meditations and enquiries. It excluded the world with its ambitions, distractions, sensuous enjoyments and aims, and provided a daily panorama of the eternal world; but it did not stimulate either the questions which he sought to answer or—except by accident—the answers which he was able to find.

And yet here too there is a paradox. Despite the daily exclusion of the world and mundane pleasures from his life, no one has ever described the joys of Paradise in such physical terms. In a sermon to the monks of Cluny, which Eadmer avidly reported, and which (he tells us) Anselm corrected, he described the fourteen joys of Heaven. They consist of the beauty of limitless light, speed, strength, liberty, health, taste, smell, feeling, combined with everlastingness, wisdom, knowledge, concord, friendship, and power commensurate with desire and joy. As for his life in this world, we hear nothing of extraordinary austerities. He ate almost nothing, but he liked to see others eating well, and once, when he was ill, on being asked if there was anything he would like, he rather surprisingly said he would like a partridge. We are only told this by Eadmer because it was the occasion of a minor miracle: a dog appeared almost at once with a partridge in its mouth, but perhaps we may value the miracle less than the characteristic precision of his choice.

Eadmer would dearly have liked to see many more and grander miracles than this, but though he did his best to make a collection such as would bring general acknowledgment of Anselm's sanctity, he was left in the end with a very poor little list—a few visions, a few cures with the aid of Anselm's belt, the mystery of the boat in which they crossed the Channel having a large hole without letting in water. These little anecdotes failed to impress the younger generation of Canterbury monks and there was a considerable possibility that Anselm would never formally be recognized as a saint. In the end, it was the radiance of his life, and of his prayers and meditations and his accounts of the great doctrines of the Christian religion which, slowly and uncertainly, but in the end universally, brought about recognition of his sanctity. Characteristically, it was the ordinary people of Canterbury who, when the likelihood of official canonization was diminishing, banded themselves together in a society which called itself the 'Dionysians of St Anselm'. By about 1160 there were a hundred and fifty of them from the port-reeve to miscellaneous cobblers and blacksmiths. This Anselmian society disappeared when the miracle-working powers of Thomas Becket took the world by storm and made Canterbury famous throughout Europe. But it is no disparagement of Thomas Becket to say that his work was for his own time, whereas Anselm's was for reconciliation and understanding in the present and always. Perhaps the time has come to restore the fellowship of the Dionysians of St Anselm in recognition of his timeless message for every today.

A twelfth-century manuscript listing members of the Canterbury 'Dionysians of St Anselm' (see pp. 32-33), reproduced by permission of the British Library. The list is printed in full on the facing page. B.L. Cotton Nero C, IX fo. 22v.

List of Members of the Canterbury Guild of St Anselm, c. 1166?
with an addition after 1170

[line 1] Isti sunt fratres et sorores dionisiorum sancti Anselmi. [2] Walterius filius Simon ; aldermon. & Eadwardus socius suus alter. Willelmus filius Pagani. [3] et uxor eius. Johannes filius Uiuiani. Joseph filius Gelgewini. Fredemundus. et uxor eius. [4] Osbertus Curteis. et uxor eius. Baldewinus de bracino. uxor eius. Jurdanus cocus. [5] Simon de Clara. Petrus. Hordwi. Prior & uxor eius. Aldiua & filia eius. [6] Baldewinus de Flandria. & uxor eius. Senllingus et uxor eius. Engnulfus. [7] Salomon filius Rogerii. Coffinus. Goscelinus. Reinoldus. del bracin. Vxor Walterii. [8] Willelmus filius Sefugel. Osbertus homo Geruasii. Elgarus homo Eadwordi. [9] Edwordus le uaneur. Liwinus homo Eadwordi. Durandus Bataille. et uxor eius. [10] Rodbertus Feld. Rogerus bunetir. et uxor eius. Baldewinus. Harpir. Purcaz. [11] Eadwordus. Salomon pistor. Wluiua uxor Eadwordi. Samuhel & uxor eius. [12] Adelice mater Walterii. Witelardus. Osbertus clericus. Johannes. Sedegos. Wlfbaldus. [13] Mathias. Willelmus Pungnant. Phylippus. Uxor Elgari. Eadilda. Wlfsi et Uxor eius [14] Simer. Wluredus. Vauasur. Picot. Eilwecer diaconus. Lifwinus. Rodbertus urser. [15] Tomas. Butor. Mahald. Radulfus. Stanburhe. et Rodbertus. Adelice. Aldib. [16] Elwinuses. [sic] de pistrino. Symon. Goldwenna. Wlmer et uxor eius. Robertus. [17] Ricardus et uxor eius. Wluordus de Niwintune et uxor eius. Elmerus de Tropham. [18] et uxor eius. Eluredus. Baldewinus. et uxor eius. Wluiua et filia eius. Fulco. [19] Hagenilda. uxor Geruasii. Elesmod. et filia eius. Adam filius Elfsi. Warinus. Elfsi de [20] fonte. et uxor eius. Brictiua. Beatrix. Elfwinus parmenter et uxor eius. [21] Wimundus. filia Fretemundi. Bricwen. Hugo de bracino. Irilda. Joewi. [22] Tidberga. Eadwinus. Gosfridus. Godwinus. Cripup. et uxor eius. Wlmerus. Coleman. [23] et uxor eius. Wiffinus. et Eluiua. Liuit. Paganus. et uxor eius. Liuricus. Picot [24] le mulner. Wido. Crane. Semerus ianitor. Sibilia. Eadmerus. Edit.
[25] Makepad. Swar.
[26] Dominum Othonem de Franche et Beatricem vxorem suam et liberos suos. recepimus in societatem nostram [27] et participes omnium beneficiorum nostrorum constituimus. et dedit quamdiu uixerit in honorem Thome annuatim [28] corone eiusdem martiris. dimidiam marcam argenti. uel per se uel per fidelem nuncium.

Part I
ANSELM AND HIS ANTECEDENTS

PROSLOGION 1: FORM UND GESTALT

Klaus Kienzler

1. *Die Confessio theologica des Johannes de Fécamp:*
Brücke von den Confessiones des Augustinus zum
Proslogion des Anselm von Canterbury

Sofia Vanni Rovighi hat auf die Nähe der *Confessio theologica* (ca.
1017) des Johannes de Fécamp zu *Proslogion* 1 hingewiesen.[1] Sie hat
eine Reihe von Verwandtschaften zwischen dieser *Confessio* und dem
Proslogion c. 1 (= P1) benannt. Der Text des Johannes de Fécamp
wurde teilweise von André Wilmart in *Auteurs spirituels et textes dévôts*
(Paris, 1932 bzw. 1971) ediert und besprochen.[2] A. Wilmart stellt dort
die Verbindungslinie von der *Confessio theologica* zu den *Confessiones*
des Augustinus her. Hauptzeuge dafür ist ein Stück aus der *Confessio*,
das deutlich an eine der bekanntesten Textpassagen der *Vision von*
Ostia erinnert:

1. S. Vanni Rovighi, *S. Anselmo e la filosofia del secolo XI* (Bari, 1987),
pp. 19ff.; cfr. P. Gilbert, *Le Proslogion de S. Anselme* (Roma, 1990), pp. 34ff. Der
Text der *Confessio theologica* wird im folgenden nach der Edition, die von Jean
Leclercq besorgt wurde, wiedergegeben: *Giovanni di Fécamp, Pregare nel Med-*
ioevo. La Confessio Theologica e altre opere. Introduzione di Jean Leclercq
(Mailand: Jaca Book, 1985), pp. 179-258.
2. A. Wilmart, *Auteurs spirituels et textes dévôts* (Paris, 1971), pp. 135-36.
Teile der *Confessio theologica* ('Finale') sind in der 'Praefatio' des 'Manuale' des
Augustinus (*PL* 40, 951) enthalten. A. Wilmart (ebd. 126-37) schreibt andere Texte
Johannes de Fécamp zu wie ein Großteil des *Liber meditationum* (*PL* 40, 901-42),
d.i. die Bücher 12-25, 27-33, 35-37 (resp. 'Libellus de scripturis et verbis patrum
collectus...' = 1.Buch der Handschrift Ms. 245 von Saint-Arnoul de Metz); sodann
die 'Confessio fidei' (*PL* 101, 1027ff.), das 'Manuale' (*PL* 40, 951ff.) und das
'Speculum' (*PL* 40, 967ff.). Es könnte gezeigt werden, wie ähnlich die Texte in
diesen Büchern oft sind und wieviele Erinnerungen an Anselm in ihnen enthalten
sind.

Dicebamus ergo: Si cui *sileat* tumultus carnis, *sileant* phantasiae terrae et aquarum et aeris, *sileant* et poli et ipsa sibi anima *sileat* et transeat se non se cogitando, *sileant* somnia et imaginariae revelationes, omnis lingua et omne signum et quidquid transeundo fit si cui *sileat* omnino... his dictis si iam taceant, quoniam erexerunt aurem in eum, qui fecit ea, et loquatur ipse solus... (*Confessiones* = C IX,10,25).

Der entsprechende Passus lautet bei Johannes de Fécamp folgendermaßen:

O pax, o requies, o gaudium, quibus tunc temporis fruitur anima tibi intenta. Ecce, dum divinae theoriae mens mea suspirat et tuam, domine, pro captu suo meditatur et loquitur gloriam, ipsa carnis sarcina minus gravat; cogitationum tumultus cessat; pondus mortalitatis et miseriarum more solito non hebetat.

Silent cuncta, tranquilla sunt omnia. Cor ardet, animus gaudet, memoria viget, intellectus lucet; et totus spiritus ex desiderio visionis tuae accensus, in invisibilium amorem rapi se videt.[3]

Die Abhängigkeit dieses Textes von Augustinus hat A. Wilmart deutlich herausgestellt. Weitere verwandte Stellen der *Confessio theologica* zur Passage der *Vision von Ostia* können dies nur unterstreichen,[4] wie etwa folgende:

Tu mihi cor tene, mentem rege, intellectum dirige, amorem erige, animum suspende et in superna fluenta os sitientis te spiritus trahe. *Taceat*, queso, tumultus carnis; *conticescant* phantasiae terrarum et aquarum et aeris et poli; *taceant* somnia et imaginariar revelationes, omnis lingua, omne signum et quicquid transeundo fit; *sileat* sibi et ipsa anima et transeat a se, non cogitando se, sed te, Deus meus.[5]

Ich selbst habe auf die Nähe des Anfangs von P1 zu dem zitierten Passus des Augustinus in der *Vision von Ostia* immer wieder aufmerksam gemacht.[6] Mit der *Confessio theologica* des Johannes de

---

3. *Confessio theologica* III 65. A. Wilmart, a.a.O. 135f. Text auch im *Manuale* c.3 (*PL* 40, 953 1.5ff.); cfr. *Meditationes* c.37 §3 (*PL* 40, 935) und 'Confessio fidei' I §30 (*PL* 101, 1046D).

4. Ebd., 135 Anm.1.

5. *Confessio theologica* III 57.

6. K. Kienzler, 'Zur philosophisch-theologischen Denkform bei Augustinus und bei Anselm von Canterbury', *Anselm Studies* 2 (ed. J. Schraubelt, F. Van Fleteren *et al.*; New York: Kraus International Publications, 1988), pp. 353-89; ders. 'Das "Proslogion"-Argument Anselms und die "Confessiones" des Augustinus', in J. Zumr, V. Herold (eds.), *The European Dimension of St. Anselm's Thinking* (Prag, 1993), pp. 137-63.

Fécamp könnte eine literarische Brücke von Anselm zu Augustinus geschlagen sein, auf die Sofia Vanni Rovighi hingewiesen hat. Paul Gilbert führt in seinem Buch *Le Proslogion de S. Anselme* (1990) diese Zusammenhänge ebenfalls an. Allerdings legt er dabei mehr Gewicht auf die Unterschiede zwischen Augustinus und Johannes de Fécamp einerseits und Anselm andererseits.[7]

Einen solchen Zusammenhang herzustellen zwischen Johannes de Fécamp und Augustinus einerseits und Anselm andererseits, hat eine starke Plausibilität für sich. Denn Johannes de Fécamp (nach 990–1078) war ohne Zweifel eine der großen Reformäbte zur Zeit Anselms, der zudem von 1028 bis 1078 dem normannische Kloster La Trinité von Fécamp vorstand und daneben eine Reihe anderer wichtiger Klöster der Normandie u.a. wie St Bénigne, Evreux und Bernay leitete. Daneben war er ein sehr fruchtbarer Schriftsteller, der so sehr von Augustinus angeregt war, daß seine Werke vor allem demselben Augustinus zugeschrieben wurden und heute unter den 'Spuria Augustiniana' zu finden sind.[8] Erst sehr spät begann man, Johannes de Fécamp sein Werk nach und nach wieder zurückzugeben. Zudem genossen seine Hauptwerke, die vor allem aus Sammlungen von 'Gebeten' und 'Meditationen' bestanden, eine kaum zu überschätzende Popularität, die durchaus mit jener der Meditationen des Anselm später und sodann der spirituellen Literatur des Bernhard von Clairvaux zu vergleichen ist. Es ist durchaus anzunehmen, daß Anselm Texte seines großen 'Kollegen'-Abtes Johannes de Fécamp kannte, was im übrigen auch erwiesen erscheint.[9]

Ich möchte die Anregung Sofia Vanni Rovighis in der Weise aufnehmen, daß ich den Zusammenhang von Augustinus und Anselm nicht nur an dieser einen, wenn auch sehr signifikanten Stelle fest-machen will, sondern versuchen werde, das ganze *Proslogion* 1 von den *Confessiones* des Augustinus her zu lesen. Der Katalysator dieser Lesart sozusagen sind dabei die *Confessio theologica* des Johannes de Fécamp sowie andere vom selben Autor stammende Texte, soweit sie A. Wilmart identifiziert hat. Bei diesen Werken fällt besonders der beständige Rück-griff auf die *Confessiones* des Augustinus auf, vor allem neben der schon erwähnten *Vision von Ostia* die häufige Zitation von Formulierungen

---

7. P. Gilbert, a.a.O.
8. S. oben Anm.2.
9. Cfr. S. Vanni Rovighi, a.a.O., und P. Gilbert, a.a.O.

und Motiven aus dem Anfang der *Confessiones* (C I, 1,1–5,6).[10] Im Rückblick auf einige zentrale Texte der *Confessiones* scheint es möglich, den Text des *Proslogion* 1 von den Hauptgedanken des Augustinus her neu zu strukturieren. Dazu lege ich einen Vorschlag vor. Er unterscheidet sich offensichtlich von der Anordnung, die Franziskus Salesius Schmitt in seinen Editionen zugrunde legt, und auch von derjenigen Paul Gilberts, der F.S. Schmitt darin offensichtlich folgt.[11] Damit sind weitere Bezüge anderer Autoren und Texte zum *Proslogion* des Anselm von Canterbury nicht ausgeschlossen. Es fällt aber die besondere Nähe von P1 zu dessen *Confessiones* auf.

2. *Die Form des kontemplativen Gebetes P1*

Der oben zitierte Text der *Confessio theologica* hat bei Johannes de Fécamp eine interessante Einführung, die lautet:

> Multa igitur sunt contemplationum genera, quibus anima tibi, Christe, devota delectatur et proficit; sed in nullo earum ita gaudet mens mea sicut in illa quae, *cunctis remotis, in te solum deum* attolit *simplicem puri cordis intuitum.*[12]

Die *Confessio theologica* spricht sich mit anderen Worten über die Form der 'Kontemplation' aus und hebt dabei die im Verständnis von Johannes de Fécamp höchste Form heraus. Diese wird aber dann im folgenden Text mit der ekstastischen Kontemplation der *Vision von Ostia* des Augustinus identifiziert, wie oben gezeigt wurde. Dieser Sachverhalt ist von großem Interesse, da hier auf ausdrückliche Weise die augustinische Form ekstatischer Kontemplation mit jener identifiziert wird, die in den *Meditationes* des Johannes de Fécamp vorliegt und die offenbar mit der des *Proslogion* eng verwandt ist. Darauf machen schon Wendungen wie 'cunctis remotis' oder 'simplex puri cordis intuitus in te solum deum' aufmerksam.

Ein Hauptargument von P. Gilbert etwa ist der unterschiedliche Charakter des Gebetes Anselms in P1, das eine *Meditation* darstellt, von der 'Ekstase', wie sie in der *Vision von Ostia* des Augustinus vorliegt. Aber der angeführte Text der *Confessio theologica* des Johannes de Fécamp könnte gerade verdeutlichen, wie der ekstatische Text des

---

10. Dies wird bei den 'invocationes' der Bücher des Johannes de Fécamp besonders deutlich.
11. Ebd. 36-47.
12. *Confessio theologica* III 65.

Augustinus zur Grundform der *Meditation* transformiert werden konnte.

Diese große Nähe zu Anselm von Canterbury wird durch eine ähnliche Überlegung des Johannes de Fécamp in den *Meditationes* bestätigt. Auch dort reflektiert er auf die höchste Form der Kontemplation:

> Multae denique sunt contemplationes, quibus anima tibi devota mirabiliter pascitur: sed in nulla earum ita *requiescit* et delectatur anima mea, sicut *quando se solum cogitat et contemplatur.* Quam magna multitudo dulcedinis tuae, Domine (Ps 30,20), quam mirabiliter inspiras cordibus amatorum tuorum. Quam mira suavitas amoris tui, quo perfruuntur illi qui *nihil* praeter te diligunt, *nihil quaerunt, nihil* etiam *cogitare* concupiscunt. Felices illi quibus tu solus spes es, et *omne opus oratio. Beatus qui sedet solitarius et tacet,* et stat super custodiam suam jugiter nocte et die; ut adhuc in hoc *fragili corpusculo* positus, praelibare valeat aliquatenus dulcedinem tuam.[13]

Ohne Zweifel ist hier die Form und der Gestus des 'Gebetes (oratio)' und der 'Kontemplation' des Anselm von Canterbury im *Proslogion* 1 auf frappierend ähnliche Weise beschrieben.

3. *Der Gehalt von Proslogion 1—im Spiegel der Confessiones*

Für das Verständnis der *Confessiones* ist unfraglich der Anfang und Auftakt des Buches entscheidend. In ihm gibt Augustinus das Thema der Schrift an. Er scheint auch für Anselm bedeutsam zu sein. Er lautet:

(A) (1) 'Magnus es, domine, et laudabilis valde' (Ps 144,3)
        (2) 'magna virtus tua
             (3) et sapientiae tuae non est numerus' (Ps 146,5).

(B) (R) Et laudare te vult homo, aliqua portio creaturae tuae,
        (1) et homo circumferens mortalitatem suam
             (2) circumferens testimonium peccati sui
                (3) et testimonium, quia 'superbis resistis'.

(C) (R) Et *tamen* laudare te vult homo, aliqua portio creaturae tuae.
        (1) Tu excitas, ut laudare te delectet,
             (2) quia fecisti nos ad te
                (3) et inquietum est cor nostrum, donec requiescat in te. (C I, 1,1)

Es sei nur nebenbei angemerkt, wie sehr die *Confessio theologica* oben auch an diese Eröffnung erinnert ('pax', 'requies', 'pondus mortalitatis', 'miseriae'). An dieser Ouverture der *Confessiones* ist mir aber ein

---

13. *Meditationes* c.37 (*PL* 40, 935).

Zweifaches wichtig im Hinblick auf meine Untersuchungen zu Anselms P1: einmal das Thema und zum anderen die Form der Dialektik, in der das Thema vorgetragen wird. Es könnte gezeigt werden, daß Augustinus mit diesem großen Auftakt einen Vorblick auf die ganze Schrift der *Confessiones* gibt, nämlich gerade auf ihre großen Themen und ihre innere Dialektik.

Die Ouverture gibt aber auch vor, was Augustinus einführend im Buch I den *Confessiones* voranstellen will. Augustinus beginnt das Thema der *Confessiones* mit einer 'invocatio', dem Lobpreis Gottes oder mit einem rühmenden Gebet über die Größe Gottes (A): die *Confessiones* werden den Charakter der 'confessio laudis' haben. Aber dieses christliche Selbstverständnis wird sogleich problematisiert (B): Wie vermag der Mensch Gott zu loben, da er doch nur ein kümmerlicher Abriß von Gottes Schöpfung ist ('aliqua portio creaturae tuae'). Aber schlimmer noch: Durch den Sündenfall ist seine Situation die des Unheils ('testimonium peccati sui'). Die innerste christliche Problematik ist von allem Anfang an offengelegt. Es ist die Problematik christlicher Rede bzw. Betens schlechthin. Damit ist zugleich eine intrikate Dialektik verbunden. Zwar erscheint die erste Selbstverständlichkeit des Betens, die 'confessio laudis', durch den Hinweis auf den Stand des Menschen, die 'confessio peccati', unmöglich geworden, doch weist ein 'tamen (dennoch)' sogleich darauf hin, daß der Mensch Gott trotzdem preisen soll, wenn er auch nur ein kümmerlicher Abriß der Schöpfung ist (C). Diese Dialektik ist durch die stanzenartige Wiederholung der Aussage, der Mensch solle Gott preisen, obwohl er nur eine gebrochene Natur ist, deutlich herausgehoben (R). Thema der *Confessiones* wird also die 'confessio laudis' sein, die Preisung der Größe Gottes. Aber es wird zugleich auch die 'confessio peccati' sein. Diese ergibt sich aus der Zustandsbeschreibung des konkreten Menschen, aus der christlichen Anthropologie des Augustinus, die einmal die ursprünglich Schöpfung des Menschen durch Gott erkennt und zum anderen den Fall der Menschheit in Adam ernst nimmt. Mit kurzen Sätzen hat also Augustinus programmatisch gleich zu Anfang das augustinische Thema der *Confessiones* angekündigt. Daraus folgt nicht nur der Einsatz für die nächsten Aussagereihen, sondern es ist im Grunde auch der Ausgang für die *Confessiones* insgesamt.

Ich würde diesen ersten Anfang der *Confessiones* als eine Vergewisserung der 'Glaubens'-ordnung des Menschen durch Augustinus charakterisieren. Sie hat ihre Entsprechung am Anfang des *Proslogion*.

Beidemal handelt es sich um eine Zustandsbeschreibung, wie es um den Menschen steht. Wir werden sehen, daß auch Anselm P1 nach diesem Muster gestaltet, indem er der 'invocatio' (I.)[14] die 'confessio peccati' folgen läßt in der Form, daß er zuerst über die 'Schöpfung' und den 'Sündenfall' meditiert (II.), sodann betend die Hoffnung auf 'Erlösung' vorträgt (III.).

Der nächste Abschnitt der *Confessiones* ist aber für Anselm nicht weniger bedeutsam: 'Laß mich, Herr, wissen und erkennen... ("da mihi, domine, scire et intelligere...")'.[15] Unüberhörbar ist der Schluß von P1 angesprochen (IV.). Es ist das 'Erkenntnis'-Interesse, das für Augustinus wie für Anselm so charakteristisch ist, wissen und erkennen zu wollen, was der Glaube am Anfang sagt. Ich muß es mir versagen, den Übergang vom 'Glauben' zum 'Erkennen' präzise mit Augustinus nachzuvollziehen; es kann nur darauf hingewiesen werden, daß er bei Augustinus wie in der entsprechenden Passage von P1 durch das Einführen der Grundworte von 'suchen' ('quaerere') und 'finden' ('invenire') und durch ihr wiederum dialektisches Verhältnis geschieht. Auf die Bedeutung dieser Grundworte bei Augustinus wie bei Anselm ist immer wieder genügend hingewiesen worden.

Nun aber zur Durchführung des großen Themas des Augustinus in P1 des Anselm im einzelnen. In einem ersten Schritt möchte ich zeigen, daß das Thema der Ouverture des Augustinus tatsächlich die Großstruktur von P1 abgibt. In einem zweiten Schritt werde ich dann die dialektische Durchführung des Themas im einzelnen aufzeigen.

I. *Invocatio—Einstimmung in das Gebet*
Anselm (Op. Om. I, 97,4-10):

> Eia, nunc homuncio,
> *fuge* paululum occupationes tuas,
> *absconde* te modicum a tumultuosis cogitationibus tuis
> *Abice* nunc onerosas curas, et
> *postpone* laboriosas distentiones tuas.
> *Vaca* aliquantulum Deo, et
> *requiesce* aliquantulum in eo.
> 'Intra in cubiculum' mentis tuae,

14. Ein schönes Beispiel für die Nähe der Texte findet sich in c.3 des *Manuale*. Es ist eine 'invocatio'. Es zeigt sich, daß Johannes de Fécamp die invocationes seiner Bücher mit Vorliebe aus Texten des Anfangs der *Confessiones* des Augustinus und aus jenen der *Vision von Ostia* gestaltet.

15. C I,1,1 (*PL* 32, 661).

exclude omnia praeter Deum et quae te iuvent
ad quaerendum eum, et
'clauso ostio' (Mt 6,6) quaere eum.
Dic nunc, totum 'cor meum'
dic nunc Deo:
'Quaero vultum tuum,
vultum tuum, Domine, requiro (Ps 26,8)

Auf den Unterschied der beiden Texte von Augustinus und Anselm habe ich schon hingewiesen. Augustinus formuliert so den Ausgang der *Vision von Ostia*, also die Einstimmung in eine ekstatische Erfahrung. Anselm formuliert auf seine eigene Weise die Einstimmung in ein meditatives Gebet, das er dem *Proslogion* voranstellt. Aber Johannes de Fécamp konnte zeigen, daß der Übergang zur Zeit Anselms tatsächlich vollzogen worden ist.[16] Deshalb ist auf die große Ähnlichkeit beider Texte noch einmal zurückzukommen. Sie besteht m.E. besonders darin, daß Augustinus wie Anselm sieben Mal zum Schweigen auffordern; Augustinus durch eine Variation des Verbs 'silere', Anselm durch eine siebenfache Variation der Aufforderung zum 'Schweigen'. Es sei noch einmal der Text des Augustinus daneben gestellt:

Augustinus (C IX,10,25; *PL* 32, 774):

> Dicebamus ergo: Si cui *sileat* tumultus carnis, *sileant* phantasiae terrae et aquarum et aeris, *sileant* et poli et ipsa sibi anima *sileat* et transeat se non se cogitando, *sileant* somnia et imaginariae revelationes, omnis lingua et omne signum et quidquid transeundo fit si cui *sileat* omnino... his dictis si iam taceant, quoniam erexerunt aurem in eum, qui fecit ea, et loquatur ipse solus...

Darüber hinaus fällt auf, daß der Anfang von P1 ebenso an den Anfang der *Confessiones* des Augustinus erinnert. Die Erklärung dazu könnten die 'invocationes' des Johannes de Fécamp bieten, der in ihnen vornehmlich Motive aus dem Anfang und der *Vision von Ostia* der *Confessiones* verwendet.[17] Den Gestus des kontemplativen Beters von P1 trifft ganz jene schon oben zitierte Passage aus den *Meditationes* c.37:

---

16. Gerade für den Anfang von P1 gibt es eine Reihe von schönen Entsprechungen bei Johannes de Fécamp; cfr. *Meditationes* c.33 (*PL* 40, 926) u.a.

17. Cfr. die 'invocationes' in *Manuale* (Praefatio, *PL* 40, 952), *Speculum* c.1 und c.2 (*PL* 40, 969 bzw. 970) und *Confessio fidei* c.4 (*PL* 101, 1030).

Multae denique sunt contemplationes, quibus anima tibi devota mirabiliter
pascitur: sed in nulla earum ita *requiescit* et delectatur anima mea, sicut
quando se solum cogitat et contemplatur. Quam magna multitudo
dulcedinis tuae, Domine (Ps 30,20), quam mirabiliter inspiras cordibus
amatorum tuorum. Quam mira suavitas amoris tui, quo perfruuntur illi qui
nihil praeter te diligunt, *nihil quaerunt, nihil* etiam cogitare concupiscunt.
Felices illi quibus tu solus spes es, et *omne opus oratio. Beatus qui sedet
solitarius et tacet,* et stat super custodiam suam jugiter nocte et die; ut
adhuc in hoc *fragili corpusculo* positus, praelibare valeat aliquatenus
dulcedinem tuam.[18]

II. *Die Schöpfung des Menschen—Urstand und Fall*

Teil II und III von P1 haben offensichtlich die christliche Anthropologie
zum Thema und zwar im Stil des Augustinus. Deshalb erkenne ich in
den folgenden Aussagen die Themenangabe des folgenden P1:

Anselm (Op. Om. I, 98,13-15):

> Tu me fecisti et refecisti
> et omnia bona tu mihi contulisti—
> et nondum novi te.
> Denique ad te videndum factus sum—
> et nondum feci, propter quod factus sum.

Augustinus. Es bedarf keiner großen Erläuterungen, daß das Thema der
Schöpfung des Menschen im Urstand und Fall der Theologie des
Augustinus entspricht. Es sei nur an die große Ouverture oben erinnert
(s. oben Eröffnung B, 1-3).

Bei Augustinus ist das Schöpfungsthema eines der zentralen theologischen Themen, mit denen er sich in den *Confessiones* beschäftigt. Das
gilt nicht nur für die letzten philosophisch-theologischen Bücher, sondern
bei genauem Hinsehen ist das Thema der ersten und zweiten Schöpfung
schon unübersehbar an ihrem Anfang präsent: 'quia fecisti nos ad te'
(C I, 1,1; 2,2) steht gleich zu Beginn und der letzte Teil der Einführung
steht unter dem Thema 'refice...' (C I, 5,6).

III. *Die Schöpfung des Menschen—Eschatologie*

Anselm (Op. Om. I, 99,15-18)

> Et o 'tu, Domine, usquequo?
> Usquequo, Domine, oblivisceris nos,
> usquequo avertis faciem tuam a nobis' (Ps 6,4)?

---

18. *Meditationes* c.37 (*PL* 40, 935).

Quando 'respicies et exaudies' nos?
Quando 'illuminabis oculos' nostros et 'ostendes' nobis 'faciem tuam'?
Quando restitues te nobis? (Ps 79,4.8) [19]

Aber Anselm weiß auch, daß Hoffnung nicht mehr vom Menschen, sondern allein von Gott kommen kann. Es muß zur großen Wende durch Gott kommen. Gott selbst muß eingreifen, den Menschen erlösen und restituieren. Augustinus hatte den Sachverhalt mit einem 'dennoch' signalisiert. Wenn es bei Augustinus aber eine Beschreibung der notwendigen Umkehr ('conversio') gibt, dann sicher ist keine so eindrucksvoll wie die seiner eigenen Bekehrung im VIII. Buch der *Confessiones*. Augustinus hat die Hoffnung auf ein Eingreifen Gottes dort grandios komponiert und mit Aussagen wie folgenden gestaltet:

Augustinus (C VIII,12,28):

Ego sub quadam fici arbore stravi me nescio quomodo et dimisi habenas lacrimis... et non quidem his verbis, sed in hac sententia multa dixi: 'Et tu, domine, *usquequo*? *Usquequo*, domine, irasceris in finem? Ne memor fueris iniquitatum nostrarum antiquarum' (Ps 6,4; 78,5.8). Sentiebam enim eis me teneri. Iactabam voces miserabiles: '*Quamdiu, quamdiu*, cras et cras? Quare non modo? Quare non hac ora finis turpitudinis meae'...

Es ist mir nicht möglich, das Thema des III. Teils von P1 zu lesen, ohne an jenen berühmt gewordenen Bericht des Augustinus erinnert zu werden. Das dreifache 'usquequo' und 'quando' sind dafür zu auffällig. Die Klage ist zu ähnlich. Die Gestaltung der Szene bei Augustinus wie ihre Adaptation durch Anselm mit Zitaten der gleichen Ps 6,4 und Ps 78 bzw. 79,4-8 geben diesem Eindruck die größte Gewißheit.

IV. *Glauben und Erkennen*

Anselm (Op. Om. I, 100,15-19):

...Non tento, Domine, penetrare altitudinem tuam, quia nullatenus comparo illi intellectum meum; sed desidero aliquatenus *intelligere* veritatem tuam, quam *credit* et amat cor meum. Neque enim quaero *intelligere* ut *credam*, sed *credo* ut *intelligam*...

Am Schluß von P1 schlägt der 'Glaube' in den Wunsch nach 'Erkennen' um. Der Übergang vom einführenden Gebet zum philosophisch-theologischen Text des *Proslogion*s danach ist bekannt.

---

19. Eine Entsprechung findet sich in der *Confessio theologica* III 11 (*PL* 40, 934).

Nicht anders der Übergang bei *Augustinus* vom rühmenden Lob zu dem Anliegen, das ihn in den *Confessiones* über weite Strecken leitet: 'da mihi, domine, scire et intelligere...' (C I, 1,1).

4. *Die Gestalt von Proslogion 1—die Durchführung des Themas*

Nachdem ich das Thema von P1 im Rückblick auf die *Confessiones* des Augustinus betrachtet und daraus die Großstruktur des Gebetes gewonnen habe, möchte ich in einem weiteren Schritt auf die Entfaltung des Themas in P1 im einzelnen eingehen. Es ist des näheren die Form der Dialektik, die immer schon aufgefallen ist und die nun näher zu bestimmen ist.

Zur Erörterung der Gestalt des Textes bei Anselms ist aber ein weiterer Rückblick auf Augustinus nützlich. Augustinus hat die innere Dialektik des Menschen vor Gott in einer dreifachen Stufung formuliert und ihre Auflösung in einer ebenfalls dreifachen Stufung angedeutet (s. oben 'Ouverture'): Der Mensch ist nicht nur eine gebrochene Schöpfung oder ein Sterbewesen, sondern er hat seinen Zustand noch durch seine eigene Sünde und seinen Fall verschlimmert und er verharrt darüber hinaus seither in seinem sündigen Hochmut vor Gott (B, 1-3). Deshalb muß Gott selbst den Anfang machen, damit der Mensch Gott wieder loben kann; Gott hat den Anfang dadurch schon gemacht, daß er den Menschen zu sich hin geschaffen hat, und daß er den Menschen nicht los läßt, bis sein ruheloses Herz in Gott Ruhe findet (C, 1-3).

Es wird sich zeigen, daß Anselm in P1 diese programmatische Zustandsbeschreibung des Augustinus breit extemporiert, indem er auf ähnliche Weise die innere Dialektik christlichen Selbstbewußtseins entfaltet: Der Mensch ist noch nicht einmal dem nachgekommen, wozu er von Gott geschaffen worden ist; schlimmer, er ist durch den Sündenfall zu einem erbarmungswürdigen Wesen herabgesunken; sein Wesen ist nun so pervertiert, daß er nur durch Gott eine Erneuerung erhofft werden kann. Gott ist es also, der den Menschen wiederschaffen, erlösen und von Grund auf erneuern muß.

Mein folgender Vorschlag trägt dieser dialektischen Form in P1 Rechnung: Als Ergebnis davon will ich meinen bisherigen Vorschlag vervollständigen und erläutern, warum ich innerhalb der 4 Teile von P1, nachdem Anselm das Thema in der nun bekannten Form vorangestellt hat, jeweils einen Dreischritt A-B-C der Entwicklung des Themas erkenne.

(I) *Invocatio—das Thema*
Das Thema wird in I.–IV. jeweils in Dialogform, also in der direkten Anrede an Gott, vorgetragen. Um noch einmal das Thema des I. Teils zu nennen, so wird es von Anselm mit Ps 26,8 formuliert:

Anselm (Op. Om. I, 97,9-10):

> Quaero vultum tuum, vultum tuum, domine, requiro (Ps 26,8). Vgl. P18 (Op. Om. I, 114,9-10).

Augustinus: Für Augustinus ist dieses Thema nicht weniger zentral, was deutlich wird, wenn man erkennt, daß derselbe Psalm den ersten großen biographischen Teil der *Confessiones* rahmt: Am Ende des I. Buches heißt es: 'cor dicit tibi: "quaesivi vultum tuum; vultum tuum, domine, requiram": nam longe a vultu tuo in affectu tenebroso' (C I, 18,28). Am Anfang des letzten biographischen Buches: 'tibi dixit cor meum, quaesivi vultum tuum; vultum tuum, domine, requiram' (C IX, 3,6).

(A) *Suche nach Gott.* Der Wunsch des Beters richtet sich zunächst an Gott. Gott ist für den Beter der erste Ansprechpartner. Der Wunsch, Gott von Angesicht zu Angesicht zu sehen, bringt aber eine bezeichnende Dialektik hervor, die Anselm mit folgenden Worten beginnt:

Anselm (Op. Om. I, 98,1-3):

> Eia nunc ergo tu, Domine Deus meus, *doce* cor meum
> ubi et quomodo *quaerat*
> ubi et quomodo te *inveniat*.
> Domine, si hoc non es,
> ubi te quaeram absentem?
> Si autem ubique es,
> Cur non video praesentem?

Es ist ohne Zweifel richtig, was Paul Gilbert zu diesem Passus ausgeführt hat, daß Anselm die christliche Dialektik in die Worte von 'docere'—'quaerere'—'invenire' faßt. Es ist auch richtig, ihr Verständnis aus Anselms *Proslogion* zu entwickeln.[20] Aber der Ursprungsort dieser Grundverben und ihrer Dialektik dürften ohne Zweifel die *Confessiones* des Augustinus sein. Ein Blick auf den Anfang dort machen darauf aufmerksam: 'Et laudabunt dominum qui requirunt eum (Ps 21,27). Quaerentes enim invenient eum et invenientes laudabunt eum' (C I, 1,1). Diese Grundworte werden durch die gesamte Schrift

---

20. P. Gilbert, a.a.O. 38ff.

entfaltet bis hin zu dem dafür signifikanten Schluß, nämlich nun die ausdrückliche Zitation von Mt 7,7: 'A te petatur, in te quaeratur, ad te pulsetur: sic, sic accipitur, sic invenietur, sic aperietur'. Im übrigen hat Paul Gilbert die dialektische Situation von P1 sehr gut beschrieben, so daß ich mich voll und ganz seiner Beschreibung anschließen kann.

(B) *Gott—unzugängliches Licht.* Anselm stellt seinem Suchen den Einwand entgegen: '*Sed* certe habitas *lucem inaccessibilem...*' (1 Tim 6,16).

Dem starken Wunsch nach dem Angesicht Gottes tritt als Antipode— ein 'sed' kennzeichnet den Wandel der Perspektive—der Mensch entgegen: 'Aber' wie soll das geschehen, da Du doch in 'unzugänglichem Licht' wohnst. Damit ist die ganze dialektische Situation des Anfangs offengelegt: Der Mensch hat den ehrenwerten Wunsch, Gott zu finden; das erscheint aber völlig unmöglich, wenn Gott grundsätzlich unzugänglich ist.

Die bei Anselm hervortretende Dialektik entspricht prägnant jener der ekstatischen Versuche des Augustinus im VII. Buch der *Confessiones* und schließlich der diese vollendenen *Vision von Ostia.* Das Motiv des 'unzugänglichen Lichtes' ist dort zentrales Thema. Etwa:

Augustinus (C VII, 10,16):

> Intravi et vidi qualicumque oculo animae meae supra eundem oculum animae meae, supra mentem meam *lucem inconmutabilem,* non hanc vulgarem et conspicuam omni carne nec quasi ex eodem genere grandior erat, tamquam si ista multo multoque clarius claresceret totumque occuparet magnitudine. Non hoc illa erat, sed aliud, aliud valde ab istis omnibus.[21]

(C) *Die Aporie des Anfangs.* Die aporetische Situation des Menschen vor Gott ist somit fürs erste offengelegt. Anselm faßt sie in antithetischen oder dialektischen Aussagen zum Schluß dieses Teils noch einmal zusammen. Es sei nur darauf hingewiesen, daß dabei wiederum die Grundverben von 'quaerere' und 'invenire' eine dominierende Rolle spielen. Es sei auch schon vorweggenommen, daß dieselben Grundverben jeweils die beiden übrigen Schlüsse—also wie I.C. auch II.C. und III.C.—prägen werden:

---

21. Cfr. Johannes de Fécamp, *Meditationes* c.29 (*PL* 40, 922), *Manuale* c.1 (*PL* 40, 952), *Speculum* c.6 (*PL* 40, 971s) u.a.

Anselm (Op. Om. I, 98,9-13):

> Anhelat videre te—et nimis abest illi facies tua.
> Accedere ad te desiderat—et inaccessibilis est
> habitatio tua.
> *Invenire* te cupit—et nescit *locum tuum.*
> *Quaerere* te affectat—et ignorat vultum tuum.
> Domine, Deus meus es et Dominus meus es—
> et numquam te vidi.

Die aporetische Situation dieser Beschreibung erinnert wiederum an den Anfang der *Confessiones*, wo Augustinus die anfängliche 'Ort'-losigkeit des Menschen auf ähnliche Weise artikuliert. Die folgende Aussage am Anfang der *Confessiones* ist programmatisch zu verstehen, da die festgestellte 'Ort'-losigkeit die Dialektik bei Augustinus im folgenden weitertreibt.

Augustinus (C I, 2,2):

> Et quomodo invocabo deum meum, deum et dominum meum, quoniam utique in me ipsum eum vocabo, cum invocabo eum? Et quis *locus* in me, quo veniat in me deus meus? Quo deus veniat in me, deus, qui 'fecit caelum et terram'?

(II) *Das Schöpfungsthema*

Das Thema des II. Teils sei auch nur noch einmal wiedergegeben. Es ist das Thema der Schöpfung. Auch dieses Thema wird in direkter Anrede an Gott vorgetragen:

Anselm:

> Tu me fecisti et refecisti
> et omnia bona tu mihi contulisti—
> et nondum novi te.
> Denique ad te videndum factus sum—
> et nondum feci, propter quod factus sum.

(A) *Der Fall der Menschheit. Anselm* wird sogleich des Sündenfalls bewußt: 'O misera *sors hominis*, cum hoc perdidit, ad quod factus est...' (Op. Om. I, 98,16).

Die aporetische Situation des Menschen vor Gott ist bereits dargelegt. Sie wird aber noch einmal schlimmer durch die Erkenntnis der Sünde und des Falls Adams und in ihm aller Menschen. Der Einschnitt in die Geschichte des Verhältnisses von Gott und Mensche ist dabei verheerend. Paul Gilbert hat auf eine stilistische Feinheit hingewiesen: Der Dialog ist im folgenden unterbrochen. Der Mensch stellt sich reflekierend die Unheilssituation vor Augen. Gott wird nicht direkt angesprochen; er wird in der dritten Person genannt. Der Dialog mit Gott ist in diesem Zustand nicht möglich.

Augustinus hat die gleiche Situation nicht nur in seiner Ouverture bereits unüberhorbar angekündigt (C I, 1,1). Ab *Confessiones* I, 5,5f hat er sie eigens thematisiert und zum Gegenstand der Klage über die Lage der Menschheit gemacht. Gegenstand der Klage ist der Mensch, der an dem Unheil schuld hat.[22]

(B) *Unser Unheil. Anselm* richtet sich mit seiner Klage an Gott: 'Cur non *nobis* custodivit...—a patria in exilium...' (Op. Om. I, 98,25–99,7).

Wie ist aus der Situation des Unheils herauszufinden? Anselm antwortet wiederum mit einem Perspektivenwechsel. Stand das Unheil, das durch den Menschen kam, bisher im Vordergrund, so wendet sich der Blick nun Gott zu: Warum hat Gott das an uns Menschen geschehen lassen? Wie gesagt wird von Gott in der dritten Person gesprochen.

Bei *Augustinus* und bei Johannes de Fécamp finden sich eine Reihe von entsprechenden Aussagen über den Zustand des 'exiliums', dem Ort der Ferne von der 'patria'.[23]

(C) *Die Aporie der Unheilssituation. Anselm.* Wiederum faßt Anselm die größer gewordene Unheilssituation in antithetischen bzw. dialektischen Aussagen zusammen (Op. Om. I, 99,9-14):

> Quaesivi bona—et ecce turbatio...
> rugire a gemitu cordis mei (Ps 37,9)...

Bei Augustinus ist das Motiv der 'turbatio' im Anschluß an die Klage Hiobs ein wiederholtes Motiv. Ebenso ist der Ps 37,9 vertreten.[24] Bei Johannes de Fécamp findet sich in den *Meditationes* genau die entsprechende Formulierung: '*Quaesivi bona, et ecce turbatio...*'[25]

---

22. Zu diesem Teil von P1 cfr. die schöne Entsprechung in den *Meditationes* c.39 des Johannes de Fécamp (*PL* 40, 937).

23. Cfr. C VII, 21,27 und *Manuale* c.4 (*PL* 40, 953-54).

24. C VII,7,11; X,37,60.

25. *Meditationes* c.39 (*PL* 40, 937).

(III) *Das Thema der Eschatologie*
Eines ist Anselm ebenso wie Augustinus klar: die Unheilssituation kann nur durch Gott behoben werden. Deshalb der heiße Wunsch und die sehnliche Erwartung: Wann wird Gott selbst eingreifen? Der Beter kehrt zur direkten Anrede an Gott zurück. Das Thema ist die Bitte um ein baldiges Eingreifen Gottes.

Anselm hatte die Bitte mit einem dreifachen 'usquequo' und 'quando' (Ps 12,1 bzw. 4) eindringlich vorgetragen. Er hatte damit an die 'Bekehrung' des Augustinus erinnert (s. oben).

(A) *Das Heil kommt nur von Gott. Anselm* fordert Gott auf (Op. Om. I, 99,18-21):

> Respice, domine, exaudi, illumina nos, ostende nobis teipsum...
> Restitue...
> Miserare...

Weil alles Heil nun von Gott abhängt, deshalb ist es hier wiederum Gott, der zuerst bittend angesprochen wird. Mit Gott ist neu anzufangen; Gott selbst muß einen neuen Anfang machen. Erstaunlich dabei ist, daß der Beter nach dem Bewußtsein des Verlustes des Dialoges durch die Schuld des Menschen wieder zur direkten Ansprache Gottes zurückkehren kann. Paul Gilbert hat wiederum auf die stilistische Feinheit aufmerksam gemacht: Anselm vermag dies, weil er nun mit den Worten des Psalmisten spricht. Das Wort der Schrift, das Gott den Menschen gegeben hat, befähigt nun auch den sündigen Menschen, sich direkt an Gott zu richten. Die folgenden Aussagen sind alle verschiedenen Psalmen entnommen.

(B) *Inständiges Gebet um Erlösung. Anselm* Gebet wird beschwörend (Op. Om. I, 99,21–100,8):

> Obsecro, domine—obsecro—obsecro...

Der Mensch aber kann nur eines tun, Gott inständig um sein Kommen und Eingreifen zu bitten. Der entsprechende Gestus ist deshalb nun die des inständigen Beters, der sich nun in beschwörender Weise an Gott um Hilfe wendet.

(C) *Die Aporie bleibt. Anselm* (Op. Om. I, 100,8-12):

> *Doce* me quaerere te et
> ostende te quaerenti; quia

nec *quaerere* te possum, nisi tu doceas,
nec *invenire*, nisi te ostendas.
Quaeram te desiderando, desiderem quaerendo
Inveniam amando, amem inveniendo.

Anselm schließt sein Gebet mit der nun ausdrücklichen Bitte, daß nichts
hilft und nichts bleibt, wenn Gott nicht seinen Beistand gibt. Die dialektische Situation ist zu Ende geführt. Die abschließenden Aussagen bilden
im Grunde eine Inklusion mit dem Anfang II.A. Die Grundverben von
'docere'—'quaerere'—'invenire' kommen wieder. Nun ist die Aussage
aber ganz dialektisch im augustinischen Stil formuliert; ohne Zweifel
könnte sie so auch in den *Confessiones* stehen.

(IV) *Aporie des Glaubens—Aporie des Erkennens*
Augustinus hat im Anschluß an seine Ouverture um 'Erkenntnis'
gebeten: 'da mihi, domine, scire et intelligere...' (C I, 1,1).
    Anselm tut desgleichen (Op. Om. I, 100,12-19):

> Fateor, Domine, et gratias ago, quia creasti in me hanc '*imaginem tuam*'
> (Gen 1,17), ut tui memor te cogitem, te amem.
> Sed sic est abolita attritione vitiorum,
> sic offuscata fumo peccatorum,
> ut non possit facere, ad quod facta est, nisi tu renoves et reformes eam.
> Non tento, Domine, penetrare altitudinem tuam, quia nullatenus comparo
> illi intellectum meum; sed desidero aliquatenus intelligere veritatem tuam,
> quam credit et amat cor meum. Neque enim quaero intelligere ut credam,
> sed credo ut intelligam. Nam et hoc credo: quia '*nisi credidero, non
> intelligam*' (Is 7,9).

Zum Schluß besinnt sich Anselm auf den Menschen als 'Bild' Gottes.
Das Motiv der 'imago' und 'similitudo' ist in den *Confessiones* des
Augustinus ohne Zweifel eines der bedeutsamsten, das ihn aufgrund der
Predigten des Ambrosius zum christlichen Glauben geführt hat (C VI
und VII) und in den letzten Büchern immer eindringlicher vorgetragen
wird.[26]
    Die Formulierung der Triade 'ut tui memor te cogitem, te amem' ist
nun ganz augustinisch und könnte ebenso im XIII. Buch der
Confessiones stehen.

---

26. Cfr. Johannes de Fécamp 'imago' in *Meditationes* c.39 (*PL* 40, 936) und
Manuale c.18 (*PL* 40, 969).

Auf das Verhältnis von 'credere'—'intelligere' und auf den Topos von Is 7,9 bei Augustinus ist immer schon hingewiesen worden. Anselm bewegt sich hier ganz auf den Spuren seines Vorbildes.[27]

5. Anselm—Johannes de Fécamp—Augustinus

Im vorhergehenden hat sich eine Fülle von Bezugspunkten des *Proslogion*-Gebetes P1 zu den *Confessiones* des Augustinus und den verschiedenen Schriften des Johannes de Fécamp ergeben. Dabei wurde auf die Entsprechungen und Ähnlichkeiten geachtet. Die Unterschiede kamen dabei weniger zur Sprache. Doch ist zum Schluß festzuhalten, daß Form und Gestalt von P1 selbstverständlich in der unverwechselbaren Art des Anselm von Canterbury nirgendwo anders anzutreffen sind. Es kann zusammengefaßt werden, daß die materialen Entsprechungen groß sind, aber die systematische Form und die gedankliche Konsequenz von P1 ganz und gar die Leistung des Abtes und Bischofs von Canterbury darstellen.

27. Cfr. bei Johannes de Fécamp etwa *Confessio theologica* 13; *Meditationes* c.29 (*PL* 40, 922); *Confessio fidei* c.16 (*PL* 101, 1038).

AUGUSTINE'S INFLUENCE ON ANSELM'S *PROSLOGION*

Frederick Van Fleteren

The first systematic demonstration of God's existence from reason in the annals of recorded Christian thought occurs in Augustine's *De libero arbitrio* II.[1] But that is not to say that Augustine's reasoning is not anticipated in Hellenic and Hellenistic thought. In *Physics* VIII, for example, Aristotle demonstrates the existence of an unmoved and primary mover, a demonstration of which Augustine was no doubt unaware. Plato mentions the Good several times in *Republic* VI,[2] and in *Republic* VII[3] describes a programme of the liberal arts by which the human mind might attain this Good. In *Symposium*,[4] in the section where Socrates speaks with the priestess Diotima, we find an ascent of the mind to Beauty itself. Several interpretations of the One occur in *Parmenides*, not to mention various commentaries upon it. In *Timaeus*, Plato establishes the existence of a Demiurge, a Craftsman, God in his primary causative function. Certainly, in *Enneads* I.6, *Peri Kalou*, Plotinus attempts to reach the divine, and most of the sixth *Ennead* is an attempt to describe the ineffable. Porphyry's *De regressu animae*, which so influenced Augustine, is not longer extant, but from surviving fragments in Augustine and elsewhere we may surmise that it contained an ascent of the mind to God by means of study of the liberal arts. These well-known passages in the Platonic tradition, however, are not attempts to demonstrate God's existence, no matter what they may name that highest being. Rather, Aristotle aside, each of these philosophers assumes as evident the existence of a highest good or supreme one, and then gives a method by which the human mind might ascend to it, or attain union with it.

1. *De libero arbitrio* II.iii.xv.39.
2. *Republic* VI.505a-c, 507b, 508e, 509b.
3. *Republic* VII.514a-534c.
4. *Symposium* 201d-212a.

Although such theses as a hierarchy of being, the existence of eternal truth, and the supremacy of the human mind over animal sensation are commonly debated, and not infrequently asserted, before the time of Augustine, he is the first thinker in recorded intellectual history to attempt a demonstration of God's existence from these premises. It is therefore not surprising that, when some seven centuries later Anselm attempts to demonstrate God's existence in *Monologion*, and later in *Proslogion*, we apparently find him using Augustine's writings as a model. Although there are many Augustinian passages in which the ascent of the soul to the divine dominate,[5] only a few represent actual attempts at a demonstration of God's existence. *De trinitate* VIII.ii.3-4 is one such passage, an argument from the goodness of inferior reality to a highest good. Even here, however, an ascent motif is not completely lacking. The mystical implications of *Confessiones* VII.x.16 and xvii.23 have been acknowledged by a majority of Christian interpreters throughout history, though a minority still takes these passages to be a mere rational demonstration. *De libero arbitrio* II.iii.7-xv.9 is universally understood as a rational demonstration of God's existence. The similarity between Augustine's ascents of mind to God and his rational demonstrations of God's existence is readily apparent.

In the *Prooemium* to *Proslogion*, Anselm tells us that he himself happened upon this one argument (which in his opinion clearly demonstrated the existence of God) only after long periods of thought, and perhaps even despair. The conditions under which Anselm came upon this argument and its clear originality should not lead us to conclude, however, that antecedents in Augustine's writings do not exist. On the contrary, and with some degree of probability, literary and thematic antecedents from various works of Augustine can be shown to exist. Indeed, in Anselm's other work which is devoted to the existence of God and his attributes, *Monologion*, some passages can be interpreted as précis of arguments found in considerably more detail in Augustine's *De trinitate* and other passages could be construed as supplying demonstrations for statements made in passing in *De trinitate*.[6]

---

5.   For a complete discussion of the ascent motif in the writings of Augustine, see *Augustine: Mystic and Mystagogue* (Collectanea Augustiniana; ed. F. Van Fleteren and J. Schnaubelt; New York: Peter Lang, 1994).

6.   F. Van Fleteren, 'The *Monologion* of Anselm and Augustine's *De trinitate*' (paper delivered at the Colloque international du CNRS in Paris in 1990, to be

A fuller investigation of Anselm's *Proslogion* and its sources in Augustine is therefore in order.

To be sure, this is not a completely new study. For example, Professor Klaus Kienzler explicated his understanding of the relationship between Anselm's *Proslogion* and various of Augustine's writings.[7] In particular, Professor Kienzler has noted a similarity of atmosphere in some of Augustine's works, especially *Confessiones*, and Anselm's *Proslogion* with particular reference to a *christliche Dialogik* occurring in both. Inevitably, Anselm's extensive familiarity with the works of Augustine often makes an ascription to any one Augustinian source virtually impossible. Nevertheless, Professor Kienzler's opinions are valuable in searching for Augustinian influences on *Proslogion*. Moreover, one of the more disastrous fault-lines introduced into western thought, whether in the late Middle Ages or in the scholastic revival of the nineteenth and twentieth centuries, is the separation of prayer and spirituality from theology. No such separation exists in either Augustine or Anselm. We owe a debt of gratitude to Professor Kienzler when he emphasizes the dialogue nature of both *Confessiones* and *Proslogion*.

Prooemium

In the *Prooemium* to *Proslogion*, written some time after the work itself, Anselm outlines his intentions:

> I began to seek within myself if perhaps one argument could be found which was in need of no other than itself to be probative and alone would suffice to furnish a proof that God truly exists, that he is the highest good in need of no other, and how all things need him to exist and be happy, and whatever else we believe concerning the divine substance.[8]

Anselm sketches a fourfold purpose for his argument: to construct an argument, in need of no other and alone by itself sufficient to prove that (1) God truly exists; (2) he is the highest good in need of no other; (3) all other things owe (a) their existence and (b) their happiness to him; and (4) whatever else we believe concerning the divine substance. The

published as part of the *Anselm Studies* series with the title, *Saint Anselme, Penseur d'hier et d'aujourd'hui*).

7.   K. Kienzler, 'Zur philosophisch-theologischen Denkform bei Augustinus und bei Anselm von Canterbury', *Anselm Studies*, 2 (ed. J. Schnaubelt, F. Van Fleteren *et al.*; New York: Kraus International Publications, 1988), pp. 353-87.

8.   *Proslogion, Prooemium* (Schmitt, I, p. 93).

attempt to show that God truly exists occurs in *Proslogion* II-IV. Creation is treated very much in passing in *Proslogion* V. Human happiness through the highest good is treated in *Proslogion* XXV-XXVI. God being the highest good in need of no other good is treated in *Proslogion* XXIII-XXIV. Finally, a demonstration of the existence of various divine attributes is found in *Proslogion* VI-XIII, XV-XXII.

Elsewhere in the *Prooemium*, Anselm summarizes the purpose of *Proslogion* in a different, though not inconsistent, manner:

> Thinking therefore that my joy in having found this would be pleasing to some reader if I were to write it down, I wrote the appended small work concerning this argument itself and some other matters under the person of (1) one attempting to raise his own mind to contemplating God and of (2) one seeking to understand what he believes.[9]

The purpose of the first four chapters is well described as an attempt to raise the mind to God, the last twenty-one as an *intellectus fidei*. Both are purposes which are Augustinian to the core.

Several parallels between the *Prooemium* of *Proslogion* and the works of Augustine should be mentioned. How many passages of Augustine's writings could be described as an ascent of the mind to God? The title, *Fides quaerens intellectum*, is fundamentally Augustinian.[10] The Augustinian basis for rendering *Monologion* as 'Soliloquium' and *Proslogion* as 'Alloquium' is apparent. The phrase 'vere esse' had achieved technical status—perhaps the phrase 'bene esse' had also by the time of Anselm—undoubtedly because of its extensive technical use by Augustine.[11] More important perhaps is the designation of God as the 'summum bonum nullo alio indigens et quo omnia indigent ut sint et ut bene sint'. The phrase 'nullum bonum indigens' is used by Augustine to describe God.[12] Ps. 15.2 'Deus meus es tu, quoniam bonorum meorum non eges' is cited or referred to not

---

9. *Proslogion, Prooemium* (Schmitt I, pp. 93-94).
10. *Proslogion, Prooemium*; see, for example, *De trinitate* IX.i.1.
11. The phrase 'vere esse' and its cognates, for example 'vere est', are used literally hundreds of times in the writings of Augustine to signify divine existence. The phrase 'bene esse', which I have translated 'to be happy', does not occur often in Augustine. He uses the term 'beata' and its cognates to express terminal happiness.
12. See, for example, *Confessiones* XIII.xxxviii.53; *De genesi ad litteram* IV.xvi.27; *Enarratio in Psalmum LXV* 19; *Enarratio in Psalmum LXX, Sermo II*, 6; *Enarratio in Psalmum CXXXIV* 4.

infrequently in Augustine's works.[13] God as the source of being and happiness for humankind is, of course, an Augustinian constant from *De beata vita* onward. Anselm's entire project is—we can see—of Augustinian origin.

Invocatio

Anselm invokes divine help for his theological enterprise in *Proslogion* I. In this endeavour, he is influenced by Christian antiquity's most famous of invocations, *Confessiones* I.i.1-v.6. Professor Kienzler has pointed out the similarity of atmosphere between the invocation to *Confessiones* and *Proslogion* I.[14] 'Similarity of atmosphere', however, is not the only affinity of these two passages; specific thematic and philological similarities exist between Anselm's text and Augustine's writings. The movement from the exterior, in Anselm's case from occupations and cares, to the interior is a common Augustinian theme,[15] derived from Neoplatonism, and more particularly *Enneads* I.6. Ps. 26.8 ('faciem tuam, Domine, requiram') occurs in the *Confessiones* and elsewhere,[16] though not precisely in the invocation. The importance to Anselm of Augustine's justly famous passage concerning his restless heart at the beginning of *Confessiones* can not be overemphasized. Anselm's use of 'cor' is fundamentally Augustinian, in turn biblically inspired. In Hebrew thought, the heart is the seat of intelligence. Therefore, Anselm's allusion to the heart at the beginning of a work devoted to a rational demonstration of God's existence and attributes is not as strange as it may sound to some contemporary ears. The reference to 'rest' is parallel to *Confessiones* I.i.1, and finds its ultimate source in the West in the categories of Plato's *Sophist*.[17]

---

13. See, for example, *Confessiones* VII.xi.17; *Epistula CII* 17; *Epistula CXXXVIII* 1,7; *De doctrina christiana* I.xxxi.34; *De civitate dei* X.5; XIX.23; *De patientia* XV.12; *Sermo CCCXXXI* 3; *Enarratio in Psalmum XXXIV* 19; *Enarratio in Psalmum XV* 7; *Enarratio in Psalmum XLIX* 19; *Enarratio in Psalmum LXVIII* 7; *In Epistulam Ioannis ad Parthos* VIII.14; *Tractatus in evangelium Iohannis* XI.5; *De genesi ad litteram* VIII.xi.24.

14. See Kienzler, 'Zur philosophisch-theologischen Denkform', pp. 358 ff.

15. See, among many other places, *Confessiones* VII.x.16; xvii.23; *De vera religione* 45.

16. See, *inter alia*, *Confessiones* I.xviii.28; IX.iii.6; *Enarratio in Psalmum XXVI* I.8; II.15; *Sermo LIII* VII.7.

17. *Sophist* 249c ff.

The presence and absence of God, a theme underlying the invocation of both *Proslogion* and *Confessiones*, is found throughout the entire Augustinian corpus.[18] At its core, Augustine's struggle towards conversion centred on his inability to conceive spiritual existence and the notions of presence so intimately connected with it. His encounter with the Platonist books effected his intellectual conversion. This encounter gave Augustine, *inter alia*, an understanding of spiritual existence and omnipresence. That God is 'ubique totus' and yet humankind does not see him, that God is present, but humankind is absent, is a theme found in *Confessiones* and throughout Augustine's works. (The source for Augustine's views on spiritual existence is disputed, Porphyry being the most likely.)

The reference to God as light is among the earliest in Augustine's corpus. In the philosophical West, the reference goes back at least as far as *Republic* VI and VII. It is found also in Ps. 26.1 ('Dominus illuminatio mea et salus mea: quem timebo'). That God dwells in inaccessible light ('qui solus immortalitatem et lucem inaccessibilem; quem nullus ominum vidit, sed nec videre potest', 1 Tim. 6.16) is found several times in Augustine's writings, though not in *Confessiones* itself.[19] The majority of Augustine's references to God as dwelling in inaccessible light stem from his later writings when Augustine was less sanguine about humanity's ability to understand the Godhead.

That humanity is destined for the vision of God of course runs through the whole of Augustine's writings from *De beata vita* through to *De civitate dei* with important stops in *De trinitate* and *Epistulae CXLVII–CXLVIII*. That the vast majority of human beings has not yet achieved this status is apparent to Augustine.[20] From the beginning of his works, Augustine presented a programme by which humanity can

18. The phrase 'totus ubique', as describing God, appears often in the Augustine corpus, for example, *Confessiones* I.iii.3; III.vii.12; VI.iii.4; *De moribus ecclesiae catholicae* XI.19; *Epistula CXVIII* IV.23; *Epistula CXX* III.16; *Epistula CXL* III.6; *Epistula CXLVIII* I.1; V.17; *Epistula CLV* IV.13; *Epistula CLXII* 9.

19. *Epistula XCII* 3; *Epistula CXLVII* XV.37; XVI.39; XVII.44; XIX.46; *De genesi ad litteram* VIII.xix.38; *Enarratio in Psalmum VI* VI.8; *Enarratio in Psalmum CXVIII, Sermo VI* 2; *Sermo LXV* III.4; *Contra Adimantum* 10; *Contra Faustum* XX.2; XX.7; XXII.9, 21; *De trinitate* I.vi.9; II; II, *prooemium*; viii.14; ix.15; *Contra Maximum* II.xii.2.

20. See F. Van Fleteren, 'Augustine and the Possibility of the Vision of God in this Life', *Studies in Medieval Culture*, 11, p. 91.

attain this vision, for a few even in this life.[21] Augustine eventually abandoned such a programme for terminal vision and found that, except for
a very few who possessed a direct, but temporary, divine vision through
the grace of God, humankind could see God only 'per speculum et in
aenigmate' in this life.[22] Although God's help played a role in this ascent
from the very beginning, Augustine progresses to the view, finalized in
396, that only through the grace of God is direct vision possible.[23] In
both Augustine and Anselm, vision and full knowledge of God and other
matters are equated; humankind does not yet see God, nor do we have
adequate understanding of theological matters. 'Tuus longinquus exsul'
is a reference to the prodigal son, a parable cited often in *Confessiones*.[24]
Likewise, the term 'proiectus', taken possibly from Ps. 50.13, is not
infrequently found in the Augustinian corpus.[25]

In the invocation, Anselm now turns to humankind's unhappy lot in
this life: human beings have lost that for which they were created and
destined—the vision of God. The theme of fall and return of humanity,
common throughout the ancient world, is found often in Augustine's
writings; its precise meaning, and its sources, have been the linchpin of
much commentary over the past thirty years.[26] Human *miseria*, especially as it contrasts with divine *misericordia*, constitutes perhaps the
fundamental theme of *Confessiones*. The phrase 'filius Adae' is found
several times in the works of Augustine, specifically three times in

21. See *De ordine* II.ix.26-xix.51; *Retractationes* I.6, 9.

22. See n. 20 and F. Van Fleteren, '*Per speculum et in aenigmate*: 1 Corinthians
13:12 in the Writings of St. Augustine', *Augustinian Studies* (1992), pp. 69-102.

23. For a full discussion of Augustine's mysticism, see Van Fleteren and
Schnaubelt (eds.), *Augustine: Mystic and Mystagogue*.

24. See *Confessiones* I.18; IV.16; XII.11.

25. See, for example, *Adnotationes in Iob* 9; *Quaestiones evangeliorum* II,
quaestiones 33, 45, 51; *Enarratio in Psalmum CXVIII, Sermo V* 2; *Sermo VIII* 2;
Enarratio in Psalmum CXIX 6; *Enarratio in Psalmum CXXIII* 9; *Enarratio in
Psalmum CXXXI* 12; *Enarratio in Psalmum CXXXVIII* 5, 6, 9, 10; *Retractationes*
I.8.

26. Most of this discussion has taken place with R. O'Connell. His views on the
subject appear in several volumes: *St Augustine's Early Theory of Man* (Cambridge,
MA: Belknap Press, 1968); *Confessions: The Odyssey of Soul* (Cambridge,
MA: Belknap Press, 1968); *The Fall of the Soul in the Later Works of St Augustine*
(New York: Fordham University Press, 1987). G. Madec has thoroughly reviewed
O'Connell's works in the various volumes of the *Revue des Etudes Augustiniennes*.
The most recent continuation of the controversy appeared in *Augustinian Studies*
1 (1990).

Confessiones.[27] The phrase 'filius Evae' is found only once in the entire Augustinian corpus, and that in *Confessiones.*[28] The phrase 'panis angelorum', found in Ps. 77.25 ('Panem angelorum manducavit homo; cibaria misit eis in abundantia') is also encountered several times in Augustine.[29] The description of humanity's lot as 'tribulationem et dolorem', is biblical ('Circumdederunt me dolores mortis; et pericula inferni invenerunt me. Tribulationem et dolorem inveni', Ps. 114.3; see also Ps. 106.39) and likewise appears in Augustine's writings.[30] Finally, that humanity was made in God's image, an image residing principally in the human intellect, Augustine received from Ambrose; its use is detected in the earliest of Augustine's writings. That this image allows humans to remember God is certainly a theme of *Confessiones* and many other writings, not the least important of which is *De trinitate.*

Proslogion II-IV

Putting aside the very notion of a demonstration of the existence of a deity (which was treated above), several other similarities between Augustine's demonstration and Anselm's remain. They make it apparent that Augustine directly influenced Anselm. The first similarity is the citation of Isa. 7.9 as scriptural basis for an *intellectus fidei*. Augustine cites it as: 'Nisi credideritis, non intellegetis', Anselm as: 'Nisi credidero, non intelligam', both translations reflecting the Septuagint version. A translation of the Hebrew, however, reads, 'Unless you believe, you shall not remain', a translation reflected in Jerome's Vulgate. Augustine is aware of the two translations and uses them as an example of the fruitfulness of various translations of the Bible.[31] Together with several other

27. See *Confessiones* I.ix.14; VIII.ix.21; XIII.xxi.30.
28. *Confessiones* I.xvi.25.
29. *De libero arbitrio* III.x.30; *Tractatus in Ioannis evangelium* XIII.4; *In epistolam Iohannis ad Parthos* I.1; *Enarratio in Psalmum XXXIII, Sermo I* 6; *Enarratio in Psalmum LXXVII* 17; *Enarratio in Psalmum CIX* 12; *Enarratio in Psalmum CXXX* 9; *Enarratio in Psalmum CXXXIV* 5; *Enarratio in Psalmum CXLIII* 10; *Sermo CXXVI* V.6; *Sermo CXXX* 2; *Sermo CXCIV* II.2; *Sermo CXCVI* III.3; *Sermo CCXXV* II.3; *De utilitate ieiunii* I.1.
30. Ps. 114.3; See *Expositio quarumdam propositionum ex Epistula ad Romanos* 46; *Enarratio in Psalmum XLV* 4; *Enarratio in Psalmum XLIX* 22; *Enarratio in Psalmum L* 4; *Enarratio in Psalmum LXXXII* 5; *Enarratio in Psalmum CXIV* 4; *Enarratio in Psalmum CXXXVI* 5; *Enarratio in Psalmum CXXXVII* 12; *Sermo CXII.*
31. *De doctrina christiana* II.12.

Church Fathers, the bishop of Hippo uses this verse as the biblical locus upon which to found the theological enterprise. More importantly, from this biblical passage both Augustine and Anselm assert the temporal priority of belief over understanding. Belief is an indispensable precondition to demonstration: the very purpose of reasoning is to support what we know from faith. That the purpose of Christian philosophy is to provide a rational basis for what we believe in faith is an Augustinian (and Anselmian) *donnée* to the western world.

A second parallel in this section between Augustine and Anselm lies in the citation of Ps. 13.1 or Ps. 52.1. Both Augustine in *De libero arbitrio* and Anselm in *Proslogion* cite the verse as follows: 'Dixit insipiens in corde suo: non est deus'. Augustine and Anselm use the verse differently. Augustine sees the 'insipiens' as one who might want to pursue the notion of demonstrating God's existence, in which the other believes. Anselm, on the other hand, uses the scriptural verse to show that no one can be ignorant of the signification of the word 'God'. Augustine cites this verse infrequently. *De libero arbitrio* II is the only place in the entire Augustinian corpus where the verse is cited with 'insipiens'; in all other places, the words 'imprudens' or 'stultus' are used. The Vulgate uses 'insipiens', which stems from 'insapiens'. The relation of the Latin *sapientia* and *prudentia* as translations of the Greek *phronesis* (practical wisdom) lies, of course, in the background here. Thus, the use of 'insipiens' by both is another indication that Anselm had read Augustine's demonstration of the existence of God before writing the first chapters of *Proslogion*.

A third parallel between Augustine and Anselm is the definition of God. Anselm's justly famous definition reads as follows: 'te esse aliquid quo nihil maius cogitari possit'. A similar definition of God occurs in Seneca (*Quaestiones naturales* I.i, *Praefatio*). In Augustine's works, similar phrases occur in *De libero arbitrio* II.vi.14, *De doctrina christiana* I.vii.7, *De moribus ecclesiae catholicae et de moribus manichaeorum* II.xi.24, and *De diversis quaestionibus LXXXIII* 18. The closest parallels to this definiton appear in *De moribus* and *De doctrina christiana*. Du Roy is certainly correct in saying that Augustine has introduced a conception of God in which Anselm participates.[32]

A fourth similarity between the *De libero arbitrio* and Anselm's *Proslogion* has to do with the justification of the theological enterprise

---

32. O. du Roy, *L'Intelligence en la foi en la trinité selon saint Augustin* (Paris: Etudes Augustiniennes, 1966), p. 214 n. 3.

by the use of Mt. 7.7 ('Quaerite et invenieritis'). This verse is widely used by Augustine and other authors, for example Tertullian, to justify their search for an *intellectus fidei*.

None of these parallels, each taken in itself, indicates that Anselm had read Augustine's *De libero arbitrio*. But taken together, in the light of the clear originality in Christian antiquity of Augustine's attempting to demonstrate God's existence, these parallels should persuade us of the likelihood that Anselm had read *De libero arbitrio* before writing *Proslogion*.

Proslogion V-XXII

Proslogion V-XXII comprises the fourth part of Anselm's work. Chapters V-XIV are an excursus on the apparently paradoxical nature of some of the divine attributes, chapters XV-XXII on the incomprehensibility of some divine attributes to the human mind. Taken together, these chapters constitute Anselm's attempt to fulfil his intention of demonstrating what he believes concerning the divine nature. Chapter V and the beginning of chapter VI of *Proslogion* provide a transition from the demonstration of God's existence to problems of knowing the perfections of the divine nature. In traditional terminology, Anselm moves from the question that God is to the question what God is. Since God is 'quod maius non potest cogitari', he must have all perfections, that is, whatever is better to be than not to be.

Proslogion VI-XIII as a whole treats themes and questions found often in the Augustinian corpus. The sixth question (*Proslogion* XIV) in which Anselm ponders the possibility of human vision of God in this life presents us with a preponderance of Augustinian themes. Anselm refers to 1 Jn 3.2: 'When he appears, we shall see him as he is'. In this life, however, we do not see God as he is; we do not see him directly. This verse is key for Augustine on the subject of humankind's inability to see God in this life. The latter uses this verse, together with 1 Cor. 13.12, as the scriptural basis for excluding complete human knowledge of God in this life.[33] The analogy between divine intelligible light and the human intellect on the one hand, and the sun and the senses on the other, a comparison found also in *Proslogion* XIV,[34] has been a philosophical

---

33. For a list of passages in the writings of St Augustine where 1 Cor. 13.12 appears, see Van Fleteren, *'Per Speculum et in Aenigmate'*.

34. *Proslogion* XIV, XVI.

commonplace since the time of *Republic* VI-VII. This analogy serves as the very basis for Augustine's discussions of his own mystical experiences in Milan. The language, theme and motif of *Proslogion* is reminiscent of *Confessiones* VII. We do not see God in all his splendour; the human mind sees only darkness. The mind's eye is infirm and therefore shaken by God's brightness. Nevertheless, the human mind sees whatever it does see through this divine inaccessible light. Whether Anselm holds Augustinian illumination theory in all its particulars may at present be moot. Resonances of that theory are apparent here. An explicit comparison to the human eye, found in several places in Augustine,[35] is drawn. The ultimate source of this analogy lies, of course, in *Republic* VII. Anselm uses the word 'reverberare' to describe the inability of the human mind to see God. 'Reverberare' and its cognates appear seventeen times in the Augustinian corpus, usually in a description of the human mind's inability to comprehend God directly.[36] Significantly, 'reverberare' is found in both mystical passages in *Confessiones*, the ascents at Milan and the vision of Ostia. The similarity between *Proslogion* XIV and *Confessiones* VII is clear.

In Anselm's excursus on those divine attributes which are incomprehensible to humanity (*Proslogion* XV-XXII), *Proslogion* XVIII stands out in its allusions to Augustine. The antimony between *satietas* and *egestas*, found for the first time in literary history in Socrates' description of 'Poros' and 'Penia' at Aphrodite's birthday party in *Symposium*, appears throughout the *Confessiones* and other places. The analogy of attempting to rise to God but falling back is found specifically in

---

35. *Soliloquia, passim*; *Confessiones* VII; *De libero arbitrio* II.13; III.14; *De moribus ecclesiae catholicae et de moribus manichaeorum* II (1351); *Epistula CXLVII*; *De Genesi contra Manichaeos* I.176; *In Ioannis epistulam ad Parthos* VII, (2033) (56). *Enarratio in Psalmum LXVII* 3; *Sermo LIII*; *Sermo LVIII*; *Sermo LXXVIII*; *Sermo LXXXVIII*; *Sermo CCCXVII*; *Contra duas epistolas Pelagianorum* IV.xi.31.

36. Augustine uses the term 'reverberare' in the following passages in a mystical or illumination context: *Confessiones* VII.x.16; IX.xi.24; *De quantitate animae* 75; *De libero arbitrio* II.16; *De moribus ecclesiae catholicae et de moribus manichaeorum* I (1315); *Epistula CXLIV* 1; *Tractatus in Ioannis evangelium* XVIII.2; *Enarratio in Psalmum V* 6; *Contra mendacium* XVIII.36; *De trinitate* XII.14; XV.6. In the following passages, he uses 'reverberare' in other contexts: *Enarratio in Psalmum LXXII* 16; *Sermo CCCLVII*; *De sancta virginitate* XXXIX.40; *De utilitate ieiunii* 10; *Contra Faustum* XV.8.

Confessiones VII.[37] The mention of Ps. 50.7 ('Ecce enim in iniquitatibus conceptus sum. Et in peccatis concepit me mater mea') as a statement concerning the human condition occurs in *Confessiones*[38] and elsewhere and its connection with that most famous and controversial of Pauline texts, Rom. 5.12 ('Propterea sicut per unum hominem peccatum in hunc mundum intravit, et per peccatum mors, et ita in omnes homines mors pertransiit, in quo omnes peccaverunt') is also Augustinian.[39] The ground for the human failure to see is sin. The phrase 'oculus mentis', found regularly in the Platonic tradition, is used often in Augustine.[40] The parallels between Augustine and Anselm on the failure of human vision of God in this life, particularly between *Proslogion* and *Confessiones* VII, are apparent.

Proslogion XXII-XXV

The final three chapters of *Proslogion* treat the nature of human salvation with God in eternity. In *Proslogion* XXV, Anselm attempts to understand what the enjoyment of the afterlife will be like. He uses the term *frui* which is the technical term employed by Augustine for human terminal love of God. The passage is a concatenation of scriptural texts: 1 Cor. 2.9 ('Quod oculus non vidit, nec auris audivit, nec in cor hominis ascendit quae praeparavit Deus iis qui diligunt illum'); Mt. 13.43 ('Tunc iusti fulgebunt sicut sol in regno Patris eorum'); 22.30 ('Sed erunt sicut angeli Dei in caelo'); 1 Cor. 15.44 ('seminatur corpus animale, surgit corpus spiritale'); Wis. 5.16 ('Ego erravimus a via veritatis; et iustitiae lumen non luxit nobis. Et sol intelligentiae non est ortus nobis'); Ps. 36.39 ('Salus autem iustorum a Domino; Et protector eorum in tempore tribulationis'); Ps. 16.15 ('Ego autem in iustitia apparebo conspectui tuo; satiabor cum apparuerit gloria tua'). There humankind will possess what it desires: beauty, the resurrected body, eternal salvation, satiety, true inebriation, true harmony, wisdom, concord, power, honours and riches, and true security. Many of these terms occur in

---

37. *Confessiones* VII.x.16; xvii.23, xx.26.

38. *Confessiones* I.7.

39. Augustine cites Rom. 5.12 some 124 times, almost exclusively in anti-Pelagian works.

40. *De ordine* II.4; *De quantitate animae* IV.6; *De libero arbitrio* II.16; *Epistula CXL* 6; *Epistula CXLVII* 23; *Epistula CXLVIII* 2, 5; *Epistula CCXLII* 3; *De vera religione* XIX; *In Ioannis evangelium Tractatus* LXXVII.1.

Augustine's works; 'securitas' is of particular interest.[41] The word itself derives from 'sine cura' (without cares). 'Securitas' means that, when man is ultimately happy, he can not lose that which causes that happiness. From the very beginning in *De beata vita*, Augustine characterizes true happiness by, among other things, indicating that it is that which cannot be lost.[42] True security therefore only comes when man possesses the highest good in a way that he cannot lose it. In *De civitate dei* and elsewhere, Augustine accuses Plato and some of his followers of not realizing this and positing eternally recurring cycles.[43] In *Retractationes* Augustine also criticizes his use of the phrase 'securior rediturus in caelum' in *Contra academicos*, perhaps because of its Porphyrian resonances.[44]

Happiness in heaven, according to *Proslogion* XXV, will be communal. One will not rejoice more over one's own happiness than over the happiness of others. In fact, one's own joy will be doubled since one will rejoice in the happiness of others as well as one's own. One will rejoice more in God's happiness than in one's own and others. The theme of communal happiness occurs in several of Augustine's works, notable among them *De libero arbitrio*, at the culmination of the demonstration of God's existence.[45] Like Augustine in several places, Anselm uses Mt. 22.37 ('Diliges Dominum Deum tuum ex toto corde tuo, et in tota anima tua, et in tota mente tua'), itself a citation of Deut. 6.5, to express the fullness of love which humankind will bring to God.

Conclusions

In demonstrating Augustine's influence on later thought, and *a fortiori* on Anselm, a scholar may be making but an elaboration of the obvious. And yet the value of literary and thematic research lies in its ability to relate one author to another while showing the individuality and originality of both. There can be no question that Augustine influenced the entire tradition of western Christian thought until the present day. The precise nature of that influence and how it was mediated is a matter of

41. The word 'securus' and its cognates occurs 1,194 times in the Augustinian corpus.
42. *De beata vita* III.27.
43. *De civitate dei* XII.11-13, 26.
44. *Retractationes* I.i.3.
45. *De libero arbitrio* II.x.28.

continuing study. Recent computerization of texts helps scholars enormously in the accurate determination of the nature of Augustine's influence.[46] By the prudent use of this mechanical means, we can perhaps avoid the excesses of some recent scholarship so that both Augustine and Anselm will retain their rightful places in the history of thought.

That Augustine influenced Anselm in the matter of demonstrating God's existence is clear. That Anselm remains original in his demonstration is equally clear. Although some may contest the probative nature of either Augustine's or Anselm's demonstration, we may all agree that neither of them strayed so very far from the mainstream of the philosophical West.

---

46. The *Thesaurus Patrum Latinorum* in the *Corpus Christianorum, curante* CETEDOC (Brepols Publishers, Turnhout), available at the Augustinian Historical Institute at Villanova University, has been helpful in writing this essay.

VERITAS ORATIONIS SELON LE *DE VERITATE*

Paul Gilbert, SJ

1. *Introduction*

Le début du *De veritate* (1:176,8-19) cite le troisième paragraphe du ch. 18 du *Monologion* qui traite de l'éternité de la vérité (17:33,11-22). Le ch. 10 du même dialogue (10:190,15-16) cite de nouveau ce paragraphe, mais brièvement (17:33,11-12). A chaque fois, Anselme précise qu'il méditera sur la *veritas orationis* (1:176,6-7; 10:190,15). En principe donc, l'analyse de cette *veritas* devrait affiner l'intelligence des affirmations du ch. 18 du *Monologion*. Nous allons voir comment.

Après avoir esquissé le plan de la première partie du *De veritate*, nous en analyserons les chapitres extrêmes (1 et 10) qui reflètent la forme traditionnelle de l'*oratio*. En commentant ensuite les ch. 2 et 9 de ce même dialogue, nous ferons référence au Stagirite pour préciser les termes anselmiens d'*enuntiatio* et de *significatio*. Nous pourrons ainsi entendre correctement le sens des catégories qui supportent la pensée anselmienne sur la vérité éternelle.

2. *Le Plan du De veritate*

Le *De veritate* n'argumente pas de manière linéaire. Il revient souvent sur ses pas (9:188,27; 11:191,3) en déterminant des unités littéraires qui divisent l'opuscule en lui assurant sa progression. Les ch. 1 à 10 font inclusion. Le début du ch. 11 (11:191,3), où Anselme définit la vérité (11:191,19-20), invite en effet à revenir là où la recherche avait commencé, au ch. 1 qui avait demandé cette définition (1:176,19-20). Les ch. 1 à 10 préparent donc la définition de la vérité en mettant en exergue ses éléments essentiels (11:191,4) qu'ils portent au coeur de la vérité souveraine, laquelle, disait le *Monologion*, n'a ni principe ni fin (1:176,6-7; 10:190,13-15). Les ch. 2 et 9 du *De veritate* précisent l'angle sous lequel ces éléments sont vus. Ils font eux-mêmes inclusion au sein des ch. 1 et 10. Au début du ch. 9 (cfr. 9:188,27), Anselme invite en effet à revenir à la *veritas significationis* vers laquelle le ch. 2 avait orienté sa méditation (2:179,32). Les ch. 1 à 10 forment ainsi comme un candélabre, les premiers chapitres correspondant en ordre inverse aux derniers. Les ch. 3 à 8, au centre de ce candélabre, ne sont pas organisés de manière concentrique. Leur suite est plutôt linéaire. Les ch. 3 à 7 traitent de divers lieux ou 'signes' (2:180,2) où on trouve la vérité. Tous ces lieux forment une progression évidente, qui conduit jusqu'à ce qui unit nos puissances humaines de la façon la plus large.

La *significatio* reçoit de ces développements une entente que la seule analyse du langage ne manifeste pas. Selon les ch. 3 à 7, chaque genre de 'signe' reçoit sa signification de sa *rectitudo*, qu'on définit comme une 'action conforme à ce qu'il faut'.[1] Le ch. 8 articule ensuite les catégories de l'action et de la passion dans le cadre du devoir et du pouvoir. Tous les 'signes' énumérés du ch. 3 au ch. 7 comportent une intention qu'ils doivent pratiquer droitement. Il faut entendre les affirmations du *Monologion* sur l'éternité de la vérité dans ce contexte de la signification droite.

3. *Veritas orationis*

1. *Etudes aristotéliciennes sur l'oratio*
L'histoire littéraire du Moyen-Age ne peut pas ignorer l'influence exercée par Cassiodore et Isidore de Séville,[2] dont les ouvrages ont transmis des définitions quasi canoniques de l'*oratio* et de l'*enuntiatio*. Toutefois, ces documents résonnèrent chez Anselme plus par leur esprit que par

1. Cette expression, ou une semblable, se trouve dans tous les chapitres précédents: *De veritate* 2:179,2; 3:180,15; 4:181,4; 5:181,30; 6:185,1; 7:185,28. Les mots 'devoir' et 'pouvoir' jouent des rôles importants dès avant le *De veritate* (cfr. P. Gilbert, *Le Proslogion de saint Anselme. Silence de Dieu et joie de l'homme* [Roma: Pontificia Università Gregoriana, 1990], pp. 115-20). Par contre, le mot 'rectitudo' et ses apparentés sont inconnus avant ce dialogue (sauf le terme 'recte' qui vient trois fois dans le *Monologion* [e:5,10; 8:23,11; 28:46,29], une fois dans la réponse à Gaunilon [5:135:31] et sept fois dans le *De grammatico* [12:156,33; 16:162,13; 18:164,5; 21:167,6,9,22; 168,7]).

2. Cassiodori Senatoris, *Institutiones* (ed. R.A.B. Myniors; Oxford: Clarendon Press, 1961), p. 115; Isidori Hispalensis Episcopi, *Etymologiarum sive originum* (ed. W.M. Lindsay; Oxford: Clarendon Press, 1981), sans pagination (II.xxvii.5).

leur lettre. Il est peu probable qu'il les eut en mains. Malgré tout, il n'est pas inutile de s'intéresser à Boèce et aux vulgarisateurs de la culture antique pour comprendre Anselme. Boèce, en transcrivant les définitions de l'*oratio* et de l'*enuntiatio* forgées par le ch. 4 du *Peri hermeneias*, parle de l'*oratio* avec une fidélité plus littérale à Aristote que Cassiodore et Isidore. 'Oratio autem est vox significativa, cuius partium aliquid significativum est separatum, ut dictio, non ut affirmatio, vel negatio' (*PL* 64, 311 et 434).[3] Relevons ici trois termes importants: *oratio, dictio* (que Cassiodore et Isidore ignorent[4]), *affirmatio vel negatio*. L'*oratio* est la phrase en général. Boèce appelle *dictio* toute partie élémentaire mais significative de l'*oratio*, par exemple le mot 'homme'. L'affirmation et la négation posent des problèmes variés. Cassiodore et Isidore les envisagent dans le contexte de l'*oratio enuntiativa*, tandis que Boèce les situe aussi dans celui de la *vox significativa*.[5] En fait, on peut les envisager aussi bien comme des opérateurs d'attribution selon la signification que comme des propriétés de l'*enuntiatio*.

Le vocabulaire d'Anselme est plus souple que celui du premier Moyen-Age. Pour le ch. 2 du *De veritate*, la *veritas enuntiationis*, ou *orationis* dans notre texte, possède deux valeurs de *significatio*, formelle et intentionnelle. Anselme n'oppose donc pas *significatio* et *enuntiatio*; il considère plutôt deux *significationes* de l'*enuntiatio*. La valeur formelle de la *significatio enuntiationis* résulte de sa bonne forme grammaticale, tandis que sa valeur intentionnelle ou véritative exerce 'ce pour quoi l'énonciation a été faite'. Par exemple l'énonciation: 'Nous sommes vendredi' a une valeur formelle puisqu'elle est bien formée, et une valeur intentionnelle vraie si nous sommes vendredi ou fausse dans le cas contraire. Dans la suite de notre exposé, pour la commodité, nous distinguerons la *veritas significationis* formelle et la *veritas enuntiationis* intentionnelle ou véritative de l'*oratio*.

Nous allons nous arrêter maintenant à Aristote. Le *logos* d'Aristote, ou l'*oratio*, résulte d'une composition de plusieurs *voces significativae*

---

3. *Oratio = logos*, *vox = phônè*, *dictio = phasis* et *affirmatio vel negatio = kataphasis è apophasis*.

4. Quant à Anselme lui-même, il utilise rarement le mot 'dictio' (*Cur deus homo* 10:106,26, *De processione* 17:198,9 et 2 fois dans *Fragmenta* 2:340, 17 et 24), et sans en tirer un catégorie philosophique digne d'étude.

5. En traduisant Aristote, Boèce distingue l'*oratio significativa* et l'*oratio enuntiativa*: 'Enuntiativa vero non omnis, sed illa [oratio] in qua verum vel falsum est' (*PL* 64, 313 et 441).

unies par un verbe, comme en témoigne l'exemple donné par Cassiodore, 'Socrate discute'. Il peut aussi être un mot isolé, 'homme' (16b28). Dans ce cas, nous sommes en présence d'un *logos* élémentaire, d'une *dictio*. Il est intéressant de préciser la portée significative de la *dictio*. Le ch. 1 du *Peri hermeneias* donnait cet exemple: le 'bouc-cerf' (16a16-17), un mot composé d'autres mots significatifs tout en ayant lui-même une signification originale. Pour Aristote, chaque mot simple (bouc et cerf) utilisé pour créer un mot composé signifiant ('bouc-cerf') doit être signifiant par lui-même. Toutefois le mot composé signifie quelque chose de neuf par rapport à ses éléments. Le mot 'bouc-cerf', sans être élémentaire du point de vue de la *dictio*, a une signification qui, indivisible et élémentaire, ne résulte pas de l'addition des éléments qui ont servi à sa fabrication.

Avec plusieurs *voces significativae*, nous formons des phrases, des *orationes*. Comme dans le cas du mot composé, chaque élément de la phrase doit être significatif pour que la phrase toute entière ait une unité de signification. L'unité significative de la phrase ne résulte pas de l'addition de ses *voces significativae*. La signification de l'*oratio*, 'Socrate discute' réside en effet dans l'unité intelligible de l'événement signifié. Enfin, comme pour la *vox significativa* composée, la proposition peut posséder une signification même si la réalité exprimée ne subsiste pas. On affirme en effet la fausseté d'une telle proposition à condition de lui accorder une signification intelligible.

Il y a donc dans le langage un étagement de significations qui, bien qu'exprimées de manière de plus en plus complexes, ne manquent pas d'unité. Le *Peri hermeneias* apporte enfin une considération importante: la question de la vérité de l'*oratio* doit être étudiée ailleurs, dans la *Métaphysique* en fait. Le Stagirite distingue ainsi la signification connotative et le sens dénotatif. D'une part, la signification d'une *dictio* ou d'une *oratio* est constituée par sa relation à d'autres unités dans un même système linguistique. D'autre part, la dénotation ou le sens intentionnel ou véritatif d'une *oratio* renvoie à un événement. Le *Peri hermeneias* est consacré à la question de la signification de l'*oratio*, dont la vérité, qui réside dans l'affirmation dénotative,[6] doit être manifestée ailleurs. L'*oratio* bien formée jouit donc d'une consistance indépendante de sa dénotation, mais déjà digne d'étude. Ajoutons que la dénotation ne

6. Le mot 'signifie bien quelque chose, mais il n'est encore ni vrai ni faux, à moins d'ajouter qu'il est ou qu'il n'est pas, absolument parlant ou avec référence au temps' (*Peri hermeneias* 1, 16a16-18). Voir aussi 16b28-30.

fonctionne bien que si une telle signification connotative est donnée préalablement, l'inverse n'étant pas nécessaire.

2. *L'Eternité de la vérité*

Nous ne pouvons certes pas retrouver chez notre auteur la lettre du Stagirite, mais au moins des traces de son héritage: en question de langage, il convient de distinguer la signification connotative des mots et leur sens dénotatif. Les ch. 1 et 10 du *De veritate* s'inscrivent dans une perspective qui approfondit la signification formelle de l'éternité de la vérité, à laquelle le *Monologion* avait déjà dédié quelques moments de sa méditation. Toutefois, maintenant, la réflexion connotative va déboucher déjà sur des affirmations dénotatives ou ontologiques.

Du Monologion au De veritate. Le ch. 1 du *De veritate* engage une réflexion sur le mot 'vérité' en soulignant les notes impliquées par son usage. La première de ces notes est l'éternité. La réflexion n'envisage plus l'éternité de l'Essence souveraine à partir de son unité idéale, comme elle le faisait dans *Monologion*, mais à partir de ce que nous entendons quand nous parlons de vérité. Anselme construit son argument en deux temps. Premièrement: nous utilisons des expressions qui impliquent le savoir d'une durée irréductible à un temps divisible en moments distincts. Par exemple, lorsque nous disons: 'quelque chose était futur', nous sommes incapables de situer à un moment du passé l'instant à partir duquel cette proposition, de fausse, serait devenue vraie. Semblablement, mais à l'inverse, quand nous disons: 'quelque chose sera passé'. Ces usages linguistiques manifestent notre intelligence d'une durée continue et indivisible, que nous attribuons à la vérité dans un second temps. Anselme, méditant sur les implications de l'idée de vérité considérée en elle-même, en manifeste la continuité atemporelle. Si par hypothèse la vérité commençait ou si elle finissait, il serait vrai qu'à un certain moment, avant qu'elle commença ou après qu'elle finira, elle n'était pas encore ou elle ne sera plus. Mais il est absurde de dire qu'en toute vérité la vérité n'était pas avant qu'elle commença ou qu'elle ne sera plus après qu'elle finira. L'atemporalité de la vérité s'impose donc à la pensée.

Ces conclusions formelles laissent toutefois perplexes. En effet, en indiquant que la vérité est atemporelle, elles suggèrent qu'elle se présente dans toutes nos affirmations. Et si la vérité se présente dans toutes nos *enuntiationes*, toutes nos *enuntiationes* sont vraies. Qu'en est-il, dans ces conditions, non seulement de nos erreurs (problème qu'Anselme n'envisage pas ici), mais de la transcendance de la vérité? Les ch. 20 à 24 du *Monologion* se débattaient dans ce problème. Avec une grande virtuosité, ils modifiaient le vocabulaire appliqué à l'Essence souveraine; 'en tout temps' devenait 'toujours' et 'en tous lieux' 'partout'. Mais ces remplacements de mots ne montraient pas la transcendance de la vérité. Ils n'étaient même pas proportionnés à la simplicité de l'Essence souveraine. Le *De veritate* n'accepte plus ces solutions faciles et sans doute seulement verbales. Le tout début de ce dialogue évoque en effet le problème comme s'il était resté irrésolu: si Dieu est vérité, est-ce que je dis Dieu quand je dis une proposition vraie (cfr. *De veritate* 1:176,5-6)?

Le *Monologion* était sinueux, trop dépendant des modèles imaginés par la Patristique, pas assez soucieux de la forme intérieure de son argumentation. En allant du *Monologion* au *Proslogion*, l'intelligence engage une réflexion sur son mystère. Le *De grammatico* accentue cette orientation en accueillant la logique comme un exercice de la pensée responsable de soi. L'*oratio* est un événement linguistique qui a une signification autosuffisante. Dans le *De veritate*, l'éternité de la vérité s'inscrit d'abord dans ce contexte de la pure signification.

Dans le De veritate. En parlant de la *veritas orationis*, le ch. 1 énonce le thème général de la première partie du traité et l'insère dans la question de l'éternité de la vérité. Le ch. 10 revient sur le même thème. Ses différences d'avec le ch. 1, qui résident essentiellement dans l'introduction de la catégorie de causalité, manifestent le progrès réalisé depuis le début du dialogue et le principe de la solution donnée au problème initial.

Le ch. 10 affirme tout d'abord (10:190,1-3) que la rectitude de la Vérité souveraine est d'un autre ordre que celle que nous signifions dans nos diverses activités humaines. La rectitude de ces activités leur est en effet imposée comme un devoir qui résulte de leur manque d'être. Leur vérité de signification leur est accordée par ce qu'elles ne possèdent pas d'elles-mêmes. Par contre, Dieu, pleinement uni à soi, est à l'origine de sa rectitude. Sa rectitude exprime sa liberté surabondante et agissante, que le ch. 15 du *Proslogion*, juste avant de méditer sur l'éternité, disait 'maius quam cogitari possit' (15:112,15). La vérité de Dieu est l'excès de son activité intérieure.

Pour articuler la vérité éternelle et la vérité créée, Anselme utilise la catégorie de causalité. La rectitude divine, dit-il, est 'la cause de toutes les autres vérités et rectitudes, et rien n'est sa cause' (*De veritate* 10:190,6-7). L'utilisation de la catégorie de causalité pose de nombreux problèmes. Qui adhère aux ch. 5 et 6 du *Monologion* voit en Dieu un rapport causal, car Dieu y est dit *per se* et *ex se*. Mais ce rapport causal embarrasse s'il impose de séparer en Dieu une cause et un effet. En toute rigueur, l'absolue simplicité de Dieu interdit de lui attribuer une forme quelconque de division. Quand donc le *De veritate* exprime la relation entre la vérité du créé et celle du Créateur en utilisant la causalité, il considère seulement la signification créée de la causalité.

Tels sont les accents nouveaux mis par le ch. 10 du *De veritate* quant aux thèmes antérieurs du *Monologion*. L'*oratio* n'est pas l'origine de sa signification. Le paragraphe cité du *Monologion* l'avait déjà indiqué: la signification s'impose au langage, qui n'en dispose pas. Mais le premier texte d'Anselme exposait son lecteur à y entendre des notes panthéistes. La vérité originaire donne au langage d'être vrai, mais non pas immédiatement. Une série de médiations causales la fait advenir dans nos *enuntiationes*. La vérité qui se trouve dans l'existence des choses (cfr. *De veritate* 10:190,9-10) cause la connaissance que nous en avons, tout en étant elle-même l'effet de la Vérité souveraine. La vérité dans la pensée cause à son tour la vérité de nos énonciations. La vérité de *l'enuntiatio* résulte donc de la Vérité souveraine à laquelle elle est liée par un enchaînement de médiations causales.

Il faut entendre droitement ces médiations et leur forme causale. Une réflexion sur l' 'existence' des choses y aidera. L'existence n'est pas un fait empirique. L'existant, que détermine intérieurement la signification, jouit d'un dynamisme que le mot 'fait', un participe passé passif, masque. Pour Anselme, l'existant exerce une extase active, répondant ainsi au don qui lui est fait d'être. Le ch. 6 du *Monologion* (6:20,16-19) avait situé l'existant au terme du dynamisme de l'Essence originaire. Il est comme le participe présent (*lucens*) qui résulte de l'activité indéfinie (*lucere*) de la substance originaire (*lux*). La signification immanente de l'existant coïncide avec son acte d'ouverture à la transcendance. La signification de l'existant est abstraite de sa vérité quand elle n'est pas rapportée à son origine active réelle. Le rapport causal doit être interprété dans ce contexte. Le ch. 9 dit qu' 'il y a une signification vraie et fausse de l'existence des choses' (*De veritate* 9:189,24-25). En se tournant vers son origine, l'existant répond à la cause qui lui donne d'être. Son existence acquiert ainsi la vérité de sa signification. En exerçant sa vérité extatique, en existant vraiment, il indique l'origine ou la cause de son essence. La médiation causale est assurée par l'acte dynamique de l'existant, dont elle fonde la signification.

Cette forme causale éclaire la structure du jugement. Le jugement n'est pas fondé sur la contemplation des formes idéales à la manière de Platon, mais sur une participation de notre acte d'affirmer à l'acte de ce qui est affirmé. L'affirmation laisse transparaître la vérité non pas quand elle reflète la forme du dit mais quand elle dit en acte ce qui est en acte. De là, à fin du ch. 10 du *De veritate*, l'affirmation qu''on ne peut pas entendre quand la vérité manquerait à l'*oratio*' (10:190,18) selon laquelle 'il est vrai que quelque chose était future'. La nécessité de ce jugement ne se fonde pas sur la forme qui y est exposée, mais sur la réalité indisponible qui s'y présente. Le savoir de la nécessité de cette *oratio* rend témoignage au savoir de l'origine immuable en son acte.

Anselme indique ainsi l'essence ultime de la *veritas orationis*. Selon le ch. 1 du *De veritate*, la vérité appartient à l'*oratio*, dont on peut entreprendre une analyse qui écarte tout risque de panthéisme. En commentant les ch. 2 et 9 du *De veritate*, nous allons préciser maintenant la relation causale, en réalité si rare chez Anselme,[7] qui articule la *veritas orationis* comme une relation d'actes.

4. Enuntiatio et significatio

Réfléchissons maintenant sur la rectitude immanente à nos *orationes*, sceau de leur sens.

1. La vérité chez Aristote

L'*oratio enuntiativa* est composée de *voces significativae* liées affirmativement ou négativement. Le *Peri hermeneias* présente la logique pure de ces propositions, sans s'attacher à leur vérité ou à leur fausseté. Certes, l'analyse des formes propositionnelles sert déjà la vérité. Elle permet en effet d'assurer la déduction de propositions vraies. Mais cette analyse suppose, sans plus, que vérité il y a. La science aristotélicienne du syllogisme n'est pas une théorie de la vérité. Selon la *Métaphysique* (VI 4, 1027b20-22), la vérité advient dans une proposition quand celle-ci exprime les articulations de la réalité. La vérité réside donc dans une médiation entre ce qui est dit et son expression. Certes, Aristote assimile l'être par accident et l'être vrai, les qualifiant d'affections de la

---

7.   Le mot 'cause' et ses apparentés viennent 14 fois avant le *De veritate* et 11 fois dans ce dialogue, dont 8 à la page commentée ici (10:190).

pensée (cfr. *Métaphysique* IV 4, 1027b34-1028a2). Mais, ajoute-t-il, 'tu n'es pas blanc parce que nous pensons d'une manière vraie que tu es blanc, mais nous disons la vérité quand nous disons que tu es blanc parce que tu l'es' (*Métaphysique* IX 10, 1051b6-8). Dire que la vérité est une affection de la pensée revient donc à responsabiliser notre intelligence. La vérité réside dans un consentement intellectuel qui dit ce qui est. Aristote ouvre ainsi l'espace d'une entente spirituelle de la vérité.

La *Métaphysique* n'était pas connue du premier Moyen-Age. Cependant, à partir du XIe siècle et avant que les grands traités aristotéliciens soient divulgués, les oeuvres logiques du Stagirite devinrent l'objet d'études attentives. Elles orientèrent la réflexion dans les directions nouvelles d'une pensée responsable de ses démarches. La vérité de la proposition, fondée traditionnellement sur la participation, fut dès lors envisagée à partir de l'acte de penser, du jugement exercé. La réflexion anselmienne sur l'essence de la vérité se déploie dans ce contexte.

2. *Le ch. 2 du De veritate*

Le ch. 2 du *De veritate* s'attache à la proposition qui relie ou sépare plusieurs *voces significativae*. Il distingue les valeurs formelle et intentionnelle. L'analyse formelle de l'*oratio*, ou la *veritas significationis*, n'en épuise pas toute l'intention, qui vise une unité réelle. Pour réfléchir sur celle-ci, Anselme recourt à la catégorie classique, mais rare chez lui,[8] de la participation, en lui donnant une portée nouvelle.

Dans la tradition platonicienne, la participation établit une continuité entre le participant et le participé, ici entre la proposition énoncée et la forme idéale. La psychologie de l'illumination permettait à Augustin d'articuler cette continuité. Anselme s'écarte de cette mentalité mais sans perdre son horizon spirituel, et il s'approche d'Aristote pour qui la vérité de la proposition réside dans son énonciation. La vérité s'atteste dans l'énonciation et son accès résulte d'un travail spirituel. Anselme reconnaît entre la proposition et la vérité une médiation spirituelle. 'Il ne me paraît pas que la vérité doive être recherchée ailleurs que dans l'*oratio*' (*De veritate* 2:177,18-19), mais non pas dans un de ses éléments matériels (cfr. 2:177,20-21, ces noms ou ces verbes que mentionne le *Peri hermeneias* [ch. 5, 17a17]), ni non plus dans sa

---

8. Les mots de la 'participation' viennent trois fois avant le *De veritate* (*Monologion* 16:30,9; 25:43,11 et *De Grammatico* 16:162,1) et une fois dans ce dialogue (*De veritate* 2:177,16).

significatio formelle. Elle réside dans le signe linguistique qui jouit d'un horizon intentionnel, dans l'*enuntiatio*.

'La vérité est dans le langage qui signifie qu'est ce qui est' (2:178,6-7). Qu'est-ce que signifier? Le *De grammatico* avait distingué la *significatio* connotative et l'*appellatio* dénotative. Cette distinction joue certainement un rôle dans le *De veritate*. Sans doute, elle n'y apparaît pas littéralement, ni non plus dans la suite du *corpus* anselmien. Sans doute le mot *oratio* ne vient que quatre fois dans le *De grammatico* et le mot *enuntiatio* jamais. Mais le *De veritate* assume le traité précédant en corrigeant les caricatures qu'imposait son entente trop rude. La *significatio* posait en effet le problème grave de son arbitrariété si aucune *res* ne lui correspond. Certes l'*oratio* peut signifier qu'est ce qui n'est pas (*De veritate* 2:178,32-33); mais pour toucher la vérité, nos jugements doivent posséder, outre cette vérité formelle, une vérité dénotative. Seule la mise au jour d'une *appellatio* ou *veritas enuntiationis* répond à la question de l'essence de la vérité.

Anselme doit donc indiquer la *res* qui rend les *orationes* vraies lorsque nous formulons des *enuntiationes*, mais sans se contenter pour cela des seules références sensibles déterminées. Il pourra ainsi justifier des *enuntiationes* du genre de celle du *Proslogion*: 'id quo maius cogitari nequit'. La *res* originale à laquelle nos *orationes* participent pour être vraies, nous la découvrons à partir de l'intention qui les finalise. Nos *orationes* réalisent ce pour quoi elles ont été faites quand elles font signe vers ce qui est en général. Leur vérité résulte de leur rectitude (*De veritate* 2:178,26), c'est-à-dire de leur orientation droite vers une *res* primordiale.

Pour mettre en évidence la *res* qui accorde sa vérité à l'énonciation particulière, Anselme se réfère à notre *usus* (2:179,5 et 15) linguistique.[9] Non pas celui, conventionnel, qui attribue telle signification à telle séquence de signes vocaux, mais celui, effectif, qui exerce une intention spirituelle. 'L'usage dit que l'énonciation est droite et vraie en fonction de la rectitude et de la vérité par laquelle elle signifie qu'est ce qui est' (2:179,4-6). L'*oratio* possède plusieurs intentions, mais aussi une ouverture à ce qu'Anselme nomme un *plus* (2:179,7) sensé. Eclairés par ce *plus* de la *res* intentionnée, nous voyons dans l'*oratio* un événement qui est *plus* qu'une simple unité formelle significative et *plus* qu'une simple

9.   E. Briancesco, *Un triptyque sur la liberté. La doctrine morale de saint Anselme* (Paris: Cerf, 1982), pp. 30-33, met en exergue l'aspect 'finalisant', nous dirions dynamisant, qui caractérise l'*usus* dans le ch. 2 du *De veritate*.

intention de réalité, qui est ce au nom de quoi nous pouvons affirmer qu'est ce qui est comme il est. En ultime analyse, ce *plus* indique la fondation en Dieu créateur de l'existant visé par notre énonciation particulière.

En portant cet argument à sa limite, nous voyons ce *plus* resplendir dans la proposition bien formée où nous l'exprimons.[10] En son acte d'énonciation, cette proposition exerce en effet son état de créature. Par cette cohérence ultime, elle se rend intérieure à ce qu'elle affirme quand elle dit l'éternité de la vérité. Nos propositions sont mues par le devoir d'énoncer ce qui doit être signifié parce qu'elles ont été faites pour cela (*De veritate* 2:179,11). L'affirmation thématique de l'éternité de la vérité réalise ce devoir et fonde toutes nos propositions vraies.

Il convient donc d'articuler dans le langage deux vérités ou rectitudes. Cette articulation est aisée à réaliser quand la vérité formelle exprime une vérité intentionnelle évidente, par exemple 'quand nous disons que "l'homme est un animal" ou qu'"il n'est pas une pierre"' (*De veritate* 2:179,21). Mais lorsque nos énoncés débordent le domaine de l'évidence empirique, ils visent le *plus* dont nous venons de parler et conduisent dans un monde tout autre, où s'exerce le dynamisme de la relation créatrice. Les ch. 3 à 8 du *De veritate* articulent l'intention spirituelle qui anime précisément la *veritas enuntiationis* et qui exerce à sa façon l'action créatrice.

3. *Du ch. 2 au ch. 9 du De veritate*
Selon le Père Schmitt, le *postea* de la fin du ch. 2 (cfr. 2:179,28 note) renvoit au ch. 5 dont le titre distingue la vérité de l'action naturelle et la vérité de l'action qui ne l'est pas. Quant au corps du ch. 5, il distingue l'action irrationnelle (cfr. 5:182,1) accomplie 'ex necessitate' (5:182,8) et l'action rationnelle (cfr. 5:181,31) par laquelle 'non ex necessitate facit homo rectitudinem et veritatem' (5:182,9). La confrontation de ces deux séries de textes invite à entendre que la vérité formelle ou naturelle est irrationnelle mais nécessaire tandis que la vérité intentionnelle ou de l'action est rationnelle mais sans nécessité. En d'autres termes, la veritas

---

10. 'L'énoncé s'efface ici devant l'énoncer (…): la vérité est dans l'énonciation *quand* l'énoncer énonce qu'est ce qui est (…). L'énoncé de l'énoncer est décrit comme le redoublement du verbe être, le contraire d'un contenu déterminé et figé (…). Le redoublement *linguistique* est comme tel renvoi à un *redoublement ontique* que l'on est en droit de nommer *auto-position de l'être*' (M. Corbin, *L'Inouï de Dieu. Six études christologiques* [Paris: Desclée de Brouwer, 1979], p. 70).

enuntiationis met en jeu la liberté à laquelle la *veritas significationis* ne laisse en fait guère d'espace.

Le ch. 2 caractérise l'ordre intentionnel par l'*usus* que le ch. 5 conçoit donc comme une visée libre et rationnelle de la vérité. La *res* de l'énonciation concorde alors avec une action, qui est aussi une passion (5:182,18) ou un devoir, et qui réside dans la sphère de l'agir réfléchi plutôt que du savoir descriptif. A l'horizon de l'énonciation, la *res* ne résulte pas d'une action purement dépendante de notre vouloir, mais d'une intention libératrice qui répond à un appel créateur et qui concorde avec l'être-même de l'existant. L'expression: 'faire ce qu'on doit' exprime ainsi l'alliance de l'action et de la passion dans l'intention qui oriente l'existant créé vers son Créateur. L'*usus* ainsi entendu exerce l'acte libre d'où naît l'énonciation droite.

4. *Le ch. 9 du De veritate*

Le ch. 9 revient sur la *veritas enuntiationis*. Les ch. 3 à 7 montrent comment nos diverses activités exercent un devoir, que le ch. 8 articule sur notre pouvoir. Anselme considère maintenant l'essence de l'action intentionnelle ou du 'faire' qui appartient au devoir. Il lie ainsi la vérité et l'action. 'Si quelqu'un doit faire ce qu'il fait, il dit le vrai; s'il ne le doit pas, il ment' (9:189,6-7).

Comment comprendre cette assomption du vrai dans l'action? Anselme propose un exemple trivial. Si quelqu'un fait le contraire de ce qu'il dit, il faut penser que, pour lui, est vrai et droit ce qu'il fait et non pas ce qu'il dit. Anselme élargit cet exemple à tout ce qui existe: 'il y a aussi une signification vraie ou fausse dans l'existence de la chose parce que, du simple fait qu'elle est, elle dit qu'elle se doit d'être' (9:189,24-25). On attribue ainsi à l'existant une action intérieure qui résiste à nos jeux verbaux. Nos vérités de signification peuvent certainement se contenter de pures formalités, par exemple lorsque nous disons qu'est ce qui n'est pas. Mais la vérité, qui, selon l'*usus*, anime la signification pour en faire une énonciation, surmonte nos formes rationnelles. La vérité naît d'au-delà de nos mots. Elle est l'exister qui se présente en acte dans nos *enuntiationes*.

Cet élargissement de la perspective, qui scelle la *veritas enuntiationis* dans l'existence, est à entendre droitement. En effet, si l'existant 'dit' ce qui doit être, tout ce qui existe dit ce qui doit être. Donc il n'y a qu'un sens vrai de l'existant, la fausseté n'existant pas. Pour ne pas tomber dans des sophismes, il faut rappeler le ch. 10 du *De veritate*: l'existant est moins un fait qu'un faire, une existence qu'un existant. L'insistance sur le participe présent conduit à reconnaître en ce qui doit être ce qui le fait être. Anselme oriente ainsi sa méditation vers l'origine créatrice de nos affirmations vraies, qui sont elles-mêmes des actions plus que des faits de langage. La fausseté apparaît alors en dehors de l'existant, comme un néant.

L'intelligence de la proposition comme action est confirmée par les exemples du ch. 9 du *De veritate*. Une existence peut avoir un sens faux, de la même manière que nos intentions peuvent ne pas exercer ce qui constitue leur essence. On entend alors par sens faux l'abandon par l'énonciation de sa tension vers son origine, le *plus*. 'Si tu voyais la volonté et la pensée de quelqu'un', dit Anselme, 'il te serait signifié par son oeuvre de vouloir et de penser qu'il doit penser et vouloir. S'il le doit, il dit vrai; si non, il ment' (9:189,22-24). Le 'dire' vrai exprime l'acte qui le fait être. Le 'dire' faux, par contre, n'exerce pas l'intention intérieure, le devoir du créé, qui donne d'être.

5. *Conclusion*

La *veritas orationis*, qui abrite le sens ultime de l'expression: 'La Vérité souveraine n'a pas de principe ni de fin' (*De veritate* 1:176,7), n'atteste pas par sa seule description linguistique ce pour quoi elle a été faite. Elle atteint son terme, la vérité, quand elle assume ses conditions dans l'acte de la dire droitement et en laissant voir comment l'esprit qui la dit y engage l'essence de son exister. En affirmant l'éternité de la Vérité, la liberté créée se reconnaît en son alliance.

Part II
ANSELM AND HIS CONTEMPORARIES

RAGIONI E NON-RAGIONI DI UN ESILIO

Inos Biffi

In due tempi diversi Anselmo trascorse in esilio quattro anni del suo episcopato cantuariense, durato sedici anni: una prima volta dal maggio 1099 al settembre 1101, e una seconda volta dal dicembre 1103 al settembre 1106. Per Anselmo esso rappresentava il segno chiaro e l'esigenza imprescindibile della coerenza alla propria coscienza, e quindi alle ragioni della verità o della rettitudine, sulle quali egli intendeva fondare, senza compromessi, tutto il suo comportamento; per i suoi monaci di Christ Church e per i vescovi dell'Anglia era invece l'indice di una incomprensibile ostinazione e di una grave insensibilità ai bisogni spirituali della Chiesa d'Inghilterra, di cui era il primate, e specialmente della Chiesa di Canterbury, della quale era vescovo. Così, mentre nel giudizio di Anselmo l'essere esule mostrava una passione e amore sofferto per la Chiesa, per gli altri, al contrario, denunziava disinteresse e disamore.

La divergenza riguardò in particolare il secondo esilio, col suo increscioso e insopportabile prolungarsi. Ciò che colpisce, al riguardo, è da un lato la forza delle argomentazioni opposte al prosieguo della condizione di esule dell'arcivescovo, e dall'altro la convinzione tranquilla, quasi implacabile, del medesimo arcivescovo di essere nel giusto. Si potrebbe dire che Anselmo applica alla sua prassi la linearità lucida e puntigliosa, e insieme l'ardua sottigliezza del suo pensiero.

Il primo esilio

Dopo i primi anni di episcopato—passati 'in pace e frustrazione'[1]—e più in frustrazione che non in pace, Anselmo intraprende il suo primo viaggio a Roma, che si concluderà con il non ritorno in Inghilterra e con l'esilio. A questo esilio Anselmo aveva da tempo manifestato la propria

---

1. R.W. Southern, *Saint Anselm: A Portrait in a Landscape* (Cambridge: Cambridge University Press, 1990), p. 274.

disponibilità di fronte all'impossibilità di attuore la sua comunione col vescovo di Roma. 'Preferisco lasciare la tua terra—aveva dichiarato al re Guglielmo II—e uscire in attesa che tu riconosca il papa, piuttosto che, anche per un momento solo, rifiutare la mia obbedienza al beato Pietro e al suo vicario.'[2] E non esiterà a manifestare il proprio crescente desiderio di 'vivere fuori dall'Inghilterra invece che dentro' dopo i primi anni di episcopato, trascorsi sterilmente 'fra tribolazioni immense ed esecrabili per l'[...]anima'.[3]

Ma non è il primo esilio—come pare—a suscitare perplessità e reazioni e a essere oggetto di critiche, ma il secondo, anche se tutt'e due identicamente giustificati alla coscienza di Anselmo da ragioni teologiche: la comunione con il vescovo di Roma, il primo, e la fedeltà alle decisioni pontificie del concilio romano del 1099, il secondo: ragioni risolventesi nella 'episcopalis libertas'.[4]

Il secondo esilio

Di ritorno dall'inconcludente secondo viaggio alla sede apostolica di Roma, deciso a non accettare una limitazione all'esercizio pieno e incondizionato della 'potestas' del suo 'officium'—imposta invece da Enrico I—Anselmo si stabilisce in un nuovo esilio. Sono, al riguardo significative, le parole di Eadmero:

Trattenute con sé alcune sue poche cose, egli con somma pace e serenità stabilì la sua residenza a Lione, abitando nella casa dell'arcivescovo [Ugo], in attesa dei suoi legati, non allontanandosi neppure per un'ora, nelle parole e nelle azioni, dalle cose riguardanti Dio.[5]

2. Eadmeri, *Historia Novorum* (ed. M. Rule; London: HMSO, 1884; Kraus Reprint Ltd, 1965), p. 53 (abbrev. *HN*).

3. *Ep.* 206; Anselmo d'Aosta arcivescovo di Canterbury, *Lettere*, I (ed. Inos Biffi e Costante Marabelli; Milano: Jaca Book, 1990), pp. 264-65.

4. *Ep.* 206, pp. 264-65. Cfr. I. Biffi, *Anselmo dal Bec a Canterbury: riluttanza e coscienza episcopale. Gli inizi*, in *Lettere*, I, pp. 80-81. Le nostre introduzioni all'epistolario sono ora edite in I. Biffi, *Protagonisti del medialto* (Milano: Jaca Book, 1996).

5. *HN*, p. 158: 'His ita gestis, ipse, paucis de suis secum retentis, Lugduni resedit in summa pace et quiete, propriam praedicti pontificis domum inhabitando, nuncios suos expectans, et ne ad horam quidem ab iis quae Dei sunt verbo se vel actu elongans.'

Francamente questa pace e questa serenità, di cui parla Eadmero, non mancano di lasciarci piuttosto sorpresi, così come lo furono i suoi stessi amici, ai quali—osserva Richard Southern—'egli parve essere inattivo. Essi pensavano che troppo facilmente si rassegnava alla sua posizione e che aveva sviluppato il gusto dell'esilio come una sottrazione alle proprie incombenze.'[6]

Le reazioni al secondo esilio di Anselmo

Prendiamo in considerazione precisamente quelle degli amici, ossia di coloro che maggiormente avrebbero dovuto capire e condividere le motivazioni dell'arcivescovo, comprendendo tra questi 'amici', anche i vescovi dell'Anglia, anche se in realtà non tutti, o all'inizio, pochi lo erano.

1. Veramente, l'insistenza per il ritorno non proviene soltanto da questi amici. Specialmente possiamo ricordare l'assillante invito ad abbandonare l'esilio rivolto ad Anselmo dalla regina Matilde,[7] la quale riceverà sempre il più fermo rifiuto, anche di fronte ai richiami, un po' ingenui e un po' enfatizzati della regina, che ricorderà all'arcivescovo l'esempio di Gesù e di Paolo:

> Che cosa farà dunque il figlio della misericordia, il discepolo di colui che, per redimere i servi, si offrì spontaneamente alla morte? Tu vedi, ecco, tu vedi i tuoi fratelli, i tuoi compagni di servizio, il popolo del tuo Signore, già in balìa del naufragio, anzi già prossimo a perire: non lo soccorri, non gli porgi la destra, non ti opponi al pericolo? Non desiderava l'apostolo essere anatema, separato da Cristo, a vantaggio dei fratelli?[8]

—richiamo d'altronde a cui Anselmo rimane assolutamente insensibile, guidato com'è nel suo comportamento dall' 'amor iustitiae Dei'[9] e ancorato al principio, che andrà ripetendo a tutti:

6.   Southern, *Saint Anselm*, pp. 298-99.

7.   Cfr. I. Biffi, *Anselmo arcivescovo e monaco: le tribolazioni per la 'libertas Ecclesiae'. L'azione pastorale. Il tramonto a Canterbury*, in Anselmo d'Aosta arcivescovo di Canterbury, *Lettere*, II (ed. Inos Biffi e Costante Marabelli; Milano: Jaca Book, 1993), pp. 49-52.

8.   Cfr. *Lettere*, II, pp. 176-81: 'Quid ergo faciet misericordiae filius, discipulus eius qui, ut servos redimeret, ipse in mortem se obtulit? Vides, ecce vides fratres tuos, conservos tuos, populum Domini tui iam naufragia sustinentem, iam labantem in ultimis, nec succurris, nec porrigis dexteram, nec obiectas te discrimini? Nonne optabat apostolus "anathema esse a Christo pro fratribus" suis?' (p. 178).

9.   *Ep.* 321; *Lettere*, II, pp. 190-91.

A motivo di quanto ho con le mie orecchie udito a Roma, non potrei senza gravissima colpa fare ciò che [...] mi si richiede [...]. Se non ne tenessi conto, certo agirei contro la legge divina.[...]. Io devo piuttosto osservare la costituzione apostolica ed ecclesiastica a tutti nota, in cui, quando è promulgata a sostegno della religione cristiana, si ritrova sicuramente la legge di Dio.[10]

2. A sorprendere sono però le obiezioni all'esilio provenienti dagli 'amici'—come li chiamava il Southern—e primi tra questi i monaci di Canterbury. Questi non comprendono e non condividono la fondatezza delle giustificazioni dell'arcivescovo—e vi reagiscono apertamente e con insistenza: prima di tutto il priore di Christ Church, Ernulfo, che invia ad Anselmo una lettera estremamente dura e circostanziata, con delle accuse precise.[11] Secondo Ernulfo la presenza dell'arcivescovo a Canterbury sarebbe più utile che non la sua, noi diremmo, ideologica assenza: essa mostrerebbe la sua partecipazione al rischio e alle molestie che i monaci devono sopportare, mentre l'assenza fa pensare a una sua dimenticanza dell'offesa subita da loro e dalla Chiesa. Ma il giudizio si fa più grave e sferzante: 'spontaneamente, proprio senza che alcuno ti costringesse, ti sei defilato dai nostri rischi, forse per non vedere ciò che siamo costretti a tollerare e, peggio, a guardare da spettatori',[12] ossia la condizione miserevole di ingiustizie, di soprusi, di disonore a cui è ridotta la Chiesa di Canterbury. Il rilievo che segue è ancora più grave: Anselmo si trova quindi in esilio senza che ce ne sia un'effettiva e convincente ragione; è una scelta, quasi un capriccio suo, poiché nessuno ve lo costringe. Se poi—continua la lettera—'avessi attentamente esaminato il criterio di comportamento della Chiesa e la sua norma tradizionale, tu non avresti trovato alcun motivo valido per andare in esilio, e gli altri non sarebbero incorsi in così gravi pericoli per la tua assenza'.[13] In più:

---

10. *Ep.* 346; *Lettere*, II, pp. 212-13: 'Quod a me [...] requiritur [...] ego propter hoc quod auribus meis Romae audivi, facere nequeo absque gravissima offensione. [...] potius debitor [...sum] apostolicam et ecclesiasticam cunctis notam servare constitutionem. In qua lex Dei sine dubio intelligitur, cum ad christianae religionis firmamentum promulgatur' (p. 212).

11. *Ep.* 310; cfr. *Ep.* 307; *Lettere*, II, pp. 156-61; *Lettere*, I, pp. 476-79.

12. *Lettere*, II, p. 159 ('Sponte tua, nullo penitus cogente, ereptus es periculis nostris, fortasse ne sentires quae nos perpeti et, quod gravius est, spectare cogimur', p. 158).

13. *Lettere*, II ('Quod si dispensationis ecclesiasticae regulam et antiquae consuetudinis ordinem sollicita studuisses consideratione pensare, nec tibi aliqua exulandi

la scelta di Anselmo non serve alla causa, poiché non riesce a piegare i suoi oppositori. Ma viene ora l'accusa più grave: Anselmo è fuggito pavidamente e indecorosamente di fronte a chi gli si opponeva; non ha avuto il coraggio, per esempio di un sant'Ambrogio, di resistere e di opporsi alla prepotenza; è stato un timido, privo di 'talis affectus et talis constantia'; al tribunale di Cristo 'i fortissimi arieti del gregge divino, che né il lupo danneggiò né alcuno, incutendo spavento, mise in fuga',[14] guideranno le schiere delle anime, mentre l'arcivescovo di Canterbury, forse, si dovrà vergognare per aver abbandonato il campo. Tanto più che egli non era stato né incarcerato né torturato né privato della sua sede—ragioni, d'altronde, che non avrebbero giustificato un suo dileguarsi: a risolverlo per la fuga è bastato un futile motivo: la parola di 'un Guglielmo qualsiasi'—Guglielmo di Warelwast—per la parola di un Guglielmo 'hai deciso di fuggire e, abbandonato il nemico, hai lasciato allo strazio degli empi le tue pecore':[15] la capitolazione generale che conseguì a tale assenza e mancanza di guida era inevitabile. L'esortazione è a ritornare prontamente, affinché venga tolto 'il disonore della santa madre Chiesa'.[16] Non sono facilmente pensabili accuse più pesanti.

D'altra parte, le richieste del ritorno e la discordanza sulla buona fondatezza dell'esilio verranno riprese dai suoi monaci.[17] E, in particolare, sotto forma di composizione poetica, da Gilberto Crispino, abate di Westminster, discepolo e amico di Anselmo. E' il lamento appassionato di una zampogna, che prima tesseva l'elogio del pastore, e ora si domanda: 'Perché dal vostro ovile state lontano?' e constata con tristezza che 'senza una guida il gregge errabondo è in cerca di pascoli, né vi è chi lo salvi', e, 'non conoscendo le erbe buone, si nutre di quelle cattive e così tutto si ammala, ed è lì per morirne', in preda al furore del lupo; e, d'altra parte, 'il creditore di ciò chiederà conto [...], e rivorrà certamente i beni infiniti che con l'ovile a voi affidato vanno in rovina'.[18]

causa surriperet, nec alii occasione tuae absentiae tam grave discrimen incurrerent', p. 158).

14. *Lettere*, II ('Tunc fortassis pro sola voluntate invidentium fugisse pudebit, cum videris ante tribunal Christi, ducentes choros animarum, illos fortissimos divini gregis arietes, quibus nec lupus nocuit nec alicuius terror in fugam vertit', p. 158).

15. *Lettere*, II, p. 161 ('Pro uno verbo cuiusdam Willelmi fugere decrevisti, et relicto hoste dilacerandas impiis oves tuas dimisisti', p. 160).

16. *Lettere*, II. ('Sanctae matris Ecclesiae depellas opprobrium', p. 160).

17. Cfr. *Epp.* 336, 355, 364; *Lettere*, II, pp. 230-33; 270-75; 290-95.

18. *Lettere*, II, pp. 298-303 ('Unde vos ab ovili, pastor, abestis? Grex duce nullo

3. All'esilio di Anselmo si oppongono non solo i suoi monaci, ma anche i vescovi dell'Anglia. Tra questi ricordiamo anzitutto Gondulfo di Rochester, l'antico monaco di Le Bec. Forse è sua una lettera anonima e autorevole,[19] che definisce—e tale deve apparire a chiunque sia dotato di ragionevolezza—tutta la questione tra Anselmo e il re una 'diabolicae fraudis illusio' ('un inganno della perfidia diabolica'), e quindi 'illudens' ('ingannevole') la 'dilatio' del ritorno: tutto è mirato a un 'quotidiano dissolvimento e definitivo annientamento di tutta quanta la Chiesa e di tutta la religiosità e la legge cristiana in Inghilterra': Anselmo sta lontano dal regno affatto immotivatamente, per nulla: 'pro nihilo abestis'; le sue convinzioni e giustificazioni non hanno arrecato nessun vantaggio, anzi hanno provocato solo mali:

> Tutto ciò ricade senza dubbio solo su di voi ed è da imputarsi alla santità vostra [...]. Domandatevi [è chiesto sarcasticamente] se il vostro cuore è così esclusivamente dedito a Dio e se la vostra vita gode già di così grande sicurezza da non dovere con ben altra vigilanza chinarvi su tali miserie spirituali.[20]

A richiamare Anselmo ai suoi doveri di pastore saranno, infine, i vescovi, o almeno un gruppo di essi,[21] che lo stimoleranno a rompere gli indugi del ritorno: 'Non devi più indugiare. Perché te ne stai lontano, mentre le tue pecore, prive di pastore, periscono? Ormai non ti rimane presso Dio nessuna scusa [...]. Torna a noi, torna subito.'[22]

Come si vede, siamo di fronte a una svalutazione concorde della determinazione di Anselmo a scegliere la via dell'esilio e a permanervi: il

---

devius errat: nemo reducit, pascua quaerit; et, quia quae sunt commoda nescit, noxia sumit; morbidus ergo et moribundus omnis habetur [...] Creditor [...] milia quippe requirit, quae sub ovili credita vestra perdita fiunt', pp. 300, 302).

19. *Ep.* 365; *Lettere*, II, pp. 294-99.

20. *Lettere*, II, pp. 297, 299 ('Videtur [...] omni fere homini sano sensu sapienti omnino nihil aliud esse id quod inter vos et regem sub tam morosa expectatione agitur, nisi diabolicae fraudis illusio et illudens dilatio, et, ut manifestius dicam, totius Anglorum Ecclesiae ac religionis et legis christianae cotidiana diminutio et summa destructio [...]. Haec autem omnia procul dubio vos solum respiciunt et vestrae sanctitati imputantur [...]. Considerate quoque, si vobis placet, si cor vestrum ita soli Deo vacat et si in tanta securitate vestri iam conversamini, ut talibus animarum miseriis alia vigilantia condescendere non debeatis' (pp. 296, 298).

21. *Lettere*, II, pp. 334-37.

22. *Lettere*, II, p. 337 ('Sed iam non est tibi pigritandum. Ut quid enim peregrinaris, et oves tuae sine pastore pereunt? Iam apud Deum nulla tibi remanet excusatio [...]. Veni ergo ad nos, veni cito', p. 336).

suo comportamento viene ritenuto senza fondamento, e anzi attribuito alla sua insensibilità pastorale. L'arcivescovo si trova così nell'isolamento interiore più assoluto, che tuttavia non riesce minimamente a smuoverlo dalla certezza non solo della legittimità ma della necessità dell'esilio: rinunziarvi significherebbe per lui venir meno a un obbligo preciso e imprescindibile della coscienza.

La risposte e le giustificazioni dell'arcivescovo

Di fronte alla serie delle critiche gravissime, ripetute e autorevoli, che riceve, Anselmo non si lascia smuovere in alcun modo, e la sua risposta è sempre la medesima: ritornare, senza che sia risolta la questione, che al suo giudizio è quella stessa della 'libertas Ecclesiae'[23] sarebbe un 'distaccarsi dalla verità'—'a veritate avertere'. Alla sollecitazione dei vescovi per il suo ritorno egli risponde:

> Sono addolorato con voi e condivido nell'animo le prove da voi sopportate e dalla Chiesa dell'Anglia, però non posso per il momento, secondo i desideri miei e vostri, porvi rimedio [...], perché il re tuttora non vuole che io mi stabilisca in Anglia, se non a patto di consentire con il suo volere e dissentire agli ordini del papa [...]. In Dio spero che, per quanto mi è dato di capire, nessuno potrà separare il mio spirito dalla verità.[24]

'Per amore della libertà della Chiesa' aveva scritto al vescovo di Tuscolo e al cardinale Giovanni—'io sono esule dalla mia diocesi e spogliato di tutti i miei averi'.[25]

Sono esattamente i termini delle sue risposte ai suoi monaci, con la precisa protesta che egli non è insensibile ai suoi doveri pastorali, che non è il timore a trattenerlo lontano dalla sua Chiesa sensibile e con il rilievo che il suo ritornare incondizionato sarebbe, in ogni caso, un male maggiore di quelli che stanno avvenendo in sua assenza. Lo dichiara alla dura lettera del priore Ernulfo:

23. *Ep.* 239; *Lettere*, II, p. 236.

24. *Ep.* 387; *Lettere*, II, p. 339 ('Condoleo et mente compatior tribulationibus, quas vos et Ecclesia Angliae sustinetis; sed ad praesens secundum meam et vestram voluntatem subvenire nequeo [...], quia rex non vult me esse in Anglia adhuc, nisi discordem a iussione papae et eius concordem voluntati [...]. Spero [...] in Deo quia nullus cor meum a veritate, inquantum cognoscam, poterit avertere', p. 338).

25. *Ep.* 339; *Lettere*, II, pp. 237, 239 ('Domnum Baldewinum [...] mitto ad vestigia domini papae pro causa, quae est inter regem Anglorum et me, immo inter illum et libertatem Ecclesiae Dei, pro qua sum exul ab episcopatu meo et rebus omnibus exspoliatus', pp. 236, 238).

Quanto al fatto che dò l'impressione di tralasciare senza alcun motivo i miei còmpiti di pastore, non è questo il giudizio di uomini saggi e pii ai quali presento la cosa, né io così la intendo. Poiché, per quanto sta in me, non sono io a tralasciarli, piuttosto, come a un'attenta considerazione potete riconoscere, non mi è dato di vivere là dove dovrei svolgerli,

—e dove, invece, Anselmo dovrebbe inevitabilmente compiere atti di comunione con gente scomunicata.

Si dice, d'altro canto, che per una sola parola andasse esule chi avrebbe dovuto effondere il proprio sangue per le sue pecore e per la Chiesa di Dio: dico che non bisogna sottovalutare una parola includente i gravi mali già detti, a cui non mi potrei comunque prestare senza mio grave rischio spirituale e senza danno per la Chiesa a me affidata. Infine, non temo l'effusione del sangue o qualsiasi pena corporale o perdita materiale. Se la mia persona avesse a soffrirne, volentieri acconsentirei in difesa della verità [...], ma, qualora fossi in Anglia in conflitto col re, una tanto tremenda quanto inutile violenza annienterebbe la nostra Chiesa [...]. Mi sembra dunque preferibile che, se non si può evitare, qualunque tribolazione imperversi in Anglia in mia assenza, piuttosto che la mia tollerante presenza confermi per il futuro qualunque malvagia consuetudine.[26]

E se è reale il danno spirituale provocato dalla lontananza di Anselmo, non per questo—egli afferma—'si dovrebbe fare il male perché ne venga un bene',[27] e per lui sarebbe un fare il male trasgredire il dettato

26. *Ep.* 311; *Lettere*, II, pp. 161, 163 ('Quod pastoralem curam sine ulla ratione relinquere videor, non hoc aestimant sapientes religiosi, quibus rem ostendo, neque ego intelligo. Non enim eam, quanto in me est, relinquo, sed ibi, ubi eam me exercere oporteret, conversari, sicut vos, si diligenter intenditis, cognoscere potestis, nequeo. Audistis enim quibus ex praecepto apostolici communicare non possum sine animae meae periculo [...]. Quod autem dicunt quod non oportuerit eum pro uno verbo fugere, qui suum sanguinem pro ovibus suis et pro Ecclesia Dei debuerit effundere: dico quod non est parvipendendum illud verbum, in quo tanta gravia mala continentur [...], in quae sine periculo animae meae et sine detrimento Ecclesiae mihi commissae nullatenus me possum ingerere. Denique non timeo sanguinis effusionem aut quamlibet corporis mei destructionem aut rerum amissionem. Quae si personae meae evenirent, libenter paterer propter veritatis assertionem. At nihil horum super me caderet, sed et Ecclesiam nostram et homines ad eam pertinentes, si in Anglia cum rege contenderem, gravis oppressio frustra contereret, et multitudo vexatorum ad culpam meam aerumnas suas me execrando converteret. Melius itaque mihi videtur ut, me absente, quaelibet tribulatio, si vitari nequit in Anglia debachetur, quam per meam praesentiam et tolerantiam quaelibet prava consuetudo in futurum confirmetur, aut multitudo hominum me aspiciente propter me tribulationem se pati lamentetur', pp. 160, 162).

27. *Lettere*, II, p. 163 ('Non debemus facere mala ut veniant bona', p. 164).

del concilio di Roma e l'entrare in comunione con quanti sono fuori dalla comunione. Per cui non rimane che 'aspettare la disposizione di Dio e affidare la questione al suo giudizio', nella decisa volontà a 'non prestare l'*hominium* a qualsivoglia mortale e a non giurare fedeltà a nessuno'.[28] Per Anselmo vale quindi il principio—sentito come imperativo in coscienza e come criterio per essere nella verità e nella volontà di Dio—dell'obbedienza alla decisione conciliare romana, a cui si accompagna la convinzione che un suo ritorno dall'esilio ambiguo o di compromesso produrrebbe mali spirituali non inferiori a quelli che si verificano in sua assenza e che, essendo un male, non va comunque intrapreso.

Sostanzialmente negli stessi termini Anselmo continuerà a rispondere alle altre richieste di ritornare alla sua sede. Egli dichiara di non vedere come la possa riprendere 'rationabiliter', non mancando di sottolineare di essere oggetto di calunnie, e di affermare perentoriamente a quanti sono persuasi che egli non si dia molto pensiero del suo ritorno: 'Dacché lasciai l'Anglia, non ho mai intravisto come potervi fare ritorno a giuste condizioni':[29] in caso contrario esso non sarebbe 'secundum scientiam' né gradito a Dio. Nessuno che sia 'rationabilis intellectus' potrebbe concepire un ritorno onorifico per Dio e per la Chiesa di Canterbury e tale da permettere la salvezza dell'anima ad Anselmo, se mancasse la possibilità di un esercizio dell'ufficio episcopale nella libertà e senza la costrizione a relazioni condannate da Roma.[30] Dinanzi ai patimenti della sua Chiesa Anselmo dichiara che è suo dovere farli propri, rimettendosi a Dio, cui solo tocca intervenire: 'meum est secundum divinam dispositionem solum compati, et solius Dei est subvenire'.[31]

Conclusione

E' arduo dare una valutazione al comportamento di Anselmo, che ci appare immediatamente così 'testardo' e sordo alle plausibili ragioni di un ritorno, a cui del resto si rassegnerà, alla fine, non del tutto persuaso della bontà della conciliazione trovata. Si sarebbe indotti a parlare di una

---

28. *Lettere*, II, p. 165 ('Hoc autem scitote quia voluntas mea est, ut adiuvante Deo nullius mortalis homo fiam nec per sacramenta fidem alicui promittam', p. 164).

29. *Ep.* 336; cfr. *Ep.* 327; *Lettere*, II, p. 233 ('Postquam de Anglia exivi, numquam intellexi quomodo rationabiliter redire possem', p. 232).

30. *Ep.* 355; *Lettere*, II, pp. 270-75.

31. *Ep.* 357; *Lettere*, II, p. 276.

certa astrattezza nella proclamazione dei principî, di una mancanza di duttilità, di una lettura inadeguata e parziale degli aspetti coinvolti nella questione, in particolare quelle derivanti alla Chiesa inglese. Richard Southern riconosce che forse qualche verità c'era nell'accusa fatta dagli amici inglesi di una 'inattività' di Anselmo, di un suo troppo facile accomodamento alla sua situazione, di un gusto dell'esilio e di un disimpegno.[32]

Ma per parte sua Anselmo sentiva come più impellente e come inevitabile la sua obbedienza al dettato di Urbano II e quindi il vincolo, percepito come incondizionato, della sua coscienza alla volontà di Dio, fatta coincidere con tale obbedienza, qualunque fossero le conseguenze negative pratiche di tale fedeltà: 'salva reverentia voluntatis eius'.[33] Una volta ancora sant'Anselmo risalta nella solitudine e nel valore, alto e inestimabile, della sua 'rectitudo', quand'anche il giudizio pratico di altri—o anche nostro—possa essere divergente, e quand'anche quella coerenza non abbia mutato, in prospettiva, la situazione e non abbiano ottenuto nulla.[34] Una simile fedeltà ha valore per se stessa.

32. *Saint Anselm*, p. 299.
33. *Ep.* 376; *Lettere*, II, p. 320. Cfr. I. Biffi, 'La coscienza drammatica di Anselmo d'Aosta', *Studi Cattolici* 38 (1994), pp. 556-62.
34. Cfr. Southern, *Saint Anselm*, p. 439.

'IN PRIMIS...OMNIS HUMANAE PRUDENTIAE INSCIUS ET EXPERS PUTARETUR': ST ANSELM'S KNOWLEDGE OF CANON LAW*

Mark Philpott

St Anselm is famously ignorant of canon law. The prevailing view among historians is Sir Richard Southern's that, 'Anselm set no great store by an extensive knowledge of canon law'.[1] Although only a small trait in Southern's portrait, Anselm's indifference to the canons is nonetheless significant; for example, it forms part of his depiction as so centred on his search for God as to be uninterested in merely worldly matters and incapable of dealing with them. It is also an important element in the fundamental contrast drawn between Anselm and his master, Lanfranc, who was, for Southern, a consummate lawyer.[2] However, by re-examining Anselm's correspondence, this paper will suggest that his knowledge of the canon law was substantial, and that he used it in similar ways to his contemporaries.

Perhaps the best place to start is Anselm's letter 65, written when he

---

*   I owe this quotation to Eadmer, *Historia Novorum* (ed. M. Rule; Rolls Series, 1884), p. 62; inspiration to think about Anselm to the works of Sir Richard Southern; and encouragement in my work to the Reverend H.E.J. Cowdrey, Dr Julia Barrow, and all who commented on the first version of this paper at the Canterbury conference, especially Sir Richard Southern, Professor Vaughn, Dr Martin Brett and Professor Fröhlich. I must also thank Professor David Luscombe, Dr Matthew Kempshall and Dr Robert Simpson for practical help. Nonetheless all mistakes and misjudgments are my own exclusive property.

1.   R.W. Southern, *St Anselm: A Portrait in a Landscape* (Cambridge, 1990), especially pp. 255-58. Among those who have had a different view of Anselm's legal capacities are D.P. Henry, 'St Anselm and Paulus', *Law Quarterly Review* 79 (1963), pp. 30-31; and S.N. Vaughn, *Anselm of Bec and Robert of Meulan: The Innocence of the Dove and the Wisdom of the Serpent* (Berkeley, 1987), pp. 11-12, 17, 131 n. 93, and *passim*.

2.   Southern, *St Anselm: A Portrait*, especially pp. xvi, 439, 14-15, 438 and 355-56.

was prior of Bec in reply to difficult questions of ecclesiastical discipline put to him by an Abbot William.[3] Although it is now impossible to identify William, the warmth of Anselm's letter suggests that they knew one another well. Since Anselm held no position at this time which would have made him a source of official advice, or placed at his disposal learned advisers, the abbot must have consulted Anselm because he thought that he would be able to help him. The answer he received justified his confidence. Anselm's advice was clear, politic and wholly in accordance with the canons. A count who was excommunicate, but still attended mass in William's abbey, was to be humbly admonished not to be contemptuous of the sentence given against him by those 'in quibus deus affirmat se audiri cum audiuntur et sperni cum spernuntur, se ligare cum ligant et solvere cum solvunt', for this would surely worsen the 'dei iudicium' against him. The abbot must either act 'secundum iam prolatam apostolicam sententiam', or consult 'ipsum apostolicum sive aliquem eius vices gerentem' anew. If the count rejected his admonition, William was to remember that 'plus est deus timendus quam homo'.[4] Similarly, on the problem of whether an unchaste priest should be allowed to resume his ministry after confession, Anselm urged the enforcement of the full rigour of the rules, while taking account of pastoral necessities.[5]

For Southern, Anselm's letter 'belongs in spirit to the confessional manuals of the thirteenth century rather than the legal compilations of his own time'.[6] Nonetheless, it bears a strong resemblance to contemporary attempts to solve canonical problems. For example, Southern points out that Anselm 'argued from general principles', only making a 'somewhat cursory' reference to his authorities before returning to 'the more congenial task of elaborating his argument'. This is very much like several of Lanfranc's letters. Giving a decision to Bishop Herfast, Lanfranc simply asserted that it was 'divina fultus auctoritate'.[7] Consulted by Bishop Walcher of Durham on a point of clerical discipline, Lanfranc summarized in one sentence what he claimed to be the teaching of the 'canones...decretaque sanctorum patrum', and added, 'Qui si

3. *Ep.* 65: Schmitt, III, pp. 181-85: 1-120.
4. *Ep.* 65: Schmitt, III, p. 182: 15-31.
5. *Ep.* 65: Schmitt, III, p. 185: 105-106.
6. Southern, *St Anselm: A Portrait*, p. 256 and n. 2.
7. *The Letters of Lanfranc, Archbishop of Canterbury* (ed. H. Clover and M. Gibson; Oxford, 1979), no. 43, p. 138.

vobis obtemperare noluerit, evangelica auctoritate utimini quae ait, "Compelle intrare."'[8] To Southern, Anselm's comment that he was quoting the canon law for those 'who would not be persuaded by any other argument than authority' suggests 'how little he was in the habit of being guided by it'. However, Lanfranc was instructed at the 1050 Roman Synod to defend himself, 'expositam plus sacris auctoritatibus quam argumentis probarem'.[9]

The interest Southern finds in 'individual psychology, the effect of various judgments on the penitent' in Anselm's opinion on the unchaste priest was also in line with contemporary canonical practice. Lanfranc, for example, was reluctant to advise the archdeacons of Bayeux about a homicidal priest. He could only make suggestions 'periculose', 'cum reus reique vita a me penitus ignoretur', and so told them to act according to the results of their own examination of the penitent's life.[10] Similarly, Gregory VII told Remigius of Lincoln to examine a penitent homicidal priest for the fruits of penance.[11] Indeed, the Preface to Ivo of Chartres' *Decretum* made it a principle of canon law that the circumstances and personality of the malefactor would determine the appropriate canonical action: 'spirituales medici, doctores videlicet sanctae Ecclesiae, nec a se, nec inter se dissentiunt, cum illicita prohibent, necessaria iubent, summa suadent, venialia indulgent: cum secundum duritiam cordis delinquentium pro correctione eorum, vel cautela caeterorum severas poenitentiae leges imponunt; vel cum secundum devotionem dolentium et resurgere volentium, considerata fragilitate vasis quod portant indulgentiae malagma superponunt.'[12]

An examination of the authorities used by Anselm in letter 65 also tells us much about his approach to canon law. He cited three;[13] the first two supported his opinion 'quae ad sacri ordinis officium reditum post lapsum concedit', the other, he admitted, 'studiose prohibet'. Anselm reconciled the views with high confidence, 'de apertis quidem prohibuisse, de occultis vero post dignam paenitentiam concessisse

8.   Lanfranc, *Letters*, no. 45, p. 142.

9.   Lanfranc, *Liber de Corpore et Sanguine Domini*, quoted from Oxford, Bodleian Library, MS Bodley 569, f. 4[r-v], in *PL* 150, 407-42 (413).

10. Lanfranc, *Letters*, no. 51, p. 162.

11. *Gregorii VII Registrum* (ed. E. Caspar; *MGH, Epistolae Selectae*, 2; Berlin, 1920-3), I.34, p. 55.

12. Ivo of Chartres, *Decretum*, Preface, in *PL* 161, 48.

13. *Pace* Southern, *St Anselm: A Portrait*, p. 256.

intelligitur'.[14] According to Southern, Anselm found his texts in the canon law collection which Lanfranc later took to Canterbury.[15] If this manuscript was still at Bec when Anselm wrote his letter,[16] he would have been able to find in it the first two of his texts.[17] However, he might also have used one of the other copies there seem to have been at Bec of the materials that made up 'Lanfranc's collection'.[18] Indeed, it seems likely that he must have used a different type of manuscript, for in none of Brooke's Bec manuscripts, nor in Lanfranc's volume, would Anselm have found his third authority.[19] All three are found, with helpful marginal titles, in a version of 'Lanfranc's Collection' including excerpts from the Register of Gregory the Great, which Southern believed to be the ultimate source of Anselm's reference to the canons in the later letters 161 and 162.[20] However, if this was Anselm's source

14. *Ep.* 65: Schmitt, III, pp. 183-84: 59-66.

15. On this manuscript, now Cambridge, Trinity College, MS B 16 44, and the collection which it contains, see Z.N. Brooke, *The English Church and the Papacy* (Cambridge, 1931), pp. 59-83; and M. Philpott, 'Lanfranc's Canonical Collection and "the Law of the Church"', in G. d'Onofrio (ed.), *Lanfranco di Pavia e l'Europa del secolo XI* (Rome, 1993), pp. 131-47. In referring to the manuscript (henceforward, 'TCC B 16 44') I give the folio and chapter (if any), followed by a reference to *Decretales Pseudo-Isidorianae et Capitula Angilramni* (ed. P. Hinschius; Leipzig, 1863) (henceforward, 'Hinschius') by page, title and chapter (if any). Because of the inadequacies of Hinschius's edition, references to the pseudo-Isidore are corroborated, where appropriate, by a reference to TCC B 16 44.

16. Neither Schmitt, nor C. Marabelli in Anselm, *Lettere*. I. *Priore e Abbate del Bec* (Milan, 1988), p. 242, was able to date letter 65.

17. TCC B 16 44, f. 20^r part of ch. V (Hinschius, pp. 141-42, chs. XIX-XX); and f. 97^r-97^v ch. III (p. 737).

18. See Brooke, *The English Church and the Papacy*, pp. 66-67, 58-7 and 231-37.

19. Brooke argued that Eton College, MS 97 and British Library, Cotton Claudius E v were copied directly from the Bec parent manuscript. Since neither of them contains these Gregorian texts, we seem entitled to assume that the parent did not either. Certainly, TCC B 16 44 does not.

20. R.W. Southern ('St Anselm and Gilbert Crispin, Abbot of Westminster', *MARS* 3 [1954], pp. 78-115 [90-91 and 102-103 n.]) suggests that Gilbert quoted canons from Durham Cathedral, MS B IV 18 (or a similar one like Lambeth Palace Library, MS 351) in his 'On the Monastic Life', which Anselm then re-used in letters 161 and 162. The first two authorities of letter 65 are on the Durham manuscript's f. 6^v and f. 16^r-16^v; the third, f. 51^r and f. 52^r. See Gregory I, *Registrum Epistolarum* (ed. P. Ewald and L.M. Hartmann; *MGH, Epistolae* I; Berlin, 1891) IV.26, p. 261 ll. 15-19; V.4, p. 284 ll. 10-17; V.5, p. 285 ll.13-19 (with some editing); and V.17, p. 288 ll. 21-8.

in letter 65, it is no longer clear that the quotations in letters 161 and 162, 'as archbishop, his only quotations from Lanfranc's collection of canon law', were 'taken at second hand from a treatise of his friend Gilbert Crispin'.[21] If Anselm already knew the collection, he might have drawn the texts to Gilbert's attention.

Another letter discussed by Southern sheds much light on Anselm's knowledge of canon law.[22] The question which had been referred to Anselm—if an altar which had been moved had to be reconsecrated, or indeed whether it could be reconsecrated—was not an easy one to answer. It is therefore striking that an abbot should have sought Anselm's opinion, especially as he also seems to have consulted the famous canonist, Ivo of Chartres.[23] We must either suppose that the abbot wrote, in the midst of extensive building works, a letter to various hierarchs regardless of their knowledge of the canons, or that he expected to receive a sensible answer from Anselm.

Some near-contemporaries certainly thought he did, since the gist of the reply is preserved in two twelfth-century English manuscripts under the imposing title, 'Sententia Anselmi archiepiscopi de motione altaris.'[24] Indeed Anselm's letter and Ivo's are extremely similar. Ivo claimed to advise 'ex auctoritate et ratione'.[25] Anselm struggled to provide authorities. He racked his memory of the canons, he noted that another bishop had mentioned a relevant decision 'in decretis egini papae', he had even canvassed the opinions of Urban II and his court. Since this produced contradictory answers, Anselm had to turn more to 'ratio' than Ivo to reconcile them.[26] Anselm did not plead ignorance of the canons; he

---

21. Southern, *St Anselm: A Portrait*, pp. 256-57.

22. See Southern, *St Anselm: A Portrait*, pp. 257-59. Anselm, *Epistolae*, Book 3, no. 159, in *PL* 159, 194-95. In order to check the *PL* edition, I have collated its readings with Oxford, Bodleian Library, MS Digby 158, f. 91^r-91^v, a twelfth-century manuscript from (*pace* Southern, *St Anselm: A Portrait*, p. 257 n. 4) Reading. I owe this last point (and much else) to Dr Martin Kauffmann of the Bodleian Library.

23. Ivo of Chartres, *Epistolae*, no. 80, in *PL* 162, 101-103 to William, abbot of Fécamp, in which he rehearses almost all of no. 72 (col. 92) to G., abbot of St-Wandrille.

24. Oxford, Bodleian Library, MS Digby 158, f. 90^v and Hereford, Cathedral Library, MS O 1 vi, f. 43^r.

25. Ivo, *Epistolae*, no. 80, in *PL* 162, 102A.

26. Anselm, *Epistolae*, Book 3, no. 159, in *PL* 159, 194-95.

implied that, if there were a clear answer in the decretals and canons, he would know it. Indeed, Anselm not only seems aware of a broader range of canonical opinions than Ivo, he also attributed correctly a text which Ivo misattributed. The sentence was really 'in decretis egini papae',[27] but Ivo wrote that it was 'in collectionibus autem Burchardi Wormacensis episcopi, ex concilio Meldensi capitulo quinto'.[28]

A striking, seemingly unscientific, element in Anselm's letter is his attempt to deal with the issue 'de moto altari iterum consecrando'. His argument was that the altar 'vicem fidei christianae tenet', and since the faith moved from its foundation in Christ is no longer the faith, 'ita altare motum a suo fundamento iam non est altare.' Therefore, it was necessary to consecrate a new altar which could either be made entirely from the material of the old one or from new material.[29] This might seem desperate, but in Ivo's letter the same metaphor bore similar weight, 'cum signa similitudinem habeant earum rerum, quarum signa sunt, sicut fides...immobilis debet manere in credente, sic visibile altare, quod figuram gerit fidei, debet manere immobile. Et sicut a fundamento fidei, si quis motus fuerit, per manus impositionem, corpori Christi, quod est Ecclesia, reconciliandus est; sic mensa altaris fidei typum gerens, si mota fuerit, iterum sacris mysteriis imbuenda est.'[30] Our comparison of their letters shows that it was no accident that Anselm and Ivo reached the same conclusion, and that Anselm's sources and methods were very close to those of 'the greatest authority on Canon Law in northern Europe'.[31]

27. *Pace* Southern, *St Anselm: A Portrait,* p. 257, 'egini' was the correct reading. See Oxford, Bodleian Library, MS Digby 158, f. 91[r]; Hereford, Cathedral Library, MS O 1 vi, f. 43[r]; TCC B 16 44, f. 15[v] (Hinschius, p. 113) and Durham, Cathedral Library, MS B IV 18, f. 4[v]. Only Anselm, *Epistolae*, in *Opera Omnia* (ed. J. Picard; Cologne, 1612), Book III, letter CLIX, (reproduced in *PL* 159, 194-95) is incorrect. On this edition, contrast R.W. Southern, *St Anselm and his Biographer. A Study of Monastic Life and Thought 1059–c.1130* (Cambridge, 1963), p. 125 n. 2, and his *St Anselm: A Portrait,* p. 257 n. 4.

28. Ivo, *Epistolae,* no. 80, in *PL* 162, 101. See Burchard of Worms, *Decretum,* Book III, ch. xi, in British Library, MS Cotton Claudius C vi, f. 52[r] (in *PL* 140, 675) 'ex decretis Ygini papae cap. IIII'. In *PL* (but not the Cottonian manuscript) ch. x is 'ex concilio Meldensi'.

29. Anselm, *Epistolae,* Book 3, no. 159, at *PL* 159, 195B (compare MS Digby 158, f. 91[r]-91[v]).

30. Ivo, *Epistolae,* no. 80, in *PL* 162, 102.

31. Southern, *St Anselm: A Portrait,* p. 258. Note the possibility that Ivo was

This treatment of the problem of the altar also shows very close parallels to Lanfranc's approach to difficult questions of ecclesiastical discipline; for example, in a letter of his to Archbishop John of Rouen.[32] Lanfranc based his view of the correct vestments for a bishop to wear when consecrating a church on the authority of the practice of bishops of various provinces, chief among them the Pope. His sources of authority were thus similar to Anselm's reference to his bishop and then the Pope and his court; the major difference being that Lanfranc found his authorities agreed, where Anselm did not. The next issue which Lanfranc discussed with Archbishop John, the ordination of subdeacons, draws out the comparison with Anselm's letter even more clearly. John had written that the maniple was given only to the subdeacon at ordination; Lanfranc sought clarification, 'ubi hoc acceperitis rogo me vestris litteris instruatis. A quibusdam enim id fieri audio, sed utrum id fieri sacris auctoritatibus precipiatur meminisse non valeo.' The practice at Canterbury was different: 'ex antiqua patrum institutione' even 'laici' would wear maniples when vested in albs. In the absence of complete agreement in custom, Lanfranc turned to analysing the divergent texts of pontificals, just as Anselm tried to use 'ratio' to reconcile his differing authorities. Finally, Lanfranc claimed that the problem was solved by the authority of two texts, a canon of the Fourth Council of Carthage and a passage from Isidore's *De sacris ordinibus*. He might have found the canon in 'his' canon law collection, or in one of the pontificals he had just quoted.[33] But he cannot have found the Isidorian text in the canon law collection, which thus was not his sole source for sacred authorities any more than it was Anselm's.[34]

---

also a pupil of Lanfranc's; M. Gibson, *Lanfranc of Bec* (Oxford, 1978), pp. 36-37.

32. Lanfranc, *Letters*, no. 14, pp. 82-88.

33. TCC B 16 44, f. 131ʳ (Hinschius, p. 303, *Concilium IV Cartaginense* ch. V) which, however, reads 'urceum' for the 'urceolum' of Lanfranc, *Letters*, no. 14, p. 86 l. 59. The text (reading 'urceolum') is used (albeit without title) as a part of the ordination of a subdeacon in all the pontificals identified by Gibson (Lanfranc, *Letters*, p. 87 n. 7 and n. 8, and pp. 84-85 n. 2) as possible sources for Lanfranc in this letter. See London, British Library, MS Cotton Claudius A iii, f. 42ʳ (printed in *The Claudius Pontificals* [ed. D.H. Turner; Henry Bradshaw Society, 97; 1971], p. 34); *Le Pontifical Romano-Germanique du dixième siècle*, I (ed. C. Vogel and R. Elze; *Studi e Testi*, 226; 1963), p. 22; and *Le Pontifical Romain du douzième siècle* (ed. M. Andrieu; *Studi e Testi*, 86; 1938), p. 128.

34. Lanfranc, *Letters*, no. 14, p. 84 ll. 34-35. For a more extended treatment of Lanfranc's canon law sources and his use of them, see M. Philpott, 'Archbishop

A number of Anselm's other letters also have canonical interest.[35] A near-contemporary gathered a collection of Anselm's 'plusieurs réponses intéressant la jurisprudence ecclésiastique', but even this is not complete.[36] The word 'canonice', for example, occurs at least eight times in Anselm's letters.[37] Some of these allusions are made merely in passing: for example, Anselm alluded to the canonical successor to his rights over the lands of Robert of Limming.[38] However, the letters as a whole show that such allusions rest on his deep knowledge of the canons.[39] He urged Prior Ernulf to resist the king's demands for money: 'Vos scitis quomodo ipse me spoliavit rebus archiepiscopatus. Nullatenus igitur per me aliquid habebit de tota pecunia totius archiepiscopatus, nisi prius me canonice revestierit et ea quae abstulit mihi reddiderit, neque vos sponte illi sine mea iussione pecuniam dare debetis.' Further, if the king compelled the prior to give him what he wanted 'aut timore...aut ulla necessitate' from the goods of the archbishopric or the convent, Anselm threatened to appeal to God 'et iudicium eius invocabo'.[40] The canons foremost in Anselm's mind seem to have been the *exceptio spolii*, 'non est privilegium quo expoliari possit iam nudatus', which was one of the cornerstones of pseudo-Isidorian canon law. Anselm used them in a masterly fashion. His application of the doctrine is correct and relevant; his allusion graceful and precise, and carefully includes some of the most numinous words of the canons like 'sponte' and 'necessitate'.[41]

Lanfranc and Canon Law' (Oxford DPhil thesis, 1993), I, pp. 92-143.

35. *Pace* Southern, *St Anselm: A Portrait*, pp. 256-58.

36. Now Oxford, Bodleian Library, MS Laud Misc. 344, f. 36^r-40^r. D.A. Wilmart ('Une lettre inédite de S. Anselme à une moniale inconstante', *Revue bénédictine* 40 [1928], pp. 319-32) drew attention to this manuscript (quotation from p. 320), but in *St Anselm and his Biographer*, p. 124 and n. 3, Southern dismissed Wilmart's discovery and in *St Anselm: A Portrait*, p. 256, he ignored it.

37. *Ep.* 198: Schmitt, IV, p. 89: 44; *Ep.* 265: Schmitt, IV, p. 180: 12; *Ep.* 274: Schmitt, IV, p. 189: 9; *Ep.* 331: Schmitt, V, p. 266: 50; *Ep.* 349: Schmitt, V, p. 288: 7; *Ep.* 404: Schmitt, V, p. 349: 9; *Ep.* 442: Schmitt, V, p. 389: 6; and *Ep.* 464: Schmitt, V, p. 414: 27. See *A Concordance to the Works of St Anselm* (ed. G.R. Evans; New York, 1984).

38. *Ep.* 331: Schmitt, V, p. 266: 50.

39. Compare Southern, *St Anselm: A Portrait*, pp. 71-80, on Anselm's use of Augustine.

40. *Ep.* 349: Schmitt, V, p. 288: 5-12.

41. Hinschius, pp. 108-109, *Epistola II Sixti I* ch. VI (TCC B 16 44, f. 14^v

Anselm referred to the canons in a variety of contexts, and in no case are there grounds for suggesting incompetence or lack of interest. In reply to a query from Henry I about a proposed translation of Bishop Hervey of Bangor to Lisieux, Anselm gave a summary of the canonical principles which would neither have disgraced, nor surprised Lanfranc.[42] Elsewhere he alluded to the canons that forbade a nun to put off the veil, referred to those that prescribed the election of a bishop by his cathedral chapter, asserted his canonical right and obligation to conse- crate the elect of York, and insisted on those canons that reserved the consecration of a suffragan to his metropolitan.[43] On each occasion Anselm's doctrine was correct in terms of the ancient canons of pseudo- Isidore or those of his own day.[44] Nor did Anselm's judgment falter

ch. III). See also p. 201, *Epistola II Felicis I* ch. X (f. 25ᵛ-26ʳ ch. I); p. 133, *Epistola II Zeppherini* ch. XI (f. 18ᵛ ch. I); and p. 503, *Epistola Damasi ad Stephanum* ch. XII (f. 40ʳ-40ᵛ ch. V); but there are many others. Anselm had already accused Henry of disseizing him of his 'officio' without due judgment (Ep. 265: Schmitt, IV, p. 180: 12).

42. Ep. 404: Schmitt, V, p. 349: 3-14. Compare Hinschius, p. 79, *Epistola II Anacleti* ch. XXV (TCC B 16 44, f. 11ʳ ch. III); p. 152, *Epistola Anteri* ch. II (f. 20ᵛ); pp. 725-29, *Epistola Pelagii II ad Benignum* (f. 94ʳ-96ʳ); p. 29, *Canones Apostolorum* ch. XXXIV (f. 110ʳ ch. XXXIV); p. 299, *Concilium III Cartaginense* ch. XXVIII (f. 129ʳ ch. XXVIII); and p. 140, *Epistola II Calixti* ch. XV (f. 19ᵛ ch. III). Interestingly, Anselm did not mention the papal intervention required by this last decretal.

43. Ep. 177: Schmitt, IV, pp. 60-61: 4-9; Ep. 274: Schmitt, IV, p. 189: 8-9; Ep. 464: Schmitt, IV, p. 413: 3-6; and Ep. 265: Schmitt, IV, p. 180: 8-10.

44. On the question of a nun putting off the veil, see, for example, Hinschius, p. 378, *Concilium VI Toletanum* ch. VI (TCC B 16 44, f. 166ᵛ ch. VI); p. 401, *Concilium X Toletanum* ch. V (f. 178ᵛ ch. V); p. 531, *Epistola Innocentii ad Victoricum* chs. XII-XIII (f. 47ᵛ ch. XIII); and compare Lanfranc, *Letters*, no. 53, p. 166; also no. 45, p. 142. Canonical election was a lively and complex question. See, for example, the synodical decretal of Nicholas II (TCC B 16 44, f. 105ʳ, also f. 105ᵛ); Hinschius, p. 368, *Concilium IV Toletanum* ch. XVIII (TCC B 16 44, f. 161ᵛ ch. XVIII); p. 616, *Epistola Leonis I ad Rusticum* ch. I (f. 72ʳ ch. IIII); p. 560, *Epistola Coelestini I ad episcopos per Viennensem cet.* ch. V (f. 57ʳ ch. III); p. 428, *Capitula Martini Bracarensis* ch. I (f. 193ʳ ch. I); and p. 299, *Concilium III Carthaginense* ch. XL (f. 130ʳ ch. XLIII). Anselm's right to consecrate the archbishop-elect of York was established in the Councils of 1072 (Lanfranc, *Letters*, no. 3, p. 46). The reservation of a bishop's consecration to the metropolitan is very clear in canons such as Hinschius, p. 322, *Concilium II Arelatense* ch. VI (TCC B 16 44, f. 138ᵛ); and p. 428, *Capitula Martini Bracarensis* chs. II-III (f. 193ᵛ chs. II-III).

when Rannulf of Durham proposed to consecrate the bishop-elect of St Andrews before the archbishop-elect of York was consecrated. The elect of York could not 'canonice' take part in a consecration as metropolitan, nor could anyone else act for him, until he was himself consecrated. The only way that the suffragan could be consecrated first, 'si forte hoc necessitas exegerit', was by Anselm himself (acting as primate).[45]

There is no sign of Anselm disparaging the authority of the canons in his correspondence. Indeed, infringing them was enough to call down God's wrath on the malefactor.[46] In a letter to Pope Paschal in 1099–1100, Anselm strongly implied the identity of the law with the will of God, complaining that the king sought 'ut voluntatibus suis, quae contra legem et voluntatem dei erunt, sub nomine rectitudinis assensum praeberem', and later writing of 'legem et voluntatem dei et decreta apostolica' as if they were all of a piece.[47] Warning him that the church in his dominions was not given to him 'in haereditariam dominationem, sed in haereditariam reverentiam et tuitionem', and that he was to love it as his mother and honour it as the spouse and 'amica' of Christ, Anselm told Marquess Umbert to obey the 'apostolici decretis' since the pope spoke on behalf of Peter, or rather on behalf of Christ who commended his church to Peter. He was to remember that if he did what was forbidden in 'vicarii Petri, et in eo Petri et Christi decreta' he would not enter the kingdom via the gates to which Peter holds the keys: 'Omnes namque qui nolunt subiecti esse legi dei, absque dubio deputantur inimici dei.'[48] Similar notions of the importance of canon law and the idea of a consonant 'divinarum litterarum corpus' which included the Bible, the Fathers, decretals and canons informed the theology of Lanfranc.[49]

---

45. *Ep.* 442: Schmitt, V, p. 389: 3-10. This seems an odd problem altogether. However, Anselm was correct in law. 'Necessitas legem non habet' (for example, Hinschius, p. 700, *Decreta Felicis IV* [TCC B 16 44, f. 91ʳ]) was one of the canonists' maxims. Necessity therefore allowed the waiving of the strict letter of the law (Hinschius, p. 128, *Epistola I Victoris* ch. II [TCC B 16 44, f. 17ᵛ ch. I]). In this case, unless necessity required it, Anselm could not trespass on the archbishop of York's right to consecrate his suffragan.

46. *Ep.* 349: Schmitt, V, p. 288: 12.

47. *Ep.* 210: Schmitt, IV, pp. 106-107: 14-55.

48. *Ep.* 262: Schmitt, IV, pp. 177: 28-46. This seems to be an allusion to Rom. 8.7.

49. For further argument on this point, see Philpott, 'Lanfranc and Canon Law', I, pp. 56-62. The quotation is from Lanfranc, *de Corpore et Sanguine*, MS Bodley 569, f. 15ᵛ (*PL* 150, 429).

In fact, their similar approach to the canons lay at the heart of many of the resemblances between the pontificates of Lanfranc and Anselm. The precise parallels in their treatment of canonical matters suggest that Anselm was not merely following Lanfranc's precedents, but was using the same intellectual tools and resources in a similar context. The rights of the church of Canterbury in its estates outside the diocese are a good example. Just as Lanfranc brought Ethelric of Chichester, 'vir antiquissimus et legum terrae sapientissimus', to his plea at Penenden Heath 'ad ipsas antiquas legum consuetudines discutiendas et edocendas',[50] so Anselm appealed to Wulfstan of Worcester, the last surviving English bishop, to confirm that his church had 'semper' 'libere et quiete' 'in praeteritis et antiquis temporibus usque ad praesens tempus' enjoyed the 'potestatem et consuetudinem' of exercising the rights pertaining 'ad episcopale officium' wherever it had a *villa* or church.[51] As for the substantive issue, Anselm's position is very close to Lanfranc's letter to Stigand of Chichester.[52] Lanfranc insisted that 'contra morem antecessorum nostrorum atque vestrorum' he had commanded the priests of his estates within Stigand's diocese to attend the bishop's synods, but that 'sicut semper consuetudo fuit' they remained subject only to his own authority. Since this arrangement had led to abuse, he forbade any of his priests to attend any other bishop's synod in future: it was for the archbishop himself to examine them 'pastorali auctoritate'. The priests were only to receive chrism from the diocesan, and that at the usual rates, 'nanque ea quae antiquitus usque ad nostra tempora antecessores nostri habuerunt sollerti vigilantia cupimus illibata servare'.

This position shared by Anselm and Lanfranc is not the most obvious one to reach from the canon law. Custom and precedent are accorded so predominant a place that at first sight there appears to be no role for the canon law, as such, at all. Indeed, the archbishops' ruling seems to run against the thrust of pseudo-Isidorian law on the episcopacy, which makes each bishop master in his own diocese and specifically forbids primates and metropolitans to intervene in the dioceses of their

50. At least according to the Canterbury version, edited as the A text by J. Le Patourel, 'The Reports of the Trial on Penenden Heath', in R.W. Hunt, W.A. Pantin and R.W. Southern (eds.) *Studies in Medieval History presented to F.M. Powicke* (Oxford, 1948), pp. 15-26 (23). There is considerable difficulty about the dating, however.

51. *Ep.* 170: Schmitt, IV, p. 51: 7-11.

52. Lanfranc, *Letters*, no. 30, pp. 116-18.

suffragans.[53] However, at the heart of the pseudo-Isidorian conception of the church lay the maxim: 'Ne transgrediaris terminos antiquos. quos posuerunt patres tui. Terminos indubitanter transgreditur; qui statuta patrum post ponit atque confundit.'[54] Hence the importance to Lanfranc and Anselm of custom and their appeal to the Anglo-Saxon past.[55] If the extra-diocesan rights of the church of Canterbury could be shown to be part of the institution of the Fathers, it was in law their primatial duty to defend it.

In conclusion, we can say that the evidence of his correspondence suggests that Anselm was, in the terms of his own day, a perfectly competent canon lawyer. Like even the most eminent of his contemporaries, he had occasionally to work hard in the absence of obvious authorities, but the sources to which he turned, and the methods by which he sought to make sense of them, bear close comparison with those used by famous canon lawyers like Ivo of Chartres and Lanfranc of Canterbury. Indeed, like theirs, Anselm's advice was sought on canonical issues; on at least one occasion before there is any likelihood of his having had advisers to guide him. Nor does Anselm emerge as any less interested in canon law or respectful of it than his contemporaries; like them, he maintained that the canons and decretals were an essential part of God's law. Thus his search for union with God predisposed him to seek to ensure observance of the canons and decretals, since in doing so he would be fulfilling his duty to secure obedience to God's law. It is thus no wonder that Bishop William of Durham found himself defeated in canonical argument by Anselm whom he had thought 'omnis humanae prudentiae inscius et expers'.[56]

---

53. There are very many such canons; see, for example, Hinschius, p. 41, *Epistola I Clementis* ch. XXXVI (TCC B 16 44, f. 4ᵛ); and pp. 138-39, *Epistola II Calixti* chs. XII-XIV (f. 19ʳ-19ᵛ ch. III).

54. Hinschius, p. 95, *Epistola I Alexandri* ch. I (here quoted from TCC B 16 44, f. 13ʳ).

55. See Southern, *St Anselm: A Portrait*, pp. 330-51.

56. Eadmer, *Historia novorum*, p. 62.

ST ANSELM, ROSCELIN AND THE SEE OF BEAUVAIS

C.J. Mews

> We know for sure, venerable father, truly we know that your insight pro-
> ceeds by solving even those knotty problems of scripture at which most
> others fail. Therefore your diligence should not be reluctant to write to me
> and certain others what faith, simple prudence and prudent simplicity
> thinks about the three persons of the godhead for the common good of
> catholic Christians.

With these flattering words 'brother John' begs Anselm to resolve a
question which Roscelin of Compiègne had raised: 'if three persons are
merely one thing and not three individual things like three angels or
three souls in such a way that by will and power they are entirely the
same, then the Father and the Holy Spirit *has* become incarnate with the
Son.'[1] Roscelin claimed that Anselm had yielded this point in disputation, as had Lanfranc. John felt sure that this contradicted an image of
the Trinity as like the sun, a single thing endowed with both heat and
brightness, traditionally attributed to Augustine. Anselm replied to this
letter after an unspecified delay, providing a preliminary answer to an
issue which he promised to discuss more fully at a later date: 'Either he
wants to set up three gods or he does not understand what he is saying'.
Anselm apologized for being too busy to see John in person before John
returned to Rome.[2] As is widely known, Anselm then set about writing
the initial version of his *De incarnatione verbi*, addressed to those 'lords,
fathers and brothers' who might read his open letter. He also asked
Fulco, bishop of Beauvais, to reassert that he had never defended the
argument attributed to him by Roscelin.

1.   *Ep.* 128: Schmitt, III, pp. 270-71. On Roscelin's thought, see C.J. Mews,
'Nominalism and Theology before Abaelard: New Light on Roscelin of Compiègne',
Vivarium 30.1 (1992), pp. 4-33. Much of my research on Roscelin was conducted at
the Institute for Advanced Study, Princeton, where I benefited greatly from its
magnificent resources and from discussion with Giles Constable.
2.   *Ep.* 129: Schmitt, III, pp. 271-72.

St Anselm's argument with Roscelin has often been understood in doctrinal terms—the clash of a philosophical realist with an unspiritual nominalist. Anselm described his adversary as one of 'those heretics of modern dialectic who do not believe a universal to be anything more than the puff of an utterance'. The political context of the conflict has never been analysed, it being commonly assumed that we know nothing about Roscelin other than that he became the teacher of Peter Abelard. Yet there are other documents beyond the correspondence of St Anselm which shed light on the dispute.

It may be useful to begin by looking more closely at what Roscelin's critic, John, was doing at the time in France. John was a Roman cleric who had become a monk at Bec not long after Anselm became abbot there in late 1079.[3] In his first letter to Anselm, Pope Urban II observed that the abbot of Bec had caused some controversy in Rome by presuming to ordain John, 'a son of our Church', to higher orders.[4] The Pope nonetheless allowed John to assist another Bec monk, Fulco, to establish himself as bishop of Beauvais, on the proviso that he return 'within a year from this present Lent'. He seems to be writing in Lent 1089. Fulco had initially obtained the see of Beauvais directly from the king after the death of Ursio, probably in 1088.[5] After returning to Italy,

3.   Eadmer, *Historia novorum in Anglia* (ed. M. Rule; London, 1884), p. 96 and *Vita Anselmi* (ed. R.W. Southern; London, 1962), p. 106 n. 1; William of Malmesbury, *De gestis pontificum Anglorum* (ed. N. Hamilton; London, 1870), p. 98. The name 'Ioannes episcopus' occurs relatively early among those received under Anselm's abbacy, while 'Fulco episcopus' was one of the last to be received prior to Herluin's death in September 1078, according to the list of Bec monks in Vat. Reg. 499; A. Porée, *Histoire de l'abbaye de Bec* (Evreux, 1901), I, p. 630.

4.   *Ep.* 125: Schmitt, III, p. 266.

5.   There is no firm evidence that Ursio died in 1089, as assumed by L.-H. Labande, *Histoire de Beauvais et des institutions communales jusqu'au commencement du XVe siècle* (Paris, 1892), p. 52 n. 5. All we know of him is that he signed a royal privilege at Compiègne in 1085 (M. Prou, *Recueil des Actes de Philippe Ier, Roi de France [1059–1108]* [Paris, 1908], p. 299, no. 117). The martyrology of Beauvais indicates only that he died on 18 April. No bishop of Beauvais was present when the king confirmed a prebend of Saint-Quentin in 1089 (Prou, *Recueil des Actes*, pp. 303-304, no. 119 [with a corresponding document from Saint-Quentin edited at n. 1]). Ewald argued that Fulco's submission to the Pope, recorded in the *Collectio Britannica*, took place before the council of Melfi, September 1088, like other events it recorded ('Die Papstbriefe der Britischen Sammlung', *Neues Archiv* 5 [1880], p. 360). In his edition of the notice, D. Lohrmann (*Papsturkunden in Frankreich. VII. Nördliche Ile-de-France und*

John was appointed abbot of San Salvatore, Telese by Urban II; by 1100 he had become John IV, cardinal bishop of Tusculum, and was papal legate to France and England.[6] John's deposition of Hugh, abbot of Flavigny, in 1100–1101 on behalf of Norigaud, bishop of Autun, provoked Hugh to comment sarcastically about John: 'I am amazed that the seriousness of such a man, famous for his unbounded goodness and honest reputation, whose constancy the Gallican Church reveres, could be deceived by one person [Norigaud], with the result that he now holds, watches over and protects its regions with his hand, yet is the only person in our world who thinks good and right things about that man, since general opinion even of the absent and the ignorant is hostile to his judgement.'[7] Hugh, already disillusioned by what he saw as the hypocritical reform rhetoric of Roman cardinals, then berated John's high-handed attitude in excommunicating canons of Autun and reports otherwise unknown information about Roscelin's critic: John had been a regular canon at Saint-Quentin, Beauvais, but had abandoned his religious habit for the world; only after he had been unable to make some unspecified accusation did John become a monk of Bec.[8] This detail helps explain why Fulco asked Urban II for John's help: Fulco wanted someone who knew Beauvais.

John was wanting Anselm to assert himself as an authoritative Christian teacher at a time when there was no clear spiritual leadership in the city. He was assisting a monastic bishop then facing widespread

Vermandois [Göttingen, new edn, 1976], p. 23 n. 17 and pp. 246-47, no. 13, following JL 5046) notes that the date cannot be established more exactly than between March 1088 and July 1089. He suggested July 1089 as the most likely date for Fulco's submission on the authority of the 1 August date appended to Urban's letter of indulgence in Paris, BN *lat.* 14146 f. 164[v]. However, as M. Horn ('Zur Geschichte des Bischofs Fulco von Beauvais [1089-1095]', *Francia* 16.1 [1989], pp. 176-84 [179]) points out, the rubric is contradicted by Urban's statement that he was writing during Lent. J.R. Somerville queries the 1088 date for Fulco's submission without realizing that the 1089 date for Ursio's decease was only approximate ('Mercy and Justice in the Early Months of Urban II's Pontificate', in *Chiesa, diritto e ordinamento della 'Societas christiana' nei secoli XI e XII: Atti della nona Settimana internazionale di studio, Mendola, 1983* [Milan, 1986], pp. 138-54 [50-1], reprinted in *Papacy, Councils and Canon Law in the 11th-12th Centuries* [London, 1990]).

6.   R. Hüls, *Kardinäle, Klerus und Kirchen Roms 1049–1130* (Tübingen, 1977), pp. 141-42. John IV died in 1119, MGH SS 20.74.

7.   *Chronicon*, MGH SS 8.494.

8.   *Chronicon*, MGH SS 8.494.

opposition to his authority. Anselm complained to the Pope that 'the canons and priests of his diocese, with very few exceptions, and certain laymen are so angry with him and so inflame any strangers they can by whatever means, that they curse not only him [Fulco] but also those who offer him some consolation'—presumably an allusion to John.[9] Anselm blamed this resistance on hostility to Fulco's efforts to prohibit clergy from associating with women and promoting their sons to prebends (in other words for enforcing the canons of Melfi).[10] He claimed that Fulco was resisting lay appropriation of ecclesiastical property.

A letter from the Pope to Rainaud of Rheims chiding the archbishop for his continued hostility to Fulco in 1090–1091 suggests a different picture: widespread suspicion that Fulco's father had bought the bishopric from the king.[11] Lancelin I was an ambitious Beauvais *miles* who had married his eldest son, Lancelin II, to Adelaïde, daughter of Count Hugh of Dammartin.[12] Another son, Radulfus, had been cathedral treasurer of Beauvais in 1078 before becoming a monk at Bec.[13] Anselm supported Fulco's appointment to Beauvais with the approval of the king, even though Fulco had then to renounce his position and receive it back directly from the Pope, at the same time as Henry of Soissons, an 'ecclesiastical adventurer' similarly tainted by irregular appointment.[14] Fulco was not reinstated with full episcopal rights on this first visit to Rome.[15] He had to make a second trip to Rome to swear on the Gospels

9. *Ep.* 126: Schmitt, III, p. 267.

10. *Ep.* 126: Schmitt, III, pp. 267-68. If the *Collectio Britannica* is correct in implying that Fulco submitted to the Pope before the council of Melfi, then Fulco is likely to have been present at this council in September 1088 if he did not return to Beauvais until the following Lent.

11. JL 5522; *PL* 151, 388B-389. A. Lohrmann corrects to 13 May 1090 Jaffé-Loewenfeld's dating of this letter to this date in 1094 (*Papsturkunden*, VII, p. 23 n. 19). Horn distinguishes two visits of Fulco to Rome, and assigns the Pope's letter to 13 May 1091 (n. 5 above).

12. O. Guyotjeannin, *Episcopus et comes. Affirmation et déclin de la seigneurie épiscopale au nord du royaume de France (Beauvais-Noyon, X^e-début XIIIe siècle)* (Geneva, 1987), pp. 73-74, 102-104 and 263.

13. *Ep.* 117: Schmitt, III, p. 254; see too *Ep.* 99 and *Ep.* 115: Schmitt, III, pp. 229-30 and 251.

14. Lohrmann, *Papsturkunden*, VII, pp. 246-47; see C. Clark, '"This ecclesiastical adventurer": Henry of Saint-Jean d'Angély', *English Historical Review* 34 (1969), pp. 548-60.

15. Horn, 'Zur Geschichte des Bischofs Fulco', p. 179.

with his father that no simony had taken place, bringing with him Anselm's letter of recommendation. Fulco also had the support of Ivo of Chartres, who blamed the hostility towards him on jealousy and thought it wrong for Fulco to be criticized when already pardoned by the Pope.[16]

The archbishop of Rheims nonetheless remained hostile to Fulco. The council of Soissons was called some time between 1090 and 1092 not just to judge Roscelin of Compiègne's orthodoxy, but to settle Fulco's legitimacy within the archdiocese and resolve complaints about his father's behaviour.[17] Before the assembled bishops, the elderly Lancelin I had to restore to the church of Beauvais the properties of Longueil and Berthecourt. Helinand of Laon reminded Lancelin of his excommunication on that account and of a submission he was supposed to have effected at a council in Paris, and challenged him to a duel.[18] Because Roscelin was present at Bayeux on 7 May 1092, before embarking for England, the council of Soissons must have taken place before this date.[19]

By December 1093 Fulco's position at Beauvais had deteriorated so much that Anselm asked Urban to relieve him of his bishopric.[20] In February 1094 Urban charged Fulco with complicity in no less than murder and treason.[21] Fulco had imprisoned the brother of the bishop of Sens for financial gain, delivering him as a captive to the king, and had ignored the judgment of his fellow bishops; he had also usurped possessions of Odo, castellan of the church of Beauvais, guaranteed by Pope Gregory in the time of his predecessor, Bishop Guy. Fulco had acted in

16. *Ep.* 3 (b), *PL* 162, 13C-14B.

17. P. Louvet, *Histoire de la ville de Beauvais* (Rouen, 1614), pp. 487-89; and M. Hermant, *Histoire ecclésiastique et civile de Beauvais et du Beauvaisis*, BN fr. 8579, pp. 448-50.

18. Guyotjeannin, *Episcopus et comes*, pp. 72-74, 103; and Labande, *Histoire de Beauvais*, p. 53; see a notice copied from the cartulary of St Pierre, Paris, BN Duchesne 22, ff. 249-50.

19. *Antiquus Cartularius Baiocensis*, no. 22 (ed. V. Bourrienne; Rouen-Paris, 1902), I, pp. 30-31: 'Rotselino Compendiensi'.

20. *Ep.* 128: Schmitt, III, p. 269. While Schmitt dates this letter to 1091, Lohrmann (*Papsturkunden*, VII, p. 23) dates it to about May 1094. Horn ('Zur Geschichte des Bischofs Fulco') notes that the letter must be before Anselm's consecration as archbishop (4 December 1093), and that it must have been written between 1091 and 1093.

21. *PL* 151, 378B-379C (JL 5509; Lohrmann, *Papsturkunden*, VII, p. 23 n. 20).

concert with his brother, Lancelin II, to try to seize Odo, snatching from him the keys of the city, which Odo held by right, and had encouraged members of Odo's household to betray their master. The Pope required Fulco to submit himself either to the archbishop of Rheims within a fortnight or to himself within three months.[22] Ivo of Chartres counselled Fulco not to resist the edicts of the papal legate, Hugh of Die.[23] Although Anselm wrote to Urban once again on Fulco's behalf after 27 May 1095, Fulco must have either died, renounced his position or have been suspended, since a new bishop of Beauvais, Roger, obtained a papal privilege for the collegiate church of St-Vaast, Beauvais, at La Chaise Dieu on 19 August 1095.[24] Recalling the establishment of canons at this church by Bishop Guy in 1072 at the request of Roscelin and Nevelo of Compiègne, the charter permitted its expansion, explicitly protecting St-Vaast from any depredation of the bishop of Beauvais.[25] This was the only known action of the bishop who replaced Fulco.

Is this Roscelin the same person as Roscelin of Compiègne? It is not a common name. Much is explained about the opposition from canons and priests in Beauvais that Fulco and John faced in 1089 if this is so. Despite the accusations against Fulco, Anselm stayed loyal to his protégé through the next five years, either not knowing or deliberately ignoring the fact that he was effectively providing spiritual legitimacy for an ambitious Beauvais family. Anselm saw nothing wrong in supporting Fulco's accession to the see, one of the most lucrative and sought after positions within the Ile-de-France. Bec had acquired some significant properties in France since 1080. Anselm's interests coincided with those of Fulco's family. The bishopric conferred effective government of the

---

22. In another missive to the clergy and people of Beauvais, Urban II confirmed existing privileges of Odo, castellan of Beauvais, against the ambitions of Fulco, *PL* 151, 379D-380A (JL 5510; Lohrmann, *Papsturkunden*, VII, p. 33 n. 5). Lohrmann's assumption that this was sent at the same time as the letter to Fulco (i.e. 14 February 1094), is questioned by Horn ('Zur Geschichte des Bischofs Fulco', p. 183); he thinks that it might belong to early in Fulco's career because it does not mention Fulco's actions. The original confirmation of Odo's possessions, then disputed by Bishop Guy (1075–79), is edited by Lohrmann, *Papsturkunden*, VII, p. 244.

23. *Yves de Chartres. Correspondance*, no. 30 (ed. J. Leclercq; Paris, 1949), pp. 127-29.

24. *Ep.* 193: Schmitt, IV, p. 82; A. Becker, *Papst Urban II (1088–1099)* (Stuttgart, 1964, 1974), II, p. 436.

25. Edited by Lohrmann, *Papsturkunden*, VII, pp. 251-52.

city and its surrounding countryside in the name of the king of France.[26] Through his two sons, the elderly Lancelin had effectively taken power over Beauvais at the same time as Bec was consolidating its position in the Ile-de-France.

The bitter antagonist of Lancelin I was Guy, bishop of Beauvais from 1063 until 1085. Guibert of Nogent remembered Guy fondly as an aristocratic figure who relished the intimate company of close companions.[27] Unlike Lancelin, Guy was an outsider to Beauvais. A former dean of Saint-Quentin-en-Vermandois and archdeacon of Laon who had been consecrated by Archbishop Gervaise of Rheims in 1063–64 (during the minority of Philip I), Guy continued Gervaise's policy of establishing collegiate churches outside the cathedral's jurisdiction to serve an expanding urban community.[28] The most famous of these was Saint-Quentin, named in honour of his former church in the Vermandois, where canons followed the Augustinian Rule, introduced by Gervaise in Rheims in 1067. In a solemn ceremony attended by many French bishops and a large crowd from the city, Guy transferred the relics of St Romana from the cathedral to the new church in 1069, deliberately weakening the monopoly of the cathedral chapter by directing popular devotion to a church outside the *urbs*.[29] Guy used the occasion to humiliate Guarinus, the treasurer of the cathedral, whom he

26. Guyotjeannin, *Episcopus et comes*, pp. 3-31, 62-66. On properties of Bec in France, see V. Gazeau, 'Le domaine continental du Bec. Aristocratie et monachisme au temps d'Anselme', in *Les Mutations socio-culturelles au tournant des XIe et XIIe siècles* (Paris, 1984), pp. 259-71.

27. *Autobiographie* I.15 (ed. E.-R. Labande; Paris, 1981), pp. 120-22.

28. *Vita S. Romanae virginis* 10, *Acta Sanctorum* (Paris, 1866), October 2, p. 138 and *Recueil des historiens de la France* 14.29; see A. Fliche, *Le Règne de Philippe Ier* (Paris, 1912), pp. 338-39; and Guyotjeannin, *Episcopus et comes*, pp. 70-72. J.-F. Lemarignier documents the increase of collegiate foundations during the eleventh century, often with royal support in 'Aspects politiques des fondations de collégiales dans le royaume de France au XIe siècle', in *La Vita Comune del clero nei secoli XI e XII. Atti della Settimana di studi: Mendola, settembre 1959* (Miscellanea del Centro di Studi Medievali III, Pubblicazioni dell'Università Cattolicà del S. Cuore III. 2; Milan, 1962), pp. 19-40, with discussion pp. 41-49. He observes that the strongest concentration of collegiate churches, standing up to the monastic federations of Bec, Cluny and Marmoutiers, was in the archdiocese of Rheims.

29. *Acta Sanctorum* Oct. 2, pp. 138-39, with valuable introduction on pp. 134-37.

accused of purloining half the tithe of the city of Beauvais for personal advantage.[30]

In 1072 Guy increased the number of canons at the church of Saint-Vaast, 'at the request of Roscelin, cantor of Saint-Pierre and Nevelon, canon of Compiègne so that by an increased number of ministers, the service of religion might be multiplied'.[31] His charter described this ancient church, now called Saint-Etienne, as 'by its antiquity in the burg of Beauvais like the mother and head of the other churches placed both in the city and the suburb'. It assured them 'the same liberty and dignity as other canons in the city as in the suburb'. The bishop's anathema against anyone who removed the stipends of these canons suggests resistance from the cathedral chapter to the development. Leading the signatories to this charter, after the Benedictine abbots of Saint-Lucian and Saint-Symphorian, was Ivo, described here as abbot of Saint-Quentin.[32] Ivo's presence at Saint-Vaast, hitherto unnoticed in discussion of the

30. Labande, *Histoire de Beauvais*, p. 260, pièce justificative no. 2. By 1072 a new treasurer had been appointed, named Gualterius.

31. The original foundation charter of Saint-Vaast was edited by Louvet, *Histoire de la ville de Beauvais*, pp. 480-82 and *Histoire et antiquitez du païs de Beauvaisis* (Beauvais, 1631–35), I, pp. 694-95: 'Guido Dei gratia Belvacensis Episcopus omnibus tam futuris quam praesentibus notum sit. Quod nos considerantes Domini Roscelini Cantoris Ecclesiae S. Petri et Nevelonis Compendiensis Ecclesiae Canonici religiosam devotionem collaudamus, et sicut dignum est comprobamus. Hi siquidem Ecclesiam B. Vedasti quae in Belvacensi Burgo sita pro antiquitatis dignitate quasi mater, et caput et coeterarum Ecclesiarum tam in urbe quam in suburbio positarum sub nomine personae possidentes cum duo tantum in ea presbyteri deservirent nostrae mansuetudinis licentiam postularunt, ut in praedicta Ecclesia plures apponi Canonicos concederemus: quatinus augmentato numero ministrorum multiplicaretur quoque religionis obsequium. Quorum laudabilem petitionem libenter amplectentes in praedicta B. Vedasti Ecclesia Canonicos institui decrevimus, id etiam constituentes ut Canonici illi iam dictam Ecclesiam, necnon et Ecclesiam S. Salvatoris sine calumnia possideant, cum omnibus quae ad utramque Ecclesiam pertinentia in ea die qua Canonici constituti sunt, Roscelinus et Nevelo possidebant. Id etiam decernimus et praesenti pagina sancimus ut iam dictae Ecclesiae Canonici ea dignitate et libertate vigeant quam caeteri qui vel in suburbio sunt Canonici obtinent. Ut autem haec Canonicorum institutio rata in posterum et stabilis permaneat illam cartae praesentis attestatione et sigilli nostri assignatione corroboramus. Illud postremo adiicientes ut si quis Canonicorum redditus et stipendiae vel Ecclesiae ornamenta violenter aut fraudulenter et perperam detrahere, corrumpere aut alienare praesumpserit anathema sit.'

32. The dozen clerics who signed included Hugh (dean of Saint-Pierre), Walter (treasurer), Roger and Goscelin (archdeacons); among the dozen lay signatories was the castellan Odo, with whom Fulco entered into conflict.

date of his arrival in Beauvais, confirms that he had already been invited by Guy to introduce a reformed canonical life at Saint-Quentin at its foundation (not in 1078, as had been thought).[33] One of the twelve prebends of Saint-Vaast was controlled by Saint-Quentin.[34]

Guy's sense of the educational role of his collegiate foundations and outrage at clerical malpractice is clarified by his charter for Saint-Nicolas in 1078. Its establishment had been prompted not just by certain clerics, but by 'helpers of the lay order'.[35] Its prebends could not be acquired by an outside cleric who simply paid for a deputy (reported to be a common practice). To avoid the pernicious practice of able clergy being driven out of the church by poverty at the expense of the idle rich, the canons of the cathedral had to grant a prebend without cost to maintain a treasurer, charged with educating boys and maintaining the fabric of the church.[36] Saint-Vaast would have had a similar educational role. Standing at the heart of the commune of Beauvais, the church came to be endowed by the burghers, often textile merchants, of the city.

Guy's patronage of collegiate churches brought him into conflict with the cathedral chapter. Only a year after establishing canons at Saint-Vaast, Guy was accused of despoiling episcopal property for the sake of his new foundations.[37] Gregory VII insisted that the canons receive Guy back to the city.[38] Guy was also in conflict with Lancelin I, whom he had excommunicated for seizing episcopal properties at Longueil and

33. The 1078 date for Ivo's invitation to Beauvais is based on a Beauvais version of Sigebert's *Chronicon*, *PL* 160, 388B; MGH SS 6.461-2: 'Ab hoc tempore coepit reflorere in ecclesia beati Quintini Belvacensis canonicus Ordo, primum ab Apostolis, postea ex beato Augustino episcopo regulariter institutus, sub magistro Ivone, vener-abili eiusdem ecclesiae praeposito, postea Carnotensium episcopo.' The date is debated in the Bollandist introduction to the *Vita S. Romanae, Acta Sanctorum* Oct. 2, p. 135.

34. Confirmed in 1116; see Lohrmann, *Papsturkunden*, VII, p. 266.

35. Louvet, *Histoire et antiquitez*, pp. 689-90 (*Histoire de la ville de Beauvais*, p. 492).

36. *Histoire et antiquitez*, pp. 690-91 (*Histoire de la ville de Beauvais*, pp. 493-94).

37. *Acta Sanctorum* Oct. 2, p. 139. The editors suggest (p. 136) that Guy's expulsion may have been provoked by his generosity to the newly founded church of Saint-Quentin, for whose sake he despoiled existing churches, a point reiterated by Labande, *Histoire de Beauvais*, p. 48.

38. Gregory VII, *Registrum* I.74-75 (JL 4854-5), *PL* 148, 347C-8D, dated 13 April 1074; *Papsturkunden*, VII, pp. 23 n. 12 and 32 nn. 1-2.

Berthecourt.[39] In 1074 Gregory VII had urged the archbishops and bishops of France to protest against the king's harassment of merchants and pilgrims, and singled out Lancelin of Beauvais as a brigand for taking hostage a pilgrim from Rome, Fulcher of Chartres.[40] Lancelin's son, Radulfus, had become cathedral treasurer by 1078, when Guy was accused by the papal legate, Hugh of Die, of selling prebends (probably alienating cathedral prebends for collegiate foundations).[41] In January 1079 Guy succeeded in obtaining royal confirmation at Gerberoy that Saint-Quentin fell under his jurisdiction alone. Radulfus was still treasurer when he attended that august assembly, which gathered the kings of England and France, as well as Anselm of Bec, Ivo of Saint-Quentin and Lancelin.[42] Not much later Radulfus left Beauvais for Bec. Fulco's future assistant, John, also left Saint-Quentin for Bec about this time. According to Guibert of Nogent, Guy's subsequent ousting in 1085 was engineered by those he had promoted within his diocese.[43] After Guy was officially deposed by Hugh of Die in 1085, he became a monk at Cluny, where the prior was Ivo, a monk from Saint-Quentin-en-Vermandois who had been with him in Beauvais.[44] It is difficult to avoid surmising that Lancelin I, Radulfus and John were all involved with Hugh of Die in the conspiracy against Bishop Guy. An alliance between Bec and a local Beauvais dynasty was forged.

After the short spell of Ursio as bishop of Beauvais (1085–88?), the accession of Fulco marked a clear victory for the elderly Lancelin.[45] It

39. Gregory lifted Guy's excommunication against Lancelin according to a document printed by Louvet, *Histoire de Beauvais*, pp. 486-7 (*PL* 148, 658BC); Lohrmann (*Papsturkunden*, VII, p. 32 no. 3) notes Jaffé's opinion (*Bibliotheca rerum Germanicarum*, II, p. 520 n. 1) that this was a forgery, presumably on the grounds that Lancelin was still excommunicated on his deathbed in 1092. See Guyotjeannin, *Episcopus et comes*, p. 74 n. 29 and Labande, *Histoire de Beauvais*, pp. 48-49, 53.

40. *Registrum* II.5 (*PL* 148, 363A-365D).

41. Hugh of Die, MGH SS 8.419; Lohrmann, *Papsturkunden*, VII, p. 23 n. 15. Anselm's earliest letter to Hugh, E100 (Schmitt, III, pp. 131-32), written soon after 1082, when Hugh was appointed archbishop of Lyons, indicates that they were already friends.

42. Prou, *Recueil des Actes*, no. xciv, pp. 242-45. Lancelin was described as *casatus* of the church of Beauvais, having taken over the role from Odo, castellan in 1072.

43. *Autobiographie* I.14 (ed. Labande), p. 100.

44. Guibert de Nogent, *Autobiographie* I.15 (ed. Labande), p. 118.

45. *Lancelinus senex* witnessed an undated judgement of Fulco (Paris, BN

was advantageous for Bec to have such high-placed contacts in France. Either the older or the younger Lancelin witnessed a royal privilege for possessions of Bec in France in 1077. One or other is likely to be the Lancelin who was *buticularius* to the king some time between 1086–90/91 when Bec monks were granted exemptions from tax in Paris, Pontoise, Poissy and Mantes.[46] The first and only known action of Roger, Fulco's successor at Beauvais, was to obtain from Pope Urban II at La Chaise-Dieu in 1095 papal confirmation of the privileges of Guy's foundation at Saint-Vaast from episcopal interference.[47] Roger's charter specifically recalled the initiative of Roscelin and Nevelon of Compiègne in establishing the community. The privileges of another foundation of Guy, at Bury, were also confirmed by Urban II at this time, with the support of the canons of Beauvais.[48]

Given that John was in Beauvais for less than a year, engaged in controversy with 'nearly all' the canons and priests of the diocese and that Anselm subsequently addressed his letter about Roscelin to Fulco, it seems logical to assume that John argued with Roscelin of Compiègne in that city. After the council of Soissons, Roscelin made contact with

Baluze 71, ff. 19-19ᵛ) cited by Prou, *Recueil des Actes*, p. cxxxvii n. 9. On the date of Lancelin I's death, see Labande, *Histoire de Beauvais*, p. 53 n. 4.

46. Guyotjeannin, *Episcopus et comes*, p. 102 n. 153; and J.-F. Lemarignier, *Le gouvernement royal aux premiers temps capétiens (987–1108)* (Paris, 1965), p. 157 n. 95 and appendix; Prou, *Recueil des Actes*, nos. xc, pp. 232-34 and cxxii, pp. 308-10; the latter privilege for Bec was extended by Philip and Louis conjointly some time between 1092 and 1108, Prou, *Recueil des Actes*, no. clxvii, pp. 410-11 (no witnesses cited), and J. Dufour, *Recueil des Actes de Louis VI*, I (Paris, 1992), no. 18, pp. 31-32. Lancelin is mentioned as *pincerna regis* in 1086, Prou, *Recueil des Actes*, no. cxvii, pp. 301-302, and as *buticularius* to the king in 1089 in a charter granting privileges to the canons of Sainte-Croix of Orléans, *Cartulaire de Sainte-Croix d'Orléans (814–1300)* (ed. J. Thillier and E. Jarry), no. xlvii, pp. 95-96.

47. Ivo did not officially relinquish his position at Saint-Quentin until 1094, even though he was elected to the see of Chartres in November 1090, *Yves de Chartres. Correspondance* (ed. Leclercq), no. 31, pp. 126-28.

48. Guy's last major action had been to confirm the establishment of a community at Bury in 1084–85, originally established in 1079–80 at the request of a certain Albert for more canons to serve the needs of the local community. It was then transformed into a monastery belonging to Saint-Jean d'Angély, *Le Cartulaire de l'Abbaye Royale de Saint-Jean d'Angély* (Archives Historiques de la Saintonge et de l'Aunis XXX; Paris, 1901), no. xv, pp. 36-38, confirmed by Philip I in 1085, no. xvi, pp. 39-40; for the confirmation by Pope Urban II, see no. xiv, p. 35. See Guyotjeannin, *Episcopus et comes*, p. 71.

Ivo of Chartres, formerly dean of Saint-Quentin, Beauvais, but was warned by Ivo that a visit to Chartres would be compromising for himself. He suggested Roscelin issue a retractation to clear his name.[49]

Roscelin was a native of the region of Compiègne, not a canon of that town.[50] In a letter to Abelard, Roscelin rejected the claim that he had been exiled by the churches of Soissons and Rheims 'where I was born and brought up'. He boasted of holding canonries at Loches, Tours and Besançon, even of being received favourably in Rome (perhaps a reference to reception by Urban II, formerly of Rheims, during his travels in France 1095–96, rather than to any visit to Rome).[51] Roscelin was an old man when he wrote that letter to Abelard (c. 1119–20). He could have been a young cantor at St-Pierre in 1072, invited to the post by a reforming bishop from outside Beauvais, eager to employ a promising teacher.

According to an entry added in the early twelfth century to an eleventh-century martyrology of Beauvais cathedral a *Roscelinus grammaticus* bequeathed to the chapter at his death (9 July of an unknown year) fourteen books, of grammar, logic and rhetoric, with some theology: 'Roscelinus grammaticus dedit libros suos Sancto Petro: Augustinum super Johannem, Augustinum de doctrina christiana, Prissianum, Macrobium, Arismeticam, Dialecticam, Rethoricam de inventione, Boetium de consolatione, Virgilium, Oratium, Juvenalem, Ovidium metamorphoseon, Statium Thebaïdos, et troparium.'[52] This Roscelin also bequeathed his house in the cathedral cloister and eight *arpenni* of vines at Hosdenc, eight kilometres from Beauvais.[53] The

49. *Yves de Chartres. Correspondance*, no. 7 (ed. Leclercq), pp. 22-24.

50. *Ep. ad Abaelardum*, in *Der Nominalismus in der Frühscholastik* (Beiträge zur Geschichte der Philosophie der Mittelalters 8.5; ed. J. Reiners; Münster, 1910), pp. 64-65.

51. *Ep. ad Abaelardum* (ed. Reiners), p. 65.

52. L. Delisle, 'Notice sur un manuscrit de l'abbaye de Luxeuil copié en 625', *Notices et extraits des manuscrits de la bibliothèque nationale* 31.2 (Paris, 1886), pp. 149-64 (160); see also H. Omont, *Recherches sur la bibliothèque de l'église cathédrale de Beauvais* (Paris, 1914), pp. 2-3. I am indebted to Françoise Gasparri for confirming an early twelfth-century date (c. 1120), rather than eleventh-century, as judged by Delisle.

53. Delisle, *Notices*, p. 160: 'Nonis julii. Obiit Roscelinus gramaticus, qui dedit nobis suam domum in claustro, et octo arpennos vinearum in hosdenco, et libros suos numero quatuordecim.' Delisle suggested that this Roscelin was the same person as the cantor Roscelin, but repeated the confused statement in *Histoire*

presence of the book of tropes points to this being the same Roscelin as was cantor in 1072.

Roscelin the grammarian did not leave any identifiable annotation to the most precious item in his bequest to Beauvais, an uncial exemplar of Augustine's homilies on the Johannine epistles copied at Luxeuil in the seventh century (our earliest extant copy of the homilies). Also among his books was a tenth-century Horace.[54] The collection reminds us that a late eleventh-century *grammaticus* was expected to teach not just grammar, but dialectic and rhetoric as well as theology. It is particularly valuable because the books seem deliberately chosen to cover the whole curriculum. This collection would have been available later in the twelfth century to Ralph of Beauvais, who used classical authors extensively in his grammatical teaching and quoted approvingly the opinion of *nominales* that 'man' denoted the status of being a man, both special and general.[55] From his books, *Roscelinus grammaticus* seems to have been a master of great learning and erudition.

In his letter to Abelard, Roscelin insisted that he remained in good standing with the churches of Rheims and Soissons.[56] If, as Abelard implied, Roscelin had become unpopular at Tours, then it is not implausible that he should have wished to bequeath some of his books to the cathedral where he spent his first twenty years as a teacher. There is no reason for him to have lost whatever property he owned in the archdiocese of Rheims after the accusations raised at the council of Soissons.

While the evidence for identifying Roscelin the grammarian and Roscelin the canon at Saint-Vaast (and ally of Nevelo of Compiègne)

littéraire de la France, IX (Paris, rev. edn, 1868), p. 364, that Roscelin and Nevelon founded a community of canons regular in Saint-Vaast, Soissons. He cites Mabillon's authority for distinguishing the cantor of Beauvais from Roscelin of Compiègne, but I have been unable to identify the passage to which he alludes.

54. New York, Pierpoint Morgan Library no. 334 (see E.A. Lowe, *Codices Latini Antiquiores*, IX [Oxford, 1966] no. 1659, p. 23) and Leiden, Universiteits-biblioteek, Bibl. pub. lat. 28; there is extensive grammatical commentary in this, according to a communication from J. Dijs, but it remains as yet unstudied.

55. On Ralph of Beauvais, see the pioneering discussion of R.W. Hunt, 'Studies on Priscian in the Twelfth Century', *Mediaeval and Renaissance Studies* 2 (1950), pp. 1-56, reprinted in his *Collected Papers on the History of Grammar in the Middle Ages* (ed. G.L. Bursill-Hall; Amsterdam, 1980), pp. 39-94, and Ralph's *Glose super Donatum* (ed. C.H. Kneepkens; Nijmegen, 1982), p. 21 (with comment on p. xxv).

56. *Ep. ad Abaelardum* (ed. Reiners), p. 63.

with Roscelin of Compiègne is inevitably circumstantial, it is hard to believe that the political arguments with Beauvais clergy in which Fulco and John were involved were not related to their doctrinal dispute at exactly this time with Roscelin of Compiègne. John's accusation that Roscelin was preaching heresy makes sense as an attempt to counter criticism raised about himself and Bishop Fulco. By supporting Fulco, Anselm was drawn unwittingly into an acrimonious local dispute. Both Roscelin and John claimed the authority of Anselm in their argument about the Trinity, an argument sharpened by bitter controversy surrounding Fulco's appointment. Roscelin of Compiègne's zeal for reform, notably his attacks on the ordination of sons of priests, provoked criticism from Theobald of Etampes, when he travelled briefly in England in 1092–93.[57] New collegiate foundations, much more numerous in the archdiocese of Rheims than in Normandy or England, provided a vital educational resource for prosperous towns, but their influence could be resented by monks as too sharply committed to new ideas about theology. Roscelin of Compiègne, who had studied at Rheims in the reform-minded atmosphere encouraged by Archbishop Gervaise, issued from such a world.

---

57. Theobald, *Epistola ad Roscelinum*, in T. Boehmer (ed.), MGH *Libelli de lite* (Hannover, 1897), III, pp. 603-607 (*PL* 163, 767-70); *Defensio pro filiis presbyterorum* (ed. Boehmer), in *Libelli de lite*, III, pp. 579-83.

THE REALISM OF ANSELM AND HIS CONTEMPORARIES

Iwakuma Yukio

The gist of realism is the assertion that universals are *res* no matter what the *res* may be. It is a traditional and authoritative view, since Porphyry himself calls five predicables *res*.[1] In the late eleventh century *vocales* or early nominalists proposed a new theory, that universals are *voces*, to provoke a controversy on universals.[2] The point of the dispute was whether universals are *res* or *voces*. Anselm's contribution to realism lies not, as is often said, in asserting any Platonic ideas,[3] but in proposing a theory to explain what *res* universals are.

1. *Ps-Rabanus on Universals*

Ps-Rabanus's commentary on Porphyry, P3,[4] is the earliest so far known that is more than a patchwork of Boethius's commentaries. It

1. See *Isagoge*, in *Aristoteles Latinus* I.6-7 *Categoriarum supplementa* (ed. L. Minio-Paluello; Leiden, 1966), p. 5.6: 'ad ea quae in divisione vel demonstratione sunt utili hac istarum *rerum* speculatione.'
2. As for the *vocales*, see Iwakuma Yukio, '*Vocales*, or Early Nominalists', *Traditio* 47 (1992), pp. 37-111.
3. The association of the Anselmian theory with Platonism began with V. Cousin, *Ouvrages inédits d'Abélard* (Paris, 1834), p. ci ff., and was continued in one way or another by the main researchers. Thus see B. Hauréau, *Histoire de la philosophie scolastique*, I (Paris, 1872), p. 273; K. Prantl, *Geschichte der Logik im Abendland*, II (Leipzig, 2nd edn, 1885), pp. 9-10; M. De Wulf, *History of Medieval Philosophy* (London, 3rd edn, 1909), pp. 150-51. Very recently, again, P. King discusses Anselm's universals theory as Platonic in his otherwise brilliant *Peter Abailard and the Problem of Universals* (2 vols.; Michigan, 1990), I, pp. 128ff. An exception might have been J. Reiners, who says 'Diese beiden Männer [= Anselm of Canterbury and Odo of Cambrai] werden mit Unrecht als extreme Realisten angesehen' (see his *Der aristotelische Realismus in der Frühscholastik* [Bonn, 1907], p. 62), but this part of his dissertation remains unpublished and it is unclear what he meant by that.
4. All the Porphyry commentaries so far known are listed, except one (see n. 40

exists in several manuscripts from the twelfth century: a remarkable fact since other texts on logic from the period are usually preserved in only one manuscript. Every manuscript contains heavy emendations and additions, suggesting that it was eagerly copied and studied until the twelfth century.

I date this commentary to the 1060s or 1070s because Ps-Rabanus and Anselm employ different terminology as I shall show below. This fact indicates that they developed their theories independently from each other. Anselm began his studies at Bec in 1059, and his works began to be circulated in the late 1070s.

Ps-Rabanus faithfully summarizes Boethius's second commentary as to the theory of universals. A closer examination, however, shows that Ps-Rabanus formulates some ideas not very explicit in Boethius's arguments, which ideas were to survive in later theories. One of the ideas is that universals are nothing in a sense, or in other words, nothing actually exists except individuals.

> Itaque genera et species inquantum sunt universalia nihil dicuntur esse, quia nusquam pura inveniuntur. Nulla enim essentialiter existunt nisi sola individua. (*O* f. 10ra; *A* f. 6vb; *P* f. 216va)[5]

The second idea is that the same things are individuals and universals.

> Hic innuit Boethius quod *eadem res est individuum et species et genus, non esse universalia in individuis quasi quoddam diversum, ut quidam* dicunt, sed *speciem nihil aliud esse quam genus formatum, et individuum nihil aliud esse quam speciem formatam.* Aliter autem non diceretur universalitas et singularitas eidem subiecto accidere. (*O* f. 10ra; *A* 6vb; *P* 216va)

These two ideas, however, are not compatible with each other. What is the same thing that is individual and universal at the same time? From the next sentence 'universals do not exist in individuals as something different', and the first idea, that is, 'nothing actually exists except individuals', the 'same thing' appears to mean individuals. But if so, then the following problem occurs. The species *homo* in Socrates is the same

---

below), in J. Marenbon, 'Medieval Latin Glosses and Commentaries on Aristotelian Logical Texts, Before c. 1150 AD', in *Glosses and Commentaries on Aristotelian Logical Texts* (ed. Charles Burnett; London, 1993), pp. 77-127. Hereafter commentaries are mentioned with his numeration 'P*'.

5. *O* = MS Oxford, Laud. *lat.* 67; *A* = MS Assisi 573; *P* = MS Paris BN *lat.* 13368.

thing as the individual Socrates, and the species *homo* in Plato is the same thing as the individual Plato. Then since Socrates and Plato are different things, the species *homo* in Socrates and that in Plato cannot be the same thing. This problem, however, was not noticed until the controversy between Peter Abelard and William of Champeaux. Ps-Rabanus, indeed, shows no hesitation in asserting the traditional view that different individuals, Socrates and Plato, have the same species *homo*.[6]

According to Aristotle, Porphyry and Boethius, a species is constituted by a genus and differences, and an individual by a species and accidents peculiar to the individual. The same idea is often formulated around 1100, that genus and species are *materiae* of species and individuals respectively, and differences and accidents peculiar to an individual are *formae* of the species and the individual respectively. The sentence 'speciem nihil aliud esse...' in the passage cited above is the earliest record of that terminology. Porphyry does make an analogy between genus/differences and *materia/forma*, but he never identifies them simply.[7] This terminology is found in no texts earlier than Ps-Rabanus, nor in Anselm. One may conclude then that this terminology became popular under Ps-Rabanus's influence.

2. *Anselm on Universals*

As I have argued above, Ps-Rabanus draws from Boethius's arguments the thesis 'nothing actually exists except individuals', incompatible with another aspect of the traditional theory: universals are one and the same thing common to many different individuals. By contrast, if one lays stress on the commonness of universals, one cannot but weaken the first thesis. The theory of Anselm takes this very direction. As a theologian, Anselm has a special reason to stress the commonness of universals. In order to develop the theory on the incarnation, on original sin and so on,

---

6.   For example, Ps-Rabanus comments on Porphyry's words 'participatione enim speciei plures homines unus, particularibus autem unus et communis plures', as follows (*O* 12ra-b, *A* 10ra, *P* 219va): 'sic enim dictum est homo, quod in natura unum est, per participationem accidentium Plato efficitur atque Socrates, qui diversi sunt atque plures'.

7.   See *Isagoge* (ed. Minio-Paluello), p. 18.9-15. Probably the origin of this terminology is Boethius's *De divisione* (*PL* 64, 879C12-15). Boethius often says in the second commentary on Porphyry that *differentiae formant* (or *informant*) *speciem* (see the Index in the Brandt edition [CSEL 48; Vindobonae/Lipsiae, 1906]).

it is indispensable to have the concept of *homo* common to Adam, to his descendants, and to Jesus.

This is the famous passage in which Anselm attacks Roscelin:

> Cumque omnes ut cautissime ad sacrae paginae quaestiones accedant, sint commonendi: illi utique nostri temporis dialectici, immo dialecticae haeretici, qui non nisi flatum vocis putant universales esse substantias, et qui colorem non aliud queunt intelligere quam corpus, nec sapientiam hominis aliud quam animam, prorsus a spiritualium quaestionum disputatione sunt exsufflandi. In eodem quippe animabus ratio, quae et princeps et iudex debet omnium esse quae sunt in homine, sic est in imaginationibus corporalibus obvoluta, et ex eis se non possit evolvere, nec ab ipsis ea quae ipsa sola et pura contemplari debet, valeat discernere.
>
> Qui enim nondum intelligit quomodo plures homines in specie sint unus homo: qualiter in illa secretissima et altissima natura comprehendet quomodo plures personae, quarum singula quaeque perfectus est deus, sint unus deus?...
>
> Denique qui non potest intelligere aliquid esse hominem nisi individuum, nullatenus intelliget hominem nisi humanam personam. Omnis enim individuus homo est persona. Quomodo ergo iste intelliget hominem assumptum esse a verbo, non personam, id est naturam aliam, non aliam personam assumptam esse?[8]

On the basis of this passage it has often been asserted that Anselm holds to a so-called 'extreme realism' which somehow has affinity with ancient Platonism. In my view, however, Anselm asserts here nothing new, but repeats what Porphyry or Boethius says.

First, according to Anselm, it is because Roscelin's reason is covered with corporeal imaginations ('imaginationes corporeales') that he falsely thinks that there exist only individuals. Turning over his sayings, one may say that Anselm concedes at least that there exist only individuals in the world perceptible with corporeal imaginations, that is, in the sensible world. Boethius concludes in his second commentary that universals are intelligible and individuals are sensible.[9] From there Ps-Rabanus draws the thesis that 'nothing exists except individuals'. By contrast Anselm accepts the assertion in a weaker formula, 'there exist only individuals in the sensible world'. Moreover Anselm's weaker formulation is more faithful to Boethius's conclusion than Ps-Rabanus's.

Second, Anselm never assumes a world apart from and beyond the sensible world as Plato does. This is clear from this passage:

8. *Epistola de incarnatione verbi* (Schmitt, I, pp. 9:20-10:13).
9. See p. 167.5-7 (ed. Brandt).

> Quod sic quoque facile animadverti posse existimo. Nempe si cuilibet substantiae, quae et vivit et sensibilis et rationalis est, *cogitatione* auferatur quod rationalis est, deinde quod sensibilis, et postea quod vitalis, postremo ipsum nudum esse quod remanet: quis non intelligat quod illa substantia quae sic paulatim destruitur, ad minus et minus esse, et ad ultimum ad non esse gradatim perducitur?[10]

He says that if any substance that is alive, sensible and rational, that is an individual *homo*, is deprived of the difference *rationale*, then there remains the genus *animal*; of the difference *sensibile*, then there remains the genus *corpus animatum*, and so on. It is also said that this deprivation is made by *cogitatio*, or by reason. It concludes, then, that according to Anselm universals can be grasped by reason only in the sensible world itself. Again, this theory agrees well with Boethius's sayings.

Third, it is asserted in the quotation above that 'plures homines in specie sint unus homo'. This is nothing more than a paraphrase of Porphyry's words: 'participatione enim speciei plures homines unus'.[11]

Fourth, it is also asserted that something is man other than individuals. Here again Anselm never assumes any man as *choris einai*. When he says 'something is man other than individuals', he means by 'something' the human nature common to every individual human being, and Anselm considers that human nature exists only in individual human beings, never apart from them.

> Nam cum profertur 'homo', natura tantum quae communis omnibus est hominibus significatur. Cum vero demonstrative dicimus 'istum *vel* illum hominem' vel proprio nomine 'Iesum', personam designamus, quae cum natura collectionem habet proprietatum, quibus homo communis fit singulus et ab aliis singulis distinguitur.[12]

The idea that universals are *naturae* common to individuals is taken from Boethius,[13] and the idea that the common human nature becomes various individual human beings because of the *proprietatum collectio* comes from Porphyry.[14]

It is true that Anselm's theology is full of neo-Platonic elements which he mainly learnt from Augustine. However, in purely logical matters

---

10. *Monologion* 30 (Schmitt, I, pp. 49:24-50:1).
11. *Isagoge* (ed. Minio-Paluello), p. 12.18-19.
12. *De incarnatione verbi* (Schmitt, II, p. 29:5-9). Cf. also *De conceptu virginali et de originali peccato* (Schmitt, II, pp. 140:18-21 and 165:20).
13. See p. 165.12-14 (ed. Brandt).
14. See *Isagoge* (ed. Minio-Paluello), pp. 13.24-14.2.

incorporated into his theology he faithfully follows Porphyry and Boethius, and the latter two explicitly declare allegiance to the Peripatetic tradition.[15] Anselm would never have considered himself to be a Platonist in any sense in developing his universals theory.

3. Anselm and essentia

How and why can a universal be one and the same thing common to many different individuals, although there exist only individuals in the sensible world and universals are in the individuals? Anselm answers this question, introducing the concept of *essentia*.

> Nempe cum omnis substantia tractetur aut esse universalis, quae pluribus substantiis *essentialiter* communis est, ut *hominem esse* commune est singulis hominibus; aut esse individua, quae *universalem essentiam communem* habet cum aliis, quemadmodum singuli homines commune habent cum singulis, ut *homines sint*... et *cuiuslibet rei essentia dici solet substantia*...[16]

What does *essentia* mean? The term *essentia* is derived from *esse*. The verb *esse* has two different meanings. First it means for something to be or to exist; secondly, as a copula, it means to be something. Accordingly *essentia* has two meanings. First it can mean some being or existing thing. According to Anselm, however, only God is that which absolutely exists, or in Anselm's words 'quaedam natura, per quam est, quicquid est, et quae per se est, et est summum omnium quae sunt'.[17] Therefore, when Anselm uses the term *essentia* to mean some existing thing, it always stands for God, often used in the form *summa essentia*. By contrast, creatures can be said to be non-existing things in a sense, 'nec tamen omnino non sunt, quia per illum, qui solus absolute est, de nihilo aliquid facta sunt'.[18] That is to say, creatures exist in such a restricted way as being something, not being simply. Therefore, when *essentia* is used concerning creatures, it has a meaning corresponding to *esse* as a copula. One may paraphrase this second meaning of *essentia* as the X in the answer 'It is X' to the question 'What is the creature?' Likewise the term *essentialiter* means 'in the point what it is'.

---

15. See *Isagoge* (ed. Minio-Paluello), p. 5.15-18, and Boethius's second commentary (ed. Brandt), p. 167.18-20.
16. *Monologion* 27 (Schmitt, I, p. 45:6-12).
17. *Monologion* 3 (Schmitt, I, p. 15:25-26).
18. *Monologion* 28 (Schmitt, I p. 46:30-31).

Now Anselm asserts that a universal is *essentialiter* common to many substances. He also gives an example that to be *homo* is common to individual human beings. It amounts to saying that what is *essentialiter* common to any individual human being is the very thing *homo* that is predicated through the copula *esse* of individual human beings. Anselm then calls the *homo* a *universalis essentia*. So, the *universalis essentia* is in this case the very thing *homo* in so far as it is predicated through the copula *esse* of individual human beings.

According to Anselm, the reason why *homo* is a universal essence common to individual human beings is the fact that the state of affairs *esse hominem* holds in every individual human being. The *homo* which is predicated of Socrates in the proposition 'Socrates est homo' and the *homo* which is predicated of Plato in the proposition 'Plato est homo' cannot be different things. For the term *homo* is not used equivocally in the two propositions. It follows then that Socrates and Plato have one and the same *essentia* or species. It thus turns out to be self-evident that a universal *essentia* is one and the same thing while existing in many different individuals.

As I stated above, the term *essentialiter* can be paraphrased as 'in what it is'. 'What it is' is a very Aristotelian definition of substance. And indeed, in the quotation above, Anselm identifies *essentia* with *substantia*. The same assertion is implied in another passage.

> Quemadmodum itaque unum est quidquid essentialiter de summa substantia [= God] dicitur, ita ipsa uno modo, una consideratione est quidquid est essentialiter. Cum enim aliquis homo [for example, Socrates] dicatur et corpus et rationalis et homo, non uno modo vel consideratione hæc tria dicitur. Secundum aliud enim est corpus [viz. genus], et secundum aliud rationalis [viz. difference], et singulum horum non est totum hoc quod est homo [viz. species]. Illa vero summa essentia nullo modo sic est aliquid, ut illud idem secundum alium modum aut secundum aliam considerationem non sit; quia quidquid aliquo modo essentialiter est, hoc est totum quod ipsa est. Nihil igitur quod de eius essentia vere dicitur, *in eo quod qualis* vel *quanta*, sed *in eo quod quid sit* accipitur. Quidquid enim est quale vel quantum, est etiam aliud in eo quod quid est; unde non simplex, sed compositum.[19]

Here Anselm implies that in the case of creatures only genus, species and differences are predicated of individuals *essentialiter*, or *in eo quod quid est*. Here again, his terminology is very Aristotelian.

---

19. *Monologion* 17 (Schmitt, I, pp. 31:25-32:4).

4. *Odo of Cambrai on Universals*

The theory of original sin developed in Odo of Cambrai's *De peccato originali* is substantially the same as that which Anselm developed in his *De conceptu virginali et de originali peccato*. We, descendants of Adam and Eve, inherit original sin through the *humana natura* common to us, because the *natura* was corrupted by our first ancestors. In accepting *natura* as common to many individuals Odo simply follows the Boethian tradition, as does Anselm. Odo also follows Porphyry's and Boethius's idea that the one and the same *natura* becomes many individuals with accidents peculiar to each.

> Individua vero nihil habent substantialiter plus quam species, nec aliud sunt substantialiter, aliud Petrus quam homo. Quod autem sub una specie plura sunt individua, non facit hoc aliquod substantiale, sed accidentia. . . Qui individuus est *propter collectionem accidentium*, sicut homo species, quia potest esse multorum communis individuorum. (*PL* 160, 1079A-B)

Lastly Odo follows Boethius's conclusion in his second Porphyry commentary that individuals are objects of sense of perception, universals of reason.

> Ex genere et differentiis speciem ratio capit, ex proprietatibus accidentium individuum sensus agnoscit. Ad universalia valet ratio rationis interior, ad singularia vero cognitio sensualis exterior. Individua sentimus corporaliter, universalia percipimus rationaliter. (*PL* 160, 1079B-C).

Just like Anselm, Odo fully belongs to Porphyry's and Boethius's tradition.
The originality of Odo appears in another passage.

> Similiter incorporalia cuncta sine suis formis esse non possunt, ut omnes species et individua differentias et proprietates accipiunt *formas*, quibus existunt. Prima vero rerum genera *essentiam* accipiunt pro *forma*. Nam quemadmodum formae suis rebus dant esse, ita genera summa nisi per essentiam non possunt esse. Et ceterae formae omnes suae sunt suarum rerum, essentia vero communis et universalis est omnium rerum. Aliae formae suas res faciunt aliquid esse, essentia vero facit omnes res simpliciter esse. Et cum res omnes habeant proprias formas quibus formantur ad aliquid esse, prima genera rerum habent essentiam qua formantur ad esse. Ceterae formae suas res faciunt quid sunt. Et cum aliud sit aliquid esse, aliud esse, aliae formae pertinent ad aliquid esse et non ad esse. . . Est autem essentia primum in primis generibus, ut prima genera principaliter sint, ut per essentiam primo loco formentur ad esse, inde habent

> inferiora per formas aliquid esse, ut corpus habet substantiam esse per
> corpoream formam. Sunt igitur formae causae rerum omnium, nam
> ceterae formae omnes causa sunt suis rebus ut aliquid sint; essentia vero
> causa est omnibus ut sint. (*PL* 160, 1098B-C)

Odo shares the term *essentia* with Anselm as well as *forma* with Ps-
Rabanus. However, there is divergence from them. First, the term
essentia has the meaning derived from *esse* to exist, not from *esse* as a
copula. Secondly, while according to Anselm *essentia* is only substance,
Odo considers that *essentia* is received by the *prima rerum genera*, that
is, the ten *genera generalissima*. Thirdly, although like Ps-Rabanus Odo
calls differences and accidents peculiar to an individual *formae* of the
species and the individual respectively, unlike Ps-Rabanus Odo does not
identify genus and species with *materiae* of species and individuals.[20]

5. William of Champeaux on Universals

As is well known, Peter Abelard records in his *Historia calamitatum*
that he forced William of Champeaux to revise his material essence
theory into the *indifferentia* theory.[21] No text is extant that adheres to
the material essence theory. However, we have many reports of the
theory from its opponents.[22] Since they all coincide with each other,
they are reliable enough.

Abelard begins his introduction of the theory in his *Logica
'Ingredientibus'* as follows:

> Quidam enim ita rem universalem accipiunt, ut in rebus diversis ab
> invicem per *formas* eandem *essentialiter* substantiam collocent, quae

---

20. Odo puzzles over what *materia* is. 'Et materiae natura substantiali priores sunt
formis, formae vero si respicias ad esse materiis priores sunt quod eas esse faciunt,
multas digressiones facimus et longas in hoc opere. Ad multas nos cogit proposito-
rum difficultas quae quaestiones multimodas generat... Ad longas vero nos impellit
subtilitas quaestionum, quae vix ad intelligentiam perducuntur etiam multiplicitate
verborum. Et cum quasi hydrae vivae caput unum abscidimus, quandoque renascun-
tur multa, quae nisi cum magno molimine non auferimus' (*PL* 160, 1098C-D). Odo
never solves the question in this work.

21. Abelard, *Historia calamitatum* (ed. Monfrain; Paris, 1978), pp. 65, 81-91.

22. Abelard, *Logica 'Ingredientibus'*, pp. 10.17-13.17 (ed. Geyer); *idem, Logica
'Nostrorum petitioni sociorum'*, pp. 515.14-518.8 (ed. Geyer); Anonymous, *Tractatus de generali et speciali statu rerum universalium*, pp. 94-103 (ed. Dijs = pp. 299-
312, ed. Hauréau); and Ps-Jocelin's *De generibus et speciebus*, pp. 151-60 (ed.
King = pp. 513-18, ed. Cousin).

singularium in quibus est *materialis* sit *essentia*, et in se ipsa una, tantum per *formas* inferiorum sit diversa. Quas quidem formas si separari contingeret, nulla penitus differentia rerum esset, quae formarum tantum diversitate ab invicem distant, cum sit penitus *eadem essentialiter materia*. Verbi gratia in singulis hominibus numero differentibus eadem est hominis substantia, quae hic Plato per haec accidentia fit, ibi Socrates per alia.

Quibus quidem Porphyrius assentire maxime videtur, cum ait [*Isagoge* p. 12.18-19] 'Participatione speciei plures homines unus, particularibus autem unus et communis plures'. Et rursus [*Isagoge* pp. 13.24-14.1] 'Individua, inquit, dicuntur huiusmodi quoniam unumquodque eorum consistit ex proprietatibus quarum collectio non est in alio'.[23]

Like Anselm, William relies on Porphyry's word in asserting that *essentialiter* one and the same *homo* is in many individuals. William adopts Ps-Rabanus's *materia/forma* terminology, too. A species is the matter, or *materialis essentia*, of its individuals, while accidents peculiar to an individual are its *forma*. Likewise, *essentialiter* one and the same genus is the matter of its species, while differences are forms of species.[24] Abelard concludes his introduction as follows.

Et cum in se sit universale, idem per advenientes formas singulare fit [*sic* MS, sit Geyer], sine quibus naturaliter in se subsistit et *absque eis nullatenus actualiter permanet* (universale quidem in natura, singulare vero actu); et incorporeum quidem et insensibile in simplicitate universalitatis suae intelligitur, corporeum vero atque sensibile idem per accidentia in actu subsistit; et *eadem, teste Boethio, et subsistunt singularia et intelliguntur universalia*.[25]

Here the idea that the same things subsist as singulars or individuals and are understood as universal is ascribed to Boethius. Such wording, however, appears nowhere in Boethius's commentaries. It must reflect Ps-Rabanus's idea that the same thing is an individual, a species and a genus. In Ps-Rabanus it is not clear what the same thing is: whether it is an individual, a universal, or something other. According to William it is clearly a universal. That which in itself is a universal becomes singular through forms.

23. *Logica 'Ingredientibus'* (ed. Geyer), p. 10.17-29.

24. 'Similiter in singulis animalibus specie differentibus unam et eandem essentialiter animalis substantiam ponunt, quae [*sic* MS] quam Geyer per diversarum differentiarum susceptionem in diversas species transit [*sic* MS] trahunt Geyer...' (p. 10.24-32, ed. Geyer).

25. *Logica 'Ingredientibus'* (ed. Geyer), p. 11.3-9.

William also inherits from Ps-Rabanus the idea that nothing actually exists except individuals, whereas Anselm and Odo assert in a weaker way that only individuals exist in the sensible world. By contrast the passage quoted above explicitly asserts that universals never persist without forms. In the first quotation above, too, the same idea is suggested by the unreal conditional: 'formas si separari *contingeret*, nulla penitus differentia rerum *esset*'. That is to say, William considers that matters, or universals, cannot actually exist separately from forms. This point is more explicit in the anonymous treatise on universals:

> Quemadmodum autem animal est una res naturaliter praeiacens ante susceptionem accidentium, sic eadem natura animalis, si omnia accidentia per quae inferioratur ab ea separarentur, una et eadem quae prius ante susceptionem accidentium remanere posset. Ideo dico 'posset' quia, *nisi prorsus desipiant, non concedunt actu remanere animal destructis omnibus accidentibus quibus inferioratur*. Si enim rationale et irrationale etc quae accidunt animali destruerentur, necessario quodlibet individuum animalis destrueretur; quod si fieret, nec animal actu remaneret, cum dicat Aristoteles [*Cat.* 5, 2b6bc] 'Destructis primis substantiis, impossibile est aliquid aliorum remanere'.[26]

One may conclude that William's material essence theory is a compilation of ideas developed in the eleventh century, using Anselm's term *essentia* and Ps-Rabanus's *materia/forma*. The conclusion is testified to by the anonymous treatise on universals which begins the introduction of the theory by saying 'Est autem antiqua sententia et quasi antiquis erroribus inveterata...'.[27] The *antiqui errores* cannot be the theories of authorities like Porphyry and Boethius. So this must mean the theories which began with Anselm and Ps-Rabanus.

6. *Essentia and Accidents according to William*

Like Odo of Cambrai, William enlarges the meaning of *essentia* to the ten categories. The introduction of the material essence theory in the *Logica 'nostrorum petitioni sociorum'* begins as follows.

> Nonnulli enim ponunt *decem res diversas* esse naturaliter secundum *decem praedicamentorum vel generalissimorum* distinctionem, cum videlicet ita dicant res esse universales, hoc est naturaliter communicabiles

---

26. *Tractatus...universalium* (ed. Dijs), §3 (= p. 299 ed. Hauréau)
27. *Tractatus...universalium* (ed. Dijs), §1 (= p. 299 ed. Hauréau).

pluribus, quod eandem rem essentialiter in pluribus ita ponunt, ut eadem quae est in hac re essentialiter sit in illa, diversis tamen formis affecta.[28]

As is shown above, for Anselm *essentia* is identical with substance. How and why, then, can the term cover the nine accidents also? William developed a theory to explain it.[29]

According to Abelard,[30] William made the following peculiar assertion. The proposition 'Socrates est albus' has different meanings in grammar and in logic. The grammatical meaning is that Socrates is the same thing as the denotation of the predicate 'albus', that is the subject of whiteness. The logical meaning is that whiteness inheres in Socrates. Therefore for grammarians the proposition 'Socrates est albedo' has a different meaning than 'Socrates est albus', since the former means that Socrates is identical with whiteness itself. For logicians, however, they have the same meaning, since they both declare that whiteness inheres in Socrates.[31] A proposition like 'Socrates est homo' means *inhaerentia essentiae* or of a substance, *homo*, in Socrates; a proposition like 'Socrates est albus' means *inhaerentia adiacentiae*, namely the inherence in Socrates of the accident, whiteness, expressed by the adjective 'albus'. And in logic, which is concerned only with predication and therefore with inherence, the term *in essentia* covers both *inhaerentia essentiae* and *adiacentiae*.

In this way for William the term *in essentia* or *essentialiter* can cover those which are formally distinguished as *essentialiter* and as *adiacenter*, that is substantially and accidentally. In his *Logica 'nostrorum petitioni sociorum'* Abelard ends the introduction of the material essence theory as follows:

28. *Logica 'Nostorum petitioni sociorum'* (ed. Geyer, p. 515.14-19.

29. As is discussed by L. Reilly (*Petrus Helias' Summa super Priscianum I-III: an Edition and Study* [Michigan, 1978], pp. 575-83), and by K.M. Fredborg ('Speculative Grammar', in P. Dronke [ed.], *A History of Twelfth-Century Western Philosophy* [Cambridge, 1988], p. 178), this theory can be traced back to a passage of the *Glosule* on Priscian minor, published by R. Hunt, 'Studies on Priscian in the Eleventh and Twelfth Centuries', *Mediaeval and Renaissance Studies* 1 (1941/43), pp 33.28-35.7 (repr. in his *Collected Papers on the History of Grammar in the Middle Ages* [Amsterdam, 1980]).

30. *Super topica glossae*, pp. 271.38-272.39 (ed. Dal Pra). I suggest the following emendations to his reading: p. 272.2 quam + attendunt MS, omitted Dal Pra; p. 272.28 qualitatem—copulat[ur] MS, qualitas—copulatur Dal Pra; p. 272.29 coniungit *scripsi*, coniungunt MS, coniungitur Dal Pra.

31. Pp. 271.38-272.35 (ed. Dal Pra).

> Et iuxta hanc sententiam praedicari de pluribus tale est, ac si diceremus: idem *essentialiter* ita inesse aliquibus rebus, per formas oppositas diversificatis, ut singulis *essentialiter* vel *adiacenter* conveniat.[32]

The first *essentialiter* is used in the broader sense, the second in the strict and traditional sense.

7. *Platonism or Aristotelianism?*

The theories of Anselm, Odo and William have usually been interpreted as 'Platonic'. In my view, however, they should rather be considered to be a stage in the development of 'Aristotelian' realism. First, as I have shown so far, they perfectly follow Aristotelian ideas, or what they believed to be such, in so far as logical matters are concerned. Secondly, their realism shows no intention of introducing what they knew to be Plato's theory. Thirdly, they are finally transformed into the *indifferentia* theory which no researchers have considered to be Platonic.

A source strengthens my claim, and tells us that contemporaries considered their theories to be essentially Aristotelian. The author, Hermann, sides with Odo of Cambrai and reproaches the vocalists as follows.

> ... in Porphyrii Aristotelisque libris magis volunt legi suam adinventitiam novitatem quam *Boethii ceterorumque antiquorum expositionem*. Denique dominus Anselmus Cantuariensis archiepiscopus in libro quem fecit de Verbi incarnatione non dialecticos huiusmodi clericos, sed dialecticae appellat haereticos: 'Qui nonnisi flatum, inquit, universales putant esse substantias', dicens eos de sapientium numero merito esse exsufflandos.[33]

It is clear that for Hermann the universals theories of Anselm and Odo follow Boethius and other ancient authors in interpreting Porphyry and Aristotle. And they must have known that Boethius himself explicitly declares that he follows the Peripatetic tradition, not the Platonic.

If one searches for 'Platonic' theory on universals, there were indeed a series of theories to be so labelled. Some texts show attempts to reconcile 'Platonism' with 'Aristotelianism'. The most primitive attempt is found in a Porphyry commentary, P16. Just like Ps-Rabanus's commentary, P16 first follows Boethius's arguments in his second commentary

---

32. *Logica 'Nostrorum petitioni sociorum'* (ed. Geyer), p. 515. 28-31.

33. *Herimanni liber de restauratione monasterii Sancti Martini Tornacensis*, MGH SS 14, p. 275.33-38.

faithfully, but it shows divergence at the end, where Boethius points out that Plato's theory is different from Aristotle's, and that Boethius follows Aristotle's.[34] By contrast, P16, deliberately neglecting the reported difference between Aristotle and Plato, says as follows:

> *Sed Plato genera et species ceteraque non modo intelligi universalia, verum esse atque praeter corpora subsistere putat.* Dicit etiam Boethius in minori commento super Porphyrium (Platonem MS) ea esse, quia *non esset de his disputatio consideratioque si non sint...* [a long quotation from Boethius' first commentary, pp. 25.22-26.25 and p. 29.16-22, ed. Brandt]...
>
> His dictis determinandum est quae res dicantur genera et species. Dicitur autem quod eadem res quae est individuum diversis modis considerata est et species specialissima et genus subalternum et etiam genus generalissimum. Si enim substantia illa, quae informata accidentibus dicitur Socrates, intelligatur spoliata suis propriis accidentibus, illa, inquam, sine illis considerata est illa species specialissima quae dicitur homo; iterum homo species sine mortalitate consideratus reducitur ad hoc ut sit illud genus quod est animal; ab animali vero 'rationali' rationalitate separata remanet animal simpliciter; iterum ab animal sensibilitate 'separata' remanet corpus animatum; a quo similiter animatione separata relinquitur 'corpus; et a corpore corporeitate separata relinquitur' substantia genus generalissimum. Ut igitur dictum est, illud quod est individuum est et species specialissima et genus subalternum et etiam generalissimum. Iterum dicitur quod substantia et quodlibet superius fit (sit MS) quodlibet suum inferius per adiectionem diversarum qualitatum. Si enim substantiae generalissimo intelligamus addi corporeitatem, ipsa fit (sit MS) corpus; et si corpori addatur animatio, fit corpus animatum; si iterum corpori animato addatur sensibilitas, fit animal; si autem animali addatur rationalitas, fit rationale animal; huic iterum addatur mortalitas, fieret 'homo'; homini vero, si addantur accidentia, fit Socrates vel aliquod individuum hominis. Spoliando igitur suis propriis qualitatibus relinquuntur superiora; si vero e contra superiora ablatis induantur qualitatibus, ex ipsis fiunt inferiora.[35]

The theory developed here is substantially the same as Ps-Rabanus's. However, the anonymous author believes it can be reconciled with what they believed to be Platonism.

Behind the deliberate neglect of the difference between Aristotle and Plato, there was a desire to introduce into the universals theory a genuinely Platonic idea: universals have something to do with exemplars in the creator's mind. Odo of Cambrai says,

---

34. P. 167.12-20 (ed. Brandt).
35. MS Munich clm 14458, f. 85rb-va.

Sic summa sapientia [= God] habet omnes formas omnium rerum. Lucent in arte summa formae plures, quia sunt in opere res plures, quia secundum diversas formas artis summae, factae sunt diversae res in opere. Ars enim summa videbat apud se intus quomodo crearentur omnia exterius et sic in essentiam omnia prodierunt,[36] ut aeternae formae monstraverunt. Ecce dicimus artis summae plures formas, cum non sint omnes in una. Quidquid est ibi, non est nisi unum et id ipsum, o Lux una, radii plures... [37]

Odo must have learnt the idea of the exemplars in the creator from the *Timaeus*, since he is known to have been keen to learn that work of Plato.[38] Moreover, he must have known that the same idea is found in Anselm's work, too (see *Monologion*, chs. 9–11). In Anselm, however, it is a purely theological matter irrelevant to his universals theory. Anselm sometimes calls the exemplars *formae*,[39] a term which has for him no relevance to universals. For Odo, however, since he inherits the term *forma* from Ps-Rabanus to apply to universals, the idea of divine forms came to play a role in his universals theory, although this Platonic element is not integrated well with Odo's otherwise 'Aristotelian' theory.

The attempt to reconcile Platonism and Aristotelianism is most explicitly stated in Adelard of Bath's *De eodem et diverso* written before 1116.[40]

36. The term *prodire* reflects the most Platonic passage in Priscian, *Institutiones grammaticae* XVII 44, p. 135.6-10 (ed. Keil).

37. *De peccato originali*, PL 160, 1101BC.

38. See the *Herimanni liber de restauratione monasterii Sancti Martini Tornacensis* (MGH SS 14), p. 276.17-18.

39. *Monologion* 9 (Schmitt, I, p. 24:14); 10 (Schmitt, I, p. 24:24).

40. After the completion of this paper, Charles Burnett drew my attention to a fragment of a Porphyry commentary in MS Cashel, GPA Bolton Libr., 1, pp. 118-120. It pays special attention to the difference between Plato's and Aristotle's theories. For example, it says on p. 118: 'Sed sciendum quod apud Platonem aliter, apud Aristotelem aliter de partibus logicae, sicut de ceteris compluribus dictum est...' And the discussion of Porphyry's questions begins (p. 20): 'Sed quia, ut dictum est, aliter innuit Plato, aliter sensit Aristoteles, Platonis et ipsius sequentium videamus sententiam. Dicebat igitur Plato genera et species esse exemplares illas rerum formas(?) quas ideas vocant, id est intellectus illos in mente divina quos de rebus singulis...' (unfortunately the following part of the manuscript is so heavily damaged as to be almost illegible). No contemporary commentaries share this style. According to Dr Burnett, this commentary is the only text to occur in the same part of the composite codex besides the curious arithmetical text written (according to the only other manuscript) by Ocreatus, a pupil of Adelard. It might have been the case,

He first develops a universal theory very like that of Ps-Rabanus and P16,[41] and then proceeds to say:

> Quoniam igitur illud idem, quod vides, et genus et species et individuum sit, *merito ea Aristoteles non nisi in sensibilibus esse proposuit.* Sunt etenim ipsa sensibilia, quamvis acutius considerata. Quoniam vero ea, inquantum dicuntur genera et species, nemo sine imaginatione presse pureque intuetur, *Plato extra sensibilia, scilicet in mente divina,* et concipi et existere dixit. *Sic viri illi, licet verbis contrarii videantur, re tamen idem senserunt.*[42]

It is noteworthy that neither P16 nor Adelard uses the term *essentia*. Presumably they developed their theories out of the Anselmian tradition. It is also noteworthy that Plato's *Timaeus* was a favourite book of Adelard as well as of Odo.

The 'Platonic' trend of universals theory is thus found only as a tributary of the main current of 'Aristotelian' realism.[43]

then, that Adelard's school was sharp on the distinction between the two ancient philosophers.

41. See *Des Adelard von Bath Traktat De eodem et diverso* (Beiträge zur Geschichte der Philosophie des Mittelalters IV-1; ed. H. Willner; Münster, 1903), pp. 11.17-12.23.

42. *De eodem et diverso*, p. 12.23-30 (ed. Willner).

43. Attempts to reconcile Platonism and Aristotelianism culminated in Peter Abelard's theory. The relation, however, between Platonism and vocalism is beyond the scope of this study.

THE MIRROR OF DIALECTICS: NAKED IMAGES IN ANSELM OF CANTERBURY AND BERNARD OF CLAIRVAUX

M.B. Pranger

1. *The Platonic Frame*

In my view there is a sense in which Anselm and Bernard, like many other twelfth-century thinkers, can be said to be 'Platonic'. By that I mean, first, that images and structures—rational and rhetorical frames— are inextricably intertwined and, second, that attempts on the part of Anselm, Bernard and others to distinguish between images and underlying structures are part of a quest for greater clarity of the entire body of images and language in preference to isolating a rational aspect of it.

There is a third feature which indeed conditions the other two, and that is the fact that, for the mind in search of its destination, its goal is present right from the beginning. Put in terms of religion, God who is the ultimate object of desire, not only governs the process of the human quest for himself but he is also involved and present in that process all along. Consequently, rather than merely being a matter of going beyond the realm of the senses and the intellect the search for God has to account for his intrinsic presence in human thought and language. And it is the very fact that this presence is both obvious and invisible and unintelligible, in other words, the fact that this presence is disguised as absence, that sets into motion a never-ending process of meditation and understanding.

2. *Anselm's Pictures*

In his *Cur deus homo* Anselm deals with the problem of images and their rationale, that is their rational subsistence, or, for that matter, their lack of it. Conceived as a written memoir containing delightful moments of contemplation about matters of faith, the treatise takes its point of departure in objections brought forward against Christian faith by the infidels, both literate and illiterate. In their view the Christian doctrine of the incarnation is needlessly complicated and, above all, vulgar.

> The infidels, deriding our simplemindedness, object that we offend God and do him injustice when we say that he descended in the womb of a woman, is born from a female, grew up being fed by milk and human food and—to pass over many other things unbecoming to God—suffered fatigue, hunger, thirst, punishment and, ultimately, the cross amongst thieves, and death.[1]

Anselm's reply is brief. The infidels would not mock the simplicity of the Christian faith if they realized that in those vulgar images God's majesty was manifested and the entire history of humankind from sin to redemption recapitulated. In accordance with Pauline and patristic tradition the vulgarity of the Lord's passion can be shown to make sense. 'Man' should be involved because through man sin had entered the world, 'woman' giving birth to this man because a woman had been the cause of our damnation, 'wood' (of the cross) because man was talked into sin by the devil who persuaded him to taste from the wood. 'And many other examples could be given,' Anselm adds, 'which would somehow demonstrate the inexpressible beauty of this special way our redemption was wrought.'

So, the first thing a closer look at the incarnation reveals is that, rather than being an incoherent picture, it contains a riddle. Read in the proper way that riddle can be solved, telling us an extraordinarily beautiful story.

However, the matter cannot be left at that. Anselm uses the infidels to keep dissatisfaction going. They, on their part, are not impressed by the solution of the first riddle because they fail to see how such an —allegedly—beautiful picture amounts to more than just a fantasy. How could it ever be rooted in reality? But what do we mean by reality? Something is real, in both Anselm's and his unbelievers' view, if it can be shown to be rational, to have subsistence and coherence, in terms of divine reality, that is, if it can be shown to be necessary. That is why Anselm, right from the beginning of the treatise, makes it clear that a discussion of pictures and images should include a discussion of the problem of potentiality, necessity and will.

This reciprocity between pictures and images on the one hand and rationality on the other raises the question as to their relationship. Does

---

1. *Cur deus homo* I, ch. 3 (Schmitt, II, p. 50).

Anselm really mean to interpret images in terms of rationality and vice versa? If so, what does rationality consist of? Is not the infidels' fear justified that such images be too insubstantial and incoherent to be taken seriously?

The answer to the first question is that Anselm indeed interprets images in terms of rationality and vice versa. The answer to the second question is that their relationship is problematic indeed. In fact, it is precisely what *Cur deus homo* is about. In other words, after having been preliminarily solved through the principle of recapitulation, the first riddle of God being a suffering man etc., is turned into a second riddle in order to bring out its *inenarrabilis pulchritudo*. The second riddle raises the following question: is there more—reason, necessity, will—to this picture of a suffering god-man than that it is the picture of a suffering god-man, and if so, what does it look like?

Although Anselm, admittedly, realized the task he had set himself to be beyond him, he also knew where to look for the key to this mystery. If a concept is to be found in which images and reason coalesce, it must be beauty. Improbable though it may sound, it is on this most evanescent of concepts that the solidity of Anselm's argumentation in *Cur deus homo* rests.

> There is another reason why I am reluctant to comply with your request. For not only is the subject-matter of a precious nature. But, just as it is about Him who is beautiful 'in appearance above the sons of man' (Psalm 44,3), so it is also marked by a splendid rationality beyond the intellectual grasp of man. For that reason I fear that, by writing in a poor style, I may be accused of the same bad taste I use to blame bad painters for because of the shapeless pictures they make of the Lord.[2]

Besides being a statement of literary modesty, this passage reveals other dimensions of the argument as well. The beauty of the incarnation has to be accounted for, regardless of the beauty of the author's style. As a matter of fact, the former's consistency is such as to wipe out the latter's scruples. As for those scruples, all that remains is Boso's irony:

> I do not think your reluctance is justified since in the same way as you will not prevent someone from writing better, you will force no one not to write more beautifully in order to please whomsoever does not like your style.

---

2.   *Cur deus homo* I, ch. 1 (Schmitt, II, p. 49).

Playful though those remarks may be, they also reflect, on a stylistic level, the outcome of *Cur deus homo*. When in Book II, 17, the necessity of the incarnation, that is, its beauty, will be proven through the application to God's *potentia* of the opposite pair of force and prevention (*coactio* and *prohibitio*), the argument is based upon an 'indifferent' moment between those two extremes. This very 'indifference' which allows God's beauty to shine through is somehow reminiscent of the one in Boso's remark allowing for the best possible style.

Let us now have a closer look at the 'inexpressible beauty of our redemption'. This beauty consists, as we have seen, of the hidden dimensions in the god-man whose suffering comprises and transforms the misery of human history, turning sin into redemption, woman into Woman, wood into Wood. But does this beauty hold out against the attacks of the unbelievers, or is it to be called just beauty?

> All these things are beautiful and should somehow be seen as pictures. However, unless they rest upon a solid foundation, they will not convince the infidels of the necessity of our belief that God has wanted to suffer the things we mentioned. For whosoever wants to make a picture, takes something solid upon which to paint to make his painting permanent. For no one paints in the water or in the air because no traces of his picture could be contained there. Hence the infidels think that we paint on a cloud when we show them the fittingness [of the incarnation] you just mentioned as certain pictures of reality. They, however, do not think that to be reality but fiction. For that reason the first task ahead is to show the solidity of the rational truth, that is, the necessity which proves that God should or could be humiliated into suffering the things we tell about Him. Next, for this very body of truth, so to speak, to shine more brilliantly, those arguments of fittingness must be expounded as pictures of this body.[3]

Now, to cut a long story short, the necessity proving that God's humiliation in the incarnation makes sense, can be summarized as follows. God's perfect plan not allowing for a breach to be permanent, demands satisfaction which should be given by man, the trespasser, and only can be given by God. Hence the necessity of a god-man who, next, is proven to have wanted to become incarnate because it was necessary and vice versa. Ultimately, all possible frictions with regard to will and necessity are being solved in the perfect freedom of God who makes necessity an intrinsic (*sequens*) affair rather than extrinsically imposed (*precedens*).

---

3. *Cur deus homo* II, ch. 4 (Schmitt, II, pp. 51-52).

So much for the solidity of rational truth, that is, its necessity. But what about the pictures? What has happened to them in the process?

To get a better grip of the problem let us once more recall the two riddles. The first one, the 'believers' one, concerns the image of the suffering God whose humiliation makes sense when seen as a manifestation of God's beauty. The second riddle, raising the problems of divine will and necessity, is meant to underpin the first one. But moving from the first to the second riddle, Anselm seems to have done away with the former's pictorial outlook. For how else are we to interpret his famous motto in the preface to *Cur deus homo*, that he will prove by necessary reasons, *Christo remoto*, Christ being removed from the process, that it is impossible to find salvation without him? True, Anselm does not apply here the method of negative theology to the presence of the divine as Scottus does. However, suspending the beautiful-ugly image of the suffering Christ, he somehow 'divests' it and faces 'nature' in its nakedness. As a result, we have a third riddle on our hands. If the first riddle raised the question how ugliness—God's suffering—could be beautiful, the second how necessity could be the same as freedom of will, the third riddle asks us to solve the problem of reading back the second into the first. How can necessity restore the outlook of a once-beautiful image?

The solution of the third riddle looks like a typically Anselmian paradox. But then it should be realized that for Anselm, arguing from the solidity of rational truth, what we call a paradox is but a proof of our incorrect use of language. It should rather be called pure logic.

At the end of *Cur deus homo* the tautological *necessitas sequens*— derived from Aristotle's 'you speak by necessity because you speak'— which proves that the faith of the prophets in the future death of Christ was true, obliging Christ to die because he wanted to do so, is so logically cogent as to leave no room to move out of the picture of the suffering Christ. Yet that is precisely what Anselm seems to have done. Hence the paradox of Christ having been removed from the picture at the beginning of *Cur deus homo* only to return in his ineluctable presence at the end.

Here the objections of the infidels are crushed. Their demand for a solid foundation underlying the vulgar imagery of Christianity is more than met. It is ridiculed. Proposing, for argument's sake, momentarily to abandon that imagery in search of a proper foundation, Anselm applies his razor. Doing so, he cuts off all superfluous talk of solid underpinning and shows it to be mistakenly imposing the concept of extrinsic necessity (*necessitas precedens*) on a fragile but self-sufficient imagery, so self-sufficient, indeed, that it can bear temporary suspension.

The effect is astonishing. Being temporarily divested does not mean that Anselm's Christ has lost its grip. On the contrary. In its absence the picture of Christ makes itself felt in its all-embracing power: *C'est Vénus tout entière à sa proie attachée.* Just as the fool's negation in the *Proslogion* is, by force of logic, drawn back, and transformed in, and by, the presence of God, so the infidels' objections are drawn within the once-offensive picture of the suffering man-god.

> By this necessity he has become man. By this necessity he has suffered what he has done and suffered. By this necessity he has willed what he has willed. And those things happened by necessity because they were to happen in the future. And they were things to happen in the future because they happened. And they happened because they happened.[4]

Thus the third riddle—how to get the solidity of necessity back into the frame of the picture—is solved by providing an answer to the second riddle (the request for the solidity of truth in the guise of the question of how free will and necessity are to be reconciled in the god-man). By removing the image of Christ altogether, Anselm forces, by reason alone, the god-man to come out. Doing so, he proves the infidels' question to have been an impossible one. When all is said and done, the only foundation for the picture of God's suffering is to be found in the picture itself. As a consequence, the question as to the difference between the image and its foundation cannot and should not be asked. Removing the image of Christ from the process of reasoning Anselm had been more radical, and more shrewd, than the infidels: he had removed Christ himself and thus made room for reason. Linking the absent Christ to the intrinsic necessity of reason he has blown up the infidels' objections. All that remains now is the extraordinary beauty of the first riddle: a god suffering 'injustice and shame, descending into the womb of a woman, growing up fed by milk and human food, bearing fatigue, hunger, thirst, punishment, the cross among thieves and death.'

3. Bernard's Argument

Generally speaking, Bernard, quite unlike Anselm, is considered to have opposed the use of rational argumentation. His fierce clashes with both

---

4. *Cur deus homo* II, ch. 17 (Schmitt, II, p. 125).

Abelard and Gilbert of Porrée have established his reputation as an anti-rational, anti-modernist and reactionary thinker. The fact that the interpretation of his writings has been firmly in the hands of those who tended to emphasize his piety and his affectionate nature rather than his artistic sophistication has further contributed to this anti-rational reputation. Of course, there is no reason not to take Bernard at his word when he rejects the logical games of Abelard and his friends. Yet there is more to his anti-rationalism than just rejection. Criticizing the modernist attempts to interpret religious problems in terms of logic does not mean, in Bernard's case, that he has moved out of the general framework of Christian Neoplatonism as described above. For him too the aim of reflection and meditation is to go beyond the images of sense experience in order to lay bare the contours of a spiritual reality untouched by the uncertainties and inaccuracies which mark unfiltered speech and thought. Clearly, to carry out that programme, he has made no use of the tools of dialectics as Anselm, Abelard and others have done. However, his refusal to apply dialectics to faith does not turn him into someone whose religious zeal has prevented him from being articulate.

Let us look, for instance, at the following passage from the second sermon on the Resurrection:

> We have learnt from the Apostle that it is through faith that Christ dwells in our hearts. Consequently, it does not seem wide of the mark if one takes this to mean that Christ lives in us as long as faith is alive. But after faith has died, there is a sense in which Christ has died in us. Further, works testify to the life of faith as it is written: 'The works which the Father has given me, testify about me'. Nor does it seem incongruent with this state of affairs to hold that faith is dead in itself when it is without works. Just as we know the life of this body from its movements, so we know the life of faith from good works. Therefore, the soul is the life of the body through which it is moved and through which it feels. But the life of faith is love because it works through love as you read in the Apostle: 'Faith which works through love'. That is why, if love cools, faith dies, just as when the soul leaves the body. But if you see a man alive, strong in good works and happily glowing in 'conversation', do not doubt that there is faith in him since you have before you the firm proof of his being alive.[5]

This text is conspicuous for its density which matches Anselm's closely knit argumentation in *Cur deus homo*. Although, admittedly, it is not

---

5. *Sermo in Resurrectione* 2.1, in *Sancti Bernardi Opera* (ed. J. Leclercq, C.H. Talbot and H.M. Rochais; Rome, 1957–1977), V, p. 95.

meant to be a real argument, its rhetorical presentation bears the stamp of the *ars dialectica*. The premise being the equation of Christ's presence in the heart with faith, the latter's absence necessarily implies the death of Christ ('consequently'). The logic of the argument having been established it can be applied to experience. Just as the movements of the body testify to the inherent presence of life, so the presence of faith, or, for that matter, its absence, can be measured from the warmth, or, coldness, produced by good, or bad, works. Thus the life and death of faith can be read as arguments (*argumenta*) proving the presence or absence of Christ.

The way this Bernardian argument runs is somehow reminiscent of the so-called 'practical syllogism' in seventeenth-century Calvinism. There the issue at stake was the 'proof' of one's being elect. Detecting in one's life the fruits of God's grace, one was led to the conclusion— which itself should be considered a manifestation of grace—that one possibly belonged to the select company of God's chosen people.[6]

Now we might object that, appearances notwithstanding, the use of logical language both in Bernard and in seventeenth-century Calvinism does not contain a real argument at all. Rather it should be taken for what it is: a statement of faith which, ultimately, cannot be proven to be either wrong or false.

If Anselm's problem with the infidels was the pictorial status of what Christians believe about Christ's suffering, we here face a discrepancy between the image of Christ's presence in a human being and the solidity of that image, or, for that matter, the lack of it. Is the presence of Christ in the soul of the believer to be seen as just a pious, imaginative statement? If so, the argumentative language about this presence would boil down to a metaphorical, inaccurate way of speaking. For an argument to make sense, however, such a discrepancy between image and

6. William Perkins (1558–1602), for one, has given the following definition of the practical syllogism in his *A treatise tending unto a declaration whether a man be in the estate of damnation or in the estate of grace*. 'Although this particular expression, I am elected, is not expressly set downe in the Scriptures, yet it is inclusively comprehended in them, as the Species in his Genus, as the Logitians speake: so that it may by just consequent be gathered out of Gods word, if we reason thus: They which truly beleeve are elected, Joh.6.35. I truly beleeve; for he which beleeveth doth know himselfe to beleeve: therefore I am elected. The first proposition is taken from Scriptures; the second from the beleevers conscience, and from them both, the conclusion is easily derived' (as quoted by R.T Kendall, *Calvin and English Calvinism* [Oxford, 1979], p. 70).

fact will not do. A basic simplicity is required which is supposed to underpin the validity of any rational argumentation. In Anselm's *Cur deus homo* this simplicity had manifested itself in a highly dramatic fashion. The seemingly unbridgeable gap between the picture of Christ's incarnation and its (lack of) rational substance turned out to be based on an optical illusion. The three riddles being solved, the suffering Christ was proven to be undistinguishable from whatever (extrinsic) compelling motive, desire or cause might underlie his suffering. At the same time it was the optical illusion itself, that is, the suggestion of Christian language being just metaphorical, image-like, that produced the dramatic effect of Anselm's argumentation.

As for Bernard, whatever the dialectical merits of his 'argument' in this passage, a basic simplicity underlies its every rhetorical amplification. Just as in *Cur deus homo* the simplicity of rational cogency is based on the unique qualities of the god-man in whom image and substance are one and the same, so in Bernard's view Christ's is the only image which is the guarantee of real, substantial life. In fact, the image is so simple and substantial as to exclude whatever happens to be outside it as belonging to the realm of disorder and death.

At this stage another *sed contra* presents itself. Is it not the case that Bernard, applying the principle of mystical tropology to the death and resurrection of Christ, creates a kind of metaphorical distance between the believer on the one hand and the latter's faith—here personified as the dying or living Christ—on the other? If so, what remains of the simplicity and cogency which are supposed to govern his 'argument'?

Here yet another comparison with Anselm's *Cur deus homo* may be helpful. Although it is the fate of humankind that is at stake in that treatise, humanity is only saved from utter destruction by the instrinsic qualities of the god-man. That is precisely what Anselm's rational argumentation is about. Establishing, by reason alone, the picture of the god-man, the human and divine minds somehow coalesce. Whatever distance remains should not be seen as being part and parcel of the usual communicative troubles between the believer and the divine object. Rather it is the impact of Christ's picture being real and substantial and humanity being part of it—that is, of its dramatic power—that can never be fully grasped in spite of its all-pervasive presence. It somehow leaves the believer—and reader—behind in a state of awe.

If with Anselm the fate of God, humanity and the creation is telescoped in the argument concerning the god-man, in Bernard's text the

latter's image is governed by the logic of the narrative. As a consequence, the most striking feature of this text is not the fact that Bernard
the author or, for that matter, the believer, associates his (lack of) faith
with the person of Christ. Within the narrow confines of the narrative
faith *is* Christ and vice versa. Consequently, if it dies, Christ dies and if it
comes to life, Christ comes to life.[7] Seen from the viewpoint of the narrative, the presence of third parties—such as a separate devotional subject—is ruled out as uneconomical. All those third parties could do is
spoil the effect of the narrative about life and death. That very same
economy makes Bernard's 'argument' univocally valid. Ultimately, it is
the rhetorical power generated by this unity of time, place and action
which performs the act of resurrection on the believer or reader in the
same way as it is the cogency produced by Anselm's reason which
forces the god-man to come out.

This economizing aspect of Bernard's 'argument' is most poignantly
expressed in his second sermon on the Song of Songs. There he pictures
the Old Testament fathers crying out for the coming of Christ:

> I therefore rightly refuse to accept any more visions and dreams, I do not
> want any more symbols and riddles. I even get tired of the pretty shapes
> of angels. My Jesus surpasses them in stature and beauty. I do not ask for
> anyone else, no angel, no man, but only for himself to kiss me with the
> kiss of his mouth.[8]

Cutting through the dense wood of symbols, riddles and images Bernard
lays bare the structure of his basic argument. It is Jesus, not as object of
faith, but as faith itself, who dominates the scene. Further on in the same
sermon Bernard does indeed describe this moment in terms of resurrection. The figure of the Old Testament fathers longing for the kiss of life
is then pictured as the dead boy from the book of Kings who is to be
resurrected by the prophet Elisha. If we transpose this imagery to the
passage from the second sermon on the Resurrection, we get an even

---

7.   Janet Coleman, discussing the implications of Abelard's logic for his view of
the past, points out that 'Abelard substituted texts for events' both past and present.
There is a sense in which the logical coherence underlying those texts, and, for that
matter, past and present, can be compared with Bernard's mystical tropology. The
validity of this mystical tropology (i.e. the simultaneity of biblical persons and situa-
tions and the monastic present) is based on its consistency, that is, the logic of the
narrative. See J. Coleman, *Ancient and Medieval Memories. Studies in the Recon-
struction of the Past* (Cambridge, 1992), pp. 272-73.

8.   *Sermo 2 In Canticum canticorum, Sancti Bernardi Opera*, I, p. 9.

more accurate picture. The logic of Bernard's argument demands the kisser and the kissed to be one. The Christ lying dead in his grave is the same as the Christ rising from the dead on his own. Through the kiss of life the prophet Elisha and the dead boy coalesce into one and the same person, leaving it to the reader to disentangle their embrace. The very indivisibility of this kiss or, for that matter, the logic of the narrative, draws the believer, who might momentarily have thought of her or himself as coming to the text as an independent subject, within the confines of the story.

In the second sermon on the Resurrection this single image of the embrace representing faith both dead and alive is consistently carried through till the very end. Nowhere is faith depicted as a separate entity outside this imagery from which the course of Bernard's tropological argument could be governed. Elaborating on the resurrection story Bernard identifies faith as the different *dramatis personae* it contains and, indeed, is. In its negative appearance it is Christ lying in his grave, the stone that closes off the tomb, the women refusing to believe that the stone can be removed. In its positive appearance, it is the women running to the grave in hopeful expectancy, God hearing the mute voice of the dead man, Christ rising from the dead. All those features coincide in the *persona* of the story-teller, the angel. Assuming in person the roles played by the different characters, he admits that it was he himself, that is, his very own faith that had been tepid, stony and wrapped in the shrouds of a dead body and was thus in need of resurrection.

4. Conclusion

Comparing Anselm and Bernard, we find in both thinkers the strong, intrinsic presence of God as a spiritual reality which has to be uncovered. The very strength of this presence—*Vénus tout entière à sa proie attachée*—is to be brought out by technical means. Cogency is the keyword to Anselm's rational adventures as well as to Bernard's rhetorical exercises. Consequently, reasoning about matters of faith as Anselm does or staging them in a theatrical manner in Bernard's fashion, is not based on separate qualities of the human mind. Things are more 'cogent' than that. Rather the mind is an intrinsic part of both the rational and theatrical performances in which the god-man Christ is forced to come out. That both thinkers dare take the risk of playing with the absence of Christ either as *Christo remoto* or as the death of faith in the soul only heightens the suspense of their respective experiments. Both deal with a 'God without qualities' who does not loosen its grip. Expansion of the divine image into meditation and argumentation, suggesting a certain degree of disappearance, serves but one purpose. Divested, images of the divine come to life if, on their way out, they find themselves mirrored in language and thought. The most the rhetoric of argumentation can achieve is to send those images back to their source. In terms of Anselm and Bernard respectively, the focus of that mirror is to be found in a single argument or a single kiss. The increasingly intense presence of the divine resulting from those 'reflections' is to be called a product of the performing arts.

SAINT ANSELM'S *IMAGO EPISCOPI*

Walter Fröhlich

Since St Anselm never wrote a treatise dealing with the office and duties of a bishop in a systematic way, any *imago episcopi* will have to be formed like a mosaic by piecing together various Anselmian statements of different times referring to the conduct or office of a bishop. They are mainly found in his correspondence during the period when he was archbishop of Canterbury.[1] A few statements from other sources may round off the picture thus gained. These Anselmian statements will in turn be related to the constitutional definitions of the office and status of bishop as embodied in the canonical tradition of the centuries before Gratian's *Decretum*.[2]

Anselm carefully selected letters for his letter collection from his vast correspondence and edited it in the years 1105 to 1108. Therefore it is not necessary to distinguish between letters he wrote and letters he received. All these letters are included in MS Lambeth 59 containing what appears to be the final and definite edition of the Anselmian correspondence.[3] These letters contain Anselm's ideal medieval *ordo* and *imago episcopi* as expressed by him between 1093 and 1108. Anselm's statements referring to *episcopus* can be most easily examined under specific headings:

---

1.   Anselm's letters are collected in vols. III–V of Schmitt's edition of his works; quotations here are taken from *The Letters of Saint Anselm of Canterbury* (trans. W. Fröhlich; 3 vols.; Kalamazoo, 1990, 1993, 1994).

2.   For an analytic synthesis of the canonistic definitions of the medieval office of bishop see R.L. Benson, *The Bishop-elect* (Princeton, 1968).

3.   For the genesis of Anselm's letter collection see Fröhlich, *The Letters of Saint Anselm*, I, pp. 26-52.

1. *Vacancy*

In August 1108, eight months before his death, Anselm wrote to Thomas, the archbishop-elect of York, that canonical authority 'prescribes that the church of a bishopric is not to remain without a pastor for more than three months'.[4] In this Anselm expressed the ecclesiastical norm, as it was to be found in *distinctio* 23 of Gratian's *Decretum*, and his wish as metropolitan and primate. Since the fulfilment of this norm did not depend on him alone, nor on the cathedral chapter alone, it was adhered to more frequently than not.

In the case in question the demand of canonical authority had been fulfilled. Archbishop Gerard of York had died on 21 May 1108. Thomas was elected as the new archbishop on 27 May 1108, thus succeeding to the *sedes vacans* within the three-month limit. Yet the elect of York delayed going to Canterbury to receive consecration and make profession of obedience to Anselm hoping that, if the ailing Anselm should die at an earlier date, he might be able to shake off the primatial claim of Canterbury during an ensuing vacancy there. ·

2. *Election*

In the same letter on the election of Thomas Anselm continues: 'Since it has pleased the King, on the advice of his barons and with our consent, that you should be elected for the archbishopric of York, the time limit thus wisely ordained should not be delayed any longer by you. I am therefore surprised that since your election you have not asked to be consecrated to the office to which you were elected.'[5] The supremacy dispute between Canterbury and York caused protracted negotiations and delayed Thomas's consecration and profession of obedience until 27 June 1109, two months after Anselm's death on 21 April.

Anselm described the interesting election procedure of May 1108. It occurred after the settlement of the investiture controversy by the concordat of London of 1–4 August 1107. This election procedure combined the lay influence of the lords temporal—king and barons—with the ecclesiastical influence of the lords spiritual—the bishops as well as the metropolitan and primate. It reflects the conflicting positions expressed by the *Decretum Gratiani* which mirrors thinking on the

4. *Ep.* 443.
5. *Ep.* 443.

constitutional history of the church in the early Middle Ages. Summing up *distinctio* 63 Gratian observed: 'By all these authorities laymen should be excluded from the election of bishops, and the necessity of obedience, not freedom of command, is enjoined on them.'[6] Yet this statement is followed by 17 *capitula* which defend various rights of rulers or lay people. Some of these chapters showed plainly that in earlier centuries emperors and kings had held and exercised wide powers of supervision and approval in ecclesiastical elections, even in papal elections. Thereupon Gratian begins his resolution of the conflict in the texts: 'By these examples...one concludes clearly that laymen should not be excluded from the election, nor princes barred from the filling of offices in the churches'.[7]

Anselm reported on the election procedure of 27 May 1108 in which he co-operated and by co-operating sanctioned; by incorporating this letter to Thomas into his letter collection—it is letter 367 in MS L 59—Anselm endorsed the procedure and established it as a precedent to be followed in future.

The king's part in the election of Thomas did not receive Anselm's censure. On the contrary, king and archbishop co-operated in electing the best candidate for York.[8] This co-operation fulfilled the Anselmian concept of kingship in this issue,[9] namely that the king and the archbishop of Canterbury as primate of all Britain should work together harmoniously as a plough team of oxen for the benefit of the church in the Anglo-Norman realm. By this action Anselm emphasized his approval of the election of Thomas. Anselm's action is supported by a canon of the Council of Nicea of 325.[10] It stresses the importance of the

6.   See Benson, *Bishop-elect*, p. 29.

7.   See Benson, *Bishop-elect*, p. 29.

8.   For Anselm's opinion on the suitability of a candidate for ecclesiastical preferment see *Epp.* 156, 157, 158, 163, 164, 165; C.W. Hollister, 'St Anselm on Lay Investiture', *Anglo-Norman Studies* 10 (1987), pp. 145-58.

9.   Eadmer, *Historia novorum in Anglia* (ed. M. Rule; London, 1884), p. 36; on kingship: W. Fröhlich, 'Anselm von Canterburys *IMAGO REGIS*, dargestellt aus seinen Briefen', in *Universität und Bildung: Festschrift für L. Boehm* (München, 1991), pp. 13-24; *idem*, 'Anselm's Concept of Kingship', in. C.E. Viola (ed.), *Saint Anselme, penseur d'hier et d'aujourd'hui: La pensée de Saint Anselme vue par nos contemporains* (Colloque international du CNRS, Paris, 1990) (*Anselm Studies*, forthcoming).

10.   *Nicaenum concilium* (Oxford, 1899–1930), pp. 116-17, 188-89, 258. See Benson, *Bishop-elect*, p. 36.

metropolitan archbishop's approval as an essential element in the promotion of any new bishop within his province.

For the period stretching from the fourth to the mid-twelfth century this canon of Nicea, one of the oldest texts in the *Decretum Gratiani*, is exemplary, since it links the metropolitan's confirmation to the consent of the other bishops of the province. Moreover, from the fifth to the seventh centuries church councils demanded the metropolitan's presence at or his consent to the consecration of a new bishop. In a similar vein Gratian insisted that the primate was also to be fully informed and to give his approval before a new bishop could be consecrated.[11]

Anselm's letter to Thomas, the elect of York, with all its canonical implications and associations, alluded to the claim for supremacy of Canterbury over York and intended to demonstrate the subordination of York to Canterbury. This Canterbury claim would be manifest to everybody when the elect of York swore his profession of obedience to the archbishop of Canterbury at his consecration. Such are the basic reasons for the ensuing, prolonged controversy between Canterbury and York,[12] and Anselm clearly demonstrated his concept of the election of bishops by his confirmation and assent to the election of this new bishop, Thomas of York.

3. *Consecration*

In two letters of 1106 and 1107 to Muirchertach, the king of Ireland, Anselm enjoined the king to secure canonical consecration of bishops in his realm. He wrote: 'bishops who ought to be a pattern and example of canonical religious practice to others are being irregularly consecrated, as we hear, either by one alone, or in places where they ought not to be consecrated' and 'It is also said that in your country bishops are elected at random and appointed without any definite place for their bishopric, and consecrated bishop by one bishop alone, just like any priest. This is of course totally against the holy canons which order that those who have been elected and consecrated in this way, as well as those who consecrated them, are to be deposed from their episcopal office.'[13]

From the church councils of the fourth century until the *Decretum*

11. Gratian, *Distinctio* 65; see Benson, *Bishop-elect*, p. 37.
12. *Epp.* 443, 444, 445, 453, 454, 455, 456, 462, 464, 465, 467, 469, 470, 471, 472, 473.
13. *Epp.* 427, 435.

Gratiani the church regarded election and consecration as the two crucial acts in the making of a new bishop.[14] Anselm based his firm advice
to the Irish king on canonical authority. He relied on the canon of the
Council of Chalcedon which had forbidden ordination of a cleric or consecration of a bishop without giving him an appropriate ecclesiastical
office. In 1095 Pope Urban II renewed this prohibition against ordination and consecration without provision for an office ('absoluta ordinatio' or 'ordinatio sine titulo'). In the middle of the twelfth-century,
according to Rufinus and Stephen of Tournai, such ordinations were
effective *with regard to the validity of the sacrament* but were null and
void *with regard to the exercise of the office.*[15]

Anselm also seems to have based his criticism of the Irish situation on
the custom of consecration followed by most twelfth-century bishops:
that metropolitans were consecrated by their suffragan bishops and that
any new suffragan bishop was consecrated by the metropolitan with his
suffragan bishops. This custom can be seen at work in the Anglo-
Norman kingdom in the second half of the eleventh century: Lanfranc
(on 29 August 1070) and Anselm (on 4 December 1093) were both
consecrated by all their suffragan bishops, with the archbishop of York
being the main consecrator. The primate and the metropolitan of York
in turn consecrated, with the assistance of their suffragans, any new
bishop of the province.

When writing about episcopal consecration it is interesting to note that
Anselm does not refer to any of the rights conferred upon the new
bishop: *plenitudo auctoritatis, plenitudo officii spiritualibus,
auctoritatis regendi et disponendi*, etc. Perhaps they were so obvious
that he did not need to mention them.

4. *A Bishop for a Diocese*

In his second letter to King Muirchertach Anselm criticized the practice
of creating a bishop without a diocese of his own. Similarly Anselm
admonished King Henry I in 1106, when the king was planning to find a
new bishopric for Bishop Hervey of Bangor, who had been driven out
of his see after the Normans had been pushed back from the western
regions of Wales at the end of the eleventh century. Anselm wrote: 'Just
as no bishop ought to be consecrated for any church without the assent

14. Benson, *Bishop-elect*, p. 24.
15. See Benson, *Bishop-elect*, pp. 52-53.

and advice of the archbishop and the other bishops of the province, so he who has been consecrated bishop cannot canonically be made a bishop in any other province without the advice and the assent of the archbishop and the bishops of that province with papal authority, nor without release by the archbishop and the bishops of the province he was consecrated in'.[16]

When criticizing King Muirchertach and admonishing King Henry I Anselm seems to have been guided by a canon of the Fourth Council of Toledo in 633. It insisted: 'He whom the clergy and the people of his own city have not elected, whom neither the authority of the metropolitan nor the assent of the provincial bishops has chosen—he shall not be chosen'. This canon was entered into *distinctio* 51 of the *Decretum* by Master Gratian. It seems to have been well known at Canterbury since Anselm quoted the Fourth Council of Toledo on a different matter in letter 161 written in October/November 1093.

5. *Confirmation of a New Archbishop*

In January 1095 Anselm wrote to Archbishop Hugh of Lyon complaining: 'If I as metropolitan archbishop, having been consecrated, neither ask to see the Pope in person, nor ask for the pallium whenever I can throughout the whole first year, then rightly I should be removed from that honour. Indeed it is far better that I reject the archbishopric than refuse to acknowledge the Pope.'[17]

When writing these lines Anselm was in a very difficult situation. He had been elected archbishop on 6 March 1093, done homage to King William II Rufus and been enthroned on 25 September, and had been consecrated on 4 December 1093. But he had not fulfilled all the canonical demands for a new metropolitan archbishop, since within a year of consecration he should have gone to Pope Urban II to receive the pallium as papal confirmation of his metropolitan rights. Anselm had not been able to do this despite repeated requests to King William Rufus to grant him leave to go to the Pope. The king repeatedly refused this permission on the grounds of William the Conqueror's *usus atque leges* which gave him the power to decide who was to enter or leave the Anglo-Norman realm.[18] William Rufus feared not only that Anselm

16. *Ep.* 404.
17. *Ep.* 176.
18. *Historia novorum*, 10, pp. 52, 53-67.

would report to the Pope on the situation of the church and morals in the Anglo-Norman kingdom, and about the king's repeated refusal to convene a reforming synod to deal with misdemeanours within the *ecclesia in Anglia*, but also that he might bring back new ideas, dangerous to *potestas regalis*, if allowed to go to Rome.

Moreover, these same *usus atque leges* also gave the king the right to decide who was the rightful bishop of Rome in the case of a schism. The anti-pope Clement III—as Archbishop Wibert of Ravenna he had been nominated by Emperor Henry IV in 1084—was at that time opposing the rightful Pope Urban II. As long as William Rufus had not decided for either claimant to the see of St Peter he could keep the collection of Romescot for the royal coffers. For these reasons Anselm was not granted royal leave to fulfil what was canonically demanded of him.

Following the practice of Urban II with regard to the pallium, Paschal defined the significance of its bestowal thus: 'With the pallium, the fullness of the episcopal office is granted, since according to the custom of the Apostolic See and of all Europe, before he has received the pallium a metropolitan is not allowed to consecrate bishops or to hold a synod'.[19]

The status of a metropolitan was more than that of a bishop: there were particular powers—the *ius metropoliticum*—pertaining exclusively to his office. His competence included the right to confirm the election of suffragan bishops in his province and to consecrate them, the right to call provincial synods and to preside over them, and also to exercise general supervision and discipline within his province. Since the earlier Middle Ages the metropolitan's right to exercise these supra-episcopal powers was dependent upon the possession of the pallium.[20] From the time of Paschal II's pontificate at the latest the newly elected metropolitan took an oath of obedience to the Pope and the effective *ius metropoliticum* dated from taking this oath as well as from the receipt of the pallium. Thus the metropolitan was called *to share in the solicitude* but not acquire the fullness of ecclesiastical power ('in partem sollicitudinis, non in plenitudinem potestatis').[21]

The receipt of the pallium made Anselm a papally confirmed metropolitan archbishop of the Anglo-Norman ecclesiastical province, and the

---

19. P. Jaffe and S. Loewenfeld, *Regesta pontificum Romanorum* (2 vols.; Berlin, 1885–88), no. 5464; see Benson, *Bishop-elect*, pp. 169-70.

20. Benson, *Bishop-elect*, pp. 168-70.

21. Benson, *Bishop-elect*, pp. 171-72.

Anselmian charter for Bishop Herbert of Norwich[22] on 3 September 1101 sums up Anselm's status perfectly. The *intitulatio* runs as follows: *Carta Anselmi archiepiscopi Cantuariensis, vicarius Paschalis Papae.* In this charter Anselm styled himself *vicarius Paschalis Papae.* This is completely congruous with the above-mentioned argument. In fact, there are doubts about the genuineness of this charter, but even if it is a forgery it is unlikely to have been produced outside the context and opinions of Anselm's chancery. Therefore, whether genuine or spurious, this charter reflects how Anselm felt, how he perceived himself to be and how he wanted to be seen.

6. *Spiritual Quality of a Bishop*

Before his consecration as archbishop of Canterbury Anselm wrote to Waleran, cantor of the church of Paris, in October/November 1093 and expressed his ideas on the ultimate spiritual essence of a bishop: 'Bishops maintain their authority as long as they are in agreement with Christ, so they have it taken from them when they are in disagreement with Christ. Every bishop who has Christ's voice is Christ. And the sheep follow him for they know his voice.'[23]

Anselm perceived the bishop to be an *alter Christus* who, like the good shepherd, cares for the sheep entrusted to him. He defends them against the attacks of enemies, robbers and wild animals. Furthermore, if one of his sheep gets lost and separated from the flock he will search for it and bring it back by lovingly carrying it on his shoulders. Moreover, Anselm conceived the bishop as the mediator between Christ the redeemer and the people entrusted to him on their pilgrimage to their celestial home.

In Anselm's view bishops are first and foremost pastors and shepherds of the flock entrusted to them. The bishop's most important task is preaching the word of God and instructing his flock so that he may assist its members in leading a divine life. The more his own conduct agrees with Christ, the more his teaching and preaching will be accepted, his word believed. Like Christ the bishop is to unite and to teach his flock. A bishop, Anselm wrote to King Muirchertach of Ireland in 1106–1107, ought to be a pattern and example of canonical religious

22. *Regesta regum Anglo-Normanorum* (ed. C. Johnson and H.A. Cronne; Oxford, 1956), II, no. 549.
23. *Ep.* 162.

practice.[24] He admonished Bishop Samuel of Dublin and told him that it pertained to the office of a bishop rather to unite what had been dispersed than to disperse what had been united.[25] Moreover, two letters from Paschal II of 21 November 1108 concerning Hervey of Bangor convey the same idea—and since these letters were incorporated by Anselm into his letter collection, they must express his own opinion. They read: 'A bishop is appointed in order to teach the people of God by his word and to form them by his life and to bring them back to the true shepherd, the Lord, a harvest of the souls entrusted to him'.[26]

7. *Potestas ligandi et solvendi*

Functioning as *alter Christus* and modelling himself on the good shepherd by teaching and setting a good example the bishop also has to have the power to punish in order to encourage the good and discourage the evil. In a letter to Pope Paschal II[27] in late 1101 or early 1102 Anselm claimed the *potestas ligandi et solvendi* for the bishop but subordinated the bishop's power to that of the Pope when he wrote: 'As it does not pertain to me to loosen what you bind, so it is not up to me to bind what you loosen'.

In Mt. 16.18-19 when Christ gave St Peter 'the keys of the kingdom of heaven' he promised him the power to bind and to loose. There was a scriptural basis for the interpretation of this gift as the power to remit sins. In this sense the 'power of binding and loosing' was an essentially sacramental prerogative belonging to any priest. Gratian accepted this traditional explanation referring the *potestas ligandi et solvendi* to the remission of sins. Discussing the pre-eminent authority of papal decretals Gratian developed an authoritative interpretation of *potestas ligandi et solvendi*. He stated: 'It is one thing to pass judgement in law cases, it is something else to expound Holy Scripture carefully. In deciding cases, not only knowledge (scientia) is necessary but also power (potestas).'[28] Gratian further explained that the *keys* are indispensable for the exercise of the power of binding and loosing. The first key consists of the *knowledge* needed for the judgment of those crimes which are tried in an

24. *Ep.* 427.
25. *Ep.* 278.
26. *Epp.* 457, 459.
27. *Ep.* 218.
28. See Benson, *Bishop-elect*, pp. 47-49.

ecclesiastical court. The second key, however, is *power* including the power to excommunicate or to reconcile. Thus, in Gratian's thought the 'power of binding and loosing' acquired a new meaning: judicial authority over the church as a society. The latter concept of *potestas ligandi et solvendi* was not alien to Anselm when he was considering excommunicating King Henry in summer 1105.

8. *Advice to Fellow Bishops*

As primate of all Britain Anselm carried out general supervision and enforced discipline within his province. At some time between 1100 and 1103 Anselm criticized Bishop Samuel of Dublin: 'I have heard that you have the cross carried in front of you along the road. If this is true, I instruct you to do it no longer since it pertains only to an archbishop confirmed by the Roman pontiff with the pallium, and it is not fitting for you to show yourself to people to be notorious and blameworthy by presuming to do anything contrary to custom.'[29]

Another example from the same letter shows Anselm acting not only as metropolitan but rather displaying his monastic training and *Weltbild*. He admonished Bishop Samuel to assist the monks to live together and encouraged him by writing: 'You are surely aware that it pertains to your office rather to unite what has been dispersed than disperse what has been united'. In the same vein Anselm, still as archbishop-elect, speaking as a monk who considered the cloister to be the place on earth closest to paradise, wrote to his fellow bishop, Geoffrey of Paris, in October/November 1093 to persuade him to allow his cantor Waleran to remain a monk at the monastery of St Martin des Champs. He criticized him: 'From there he was precipitately removed by force by your order in a manner which was not necessary at all'.[30] In the rest of the letter Anselm quoted numerous reasons and examples from scripture, patristic literature and canonical teaching supporting Waleran's desire to become a monk and urging the bishop to grant him permission to accomplish his desire. As far as we know Bishop Geoffrey did not follow Anselm's argument or carry out his request.

29. *Ep.* 278.
30. *Ep.* 161.

9. The Metropolitan's General Supervision and Discipline
within the Province

In February 1094, shortly after his consecration but long before he had received the pallium confirming his position as metropolitan, Anselm acted as metropolitan according to the requirement of canon 2 of the Council of Nicaea (325) and to ecclesiastical custom in the Anglo-Norman realm: he implored William II to grant permission to convene a reforming council which he considered most necessary.[31] Under the *usus atque leges*, however, it was a royal prerogative to grant permission or not. Since the king resented Anselm's initiative and feared moral censure he continued to refuse to convene a reforming council throughout his reign.[32]

In March/April 1106, writing from Bec, Anselm strongly criticized Henry I for by-passing the canons of the first reforming council which Anselm had held in 1102. 'I hear that your excellency is inflicting punishment upon priests in England and exacting fines from them for not keeping the canons of the Council which I, with other bishops and religious persons, held in London with your approval. Up to now this has been unheard of and unprecedented in the Church of God on the part of any king or prince. By the law of God it is not for anyone except each bishop in his own diocese to punish an offence of this kind or, if the bishops themselves are negligent in this, then for the archbishop or primate. Therefore I beseech you as my dearest lord, whose soul I love more than the present life of my body, and I advise you as a true friend of your body and soul, not to cast yourself into such a grave sin contrary to ecclesiastical custom and, if you have already begun to do so, give it up completely.'[33]

King Henry was collecting fines from archdeacons, priests, deacons, subdeacons and canons who had kept their wives after celibacy was firmly enforced by canons 4, 5 and 6 of the Council of London 1102.[34]

---

31. See R. Foreville, 'The Synod of the Province of Rouen in the Eleventh and Twelfth Centuries', in *Church and Government in the Middle Ages. Essays presented to C.R. Cheney...* (ed. C. Brooke *et al.*; Cambridge, 1976), p. 19; *Historia novorum*, p. 48.
32. *Historia novorum*, p. 49.
33. *Ep.* 391.
34. *Historia novorum*, p. 142.

The king collected money from wherever he could get it in order to equip his army for the war he was planning against his brother Robert to wrest the Duchy of Normandy from him: Anselm rebuked the royal infringement on church rulings and demonstratively stated his metropolitan rights.

This Anselm also did in a letter to King Muirchertach of Ireland in 1106 or 1107. 'We have heard,' he wrote, 'that in your kingdom marriages are being dissolved and altered without ground: that those related to each other do not fear to live together openly without reproof despite canonical prohibition, either under the name of marriage or in some other way.'[35]

Anselm pursued his metropolitan duties and obligations outside his own diocese by exhorting and firmly admonishing individual monks and nuns as well as whole communities in other dioceses.[36] He advised the fellow bishops of the *ecclesia in Anglia* to order prayers to be said for the king while at war;[37] he sent letters of instruction about the papal prohibition for monks wanting to join the crusade,[38] on the practice of celibacy[39] and on the censure of worship to a dead person not a saint.[40] He asked Pope Paschal to grant the pallium to Archbishop Gerard of York[41] and even persuaded him to write to some obdurate fellow bishop.[42] Moreover, he made his metropolitan surveillance felt throughout what he considered to be his ecclesiastical province. He patiently pursued the reform of the clergy and people of Ireland;[43] diligently investigated the ecclesiastical obedience and orders of the bishops of Wales;[44] and maintained canonical order in the creation of bishops in Scotland.[45] He even encouraged Earl Hacon of Orkney to listen to and

---

35. *Ep.* 427.
36. *Epp.* 168, 169, 184, 185, 203, 204, 230, 414, 231, 232, 233, 245, 251, 252, 267, 382, 408, 276, 183, 337, 403, 450, 405.
37. *Ep.* 190.
38. *Ep.* 195.
39. *Ep.* 254.
40. *Epp.* 236, 237.
41. *Ep.* 220.
42. *Epp.* 172, 226.
43. *Epp.* 198, 201, 202, 207, 277, 278, 426, 427, 428, 429, 435; *Historia novorum*, pp. 64, 77, 79-80.
44. *Epp.* 175, 270; *Historia novorum*, pp. 72, 76, 81, 147.
45. *Epp.* 413, 442; *Historia novorum*, pp. 126-128, 212-214.

assist his bishop[46] and cordially greeted Atser in his recently created archbishopric of Lund.[47]

Thus it can be seen that Anselm was fully aware of the canonical duties and rights of a metropolitan and pursued them even before he was bestowed with the pallium. He regarded himself as the primate of England, Wales, Scotland, Ireland and the adjacent islands and territories and acted accordingly.

10. *Possessions of a Church*

In his letter to Archbishop Hugh of Lyon of January 1095 Anselm was seriously concerned about the loss of church property. William II had taken lands which had been held by Lanfranc in demesne but were thought to have been held by English knights before the Conquest. The legal basis for William's action had been his claim that these lands once more be held by military service.

Anselm styled the king *advocatus ecclesiae* and called himself, the bishop, *custos ecclesiae*, guardian or keeper of his church in place of Christ and the saint to whom the church was dedicated. He saw the bishop as the earthly deputy of the patron, administering the earthly possession of the patron saint and leading the people entrusted to him on behalf of the patron to the heavenly kingdom. St Augustine had stated that the prelate holds ecclesiastical property as procurator of the patron saint and as proctor representing the poor, and he thereby emphasized the prelate's solemn responsibility in the administration of his church's property. This Augustinian statement is also quoted by Gratian: 'the bishop...is the proctor, not the owner, of the ecclesiastical properties'.[48]

For these reasons, not merely exercising metropolitan rights, Anselm censured Bishop Samuel between 1100 and 1103: 'I have heard that of your own accord you are disposing of and giving to strangers the books, vestments and other ornaments of the church which lord Lanfranc, the archbishop, gave to your uncle, lord Donatus, the bishop, for the use of the church over which your fraternity now presides. If this is true, I am amazed you are acting in this way since these ornaments were not given to him but to the church, as your brothers, the sons of the church of Canterbury, bear witness. Wherefore, I admonish you, and admonishing

46. *Ep.* 449; *Historia novorum*, p. 212.
47. *Ep.* 447.
48. See Benson, *Bishop-elect*, p. 84.

ask you that if any of the aforesaid articles has been bestowed outside the church you speedily have it restored.'[49]

Conclusion

The foregoing examples of Anselm's actions and thoughts while archbishop of Canterbury demonstrate that he was in harmony with the mainstream medieval concept of a bishop. His *imago episcopi* is well supported by scripture and canonical tradition. Since he hardly ever quoted authorities verbatim either in his philosophical or theological writings or in his letters his *imago episcopi* has to be deduced from his writings and actions and related to the relevant passages in scripture, patristic writings and canonical tradition. The suggestion[50] that Anselm was ill informed on canon law because there are very few citations from canon law in his writings and letters therefore carries little weight.

This paper shows that Anselm had an excellent working knowledge of the requirements of the canons and based his *imago episcopi* on his understanding of all available authorities. His perseverance in upholding what he believed to be God's plan for the *corpus Christianorum* on earth and carrying it through despite exile and frustrations until the end of his life shows that he wholeheartedly lived up to his own perception of the demands of his office.

49. *Ep.* 278.
50. R.W. Southern, *St Anselm and his Biographer* (Cambridge, 1963), pp. 124-27, 189-90; *idem, Saint Anselm: A Portrait in a Landscape* (Cambridge, 1990), pp. 149-50, 152.

ECCLESIA MATER—ECCLESIA MATER CANTUARIENSIS
CONCEZIONE DELLA MATERNITÀ ECCLESIALE DI CANTERBURY

Costante Marabelli

All'espressione 'mater ecclesia', che ricorre nell'epistolario di Anselmo, è attribuibile una molteplicità di significati, che qui di seguito cercheremo di illustrare e documentare nei loro diversi contesti.

1. *Mater catholica (ecclesia)*

Quando Anselmo, da priore e abate di Le Bec, si rivolge all'arcivescovo Lanfranco di Canterbury, non solo riconosce sempre nell'antico maestro il proprio 'dominus et pater',[1] ma ne pone in risalto di là dai rapporti personali i meriti che quegli ha acquisito sul piano della chiesa universale talora salutandolo come degno di onore da parte di tutti i 'catholici': 'Suo domino et suo patri, multum cum amore catholicis reverendo et cum reverentia amando archiepiscopo Lanfranco...',[2] o come arcivescovo che la 'mater catholica' deve tenere molto a caro e riverire: 'archiepiscopo matri catholicae amplectendo Lanfranco...'[3] Qui la 'mater catholica' è inequivocabilmente la chiesa universale. È ancora al valore di Lanfranco riconosciuto dalla chiesa universale che Anselmo si richiama quando dice che la vita dell'arcivescovo è 'necessaria' alla

---

1. Cf. *Epp.* 1, 14, 23, 25, 27, 32, 39, 49, 57, 66, 72, 77, 89, 90, 103, 124. Di seguito le lettere dell'epistolario anselmiano vengono citate dall'edizione di F.S. Schmitt; tuttavia segnaliamo qui anche l'edizione bilingue latino (con testo dello Schmitt)–italiano, con commento: I. Biffi e C. Marabelli (edd.), *Anselmo d'Aosta, Lettere*, 2 voll. / 3 tomi (Milano: Jaca Book, 1988–1993).
2. *Ep.* 1: 97, 1-2; cf. anche *Ep.* 23 e *Ep.* 77.
3. *Ep.* 25: 132, 2; cf. anche *Ep.* 32: 140, 1: 'catholicae matri amplectendo archiepiscopo Lanfranco...'; *Ep.* 39: 149, 1: 'matri catholicae cum amore reverendo...Lanfranco'; *Ep.* 66: 186, 1-2: 'reverentiae honore et amoris affectu matri catholicae colendo archiepiscopo Lanfranco'.

'mater ecclesia': 'nec solum nobis, sed et matri ecclesiae, quantum nomen vestrum extendi potest, vitam vestram necessariam esse intelligimus'.[4] Analogo riconoscimento e analoghe espressioni Anselmo riserva a un altro personaggio di alto profilo ecclesiale: l'arcivescovo Ugo di Lione, uomo che la 'mater ecclesia' deve sinceramente amare: 'matri ecclesiae sincere diligendo'.[5]

La metafora della madre nel senso di chiesa universale non è richiamata da Anselmo solo nelle sue relazioni con membri del clero, ma anche, e con più frequenza, nelle esortazioni ai principi cristiani: specialmente ai potenti è ricordato di onorare la santa chiesa come i figli una madre. Questo dovere è ricordato al re Baldovino di Gerusalemme,[6] al conte Roberto di Fiandra[7] e a sua moglie Clemenza,[8] al conte e marchese Umberto di Savoia,[9] alla contessa Matilde di Canossa.[10] La chiesa è madre in quanto è 'sponsa Dei' (o 'sponsa et amica Dei'); un testo particolarmente eloquente in proposito è quello della lettera a Umberto di Savoia: 'qualiter mater nostra, ecclesia dei, quam deus pulchram amicam et dilectam sponsam suam vocat, a malis principibus conculcatur'.[11]

Mentre in tutti i contesti che sopra abbiamo riferito l'espressione 'mater ecclesia' è sinonimo di chiesa universale, in una lettera a Urbano II essa appare piuttosto indicare la chiesa di Roma (o la sede apostolica). Al papa Anselmo manifesta di considerare la chiesa romana come il 'sinus matris ecclesiae' cui aspira a rifugiarsi in mezzo al naufragio: 'ad sinum matris ecclesiae confugero'.[12] D'altra parte però, in un contesto diverso, la metafora della madre sembrerebbe impiegata (non senza una certa ambiguità) per designare piuttosto la chiesa di Canterbury (Ecclesia Christi / Christ Church) nella distinzione dalla sede apostolica:

4. *Ep*. 124: 264, 6. Cf. anche *Monologion*, Epistola ad Lanfrancum archiepiscopum: 5, 3: 'matri ecclesiae catholicae fidei utilitatisque merito multum amplectendo Lanfranco'.

5. *Ep*. 389: 333, 2: 'Hugoni... matri ecclesiae sincere diligendo'.

6. *Ep*. 235: 143, 24: 'Qui eam sicut matrem filii tractant et honorant...'

7. *Ep*. 248: 159, 21: 'dignitatem, si sponsa dei, matris vestrae ecclesiae amatis'.

8. *Ep*. 249: 159, 11: 'Non enim principes sponsam dei, matrem suam, si Christiani sunt...'

9. *Ep*. 262: 177, 29: 'mater nostra ecclesia dei...'; *Ep*. 262: 177, 44: 'Eam ut matrem vestram amate, ut sponsam et amicam dei honorate...'

10. *Ep*. 325: 257, 23: 'quam erga matrem ecclesiam habetis...'

11. *Ep*. 262: 177, 29.

12. *Ep*. 193: 83, 50: 'ad sinum matris ecclesiae confugero'.

'ad haec omnia deo confortante paratum est cor meum pro apostolicae sedis obœdientia et matris meae, ecclesiae Christi, libertate'.[13]

2. *Ecclesia mater come chiesa di appartenenza*

Anche la comunità in cui un monaco ha fatto la sua professione monastica è considerata da Anselmo come una 'ecclesia mater'. Al giovane Lanfranco, nipote dell'omonimo arcivescovo, Anselmo ricorda con toni di rimprovero come il suo comportamento insubordinato abbia prodotto scandalo e vergogna in lui abate 'pater' e alla 'ecclesia mater' di Le Bec.[14]

Un monaco, anche quando, come nel caso di Anselmo medesimo, è chiamato ad un incarico al di fuori del monastero di professione, riserva sempre sentimenti filiali per la madre che lo ha generato, e affetto per i 'fratelli nati dallo stesso utero':

> Hoc itaque nullatenus caritati vestrae sit dubium quia sicut dilexi radicem, sic et ramos, quantumcunque multiplicentur, diligo, et omnes filios matris meae et primogenitos et post me genitos velut fratres uterinos in corde meo amplector et amo.[15]

3. *Ecclesia mater come sede episcopale*

La 'mater ecclesia' in altri contesti poi figura come sinonimo di chiesa cattedrale o sede episcopale. Intervenendo presso il vescovo Osberno di Exeter a favore dei monaci di Battle istallati nella chiesa di St Nicholas di quella città, ricorda che si può vietare loro di suonare le campane secondo le loro esigenze 'solo nel caso in cui quei monaci svolgano servizio nella chiesa madre della città'.[16] Qui l'espressione 'mater ecclesia civitatis' vale come cattedrale della città o 'maior ecclesia'.[17] Medesimo significato troviamo quando Anselmo fa richiesta a Pasquale II di istituire la nuova diocesi di Ely e chiede anche che i monaci dell'abbazia possano continuare a risiedere nella 'mater ecclesia', prendendovi il posto, come avveniva in quel tempo in altre cattedrali inglesi, di un capitolo canonicale:

13. *Ep.* 280: 195, 33-34.
14. *Ep.* 137: 282, 27: 'ego pater tuus et mater tua, ecclesia nostra, "facti sumus opprobrium vicinis nostris…"'
15. *Ep.* 205: 98, 12-15.
16. *Ep.* 172: 54, 19-20: 'nisi ubi monachi in matre ecclesia civitatis deserviunt'.
17. *Ep.* 172: 54, 20.

'monachis ibidem permanentibus, sicut sunt multi episcopatus, qui monachos in matre ecclesia habent, non canonicos'.[18]

4. *Ecclesia mater Cantuariensis*

Le circostanze in cui Anselmo si riferisce alla chiesa di Canterbury chiamandola 'mater' consentono di comprendere che, secondo il suo modo di vedere, l'espressione non ha semplicemente il significato comunemente giuridico di chiesa metropolitana, ossia di chiesa posta a capo di una provincia ecclesiastica.[19] Innanzitutto occorre notare che Anselmo rarissimamente si definisce nella sua funzione con l'aggettivo 'metropolitanus'. Troviamo un 'Cantuariensis ecclesiae metropolitanus antistes' in una lettera inviata ai vescovi di Irlanda;[20] in altre due lettere, una a Urbano II,[21] l'altra al cardinale legato Gualtiero,[22] troviamo un 'metropolitanus episcopus'. Egli preferisce altri appellativi nelle intestazioni delle lettere scritte da arcivescovo:[23] normalmente amava qualificarsi presso i suoi corrispondenti semplicemente come 'Anselmus archiepiscopus' o come 'Anselmus archiepiscopus Cantuariensis'. In poco meno di un quarto delle sue lettere[24] opta per la qualifica di 'servus ecclesiae Cantuariensis' (o 'Cantuariae').[25] L'uso dell'appellativo 'metropolitanus' nei rapporti coi vescovi irlandesi può spiegarsi come volontà di evidenziare—nella fase iniziale del suo pontificato—i rapporti tra la chiesa di Canterbury e le chiese irlandesi, le quali non avevano in Irlanda una loro riconosciuta metropoli[26] e anzi talora dipendevano

18. *Ep.* 441: 388, 15-17.
19. Etimologicamente il termine μητρό-πολις equivale a città-madre.
20. *Ep.* 198: 88, 1.
21. *Ep.* 193: 82, 3.
22. *Ep.* 194: 84, 2.
23. L'epistolario arcivescovile di Anselmo (ed. Schmitt) è costituito da 329 lettere, di cui 235 scritte da Anselmo.
24. Ovvero 57 su 235.
25. D'altronde possiamo notare che, sulla base di ciò che è rimasto del suo epistolario, anche il predecessore di Anselmo, Lanfranco da Pavia, non usa mai il titolo di 'metropolitanus', preferendo piuttosto quello di 'indignus antistes'. Cf. H. Clover e M. Gibson (eds.), *The Letters of Lanfranc Archbishop of Canterbury* (Oxford: Clarendon Press, 1979). Sull'epistolario di Lanfranco cf. anche C. Marabelli, 'Un profilo di Lanfranco dalle sue "Lettere"', in G. d'Onofrio (ed.), *Lanfranco di Pavia e l'Europa del secolo XI*, Atti del convegno—settembre 1989 (Roma: Herder, 1993), pp. 501-19.
26. Cf. *Ep.* 278: 192, 18-22, scritta da Anselmo al vescovo Samuele di Dublino,

da Canterbury per l'ordinazione dei loro vescovi.[27]

Nei rapporti con le altre chiese inglesi i termini di 'episcopus metropolitanus' erano solo parzialmente adatti per evidenziarne il primato, poiché in Inghilterra erano riconoscibili due metropoli: Canterbury e York. L'identificazione della Chiesa di Canterbury con la 'mater' è naturalmente impiegata nella interlocuzione coi vescovi suffraganei. Il vescovo suffraganeo di Londra è chiamato figlio ribelle alla Chiesa di Canterbury, sua madre, in quanto attenta al diritto e alla dignità del suo arcivescovo-primate,[28] l'altro suffraganeo di Worcester è invece il 'fedelis filius' a cui Anselmo chiede di prestare aiuto alla chiesa madre di Canterbury contro l'altro che la vuole diseredare.[29]

La 'mater ecclesia Christi' (ossia la Christ Church di Canterbury, che è madre) non ha solo per figli i vescovi suffraganei. In diverse circostanze, Anselmo ne ricorda la maternità anche a laici come Guglielmo Calvello[30] o l'influentissimo conte Roberto di Meulan.[31] È degno di nota, anche se in questo caso forse puramente casuale, il fatto che la maternità della chiesa di Canterbury non è mai richiamata nella corrispondenza coi reali inglesi. Anche l'arcivescovo di Canterbury, lo stesso Anselmo, riconosce la chiesa di Cristo a Canterbury come la propria madre.[32]

Ma c'è motivo di pensare che la metafora della 'ecclesia mater Cantuariensis' voglia assumere nel linguaggio di Anselmo, non mai casuale, una valenza che va oltre quella di 'ecclesia metropolitana' come estendendosi ad una maternità per così dire superiore, propria della 'ecclesia primas'.[33] D'altra parte era questo un sentire comune a

in cui fra le altre cose l'arcivescovo di Canterbury gli intima di non usare indebitamente le insegne arcivescovili, proprie dei metropoliti che abbiano ricevuto il pallio.

27. Cf. *Ep.* 201: 93, 19-20, scritta dal clero e dal popolo di Waterford perché Anselmo acconsenta e consacri vescovo per la loro città il monaco Malco.

28. *Ep.* 170: 52, 22-25: 'Hanc dignitatem et potestatem tam diu inconcussae ab ecclesia Cantuariensi possessam conatur hoc nostro tempore praedictus episcopus, suffraganeus scilicet archiepiscopo et primati suo, filius matri suae, auferre et annihilare.'

29. Cf. *Ep.* 170: 52, 26-28.

30. *Ep.* 358: 299, 6: 'et mihi et ecclesiae Christi, matri tuae'.

31. *Ep.* 467: 416, 5: 'verum amicum et filium matris ecclesiae Cantuariensis'.

32. *Ep.* 280: 195, 34: 'Non timeo exsilium, non paupertatem, non tormenta, non mortem, quia ad haec omnia deo confortante paratum est cor meum pro apostolicae sedis oboedientia et matris meae, ecclesiae Christi, libertate.'

33. 'Ecclesia primas' è espressione che si riscontra in Eadmero, *Historia*

Lanfranco, il quale nel corso della sua disputa con l'arcivescovo Tommaso I di York definisce Canterbury come la 'mater totius regni aecclesia'.[34]

È proprio nel contesto del contrasto insorto con l'arcivescovo eletto Tommaso II di York (1108–1109), cui appartiene anche la lettera citata sopra a Roberto conte di Meulan,[35] che Anselmo mostra inequivocabilmente di usare l'espressione 'mater ecclesia Cantuariensis' nel significato di un maternità connessa con la primazia. Il dissidio circa i diritti della chiesa 'primate' di Canterbury sulla chiesa 'metropolitana' di York non era una novità: già sotto Lanfranco si era accesa la disputa con l'arcivescovo Tommaso I, zio di Tommaso II. La partita, allora conclusasi solo con un certo vantaggio di Canterbury, si riaccese quando l'elezione di Anselmo pose termine alla lunga sede vacante seguita alla morte di Lanfranco (1089–1093). Eadmero riferisce che prima della ordinazione episcopale di Anselmo (4 dicembre 1093), durante la lettura dell'elezione scritta, l'arcivescovo Tommaso I,

dopo le prime parole, gravemente ferito, si lamentò della sua scorrettezza giuridica. Quando, infatti, udì leggere: 'Miei fratelli nell'episcopato, a voi tutti è noto da quanto tempo, per una serie di eventi, questa chiesa di Canterbury, metropolitana della Britannia, sia rimasta privata del suo pastore', interruppe dicendo: 'Metropolitana di tutta la Britannia? Se essa è metropolitana di tutta la Britannia, allora significa che la chiesa di York, che è risaputamente metropolitana, metropolitana non è. È certo che Canterbury sia la chiesa primate di tutta la Britannia, ma non metropolitana.' Si capì che quanto aveva sentenziato era stato detto con ragione e subito si corresse lo scritto: 'primate di tutta la Britannia' invece di 'metropolitana di tutta la Britannia'. La controversia si placò e lo ordinò primate di tutta la Britannia.[36]

novorum in Anglia (ed. M. Rule; London: HMSO, 1884), p. 42; cf. *infra*, nota 36.

34. Cf. *Memorandum on the Primacy of Canterbury*, in Clover e Gibson (eds.), *The Letters of Lanfranc Archbishop of Canterbury*, p. 40, l. 37: 'statutum est ad praesens debere Thomam ad matrem totius regni aecclesiam redire...'

35. Cf. *supra*, nota 31.

36. *Historia novorum in Anglia*, pp. 42-43: 'mox in rimo versu, Thomas Eboracensis, graviter offensus, eam non jure factam conquestus est. Nam cum diceretur, "Fratres et coepiscopi mei, vestrae fraternitati est cognitum quantum temporis est ex quo, accidentibus variis eventibus, haec Dorobernensis ecclesia, totius Britanniae metropolitana, suo sit viduata pastore," subintulit dicens, "Totius Britanniae metropolitana? Si totius Britanniae metropolitana, ecclesia Eboracensis, quae metropolitana esse scitur, metropolitana non est. Et quidem ecclesiam Cantuariensem primatem totius Britanniae esse scimus, non metropolitanam". Quod

Nel contesto dell'ordinazione episcopale dell'altro arcivescovo di
York, Tommaso II, Anselmo scrive all' 'electus' le lettere 443, 445, 455,
472 e al vescovo di Worcester la 464. La chiesa di Canterbury è la
'madre' da cui l'eletto arcivescovo di York deve ricevere l'ordinazione
episcopale: 'Mando itaque vobis, ut octavo Idus Septembris sitis apud
matrem vestram ecclesiam Cantuariensem, ad faciendum quod debetis,
et ad suscipiendam consecrationem vestram.'[37] Tommaso, in attesa della
sua ordinazione episcopale, si atteggiava, secondo le informazioni di
Anselmo, a metropolita[38] e già ne esibiva il titolo: 'Thomas, Eboracae
metropolis electus'.[39] Anselmo sembra insistere, nei suoi rapporti con
Tommaso, con quel concetto di maternità di Canterbury che vede anche
il metropolita di York come figlio, e quindi la chiesa di York come figlia.
Dopo ritardi, promesse di appuntamenti poi disattesi da parte di
Tommaso allo scopo di evitare che avvenisse la sottomissione di York a
Canterbury nella forma della sottomissione e promessa di obbedienza
dell'eletto arcivescovo di York ad Anselmo, nella breve lettera 455
Anselmo per due volte ritorna sul concetto di Canterbury 'mater':

> Mandavi vobis caritative plus quam semel, quatenus *ad matrem vestram,
> ecclesiam Cantuariensem*, veniretis... et non venistis. Quapropter eadem
> dilectione vobis adhuc mando, quatenus *apud ipsam matrem vestram*
> sexto Idus Novembris sitis, ut faciatis quod debetis et suscipiatis
> benedictionem vestram.[40]

La stessa cosa Anselmo esprime scrivendo a Sansone, vescovo di
Worcester e padre dell'arcivescovo eletto a York Tommaso: 'Ego tamen
ex abundantia caritatis invitavi eum bis...et tertio...ut veniret ad matrem
suam Cantuariensem ecclesiam et ad me, cui ministerium eius
commissum est.'[41]

Anselmo non riuscì a vedere la fine di questa controversia perché
morì il 21 aprile 1109. Si può dire che sia abbastanza documentato
il sentimento che egli aveva della maternità di Canterbury e il suo

---

auditum, ratione subnixum esse quod dicebat intellectum est. Tunc statim scriptura
ipsa mutata est, et pro "totius Britanniae metropolitana" "totius Britanniae primas"
scriptum est, et omnis controversia conquievit. Itaque sacravit illum ut Britanniae
totius primatem.'
37. *Ep.* 443: 390, 9.
38. Cf. *Ep.* 443: 390, 13-18.
39. *Ep.* 444: 391, 2.
40. *Ep.* 455: 404, 3-8.
41. *Ep.* 464: 413, 7-10.

desiderio che questo principio della maternità si radicasse e fosse tranquillamente accettato come un primato 'affettivo'. Rimane comunque l'ambiguità tra la metafora della madre e la figura giuridica della 'ecclesia metropolitana'. È forse significativo che lo stesso Tommaso 'Eboracensis ecclesiae consecrandus metropolitanus', all'atto della sua professione di obbedienza a Canterbury prima della sua ordinazione episcopale, dopo la morte di Anselmo, il 27 giugno 1109, sembri rigettare la metafora cara ad Anselmo per un linguaggio giuridico, che già era stato quello di Tommaso I, in cui nessuna concessione ad una qualche maternità è fatta al ruolo primaziale:

Io Tommaso, che devo essere consacrato (vescovo) metropolitano della chiesa di York, professo soggezione e obbedienza canonica [subjectionem et canonicam oboedientiam] alla santa chiesa di Canterbury e al primate della medesima chiesa canonicamente eletto e consacrato ['ejusdem ecclesiae primati canonice electo et consecrato'], e ai successori suoi canonicamente intronizzati, salva la fedeltà del mio signore Enrico re degli Angli, e salva l'obbedienza che da parte mia debbo tenere e che già il mio predecessore Tommaso da parte sua professò alla santa chiesa di Roma.[42]

42. Eadmero, *Historia novorum in Anglia*, p. 210: 'Ego Thomas, Eboracensis ecclesiae consecrandus metropolitanus, profiteor subjectionem et canonicam oboedientiam sanctae Dorobernensis ecclesiae et ejusdem ecclesiae primati canonice electo et consecrato, et successoribus suis canonice inthronizatis, salva fidelitate domini mei Henrici regis Anglorum, et salva oboedientia ex parte mea tenenda quam Thomas antecessor meus sanctae Romanae ecclesiae ex parte sua professus est.'

Part III
PHILOSOPHY AND THEOLOGY

AUTHORITY AND REASON IN SAINT ANSELM'S LIFE AND THOUGHT

Coloman Etienne Viola

Quam ampla est illa Veritas, in qua est omne quod verum est, et extra quam non nisi nihil et falsum est

Proslogion, ch. XIV

Veritatis ratio tam ampla tamque profunda est, ut a mortalibus nequeat exhauriri

Cur deus homo, Commendatio operis

... sacra scriptura omnis veritatis quam ratio colligit auctoritatem continet, cum illam aut aperte affirmat aut nullatenus negat.

De Concordia, q. III, VI

Anselm's thought is often presented as rationalistic thought and Anselm himself is considered by some historians or commentators as the 'champion' of early western rationalism.[1] This title is certainly flattering for some. The question for us is how to grasp in its vital context the place of

1. Of course, we should not forget Eriugena's rationalism. But we can presume without too much possibility of error that Anselm's thought and method was not influenced directly by Eriugena. Anselm's methodological development can be easily understood from the intellectual atmosphere which reigned in Europe in his time, especially the 'mode' of dialectic and dialectical explanations even of the sacred texts. On Eriugena's rationalism, see J. Dillon, 'The Roots of Reason in John Scottus Eriugena', *Philosophical Studies* (The National University of Ireland) 33 (1991–92), pp. 25-38. For a better understanding of Anselm's position in the twentieth-century context one can read for instance *Rationality Today* (ed. Th. F. Geraets; Ottawa: The University of Ottawa Press, 1979), especially the contribution of D. Dubarle, 'Raison et religion, raison et foi', pp. 280-306. Dubarle here considers reason in its 'état fort, pour autant donc que la raison se constitue, non seulement en faculté commune à l'humain, mais bel et bien en authentique puissance philosophique, déléguant au besoin à ce que nous appelons aujourd'hui même les sciences la force d'esprit de la rationalité. Car c'est ainsi que la raison de l'homme, non seulement vaut en et pour elle-même, mais encore se fait au sein de la communauté humaine celle qui induit et éduque une transformation de l'état d'esprit culturel, transformation qui, quoi que l'on en veuille dire, finit toujours par s'imposer à la considération sérieuse' (p. 281).

reason in Anselm's life and thought—how to render justice to him who for the first time in the history of western thinking proposed the method called 'sola ratione', in an essentially religious context comprising the whole of Christian doctrine except the dogma of incarnation. Is there any place left in Anselm's life and thought for 'auctoritas', conceived by many as the opposite or even the negation of reason?

In order to answer this question, I would like to show the place of authority in Anselm's life and thought,[2] analysing and examining this and also its historical background.[3] Then I would like to show the profound connection between 'auctoritas' and 'ratio' in order to arrive at the fundamental question: the foundation of reason in Anselm's thought, in other words the problem of 'ratio' as 'auctoritas'. In establishing the balance of these two ways of proceeding on the path of knowledge in Anselm's life, the testimonies of some of his biographers are indispensable in addition to Anselm's own writings. Indeed, the first portrait Eadmer gives of the new monk of Bec is that of one who relies firmly on the highest authority of holy scripture but who at the same time is trying to penetrate 'with the eye of reason' ('mentis ratione', with the rational faculty of the mind)[4] into the mysteries which faith proposes. Eadmer thus gives us a real 'résumé' of Anselm's life which holds firmly to authority but at the same time tries to make full use of reason to penetrate all that this authority proposes.

1. Preliminary Question: Terminology

Our meditation is based essentially on the analysis of two fundamental notions in Anselm's works: that of 'ratio'[5] and that of 'auctoritas'. But

2. The unity of Anselm's life and thought has been stressed recently by R.W. Southern, *Saint Anselm: A Portrait in a Landscape* (Cambridge, 1990), pp. 443-47.

3. For a general survey see E. Gilson, *Reason and Revelation in the Middle Ages* (New York, 1946). See also some recent studies concerning reason and authority in the eleventh century in *Lanfranco di Pavia e l'Europa del secolo XI nel IX centenario della morte (1089–1989). Atti del Convegno Internazionale di Studi (Pavia, Almo Collegio Borromeo, 21-24 settembre 1989)* (ed. G. d'Onofrio; Italia Sacra. Studi e documenti di storia ecclesiastica, 51; Roma, 1993).

4. 'mentis ratione' translated by Southern; see Eadmer, *The Life of St Anselm Archbishop of Canterbury* (ed. and trans. R.W. Southern; Oxford Medieval Texts; Oxford, 1972), I, p. 12. According to Anselm, 'ratio' is the highest faculty of 'mens'.

5. I must record here the important contribution of H. Kohlenberger, *Similitudo und Ratio. Überlegungen zur Methode bei Anselm von Canterbury* (Münchener philosophische Forschungen, Hrsg. von Max Müller, Band 4; Bonn, 1972). The

before proceeding further, I would like to give a short indication of the frequency and application of these two terms. We must notice that the word 'ratio' and its derivations such as 'rationalis', 'rationabiliter',[6] its synonymous uses or the 'rationes' themselves in their various concrete forms of argument and argumentation, can be found several times on almost every page of the *Corpus Anselmianum*. Rather than noting the frequency of their occurrence, it seems to me more important to notice that the 'rationes' in Anselm's works have very often an 'ontological' status, as Stephen Gersh has pointed out.[7] I would suggest that a great

author's main endeavour is the study of Anselm's method from the standpoint of the language, giving less importance to authority and faith which, however, condition even Anselmian linguistic procedure. Linguistic clarification, distinguishing between the ordinary way of speaking ('usus communis loquendi') and the proper sense ('sensus proprius'), is of course an important 'étape' of Anselm's method although it is not its last aim. What Anselm does is not merely *Sprachlogik* but a real metaphysical reflection.

6.   I note in passing that the term 'rationabiliter' refers not only to demonstrations and logical connections or reasons, but also to human behaviour and action as it is to be seen in Anselm's correspondence: 'Sciat pro certo vestra reverentia quia eundem animum quem habetis, ut corrigantur quae corrigenda sunt, habeo. Sed exspecto reditum domini mei regis et episcoporum et principum qui cum eo sunt, quatenus illi quae agenda sunt opportune et *rationabiliter* suggeramus, et sic deo adiuvante eius assensu et auxilio efficacius expleamus quod desideramus'. See Anselm, *Ep.* 191 (Schmitt, IV, p. 78:22-26). See also, *Ep.* 192 (Schmitt, IV, p. 79:21). Anselm suggests the same to Roscelin and also to the young Guibert of Nogent; he says also that creatures having a rational nature must always follow reason in their actions: 'Cum deus fecit Adam, fecit in eo naturam propagandi, quam subiecit eius potestati ut ea uteretur pro sua voluntate, quamdiu ipse vellet subditus esse Deo. Nam non illa uteretur bestiali et irrationabili voluptate, sed humana et rationabili voluntate. Sicut enim bestiarum est nihil velle cum ratione, *ita hominum esset nihil velle sine ratione*. Quod semper debent, quia potestatem hanc accepit Adam, et eam semper servare potuit. Dedit etiam illi Deus hanc gratiam, ut sicut quando illum condidit nulla propagandi operante natura aut voluntate creaturae *simul fecit eum et rationalem et iustum*, ita simul cum rationalem haberent animam iusti essent, quos generaret operante natura et voluntate, si non peccaret.' See Anselm, *De conceptu virginali et originali peccato*, ch. X (Schmitt, II, p. 152:1-11). Anselm shows here that Adam had been created having a perfect rational nature in which justice precisely consists. So even in the act of propagation Adam was supposed to follow the rational will ('rationabilis voluntas') and not the irrational 'voluptas'. We see from this text that for Anselm *the ideal man is the rational man*, according to his status before the fall.

7.   Gersh enumerates the different senses of 'ratio' in St Anselm's works: ontological senses (the structure of reality, 'ontological' necessity); the theological 'ratio'

number of his 'rationes' are metaphysical ones and in that sense, Anselm surpasses his contemporaries whose 'rationes' did not move outside the domain of grammar or of dialectic.[8] We must also notice that in Anselm's works, 'rationes' may be even scriptural texts or revealed truths used as arguments in a rational way ('rationabiliter') and forming part of a logical procedure.[9]

The opposite term to 'ratio' is of course 'auctoritas'. In Anselm's works—except his letters which do not constitute the matter of my considerations[10]—I found the word 'auctoritas' 36 times in various contexts

(an aspect of divine nature); epistemological senses (state of mind contrasted with faith or without reference to faith); the psychological 'ratio' (a faculty of the human soul); logical senses (as a specific argument or as an activity of debating philosophical questions in general and especially as 'logical' necessity). In conclusion he points out that 'the simple equation with the content of Aristotelian-Boethian dialectic is totally unsatisfactory as a basis of interpretation' of Anselm's writings. See S. Gersh, 'Anselm of Canterbury', in P. Dronke (ed.), *A History of Twelfth-Century Western Philosophy* (Cambridge, 1988), pp. 260ff.

8.   See Viola, 'Lanfranc de Pavie et Anselme d'Aoste', in *Lanfranco di Pavia*, pp. 558-65.

9.   Eadmer was impressed by the 'rationality' of Anselm's reply to King Rufus during the Rockingham Assembly: this rationality was nothing but a 'rational way' of using scriptural arguments, therefore 'authority': 'Requisitus [a rege] Willelmus Dunelmensis quid ipse ex condicto noctu egerit apud se, respondit nil rationis posse afferri ad enervationem rationis Anselmi; "praesertim cum omnis", inquit, "ratio eius innitatur verbis Dei et *auctoritate* Beati Petri."' See Eadmer, *Historia novorum in Anglia* (ed. M. Rule; London, 1884), I, p. 62; see also C. Viola, 'Histoire, historiographie et théologie. Saint Anselme devant l'assemblée de Rockingham (25-28 février 1095). La relativisation du pouvoir temporel', in *Mediaevalia Christiana. XIᵉ-XIIIᵉ siècles. Hommage à Raymonde Foreville* (ed. C.E. Viola; Paris, 1989), pp. 210-11; *idem*, 'Histoire, historiographie et théologie. Une approche pour comprendre le Moyen Age. Saint Anselme et l'assemblée de Rockingham (25-27 février 1095)', in *'Histoire et littérature au Moyen Age'*, Actes du Colloque du Centre d'Études Médiévales de l'Université de Picardie, Amiens, 20-24 mars 1985 (ed. D. Buschinger; Göppinger Arbeiten zur Germanistik, 546; Göppingen, 1991), pp. 457-59.

10.   I should, however, mention the important letter of Anselm (77) in which he apologizes to Lanfranc about his intention in writing the *Monologion*. Anselm explains clearly his intention: he did not want to say anything which according to him could not be defended immediately by either the canonical texts ('canonicis... dictis': the canonical texts of holy scripture) or by Augustine's texts ('dictis'). And doing this, finally he expresses his confidence in Augustine's 'authority': 'Nam haec mea fuit intentio per totam illam qualemcumque disputationem, ut omnino nihil ibi

and with different meanings. Sometimes the word 'auctoritas' appears alone without any restriction or qualification (9×);[11] in other circumstances

assererem, nisi quod aut canonicis aut beati Augustini dictis incunctanter posse defendi viderem; et nunc quotienscumque ea quae dixi retracto, nihil aliud me asservisse percipere possum. Etenim ea quae ex eodem opusculo vestris litteris inservistis et quaedam alia quae non inservistis, nulla mihi ratiocinatio mea, quantumlibet videretur necessaria, persuasisset, *ut primus dicere praesumerem.* Ea enim ipsa sic beatus Augustinus in libro *De trinitate* suis magnis disputationibus probat, ut eadem quasi mea breviori ratiocinatione inveniens eius [i.e. beati Augustini] confisus auctoritate dicerem.' See *Ep.* 77 (Schmitt, III, p. 199: 17-26). See also Viola, 'Lanfranc de Pavie et Anselme d'Aoste', pp. 550ff. In this letter, 'auctoritas' refers to the canonical texts of scripture as well as to Augustine's writings.

11. 'Quamvis enim *tanta auctoritate* asseratur et tanta teneatur utilitate, ut nullatenus propter ullam humanam rationem dubitandum sit divinam praescientiam et liberum arbitrium invicem sibi consentire: tamen quantum ad rationis considerationem quae videtur spectat, insociabiliter videntur dissentire.' *De casu diaboli*, ch. 21 (Schmitt, I, p. 266:26-30). 'Sed quoniam libero arbitrio praescientia et praedestinatio et gratia dei videntur repugnare, gratissimum mihi erit, si eas illi non tam auctoritate sacra, quod a multis satis factum est, quam ratione, quod sufficienter factum nondum me memini legisse, concordare facias. *Auctoritate* vero ad hoc non indigeo, quia illam quantum ad hoc quod quaero pertinet, sufficienter novi et suscipio. M. De praescientia et praedestinatione similis et pariter difficilior quam de gratia quaestio est.' *De libertate arbitrii,* add. T (Schmitt, I, p. 226). '. . . et sapientia est exquisitum et *auctoritate* roboratum et dilectione conditum: cum aliquid inde haurio, id me sua et dulcedine delectat et securitate satiat. Sed quoniam haec ipsa scienti loquor, his omissis, cur eorum meminerim, expediam.' *Monologion* (Schmitt, I, p. 6:1-4). 'Quod cur faciant nullam video *auctoritatem* aut rationem.' *Epistola de sacrificio azimi et fermentati*, ch. 7 (Schmitt, II, p. 231:10-11). '. . . quod nulla prohibet *auctoritas* vel ratio; aut impossibile est—ut dixi—servare quod praecipiunt, ut scilicet tot cognationes exquirantur ad unius cognationis conubia, quot sunt in illa viri et mulieres petentes coniugia. Quod autem sine omni *auctoritate* et ratione fit contra rationem, absque dubio *rationabiliter* repudiandum iudicatur.' *Epistola de sacrificio azimi et fermentati*, ch. 7 (Schmitt, II, p. 232:1-5). 'Sed si hoc praecipit propheta— ut secundum eos loquar—, illos "occidit littera", qui litteram servando de fermentato sacrificant. At si hoc exprobrando dictum est: qua fronte sacrificant quod propheta in sacrificium execratur, aut qua ratione hoc *in auctoritatem* sibi assumunt ? Quod autem hoc propheta non iubendo sed reprehendendo dixerit dubium non est, cum hoc impiae actioni associaverit. *Epistola de sacrificio azimi et fermentati*, ch. 6 (Schmitt, II, pp. 230:24-231:2). '. . . multo magis debemus huius unitatis servare consequentiam, de qua supra locutus sum, cum eam nulla aut scripto aut sensu negat *auctoritas*, nec profert aliquid quod contrarium sit aut aliquo modo repugnet. Eligant itaque Graeci unum de duobus, si aperte veritati nolunt resistere.' *De processione Spiritus Sancti*, ch. 7 (Schmitt, II, p. 199:3-6). 'Iudicent ergo ipsi quid potius suscipiendum

we have 'auctoritas' referring to the Pope's 'magisterium' in doctrinal matters (2×),[12] the apostolic authority of the papal legate[13] the
authority of Lanfranc,[14] 'divina auctoritas' (5×),[15] 'auctoritas sacra'

sit, quamvis utrumque in sacra pagina taceatur: an hoc quod nos dicimus spiritum
sanctum procedere de filio, quod ostendimus ex iis consequi quae veraciter credimus;
an quod ipsi dicunt spiritum sanctum aliter esse spiritum patris, aliter filii, quod *nec
auctoritate* nec ratione nec ex iis quae certa sunt possunt ostendere. Utique aut debent
cessare ab hac sua sententia—si tamen hoc dicunt, ut audio, quia spiritus sanctus
aliter est spiritus filii quam spiritus patris—, cum hoc nusquam legant, vel unde hoc
probent; aut saltem nos non reprehendere debent, qui dicimus spiritum sanctum procedere de filio...' *De processione Spiritus Sancti*, ch. 12 (Schmitt, II, p. 210:25-33).

   12. '...amande et cum amore reverende papa Urbane, quem dei providentia in
sua ecclesia summum constituit pontificem: quoniam nulli rectius possum, vestrae
sanctitatis praesento conspectui subditum opusculum, ut eius *auctoritate* quae ibi
suscipienda sunt approbentur, et quae corrigenda sunt emendentur.' *Cur deus homo,
Commendatio operis* (Schmitt, II, p. 41:2-5). 'Quoniam divina providentia vestram
elegit sanctitatem, cui fidem et vitam Christianam custodiendam et ecclesiam suam
regendam committeret, ad nullum alium rectius refertur, si quid contra catholicam
fidem oritur in ecclesia, ut *eius auctoritate* corrigatur; nec ulli alii tutius si quid contra
errorem respondetur ostenditur, ut eius prudentia examinetur. Quapropter sicut nulli
dignius possum, ita nulli libentius praesentem epistolam quam vestrae destino sapientiae, quatenus si quid in ea corrigendum est, vestra censura castigetur, et quod
regulam veritatis tenet, *vestra auctoritate roboretur.*' *Epistola de incarnatione verbi*,
ch. 1 (Schmitt, II, pp. 3:7-4:4). Eadmer shows clearly Anselm's obedience towards
the Pope: '...venerabilis sanctae Romanae ecclesiae summi pontificis oboedientiam
abnegare nolo...' See Eadmer, *Historia novorum*, I, pp. 61ff.

   13. 'Sed cum iam a pluribus cum his titulis utrumque transcriptum esset, coegerunt
me plures et maxime reverendus archiepiscopus Lugdunensis, Hugo nomine, fungens
in Gallia legatione Apostolica, qui mihi hoc ex *Apostolica* praecepit *auctoritate*, ut
nomen meum illis praescriberem.' *Proslogion, Prooemium* (Schmitt, I, p. 94:8-11).

   14. '...vestro mitto iudicio, ut *eius* (i.e. Lanfranci) *auctoritate* aut inepta a con-
spectu prohibeatur, aut correcta volentibus praebeatur.' *Monologion* (Schmitt, I,
p. 6:13-14).

   15. 'Fateor enim nondum alicubi excepta *divina auctoritate cui indubitanter credo,*
me legisse rationem quae mihi sufficeret ad eiusdem solutionis intellectum.' *De casu
diaboli*, ch. 21 (Schmitt, I, p. 267:17-19). 'Unde *ADAM* et *EVA* ad illam pertinuisse
redemptionem dubitandum non est, quamvis hoc *auctoritas divina* aperte non
pronuntiet. A. Incredibile quoque videtur, quando deus illos fecit et proposuit immu-
tabiliter facere de illis omnes homines, quos ad caelestem civitatem assumpturus erat,
quod illos duos ab hoc excluserit proposito. B. Immo illos maxime ad hoc fecisse
credi debet, ut essent de illis propter quos facti sunt.' *Cur deus homo* II, ch. 16
(Schmitt, II, p. 119:18-24). 'Quod *auctoritas divina* nequaquam faceret, si voluntatis
libertatem nullam in homine cognosceret. Sed nec ullo modo esset cur deus bonis vel

(5×),[16] 'auctoritas (sacrae) scripturae' (5×),[17] 'auctoritas Christiana',[18]

malis pro meritis singulorum iuste retribueret, si per liberum arbitrium nullus bonum vel malum faceret.' *De concordia*, III, ch. 2 (Schmitt, II, p. 264:2-5). 'Sed ne quis existimet *auctoritate divina* dici iustum illum vel rectum, qui non nisi propter aliud tenet rectitudinem voluntatis: dicimus iustitiam esse rectitudinem voluntatis propter se servatam.' *De concordia*, III, ch. 2 (Schmitt, II, p. 265:13-15). 'Utique si verum est spiritum sanctum procedere a filio sicut a patre, sequitur quia filii spiritus est sicut patris, et mittitur et datur a filio sicut a patre, quae *divina* docet *auctoritas* et nulla penitus sequitur falsitas. Cum autem processio spiritus sancti de filio negata tantam inducat falsitatem, ut illa ex quibus eam consequi monstravimus destruat contra fidem Christianam nec ullam generet veritatem, et asserta tantam probet veritatem, sicut ostendimus, nec aliquam ullatenus secum trahat falsitatem: cogitet cor rationale qua ratione illam excludat a fide Christiana. Denique si error est hanc credere de filio spiritus sancti processionem, ipsa divina auctoritas nos in errorem inducit, cum et illa ex quibus haec sequitur processio et quae illam sequuntur nos docet, nec alicubi aut illam negat aut quod illi repugnet aliquo modo pronuntiat. Si ergo opponitur quia nusquam eam *divina profert auctoritas*, ideo non esse dicendam: dicatur similiter, quia nusquam illam negat nec aliquid dicit quod repugnet, non esse negandam. Dicimus etiam quia satis illam affirmat, cum illa asserit unde probatur, et nullo modo aliquid significat unde negetur.' *De processione Spiritus Sancti*, ch. 14 (Schmitt, II, p. 215:11-26).

16.´ 'Sed quoniam libero arbitrio praescientia et praedestinatio et gratia dei videntur repugnare, gratissimum mihi erit, si eas illi *non tam auctoritate sacra, quod a multis satis factum est, quam ratione*, quod sufficienter factum nondum me memini legisse, concordare facias.' *De libertate arbitrii*, add. T (Schmitt, I, p. 226). 'Est igitur unde possit conici "quo maius cogitari nequeat". Sic itaque facile refelli potest insipiens *qui sacram auctoritatem non recipit*, si negat, "quo maius cogitari non valet" ex aliis rebus conici posse.' *Responsio*, ch. 8 (Schmitt, I, p. 137:27-30). 'Et si quid responderis cui *auctoritas obsistere sacra videatur*, liceat illam mihi obtendere, quatenus quomodo non obsistat aperias.' *Cur deus homo*, I, ch. 3 (Schmitt, II, p. 50:20-22). 'Quod autem iustitia sit rectitudo voluntatis, *sacra saepe monstrat auctoritas*. Qua de re sufficit unum exemplum proponere. Cum enim dixisset DAVID: "non relinquet dominus plebem suam, et haereditatem suam non derelinquet, quoadusque iustitia convertatur in iudicium": ut doceret nos quid esset iustitia, interrogando ait: "Et qui iuxta illam?" Ad quod ipse sibi respondens "omnes" inquit "qui *recto sunt corde*", hoc est qui recta sunt voluntate.' *De concordia*, III, ch. 2 (Schmitt, II, pp. 264:28-265:5). 'Siquidem ipsos motus sive appetitus, quibus propter peccatum ADAE sicut bruta animalia subiacemus, quos apostolus vocat "carnem" et "concupiscentiam", quam invitum se tolerare manifestat cum dicit: "quod odi, illud facio", id est nolens concupisco: satis ostendit *sacra auctoritas* imputari ad peccatum. Quippe cum de solo motu irae sine opere vel voce dicit dominus: "qui irascitur fratri suo, reus erit iudicio": aperte monstrat esse culpam non levem, quam tam gravis, scilicet mortis, sequitur damnatio.' *De concordia*, III, ch. 7 (Schmitt, II, p. 274:3-9).

17. '... hanc mihi formam praestituerunt: quatenus *auctoritate scripturae* penitus

'omnis veritatis auctoritas',[19] 'non parva auctoritas',[20] 'symbolum tanta

nihil in ea persuaderetur, sed quidquid per singulas investigationes finis assereret, id ita esse plano stilo et vulgaribus argumentis simplicique disputatione et rationis necessitas breviter cogeret et veritatis claritas patenter ostenderet.' *Monologion,* (Schmitt, I, p. 6:7-11). 'Si enim aperta ratione colligitur, et illa ex nulla parte contradicit—quoniam ipsa sicut nulli adversatur veritati, ita nulli favet falsitati—: hoc ipso quia non negat quod ratione dicitur, eius [i.e. sacrae scripturae] *auctoritate* suscipitur. At si ipsa nostro sensui indubitanter repugnat: quamvis nobis ratio nostra videatur inexpugnabilis, nulla tamen veritate fulciri credenda est. Sic itaque *sacra scriptura omnis veritatis quam ratio colligit auctoritatem continet, cum illam aut aperte affirmat aut nullatenus negat.*' *De concordia,* III, ch. 6 (Schmitt, II, p. 272:1-7). St Augustine expresses a similar view: '*Si enim ratio contra divinarum Scripturarum auctoritatem redditur,* quamlibet acuta sit, fallit veri similitudine; nam vera esse non potest.' See Augustine, *Ep.* CXLIII, n. 7 (*PL* 33, 588). 'Huic homini *non est respondendum auctoritate sacrae scripturae,* quia aut ei non credit aut eam perverso sensu interpretatur. Quid enim apertius dicit scriptura sacra, quam quia deus unus et solus est? Ratione igitur qua se defendere nititur, eius error demonstrandus est.' *Epistola de incarnatione verbi,* II, ch. 2 (Schmitt, II, p. 11:5-8). 'Sed et si quis legere dignabitur duo parva mea opuscula, *Monologion* scilicet et *Proslogion,* quae ad hoc maxime facta sunt, ut quod fide tenemus de divina natura et eius personis praeter incarnationem, necessariis rationibus *sine scripturae auctoritate* probari possit; si inquam aliquis ea legere voluerit, puto quia et ibi de hoc inveniet quod nec improbare poterit nec contemnere volet.' *Epistola de incarnatione verbi,* II, ch. 6 (Schmitt, II, p. 20:16-21).

18. 'At si negat tria posse dici de uno et unum de tribus, ut tria non dicantur de invicem, sicut in his tribus personis et uno deo facimus, quoniam hoc in aliis rebus non videt, nec in deo intelligere valet: sufferat aliquid quod intellectus eius penetrare non possit esse in deo, nec comparet naturam quae super omnia est, liberam ab omni lege loci et temporis et compositionis partium, rebus quae loco aut tempore clauduntur aut partibus componuntur; sed credat aliquid in illa esse quod in istis esse nequit, et acquiescat *auctoritati Christianae* nec disputet contra illam.' *Epistola de incarnatione verbi,* II, ch. 13 (Schmitt, II, p. 31:2-9).

19. 'Si enim *aperta ratione* colligitur, et illa ex nulla parte contradicit—quoniam ipsa sicut nulli adversatur veritati, ita nulli favet falsitati—: hoc ipso quia non negat quod ratione dicitur, eius *auctoritate* suscipitur. At si ipsa nostro sensui indubitanter repugnat: quamvis nobis ratio nostra videatur inexpugnabilis, nulla tamen veritate fulciri credenda est. Sic itaque *sacra scriptura omnis veritatis quam ratio colligit auctoritatem continet, cum illam aut aperte affirmat aut nullatenus negat.*' *De concordia,* III, ch. 6 (Schmitt, II, p. 272:3-6).

20. 'Nec miretur aliquis me tantum in hoc immorari, quoniam *non parvae auctoritatis erat ille inter suos,* quem sensi non sentire spiritum sanctum hoc quod est habere ex patre, nec tunc habui opportunitatem respondendi.' *De processione Spiritus Sancti,* ch. 13 (Schmitt, II, p. 188:11-13).

auctoritate (1×) taxatum',[21] 'maior auctoritas' (3×),[22] 'philosophorum
auctoritas'.[23]

Among these passages, the most important is that of *De concordia*:
'...sacra scriptura omnis veritatis quam ratio colligit auctoritatem continet, cum illam aut aperte affirmat aut nullatenus negat'.[24] Here Anselm
expresses his view about the relation between scripture as 'auctoritas',
'ratio', and truth. Anselm is firmly stating that holy scripture contains
the authority of all truth which reason is able to grasp. Here, authority

21. 'Si autem dicunt nullo modo debuisse corrumpi symbolum *tanta auctoritate*
taxatum, nos non iudicamus esse corruptionem, ubi nihil addimus quod iis quae
ibi dicta sunt adversetur.' *De processione Spiritus Sancti*, ch. 13 (Schmitt, II,
p. 211:22-24).

22. Anselm uses the expression 'maior auctoritas' in *Monologion* and he repeats
it twice more in *Cur deus homo*. It is important to observe that in his mind the rational necessity does not mean an absolute necessity ('omnino necessarium') or an
absolute 'authority' (of reason). The authority of reason is always subordinated to a
'higher authority' ('maior auctoritas'). In other words, Anselm's gnoseological procedure is a hierarchical one and his rational method is only a (lower) part of the hierarchy of knowledge. 'In quo tamen, si quid dixero quod *maior non monstret
auctoritas*: sic volo accipi ut, quamvis ex rationibus quae mihi videbuntur, quasi necessarium concludatur, non ob hoc tamen omnino necessarium, sed tantum sic interim
videri posse dicatur.' *Monologion*, ch. 1 (Schmitt, I, p.14:1-4). 'Videlicet ut, si quid
dixero quod *maior* non confirmet *auctoritas*—quamvis illud ratione probare videar—,
non alia certitudine accipiatur, nisi quia interim ita mihi videtur, *donec deus mihi
melius aliquo modo revelet*. Quod si aliquatenus quaestioni tuae satis facere potero,
certum esse debebit quia et sapientior me plenius hoc facere poterit. Immo sciendum
est, quidquid inde homo dicere possit, altiores tantae rei adhuc latere rationes.' *Cur
deus homo*, I, ch. 2 (Schmitt, II, p. 50:7-13). 'Sed memento quo pacto incepi
respondere quaestioni tuae: videlicet ut si quid dixero quod *maior non confirmet
auctoritas*—quamvis illud ratione probare videar—, non alia certitudine accipiatur,
nisi quia interim ita mihi videtur, *donec deus mihi melius aliquo modo revelet*. Certus
enim sum, si quid dico quod sacrae scripturae absque dubio contradicat, quia falsum
est; nec illud tenere volo si cognovero. Sed si in illis rebus de quibus diversa sentiri
possunt sine periculo, sicuti est istud unde nunc agimus—si enim nescimus utrum
plures homines eligendi sint quam sint angeli perditi an non, et alterum horum magis
aestimamus quam alterum, nullum puto esse animae periculum—; si, inquam, in
huiusmodi rebus sic exponimus divina dicta, ut diversis sententiis favere videantur,
nec alicubi invenitur ubi quid indubitanter tenendum sit determinent, non arbitror
reprehendi debere.' *Cur deus homo*, I, ch. 18 (Schmitt, II, p. 82:5-16).

23. 'Quod vero grammaticus sit qualitas, aperte fatentur *philosophi* qui de hac re
tractaverunt. Quorum [= *philosophorum]* auctoritatem de his rebus est impudentia
improbare.' *De grammatico*, ch. 1 (Schmitt, I, p.146:1-3).

24. *De concordia*, III, ch. 6 (Schmitt, II, p. 272:6-7).

and truth are in a close relation, and scripture is presented as the source of all truth. We must still add that in most cases, the word 'auctoritas' refers to the authority of scripture: the expressions 'divina auctoritas', and 'auctoritas sacra' can be regarded as synonymous with 'auctoritas sacrae scripturae'. Although the word 'auctoritas' appears infrequently in comparison to 'ratio' and its derivatives, nevertheless the notion of authority constitutes one of the key points of Anselm's thought and life.[25]

2. *The Primacy of Authority over Reason*

In about 1125, therefore not too long after Anselm's death, one of the historians of the pontiffs in England evokes the importance of Anselm's literary work, saying that it was based on rational method and was a real liberation for his contemporaries. William of Malmesbury writes indeed that while others were trying to extort their credulity with authority, Anselm himself tries to corroborate their faith with reason, proving with invincible arguments that all we believe is indeed so and that it cannot be otherwise. So according to this historian, Anselm accomplished a real task of liberation, the liberation of the minds of his contemporaries who were suffering under the domination of 'auctoritas'.

> Credulitatem enim nostram quam *illi* auctoritate extorquere volunt, ille ratione roborat quod credimus ita esse nec aliter esse posse invincibilibus approbans argumentis.[26]

---

25. Besides the texts given above on authority in the Middle Ages, see also J. de Ghellinck, 'Patristique et argument de tradition au bas moyen âge', in *Aus der Geisteswelt des Mittelalters* (Beiträge zur Geschichte der Philosophie und Theologie des Mittelalters, Supplementband 3.1; Münster, 1935), pp. 403-26; M.-D. Chenu, *Introduction à l'étude de Saint Thomas d'Aquin* (Paris, 1954), pp. 106-31, who gives a general survey of the sense and use of authority mainly in the thirteenth century and particularly in St Thomas's works. As may be seen from the brief analysis of Anselm's works, the problem of authority for Anselm was not confined to that of legatine authority. See Southern, *Saint Anselm: A Portrait*, p. 335. For the historical background, see A. Cantin, 'Ratio et auctoritas de Pierre Damien à Anselme', *Revue des études augustiniennes* 18.1-2 (1972), pp. 152-79.

26. See Willelmi Malmesberiensis Monachi, *De gestis Pontificum Angliae*, I (*PL* 179, 1481). See C. Viola, 'L'Influence de la méthode anselmienne. La méthode de saint Anselme jugée par les historiens de son temps', in *Wirkungsgeschichte Anselms von Canterbury* (Analecta Anselmiana 4; 1975) II, table, p. 28 note 75.

William of Malmesbury does not treat Anselm's contemporaries or predecessors very tactfully. He delivers a severe judgment using the verb 'extorquere'—extort—while drawing a very great contrast between the authoritarianism of these masters (*illi*) and the rational method of Anselm which—according to his testimony—was felt by his generation to be a real liberation of minds. Still, when reading the judgment of William of Malmesbury one cannot avoid asking whether he was conscious of the complexity which arises from the problem of the relation between authority and reason. For the time being, let us put aside this rather intricate question, the solution of which will require some philosophical reflection and, with regard to the clarification of its 'historical background', also the examination of the Augustinian doctrine of reason and authority.

Before giving a survey of these problems, let us try to see who are these 'illi'? Who are these people or masters who tried to extort the credulity of their pupils? Is it possible to identify them? But before identifying them, let me make a statement which is important in our context. When William of Malmesbury makes his rather disagreeable judgment, there is no question of him throwing away faith, there is no question of him denying or disputing the supreme authority of scripture—on the contrary, he rejoices in the fact that Anselm was reinforcing his contemporaries' faith by finding invincible arguments; he is only pointing out those who try to impose this authority without any reference to reason.

In order to understand William of Malmesbury's allusion, we must remember some important events of the period when Anselm was working. Anselm's master, Lanfranc, relates in his polemical work against Berengar of Tours his interview with Pope Leo IX (1049–1054) at Rome when he had to justify publicly his orthodoxy against Berengar's accusations. The Pope ordered him to reveal his faith, proving it rather by authority than with rational arguments.[27] The option imposed by the Pope in this controversial context was clear: the expressed will of the Pope was that in matters of faith one should rely upon the authority of holy scripture and not on reason. The word

---

27. 'Post haec praecepit Papa, ut ego surgerem, pravi rumoris a me maculam abstergerem, fidem meam exponerem, expositam *plus* sacris auctoritatibus, *quam* argumentis probarem.' See Lanfranc, *Liber de corpore et sanguine domini nostri adversus Berengarium*, ch. 6, in *Beati Lanfranci Opera quae supersunt omnia.* II. *Commentaria etc* (ed. J.A. Giles; Oxford, 1844), p. 154.

'auctoritas' is used by Lanfranc in his polemical work several times. For instance facing Berengar, he appeals to the 'authority of the entire holy church' ('auctoritas totius sanctae Ecclesiae') and of the correct explanations of the holy scriptures. We must notice that the word 'auctoritas' in Lanfranc's mind embraces not only scripture and its correct interpretation, but also the writings of the Fathers, such as Augustine, Gregory and Jerome.[28]

Of course, Lanfranc also used dialectic, dialectical reasoning and syllogisms to explain Saint Paul's epistles, in order to argue on the same level as his adversary.[29] Nevertheless, in one passage of the *Liber de corpore*, Lanfranc says that the 'righteous who lives by faith' (Rom. 1.17; cf. Hab. 2.4) does not have to search for arguments or conceive reasons in order to understand the mystery of the Eucharist:

> Quonam modo panis efficiatur caro, vinumque convertatur in sanguinem, utriusque essentialiter mutata natura: justus—qui ex fide vivit—, scrutari argumentis, et concipere ratione non quaerit.[30]

However we must also notice that the literature of the glosses (*glossae* on the 'sacra pagina') shows its misuses: very often the masters of the 'sacra pagina' did nothing else than repeat from generation to generation the same glosses, that is to say the same texts taken out of their context, which were supposed to clarify obscure and difficult passages of the Bible. This state of things continued even after Anselm's time. For these masters, of course, the reading and interpretation of scripture had to be confined to a very rudimentary explanation based only on the authorities. In this context, we can also easily understand the critical

28. '... Augustinus, Gregorius, Hieronymus, vel quilibet eorum, quos in *arce auctoritatis* positos Ecclesia Christi insigniter veneratur.' See Lanfranc, *Liber de corpore*, ch. 1, p. 148.

29. See Southern, *Saint Anselm: A Portrait*, pp. 40-43. See also G. d'Onofrio, 'Lanfranco teologo e la storia della filosofia', in *Lanfranco di Pavia*, pp. 189-228. Lanfranc—following Augustine—acknowledged the utility of dialectic even in explaining scripture: '... Quamuis beatus Augustinus, in quibusdam suis scriptis et maxime in libro *De doctrina christiana,* hanc disciplinam [i.e. dialecticam] amplissime laudet, et ad omnia quae in sacris litteris vestigantur plurimum valere confirmet.' See Lanfranc, *Liber de corpore*, ch. 7, p. 159. This is an allusion to Augustine: 'Sed disputationis disciplina ad omnia genera quaestionum quae in litteris sanctis sunt penetranda et dissoluenda plurimum valet...' See Augustine, *De doctrina christiana*, II, ch. 30 (*PL* 34, 58).

30. See Lanfranc, *Liber de corpore*, ch. 17, p. 175.

remarks of the great English theologian Robert of Melun who—after pursuing his career as a professor first in Melun and then in Paris in the *Schola artium* founded by Abaelard and where he was admired by his pupil John of Salisbury—returned to his native land to become bishop of Hereford.[31] Some years after Anselm's death Robert presents in the Preface of his *Sententiae*[32] a long meditation on the right method of reading the 'sacra pagina', with his views about exegetical problems, the literary forms of scripture and its interpretation (*sensus litteralis*, etc.), the place of rhetoric in theology and finally the problem of the 'auctoritates'. He severely criticizes those who almost put more importance on the *glossae* than on scripture itself, forgetting that the *glossae* themselves receive their authority from scripture which is the fundamental authority in theology. But at the same time, he shows that the supreme authority belongs directly to holy scripture and not to the texts one proposes for its clarification. Therefore the *glossae*—these patristic texts—have no authority in themselves but only in relation to scripture which must be considered as the supreme norm of truth.

3. Anselm's Search for Reasons

Now what was Anselm's attitude in this historical context where the primacy of authority seemed to be imposed by the Pope himself in matters of faith? In his *Vita Anselmi*, Eadmer gives us in five main texts a portrait of Anselm as a thinker. All these texts are well known to scholars of Anselm's life and thought but it is necessary to recall them if we want to have a complete view of Anselm's attitude towards the problem of authority and reason. The first portrait Eadmer gives us of Anselm after he joined the community of Bec is that of a thinker already 'wrestling with Biblical texts', as Sir Richard Southern says.

31. R.M. Martin, *Oeuvres de Robert de Melun*. I. *Quaestiones de divina pagina* (Louvain, 1932), Introduction, pp. vi-xii.

32. 'Ordinis namque doctrinalis magna confusio est et discipline intolerabilis perturbatio, secundarium principali adequare, nedum anteponere. Quod ab his fieri qua ratione negabitur qui textu et serie legendorum librorum postpositis, totam lectionis operam in studio glosularum expendunt? Neque enim huius rei hanc causam pretendere possunt, quod textus sine glosulis intelligi non valeat, aut quod glosarum cognitionem textus intelligentia necessario sequatur, quoniam utrumque sine altero tam doceri quam addisci potest.' Robert de Melun, *Sententiae, Praefatio*, in Martin, *Oeuvres de Robert de Melun*. III. *Sententiae* (Louvain, 1947), I, p. 9.

Having thus obtained a larger liberty for the service of God, he began to devote his whole self and his whole time to serving God, and he put the world and all its affairs entirely behind him. And so it came about that, being continually given up to God and to spiritual exercises, he attained such a height of divine speculation, that he was able by God's help to see into and unravel many most obscure and previously insoluble questions about the divinity of God and about our faith, and to prove by plain arguments *that what he said was firm and catholic truth.*

For *he had so much faith in the Holy Scriptures, that he firmly and inviolably believed that there was nothing in them which deviated in any way from the path of solid truth.* Hence he applied his whole mind to this end, that according to his faith he might be found worthy to see *with the eye of reason* ('mentis ratione' = with the rational faculty of the mind)[33] those things in the Holy Scriptures which, as he felt, lay hidden in a deep obscurity. Thus one night it happened that he was lying awake on his bed before matins exercised in mind about these matters; and as he meditated he tried to puzzle out how the prophets of old could see both past and future as if they were present and set them forth beyond doubt in speech or writing. And, behold, while he was thus absorbed and striving with all his might to understand this problem, he fixed his eyes on the wall and—right through the masonry of the church and dormitory—he saw the monks whose office it was to prepare for matins going about the altar and other parts of the church lighting the candles; and finally he saw one of them take in his hands the bell-rope and sound the bell to awaken the brethren. At this sound the whole community rose from their beds, and Anselm was astonished at the thing which had happened. From this he saw that it was a very small thing for God to show to the prophets in the spirit the things which would come to pass, since God had allowed him to see with his bodily eyes through so many obstacles the things which then were happening.[34]

We can see in this passage of Eadmer how authority and reason are united in the life and thought of Anselm from the very beginning of his career as a monk. In fact, his starting point is faith: the supreme authority of holy scripture which he intends to penetrate with his mind, in order to seek reasons, in order to clarify with reason things which are obscure in the sacred texts.

What Eadmer said about Anselm at the beginning of his life as a monk, Anselm himself confirmed later on: indeed in his controversy

---

33. See here note 4.
34. Eadmer, *Life of St Anselm*, I, ch. 7, pp. 12-13. See also Southern, *Saint Anselm: A Portrait*, pp. 70-71.

with Roscelin, the canon of Compiègne, he himself insists on the value of scripture considered by him as the supreme authority in discussions about questions arising from faith.

Eadmer also gives us an important description of how Anselm composed his first treatises and thus shows first of all in what way Anselm was a real thinker and also his view on the relation between authority and reason.

> Also he wrote a fourth treatise *On the Grammarian*, as he called it. This treatise was in the form of a disputation with a disciple, whom he introduced as the other disputant, and in it he both propounded and solved many dialectical questions, and expounded the different ways in which qualities and *qualia* are to be regarded. He also composed another small book, which he called the *Monologion* because in this he alone spoke and argued with himself. Here, *putting aside all authority of Holy Scripture*, he enquired into and discovered *by reason alone* what God is, and proved by invincible reason that God's nature is what the true faith holds it to be, and that it could not be other than it is.
>
> Afterwards it came into his mind to try to prove by one single and short argument the things which are believed and preached about God, that he is eternal, unchangeable, omnipotent, omnipresent, incomprehensible, just, righteous, merciful, true, as well as truth, goodness, justice and so on; and to show how all these qualities are united in him. And this, as he himself would say, gave him great trouble, partly because thinking about it took away his desire for food, drink and sleep, and partly—and this was more grievous to him—because it disturbed the attention which he ought to have paid to matins and to Divine service at other times. When he was aware of this, and still could not entirely lay hold on what he sought, he supposed that this line of thought was a temptation of the devil and he tried to banish it from his mind. But the more vehemently he tried to do this, the more this thought pursued him. Then suddenly one night during matins the grace of God illuminated his heart, the whole matter became clear to his mind, and a great joy and exultation filled his inmost being. Thinking therefore that others also would be glad to know what he had found, he immediately and ungrudgingly wrote it on writing tablets and gave them to one of the brethren of the monastery for safe-keeping.[35]

We see in this description how Anselm was almost obsessed by the search for rational solutions concerning mysteries of faith. But it is the description of the *Proslogion*'s origin which shows most clearly to what extent the search for reasons had penetrated his entire being. We can see

35. See Eadmer, *Life of St Anselm*, I, ch. 19, pp. 28-30.

here the thinker working. In this description we find in a vital unity 'quaerere', 'ratio' ('unum argumentum') and 'auctoritas' ('fides'). The movement started by faith penetrates the whole being of the thinker; it is the authority ('fides') which causes in the highest degree the movement of the mind ('ratio, intellectus'). We can also see to what extent Anselm's life is the life of a real thinker who is completely seized by the object of his rational searching.

For Anselm, treating questions of scripture was also a refuge at Canterbury from difficult worldly affairs and controversies:

> When useless uproars, controversies and altercations arose, as sometimes happens, he tried either to stem them or to get out as quickly as possible. For unless he did this, he was immediately overcome with weariness; his spirits drooped, and he even ran the risk of serious illness. When long experience had taught us this tendency of his, we drew him out of the crowd when such an occasion arose and put to him some question of Holy Scripture; and so we brought his body and mind back to their accustomed state, restored to health by this sort of wholesome antidote.[36]

In one more text, Eadmer relates Anselm's intervention in the Council of Bari:

> ...with the pope's blessing he returned to Liberi to wait there until the time of the council, which the pope was going to hold at Bari on 1 October (1098). When Anselm had presented himself at the Council, he was induced by the pope to confute the Greeks, who erred on the procession of the Holy Spirit, in asserting that He proceeded from the Father but not the Son. Having accomplished this *in a reasoned and catholic disquisition ('rationabili atque catholica disputatione')*, he was held in great honour by all and established as a man worthy of the highest veneration.[37]

In the last text of Eadmer we can see how Anselm wrestled until his death with difficult questions related to faith:

> Palm Sunday dawned and we were sitting beside him as usual. One of us therefore said to him: 'My lord and father, we cannot help knowing that you are going to leave the world to be at the Easter court of your Lord.' He replied: 'And indeed if his will is set on this, I shall gladly obey his will. However, if he would prefer me to remain among you, at least until I can settle a question about the origin of the soul, which I am turning over in my mind, I should welcome this with gratitude, for I do not know

36. See Eadmer, *Life of St Anselm*, II, ch. 13, p. 80.
37. See Eadmer, *Life of St Anselm*, I, ch. 24, pp. 112-13.

whether anyone will solve it when I am dead. Truly I think I might recover if I could eat something, for I feel no pain in any part of my body, except that I am altogether enfeebled by the weakness of my stomach which refuses food.'[38]

4. *The Anselmian Method and its Augustinian Sources*

Having reviewed briefly these texts of Eadmer, let us examine the philosophical problem of the relation between 'auctoritas' and 'ratio'. Indeed, there is a real philosophical problem involved in this relation and it is Augustine who shows us precisely its implications. We may ask the question, is it certain that when choosing the solitary way of reason we shall be able to do without authority? And another question: are there not some cases where reason itself becomes authority? How, then, can we solve the problem of the relation between reason and authority?

In order to define the problem and eventually find a solution, let us examine the new method Anselm introduces in the *Monologion*. First of all, we have to stress the double aspect of the new method. The merely negative aspect of his method consists in putting aside all authority of scripture, thus 'putting into parentheses' the *auctoritas par excellence*, because scripture is the highest authority in Anselm's mind. This aspect of the Anselmian method is the more surprising in that we saw how Anselm was wrestling with the Bible from the very beginning of his life as a monk, and how much respect he had for scripture. We can only mark the contrast between his firm and inviolable faith in scripture and his new method which consisted precisely in putting aside its entire authority. The positive aspect of his method consists in a full application of 'ratio' as a faculty ('sola ratione') whose main task is 'inter cogitationes discernere'[39]—to examine and to distinguish the various thoughts and to choose among them—in order to find 'reasons' proving that God's nature is what the true faith holds it to be, and that it could not be other than it is.

Nevertheless, in order to understand clearly Anselm's mind in introducing his new method, we must carefully examine his own text. The expression 'sola ratione' which characterizes his method positively has been consecrated by Eadmer and by all historians of Anselm's time,

38. See Eadmer, *Life of St Anselm*, II, ch. 46, pp. 141-42.
39. *De concordia*, III, ch. 11 (Schmitt, II, p. 283), add. T in note.

who depended on his literary tradition[40] and became the standard interpretation up to the present as we can see when we open commentaries on the Anselmian method. We must therefore examine Anselm's text closely. In the *Prologus*, we cannot find the expression 'sola ratione', but Anselm explains his thinking on the new method he wanted to practise when requested by his pupils:

> quatenus *auctoritate scripturae penitus nihil* in ea persuaderetur, sed quidquid per singulas investigationes finis assereret, id ita esse plano stilo et vulgaribus argumentis simplicique disputatione et rationis necessitas breviter cogeret et veritatis claritas patenter ostenderet.[41]

In the first chapter of the *Monologion* Anselm continues to explain his intention and comes to the expression 'sola ratione' which is preceded by 'saltem'; he says, '...puto quia ea ipsa ex magna parte, si vel mediocris ingenii est, potest ipse sibi *saltem* sola ratione persuadere'[42]— which means 'if somebody has an average understanding, he will be able to prove *at least (saltem) by reason alone* all that we believe about God and his nature'. Let us try to analyse the meaning of this expression in order to establish its full significance.

First of all, a question arises about Anselm's intention: did he insert the word 'saltem' by pure chance or did he have something in mind when writing it? When we think how concise Anselm's style is, not allowing any word which would seem superfluous, we must conclude that he put in the word 'saltem' on purpose.[43] In fact, by doing this, on the one hand he could stress the distinction between the path of faith and the path of reason, and on the other hand he could signify clearly the hierarchy of values which exists between faith and reason. As for Augustine, so for Anselm, faith—represented here by authority, the 'auctoritas Scripturae'—is more valuable than reason alone. This is because faith is a gift of God who is the truth while reasons are the result of human effort.

---

40. See Viola, 'L'Influence de la méthode anselmienne', p. 26, table.

41. *Monologion, Prologus* (Schmitt, I, p. 7:5-11).

42. *Monologion*, ch. 1 (Schmitt, I, p. 13:10-11).

43. It is not impossible that this restrictive word 'saltem' is due to the corrections of Anselm's text imposed (or made?) by Lanfranc. See Viola, 'Lanfranc de Pavie et Anselme d'Aoste', p. 562; *idem*, 'Le "Monologion" face à la philosophie réflexive', in *Recherche de théologie ancienne et médiévale (A Journal of Ancient and Medieval Christian Literature)* 49 (1992), pp. 97-110 (102).

In passing, we may notice that we find the expression 'sola ratione' in four more contexts in Anselm's works.[44] The most relevant is that of *Cur deus homo* when Anselm is discussing the problem of the mortality of human nature. The question is whether mortality is a part of pure human nature ('natura pura') or only the consequence of human nature having been corrupted by sin. After having tried to show by reason the ideal image of Christ which should enable him to atone for the sins of humankind, Anselm continues:

> Sunt et alia multa cur eum valde conveniat hominum similitudinem et conversationem absque peccato habere, quae facilius et clarius per se patent in eius vita et operibus, quam velut ante experimentum *sola ratione* monstrari possint.[45]

Although the whole discussion is a search for reasons—and we find indeed expressions such as 'non est dubium' (p. 110:6), 'ad hoc nos indeclinabiliter perducit ratio' (p. 110:8), 'sic sequitur' (p. 110:15), 'non possum aliter intelligere' (p. 110:17), 'ita sequitur ex supra dictis' (p. 110:24), 'hoc negari nequit' (p. 110:29), 'ad hoc nos impellit ratio' (p. 110:31), 'aliter nequeo intelligere' (p. 111:5), 'consideremus adhuc

---

44. *Cur deus homo*, II, ch. 11 (Schmitt, II, p. 111:26-29). The apologetical aim of the method 'sola ratione' is clearly stated at the end of *Cur deus homo*: 'Cum enim sic probes deum fieri hominem ex necessitate, ut etiam si removeantur pauca quae de nostris libris posuisti, ut quod de tribus dei personis et de Adam tetigisti, non solum Iudaeis sed etiam paganis *sola ratione* satisfacias, et ipse idem deus-homo novum condat testamentum et vetus approbet: sicut ipsum veracem esse necesse est confiteri, ita nihil quod in illis continetur verum esse potest aliquis diffiteri.' *Cur deus homo*, II, ch. 22 (Schmitt, II, p. 133:5-11). There are two more texts in which Anselm uses the expression 'sola ratio'. In the first context he is simply stating that there is only one *ratio* (rational faculty), i.e. only one 'instrumentum ratiocinandi': 'Voluntas igitur quae est instrumentum, una sola est; id est, instrumentum volendi unum solum est in homine, sicut *una sola ratio*, id est *unum solum instrumentum ratiocinandi*.' *De concordia*, III, ch. 11 (Schmitt, II, pp. 280:25-281:2). In the apologetical context against Roscelin Anselm uses the expression 'sola ratio' and also the expression '*pure* reason' (long before the '*reine* Vernunft' of Kant) in order to criticize the incoherence of the dialecticians of his time: 'In eorum quippe animabus *ratio* quae et princeps et iudex debet omnium esse, quae sunt in homine, sic est in imaginationibus corporalibus obvoluta, ut ex eis se non possit evolvere, nec ab ipsis ea quae ipsa [= ratio] *sola* et *pura* contemplari debet, valeat discernere.' *Epistola de incarnatione verbi*, ch. 1 (Schmitt, II, p. 10:1-4).

45. *Cur deus homo*, II, ch. 11 (Schmitt, II, p. 111:26-29).

utrum sic rationabiliter conveniat' (p. 111:6), 'non est aliquid rationabilius' (p. 111:15), 'vera sunt omnia haec' (p. 111:19)—in his conclusion Anselm shows the superiority of knowledge based on the experience of Christ's life and actions compared with what '*sola ratione* monstrari possit', with all that could be shown by reason alone. The experience of Christ, from which we know his nature and attitude, is more important than all that we can 'deduce' by reason.

The word 'experimentum' reminds us of another relevant text of the *Epistola de incarnatione verbi* where Anselm underlines the importance of experience for true knowledge:

> Nimirum hoc ipsum quod dico: qui non crediderit, non intelliget. Nam qui non crediderit, non experietur: et qui expertus non fuerit, non cognoscet. Quantum enim rei auditum superat experientia, tantum vincit audientis cognitionem experientis scientia.[46]

These passages prove clearly enough that in Anselm's mind the expression 'saltem' must have had a profound meaning. They show that in his mind there was a hierarchy of knowledge and that the highest way of knowledge is that of experience and not reason alone. It is important to make these remarks about the crucial moment when Anselm introduced his new method because—as we know—this was the first 'stumbling block' in his *milieu* and particularly for Lanfranc, his former master and now archbishop of Canterbury.

For a better historical understanding of the problem we have to go back to Augustine, Anselm's spiritual and intellectual master, whose authority he invokes in his apologia. In fact, the expression 'sola ratione' can be found in Augustine's *De quantitate animae*. This text seems to me very important first of all as a means of knowing the nature of knowledge in general, and then in particular the nature of rational knowledge according to the bishop of Hippo. In chapter VII, after having distinguished the two main ways of learning, in his dialogue with Evodius, Augustine compares like an excellent master the great advantage of one who follows authority compared with one who follows only reason. But it is interesting to notice that firstly, Augustine places authority and reason on the same level: according to him both of these ways of knowing rely finally upon a kind of faith, a 'credere'. He then makes a distinction between the two, 'Aliud est enim cum auctoritati

---

46. *Epistola de incarnatione verbi*, ch. 1 (Schmitt, II, p. 9:5-8).

credimus, aliud cum credimus rationi', in order to emphasize the advantage of believing in authority:

> there is a great advantage in believing in authority and it is without any toil: if you like it, you may read plenty of things which great and divine men said about things which seem necessary and useful for those having less experience...[47]

47. Saint Augustine discusses more than once in his various treatises the problem of *auctoritas* in relation to *ratio*. He stresses the importance of the highest authority which is that of God. Augustine's approach to this problem is conditioned by his searching after truth, but he clarifies also the importance of authority in relation to the natural process of human knowing which according to him necessarily has to start with authority. 'Aliud est enim cum *auctoritati credimus, aliud cum rationi*. Auctoritati credere magnum compendium est, et nullus labor: quod si te delectat, poteris multa legere, quae magni et divini viri de his rebus necessaria quae videbantur, salubriter imperitioribus quasi nutu quodam locuti sunt, credique sibi voluerunt ab iis, quorum animis vel tardioribus vel implicatioribus alia salus esse non posset. Tales enim homines, quorum profecto maxima multitudo est, si ratione velint verum comprehendere, similitudinibus rationum facillime decipiuntur, et in varias noxiasque opiniones ita labuntur, ut mergere inde ac liberari, aut nunquam, aut aegerrime queant. His ergo utilissimum est *excellentissimae auctoritati credere*, et secundum hoc agere vitam. Quod si tutius putas, non solum nihil resisto, sed etiam multum approbo. *Si autem cupiditatem istam refrenare non potes, qua tibi persuasisti ratione pervenire ad veritatem, multi et longi circuitus tibi tolerandi sunt, ut non ratio te adducat, nisi* ea quae *sola ratio* dicenda est, id est *vera ratio*; et non solum vera, sed ita *certa* et *ab omni similitudine falsitatis aliena*, si tamen ullo modo haec ab homine inveniri potest, ut nullae disputationes falsae aut verisimiles ab ea te possint traducere.' See Augustine, *De quantitate animae*, ch. 7 (*PL* 32, 1042). 'Naturae quidem ordo ita se habet, ut cum aliquid discimus, rationem praecedat auctoritas. Nam infirma ratio videri potest, quae cum reddita fuerit, auctoritatem postea, per quam firmetur, assumit...' *De moribus catholicae ecclesiae*, I, chs. 3-4 (*PL* 32, 1311-1312).

In other texts Saint Augustine insists on the importance of authority in learning and exalts Christ's authority: 'Nulli autem dubium est gemino pondere nos impelli ad discendum, *auctoritatis* atque rationis. Mihi autem certum est nusquam prorsus a *Christi auctoritate* discedere: non enim reperio valentiorem. Quod autem subtilissima ratione persequendum est; ita enim iam sum affectus, ut quid sit verum, non credendo solum, sed etiam intelligendo apprehendere desiderem; apud Platonicos me interim *quod sacris nostris non repugnet* reperturum esse confido.' *Contra academicos*, III, ch. 20 (*PL* 32, 957). We are reminded of the *Proslogion* when Augustine explains his desire to grasp truth ('verum') not only by faith but also by intellectual searching. *De ordine*, II, ch. 9 (*PL*, 32, 1007); here Augustine recognizes that for the greatest number of people without culture ('imperitae'), the authority of honest men ('bonorum auctoritas') seems to be more useful ('salubrior'), while *ratio* fits more

But on the other hand, Augustine points out the danger which awaits those who are not able to refrain from their greed or curiosity to know only by reason:

cultured people; nevertheless, adds Augustine, for all those who are keen to know great and hidden things, there is no other way than authority, since no human being becomes cultured without being previously uncultured. See also the definition of *ratio*: 'Ratio est mentis motio, ea quae discuntur distinguendi et connectendi potens: qua duce uti ad Deum intelligendum, vel ipsam quae aut in nobis, aut usquequaque est animam, rarissimum omnino genus hominum potest; non ob aliud, nisi quia in istorum sensuum negotia progresso, redire in semetipsum cuique difficile est. Itaque, cum in rebus ipsis fallacibus ratione totum agere homines moliantur, quid sit ipsa ratio, et qualis sit, nisi perpauci prorsus ignorant. Mirum videtur, sed tamen se ita res habet.' *De ordine*, II, ch. 11 (*PL* 32, 1009-1010). Anselm often uses the adjective 'rationabile'. It is interesting to notice the Augustinian distinction between *rationale* and *rationabile*: 'Sed quoniam solent doctissimi viri quid inter rationale et rationabile intersit, acuto subtiliterque discernere, nullo modo est, ad id quod instituimus, negligendum: nam rationale esse dixerunt, quod ratione uteretur vel uti posset; rationabile autem, quod ratione factum esset aut dictum.' *De ordine*, II, ch. 11 (*PL* 32, 1009 n. 31).

In *De utilitate credendi* Augustine speaks of divine authority: 'Haec est, crede, saluberrima auctoritas, haec prius mentis nostrae a terrena inhabitatione suspensio, haec in Deum verum ab huius mundi amore conversio. Sola est auctoritas, quae commovet stultos ut ad sapientiam festinent. [Notice the opposition between *sola ratio* and *sola auctoritas*.] ... non est desperandum ab eodem ipso Deo auctoritatem aliquam constititutam quo velut gradu certo innitentis, attollamur in Deum. Haec autem, *seposita ratione*, quam sinceram intelligere, ut saepe diximus , difficillimum stultis est, dupliciter nos movet; partim miraculis, partim sequentium multitudine.' *De utilitate credendi*, ch. 16 (*PL* 42, 89). One might notice the contrast between the Augustinian 'seposita ratione' and the Anselmian 'quatenus auctoritate scripturae nihil persuaderetur', the 'sola ratione' and the 'remoto Christo'. See also the parallelism between ch. 1 of Augustine's *De utilitate credendi* and the description of the error of Roscelin in *Ep. de Incarn.*: how men are deceived by their imagination. Ch. 14 (*PL* 42, 88) is also very important where Augustine stresses the superiority of faith in Christ against 'indubitata ratio reddita'; 'prius est credendum...'.

There is one more relevant Augustinian text which combines the problem of authority with that of searching: Hoc ergo sapiamus, ut noverimus tutiorem esse affectum vera quaerendi, quam incognita pro cognitis praesumendi. Sic ergo quaeramus tanquam inventuri: et sic inveniamus, tanquam quaesituri. 'Cum enim consummaverit homo, tunc incipit' (Ecc. 18.6). De credendis nulla infidelitate dubitemus, de intelligendis nulla temeritate affirmemus: in illis auctoritas tenenda est, in his veritas exquirenda... Hoc autem quaeramus intelligere, ab eo ipso quem intelligere volumus, auxilium precantes, et quantum tribuit quo intelligimus explicare tanta cura et sollicitudine pietatis cupientes, ut etiam si aliquid aliud pro alio dicimus, nihil tamen indignum dicamus.' *De trinitate*, IX, i, 1 (*PL* 42, 960-61).

Si autem *cupiditatem* istam refrenare non potes, qua tibi persuasisti ratione pervenire ad veritatem... Tales enim homines... si ratione velint verum comprehendere, similitudinibus rationum facillime decipiuntur, et in varias noxiasque opiniones ita labuntur, ut mergere inde ac liberari, aut nunquam, aut aegerrime queant.[48]

According to Augustine, the way of reason cannot grant us the absolute security of arriving at the truth and avoiding what he calls 'similitudines rationum': illusions or illusory reasons.[49] In fact, illusory reasons can deceive us and thus prevent us from regaining our freedom. Augustine somehow mistrusts reason. His rather prudent attitude towards reason is indeed founded on the experience of humankind attested by its history, or at least by the history of human thinking which testifies to errors and to the weakness of human opinions. We know very well that the earliest written documents of western philosophy attest that reason is subject to deviation and error. The existence of the distinction between δόξα and ἀλήθεια and the presence of the two ways in the Presocratic fragments make clear that from the very beginning western thinkers were fully conscious of the limits of the human mind (νόος) and of the danger for humans of being misled by the mind in the search after truth.[50]

We can also understand why finally Augustine places reason and authority on the same level, stating that *to believe authority as well as reason* is unavoidable. In other words, paradoxically even reason is founded on a kind of faith. If it is necessary to have faith in order to accept authority, it is also necessary to have a kind of faith in order to accept reason as a supreme guide, precisely because according to experience, reason can mislead us in our seeking for truth. This is certainly a warning against all kinds of extreme rationalism, but as Bochenski[51] points out, all rationalism must be finally based on the acceptance of a supreme authority and therefore it must by logical necessity be based on a faith.[52] Thus *no form of rationalism is completely rational.* As I wrote

48. *De quantitate animae*, ch. 7 (*PL* 32, 1042).

49. See also Augustine, *Ep.* CXLIII, n. 7 (*PL* 33, 588), cited in n. 17 above.

50. See C.E. Viola, 'Aux origines de la gnoséologie: réflexions sur le sens du Fr.IV du Poème de Parménide', in *Etudes sur Parménide. II. Problèmes d'interprétation* (ed. P. Aubenque; Paris, 1987), pp. 69-101.

51. See J.M. Bochenski, *Autorität, Freiheit, Glaube. Sozialphilosophische Studien* (Munich, 1988), pp. 56-67, 98-106

52. Pascal goes still further when he exclaims: 'Si la raison était raisonnable' (see Pascal, *Pensées*, n. 189 [ed. J. Chevalier; Paris, 1954]): '... la petite phrase de Pascal met en lumière ce qu'a d'irréel la prétention de la raison humaine à la totale

at the beginning of this paper, we see that the problem of *auctoritas* in its antagonism with *ratio* involves a difficult philosophical problem: reason becomes authority and rationalism claims faith, in other words, it claims authority.

But still Augustine predicts other dangers which await those who have chosen the way of the 'sola ratio':

> ... multi et longi circuitus tibi tolerandi sunt, ut non ratio te adducat, nisi ea quae *sola ratio* dicenda est, id est *vera ratio*; et non solum vera, sed ita *certa* et *ab omni similitudine falsitatis aliena....* ut nullae disputationes falsae aut verisimiles ab ea te possint traducere.[53]

Here we have the expression 'sola ratio' which has to be called according to Augustine 'vera ratio', and not only 'vera' but also 'certa et ab omni similitudine falsitatis aliena'. In this important text, Augustine produces a clear distinction between reason alone, 'solitary' reason, and true reason which also has to be certain and free from all resemblance to falsehood. There is also another inconvenience when walking on the path of solitary reason: we have to tolerate a great number of diversions ('multi et longi circuitus tibi tolerandi sunt') in order to find the way of true reason. Isn't this a prophecy for the future author of the *Monologion*? It is difficult not to see a parallel between the 'multi et longi circuitus' Augustine is speaking of and the 'multorum concatenatione contextum argumentorum' Anselm speaks about after having completed the *Monologion*. Yet Augustine has protected Anselm from the dangers and inconveniences of practising the method of solitary reason.

On considering this Augustinian passage, there is a question which arises spontaneously: did Anselm know this text of *De quantitate animae*? I am not sure. In order to justify his methodological choice, he appeals to the authority of Augustine, mentioning in particular *De trinitate*. Nevertheless might it be permissible to think that the presence in *De quantitate animae* of the expression 'sola ratio' identified with the 'vera et certa ratio' could have inspired Anselm to try the way of the solitary reason first in his oral teaching and then in his writing? This problem of literary influence cannot be solved easily because of the absence of any material evidence. But at least we can propose the

---

autonomie. Elle ignore la possibilité de l'erreur et le péril, que court une raison voulant être à elle-même sa propre loi, de basculer dans l'irrationnel.' See G. Cottier, 'Repères', in Jean-Paul II, *La splendeur de la vérité* (Paris, 1993), p. 192.

53. See Augustine, *De quantitate animae*, ch. 7 (*PL* 32, 1042).

following hypothesis: for Anselm, as for Augustine, the method of 'sola ratione' is that of the 'vera ratione', in the sense that 'sola ratio' preceded by 'saltem' is inseparable from 'credere' as its starting point and as its point of arrival. Indeed, on the one hand, the method of 'sola ratione' is to be achieved under the highest authority of 'credere', and on the other hand the way Anselm is pursuing with reason is parallel with that of 'credere'. It is useful to notice that long before Anselm, Augustine already knew the way of 'sola ratio' with all its inconveniences and dangers which await those who would cut it off from its root which is nothing other than faith.

Nevertheless Anselm pursued the solitary way of reason not only in his *Monologion*,[54] but in practically all his works until the end of his life: the methodological exigency 'quatenus auctoritate scripturae penitus nihil in ea persuaderetur' will give way later on in *Cur deus homo* to another exigency expressed by 'remoto Christo'. We know, in the case of the *Monologion*, that the exclusion of holy scripture, the highest authority in his meditation, caused a real crisis with a living authority: that of Lanfranc who represented for him as much the authority of the pontiff as the authority of the former master whose advice was necessary in the eyes of his pupil. This was the first dramatic clash in Anselm's life between authority and reason, occurring precisely at the moment that he expressed his intention of putting into motion the entire power of his reason while putting aside[55] the

54. In Anselm's mind, as he states it later on, both *Monologion* and *Proslogion* were written with the same intention: not to prove anything using scriptural authority: 'Sed et si quis legere dignabitur duo parva mea opuscula, *Monologion* scilicet et *Proslogion,* quae ad hoc maxime facta sunt, ut quod fide tenemus de divina natura et eius personis praeter incarnationem, necessariis rationibus *sine scripturae auctoritate* probari possit...' See Anselm, *Epistola de incarnatione verbi*, ch. 6 (Schmitt, II, 20:16-19). This statement puts in a new light Anselm's real intention in writing *Proslogion* which is full of scriptural quotations or reminiscences and prayers. According to Anselm's own judgment all this is not the 'essence' of *Proslogion*, but rather the proving with necessary reasons of God's existence and attributes.

55. We must notice that while Anselm is speaking of 'quatenus auctoritate scripturae penitus nihil in ea persuaderetur', Eadmer and other historians of Anselm's time say 'tacita omni auctoritate divinae scripturae'. In Anselm's text it is a question of not using 'persuasion' which is the aim of rhetoric. Explaining his intention about the method of the *Monologion* and the *Proslogion* Anselm says: '... quae ad hoc maxime facta sunt, ut quod fide tenemus de divina natura et eius personis praeter incarnationem, necessariis rationibus *sine scripturae auctoritate* probari possit.' *Epistola de incarnatione verbi*, ch. 6 (Schmitt, II, p. 20:17-19). At the same time Anselm insists

highest authority. This clash was about to cost him the first fruits of his meditation.[56]

5. Authority and the Foundation of Reason in Anselm's Thought

The hostile attitude of some of the authors of the eleventh century towards grammatical or dialectical reason is well known. We know also that the defenders of the value of reason replied promptly saying that the 'mens rationalis', 'ratio', is not only a creature of God, but even the 'imago Dei' and therefore we cannot have towards it a merely negative or contemptuous attitude. If Anselm is not only not hostile to reason but positively following its path, it is from a completely different motive. The search for reasons in his mind is founded in scriptural texts, therefore in authority. It is not only the inaccurate text of the 'nisi credidero non intelligam' (Isa. 7.9), which is an invitation to faith (authority) to have understanding ('intelligetis'), but the text of the First Letter of Peter which invites us to give reasons for the hope which is in us (1 Pet. 3.15: 'Always be prepared to give an answer to everyone who asks you to give the reason for the hope that you have' (ἕτοιμοι ἀεὶ πρὸς ἀπολογίαν παντὶ τῷ αἰτοῦντι ὑμᾶς λόγον περὶ τῆς ἐν ὑμῖν ἐλπίδος). This is the very text Anselm refers to at the beginning of *Cur deus homo*.[57]

also on the double aim of using the rational method: '...ad respondendum pro fide nostra contra eos, qui nolentes credere quod non intelligunt derident credentes, sive ad adiuvandum religiosum studium eorum qui humiliter quaerunt intelligere quod firmissime credunt...' *Epistola de incarnatione verbi*, ch. 6 (Schmitt, II, p. 21:1-3). According to him, the rational method is as useful against those who will not believe and reject all that faith teaches as for those who try to understand while believing firmly: Anselm thinks he can help them in their religious study. The same double purpose is also clearly stated by Anselm at the beginning of *Cur deus homo*, I, ch. 1 (Schmitt, II, pp. 47:7-48:11). Anselm insists on this double aim of using reason in his letter to Fulco, bishop of Beauvais: 'Fides enim nostra contra impios ratione defendenda est, non contra eos qui se Christiani nominis honore gaudere fatentur. Ab iis enim iuste *exigendum est ut cautionem in baptismate factam inconcusse teneant*; illis vero rationaliter ostendendum est, *quam irrationabiliter nos contemnant*. Nam Christianus per fidem debet ad intellectum proficere, non per intellectum ad fidem accedere, aut, si intelligere non valet, a fide recedere. Sed cum ad intellectum valet pertingere, delectatur; cum vero nequit, quod capere non potest veneratur.' *Ep.* 136 (Schmitt, III, pp. 280:34-281:41).

56. See Viola, 'Lanfranc de Pavie et Anselme d'Aoste', pp. 545-50.
57. *Cur deus homo*, I, ch. 1 (Schmitt, II, p. 47:10-11).

But besides the text of Peter there are also texts which invite us to search the face of the Lord.[58] In fact, looking for reasons is a real searching, a real 'quaerere' in both senses: asking questions and also searching. These are so to speak the biblical backgrounds and principles which Anselm had behind him when following the path of reason. But there is also another aspect of the problem: Anselm himself experienced being able to arrive by reason alone at the same conclusions which constitute the object of faith. He experienced reason as able to grasp truth, the same truth that he knew by faith. And—as I suggested before—we know that for Anselm experience is a very important moment in the *processus* of knowing.

a. *Authority, Reason and Truth*
There is in the *Proslogion* a certain paradox which appears precisely after Anselm has completed his argument for the existence of God: 'Gratias tibi, bone domine, gratias tibi, quia quod prius credidi te donante, iam sic intelligo te illuminante, ut si te esse nolim credere, non possim non intelligere'.[59] Let us analyse briefly the content of this thanksgiving. What Anselm believed before, he now understands in such a way that *even if he did not believe it, from now on, it is impossible for him not to understand it.* His manner of proceeding is clear: first he believed that God exists, and now he also understands what he believed. Of course, it was faith which was guiding his intelligence (reason) to understand, but now his understanding has reached such a degree of necessity that he is no longer able to doubt in his mind. In other words, the truth which was contained in faith has been transformed into a truth of reason precisely because of the effort made by reason. There is here a clear distinction between 'credere' and 'intelligere' in the perspective of the same truth: under the influence of the will ('si nolim'), of course, we can reject faith. Nevertheless, we must acknowledge what we came to understand through the initial influence of faith, even if we reject it. This paradoxical text of *Proslogion* also contains an implicit statement according to which we are able to gain access to knowledge of God's existence and its absolute necessity independently from faith.

In fact as we know, Anselm's plan consists in proving by a unique

---

58. See H. de Lubac, '"Seigneur, je cherche ton visage". Sur le chapitre XIVe du "Proslogion" de saint Anselme', in *Archives de philosophie* 39 (1976), pp. 201-25, 407-25.
59. *Proslogion*, ch. 4 (Schmitt, I, p. 104:5-7).

argument the truth of our knowledge of God: his existence as well as his nature and attributes. Of course, it is faith which gave reason the motive for searching ('fides quaerens'), but at the end of this search reason itself has acquired its autonomy, or rather, its autonomy has been guaranteed by faith. How? In reflecting on itself, reason discovers itself as a faculty capable of reaching the truth, as is shown by the fact that it was able to reach the same reality as that presented by faith. In this coinciding of the object of research there is also a paradox: while reason appears as a faculty 'capax veritatis', at the same time, faith receives a strengthening from reason through this coinciding of the objects.

Now aware of its capacity to reach the truth, reason can, so to speak, separate from faith, at least in a hypothetical way ('si...nolim credere'). Starting from faith ('credo ut intelligam'), Anselm's plan seems to go beyond the limits of faith because, for him, truth—even the truth of the existence of God which is the fundamental dogma of Christian faith—is accessible to reason. In other words, truth can be sought or established even outside faith. This statement formally denies the conception of Barth concerning immanent theology.

Before coming to the problem of the overflowing ('débordement') of truth in regard to faith, I want to mention the fact that, in *Proslogion*, Anselm passes from the 'veritas tua' to the 'tu es veritas'. In other words, he understands that the truth of God is that *he is the Truth*. It is this God-truth or Lord-truth he seeks. Thus Anselm's seeking for the truth becomes a personal search: truth is not a thing, not even a quality of the mind, but the personal God whom Anselm questions. We must understand in a personal sense Anselm's searching for truth. But what is fundamental to an understanding of the *Proslogion* is its dialectical process (method): on the one hand, through this dialectical process, faith grows in intensity by the fact that through reason, we grasp—at least 'aliquatenus', to a certain extent—what faith teaches us; on the other hand, reason itself is fortified, it acquires a real 'status of truth' by the fact that it becomes aware of its capacity to reach the truth. Of course, in this context, reason means—as Stephen Gersh has pointed out—the highest part of the soul which is equivalent to 'mens'.[60]

Let us move now to another question which arises when we approach the problem of the relation between faith and truth. We should not forget meanwhile that *faith is equivalent to authority*, or more exactly, faith represents the highest form of authority which involves the

60. See Gersh, 'Anselm of Canterbury', pp. 263-64.

authority of God-truth who speaks through faith. If there is—as we have seen—a certain convergence between 'veritas' and 'ratio', are we allowed to conclude that, according to Anselm, these two realities cover perfectly the domain of faith?

This question is not without interest, especially when we hold before our eyes Anselm's programme: the 'fides quaerens intellectum'. First of all, we have to notice carefully that for Anselm there is no question of establishing faith by reason or by 'rationes': the 'firmitas fidei' must always precede the search for reasons, as we saw indeed in Eadmer's account too. On the contrary: it is faith which imposes the search for reasons. But to what extent are humans able to search and find reasons—which anyway arise from the domain of faith—in order to show that faith is true? Anselm's answer is formal: faith overflows the domain of reason and of the rational, because the truth of faith has to be firmly asserted even if we do not find any reason to clarify its contents, even in the case where reason seems to prove the contrary of what faith is proposing. This is an extreme condition which in Anselm's view has to be deduced from the absolute superiority of faith,[61] which is based on the only absolute authority, that is to say the God-truth. Reason is

---

61. We can also see this in Anselm's letter to Fulco, bishop of Beauvais where, already abbot, he rejects Roscelin's accusations of heterodoxy: 'De me autem hanc veram omnes homines habere volo sententiam: Sic teneo ea quae confitemur in symbolo, cum dicimus: "credo in Deum, patrem omnipotentem, creatorem"; et "credo in unum Deum, patrem omnipotentem, factorem"; et: "quicumque vult salvus esse, ante omnia opus est *ut teneat catholicam fidem', et ea quae sequuntur*; haec tria Christianae confessionis principia, quae hic proposui, sic inquam haec et corde credo et ore confiteor, ut certus sim quia quicumque horum aliquid negare voluerit, et nominatim quicumque blasphemiam, quam supra posui me audisse a Roscelino dici, pro veritate asseruerit—sive homo sive angelus—, anathema est; et confirmando dicam: quamdiu in hac pertinacia perstiterit, anathema sit. Omnino enim Christianus non est. Quod si baptizatus et inter Christianos est nutritus, nullo modo audiendus est, nec ulla ratio aut sui erroris est ab illo exigenda aut nostrae veritatis illi est exhibenda; sed mox eius perfidia absque dubietate innotuerit, aut anathematizet venenum quod proferendo evomit, aut anathematizetur ab omnibus Catholicis, nisi resipuerit.' *Ep.* 136 (Schmitt, III, p. 280:16-31). Besides holy scripture, the Creed also has its supreme authority which contains the 'principles of the Christian Confession'. Anyone who denies even one of the Creed's articles is 'anathema', and is in no way a Christian. Even if he has been baptized, one does not have to listen to him; there is no question of asking him the reason(s) for his error or proposing to him the reason(s) for 'our Truth'. Anselm adopts a very firm attitude against those who deny their faith after having been baptized and 'nourished' in the faith.

therefore not the supreme critical instance of the truth; it has to submit itself to a higher criterion. And precisely at this point we can see the limits of what some historians have called the rationalism of Anselm.

Therefore, the domain of reason does not entirely cover the domain of truth; faith alone is capable of giving us the truth in its fullness. Reason has its own limits imposed by faith. That is why if we can establish an identity between *fides et veritas*, we cannot do the same with *fides et ratio*; therefore it is not possible to identify simply *veritas et ratio*, for several reasons. (1) There are arguments—or let us rather say some dialecticians such as Roscelin of Compiègne propose arguments—which are not true. Let us remember here Augustine's admonition against illusory reasons. False reasons appear as such precisely insofar as they are in opposition with the faith of the Catholic Church. (2) There are truths which we know by faith but which we cannot prove at all, or at least we are not able to prove them perfectly by reason. Therefore not everything which has been revealed by God can be proved or exhausted also by reason. And that is just what Anselm is clearly stating in *Cur deus homo*[62] and in *Epistula de incarnatione verbi*.[63] We can thus conclude that in our actual condition of humanity the only way to reach the fullness of truth is faith.

The most complete text which sheds some light on the delicate problem of the relation between faith and truth is *De concordia praescientiae*, q. 3, 6. We must insist on a certain number of principles which Anselm states in this text. First of all, the search for truth must be subordinated in an absolute way to faith, more precisely to faith in the absolute truth of scripture. Here we can remember what Eadmer said of Anselm at the very beginning of his career as a monk.[64] Anselm admits that very often our reason seems to offer us invincible arguments to prove what seems to us true, although they are in evident contradiction with faith. In that case our act of faith must guide us to understand that despite this appearance, these arguments have no foundation in truth.[65] Faith in the truth of holy scripture is the supreme source, the last criterion of any particular truth reason can offer to us. In our 'quaerere', in our search, reason has an important part and must intervene very often,

---

62. *Cur deus homo, Commendatio operis* (Schmitt, II, p. 40:4-7).
63. *Epistola de incarnatione*, ch. 1 (Schmitt, II, p. 10:14-17).
64. See n. 35.
65. See Augustine, *Ep.* CXLIII, n. 7 (*PL* 33, 588).

as we can see in all of Anselm's works.[66] Reason is a very useful means of disciminating ('rationis est inter cogitationes discernere'[67]); nevertheless reason has to be submitted to the highest authority represented by scripture.

What is therefore the nature of the relation between faith and truth? Anselm's answer is that faith and truth are closely connected: it is faith in scripture which assures the plenitude of truth. Nevertheless, the 'bond' between faith and truth opens the way to another 'bond' which connects truth and reason. Still, reason can never have the last word: it must be continuously measured with regard to faith. If there were no absolute and inseparable bond between faith and truth, reason could have been considered as the only absolute criterion, or as one of the criteria of truth, at least in its own domain.

But reason cannot be considered as the supreme criterion, because it has to be continuously in contact with faith, the only source of the plenitude of truth. As we have seen, according to Anselm, scripture contains the authority of all truth that reason would be able to grasp ('auctoritas omnis veritatis'). The 'authority' of reason comes therefore from the authority of scripture: in fact, as we have shown, reason receives its authority from scripture as far as it states clearly ('aperte') what scripture teaches us. This is evidently the case in *Monologion* and *Proslogion* and the case in the Anselmian method in general which consists in searching and finding by reason alone all that faith teaches us. Nevertheless, here Anselm goes even further: reason receives its authority from faith even in the case where it seems clear that all that reason is proposing is in contradiction with holy scripture; in other words, when there is no scriptural text to prove what reason is proposing. In this Anselmian conception we can recognize what later theologians called the 'norma fidei negativa', a principle according to which reason should not state anything which would be in evident contradiction to faith.[68] However, we may notice that the Anselmian principle is precisely the reverse: it does not take its starting point from reason but from faith. On the other

66. 'Sicut enim bestiarum est nihil velle cum ratione, ita hominum esset nihil velle sine ratione.' *De conceptu virginali*, ch. 10 (Schmitt, II, p. 152:5-6). In Anselm's thought will is connected with reason by a natural necessity.

67. *De concordia*, ch. 11 (Schmitt, III, p. 283, note).

68. See Augustine, *Ep.* CXLIII, n. 7 (*PL* 33, 588): '*Si enim ratio contra divinarum Scripturarum auctoritatem redditur*, quamlibet acuta sit, fallit veri similitudine; nam vera esse non potest.'

hand, instead of imposing any limit to reason, faith grants the true 'auctoritas' of reason. Thus Anselm gives us a very positive conception as far as the relation between faith and reason, between the truth of faith and the truth of reason, is concerned.

We have to stress in this context the extension of the domain of truth and we touch again on the problem of the 'overflowing' of faith and reason. One could say with Anselm that the domain of truth has to be defined by a double criterion: one positive and the other negative.

So we see that according to Anselm holy scripture contains the authority of all truth; scripture is supposed to be the highest authority from which derives also the 'authority' or the truth of reason. Now this conception involves a tremendous problem: if this is the case how does one solve the problem which arises continously from the fact that the sacred texts are not always clear and therefore can be interpreted in different senses, sometimes even in contradictory ways. If faith, the supreme norm of truth, contains these uncertainties, and if reason itself must rely upon this supreme norm which is faith in scripture, how can even reason solve this problem?

b. *Reason and the Interpretation of the Bible*

Living in a time of strong controversies—that of Berengar, of Roscelin and the Filioque controversies with the Greeks—Anselm could not avoid problems with the interpretation of sacred texts, of holy scripture and the Creed. He himself knew that everything is not clear in the texts, he was wrestling with difficult questions of interpretation, and he could not avoid noticing that the great disputes with Berengar or Roscelin involved textual problems. We know that Lanfranc was already conscious of the serious problem of textual interpretation in his dispute with Berengar: he specifically reproached Berengar for having given a 'perverted interpretation' of scripture.[69]

Even in the hypothesis that scripture has the plenitude of truth and the highest authority, one cannot avoid problems of interpretation which are inherent to any written text or textual tradition. Indeed scripture can be interpreted in different ways; its sense can be changed, deformed and

---

69. 'Ibi enim conquiesceret omnis versuta tergiversatio, quum *sacri codices* te audiente legerentur, vel tibi ad legendum in manus traderentur: coelestique lampade splendidius eniterent *quaedam, quae de scripturis sanctis* te sumere nonnumquam *dicis, aut penitus esse falsa, aut* aliqua ex parte, prout ratio tui negotii postulat *depravata.*' See Lanfranc, *Liber de corpore*, ch. 1, p. 148.

corrupted, not only because of the faults of the scribes who copied the texts—that is why Lanfranc and Anselm passed long nights in emending sacred texts—but also by personal approaches using new means of interpretation such as those of the grammarians and dialecticians in Anselm's time.

Anselm too was aware of the fact that the interpretation of scripture raises a problem of language. An interesting text of *De casu diaboli* shows clearly his attitude: we have to pay attention not so much to the 'improprietas verborum' which is impossible to avoid in speaking of God and his actions, but rather to the truth which is hiding in the many ways of speaking of the Bible:

> M. Vide ne ullatenus putes, cum in divinis libris legimus aut cum secundum illos dicimus deum facere malum aut facere non esse, quia negem propter quod dicitur, aut reprehendam quia ita dicitur. Sed non tantum debemus inhærere improprietati verborum veritatem tegenti, quantum inhiare proprietati veritatis sub multimodo genere locutionum latenti.[70]

We see therefore that even if one accepts scripture as the highest authority, one cannot avoid raising problems. This fact shows in some way the limits of the authority of scripture considered in itself and independently from a living body—such as the church—which should be qualified to give an authentic interpretation of those texts which are not clear enough or which are open to different interpretations. Anselm remarked in his *Epistola de incarnatione* that against Roscelin, 'auctoritas' had no weight: arguing against him with authority, even with the supreme authority of holy scripture, could not have any effect either because Roscelin did not believe in scripture or because he was interpreting the holy texts in a perverse way. The only way to discuss with him or refute him was to use 'ratio', the field he had chosen himself for the discussion. This case shows also that for Anselm 'auctoritas' had its limits even in defending the truth against his adversary. That is why Anselm set out on the path of reason in his dialogues *De casu diaboli* and *De libertate arbitrii*.

> Sed quoniam libero arbitrio præscientia et prædestinatio et gratia dei videntur repugnare, gratissimum mihi erit, si eas illi *non tam auctoritate sacra, quod a multis satis factum est, quam ratione,* quod sufficienter factum nondum me memini legisse, concordare facias. *Auctoritate* vero ad hoc non indigeo, quia illam quantum ad hoc quod quæro pertinet,

---

70. *De casu diaboli*, ch. 1 (Schmitt, I, p. 235:8-12).

sufficienter novi et suscipio. M. De præscientia et prædestinatione similis et pariter difficilior quam de gratia quæstio est.[71]

This passage is an addition in the *prior recensio* of *De libertate arbitrii*. Still the content of this text seems to me important because it shows clearly Anselm's predilection for reason in the face of authority. As in other circumstances when difficult questions arise from scripture—in this case the problem is how to reconcile freedom, divine prescience and grace—his fundamental attitude is that of acceptance when in possession of a sufficient knowledge of the problem ('sufficienter novi et suscipio'). Nevertheless Anselm does not want to stop using his mind at this stage: knowing precisely the 'status quaestionis' as it is clear in the sacred texts or in faith, he wants to seek after reasons. That is why he says there is no need of 'auctoritas' which is sufficiently known already, but we need 'rationes'. Therefore the main task is 'ratione concordare facias': it is through reason that he wants to clarify what he knows already sufficiently and what he accepts in any case by authority.

Again, in his controversy with the Greeks, Anselm recognized clearly the limits of argumentation based exclusively on the text of scripture: the fact that something is not explicitly stated in scripture does not mean that one cannot state such a thing is true, that one cannot make such a statement with certitude. It is possible to deduce some truths which scripture does not contain formally[72] on the following conditions: we can admit a new statement deduced from an explicit statement of scripture—for instance the 'Filioque'—if it is in logical harmony with the texts on the one hand, and on the other hand if this new statement is not in contradiction with any other text of scripture. There is therefore a double rule which has to guide us in explicating scripture, one positive and the other negative. One might be tempted to apply these rules, for instance, to the question of the ordination of women. There is, in fact, no one text of scripture which would propose such a practice, no one text

71. *De libertate arbitrii*, add. T (Schmitt, I, p. 226).

72. In his letter to Bishop Fulco of Beauvais Anselm states also that we have to believe not only all that the Creed contains but also all that follows from the Creed: 'quicumque vult salvus esse, ante omnia opus est *ut teneat catholicam fidem, et ea quae sequuntur*'. (*Ep.* 136, Schmitt, III, p. 280:20). In Anselm's mind there are also truths which are not contained 'explicitly' in the 'fides catholica' but which follow from it. Anselm admits that not all the truth of faith is explicit, but there are also implicit truths which the Christian equally has to 'believe in his heart and profess by his mouth' ('corde credo et ore confiteor').

which would be in 'harmony' with this practice. On the other hand, all texts speaking of the selection of the Apostles and the disciples by Jesus concern only men. Is it then possible to deduce the validity (or 'necessity'?) of the ordination of women from any other text in such a way that it be in harmony with other statements of scripture and not in contradiction with any other scriptural text?

We can say also that the problem of textual interpretation explained in all its force in Abaelard's *Sic et non* [73] was always present in some way in history and Anselm himself could not ignore it. We see also that the controversies of Anselm's time—that with Berengar or later on that with Roscelin—essentially involved problems of textual interpretation stressed especially by the use of dialectic. Because scripture—considered as the highest authority in itself—could not give the solution to all textual problems, it was logical that some people in its interpretation were looking for other means, such as dialectic, to which they granted the highest authority.

Facing these interpretations based on some kind of autonomy, like that of dialectic, Anselm stresses first the importance of some essential virtues—solid faith, a high degree of humility—for those who intend to deal with the problems of the 'sacra pagina'. He even goes so far as to state that people who do not fulfil these moral conditions should be excluded ('sunt exsufflandi') from treating questions of 'sacra pagina'. He shows also—in Roscelin's case—how the autonomous and absolute use of dialectic can lead its masters to grave errors even in their own field so that he calls them 'dialecticae haeretici': heretics of dialectic. The elevation to absolute authority of dialectic instead of scripture produces errors not only in the field of 'sacra pagina' but also of dialectic. And Anselm enumerates a certain number of philosophical errors in Roscelin's nominalism.

We have to stress also another aspect of Anselmian exegesis. Anselm encountered continuously the problem of language as such when speaking of the mysteries of faith. He is aware of the fact already in *Monologion*, that human language is not completely appropriate for expressing these mysteries. Therefore he is obliged to make a distinction between the ordinary way of speaking ('communis usus loquendi') and theological language which is the result of a purification of meaning. Augustine himself had already encountered the linguistic problem in

73. See Peter Abailard, *Sic et non* (B.B. Boyer and R. McKeon; Chicago and London, 1976–77), *Prologus*, pp. 89ff.

speaking of God: he had to eliminate and purify the Aristotelian categorical language as well as the language of participation of the Neoplatonists.[74] Of course, it would be more than an anachronism to speak in Anselm's case of an attempt at 'demythologization' in the Bultmannian sense.[75] Anselm does not touch on the 'donnés' of the Bible, but he does correct human language, that is to say our ordinary way of speaking which is most of the time not able to express correctly the truth hidden in the mysteries.[76]

Epilogue

Let us summarize in a few words what we have seen concerning the problem of authority and reason in Anselm's life and thought. First of all we must notice that for Anselm from the very beginning of his life as a monk the highest authority is faith, the Catholic faith as it is represented and contained in the holy scripture. But on the other hand, faith as the highest authority appeals to reason for its own elucidation ('fides quaerens intellectum'). Paradoxically, one of the results of reason's use for the elucidation of faith is precisely the authentication of reason by faith.

However, everything cannot be solved only by authority and in Anselm's own terms the last word goes to reason. There is therefore a kind of dialectical tension between faith and reason. Anselm himself agrees with the Augustinian view that reason cannot solve the whole

---

74. See C. Viola, '"...*hoc est enim Deo esse, quod est magnum esse*". Approche augustinienne de la grandeur divine', in *ΣΟΦΙΗΣ ΜΑΙΗΤΟΡΕΣ*. *'Chercheurs de sagesse'. Hommage à Jean Pépin* (ed. M.-O. Goulet-Cazé, G. Madec and D. O'Brien; Collection des Etudes Augustiniennes, Série Antiquité, 131; Paris, 1992), pp. 403-20. Augustine himself encountered the problem of the ordinary manner of speaking which did not—or could not—correspond to the reality it was supposed to express: 'Ideo quippe et parva atque exigua iam *communi loquendi usu* modica dicuntur, quia modus in eis aliquis restitit, sine quo non jam modica sed omnino nulla sunt.' See Augustine, *De natura boni*, ch. 21 (*PL* 42, 557).

75. In that sense Briancesco's view seems to me quite alien to Anselm's point of view. See E. Briancesco, 'Le portrait du Christ dans le "Cur Deus Homo": herméneutique et démythologisation', in *Les Mutations socio-culturelles au tournant des XIe-XIIe siècles* (Spicilegium Beccense, II; ed. R. Foreville; Paris, 1984), pp. 631-46.

76. See especially *Monologion* ch. 22.

mystery of faith: 'ampla veritas'[77] cannot be elucidated even by all human generations. Anselm has also a 'faith' in reason: that is why he makes full use of it with such 'élan'. In fact, as Augustine pointed out, authority and reason ('sola ratio') are equally based on a kind of belief. This conception makes possible an understanding of faith ('ratio fidei') and at the same time a limitation of the 'authority' of the reason.

On the other hand, Anselm's 'faith' in reason is finally based on his theology of humanity before the fall. According to him the status of humanity before the fall was that Adam was to follow in everything his 'voluntas rationabilis': 'hominum esset nihil velle sine ratione'. The ideal man is the man who does not want anything without reason. In this context, Anselm identifies even justice and rationality: the man whose will always follows reason is righteous.[78]

Further we must also stress the fact that in his search for truth and reason Anselm appeals to living authorities: he is always consulting others. He recognizes the authority of the Pope in doctrinal matters, as well as asking the Irish bishops to refer to him in doctrinal matters. In other words, for Anselm, the supreme authority of scripture is in a living relationship with the church and its head, the 'Apostolicus'. The Pope is the supreme living critical instance in doctrinal matters, he is the supreme critical instance in interpreting scripture in an orthodox sense. But Anselm is also claiming the 'traditio catholica': according to him in liturgical matters we must follow what the church follows everywhere and for all time. At the same time, he claims also the right of any local church to explain and to explicate texts, even the text of the Creed when it is necessary for its better understanding, but always observing the double criterion: this explication must be in harmony with the rest of the texts and it cannot be in evident contradiction with any other text. We can say that this is the criterion according to Anselm for the evolution of dogmas in the life of the church, and even a local church can take an initiative in this evolution, as we can see in the case of 'Filioque' which was an initiative of the Spanish church. Again, we can see here in close connection and in close collaboration authority and reason: authority (= faith) is explicated by reason, but with the proviso that reason never should contradict faith.

77. *Proslogion*, ch. 14 (Schmitt, I, pp. 111-12); *Cur deus homo, Commendatio operis* (Schmitt, II, p. 40:4-5).
78. *De conceptu virginali*, ch. 10 (Schmitt, II, pp. 151-52); see also the text in n. 6.

Sur quelques aspects annonciateurs de la littérature
sophismatique dans le *De grammatico*

Alain Galonnier

I

Parmi les singularités les plus notables que compte le dialogue entre
maître et disciple *De grammatico*[1] de saint Anselme, enquête sur la
nature catégorielle (substance ou qualité) de l'unité lexicale *grammaticus*,
la moindre n'est sûrement pas celle qui a trait au cheminement de
l'entretien. Le fil conducteur que l'on peut y percevoir d'un bout à
l'autre se suit au travers d'une argumentation volontiers houleuse et
déroutante qui représente, dans la production de son auteur, un cas sans
précédent et une expérience non réitérée. L'image du disciple docile et
passablement en retrait, cultivée dans les autres écrits dialogués
d'Anselme,[2] est ici bousculée au profit d'un *discipulus* presque hardi,
combatif et décidé, allant jusqu'à fixer une clause initiale (1.000 D.3)
destinée à préserver son temps de parole. Dans cette crainte de se voir
interrompre pour être contredit le ton de l'échange est en quelque sorte
donné. En se maintenant ainsi sur ses gardes, l'interlocuteur du *magister*
montre qu'il appréhende certaines manœuvres, et pense que se garantir
la possibilité de mener à terme chacune de ses interventions le mettra
davantage en mesure, d'abord d'être mieux instruit, mais aussi de con-
trer les manipulations dialectiques du maître qu'il craint,[3] non moins que
la volonté qu'il pressent chez lui d'en faire pour ainsi dire la victime de

---

1. Nos références seront données d'après le découpage adopté par D.P. Henry
dans *The De grammatico of Saint Anselm: The Theory of Paronymy* (Oxford:
University of Notre Dame Press, 1964) (ainsi 1.000 D.3 signifiera: troisième intervention du disciple dans la portion textuelle numérotée 1.000).
2. Voir surtout les *De libertate arbitrii*, *De veritate* et *Cur deus homo*.
3. Voir 4.14 D: 'Tu me sembles pour ainsi dire ne pas avoir cure de
m'enseigner, mais seulement de faire obstacle à mes raisonnements'.

jeux de langage.[4] Quelques-unes de ses réactions (par ex. 3.21 D.4) viendront le confirmer. L'atmosphère est donc celle de la joute oratoire,[5] à la finalité assurément formatrice et constructive, mais qui sacrifie également à une sorte de rituel de la dispute dont la technique, quoique répondant à des règles et à une méthode sous-jacentes, excède par trop souvent et de façon déconcertante les réquisits du genre. Dans ces conditions nous ne serons pas étonnés à la divulgation qui est faite du mot-clé de l'opuscule en ce domaine, ni de l'entendre dévoiler par le maître à son partenaire au moyen d'une métaphore: 'le sophisme même qui te trompe sous le manteau de la vraie raison' (3.800 M.1).

La mention de ce terme (*sophisma*) ne doit toutefois pas servir uniquement à illustrer l'aspect souligné au départ. Lui-même engage en vérité sur deux directions, à la fois autonomes et subordonnées entre elles, selon qu'intervient la considération des formes extérieures du dialogue par laquelle nous avons commencée, ou cette autre qui s'attache à ce que la première est susceptible de nous révéler concernant la problématique et les instruments confectionnés pour en traiter. Là, en effet, nous trouvons un comportement par endroits exagérément retors, mais dont on peut s'employer à rendre raison sur un plan historique; ici une réflexion revêtant une panoplie conceptuelle qui annoncerait, par divers côtés la littérature sophismatique et son vocabulaire, telle qu'elle s'édifiera au cours du XIIe siècle, dont il nous paraît opportun d'évaluer la précision et l'ampleur. En d'autres termes, dans l'épaisseur d'un propos mené avec un goût prononcé pour les raisonnements captieux se dégagerait fondamentalement une démarche intellectuelle qui prend le ou les sophismes mis au débat comme matière d'un examen plus systématique et d'une sorte de catégorisation de l'erreur, que l'on verra, dès le siècle suivant, se constituer doctrinalement à partir de nouveaux matériaux textuels. Nous touchons peut-être ici à la difficulté majeure du dialogue sur *grammaticus*, et probablement à ce qui détourne souvent de lui l'intérêt que manquent d'attacher à ses pages la plupart des historiens de la logique médiévale: le fond s'y dilue dans la forme. Anselme

---

4.   Voir 3.21 D.3: 'Je ne puis dire que (cela) ne s'ensuive pas de (mes) concessions, encore que je craigne fort (ce) à quoi je te soupçonne de tendre'.

5.   Voir sur ce sujet A. Cantin, 'Sur quelques aspects des disputes publiques au XIe siècle latin', dans *Mélanges E.-R. Labande, Etudes de civilisation médiévale (IXe-XIIe s.)* (Poitiers, 1974), pp. 89-104; et *Les Sciences séculières et la foi. Les deux voies de la science au jugement de Pierre Damien (1007–1072)* (Spoleto: Centro Italiano di Studi sull'Alto Medioevo, 1975).

met trop en scène, pour des raisons que nous allons tenter de cerner, ce qu'en la matière la rigueur des siècles postérieurs dépouillera de tout apprêt littéraire. Voilà pourquoi mieux apprécier la dispute du *De grammatico* au plan défini passe d'abord par la caractérisation de ceux qui la pratiquent.

Nous avons dit que la lecture du traité accentue progressivement un certain clivage entre les deux intervenants et contourne de plus en plus précisément le profil de chacun. Il y faut à peine la dénonciation du *sophisma* pour confirmer l'impression très tôt ressentie que la manipulation qui se met en place mêle un processus didactique à l'application de préceptes de dispute passablement marqués par l'argutie. Constamment renvoyé de l'un à l'autre registre, l'exégète ne sait pas toujours faire le départ entre ce qui tient du pur plaisir de la ratiocination et ce que régit une intention éducative. Quelle peut être la justification d'un pareil exercice?

La datation de l'opuscule est en l'occurrence un facteur non négligeable. Il n'est pas égal d'en évaluer la composition aux environs de 1080–1085, éventail présumé pour dater les trois premiers ouvrages anselmiens, comme l'a proposé F.S. Schmitt sur les indications de divers contemporains[6], ou de le situer vers 1060–1063, ainsi que l'a récemment fait R.W. Southern en fonction de critères plus intrinsèques.[7] D'après la seconde hypothèse, saint Anselme aurait pu rédiger l'opuscule alors qu'il était l'assistant de Lanfranc à l'école du Bec. Cela permet en effet de rendre compte en partie de la question soulevée, de l'idéal formateur de son traitement et de sa désignation globale comme 'introduction à la dialectique'.[8] La conjecture seule ne suffit pourtant pas à justifier l'échange sous l'angle qui nous intéresse, celui d'une procédure inhabituellement trompeuse où prédomine la volonté d'initier et d'aguerrir. Il est besoin d'une autre présomption, qui du reste

6. Voir 'Zur Chronologie der Werke des hl. Anselm von Canterbury', *Revue bénédictine* 44 (1932), pp. 322-50.

7. Voir *Saint Anselm: A Portrait in a Landscape* (Cambridge: Cambridge University Press, 1990), pp. 62-65.

8. Cette dernière appréciation a, semble-t-il, prévalu très tôt, puisque déjà Eadmer écrit à propos de notre dialogue: 'In quo cum discipulo quem secum disputantem introducit disputans, cum multas quaestiones dialecticas proponit et solvit, tum qualitas et qualia quomodo sint discrete accipienda exponit et instruit' (*Vita Anselmi*, I, 19), tout comme Sigebert de Gembloux notifiera au même moment, en parlant d'Anselme: '(Scripsit) alium librum introducendis ad dialecticam admodum utilem...' (*Liber de scriptoribus ecclesiasticis*, cap. CLXVIII).

s'accommode au mieux de la précédente. Déjà formulée,[9] elle fait valoir les possibles influences subies par Anselme en Italie du Nord, entre son départ d'Aoste et son passage en Burgondie, voire au-delà. Il aurait pu fréquenter, en ces temps où la montée des arts séculiers enflait les esprits et la griserie du discours conquérant exaltait les passions, ces professionnels du langage boursouflé qu'on surnommait *grammatici*,[10] lesquels, non contents de faire étinceler le discours par le clinquant de la rhétorique cicéronienne, enseignaient à subjuguer l'adversaire et à le tenir sous le joug des raisonnements. Ayant pu voyager parmi les cités de la plaine du Pô dans lesquelles sévissaient tout particulièrement ces curieux 'grammairiens', Anselme dut probablement subir l'ascendant de cette corporation exubérante. Le pli qu'en conservera sa pensée ne s'estompera sans doute jamais; et lorsque, éperdument épris de Dieu, il aura, devant ses élèves, à répondre au fort désir que ceux-ci éprouvent à réduire *a quia* par l'effet coercitif d'une déduction rationnelle bien menée, il se souviendra sans doute de ces techniques nerveuses devenues alors réprouvées: la violence des images,[11] le harcèlement du questionnement et la fourberie quelquefois excessive de sa méthode y trouveraient une explication. Dès lors, si le *De grammatico* est bien une *exercitatio disputandi*[12] issue de l'enseignement dispensé par un jeune et brillant moine féru de *trivium* au cours des toutes premières années de son très long séjour en l'abbaye normande, il ne le serait pas moins d'une expérience peu antérieure, qui lui aurait laissé le goût de la raison téméraire et de la controverse gratuite, en même temps d'ailleurs que le désir d'apporter à ceux qu'il enseigne les rudiments d'une *ars dialectica* aux ressources fascinantes et nécessaires. Autant de contrastes que reflètent les personnages du *De grammatico*. Ce n'est aucunement un hasard si l'on peut en trouver une spécification générale dans la définition du *sophisma* rapportée par saint Augustin en son *De doctrina christiana*:

9. Voir A. Galonnier, *L'Œuvre de S. Anselme de Cantorbéry*, II, *Introduction* (Paris: Cerf, 1986), pp. 26-34.

10. Voir *supra* n. 5 et *Pierre Damien: Lettre sur la toute-puissance divine* (Sources Chrétiennes, 191; Paris: Cerf, 1971), *Introduction*.

11. Les échanges sont d'emblée frappés du sceau de la contradiction ('contradicere') (1.000 D.3 + 4.2413 D.1 et 4.72 D.3); on y réfute en mettant en pièce ('frangere') (4.14 D.), en étouffant ('obruere') (3.6313) et en répudiant ('repudiare') (4.230), alors que se dressent ('obstruere') (4.14 D.) les obstacles et s'abat ('destruere') (1.21, 4.140, 4.83) l'erreur.

12. L'expression fait partie des derniers mots (4.14 D.) du dialogue (4.83 M.); v. aussi *De veritate, Praefatio* (Schmitt, I, p. 173:6).

Disputationis disciplina ad omnia genera quaestionum quae in litteris sanctis sunt, penetranda et dissolvenda plurimum valet. Tantum ibi cavenda est libido rixandi et puerilis quedam ostentatio decipiendi adversarium. Sunt enim multa quae appellantur sophismata, falsae conclusiones rationum et plerumque ita veras imitantes, ut non solum tardos, sed ingeniosos etiam minus diligenter attendos decipiant. Proposuit enim quidam, dicens ei cum quo loquebatur. Quod ego sum, tu non es. At ille consentit: Verum enim erat ex parte, vel eo ipso quod iste insidiosus, ille simplex erat. Tunc iste addidit: Ego autem homo sum... Quanquam etiam sermo non captiosus, sed tamen abundantius quam gravitatem decet, verborum ornamenta consectans, sophisticus dicitur (II, 117-118; CSEL, 80, p. 67: 12-29).

Les deux comportements qui nous intéressent apparaissent relativement bien rendus par les adjectifs *iste insidiosus–ille simplex*. Le maître insinue l'élément fallacieux dont il n'instruit son disciple qu'assez tard, lequel fait preuve de naïveté en prenant le discours au premier degré et en consentant ('consentire') ce que l'autre propose ('proponere'), sans soupçonner au début d'artifice. Quant à la passion de la lutte ('libido rixandi') et au spectacle qu'engendre l'abus de l'autre ('ostentatio decipiendi'), ce serait peu dire qu'ils forcent au constat.

L'instrument de prédilection de cette parade, qu'en l'occurrence Augustin ne mentionne pas, reste bien sûr le syllogisme. Structure ternaire où la pensée trouve rapidement son expression la plus contraignante, le schéma syllogistique était qualifié à peu près à la même époque d'*inevitabile*.[13] Il sert ici, comme tel, l'exécution d'un programme logique en un sens spécifiquement aristotélicien, qui conduit à découvrir et à juger au moyen de la définition, de la division et de la déduction. Anselme le connaît, notamment par le Boèce du *In topica Ciceronis*,[14] et sait que d'un même point de vue l'art, dénommé ailleurs *sillogizare*, de confectionner des syllogismes, lorsqu'il s'exerce sur une question soumise au préalable en utilisant des arguments probables et vraisemblables, s'appelle dialectique. Mais il n'ignore pas non plus que lorsque le processus logique use d'argumentations évidemment fausses ou de raisonnements apparemment déductifs, il se nomme sophistique. La vingtaine de syllogismes qui entre dans la composition du *De grammatico* n'achemine le disciple vers une conclusion qu'au prix de

---

13. Voir Papias de Pavie, *Elementarium doctrinae rudimentum* (Venetiis, 1474 et 1491), *ad verbo*.

14. *Liber* I, § 2: 6 dans *M. Tullii Ciceronis Opera. V.1. Scholiastae* (ed. C. Orelli et I.G. Baiter; I, Turici: Typis Orellii, Fuesslini et Sociorum, 1833), p. 274: 10 *sqq*.

nombreuses transformations de schémas, dont beaucoup ont délibérément une formulation erronée de facture variable, qui fait rebondir d'un raisonnement à l'autre. Par ce cheminement tortueux, le maître amène son interlocuteur à résorber la *deceptio* qui l'obnubile et à réduire la *fallacia* qui le trompe ('fallere'), celle-là même qu'il a suscitée et modelée avec sa complicité passive, le maintenant délibérément dans une certaine errance jusqu'à ce que, informé par étape, il demande à être éclairé. C'est un tel vocabulaire, auquel appartient également le substantif *sophisma*, qui, nous l'avions laissé entendre, couvre bien davantage qu'un art de l'argumentation victorieuse à dimension pédagogique. Il anticiperait, avec un demi-siècle d'avance au moins, et beaucoup plus qu'allusivement comme nous allons le voir, sur une problématique nouvelle, dans la mesure où l'éclosion de celle-ci fut majoritairement liée à la réapparition d'un texte perdu d'Aristote.

II

La redécouverte des écrits aristotéliciens indisponibles pour la *logica vetus* qui eut lieu vers 1130 à Paris,[15] divulgua entre autres les *Réfutations sophistiques* dans la traduction de Boèce. Cet accès direct à l'ouvrage du Stagirite équivalait en réalité, non point à une révélation mais à la mise à disposition d'un traité dont on possédait et le titre et l'orientation générale. Car dans le commentaire majeur au *Peri hermeneias*,[16] pièce maîtresse de l'ancienne logique, le même Boèce, non seulement fait référence, à propos de l'opposition entre affirmation et négation et des subtilités qu'elle entraîne chez Aristote (voir 17a 34-37), aux *Sophistici Elenchi*, mais profite plus loin, au sujet de la contrariété des propositions (voir 23b 8-14), d'allusions à l'erreur (ἀπάτη), pour présenter extensivement, par le biais précisément de réflexions sur la *fallacia* (ἀπάτη aussi), les processus d'engendrement

---

15. Voir L.M. De Rijk, *Logica Modernorum* (3 vols.; Assen: Van Gorcum, 1962, 1967), I, p. 24; détails dans B.G. Dod, 'Aristoteles Latinus', dans *The Cambridge History of Later Medieval Philosophy* (ed. N. Kretzmann, A. Kenny et J. Pinborg; Cambridge: Cambridge University Press, 1982), pp. 45-79; et C.H. Lohr, 'The Medieval Interpretation of Aristotle', dans Kretzmann *et al.* (eds.), *The Cambridge History of Later Medieval Philosophy*, pp. 80-98.

16. Ed. C. Meiser, *Commentarii in librum Aristotelis ΠΕΡΙ ΕΡΜΗΝΕΙΑΣ. Pars posterior secundam editionem et indices continens* (Lipsiae: Teubner, 1880); ici II, 6, pp. 132: 9 et 134: 4-5.

des formulations erronées effleurés par Aristote.[17] Il n'est pas sans
intérêt de souligner, à l'occasion de ce dernier aperçu, que l'équivalence
fallacia = ἀπάτη, à laquelle recourt Boèce surtout en ses développements sur 23b 8-14, et qui se maintiendra dans sa version des
Réfutations,[18] fait apparaître que le vocable *deceptio* lui est inconnu, du
moins en contexte logique. Le substantif ne suppléera ἀπάτη que dans
la traduction des mêmes *Réfutations* par Jacques de Venise puis dans
celle du *Perihermeneias* par Guillaume de Moerbeke, un grand siècle
plus tard.[19] En d'autres pages il eut sans doute été indiqué de s'arrêter à
cette disparité de vocabulaire, qui prive déjà l'utilisation du terme
deceptio par Anselme des précédents attendus. Au cours des premières
gloses donc (sur 17a 34-37), la *fallacia* est décrite comme ce qui donne
consistance à une contradiction (*contradictio*) apparente car factice, concernant un sujet et un prédicat identiques dans deux énoncés et jouant
sur l'opposition (*oppositio*) d'une proposition affirmative (*adfirmatio*) et
d'une proposition négative (*negatio*), dont la résolution dépend de la
considération différente de l'étendue sémantique d'un même mot: on la
dira successivement selon l'équivocité, l'univocité, la partie, la *relatio*, le
temps et le mode. Comparativement aux treize vices (à savoir six *in
dictione* [selon l'équivocité, l'amphibolie, la composition, la division,
l'accentuation et la *figura dictionis*] et sept *extra dictionem* [selon
l'accident, *quid et simpliciter*, l'ignorance de la réfutation, la conséquence, la pétition de principe, la considération d'une cause pour une
non-cause et la réunion d'une pluralité de questions sous une seule])
qu'Aristote envisage dans ses *Réfutations* (165b 24-27 et 166b 20-27
pour leur énumération), il semblerait que Boèce ait alors procédé à
une sorte d'échantillonnage, mais sans justification d'élaboration ni
d'objectif. La recherche d'une compatibilité entre ces deux listes a stim-
ulé les glossateurs dès le XIIe siècle. Ainsi, quelques-uns y ont vu une
correspondance avec certains des six modes *in dictione*, d'autres les ont
rangé sous la catégorie *extra dictionem* de l'*ignorantia elenchi*, tandis

17. VI: 14 dans Meiser, *Commentarii*, pp. 473-78.
18. Il convient de noter que sa monographie *Introductio ad syllogismos categori-
cos*, bien que relevant aussi de la *logica vetus* et s'intéressant pareillement à ces
raisonnements ambigus, certes selon une répartition légèrement différente puisqu'on
n'y retrouve pas l'univocité, n'emploie point le terme *fallacia* ; voir De Rijk, *Logica
Modernorum*, I, pp. 39-42.
19. Voir les *Indices* dans *Aristoteles latinus* II. 1-2, Bruges-Paris, 1965 et VI. 1-
3, Leiden-Bruxelles, 1975.

qu'Abélard les a réparti dans leur majorité entre ce qu'il appelle le *secundum locutionem* et l'*extra locutionem*[20]. Toujours est-il que la classification boécienne n'est sans doute pas totalement réductible au panorama complet d'Aristote, sous la réserve que son auteur ne l'eut point souhaitée simplement complémentaire, par conséquent sans projeter de suppléer le tout de l'instrumentation aristotélicienne. Et si des recoupements par conversions de schémas restent possibles, les moyens d'exécuter de tels transferts ne sont nullement donnés. Malgré ce, l'examen des critères que sont la dénomination, le montage, l'exemplification et la résolution de chaque *fallacia*, nous fait incliner, eu égard au collationnement des *Réfutations*, et sans que l'on puisse présentement le justifier, vers une volonté d'en illustrer en définitive que des formes *in dictione*, autrement dit comportant et démasquant un vice axé non point tout entier sur le construction de l'expression mais plus spécifiquement sur ses composantes. Dans quelles proportions ce balisage regarde-t-il notre propos?

On sait que la résurgence des *Sophistici Elenchi* suscita un genre littéraire propre, qualifié de sophismatique, possédant un programme (typer et classer les abus du discours au moyen des *fallaciae* et *sophismata*) et répondant à une finalité (construire une logique de la langue naturelle par la détermination systématique et l'analyse de ses modèles déductifs), qui contribuèrent à engendrer notamment la théorie de la supposition et la logique terministe.[21] Ce faisant, les penseurs qui bénéficièrent de la *logica nova*, sans délaisser l'aperçu relativement original de Boèce sur la *fallacia*, le complétèrent et le diversifièrent au moyen du riche outillage des *Réfutations*. Or Anselme, qui ne pouvait se permettre un tel élargissement, a cependant déroulé, dans le *De grammatico*, une pensée et une méthode aux affinités insoupçonnées avec les orientations définies, que ne parviendraient à justifier à eux seuls ni l'apport du Boèce de la *logica vetus*, ni le capital de cette dernière dans son ensemble. Car, sans même connaître encore le détail de l'analyse anselmienne, il se laisse deviner dès à présent, eu égard aux quelques indices dont nous disposons, que le commentaire second au *Peri*

---

20. Voir De Rijk, *Logica Modernorum*, I, pp. 44-126, 287, 378-79, 533-34. Sur les sources possibles de Boèce en ce passage voir De Rijk, *ibid.*, pp. 28-39.

21. Voir dans Kretzmann *et al.* (eds.), *The Cambridge History of Later Medieval Philosophy*, P.V. Spade, 'The Semantics of Terms', pp. 188-96; G. Neuchelmans, 'The Semantics of Propositions', pp. 197-210; N. Kretzmann, 'Syncategoremata, exponibilia,sophismata', pp. 211-45.

hermeneias offre une caractérisation terminologique et conceptuelle qui ne serait pas toujours suffisante pour étendre l'incidence à toute la mobilisation argumentative de l'opuscule sur *grammaticus*. A défaut d'espérer démontrer, en cette contribution, qu'il n'est pas exclu que son éventail de pseudo-réfutations ait été déficitaire pour qu'Anselme put y prélever celle qu'il choisit d'illustrer, on se bornera à rassembler quelques éléments d'enquête dans l'espoir de manifester la légitimité de celle-ci.

Nous commencerons par nous demander s'il existe une différence entre *fallacia* et *sophisma* qui permette de mieux cerner la première telle qu'Anselme la représente? Certains textes ne semblent en observer aucune. On trouve ainsi, comme dans le MS de Nuremberg intitulé *Excerpta Norimbergensia* (c. 1150), l'énumération des six genres de *sophismata*[22] là où Boèce parle de six cas de *fallaciae*.[23] Parfois s'établit une distinction au plan d'un découpage dans l'élaboration de la tromperie, la *fallacia* étant perçue comme la cause du *sophisma*.[24] Le *De grammatico* irait dans le sens de cette dernière nuance. Car la *fallacia*—une seule probablement, mais dédoublée—que met en scène l'opuscule, très étirée par la dispute, est introduite à point nommé par le maître pour accentuer à la fois la réfutation et l'enseignement de son disciple. L'intention nous paraît particulièrement claire si l'on s'en tient à la notion de *deceptio* qui surgit très tôt (3.234 D.); elle entrera au XIIe siècle dans la définition de la *fallacia* et du *sophisma*. Parmi les formules canoniques d'identification de la *fallacia* on rencontre effectivement celle-ci:

non provenit et est deceptio ex eo quod...[25]

Voici comment la *Dialectica Monacensis* définit la *fallacia*:

22. Voir De Rijk, *Logica Modernorum*, II, pp. 120-22.

23. La même indistinction touche *paralogismi* et *fallaciae*; voir la *Summa sophisticorum elencorum* (s. XII ex.) dans De Rijk, *Logica Modernorum*, I, pp. 287: 3-11 et le *Tractatus Anagnini* (c. 1200), dans De Rijk, *Logica Modernorum*, II, p. 328.

24. Voir *Dialectica Monacensis* (s. XII²), dans De Rijk, *Logica Modernorum*, II, p. 557: 4-5. Ph. Boehner, *Medieval Logic: An Outline of its Development from 1250-c. 1400* (Manchester: Manchester University Press, 1952), p. 8, marque davantage le clivage.

25. *Fallacie Parvipontane* (s. XII²), dans De Rijk, *Logica Modernorum*, I, p. 559: 17 *et passim* pour des formules similaires. Pour le *sophisma*, voir par exemple les *Excerpta Norimbergensia*, dans De Rijk, *Logica Modernorum*, II, p. 130: 25.

Fallacia... dicitur secundum quod est deceptio generata in anima et hoc propter inpotentiam iudicandi quid unum quid multa, quid idem quid diversum.[26]

Une comparaison avec le passage du *De grammatico* renfermant la première occurrence de la *deceptio* ne manque pas d'être instructive:

Ostende... in quo et hic et ibi tanta sit deceptio, ut cum et verae propositiones et secundum naturam syllogismorum conexae videntur, nulla tamen eorum conclusiones veritas tueatur (3.234 D.).

La *fallacia* est, selon la *Dialectica*, génératrice de *deceptio*, laquelle provoque une impuissance à juger et un égarement de l'esprit; or nous constatons que dans le *De grammatico* la *deceptio* est pareillement la résultante de l'introduction d'une *fallacia*, même si cette dernière, par pédagogie, ne sera nommée qu'en second (3. 320), et que l'abus génère une espèce d'aveuglement. Elle affecte une suite d'énoncés syllogistiques dont elle confisque en quelque sorte la pertinence, comme l'expriment notamment les *Fallaciae Londinenses*, un autre MS du premier tiers du XIIe siècle, en disant:

fallatia est *id quod verum sillogismum vel elencum obnubilat.*[27]

Dans cette notation se retrouve sensiblement la situation du disciple qui ignore où se tient le syllogisme vrai, neutralisé par la manipulation, et ne sait comment réfuter celui qui l'égare. L'obnubilation et l'incertitude traduisent approximativement les effets de la *deceptio*, lorsque celle-ci est traitée comme état psychologique de l'erreur.

Nous savons que son apparition précède de peu celle de la *fallacia*: 'adverto eius fallaciam' (3.320). Faux aperçu en réalité de la part du disciple, puisque le troisième élément—*sophisma*—intervient un peu plus loin, associé à la *fallacia* dans une métaphore vestimentaire déjà citée:

utile... tibi erit, cum ipsum sophisma quod te sub pallio verae rationis fallit, in sua fallacia nudum conspicies (3.800 M.1).

Le sophisme est un raisonnement qui trompe ('fallere'); il semblerait se distinguer ici d'un autre sophisme par sa *fallacia* qui en type l'erreur. Mettre à nu la *fallacia* ce serait déjà réfuter le sophisme, de la même façon qu'identifier la *deceptio* ce serait reconnaître la *fallacia*. Pour répondre à l'image du vêtement, nous dirons que la *fallacia* est l'habillage d'une *deceptio*, tout comme du reste le *sophisma* est l'habillage

---

26. Voir De Rijk, *Logica Modernorum*, II, p. 558: 28-31.
27. Voir De Rijk, *Logica Modernorum*, II, p. 647: 5-6.

d'une *fallacia*. La difficulté que nous avons à déterminer chaque opération ne s'estompera en rien au XIIe siècle; il pourrait être tentant, en ce qui concerne le *De grammatico*, de la mettre au compte de cette terminologie flottante dont parle Jan Pinborg[28]—si ce n'était risquer d'oublier que les règles du dialogue et de l'échange animé expliqueraient peut-être ce flottement.

La *fallacia* qui sert de support au traité anselmien est entièrement actualisée au cours des dix premiers chapitres. Les sections centrales XI–XII, où se trouve présenté, en réponse à l'hésitation primitive, l'énoncé-pivot de tout le dialogue (4.232), n'en sont que le prolongement et l'aboutissement, tandis que les chapitres XIII–XXI précisent et approfondissent ce résultat. La *fallacia* est agencée dans une suite de transformations syllogistiques, ayant pour point de départ un schéma catégorique classique de la première figure du premier mode, formé par le disciple en vue de la réfutation qu'il va se risquer à mener:

$$
\begin{array}{ll}
& \text{omnis grammaticus homo est} \\
S.1 & \text{(at) omnis homo substantia (est)} \\
& \text{(omnis igitur) grammaticus substantia est. (1.101–1.12).}
\end{array}
$$

Si Anselme avait composé un ouvrage intitulé *De fallaciis*, loin des circonvolutions dialectiques destinées à rendre le dialogue vivant et instructif, la réfutation eut été directe et abrupte, à l'image de celles qu'auraient pu confectionner les penseurs de la *logica moderna* selon des paradigmes préétablis d'invalidation. La *Summa sophisticorum elencorum* s'y emploie pour un autre paralogisme de confection semblable:

$$
\begin{array}{ll}
& \text{Socrates est homo} \\
S.2 & \text{sed homo est species} \\
& \text{ergo Socrates est species.}^{29}
\end{array}
$$

A propos de ce dernier précisément elle fait état d'une sorte de controverse touchant l'identification et la résolution dudit sophisme. En effet, dans le cadre d'une querelle se déroulant à peu près à cette époque entre *Magister Iacobus* (probablement Jacques de Venise) et *Magister Albericus* (peut-être Albéric du Mont), deux maîtres souvent opposés,

---

28. 'On ne sait pas encore très bien si Anselme a eu une influence sur la formation de la logique médiévale. En tout cas, il a abordé les problèmes de la même façon que les logiciens ultérieurs; mais sa terminologie diffère un peu des auteurs postérieurs et n'est pas encore technique'; J. Pinborg, *Logik und Semantik im Mittelalter. Ein Ueberblick* (Stuttgart: Frommann-Holzboog, 1972), p. 44.

29. De Rijk, *Logica Modernorum*, I, pp. 357: 17-19.

on l'identifiait comme étant soit *secundum accidens* (Iacobus), soit *secundum equivocationem* (Albericus). Voici les arguments de chacun tels que les rapporte la *Summa*, qui montrent l'irréductibilité de solutions voulues non cumulables par les controversistes:

> Sophisma est secundum accidens secundum illum (i.e. Magistrum Iacobum), quia 'homo' in prima propositione significat illam speciem coniunctam illi individuo, scilicet Socrati; sed postea, cum dico: 'homo est species', significat illam speciem non ut iunctam alicui individuo, sed seorsum vel separatim. Et sic dicit quia in omnibus huiusmodi fit sophisma secundum accidens.
>
> Magister Albericus vero dicit quod non secundum accidens, sed secundum equivocationem in his paralogismis fit sophisma (...) quia in prima propositione 'homo' appellat *homines*, sed in secundo appellat *illam speciem*; ergo cum in utraque propositione diversa appellat, secundum equivocationem est ibi sophisma, et non secundum accidens.[30]

S'il ne paraît point d'emblée abusif, sur la seule base d'une parenté schématique, d'amorcer un parallèle, celui-ci doit avoir à charge de marquer si l'évolution de *S.1* peut se mesurer, au cours du premier bloc argumentatif qui occupe les chapitres I à VII, à l'aune d'un sophisme contenant et répercutant soit une *fallacia* dite *secundum equivocationem*, à savoir *maior* ou *in dictione*, soit une *fallacia* dite *secundum accidens*, à savoir *minor* ou *extra dictionem*. L'intérêt d'une telle vérification tient au fait qu'elle serait susceptible de mettre à l'épreuve notre souci exégétique envers le *De grammatico* qui est, redisons-le, de chercher à identifier en creux de la démarche d'Anselme une structure conceptuelle et dialectique possiblement d'avant-garde, que lui-même n'élucide pas. Cela devient ici réalisable comparativement aux deux *solutiones* rapprochées par la *Summa*, dont l'aboutement facilite la mise en balance. Effectivement, la première énumérée, quoique coïncidants, à plus d'un titre, avec l'un au moins des six modes évoqués par Boèce dans son commentaire majeur du *Peri hermeneias*,[31] n'apparaît point opérer au premier degré, ne serait-ce que dans ses contours, parmi les méandres des raisonnements anselmiens, dans la mesure où elle ne fait affleurer qu'une distorsion d'appellation. En revanche, la seconde, que l'on aurait moins d'aisance à faire émerger de l'une des formes boéciennes, notamment parce qu'elle découvre un déséquilibre de

---

30. De Rijk, *Logica Modernorum*, I, pp. 357: 20-358:4.
31. Voir *supra*, p. 214.

signification,[32] semble bien mieux correspondre au traitement choisi par Anselme. Mais nous avons au préalable à nous souvenir de deux circonstances. D'abord que la classification boécienne n'a pas permis une identification stable de ses *fallaciae*; ensuite, et afin de ne pas attendre du *De grammatico* ce qu'il n'est pas en mesure de nous fournir, que s'il y a bien représentation répétée d'une même *fallacia* dans un *sophisma* Anselme ne procède pas à son égard aussi techniquement qu'on le fera après lui, parce qu'il a conçu un authentique dialogue et non un catalogue des raisonnements vicieux et de leurs *solutiones*. C'est pourquoi, dans ce qui serait précisément l'adaptation d'une *solutio*, la *deceptio* ne survient (3.234 D.) qu'au moment précis où le disciple, après avoir créé le syllogisme ci-après pour réfuter la majeure de *S.1*:

S.3   nullus grammaticus potest intelligi sine grammatica
        (at) omnis homo potest intelligi sine grammatica (3.101–3.102),

infère, à partir de ces prémisses: 'nullus homo animal est'. Il y parvient à l'issue d'une série de modifications au cours desquelles le terme 'animal' est substitué à 'grammaticus', dans l'intention de rendre le sophisme inopérant par flagrance (*cf.* 3.800 M.2) et d'accentuer l'absurdité de la conclusion, irrecevable—et de là naît le soupçon—quoique déduite de prémisses (voir 3.324 *in fine*) données pour définitivement vraies et sans faux pas de combinaison (3.221-3.222; 3.231-3.232). Or, cette présomption de vice se marque justement par l'intervention de la *fallacia* (3.320), dont la caractérisation coïncide avec l'amorce de sa solution. Les deux propositions de *S.3* sont reprises et ajustées:

        omnis homo potest intelligi homo sine grammatica
S.4   nullus grammaticus potest intelligi grammaticus sine grammatica
        (3.311 D.3–3.312 D.3).

L'absence de terme commun (*terminus communis*) qui est manifestée et dénoncée vient de ce que le sujet s'est trouvé rapporté à lui-même, autrement dit, ainsi que les chapitres V et suivants vont l'expliciter, a été envisagé par rapport à son être, comprenons à sa définition et à son essence. Cet effort de recentrage ontologique est commandé par la nécessité de faire en sorte que le disciple respecte et applique la règle

---

32. Sur l'importance des notions d'*appellatio* et de *significatio* dans le *De grammatico*, voir A. Galonnier, 'Le *De grammatico* et l'origine de la théorie des propriétés des termes', dans *Gilbert de Poitiers et ses contemporains. Aux origines de la* Logica Modernorum (éd. J. Jolivet et A. de Libera; Napoli, 1987), pp. 353-75 et notre *Introduction* à ce même dialogue (voir note 9), pp. 35-42.

édictée en 3.33, touchant la primauté du contenu signifiant (*sententia*) sur l'énonciation (*prolatio*) dans la confection des syllogismes. Or, en isolant le nerf de l'argumentation, on reconnaîtra dans l'objectif du *magister* une application à faire admettre qu'il est accidentel ou non essentiel à l'homme d'être grammairien tout comme il est accidentel au grammairien d'être un homme. En sorte que ce n'est point tout homme qui peut être compris grammairien sans la grammaire mais l'homme en tant qu'homme, puisque l'homme en tant que grammairien ne le peut (voir 3.6334), et ce n'est pas tout grammairien qui ne peut être compris homme sans la grammaire mais le grammairien en tant que grammairien, puisque le grammairien en tant qu'homme le peut (voir 3.6333). La procédure gagne pour nous en importance lorsqu'on effectue un recoupement avec les explications de *Magister Iacobus* consignées dans la *Summa*, où il devient possible de remplacer en *S.1* 'species' par 'substantia' et 'Socrates' par 'grammaticus' pour obtenir un raisonnement applicable à notre dialogue: le *seorsum vel separatim* oriente tout à fait vers l'ajustement en question.

Mais il y a plus pour donner à penser qu'Anselme a ici organisé son enseignement dans la ligne argumentative d'un paralogisme *secundum accidens*. On peut le vérifier en prenant pour référence la distinction tripartite que font les *Glose in Aristotelis Sophisticos elencos* (c. 1140) sur ce type de sophisme, dont elles désignent le troisième mode[33] comme étant 'secundum hoc quod convenit ex alio et non per se'. Qu'il s'agisse de *S.1* ou de sa transformation en cette première séquence de texte, il n'est pas faux de dire, croyons-nous, que le maître du *De grammatico* cherche à montrer d'une part que 'grammaticus' convient *ex alio* à 'homo' dans la majeure, de l'autre que 'substantia' lui convient *per se* dans la mineure, soit que 'grammatica' convient *ex alio* à 'homo' mais *per se* à 'grammaticus'. L'attrait de ce rapprochement tient de surcroît à ce que, par anticipation, le couple *ex alio–per se* des *Glose* rejoint, au plan tant lexical que doctrinal, les *per se–per aliud* de l'opuscule anselmien, constitutifs de la réponse proposée à l'alternative primitive: 'grammairien' signifie 'grammaire' *per se* et 'homme' *per aliud* (4.232). N'ayant point l'occasion de nous arrêter à ces deux foncteurs, on notera qu'ils concrétisent au mieux, eu égard à leurs variantes ultérieures, le balancement de point de vue que fonde une notion de dualité prédominante dans la littérature sophismatique, car c'est précisément elle qui conduit à changer la prédication selon que l'on considère le sujet en

33. Voir De Rijk, *Logica Modernorum*, I, p. 214: 16-17.

lui-même, c'est-à-dire définitionnellement ou en son essence, ou bien en fonction de ses accidents.

Néanmoins, l'existence même de la querelle entre les *magistri Iacobus* et *Albericus* met en lumière la bivalence du syllogisme concerné et par conséquent celle de sa résolution. Se vérifie-t-elle dans le cas du paralogisme *S.1* construit par le disciple du *De grammatico* et, pour mener à son terme notre conjecture, serait-il permis de dire, dans ces conditions, que l'enseignement réfutatoire du maître pourrait dépendre, tout autant et de façon plus usuelle, d'une *fallacia* de la classe *secundum equivocationem?* Au premier des trois modes de celle-ci, c'est-à-dire lorsqu'un nom quelconque signifie principalement de plusieurs manières, comme 'canis' signifie à la fois une constellation, un animal aboyant et un poisson, la même *Summa sophisticorum elencorum* assemble un syllogisme tout proche de celui d'où nous sommes partis:

	Omne gramaticum est homo
S.5	sed omnis anima est gramatica
	igitur omnis anima est homo.

La *solutio* avancée précise aussitôt:

> Equivocatio est in hoc nomine '*gramaticum*'. Dicitur enim '*gramaticum*' idest: *habens exercitium gramatice*, et hoc convenit homini tantum. Dicitur etiam '*gramaticum*', idest: *habens scientiam gramatice* ; et hoc convenit anime.[34]

Ne nous laissons point entraîner à l'extrapolation par l'intérêt de définitions similaires de 'grammairien': *habens exercitium* et *habens scientiam gramatice* pour la *Summa, habens grammaticam* pour le *De grammatico*,[35] d'où 'homme' est pareillement exclu. Le commentateur anonyme entend surtout observer une distinction sur 'gramaticum' qui dénonce deux états sémantiques incompatibles pour un syllogisme concluant, que l'on ne saurait reporter efficacement sur *S. 1*. L'ajustement des propositions en *S.4* donne en effet le sentiment de viser la manifestation d'une non-concluance davantage par un décalage dans la référence ontologique du substantif 'homme' que par stricte homonymie. Dans la majeure de *S.1* 'grammaticus' ne convient qu'à l'homme

---

34. De Rijk, *Logica Modernorum*, I, p. 291: 20-26.

35. Pour être exact: 'habens disciplinam' (4.700 D.1 *in fine*); les deux expressions sont en fait équivalentes, l'une et l'autre illustrant le 'habens qualitatem' (4.700 D.1). 'Habens grammaticam' apparaît en 4.511, mais avec une autre fonction. Le résultat définitif énoncé sur 'albus', signifiant 'habens albedinem' (4.82), est rigoureusement interchangeable avec 'grammaticus'.

grammairien, c'est-à-dire l'homme individué ayant pour qualités les accidents qui font de lui un grammairien, condition accidentelle de son essence, alors que dans la mineure 'substantia' lui convient seulement en tant qu'il est abstrait et séparé de toute individuation dans un sujet concret. Ce n'est point vraiment sur un terme 'homo' ambigu qu'Anselme paraît mettre l'accent, mais sur une disparité prédicative plus structurelle, qu'il rend tangible par *S.4* sur *S.3*, la mise en conformité étant destinée en fait, pensons-nous, à déclencher le même réflexe décisif de vérification par visée de l'essence et abstraction de l'accident.

Pour autant qu'elle se laisse ainsi juger et confronter, l'orientation adoptée par Anselme le rangerait, dans le désaccord choisi à titre comparatif, du côté de *Magister Iacobus*. Il n'est alors pas superflu de noter que le raisonnement captieux connu en toute vraisemblance par les échantillons boéciens (*secundum equivocationem*) et dont l'utilisation éventuelle, de ce fait, n'engendrerait aucune réticence, demeure plutôt incertain dans les déductions du *De grammatico*, tandis que celui plus opératoire (*secundum accidens*), qui, en raison de cet aspect, donne l'impression d'être resté en retrait de la conceptualisation accessible à l'auteur, devient assez nettement repérable. Certes, hormis le fait que la sélection de Boèce pourrait être organisée différemment, nous savons qu'Anselme n'était pas en mesure d'être totalement explicite—ce qui est susceptible de donner à notre enquête une tournure forcée par son obstination même à voir dans la trame des déductions anselmiennes le profil dialectique d'une *fallacia secundum accidens*. Toutefois, il n'est que prématuré et non point abusif de soulever la question afférente à l'embarras que nous rencontrons à vouloir expliquer comment Anselme pouvait connaître la nature d'un sophisme dont le maniement n'aurait pas été à sa portée, attendu que l'on n'est ici qu'à la première phase des développements, c'est-à-dire en chemin d'une argumentation qui va culminer avec la notification du sophisme. Durant une seconde phase en effet (chapitres VIII–X), la démarche intellectuelle va s'affermir et confirmer le recours à un type de *fallacia* théoriquement non disponible, tout en devenant plus précise sur le plan terminologique. Jugeons plutôt.

A la suite de l'application par le *discipulus* (voir 3.320-3.7211), mais avec trop peu de rigueur (voir 3.6320 M.1), de la ligne démonstrative qui lui a été tracée, et de sa nouvelle conclusion: 'nullus grammaticus homo est' (3.7211), le maître porte pour la première fois à la connaissance du disciple la présence d'un *sophisma* au cours d'une intervention capitale que nous avons rapportée (3.800 M.1). En vue de relancer l'échange, il fait intervenir dans son prolongement les notions de *simpliciter* (3.911-3.931) et de *secundum aliquid* (4.131). La façon dont sont convoqués et activés ces deux paramètres, certes mis en correspondance indirecte mais fonctionnant symétriquement dans la déduction, conduit-elle à voir entrer en jeu le type de *fallacia* dit *secundum quid et simpliciter*, c'est-à-dire 'sous un certain aspect et au sens absolu', autre variété d'énoncés ambigus dits *extra dictionem?* La *Dialectica Monacensis*, parmi d'autres MSS, la définit de cette manière:

> est deceptio proveniens ex hoc a parte nostri quod nescimus distinguere inter dictum secundum quid et dictum simpliciter.[36]

D'où l'explicitation suivante:

- *dici secundum quid* est dici cum tali determinatione in qua non salvatur dictum simpliciter nec ex ipso sequitur. Sicut est hic: 'Sor est homo albus secundum pedem'.
- *dici...simpliciter* est dici absque determinatione, ut hic: 'Sor est homo'; vel cum tali determinatione in qua sequitur et in qua salvatur dictum simpliciter. Ut hic: 'Sor est homo albus'.[37]

Le plus souvent la *solutio* d'ensemble de cette *fallacia* notifie l'inférence indue du déterminé au non déterminé:

> Est... fallacia secundum quid et simpliciter *deceptio proveniens ex eo quod aliquid cum determinatione primo proponitur, postea vero idem simpliciter et absque determinatione infertur, vel econverso.*[38]

Forts de cette règle, nous pouvons vérifier que lorsque le *magister* du *De grammatico* interprète la proposition 'nullus grammaticus homo est' (3.7211) en 'nullus grammaticus est simpliciter homo' (3.931), il donne effectivement à comprendre au disciple que l'on peut affirmer 'aucun grammairien n'est un homme' à la condition de ne pas envisager les déterminations du premier terme, soit *simpliciter*. Au contraire, *secundum (ali)quid*, entendons considéré en ses déterminations, 'grammaticus' s'impose comme une substance, puisque non seulement il n'est pas dans un sujet, mais il est espèce et genre, dit *in eo quod quid* et individuel (4.131). D'où l'impossibilité de maintenir l'affirmation qu'aucun grammairien n'est un homme.

Nous retrouvons dans le *simpliciter* tel qu'Anselme le fait intervenir (3.900–3.931) le même critère définitionnel et essentiel que celui précisément à l'œuvre dans la précédente phase de développement, où nous avions trouvé assez précisément une parenté tant de fond que de forme avec le traitement d'une possible *fallacia secundum accidens*. Cette orientation qui se confirme nous incite alors à ne voir dans les différents volets de la démonstration que le maniement d'une seule et même *fallacia*, nommément désignée par les expressions *simpliciter* et *secundum aliquid*, et distillée au gré du discours magistral. Que penser alors de la première orientation que nous avons perçue dans la dispute? Si elle ne participe point d'une exégèse artificielle, il importe que la *fallacia secundum accidens* et la *fallacia secundum quid et simpliciter* se correspondent en quelque manière. En consultant une fois de plus les *Glose* nous trouvons le libellé suivant:

> Dicitur '*secundum accidens*', *idest secundum mutationem proprietatis, ut quando aliquid attribuitur alicui sumpto cum aliqua proprietate et postea attribuitur eidem sumpto simpliciter.*[39]

On se limitera à y remarquer, dans les termes aussi, l'interaction des deux *solutiones*, que hisse à la hauteur d'un principe d'identification l'avertissement de la *Summa sophisticorum elencorum*:

> Sciendum est quod fere ubicumque est sophisma secundum quid et simpliciter, est predicatio secundum accidens.[40]

Voilà qui permettrait dès lors d'embrasser la trajectoire conceptuelle des douze premiers chapitres du *De grammatico*, et par suite de l'ensemble du dialogue. Au cours des sections que nous dirons d'approche (I-VII), *deceptio* et *fallacia* sont dénommées et progressivement instillées dans l'épaisseur de l'entretien par une réflexion centrée sur les modalités de la prédication, dont celle selon l'accident. La progression y est telle que l'on est rapidement conduit à la rapprocher d'une résolution de *fallacia secundum accidens*, qui s'articule, plus que toute autre, autour d'un décalage prédicatif:

> Est… fallacia secundum accidens deceptio proveniens ex alieno predicandi modo cum predicatur aliquid de aliquo, non eo modo quo sumi deberet, et hoc vel per se vel cum alio.[41]

39. De Rijk, *Logica Modernorum*, I, pp. 213: 33-214: 2.
40. De Rijk, *Logica Modernorum*, I, p. 373: 8-9.
41. *Fallacie Parvipontane*, dans De Rijk, *Logica Modernorum*, I, p. 593: 19-21.

Mais il ne s'agit là que de manœuvres de mise en place. Aux chapîtres VIII-X le *sophisma*, assorti de sa *fallacia*, est introduit par désignation (3.800 M.1), puis évolue en deux temps *secundum aliquid* et *simpliciter* (3.911 et 4.131) pour finalement endosser le schéma synonyme. La phase terminale d'exposition (XI-XII) achève de résoudre le paralogisme en divulguant la diade *per se–per aliud*. Celle-ci, il convient de le remarquer, n'annule pas l'alternative de départ (*substantia* ou *qualitas*) mais lui trouve une issue dialectique, qui livre en même temps la *solutio* de toutes les variantes syllogistiques.

III

Telle serait la *fallacia* qui court dans le *De grammatico*, annoncée, travaillée et improuvée tout au long de l'échange dialogué. Confrontés à sa nature approchée, à une analyse somme toute poussée du champ conceptuel qu'elle couvre et au découpage de son ambiguïté d'agencement, ainsi qu'à un vocabulaire déjà bien constitué par rapport à son élaboration prochaine, sans être figé dans des formules invariables, nous nous heurtons inévitablement au problème de savoir comment Anselme, peut-être vers 1060, put disposer de cet horizon spéculatif et le parcourir avec autant d'aisance et de recul. L'exemple du couple *fallacia-deceptio* est à lui seul éloquent. Boèce n'usait que du premier vocable pour traduire le substantif ἀπάτη, donnant l'impression d'ignorer le second, également absent de sa réflexion logique. Anselme, lui, nous l'avons vu, connaît l'un et l'autre termes et sait les contextualiser; mais il aurait déjà intégré, dans sa façon de les manier, une nuance dissociative parfois observée par les penseurs de la *logica nova*, qu'aucune antécédence, à ce que l'on sait, ne normalise entièrement. Et le constat se renouvelle d'ailleurs pour le croisement des deux modèles fallacieux *extra dictionem*, qu'il lui paraît aisé de modeler et de manipuler avec une maîtrise inopinée. Notre hypothèse de lecture est certes encore fragile, mais elle permet en un sens d'élargir la perspective exégétique. Car s'il reste permis de ne s'étonner qu'à demi de l'offensive sophistique conduite par le *magister* et lui trouver quelques justifications historiques, il n'en va point de même, à notre sentiment, pour la matière du traité. Le ferment dont il semble dépositaire déborde les cadres habituels de l'organisation du savoir. Sans doute doit-on s'abstenir de statuer trop tôt sur les divers moments d'anticipation doctrinale que nous y avons aperçus; leur troublante 'modernité' pourrait à la limite aboutir à se demander si le

De grammatico que nous connaissons et abandonnons sans réticence à saint Anselme est bien en définitive celui dont lui-même et ses héritiers nous ont informé.

THE PERFORMATIVE HEART OF ANSELM'S *PROSLOGION*

A.J. Vanderjagt

One of the things that strike the reader of Anselm of Canterbury most is his concise but evocative Latin style, which in its economy of words often seems akin to the best minimal music or poetry. Read correctly and printed on the page as it ought to be, the *Proslogion*, to a large extent, is actually a poem.[1] Deftly and with great feeling Anselm places phrases and texts from the scriptures, mainly the Psalms but also the Gospels and Epistles, on his own music staff thus making a composition that is at once intensely personal and subjective but also philosophically interesting even if it is not convincing for many today.[2] His economy with words, never using more than is strictly necessary, but always in a way that is fascinatingly direct, paradoxically makes reading Anselm extremely difficult.

In this paper, attention will be paid to the use Anselm makes in the *Proslogion* of words and images as religious performatives. The wording in itself of this theme already indicates the central position that a consideration of language will take in my remarks. If we are intent on considering Anselm's use of language, image and reality in connection

---

1. Like Boethius's *Consolatio philosophiae* earlier and Bernard Silvestris's *Cosmographia* later, Anselm's *Proslogion* is a fine specimen both of prosimetrics and prose poetry. Schmitt's standard edition does not show this and neither do most of the modern translations. Sister Benedicta Ward takes account of this aspect of Anselm's style in practice: cf. *The Prayers and Meditations of St Anselm* (trans. B. Ward; Harmondsworth: Penguin, 1973). The poetic sections are ch. 1, the middle of ch. 9, ch. 14, ch. 16 and ch. 26; prosimetrics is practised throughout the work.

2. It is this personal style that often turns philosophers away from Anselm's argumentation. Certainly the so-called 'ontological argument' belongs to the canon of courses in systematic philosophy and theology, but it is unrecognizable as the 'ratio Anselmi' because when it is presented every suggestion of personality has been radically excised from it—hence the treatment of the argument on the basis of excerpts from only a couple of chapters—and it has been completely objectified.

with his rational proof for God's existence, it will be useful first to make some general methodological remarks on ideas about the relation of language to reality in the late twentieth century.

Contemporary debates about language show two main positions,[3] one 'scientistic', the other rhetorical. According to the 'scientistic' approach, language, if used correctly, is said metaphorically to be transparent; it affords us a direct view of sensible reality whether in its ordinary corporeal aspect or the 'insightful' kind. The language user can clear up conceptual muddles by giving thought to the ins and outs of the practice of language. This means that from the outset the language should be grammatically, syntactically and semantically clear, and that any remaining problems should be able to be resolved on a consideration of its truth, correspondence, objectivity, realism and reference. Language is thus seen as an instrument that affords a *description* of the extra-linguistic reality of the senses, whether of the world around us (e.g. the natural sciences and humanistic scholarship) or, in a more complicated way, of the world within us (e.g. psychology). Language here is rather like a picture-window that must be kept bright and clean so as to be able to see the Rocky Mountains through it clearly.

The second position is the rhetorical one, usually associated with the so-called 'linguistic turn'—the idea that language should be regarded as a kind of Kantian, transcendental category that makes knowledge of the world possible. This view has for some time now been connected to the movement of anti-foundationalism—the radicalization by Richard Rorty and many others in his wake of the so-called 'linguistic turn'. The latter holds that it makes little sense to seek a foundation with regard to which language is transparent or descriptive. Language is opaque; it is like the black holes in space; it absorbs our gaze, our looking and even our entire thinking. The frontiers of language here are not only the frontlines of reality; but language itself becomes the world; language, like the black holes, inexorably draws reality into itself. Language's most important task in this view is not to describe; rather, language represents a world of its own that can be examined only on its own terms. It is like a completely self-contained novel or poem that must be interpreted, if at all possible, without reference and certainly without recourse to a real world outside itself.

---

3.   An admirable survey is F. Ankersmit, 'Retorica en geschiedschrijving', in T.A.F. Kuipers (ed.), *Filosofen in actie* (Delft: Eburon, 1992), pp. 37-50; see also his 'Historical Representation', *History and Theory* 27 (1988), pp. 205-29.

In many studies, but especially in those by Marcia Colish and Burcht Pranger, attention has been given to the exacting way in which Anselm uses words such as 'non' and other syncategorematic terms.[4] They have shown that many of Anselm's philosophical discussions and indeed arguments for the central points of Christian doctrine turn on a systematic and *univocal* use of these words that qualify nouns, verbs and statements. This is true for the *Proslogion* and the *Cur deus homo*, but no less for much in *De veritate* or *De casu diaboli*, or the *Meditations* and *Prayers*. Syncategorematic terms are of central, indeed of constitutive, importance for the declarative statements in any sort of descriptive language. Besides, in the use of rhetoric they are often the hinges on which the convincing of an audience turns.

Anselm's meaning-giving procedure in *De veritate* is a case in point for the careful grammatical analysis and astute use of central terms in his argumentation. By defining *veritas*, truth, in its different guises in propositions, acts, the will and reality adverbially in terms of signifying *vere*, *recte* and *iuste*, Anselm can redefine and reduce the *activity* of the meaning-giving process to the function of 'Veritas'. It is through this 'Veritas' that all things exist and through which they receive their being, and, as Anselm says at the end of his discussion, *in* which all things that are true exist. Anselm's definition of the true and truth is thus not nominal but verbal, predicative, that is to say dynamic. 'Veritas' thus becomes the space within which individual 'truths' can exercise their strength with regard to that of which they are the 'truth'. Or, to put it a little differently: if propositions, the will, actions and so on *function correctly* within this space they are said to be 'true'. This entire intellectual process of seeking after meaning would come to a grinding halt if the word-definitions that Anselm employs were to be semantically inconsistent, or if there were to be something wrong with the logical connections of his argumentation. *De veritate* combines the descriptive approach of 'scientific' language, albeit in an adverbial form, with the hortative aspect that is also hidden in the same adverbs.

Now, this strict procedure of Anselm's might seem to preclude the medieval mental imagery which has been so carefully described by

---

4. M.L. Colish, *The Mirror of Language: A Study in the Medieval Theory of Knowledge* (Lincoln: University of Nebraska Press, rev. edn, 1983); M.B. Pranger, *Consequente Theologie: Een studie over het denken van Anselmus van Canterbury* (Assen: Van Gorcum, 1975).

Burcht Pranger.[5] After all, mental imagery at first glance thrives on an abundance of words and evocative colourful phrases. Conducive to this imagery would be rather the work of St Bernard, St Bonaventure, or Nicholas of Cusa, but hardly the conciseness and sparsity if not parsimony of the vocabulary of Anselm.[6]

I would put the point here that it is exactly Anselm's economical procedure—and not so much the content of his argument—that makes his naming and defining of God in the *Proslogion* so cogent, and that makes his demonstration of God's existence so much more 'imaginative' and 'heart-felt' than that in the traditional proofs, such as the cosmological or physico-teleological ones. Paul Ricoeur has pointed out that the theory of metaphor that he has developed offers a new approach to the phenomenon of imagination.[7] I would like to use it in the context of Anselm. Ricoeur tells us that instead of approaching imagination by way of perception and asking if and how we can move from perception to image, his theory of metaphor and metaphorical utterance invites us to relate the imagination to a certain type of language use; more precisely, to see in it an aspect of semantic innovation characteristic of the metaphorical use of language.

The implication of this idea for the study of the *Proslogion* seems immediately clear. Consider for a moment the way traditional Aristotelian or stoical proofs for God's existence proceed. There is first a perception and statement or description of the individual causation of things in the cosmos; the awareness of this causation leads to individual study of causes and effects; this in turn allows for the construction of an unperceptible cause and this then forms the basis for a knowledge of the ultimate cause, that is to say, God. Or at least, Thomas Aquinas states at

5.   See Pranger's paper in this volume: 'Naked Images in Anselm of Canterbury and Bernard of Clairvaux'.

6.   Elsewhere I have pointed out the exacting performative procedure of St Bernard in his sermons on the *Canticle* notwithstanding the richness of his vocabulary: 'Bernard of Clairvaux (1090–1153) and Aelred of Rievaulx (1110–1167) on Kissing', in H. van Dijk *et al.* (eds.), *Media Latinitas* (Turnhout: Brepols, 1994), pp. 339-43.

7.   P. Ricoeur, *La métaphore vive* (Paris: Seuil, 1975), especially 'Métaphore et référence' and his remarks on 'language "tensionnel"' and 'Métaphore et discours philosophique', esp. pp. 380-84, 390ff. Dr Giselle de Nie pointed me in the direction of Ricoeur's important 'Imagination in Discourse and in Action', in A.-T. Tymieniecka (ed.), *The Human Being in Action* (Dordrecht: Reidel, 1978), II, pp. 3-22.

the end of each of the five ways that this it is that people generally call God. Thus it might be said that in this kind of traditional proof, knowledge is based upon an image, which itself is a kind of appendix to the primal perception that there are things in reality and the realization that all things have causes. The person who studies these traditional proofs seriously is well aware of the problem this gives. There is no guarantee that the image that one has of the causal God is 'objective': after all, it is only 'said' to be God. One might ask on whose authority is that equation made?

Ricoeur's theory of metaphor, on the other hand, puts an end to the notion that the image—in the case of the traditional proofs, the image of God—is first and foremost the result of a 'scene' being played out, so to speak, on the stage of a mental theatre for the benefit of an 'internal' spectator. Besides, Ricoeur's analysis means giving up a second assumption, namely that the mental image is a kind of stuff out of which we can construct our abstract ideas and concepts in a kind of mental alchemical process. It is at this level, for example, that the ways of Thomas Aquinas fall apart and lose their cogency. The basic problem in these traditional proofs lies in the fact that they turn on a metaphoric use of a noun, in this case the noun 'causa'. The metaphoric connection between an 'ordinary' cause and the 'Causa', with a capital letter, that is defined as God is seen simply as a 'deviant' use of names or nouns. In other words, as a deviation in denomination. This insight in fact deconstructs the traditional proofs and renders them unconvincing in the final analysis because they cannot pass over from metaphor into reality.

Now, what does this analysis of metaphor mean for Anselm's *Proslogion*? How does metaphor work there? Anselm's procedure involves not a deviation in denomination but a deviant use of predicates in the context of the sentence as a whole. This is to say, as the basis for his demonstration he does not use metaphors based on nouns which in turn are used to describe images drawing on perceptions. Anselm is arguably unique, perhaps with Raymundus Lullus and Nicholas of Cusa, in anchoring his demonstration in predication. It is useful in this context to trade in the traditional concept of metaphor, tied as it is to nomination, for that of Ricoeur's metaphorical utterance.

It is, I think, at this stage of my examination, Anselm's 'discovery' of a discursive strategy which governs the use of unusual predicates that is the heart of his demonstration of God's existence. Thus in 'id quo maius cogitari non potest' it is precisely the syntactical and grammatical

predicative use of 'non potest' and the comparative 'maius' that gives
the proof its flavour and cogency. Anselm is quite aware that he is here
'talking', so to speak, on the thin line between the grammatical construction of the comparative-plus-negation which is not the same as the
superlative-without-negation (see his reply to Gaunilo, ch. 5), on the one
hand, and the creation of a new metaphoric utterance, on the other. It is
his novel and surprising and at first sight unconventional[8] use of syntax
that here constructs the image and his faith, and not the image that is
perceived and then put into syntactically correct phrases which in turn
describe his faith in God's existence.

Anselm's production of meaning in other aspects of the *Proslogion*
follows this same gambit. One recalls that in the preface to that work he
relates externally his discovery of the unique argument. He tells us that
one day, when he was quite worn out with mulling over the problem of
philosophically proving God's existence, in the very conflict of his
thought, he found '*that* which in my distraction I had been rejecting'. I
would now pay some attention to this 'that'. Charlesworth and others
incorrectly supply 'notion' or 'idea' to the 'that' in the sentence '*that*
which in my distraction I had been rejecting'.[9] Anselm, however, himself
does his utmost not to use a noun such as 'notion', 'idea' or even
'image'—a word he uses later on only to discard it—to name his discovery. When he for stylistic reasons has to use a shorthand for our
phrase he calls it 'illa cogitatio', 'that cogitation', 'that thought'. By
translating 'that' by 'notion' or 'idea', a misunderstanding of the
uniqueness of his argument has to follow. Anselm's discovery has nothing to do with 'notions' or 'images'. As a matter of fact, Anselm dis-
cards any kind of metaphor of image explicitly in ch. 1 of the
Proslogion. He does, of course, acknowledge that God has created his
image in him so that he may remember God. But the demonstration of

8.   L.M. de Rijk has insisted that the Latin comparative-plus-negation should be
translated into modern Dutch or French (and presumably English as well) as a superlative, thus solving the problem of the Latinisms of such translated phrases. In general this is certainly the right procedure, but in resolving 'id quo maius cogitari non
potest' into 'correctly' translated grammar this way, De Rijk has, I think, missed the
point of Anselm's argument. Anselm himself, in this same context, takes Gaunilo to
task for equating the 'negative comparative' with the 'positive superlative'. Indeed,
Anselm is here forcing language to do what he wants it to do. Cf. L.M. de Rijk, *La
philosophie au moyen âge* (Leiden: Brill, 1985), p. 228.

9.   *St Anselm's 'Proslogion'* (trans. M.J. Charlesworth; Oxford: Oxford
University Press, 1979).

God's existence by way of the image is impossible, much as we might want to do it: 'sed sic est abolita attritione vitiorum, sic est offuscate fumo peccatorum, ut non possit facere ad quod facta est'. This impossibility is not one in principle but one in practice. That is to say, such an image of God is *no longer* possible because the 'image-making' faculty of human beings has been obfuscated by sin. This lost faculty cannot be the source or basis of his proof. It cannot clarify the 'image of God'. It will not be renewed and reformed until well after the proofs of chs. 2–5. In the post-Paradisal world humanity will have to make do with words and the Word, and with the questions and answers of faith and the Creed. The image of God blinds even the believer, but the negative formulation of what God is not leads to the understanding that he is greater than can be thought.

Anselm's approach is not through notions, images and nominal metaphors. Instead, Anselm's proof hinges on a metaphorical utterance in the context of faith. That is to say, it turns on a confession or credo and prayer, and the kind of language that is used in these contexts, and not on an image. The distinction is clear: an image is primordially languageless and subjective. On the other hand, confessions or credos are primordially *verbal* constructs, responses, that is to say: utterance-based and predicative and non-descriptive and audible and communicable to others, at least in principle. For this reason, Anselm insists so strongly time and again on using the verb *credere* in conjunction with his 'id quo maius' formula. He does not say 'we think that you are "id quo maius cogitari non potest"' or 'we have a notion or idea that you are "id quo maius cogitari non potest"'; he writes 'Et quidem credimus te esse aliquid quo nihil maius cogitari possit'. He uses the word 'credere', thus invoking not 'image' but 'answer', confession, speech, assertion. Besides, it is significant that he does not say 'credo'—I believe in the first person singular; his expression is 'credimus'—we believe, confess that you are 'id quo maius cogitari non potest'. Here his proof escapes the subjectivity of the individual and it becomes part of the speech act of an entire confessing community. This description of God—in the second person 'you'—as 'id quo maius cogitari non potest' is not a metaphor, an image made into a word, but an understanding and activity that stimulates to a logical analysis of its own functioning and to a movement along the hierarchy of being. It is interesting that each time that one would expect Anselm to write about his metaphorical predicative utterance 'we thus believe that you are "id quo maius cogitari non potest"' as a notion, image or denominating metaphor, he reverts to a direct approach or prayer to God. In this way he is circumventing the inexactness and 'improprietas' of descriptive language in favour of verbal activity. In fact, he is, to use Austin's expression, 'doing things with words', or making words do things, as opposed to describing reality in terms of words and the metaphorical use of words.[10] In these sequences of prayer he does not metaphorically describe God in all his qualities, but he tells God directly what he is. Thus in ch. 5: 'You are just, truthful, happy, and whatever it is better to be than not to be.' Whence this knowledge of God? This question might be answered by considering that the central place of faithful activity for Anselm is the heart, specifically his own heart: in ch. 1 he enjoins God: 'doce cor meum' and in ch. 18 there is the interesting dialogue: 'Quid es, domine, quid es, quid te intelliget cor meum?' and the immediate answer 'Certe vita es, sapientia es, veritas es...' And subsequently Anselm continues asking and giving answers to his questioning heart. His heart is in a continuous dialogue with God; there is here no static notion of God in one's intellect or mind. One might say that it is the fool's error *to say* in his heart that there is no God. He 'says', that is, he states. He is not receptive to a *dialogue* with God or to teaching by the God whom he has already decided beforehand does not exist.

I would like to close these remarks with the observation that in order to understand Anselm's demonstration of God's existence it is necessary to look at the entire sentence in which his predicative phrase occurs. It is not sufficient to look only at the description 'id quo maius cogitari non potest' and to analyse this phrase logically and thus statically in the way of examining a metaphor. One can understand Anselm's argument only if the entire sentence in which it is couched is taken into consideration.

To sum up: the 'credimus' is the language continuum in which the comparative 'maius' and its negation receive the dynamic force, which transcends the unmoving, static image of any nominal metaphor of the name of God (as 'id quo maius cogitari non potest' is usually regarded).

This brings me to a final point. Anyone who has read the *Proslogion* will remember Anselm's recurring lament, before as well as after his demonstration of God's existence, that he cannot 'see' God, that he cannot get an image of God and that he cannot describe God in terms of nouns used for mere things. He states early in the work that God

---

10. J.L. Austin, *How to do Things with Words* (Oxford: Oxford University Press, 1962).

'fulgeret mentis aciem omnino', that he flees or defies even the sharpest of thought. Now the word 'mens, mentis' is important for our purposes. Most translators translate 'mentis' in Anselm's expression in terms of an activity: thinking. But I think Anselm chooses the noun 'mens' purposely, when he says in disillusion that God escapes even the sharpest mind. The *Proslogion* traces a path from the impossibility of 'catching', so to speak, God in thought in ch. 1 to the knowing and thinking of God in action in chs. 25 and 26. Indeed, knowledge of God always escapes ideas, notions or thoughts and even generic thought. There can be no image of God because God is ultimately active. As Anselm writes nearly at the end of the *Proslogion* in ch. 24, it is not through the metaphors of life that God can be understood to be good but through the activity of life that creates; not through salvation that God is joy, but through the joyful salvation that saves; not through the metaphor of God as wisdom, but through the wisdom that has brought all things into being out of nothing.[11]

Anselm continues in ch. 25, saying that God cannot be described in terms of the goods of body and soul and that he is such that he cannot be seen by the eye, heard by the ear or conceived of by the heart. Anselm then proceeds to give a long list of the activities of God which describe him. It is this list of activities—all derived from Bible texts such as 'setting His good and faithful servants over many things', 'making his faithful servants heirs of God and co-heirs of Christ' and many more—that is necessary for Anselm to complete his so-called 'ontological' demonstration of God's existence in the early chapters of the work. Anyone not realizing that Anselm's formula 'id quo maius cogitari non potest' is not a metaphor of a perceived image, but that it is a metaphorical utterance based on the fundamental insight that faith is not logical but rhetorical, not thought but action, not statements but question and answer, not noun but gerund, will miss the central issue of his philosophy: 'credo ut intelligam', I believe in order to understand, not 'credo ut habeam notitiam imaginemque Dei'.

---

11. Anselm makes extensive use of what have been called 'verb metaphors'; for an interesting study focused on English literature, see C. Brooke-Rose, *A Grammar of Metaphors* (London: Secker & Warburg, 1958).

THE *PROSLOGION* ARGUMENT AND THE ANSELMIAN *COGITO*

T. Losoncy

> In this way, therefore, this Nature is ineffable because words cannot at all express it as it is; and yet, if by the enlightening (*docente*) of reason by 'something/another' (*per quid*) we can intimate (*aestimari*) something about it obliquely, as in conjecturing/speaking through riddles (*velut in aenigmate*), [this understanding] is not false.[1]

The above passage from Anselm's *Monologion*, ch. 65, is cited to draw attention to two currents in Anselm's thinking about God. He certainly intends to maintain that in some sense God is unknowable to the human intellect and supersedes one's human 'knowing abilities'. Yet, in another sense, God is somehow knowable by the human being. It is the making sense of these opposing themes that constitutes a large part of the *Proslogion*.

This study seeks to establish the three claims below:

1. Anselm's *Proslogion* argument rises from the rich and varied tapestry of Augustinian insights and notions about one's knowledge of God.
2. Anselm's *cogito* is developed in a fashion unique to him.
3. The *Proslogion* argument Anselm produces is innovative.

Returning, then, to the discussion of the opening quotation, one may readily recall its similarity to and connection with a quite famous passage of Augustine's *De trinitate*, XV.ix.16:

> '*Videmus nunc per speculum et in aenigmate*'... just as he wished image to be understood by the word mirror, so he wished a similitude, albeit an obscure one, difficult to perceive, to be understood by the word

---

1. 'Sic igitur illa natura et ineffabilis est, quia per verba sicuti est nullatenus valet intimari; et falsum non est si quid de illa ratione docente per aliud velut in aenigmate potest aestimari', *Monologion*, ch. 65. All quotations and references from Anselm and Gaunilo are to Schmitt's edition. The translations throughout, and the sections emphasized, are mine.

aenigma... Therefore by the words 'mirror' and 'enigma' some similitudes signified by the Apostle can be understood which are accommodated
to understanding God in the way that he can be...

In Augustine's statement above, and indeed in his writings generally, we
meet the view that human knowledge concerning God is difficult to
achieve. Even though Anselm echoes Augustine, and actually resorts to
a mirror example in the earlier part of the *Monologion* chapter quoted,
he inserts a distinction which Augustine does not make. For Anselm
adds that knowledge is impossible, not just limited, if one is thinking
about attaining a precise and comprehensive understanding of God. This
kind of knowing one simply cannot realize.[2] But one can still somehow
know God.

In a second and different instance, section 8 of Anselm's *Rejoinder*,
one discovers Anselm further imbuing this problem with his own
approach. Here, in response to Gaunilo, he argues that one can gain
some knowledge about God by means of conjecturing/puzzling out
('conicere') the existence of a being whose greater cannot be thought
from the things which are in this world. He proposes a kind of comparative ascent whether by means of a good, better, best hierarchy or a
great, greater, greater still, greatest hierarchy to the existence of God.
One may, once more, read into this account echoes of Augustine's own
famous reasoning to God's existence in Book II, ch. 15, of the *De libero
arbitrio*. Obviously, in this case, Anselm does not adhere to Augustine's
exact procedure of moving from external hierarchies of goods, to the
mind's interior good, to that good that surpasses the mind. Nevertheless,
Anselm's 'conicere ' cannot help but remind one of Augustine's own
curious ending to this particular argument. For Augustine observes:

> For it is not only indubitable, on the part of faith that one holds this, I
> think; but it is also as a matter of certainty even though we reach this by a
> *most tenuous* form of reasoning.[3]

2.   'Et saepe videmus aliquid non proprie, quemadmodum res ipsa est, sed per
aliquam similitudinem aut imaginem—ut cum vultum alicuius consideramus in
speculo. Sic quippe unam eandemque rem dicimus et non dicimus, videmus et non
videmus. Dicimus et videmus per aliud; non dicimus et non videmus per suam proprietatem. Hac itaque ratione nihil prohibet et verum esse quod disputatum est
hactenus de summa natura et ipsam tamen nihilominus ineffabilem persistere, si
nequaquam illa putetur per essentiae suae proprietatem expressa, sed utcumque per
aliud designate', *Monologion*, ch. 65.
3.   'Quod iam non solum indubitatum, quantum arbitror, fide retinemus, sed

A few comments seem warranted here in regard to Augustine's use of 'tenuissima'. One may easily relate his earlier thoughts of 'through a mirror' and 'enigmatically' to the expression here. Maybe he is once again expressing a sense of an inherent tentativeness about such knowledge. But it may also be the case that Augustine is recognizing here an intellectual procedure that is quite distinct from defining, identifying, judging and the like. In short, the reasoning process he has undertaken is not one's everyday fare, even for philosophers. In this latter Augustinian sense, Anselm's resorting to 'conicere' might simply be taken as his way of designating an unusual and special procedure on the part of the intellect. One is engaged in reasoning to, or reasoning from. Whichever the direction of the argumentation, the steps are important, difficult, and not among the ordinary everyday actions of the intellect.

One might pause here and inquire just what all of these connections between Augustine and Anselm and, moreover, Anselm's various modifications, have to do with the Anselmian *cogito*. The question is appropriate but prior to addressing it one more observation is in order. When Anselm writes section 8 of his *Rejoinder* he is responding to Gaunilo. Specifically, he is responding to Gaunilo's charge in section 4 of his *Reply on Behalf of the Fool* that, in regard to this world, there is no species of thing, no genus, no similitude, nor even the being itself, God, from which one could begin an argument leading to knowledge of God's existence. Anselm's *Rejoinder* does not necessarily deny these points explicitly. He will, however, deny that there is no way available by means of which one can argue to the existence of God.[4]

Anselm's cogito

One could sort out the numerous types of occurrences of *cogitare, cogitari, cogitatio*, etc., in Anselm's writings as one method for ascertaining how it functions in his *Proslogion* argument. Unfortunately, these

etiam certa, quamvis adhuc tenuissima forma cognitionis adtingimus', *De libero arbitrio*, II, ch. 15 (CCSL XXIX, p. 264, §155).

4. 'Item quod dicis quo maius cogitari nequit secundum rem vel ex genere tibi vel ex specie notam te cogitare auditum vel in intellectu habere non posse, quoniam nec ipsam rem nosti nec eam ex alia simili potes conicere: palam est rem aliter sese habere. Quoniam namque omne minus bonum in tantum est simile maiori bono inquantum est bonum, patet cuilibet rationabili menti quia, de bonis minoribus ad maiora conscendendo, ex iis quibus aliquid maius cogitari potest multum possumus conicere illud quo nihil potest maius cogitari', *Responsio*, §8.

usages are numerous, often merely repetitive, and otherwise too far afield for this to be very helpful. To begin in another way, Anselm's *Proslogion* surely reminds one of Augustine's own 'intellectus fidei'. Anselm pointedly announces that he seeks to know what he already believes by faith, that is, 'that God is that whose greater cannot be thought ('cogitari')'. I am unaware of any place in scripture, or even in Christian dogma and teaching, where such a formulation is proposed for belief. On the other hand, one can easily sense that this has simply become Anselm's rendition of 1 Cor. 2.9 which runs, 'neither has eye seen, nor ear heard, nor has it entered the heart of man' what those goods of the next life will be like. As Anselm repeats these words in chs. 25 and 26 of the *Proslogion* one can understand them as speaking of the enjoyment of a being, 'whose greater cannot be thought'.[5]

What is at issue here, however, is not the origin of Anselm's phrase, nor its meaning, but rather the 'thinking' that is involved. For how is it, or in what way is it, that one is 'thinking of God'? Some brief reflections on related matters will serve to bring the problem into focus. Anselm had been preoccupied at greater length with the writing of ch. 1 of the *Proslogion* than with the writing of any other chapter. In that chapter he mentions a number of specific points bearing on his enterprise. First, he emphasizes that God's existence is not self-evident. Second, he voices unremittingly his desire, his need to know of God's existence. Finally, he concedes that he would be satisfied merely to be granted 'some measure ('aliquatenus')' of knowledge about God if he cannot expect to ever know God, as God is, and as God might know

---

5. This is not intended to ignore the fact that Augustine's 'melius' of the *De libero arbitrio*, II, chs. 6 and 15 and Boethius's 'maius' of the *De consolatione philosophiae*, III, prose §10, may easily have some role in the formation of Anselm's, 'aliquid quo nihil maius cogitari possit'. What the scriptural references indicate, however, is that Anselm is making a distinction vital to his own argumentation. The claim that God is a 'being compared to which no greater can be thought' is recognized by Anselm as a status or position claim. This aspect of his thought connects him with Augustine and Boethius. When he adds the scriptural nuance he is emphasizing that the status of this being is such that its 'content' exceeds human grasp and, for this very reason, cannot be conceptualized or contained within an 'idea'. This is what permits Anselm to direct the intellect to a being that is simultaneously a being whose greater cannot be thought and a being whose very greatness is such 'that eye has not seen, nor ear heard, nor has it entered the heart of man' *what* such a being comprises. Such is what it means to speak of this being as 'ineffable'.

God.[6] Such a programme does not strike one as overly ambitious. However, is any such knowledge attainable? More importantly, by what means is one to come to such knowledge? For this reason, the *cogito* as some sort of thinking about God is of paramount importance. Whatever the *cogito* means or however it works, it and it alone holds the key to Anselm's quest.

Although many, at this point, would prefer to turn to Anselm's 'idea' of God, or his 'concept' of God as the meaning of his *cogito* such a direction does not appear supportable. Anselm himself insists that his 'painter example' in ch. 2 of the *Proslogion* was never intended to be taken as a piece of argumentation that would proceed from some thought or idea in the intellect to the extramental existence of the being contained in such a concept or idea.[7] Indeed, ch. 15 of the *Proslogion* goes so far as to proclaim that any such knowledge of God, a quidditative or conceptual knowledge, is quite out of the question: 'You are greater than can be thought'.[8] What then is the work of the *cogito* in Anselm? His first indication of its task proves extremely troublesome.

It is in ch. 3 that Anselm provides some insight into the 'thinking' at work in the *Proslogion*. Unfortunately, this insight is abrupt to the point of near non-existence, is wrapped in text laden with Augustinian overtones, and does not receive further elucidation until chs. 18-22 of the work.

6. For a fuller discussion of this matter, one might consult M.J. Adler, *How to Think about God* (New York: Macmillan Publishing, 1980), p. 70; T.A. Losoncy, 'Language and Saint Anselm's *Proslogion* Argument', in R.J. Schoeck (ed.), *Acta Conventus Neo-Latini Bononiensis* (Binghamton, NY: Medieval & Renaissance Texts & Studies, 1985), pp. 284-91; and *idem*, 'Chapter 1 of St. Anselm's *Proslogion*: Its Preliminaries to Proving God's Existence as Paradigmatic for Subsequent Proofs of God's Existence', in J. Sumr and V. Herold (eds.), *The European Dimension of St. Anselm's Thinking* (Prague: Institute of Philosophy, 1993), pp. 95-106.

7. Concerning this specific issue, see T.A. Losoncy, 'St. Anselm's Rejection of the Ontological Argument—A Review of the Occasion and Circumstances', *American Catholic Philosophical Quarterly* 64 (1990), pp. 373-85.

8. Admittedly, this strikes one as an unusual turn in Anselm's *cogito*. What he acknowledges here, however, is that his series of attempts to realize some sort of quidditative knowledge of God, an enterprise beginning at ch. 5 and running through ch. 14 of the *Proslogion*, has proven fruitless. For additional discussion of this feature of Anselm's thinking, see T.A. Losoncy, 'Did Anselm Encounter a Detour on the Way to God?', in G.C. Berthold (ed.), *Faith Seeking Understanding* (Manchester, NH: St Anselm College Press, 1991), pp. 127-33. Chapter 15 of the *Proslogion* simply states Anselm's succinct appraisal of his efforts.

And just what is this 'thinking' that Anselm proposes in ch. 3? How does it work? He expresses it in the following fashion:

> And, indeed, whatever there is other than you alone can be thought (*cogitari*) not to be. You alone, then, more truly than all, and therefore, more than all have being. For whatever else there is has being not so truly and for that reason has being less.

Surely such a passage is brief for the momentous argument it carries. And just as surely the influence of Augustine is in evidence. Had not Augustine's own argument in the *De libero arbitrio* reached a highest being as 'immutable truth'? And here too Anselm speaks of what appears to be a supreme level or degree of truth and being. And is this not precisely what is reflected in Anselm's *Rejoinder*, section 8? All this must to some extent be admitted, and yet it is not speaking to Anselm's *cogito*. For what he is proposing to the reader is a very special consideration. Is it *true* that everything in the universe of experience is such that its non-being, its non-existence is thinkable? The critical notes here are those of 'everything' and that 'their non-existence is thinkable'. Surprisingly, or perhaps not, Anselm has introduced the proposition that the entire universe enjoys a 'contingent existence'. He has accomplished this within the trappings of the Augustinian notion of 'immutable truth' and the contrasts between mutable and immutable being, contrasts which will not be enlarged upon until chs. 18-22 of the *Proslogion*. But given these Augustinian surroundings is Anselm's *cogito* developed in a way that can be said to be unquestionably his? The answer for me is 'Yes'. The uniqueness of Anselm's insight is borne out in a somewhat unexpected place and way.

Ironically, it is Gaunilo who provides the occasion for Anselm to articulate fully the *cogito*. In a highly elliptical passage near the end of his *Reply*, section 7, Gaunilo directs the following dilemma at Anselm:

> I do most certainly know of myself that I exist. Nonetheless I also know that I can have non-being. Of course, that very summit of being, God, I mean, both has being and cannot not have being: this beyond question I understand. But can I *think* I have non-being so long as I know quite certainly that I have being? I do not know whether I can or not. But suppose I *can think* I have non-being? Why should I not *think* non-being of everything which I know with the same certainty? On the other hand, if I am unable *to think* my non-being then *unthinkable* non-being will no longer be exclusively God's.[9]

9.   'Et me quoque esse certissime scio, sed et posse non esse nihilominus scio.

If one were to paraphrase it, the thrust of Gaunilo's argument/dilemma would take the following form:

> I know, with the most/greatest certainty, my own being. But suppose I could *think* my own non-being? If such is *thinkable* and my greatest certainty is of my own being—then, it must follow that God's non-being is also *thinkable*. Consequently, God is not that being whose non-being is *unthinkable* and that whose greater is *unthinkable*.

> On the other hand, if one were to insist that one cannot *think* one's own non-being since one's existence is known with the most/greatest certainty thereby making the *thought* of one's non-being impossible, then God is not the only being whose non-being is *unthinkable*. Since *unthinkable* non-being can no longer exclusively belong to God it cannot be supportive of God's existence.

This parting attack in Gaunilo's *Reply* is, perhaps, providential and, perhaps, the reason why Anselm insisted the *Reply* be published along with the *Proslogion*. If such assessments sound somewhat exaggerated, consider that the dilemma targets the heart of the issue, God's existence as it does or does not relate to that of all other beings. In fact, the dilemma accomplishes this in regard to the critical feature of the question—Can one ever be 'certain', 'know for certain' that there is some such other and exalted existence? Anselm has much to say about this.

The locus of his lengthy discussion is section 4 of his *Rejoinder*. He begins this section with a short account of what Gaunilo had argued and whether or not it was accurately put. He next proceeds to a discussion of how he distinguishes 'to understand' ('intelligere') from 'to think' ('cogitare') in which he elaborates upon just what the *cogito* of the *Proslogion*, ch. 3, was reasoning about in regards to being:

> But this objection about understanding cannot be made about thinking if the points are well weighed. For nothing which is may be *understandable* as non-being, yet everything which is is *thinkable* as non-being except that *which is* in the highest fashion. Indeed, all those things and those alone are *thinkable* as non-being which have a beginning, or which have an end, or which have a composition of parts, and (this I already said)— whatever at some place or at some time is not a whole. But that alone is *unthinkable* as non-being in which thought never discovers a beginning,

Summum vero illud quod est, scilicet deus, et esse et non esse non posse indubitantur intelligo. Cogitare autem me non esse quamdiu esse certissime scio, nescio utrum possim. Sed si possum, cur non et quidquid aliud eadem certitudine scio? Si autem non possum, non erit iam istud proprium deo', *Pro insipiente*, §7.

an end, a composition of parts, and which thought discovers always and everywhere to be a whole.

Be sure, then, that you can *think* of your own non-being so long as you are absolutely sure that you are... let one then grasp the distinction I have made in the two preceding sentences and he will understand that nothing, so long as it is known to be, can be *understood* not to be; and that everything apart from that than which no greater can be thought, even when it is known to be, can be *thought* not to be.[10]

As it turns out, the Anselmian *cogito* is assigned a major function in the human grasp of existence for Anselm. Its function is to recognize that one cannot legitimately or cogently say, 'That is not, all the time knowing that it is/exists' and this is in reference to things presently existing in this universe. All the same one is capable of recognizing that being is not of the very nature/essence of these things. They can all be thought of as not existing with reference to the past, the future, change or decomposition. In fact, their existence is not necessary.

Anselm's Proslogion Argument

From such an understanding of the Anselmian *cogito*, what should one make of his famous *Proslogion* argument? Certainly, it emerges out of an Augustinian ancestry. Moreover, the metaphysical role assigned the *cogito* is very much Anselm's own innovation. It enables the metaphysician to engage two fundamental features of the question, 'Does God exist?' They are, of course, to remember that the question is about the 'existence' of God and second that one only knows through experience the beings of this universe which one observes and one's own existence. Keeping within the parameters of the problem Anselm is able to

10. 'Sed hoc utique non potest obici de cogitatione, si bene consideretur. Nam et si nulla quae sunt possint intelligi non esse, omnia tamen possunt cogitari non esse, praeter id quod summe est. Illa quippe omnia et sola possunt cogitari non esse, quae initium aut finem aut partium habent coniunctionem, et, sicut iam dixi, quidquid alicubi aut aliquando totum non est. Illud vero solum non potest cogitari non esse, in quo nec initium nec finem nec partium coniunctionem, et quod non nisi semper et ubique totum ulla incenit cogitatio.

Scito igitur quia potest cogitare te non esse, quamdiu esse certissime scis—quod te miror dixisse nescire... Si quis igitur sic distinguat huius prolationis has duas sententias, intelligit nihil, quamdiu esse scitur, posse cogitari non esse, et quidquid est praeter id quod maius cogitari nequit, etiam cum scitur esse, posse non esse cogitari', *Responsio*, §4. My emphasis is intended to highlight the two terms, 'understanding' and 'thinking'.

discern, and portray for the reader, the contingency within all the beings of one's experience and to point the way to another manner of being or, if one prefers, to direct the intellect to God.

Nor should one be distracted by all of Anselm's vibrant depictions of this situation. For a being 'whose greater cannot be thought', a being without beginning or end, a being with no parts, a being that is everywhere one and the same, a being whose non-being is unthinkable is simply the one being whose existence is necessary. Is it not only appropriate then to designate Anselm as the first thinker of the Latin Christian West to formulate an argument from the contingency of beings to the existence of God, regardless of his colourful terminology, as 'Necessary Being'?

VOLONTÉ ET LIBERTÉ DANS LE *DE LIBERTATE ARBITRII* DE S. ANSELME DE CANTORBÉRY

Jeannine Quillet

En quels termes le problème de la volonté et de ses rapports avec la liberté humaine se pose-t-il dans la doctrine de saint Anselme?[1] On l'a souvent signalé, le *De libertate arbitrii* constitue, avec le *De veritate*, et le *De casu diaboli*, un tout que leur auteur appelle 'les trois traités qui appartiennent à l'étude de l'Ecriture sainte',[2] dans la ligne générale de la programmatique de son oeuvre: l'*intellectus fidei*.

Une telle entreprise comporte en effet l'ambition de définir la vérité et de dégager le lien avec la foi avant d'aborder le thème essentiel de la volonté et de la liberté humaine. Qu'est-ce en effet que la vérité? C'est d'abord une pensée vraie, qui exerce la fonction pour laquelle elle est faite; c'est une pensée droite, qui dit que ce qui est, est, et ce qui n'est pas, n'est pas.[3] Où l'on voit déjà l'importance fondamentale de la *rectitudo* dans la pensée et l'énonciation de la vérité, mais aussi pour définir la liberté de la volonté dans le traité *De libertate arbitrii*. En effet, on ne saurait comprendre ni interpréter l'Ecriture si on ne mettait pas à sa disposition l'instrument rationnel dont dispose la créature, ni si on ne soumettait à l'examen de la raison les concepts fondamentaux de vérité et de liberté. Telle est la méthode anselmienne.

Définir la vérité comme *rectitudo*, c'est la désigner comme l'opération 'qui consiste à faire se correspondre ce qui est à ce à quoi il est fait'. Nous verrons que la liberté a également partie liée avec la *rectitudo*, comme le confirme Anselme lui-même dans la préface au *De veritate*:[4]

---

1. S. Anselme de Cantorbéry, *Oeuvres* (trad. M. Corbin et R. de Ravinel; Paris, 1986), pp. 180-247. Nous donnons la concordance avec l'édition F.S. Schmitt.

2. Corbin (trad.), *Oeuvres*, t.II, p. 9, *Avertissement*.

3. E. Gilson, *Etudes médiévales, Sens et nature de l'argument de S. Anselme* (Paris, 1986), pp. 53-99.

4. Schmitt, I, p. 173; Corbin, I, p. 125.

'Le premier des trois traités est *Sur la vérité*, à savoir, qu'est-ce que la vérité, en quelles choses a-t-on coutume de la dire, et qu'est-ce que la justice?'

Remarquons d'emblée le lien étroit qu'établit Anselme entre justice et vérité, et la connotation scripturaire du concept de vérité dans ce contexte, puisque, outre le traité *Sur la liberté de choix*, mentionné en second lieu, qui définit aussi cette dernière par la *rectitudo*, connue par la créature raisonnable, il fait en somme de la vérité le contraire du mensonge, selon le verset johannique, 8, 44: 'Le diable était homicide dès le commencement et n'était pas établi dans la vérité, parce qu'il n'y a pas de vérité en lui; quand il profère le mensonge, il parle de son propre fonds, parce qu'il est menteur et père du mensonge'.[5]

Une telle perspective justifie pleinement le lien entre les deux premiers traités et le troisième, le *De casu diaboli* où est interprété le péché des mauvais anges, et dont on voit bien combien il se rattache au problème de la liberté et à celui de la vérité ressentie ici dans toute l'ampleur de son concept.

Avant d'entrer dans la problématique de la liberté et de son rapport à la volonté, nous nous attarderons sur celle de la vérité afin de mettre en lumière son caractère fondamental dans l'analyse de la liberté.

Dès l'abord, Anselme définit la vérité comme étant Dieu lui-même, selon la parole de Jean 14, 6: 'Je suis le chemin, la vérité et la vie.' Toute autre vérité qu'affirme une énonciation participe de cette Vérité même; on dira qu'elle est vraie lorsqu'elle est droite, c'est-à-dire lorsqu'elle signifie ce qu'elle doit signifier, par exemple 'qu'est ce qui est'.[6] La *rectitudo* étant en quelque sorte, la finalité de la pensée vraie, elle n'est pas seulement cette conformité à sa finalité, en quelque sorte, ontologique: elle est en liaison intime avec la volonté. En effet, si le diable 'ne s'est pas tenu dans la vérité', c'est que cette dernière a partie liée avec la volonté qu'une définition préliminaire va identifier avec la droiture elle-même, c'est-à-dire encore la volonté de vouloir ce qu'on doit ('quoniam sive veritas sive rectitudo non aliud in eius voluntate fuit quam velle quod debuit').[7]

En approfondissant davantage la signification de la vérité, Anselme place de nouveau le dialogue sous l'autorité de Jean 3, 20–21: 'quiconque connaît le mal hait la lumière de peur que ses oeuvres ne

5. Corbin, II, p. 125, note a.
6. Schmitt, I, p. 178; Corbin, II, p. 135.
7. Corbin, II, p. 181: *Introduction* au *De libertate arbitrii*.

soient démontrées coupables, mais celui qui fait la vérité vient à la lumière, afin de manifester que ses oeuvres sont faites en Dieu'.[8]

Le recours à cette autorité scripturaire permet le glissement—tout platonicien—du vrai au bien: 'mais c'est l'avis de tous que celui qui fait ce qu'il doit, fait bien et fait la droiture...car il est établi que faire la vérité est bien faire et bien faire faire la droiture'[9] ('...facere veritatem esse bene facere et bene facere esse rectitudinem facere'). Etre dans la vérité, c'est, par la médiation du faire, agir en conformité avec la justice, en sorte que dire le vrai, le bien, le juste équivaut à dire le même. 'Ainsi, la vérité est la droiture perceptible au seul esprit' ('veritas est rectitudo mente sola perfectibilis').[10] Mais la justice, qui en est l'homologue, ne peut se définir que par la médiation de la volonté: 'quiconque fait ce qu'il doit n'est pas juste s'il ne *veut* ce qu'il fait',[11] et de la volonté d'une nature raisonnable. La justice est donc partie intégrante de la droiture de la volonté; elle est 'la droiture de la volonté gardée pour elle-même' ('voluntas ergo illa justa est quae sui rectitudinem servat propter ipsam rectitudinem').[12] La *rectitudo* de la volonté humaine considérée dans sa nature, dans son contexte ontologique, son défaut et sa restauration est un concept porteur de l'ensemble de l'oeuvre d'Anselme.[13]

L'économie du *De veritate* préside à l'intelligibilité du *De libertate arbitrii*, à l'analyse de la volonté et de la liberté dans un contexte théologique, car Anselme tente de résoudre dans ce dialogue le problème du lien entre la liberté humaine et l'esclavage du péché, dans la perspective du verset johannique 8, 34: 'En vérité, en vérité je vous le dis, celui qui commet le péche est esclave du péché.' Il ne s'agit donc point seulement d'une analyse anthropologique de la liberté humaine mais du traitement de ce concept et de celui de la volonté dans le contexte de la problématique scripturaire, avec, à l'horizon, le rapport entre liberté humaine et liberté divine, entre le péché et la grâce.

Il y a pour Anselme un paradoxe de la volonté, à savoir que 'la volonté qui ne peut pas (sous-entendu: pécher) est plus puissante que la

8. Corbin, II, p. 141.
9. Corbin, II, p. 141.
10. Schmitt, I, p. 191; Corbin, II, pp. 160-61.
11. Schmitt, I, p. 192; Corbin, II, p. 163.
12. Schmitt, I, p. 194; Corbin, II, p. 167.
13. E.R. Fairweather, 'Truth, Justice and Moral Responsibility in the Thought of S. Anselm', dans *L'Homme et son destin d'après les penseurs du Moyen-âge* (Louvain: Nauwelaerts, 1958), pp. 385-91.

volonté qui peut'[14] Est-ce là un libre choix, et comment faut-il l'entendre?

Il faut bien voir que 'l'ange et le premier homme...ont péché par leur propre choix qui était libre', nous dit Anselme.[15] Il y a en effet une liberté naturelle de choix: raison et volonté en sont les deux dimensions. Tout homme qui veut, veut précisément son propre vouloir; il en a, en quelque sorte, le pouvoir, si bien qu'il faut distinguer deux sens de vouloir: faire malgré soi, en ne voulant pas et par nécessité, ce qu'on fait cependant en voulant. Il s'agit là d'un pouvoir naturel qu'il faut distinguer du consentement à la volonté qui, lui, n'est pas de l'ordre de la nature. En d'autres termes, ce consentement est précisément la *rectitudo* de la volonté, qu'aucune tentation ne peut vaincre; à l'opposé, la volonté comme pouvoir naturel d'agir ou de ne pas agir n'est vaincue que par son propre pouvoir.[16]

Comment rendre compte de ce lien entre volonté et *rectitudo*? En recourant à la deuxième dimension en oeuvre dans l'exercice de la liberté humaine, à savoir à la raison. En effet, n'y a-t-il pas une sorte d'impuissance de la volonté lorsque, par exemple, l'homme cède à la tentation? En vérité, une telle impuissance ne veut pas dire impossibilité, mais difficulté, laquelle n'anéantit pas la liberté de la volonté.[17] La difficulté est celle qui consiste à ne pas maintenir la *rectitudo*, alors que la volonté a un tel pouvoir de persévérer en elle. Il faut bien voir en effet que le mot 'volonté' est ambigu: il y a d'une part la volonté, instrument même du vouloir qui est dans l'âme, que nous orientons à vouloir telle ou telle chose, et la volonté considérée comme 'quelque chose'[18] de l'âme, qui persiste même quand aucun objet ne la sollicite, de la même façon qu'il faut distinguer la vue comme pouvoir et la vision comme instrument.

En d'autres termes: 'Lorsqu'un homme abandonne la droiture de la volonté qu'il possède quand survient quelque tentation, aucune force étrangère ne l'en arrache mais c'est sa volonté qui d'elle-même se tourne vers ce qu'elle veut avec plus de force'.[19] C'est pourquoi elle

---

14. Corbin, II, pp. 188 sq.

15. Schmitt, I, p. 210; Corbin, II, p. 215.

16. Schmitt, I, pp. 213-14; Corbin, II, pp. 221-23.

17. Schmitt, I, p. 218; Corbin, II, p. 231.

18. 'Non enim est ratio vel voluntas tota anima, sed unaquaeque aliquid in anima', *De concordia*, *cit.* par Fairweather, 'Truth', p. 388.

19. Schmitt, I, p. 218; Corbin, II, pp. 231 sq.

pèche en quelque sorte librement. Dieu lui-même[20] ne peut non plus enlever la droiture de la volonté; la volonté droite est juste, c'est-à-dire qu'elle est gardée pour elle-même, et il n'est de volonté juste sinon celle qui veut ce que Dieu veut qu'elle veuille.

Rien, donc, n'est plus libre que la volonté droite: elle est la liberté même; rien ne peut l'entraver sinon elle-même. On ne saurait affirmer avec plus de force l'unité et l'autonomie du sujet humain comme tel.[21]

Comment, dans ces conditions, celui qui pèche est-il esclave du péché, étant entendu que 'la nature raisonnable a toujours le libre choix'? En réalité, l'homme pécheur conserve sa liberté, entendu comme son pouvoir d'agir, mais il en perd la norme, à savoir la *rectitudo* qu'il ne peut recouvrer désormais par lui-même, mais que Dieu peut lui octroyer par grâce. Servitude et liberté sont en effet dans la volonté, et de la volonté dépend que l'homme soit libre ou esclave. Sans la *rectitudo* qu'il a perdue, l'homme est à la fois, sans contradiction, esclave et libre. L'essence de la liberté, c'est le pouvoir de la garder quand l'homme la possède; mais il n'a pas le pouvoir de la posséder quand il l'a perdue: 'Par nature il (l'homme) est toujours libre de garder la droiture, s'il l'a, et même quand il ne l'a pas à garder'.[22]

En définitive, le pouvoir est le genre auquel appartient la liberté: la vraie liberté est cette liberté de choix, pouvoir de garder la droiture de la volonté pour la droiture elle-même. Enfin, la liberté est commune à la créature raisonnable et à Dieu; elle diffère cependant de celle de Dieu en ce sens que cette dernière est par soi, alors que celle de l'homme est reçue de Dieu, qui la lui a donnée pour faire le bien et non le mal. Le libre arbitre renvoie à la spontanéité de la volonté,[23] ce que Descartes appellera plusieurs siècles plus tard la liberté d'indifférence. La liberté est son bon usage, dans la ligne de la doctrine augustinienne du *De libero arbitrio*:[24] Le mauvais usage du libre arbitre ne détruit pas la nature, cependant que le bon usage qu'on en fait définit la liberté même. Pour Augustin, comme le rappelle E. Gilson, *liberum arbitrium* suppose la liberté de faire le mal, cependant que *libertas* désigne l'état de celui qui

20. Schmitt, I, p. 220; Corbin, II, p. 235.
21. Schmitt, I, pp. 221-22; Corbin, II, pp. 237-39.
22. Schmitt, I, p. 223; Corbin, II, p. 241.
23. F.J. Thonnard, 'La Personne humaine dans l'augustinisme médiéval (S. Anselme et S. Bonaventure)', dans *L'Homme et son destin*, pp. 163-72.
24. E. Gilson, *Introduction à l'étude de S. Augustin* (Paris, 3e ed., 1949), p. 212, n. 2.

est *liberatus*, 'la *libertas* est en chacun beaucoup plus grande qu'il est plus complètement *liberatus*'.[25] Et l'historien ajoute: 'La terminologie augustinienne s'est clarifiée et fixée chez saint Anselme: il substitue à *liberum arbitrium* l'expression *libertas arbitrii*. L'homme a toujours un *arbitrium* mais qui n'est pas toujours *liber*... *Libertas* est alors synonyme de *potestas non peccandi.*'

C'est ce que développe aussi le *De concordia praescientiae et praedestinationis et gratiae Dei cum libero arbitrio*, ainsi que le *De casu diaboli*.[26] En effet, l'existence du mal suppose son remède, c'est-à-dire la grâce, que peut restituer au pécheur qui se repend la *rectitudo* qu'il a perdue. En outre, autre obstacle qui se dresse devant la définition anselmienne de la liberté, on peut se demander si elle est compatible avec la prescience et la prédestination divine. Comment, si Dieu sait tout par avance, ne pas mettre sur le compte de la nécessité ce que nous pensons être l'exercice de notre liberté et notamment lorsque l'homme est pécheur? La réponse d'Anselme consiste à écarter toute présomption de nécessité en précisant son sens obvie: 'Nécessité semble évoquer contrainte (*coactio*) ou empêchement (*prohibitio*)',[27] mais il s'agit en réalité d'une impossibilité logique, en quelque sorte: le fait que Dieu sache d'avance si l'homme pèche ou non dans le futur n'exclut pas l'hypothèse selon laquelle il le fait librement: 'Cette nécessité, en effet, ne signifie pas autre chose que (ceci): ce qui sera ne pourra pas en même temps ne pas être'; en d'autres termes, il s'agit d'une nécessité séquente, *neccesitas sequens*, non d'une contrainte.

Dieu sait donc d'avance que certaines choses ou actions seront dans le futur 'par la libre volonté de la créature raisonnable'. Revenant alors à la définition de la liberté de choix, le Docteur magnifique distingue le choix de la liberté (*arbitrium*, et *libertas*), dans la perspective du salut et donc de la justice, dont nous avons vu l'importance pour la définition de la vérité, et qui joue également un grand rôle dans la doctrine de la liberté.

La justice se définit comme 'la droiture de la volonté gardée pour elle-même' ('rectitudo voluntatis propter se servata'), cependant que la liberté se définit comme 'le pouvoir de garder la droiture de la volonté pour la droiture elle-même' ('potestas servandi rectitudinem voluntatis propter ipsam rectitudinem').[28] Mais, alors que la liberté comme pouvoir

25. Gilson, *Introduction*, p. 213, même note.
26. *De concordia...* Corbin, V, pp. 15 sq, *Introd.*, de M. Corbin.
27. Schmitt, II, p. 247; Corbin, V, p. 161.
28. Schmitt, II, p. 256; Corbin, V, p. 179.

est naturelle et inséparable de la nature humaine, la justice, elle, est séparable; elle est cette *rectitudo voluntatis*, en sorte que celui qui la possède 'veut ce que Dieu veut qu'il veuille' ('cum ipse vult quod Deus vult eum velle'). En d'autres termes, la liberté 'est le pouvoir de garder la droiture de la volonté pour la droiture elle-même. C'est par cette liberté de la nature raisonnable qu'on dit libre le choix et libre la volonté',[29] qui, entreprend de montrer Anselme, abordant la dimension proprement sotériologique de son analyse, coexiste avec la grâce,[30] car, en réalité, la droiture de la volonté n'est pas la fruit de la conjonction, en l'homme, de la raison et de la liberté; elle a besoin du secours de la grâce pour exister: 'S'ensuit que nulle créature ne tient la droiture de volonté que j'ai dite (autrement) que par grâce de Dieu; mais elle la conserve par libre choix.'[31] Grâce et libre choix coopèrent étroitement pour le salut de l'homme dans l'exacte perspective de l'*intellectus fidei*, où l'Ecriture s'accorde avec les données de la raison humaine.

Nous avons déjà vu qu'Anselme définit la volonté comme 'quelque chose qui est dans l'âme'.[32] Il faut distinguer en ce quelque chose ce en quoi elle est instrument, ses aptitudes et ses usages. On dira des aptitudes qu'elles sont des 'affections'; considérée comme instrument, la volonté est 'affectée par ses aptitudes en vue du vouloir'. Ce triple sens de volonté manifeste son équivocité: l'instrument du vouloir diffère de ce qui affecte l'instrument, dont l'usage sera différent en fonction des diverses affections.

C'est à une réconsidération des rapports de la volonté et de la liberté que nous convie le *De concordia* en approfondissant et en enrichissant les analyses précédentes. L'instrument du vouloir est cette force de l'âme (*vis illa animae*) dont nous usons pour vouloir; de même que la raison est l'instrument dont nous usons quand nous raisonnons.[33] Cette force vient à être actualisée en fonction des besoins. Son usage n'intervient...'que lorsque nous pensons ce que nous voulons'. Il y a un double usage de la dimension instrumentale de la volonté; l'un a pour finalité la commodité et le bonheur, l'autre la droiture et la justice. De telles précisions ne dissipent pourtant pas l'équivoque: 'Ainsi affirme-t-on que veut et celui qui use de l'instrument du vouloir en pensant ce qu'il veut et

29. Schmitt, II, p. 257; Corbin, V, p. 181.
30. Schmitt, II, p. 264; Corbin, V, p. 195.
31. Schmitt, II, p. 266; Corbin, V, p. 199.
32. Schmitt, II, p. 279; Corbin, V, p. 225.
33. Schmitt, II, p. 279; Corbin, V, p. 225.

celui qui n'en use pas parce qu'il possède l'affection c'est-à-dire l'aptitude à vouloir.'[34]

C'est à partir de l'analyse des dimensions de la volonté et du libre choix qu'Anselme introduit dans sa doctrine la notion de mérite. C'est en même temps, selon le Docteur magnifique, que la nature raisonnable a reçu la volonté de bonheur et la volonté de justice, c'est-à-dire la droiture qui est la justice même, et le libre choix sans lequelle 'elle n'était pas capable de garder la justice',[35] et 'en vue de son honneur'.

Ainsi la volonté instrument a été créée bonne mais c'est par libre choix qu'elle s'est faite mauvaise, en abandonnant la justice de son plein gré pour se tourner vers ce qui peut satisfaire des 'appétits bestiaux'. Comme nous l'avons vu, si la volonté a perdu la justice par libre choix, elle n'a plus le libre choix de la vouloir, alors qu'elle le possède quand elle l'a gardée; il lui faut l'aide de la grâce pour la recouvrer. La liberté est donc le pouvoir de garder la justice; la droiture perdue, la volonté trébuche dans le péché en perdant le pouvoir véritablement libre. La perte de la droiture rend la volonté esclave de ses appétits: ce n'est pas la chair qui est en elle-même mauvaise; c'est parce qu'elle ne doit pas être dans la nature raisonnable qu'elle est dite injuste ou mauvaise. Telle est l'étendue de la faute.

Il y a donc une volonté sans justice: l'homme seul est responsable de son abandon; c'est ce qu'Anselme appelle sa 'volonté propre' c'est-à-dire injuste. Ainsi se réalise l'accord entre volonté et liberté dans la créature: refuser d'abandonner l'injustice en est la cheville ouvrière. Tout ce qui vient de Dieu est positivité, ou bien; le mal est négation, réfus, néant.

Le *De casu diaboli* revient sur la question de la possibilité, pour la créature douée de libre choix, de succomber au mal; il y a une irréversibilité de la chute, sauf recours à l'aide divine; mais comment une volonté bonne peut-elle devenir mauvaise? Ce n'est qu'avec la seule 'permission divine'.[36]

Comme pour Augustin, la liberté est pour Anselme au fondement de la vie morale; comme pour le Docteur africain, le libre arbitre de l'homme le rend semblable à Dieu et, de la même façon, le péché la prive de sa liberté et le rend esclave de ses désirs et de ses tentations. En tout état de cause, le libre arbitre est attaché à la condition de la créature mais la liberté véritable est celle par laquelle l'homme participe à la

34. Schmitt, II, p. 282; Corbin, V, p. 231.
35. Schmitt, II, p. 286; Corbin, V, p. 239.
36. Schmitt, II, p. 245; Corbin, II, p. 307.

liberté divine, c'est-à-dire s'est complètement affranchi du péché.

On le voit, la réflexion anselmienne sur la liberté dans son rapport à la volonté fait un large usage de la dialectique qui, du reste, est déjà à son époque partie intégrante de la culture monastique et met en lumière un genre spécifique de connaissance religieuse. Il y a chez le Docteur magnifique 'une authentique doctrine monastique'[37] dont l'analyse de la liberté dans son rapport avec la grâce est un moment essentiel. Le pivot en est le concept de *rectitudo* qui n'est rien de moins que le premier effet de la grâce, cependant que le péché est la privation de la *rectitudo*.[38]

S'il est vrai que 'le don de la grâce ne se conçoit qu'en fonction des maux dont elle est le remède'[39] on en concluera à la liberté finie de l'homme qui, tiré du néant par la création, n'en participe pas moins de lui en succombant au pouvoir du péché et en perdant la *rectitudo* qui définit en lui une authentique liberté.

37. J. Leclercq, *Initiation aux auteurs monastiques du Moyen-âge* (Paris, 1957), p. 204.

38. Fairweather, 'Truth', *passim*.

39. Gilson, *Introduction*, p. 184.

THE CONCEPTUAL ROOTS OF ANSELM'S SOTERIOLOGY

Richard Campbell

In scholarly discussion of Anselm's *Cur deus homo* there continue to be proponents of the view that the notions of *debitum* and satisfaction, so crucial to his soteriology, are grounded in the structure of feudal society and its legal system. This view still persists despite John McIntyre's argument of forty years ago that the notion of satisfaction finds its proper place in Anselm's description of God's act of salvation rather than in the setting of Roman law or Teutonic *Wergild*.[1] In this paper I wish to challenge such sociological and juridical readings, which I find not only superficial but also impediments in the way of understanding how his thinking worked.

Lest it be thought that I am attacking a straw man, let me quickly run through some of the recent literature on the subject. P. Fiddes, in *Past Event and Present Salvation*, sees Anselm's account as reflecting the structure of the feudal hierarchy. Justice in the medieval period was a matter of the rights of the great overlords, and any crime at all was an infringing of their personal honour, demanding the alternatives of either satisfaction or punishment. Fiddes goes on to portray Anselm's God as 'our feudal Overlord', with human beings as 'his servant-subjects who have offended against his honour'.[2]

Gillian Evans notes that for Anselm sinning is defined as not rendering to God what one ought, and that satisfaction for sin involves not only paying what was originally owed, but also a restoring of honour where there has been insult. On this basis, she argues that Anselm 'is unconsciously adopting a feudal frame of reference, in which

---

1. J. McIntyre, *St Anselm and his Critics* (Edinburgh: Oliver & Boyd, 1954), p. 89.
2. P. Fiddes, *Past Event and Present Salvation* (London: Darton, Longman & Todd, 1989), p. 97.

the notion of the honour due to a lord is mixed in with the Biblical concept of God as Lord'.[3]

Similarly, P. McKenzie in *The Christians* talks about 'the injured honour of God' and suggests that 'it is possible that germanic juridical views lived on in this theory'.[4] F. Herzog in *God-Walk* is even more severe on Anselm. He writes that his notion of satisfaction,

> reminds one of a duel. Not long ago, men who felt that their honour had been tampered with challenged the insulted person to a duel. The medieval 'theo-logic' apparently implied a similar notion of honour. Anselm's social location cannot be disregarded. He does not argue here with biblical categories.[5]

More judicious is G. Daley, who announces that,

> the advent of feudalism enabled certain refinements to be made to the understanding of redemption... This is not to say that feudalism created a new soteriology; it merely supplied refinements to a model which the Fathers had already constituted from biblical materials.

Turning specifically to Anselm, Daley comments,[6]

> The immediate cultural background was feudal, but by Anselm's time its epic character was beginning to wane. The courtroom replaced the battlefield. Anselm's soteriological thinking is dominated by reflection upon the damage done to God's majesty and honour by sin.

Daley is careful, however, not to be too sociological in his interpretation. He goes on to say,

> Anselm's soteriology was thus a striking essay in theological relevance to his own age. It is perhaps too easy to react in disfavour today against precisely those elements in the feudal theory which were most relevant to their time. They spoke to their age about realities which transcend the ability of any age to give them permanent expression.

But at the same time, Daley continues,

> The trouble is that words like 'justice', 'honour' and 'satisfaction' can sound grimly calculating when they are detached from the culture which provided them. Especially do they lose their austere grandeur when they

---

3. G.R. Evans, *Anselm* (London: Geoffrey Chapman, 1989), p. 76.
4. P. McKenzie, *The Christians* (London: SPCK, 1988), p. 270.
5. F. Herzog, *God-Walk* (Maryknoll, NY: Orbis, 1988), p. 112.
6. G. Daley, *Creation and Redemption* (Dublin: Gill & Macmillan, 1988), p. 190.

are thought of not as martial and governmental, but as commercial models...

Even Colin Gunton, who resists the contention that Anselm likens the deity to an arbitrary and oppressive ruler, suggests that Anselm's God is to be understood as operating analogously to the way a feudal ruler had a duty to maintain the order of rights and obligations without which society would collapse.[7]

So much for those who espouse sociological or juridical understandings of Anselm's key concepts. To be fair, there have recently been other scholars who have resisted these kinds of readings. B. Eckhardt, for instance, argues vigorously that an aesthetic vision is crucial to Anselm's approach. An essential theme in the *Cur deus homo* is that it would not be 'fitting' for God to forgive sin which is unpunished; Eckhardt contends that the notion of being 'fitting' is an aesthetic notion, inasmuch as beauty is fitting and the lack of it unfitting.

My own view is that, for all that it is fashionable for scholars to 'explain' an author's key concepts in sociological or juridical terms, in this case such analyses are shallow and lacking in scholarly penetration. Of course, Anselm's use of terms such as *justitia, honor* and *debitum* would have had resonances with the legal and social structures of his day, and thereby would have seemed readily understandable and relevant to his contemporary audience, as Gunton has pointed out. To deny that would be silly. But I am wanting to argue that, while those resonances must surely have been powerful in their day, all these interpretations suffer from a failure to recognize the deeper conceptual roots of Anselm's key terms.

The thesis of this paper is that while the key notions in the *Cur deus homo* may have been evocative of the feudal and legal concepts of Anselm's day, they are fundamentally metaphysical rather than sociological in character, and derive from a centuries-long synthesis of ancient Greek and biblical themes. To be specific, the core idea in that dialogue of the *debitum* which humans owe to God is rooted in his earlier dialogues, especially *De veritate*, where it emerges that everything is created with a proper function to fulfil. In order to substantiate this claim, let me summarize the argument of *De veritate*.

The ostensible question of this teacher–student dialogue is whether we

---

7.   C. Gunton, *The Actuality of Atonement* (Edinburgh: T. & T. Clark, 1988), p. 89.

ought to believe that truth in all its forms is God, but the argumentation begins with the teacher's asking what truth is 'in' a proposition. The student can make only a little headway with this question, so the teacher soon takes over, leading him to see that, since a proposition is true when it signifies correctly, as it ought, truth in a proposition is correctness ('rectitudo').

The teacher further develops this idea through a fascinating discussion of a difficulty presented by the student, namely, how to answer someone who says that a statement ('oratio') signifies as it ought even when it signifies as being the case what is *not* the case. For, he points out, a statement has the function of signifying as being ('accepit significare esse') both what is and what is not the case.[8] And if it does that, it does what it ought, and so it is true.

To this, the teacher replies that it is not usual to call true a proposition which signifies as being what is not. Yet it does have a certain truth and correctness. When it signifies as being what is, it does what it ought in *two* ways: for it signifies both what it has the function of signifying and that towards which ('ad quod') it was made. But, he says,

> a statement is usually said to be correct and true in accordance with this latter truth and correctness, by which it signifies as being what is. For it does what it ought more with respect to what it has the function of

8. In an earlier paper on Anselm's theory of truth ('Anselm's Background Metaphysics', *Scottish Journal of Theology* 33 [1980], pp. 317-43), I rendered 'accepit significare esse' as 'has the proper function of signifying to be'. Jasper Hopkins, with characteristic asperity, has objected to this translation on the grounds that it is linguistically inaccurate and renders my exposition inconsistent. (See his *Nicholas of Cusa's Dialectical Mysticism* [Minneapolis: Arthur J. Banning, 1985], pp. 319-20.) I readily confess that, as a translation, my rendering is interpretative rather than pedantic—but then, in an interpretative article that was appropriate. In his *Anselm of Canterbury*, II (Toronto and New York: Edwin Mellen, 1976), Hopkins himself translates the phrase as 'has received the capability of signifying that... is'. But I must also confess that I cannot make much sense of that. Clearly, 'accepit' is used by Anselm sometimes to mean 'receive', for example in *De casu diaboli*. However, in a very relevant parallel passage in *De veritate* ch. 5 Anselm's student says, 'Si ignis ab eo a quo habet esse accepit calefacere: cum calefacit facit quod debet'. Hopkins translates this as 'If fire has received the power to heat from Him from whom it has its being, then when it heats it does what it ought'. This translation has shifted from rendering 'accepit' as 'has received the capability of' to 'has received the power to', no doubt because the former would have rendered Anselm's argument patently fallacious—unless his argument be supposed to depend on the manifestly false assumption that whatever something *can* do, it *ought* to do!

signifying than with respect to what it does not have the function of signifying.[9] For it does not have the function of signifying that a thing is when it is not, or is not when it is, except that it could not be restricted to signifying that it is when it is, or that it is not when it is not. Therefore a proposition has one correctness and truth when it signifies what it was made to signify, and another by which it signifies what it has the function of signifying.

The point is: despite its having the function of signifying *what* is the case *when* it is the case, a proposition can be used wrongly, to signify something that is *not* the case. It can be so used because its having that function does not guarantee that it will always be used properly.

Consider, for example, the proposition 'it is day'. It is designed to point our attention towards the daylight. So when that proposition is asserted during daytime, it signifies as being what is, and so it is true. But although that is what it is made for, it can be asserted at night-time. When that happens what it has the function to do is not being fulfilled. Its role is still to signify that it is day, but in these circumstances it is not signifying as it ought.

This is not the place to work through the detail of this theory.[10] What is important for our current purposes is the way Anselm locates this theory of truth in a much wider context. For him, all sorts of things have natures which define their proper ends. For instance, a fire 'does what it ought' when it heats, because heating is the function it has received ('accepit') from him from whom it has its being. So it does not seem unfitting to say that fire does the truth and what is right when it does what it ought, namely heats.

What we have to deal with here is a thoroughgoing immanent teleology of created natures, in which all creatures have proper functions to perform, and when they do so, they do what they ought. In typical medieval fashion, he easily speaks of both rational and non-rational actions. The natures of things have been created in such a way that what they ought to do is naturally given; their natures define the actions they have it in them to perform. In the case of non-rational things, like fire,

9.   Hopkins translates 'accepit significare' here as 'designed to signify', whereas previously he had used that English phrase to translate 'ad quod facta est', thereby confusing the two senses which Anselm has just carefully distinguished. Of course, this completely muddles Anselm's argument.

10.   I have discussed this theory in detail in the aforementioned article and in chapters 6 and 18 of my *Truth and Historicity* (Oxford: Clarendon Press, 1992).

the exercise of the powers defined in their natures is a matter of necessity, provided nothing else interferes. In the case of voluntary agents and the things they use, the same necessity does not invariably obtain; we can do what we ought not.

From these considerations in *De veritate* Anselm derives his definition of truth as '*rectitudo* perceived by the mind', the qualifying phrase added to distinguish it from the straightness ('rectitudo') of a stick. And in ch. 12 he derives his definition of justice as '*rectitudo* of will kept for its own sake'. So already in this early dialogue we have the conceptual connections between *iustitia* and *debitum* established via the startling yet powerful notion of truth as *facere quod debet*.

Underpinning it all is what I have called a teleology of created natures. The teleology of this goes back to the Greeks—to Aristotle and those before him, since Aristotle was systematizing and developing ideas deeply entrenched in the ancient Greek tradition, indeed in its very language. For Aristotle, change is involved in the very entity of a natural being, and this change is not just any alteration, but its continuous transition from its origin to the achievement of an end-state. Kinesis is that process of attaining the specific end-state which a natural thing has it in it to attain.

Yet that Greek view of natural necessity has been modified by its synthesis with the radical character of the biblical picture of creation, in which everything that is not God is a creature of God: as the creeds put it God is 'creator of all things visible and invisible'. Anselm himself is aware of the tensions generated by this synthesis; in *Monologion* ch. 9 he explains that before the things which were created out of nothing came to be, there was in the mind of the Creator some model, or likeness, or rule. This craftsman analogy sits comfortably enough with the Greek metaphysical picture, as we find it for example in Plato's *Timaeus*. But in *Monologion* ch. 11 Anselm recognizes that the analogy has severe limitations: a craftsman cannot conceive anything in his imagination except what he has somehow learnt from other realities, and he cannot make anything without pre-existing material. Centuries later this very point was to generate such powerful tensions that they blew apart this Greek-Christian synthesis, but that is another story.[11] In Anselm's thinking the Greek teleological metaphysics is still comfortably embedded within an orthodox view of creation.

There are two special twists which Anselm put upon this familiar

11. This story is developed in *Truth and Historicity*, ch. 8.

metaphysical account. One is his describing a thing's performance of those natural functions for which it was made as its doing what it ought, *facere quod debet*. The second is his proposing that that is what is at the core of truth. From all this, it emerges that when a thing does the truth it does what it ought. The concept of *debitum* is deeply rooted in this Christianized teleology.

It is this conception, first sketched in Bec, which Anselm subsequently put to work when in Canterbury he wrote the *Cur deus homo*. Humans have an original *debitum* freely to obey God's will, thereby honouring him. This requirement is no insistence of some feudal overlord with a tender ego. It arises from the very purpose of God's creation of 'Adam's race', which was to maintain the perfect number of rational creatures in proper relation to himself. Secondly, in view of humankind's failure to obey God, by willing what should not be willed, not only does the original *debitum* remain outstanding, but something of appropriate value, not justly required before the offence, needs to be performed if proper order is to be maintained. These are the two elements in satisfaction. This second requirement is no arbitrary addition; it is what is required to make good the failure to fulfil the first. As Steven Asperson has recently argued,[12] the fact of human sin has incurred two debts, one which he calls societal and one personal, both of which need to be discharged. The 'societal' debt which Anselm has identified—a debt which has nothing to do with the sociological models I earlier dismissed—is to be understood as follows. The dishonour of God by no one's conquering the devil is redressed only by someone's making satisfaction, that is, a member of Adam's race returns to God what Adam and his descendants took by disobeying. Asperson calls it a 'societal' debt because the vindication of God, owed by Adam's race, is required of someone, but no particular person. He likens it to political obligations:

> ... the Constitution of the United States, playing the role of a codification of the requirements of justice, obligates each citizen to supply someone to fill the office of President but does not hold any citizen guilty of violating that obligation if he himself does not exercise supererogation in societal action by becoming President.

Christ discharged that debt and so made satisfaction on that score. On the other hand, the *personal* debt is discharged by God's acceding to

12. S. Asperson, 'In Defense of Anselm', *History of Philosophy Quarterly* 7 (1990), pp. 33-45.

Christ's prayer that he forgive the penitent. That is Christ's reward for discharging the societal debt owed by man, that *someone* conquer the devil.

The discharging of these two *debita* amounts to the restoration of *rectitudo*. It is essential to the logic of Anselm's position that this restoration of *rectitudo* be *for its own sake*, and not just to assuage God's injured sense of honour, as some critics would have it. Only *rectitudo* of will kept for its own sake is *iustitia*; that had been established in *De veritate*. And that understanding of *iustitia*, as we have seen, is grounded in his own development of a teleological metaphysics, itself the outcome of more than a millenium of philosophical and theological reflection. Unless we recognize that this is the soil in which the key concepts of his soteriology are rooted, we will fail to appreciate how his theological vision grew and flourished.

PHILOSOPHISCHE ÜBERLEGUNGEN ZU ANSELM VON CANTERBURY:
CUR DEUS HOMO

Adolf Schurr

Vorbemerkung

Die Formulierung der Thematik, daß zu einer vorliegenden Problemerörterung *philosophische* Überlegungen angestellt werden, könnte die
Vermutung nahelegen, daß ein Sachverhalt in Betracht gezogen wird,
der allenfalls philosophische *Marginalien* erlaubt, dem Zugriff einer
philosophischen *Reflexion* und *Argumentation* jedoch entzogen wäre.

Ein solcher Vorbehalt scheint in der Thematik des Spätwerks Anselms
selbst beschlossen zu liegen. Kann die Frage *Cur deus homo*—Warum
ist Gott Mensch geworden?—zum Gegenstand einer *philosophischen*
Untersuchung gemacht werden? Wie sollte es möglich sein, ein solches
Geschehen im 'Warum' seines Sichereignens verstehend einzuholen?
Führt eine solche Fragestellung nicht in den Bereich des Irrationalen, in
einen Bereich also, der dem Zugang der Ratio gänzlich verwehrt ist?

Wenn dies zuträfe, daß eine Menschwerdung Gottes dem Zugriff der
Ratio gänzlich entzogen wäre, dann würde Anselms Spätwerk *Cur deus
homo* jede *philosophische* Reflexion ausschließen—aber nicht nur dies.
Ohne Ratio als integrales Moment könnte sein Werk auch nicht den
Anspruch einer theologischen Problemerörterung erheben.

Thematisiert das Werk *Cur deus homo* den grundlegendsten und
zentralsten Sachverhalt christlich-religiöser Glaubensüberzeugung,
dann wird mit der *Beantwortbarkeit* von Anselms Fragestellung nicht
nur unter *wissenschafts-theoretischen*, sondern darüber hinaus unter
existentiell-relevanten Aspekten über das Selbstverständnis des christlichen Glaubens entschieden.

Akzentuiert formuliert: Unter prinzipiellen Aspekten sind nur zwei
Möglichkeiten denkbar: Der christliche Glaube ist entweder *blinder* oder
rational ausweisbarer Glaube.

Es ist unmittelbar einsichtig, welche Bedeutung der Entscheidung dieser Alternative für den christlich-religiösen Existenzvollzug zukommt: Im ersten Fall wäre der Existenzvollzug einer (wie auch immer gearteten) *Willkür* ausgeliefert—im zweiten Fall dagegen fiele er in die *Verantwortbarkeit* der menschlichen Freiheit.

Umso drängender wird die Frage: Mit welch wissenschafts-theoretischer Konzeption wird die Problematik von Anselm angegangen und erörtert?

Anselms Intention und wissenschafts-theoretische Konzeption
einer Erörterung der Frage: Cur deus homo?

Eine für jede Anselm-Rezeption höchst bemerkenswerte Tatsache liegt in dem Umstand beschlossen, daß sich Anselm bereits vor dem Eintritt in die Problemerörterung über deren Intention und insbesondere über deren methodische Verfahrens- und Argumentationsweise erklärt.—Ich selbst könnte keinen Grund benennen, warum die Prolegomena seines letzten Hauptwerkes nicht genau so gelesen und verstanden werden könnten wie sie niedergeschrieben sind.

Hinzu kommt, daß beides—sowohl die Artikulation der *Intention* als auch die Bestimmung der *methodischen Verfahrensweise*—im Gang der Problemerörterung selbst aufgegriffen und präzisiert wird.

Anselm postuliert nichts anderes als die Realisation eines Vermögens, über das jeder Mensch verfügt, nämlich seine Vernunftbegabtheit. Angesichts dieser fraglosen Implikation des Menschseins kann und muß ganz einfach gesagt werden: 'es scheint mir eine Nachlässigkeit, wenn wir [...] uns nicht zu verstehen bemühen, was wir glauben'.[1] Aufgrund der Vernunftbegabtheit des Menschen kann die postulierte reflexive Einholbarkeit des *christlichen* Existenzvollzuges nicht bereits anfänglich ausgeschlossen werden. Bei einer gegenteiligen Annahme müßte der Nachweis der Irrationalität des christlichen Offenbarungs-Anspruchs geführt werden.

Nun ist unmittelbar einsichtig, daß die gestellte Alternative—den christlich-religiösen Glauben entweder als reflexiv einholbar oder als irrational zu veranschlagen—legitimerweise nur im Medium von Erkenntnis und nicht auf dem Wege von Vorurteilen entschieden werden kann.

Kann die Frage, ob der christliche Glaube der Vernunft widerspreche

---

1. *Cur deus homo* 1: Schmitt, II, p. 48:17-18: 'negligentia mihi videtur, si [...] non studemus quod credimus intelligere'.

oder nicht, einzig und allein durch die Vernunft selbst entschieden werden, dann handelt es sich um eine Problemerörterung, die auch dem Ungläubigen unter prinzipiellen Aspekten nicht verschlossen ist. Anselm kann daher zurecht konstatieren: 'Obschon nämlich [die Ungläubigen] nach Gründen fragen, weil sie nicht glauben, wir dagegen, weil wir glauben, so ist es doch ein und dasselbe, wonach wir forschen.'[2] Wie muß eine Problemerörterung unter wissenschafts-theoretischen Aspekten bestimmt werden, damit Zugang und Nachprüfbarkeit jedes Argumentations-Schrittes jedem möglich ist, der sich darauf einläßt?

In die erfragte wissenschafts-theoretische Bestimmung des Erkenntnisbemühens darf im Hinblick auf die Voraussetzungen nur das eingebracht werden, ohne das keine Problemerörterung denkbar wäre. Das heißt: als Argumentationsbasis kann nur das veranschlagt werden, was sich für jede Reflexion als denknotwendig erweist. Dies aber wäre—in einer äußersten Abstraktion gefaßt—einzig und allein die Artikulation des Denkens selbst.

Was aber verbleibt für die Reflexion und deren Argumentation, wenn das Denken sich auf sich selbst zurücknimmt und damit jegliche Erfahrung—im Falle der Fragestellung Anselms insbesondere die religiöse Glaubenserfahrung—als Argumentationsbasis eingeklammert wird?—Es verbleibt in der Tat nur das, was in der *Praefatio* des Spätwerks unmißverständlich festgeschrieben wird: 'mit Beiseitesetzung Christi, so, als ob niemals etwas von ihm gewesen wäre, beweist es mit zwingenden Gründen'.[3] Was hier unter wissenschafts-theoretischen Aspekten formuliert wird, ist eine höchst bemerkenswerte These: Für die Begründung von Erkenntnis werden *nur rationes necessariae* zugelassen; aber nicht nur dies: mit Hilfe 'denknotwendiger Vernunftgründe' soll darüber hinaus die Problematik einer *Inkarnation Gottes* erörtert werden.

Daß erfahrungs-unabhängige Erkenntnis-Aussagen möglich sind und daß es aufgrund solcher Erkenntnis-Aussagen Wissenschaften gibt, deren Kriterien einzig und allein im Denken selbst liegen, dokumentiert die Möglichkeit *apriorischer* Erkenntnis und die Tatsache reiner Geisteswissenschaften, wie sie in der Mathematik und Logik vorliegen.

---

2. *Cur deus homo* 3: Schmitt, II, p. 50:18-20: 'Quamvis enim [infideles] ideo rationem quaerant, quia non credunt, nos vero, quia credimus: unum idemque tamen est quod quaerimus'.

3. *Cur deus homo* P: Schmitt, II, p. 42:12-13: 'remoto Christo, quasi numquam aliquid fuerit de illo, probat rationibus necessariis'.

Erweist die Möglichkeit apriorischer Erkenntnis überhaupt aber bereits die Möglichkeit einer erfahrungs-unabhängigen Problemerörterung einer Inkarnation Gottes?—Niemand wird diese Frage ohne zusätzliche Voraussetzungen bejahen; denn es ist unmittelbar einsichtig, daß allein schon eine sinnvolle *Artikulation* der Fragestellung Anselms bereits die *Wirklichkeit* Gottes oder zumindest den *Begriff* Gottes voraussetzt.

Was bedeutet die denknotwendige Implikation der Fragestellung von *Cur deus homo*, daß für das Verstehen der Frage der Begriff oder die Wirklichkeit Gottes bereits vorausgesetzt werden muß?

Wenn das, was erörtert wird, für den Glaubenden und den Nicht-Glaubenden als 'ein und dasselbe' veranschlagt wird, so muß die Problemerörterung von *Cur deus homo* auch dann nachvollziehbar sein, wenn lediglich der *Begriff* Gottes als einer 'schlechthin absoluten Wirklichkeit' vorausgesetzt wird.

Anselm nimmt die Möglichkeit eines Begriffs des 'Absoluten' auf das Vermögen reinen Denkens zurück und bestimmt das mit dem Begriff Gemeinte als 'etwas worüber hinaus nichts Größeres gedacht werden kann'.[4] Mit dem Begriff des Absoluten sieht sich das Denken, so gewiß es sich in seinem Sein nicht selbst als Absolutes begreifen kann, über sich hinausverwiesen:

entweder—nach der Überzeugung des Glaubenden—
auf eine *wirkliche* Wirklichkeit des Absoluten;

oder—nach der Überzeugung des Nicht-Glaubenden—
auf eine *bloß vorgestellte* Wirklichkeit des Absoluten.

In beiden Fällen kann die Frage der theoretischen Ausweisbarkeit der lebensmäßigen Überzeugung zum Gegenstand des Erkenntnisbemühens gemacht werden; das Erkenntnisvermögen muß geradezu angestrengt werden, wenn man die beiden entgegengesetzten Lebensüberzeugungen nicht einfach unbefragt nebeneinander stehen läßt.

---

4. *Proslogion* 2: Schmitt, I, p. 101:5: 'aliquid quo nihil maius cogitari possit'. Bei diesem Begriff des Absoluten handelt es sich um das 'unum argumentum' des sogenannten 'ontologischen Gottesbeweises', das von Anselm in einem dreifachen Explikationsschritt entfaltet wird: (1) 'zur *Wirklichkeit* des Absoluten'; (2) 'zur *Undenkbarkeit des Nichtseins* des Absoluten'; (3) 'zum Denken der *Unbegreiflichkeit* des Absoluten'. (Siehe meine Arbeit: *Die Begründung der Philosophie durch Anselm von Canterbury. Eine Erörterung des ontologischen Gottesbeweises* [Stuttgart, 1966], pp. 86-120).

268   *Anselm: Aosta, Bec and Canterbury*

Unter wissenschaft-theoretischen Aspekten ist entscheidend, daß eine grundlegende Problemerörterung von beiden entgegengesetzten Positionen aus möglich ist. Eine Differenz liegt dem Bemühen um Erkenntnis zwar in der Implikation des Ausgangspunktes beschlossen:

> Dem Glaubenden gilt eine *Negation* der Wirklichkeit Gottes
> als *bloß hypothetischer* Ausgangspunkt;
> dem Nicht-Glaubenden gilt die *Affirmation* der Wirklichkeit Gottes
> als *bloß hypothetischer* Ausgangspunkt.

Die reflexive Ermittlung und Entscheidung darüber jedoch, wie Gott als schlechthin absolute Wirklichkeit gedacht werden muß—entweder als *bloß vorgestellte* oder als *wirkliche* Wirklichkeit—ist vermittelst denknotwendiger Vernunftgründe für beide Ausgangspositionen gleichermaßen möglich.

Der Durchvollzug der Reflexion könnte anfänglich bloß hypothetisch Veranschlagtes in apodiktisch Gewisses transformieren: Die Hypothese einer bloß vorgestellten, aber nicht wirklichen Wirklichkeit des Absoluten könnte in die apodiktische Gewißheit der wirklichen Wirklichkeit des Absoluten umschlagen, so daß mit Anselms Worten gesagt werden müßte: 'was ich zuvor [...] geglaubt habe, sehe ich jetzt [...] so ein, daß ich, wollte ich es nicht glauben, daß Du existierst, es nicht nicht einsehen könnte'.[5]

Die apodiktische Erkenntnis, zu der Anselms Reflexion auf die Glaubensüberzeugung: '*Daß Gott in Wahrheit existiert*'—'*Quod vere sit deus*',[6] zu führen vermag, ist auch dem nicht verwehrt, der die Wirklichkeit Gottes anfänglich als bloße Hypothese betrachtet, da es sich um einen Sachverhalt handelt, der am Ende einer streng rational geführten Argumentation 'dem vernunftbegabten Geiste offen zutage liegt'.[7]

Die Differenzierung der wissenschafts-theoretischen Konzeption unter dem Aspekt von apodiktisch und bloß hypothetisch veranschlagten Voraussetzungen einer Problemerörterung erfolgte aus zwei Gründen:

1. Es sollte darauf verwiesen werden, daß die Negation des Wahrheits-Anspruchs einer religiösen Glaubensüberzeugung—und zwar der grundlegendsten Überzeugung von der Wirklichkeit Gottes—nicht daran hindert, die Wirklichkeit des Absoluten als bloß hypothetische

---

5. *Proslogion* 4: Schmitt, I, p. 104:5-7: 'quod prius credidi [...], iam sic intelligo [...], ut si te esse nolim credere, non possim non intelligere'.

6. *Proslogion* 2: Schmitt, I, p. 101:2.

7. *Proslogion* 3: Schmitt, I, p. 103:10: 'cum [...] in promptu sit rationali menti'.

Voraussetzung in eine Problemerörterung einzubringen, ohne daß dadurch die Stringenz der Argumentation aufgehoben würde. 2. Aus der benannten wissenschafts-theoretischen Tatsache kann m.E. darüber hinaus zurecht gefolgert werden, daß auch durch die hypothetische Voraussetzung zusätzlicher, noch unreflektierter denknotwendiger Implikationen der grundlegendsten Glaubensüberzeugung die Stringenz einer weiterführenden Problemerörterung nicht aufgehoben wird.—Die Richtigkeit der angezeigten Konsequenz kann sich nur daraus ergeben, daß die Implikationen benannt werden, ohne welche die Frage: *Cur deus homo?* weder angegangen noch erörtert werden könnte, um aus der Problementwicklung selbst deren mögliche argumentative Stringenz entweder bejahen zu können oder verneinen zu müssen.

Voraussetzungen und Fragestellungen von Cur deus homo

Voraussetzungen
Eine Problemerörterung der Frage '*Cur deus homo?*' hat eine dreifache Voraussetzung:

1. die Vorstellung Gottes als einer schlechthin absoluten Wirklichkeit;
2. das Sein und die unmittelbare Selbsterschlossenheit des Vorstellenden;
3. die Bestimmbarkeit der Relation beider als Interpersonal-Relation.

Fragestellungen
Die Problemerörterung selbst läßt sich in die beiden Fragen fassen:

1. Wie müßte die Ideal-Realisation einer Interpersonal-Relation zwischen Gott und dem Menschen gedacht werden?
2. Wie müßte—bei einer Verfehlung der Ideal-Realisation—eine Wiedereröffnung der Möglichkeit einer Ideal-Realisation gedacht werden?

Die Voraussetzungen der Problemerörterung und deren Implikation

Ehe die Problemerörterung selbst aufgegriffen wird, bedarf es einer Präzisierung der dreifachen Voraussetzung und einer Reflexion auf deren Implikationen.

Eine Reflexion, die nicht bereits voraussetzt, was allererst erwiesen werden soll, sieht sich zunächst einzig und allein auf die Artikulationsweisen des menschlichen Bewußtseins zurückverwiesen.

Reflektiert man auf *die* Artikulationsweise, die als '*absolut*' begriffen werden muß, dann sieht sich die Reflexion auf die Artikulation der *Freiheit* verwiesen; denn unter dem Begriff der Freiheit kann nur ein ausschließliches *Durch-sich-sein* und insofern ein *absolutes Grund-sein* gedacht werden.

Wird als ausgezeichnetstes Vermögen des Menschen dessen Freiheit als absolutes Grund-sein-Können veranschlagt, so stellt sich die Frage: Wie müßte eine Realpräsenz Gottes im menschlichen Bewußtsein gedacht werden?

Die Konzeption einer *Realpräsenz Gottes im menschlichen Bewußtsein* kann nur auf folgende Weise gedacht werden:

Unter *formalen Aspekten* kann eine Realpräsenz Gottes im menschlichen Bewußtsein nicht anders gedacht werden als die Realpräsenz irgend einer anderen Freiheit als Freiheit: nämlich im Modus eines zu freier Selbsttätigkeit aufrufenden *Sollens*.

Die Konzeption einer Realpräsenz Gottes im menschlichen Bewußtsein unter *material-inhaltlichen Aspekten* ist jedoch ohne eine Bestimmung dessen, was mit den Worten 'Gott' oder 'schlechthin absolute Wirklichkeit' oder 'das Absolute' gemeint ist, gar nicht möglich.

Anselm hat die Begriffsbestimmung des 'Absoluten' zu einer streng rationalen Erörterung der Gottesfrage[8] in seinem 'unum argumentum'[9] des sogenannten 'ontologischen Gottesbeweises' festgeschrieben als 'aliquid quo nihil maius cogitari possit'[10]—als: 'etwas worüber hinaus nichts Größeres gedacht werden kann'.

Welche Implikationen hat Anselms Begriffsbestimmung des Absoluten für die Konzeption einer Realpräsenz des Absoluten im menschlichen Bewußtsein?—Eine Beantwortung der gestellten Frage läßt sich nur dadurch angehen, daß das unter dem Begriff des Absoluten zu

---

8. Bereits in seinem Erstlingswerk hat sich Anselm klar und eindeutig zu seiner methodischen Verfahrensweise geäußert: 'auctoritate scripturae penitus nihil in ea [meditatione] persuaderetur'—'nichts solle durch die *Autorität der Schrift* zur Überzeugung gebracht werden'; zur *Erkenntnis* ('veritatis claritas') soll nichts anderes führen als die '*Notwendigkeit der Vernunftüberlegung*' ('rationis necessitas') (*Monologion* P: Schmitt, I, pp: 7,7-8 und 7,10-11).

9. *Proslogion* P: Schmitt, I, p. 93:6.

10. *Proslogion* 2: Schmitt, I, p. 101:5.

Denkende im Denken und durch das Denken selbst weiterbestimmt wird.

Anselm faßt das unter dem Begriff des Absoluten zu Denkende nicht nur als schlechthin unbedingtes Durch-sich-Sein, als: 'solus existens per se'—als: 'allein durch sich bestehend'; die höchst bemerkenswerte Weiterbestimmung des zu Denkenden erfordert, das Absolute als das zu denken: 'quidquid melius est esse quam non esse'[11]—'was besser ist zu sein als nicht zu sein'.

Aufgrund der implikativen Weiterbestimmung des Begriffs kann das Absolute nicht als wertneutrale Wirklichkeit gedacht werden, ohne dessen Begriff zu verfehlen; das Absolute kann nur gedacht werden als ein solches Durch-sich-Sein, das aufgrund einer alles menschliche Denken ins Unendliche übersteigenden Wertqualitas die Frage nach dem *Warum* seines Seins gegenstandslos macht: es kann nur gedacht werden als fraglose Positivität nicht mehr hinterfragbarer in sich gründender Selbstbegründetheit.

Was bedeutet die implikative Weiterbestimmung des Begriffes des Absoluten für die Konzeption einer Realpräsenz des Absoluten im menschlichen Bewußtsein? Wie müßte eine Realpräsenz des Absoluten unter material-inhaltlichen Aspekten gedacht werden?

Es versteht sich von selbst, daß die Frage nach einer *material-inhaltlichen* Bestimmung von etwas, das *sein soll*, auf rein begrifflichem Wege ebenso wenig möglich ist wie die qualitative Bestimmung von etwas, das *ist*. Die Erschlossenheit der *qualitativen* Bestimmtheit bedarf in beiden Fällen der Anschauung; dennoch aber ermöglicht der Begriff des Absoluten die Formalbestimmung eines Sollens, das als *absolutes* Sollen begriffen werden könnte und begriffen werden müßte.

Eine Realpräsenz des Absoluten in einem absoluten Sollen wäre im menschlichen Bewußtsein überhaupt und immer dann gegeben, wenn sich einem Sollens-Gehalt die Evidenz eines fraglosen, sich in und durch sich selbst begründenden Sein-Sollens verbände.

Was müßte aus der Möglichkeit, daß sich dem menschlichen Bewußtsein eine sich fraglos selbstbegründende Wertevidenz von Gesolltem verbinden könnte, für dessen Selbstverständnis gefolgert werden?

In einer Bestimmung des erfragten Selbstverständnisses müßte eine argumentative Fragebeantwortung folgendermaßen verfahren:

---

11. *Proslogion* 4: Schmitt, I, 104:9-10.

1. Wenn sich dem Bewußtsein die Evidenz eines sich fraglos selbst begründenden Sollens-Gehaltes verbände,
2. wenn das menschliche Bewußtsein außerstande wäre, einen sich fraglos selbst begründenden Sollens-Gehalt zu kreieren,
3. dann könnte das menschliche Bewußtsein nicht anders gedacht werden als immer schon eingelassen auf eine interpersonale Relation seiner selbst als nicht-absoluter Wirklichkeit auf eine absolute Wirklichkeit.

Als Resultat der bisherigen Überlegungen ergäbe sich der für das menschliche Selbstverständnis grundlegende Sachverhalt:

Aufgrund eines sich dem Bewußtsein verbindenden absoluten Sollens müßte für den Selbstvollzug des menschlichen Bewußtseins eine *konstitutive* Bezogenheit auf eine personal zu konzipierende absolute Wirklichkeit veranschlagt werden.

Kann eine konstitutive Bezogenheit nur als *apriorische* Bezogenheit gedacht werden, dann sähe sich das menschliche Bewußtsein in der Apriorität eines absoluten Sollens auf eine nicht selbst verfügte und zugleich unaufhebbare *Normativität* seines Wollens und Handelns bezogen.

In der Normativität eines absoluten Sollens, dessen Sollens-Gehalt sich fraglos selbst begründet, läge zugleich die Möglichkeit einer in Wahrheit begründbaren *Sinn-Realisation* des menschlichen Daseins überhaupt beschlossen.

Es wurde der Versuch unternommen, die dreifache Voraussetzung der Frage 'Cur deus homo?' zu präzisieren, wobei

1. die explizite Fassung des Gottesbegriffes,
2. die Reflexion auf das eigentliche Vermögen des menschlichen Existenzvollzuges, und
3. die Reflexion auf die grundlegendste Interpersonal-Relation menschlichen Daseins

jedem radikalen Erkenntnisverlangen einen m.E. unverstellten Zugang zu Anselms Problemerörterung eröffnen müßten.

Die Erörterung der tiefgreifendsten Fragen von Cur deus homo

Die zentrale Problematik von Anselms *Cur deus homo* ist bereits in die beiden Fragen gefaßt worden:

1. Wie müßte die Ideal-Realisation einer Interpersonal-Relation zwischen Gott und dem Menschen gedacht werden?
2. Wie müßte—bei einer Verfehlung der Ideal-Realisation—eine Wiedereröffnung der Möglichkeit einer Ideal-Realisation gedacht werden?

1. Die Konzeption einer Ideal-Realisation der Interpersonal-Relation zwischen Gott und dem Menschen
Die erfragte Bestimmung der Ideal-Realisation könnte aufgrund der bisherigen Überlegungen in nichts anderes gesetzt werden als in die Realisation eines konstitutiven absoluten Sollens. Eine Verwirklichung der Ideal-Realisation bestünde darin, sich fraglos selbst Begründendes zur alleinigen Norm des Wollens und Handelns zu erheben und ausnahmslos zu verwirklichen.—Eine umfassendere Bestimmung der erfragten Ideal-Realisation bedarf jedoch einer Reflexion auf die Implikationen einer Interpersonal-Relation überhaupt.

Ohne Zweifel liegt der Artikulationspunkt einer Interpersonal-Relation im Begriff des *Sollens*; denn ein Sollen impliziert das Ineinandergreifen zweier Freiheiten: eine das Sollen setzende Freiheit und eine das Sollen realisierende Freiheit. Die Realisation des Gewollten *einer* Freiheit durch eine *andere* Freiheit bedeutet das freie Sich-Zusammenschließen *zweier* selbständiger und selbsttätiger Willen zu *einem* gemeinsam-identischen Wollen.

Wie müßte über die elementarste Strukturiertheit der Interpersonal-Relation hinaus die Realisation eines *absoluten* Sollens gedacht werden?

Unter prinzipiellen Aspekten müßte zur Bestimmung der erfragten Ideal-Realisation Folgendes gesagt werden:

1. Die Bestimmung eines absoluten Sollens-Gehalts wäre der Willkürfestsetzung entzogen.
2. Durch die Realisation eines absoluten, sich in seinem Seinsollen fraglos selbst begründenden Sollens verwirklichte die Freiheit die Ideal-Realisation ihres eigentlichsten Seinkönnens.
3. Die Evidenz einer fraglosen Selbstbegründung absoluten Sollens wäre einsichtigerweise nur aufgrund eines wechselseitigen Zusammenwirkens von Freiheiten im interpersonalen Nexus, d.h. nur aufgrund von Erfahrung möglich.

Die Frage nach der Möglichkeit einer *inhaltlichen* Bestimmung der Ideal-Realisation könnte demnach nur folgendermaßen beantwortet werden:

Für die material-inhaltliche Bestimmbarkeit dessen, worin die Ideal-Realisation als *Sinn-Realisation des Menschseins überhaupt* bestünde, sähe sich die Reflexion auf das wirkliche Geschehen interpersonaler Erfahrung verwiesen.

Anselm setzt die Sinn-konstituierende material-inhaltliche Bestimmtheit der Ideal-Realisation in die Wechselwirksamkeit der *interpersonalen Liebe*.

Wissenschafts-theoretisch gesehen ist es höchst bemerkenswert, daß Anselm bei der Bestimmung der Ideal-Realisation auf nichts anderes zurückgreift als auf das Urteilsvermögen des Menschen als Vernunftwesen:

> Schließlich bedeutet der vernünftigen Natur vernünftig sein nichts anderes, als das Gerechte vom Nicht-Gerechten, das Wahre vom Nicht-Wahren, das Gute vom Nicht-Guten, das Bessere vom weniger Guten unterscheiden zu können. [...] Es ist also klar, daß das vernünftige Geschöpf sein ganzes Können und Wollen aufwenden muß, um des höchsten Gutes sich bewußt zu sein und es zu erkennen und zu lieben, zu welchem Zwecke es gerade, wie es weiß, sein Dasein hat.[12]

Die Ideal-Realisation menschlichen Daseins gründet in der ganzheitlichen Liebe zum Absoluten als der schlechthin absoluten Liebe, 'weil sie gut durch sich ist und nichts anderes gut ist außer durch sie'.[13]

Dies bedeutet: Allein die Liebe des Absoluten kann als sinn-stiftendes Prinzip der Sinn-Realisation menschlichen Daseins gedacht werden. Allein die Liebe des Absoluten kann und muß—aufgrund ihres absoluten Durch-sich-Seins—als das gedacht werden 'worüber hinaus nichts *Besseres* gedacht werden kann': 'Denn wenn ein Geist etwas Besseres [...] denken könnte, erhöbe sich das Geschöpf über den Schöpfer [...], was ganz widersinnig ist.'[14]

Kann das Absolute nur als absolute Liebe gedacht werden, dann kann

---

12. *Monologion* 68: Schmitt, I, pp, 78:21-23, 79:6-9: 'Denique rationali naturae non est aliud esse rationalem, quam posse discernere iustum a non iusto, verum a non vero, bonum a non bono, magis bonum a minus bono. [...] Clarum ergo est rationalem creaturam totum suum posse et velle ad memorandum et intelligendum et amandum summum bonum impendere debere, ad quod ipsum esse suum se cognoscit habere'.

13. *Monologion* 68: Schmitt, I, p. 79:4-5: 'quia illa [scil. die 'höchste Wesenheit' als absolute Liebe] est bona per se, et nihil aliud est bonum nisi per illam'.

14. *Proslogion* 3: Schmitt, I, p. 103:4-6: 'Si enim aliqua mens posset cogitare aliquid melius [...] ascenderet creatura super creatorem [...]; quod valde est absurdum'.

ein der menschlichen Freiheit zugrundeliegendes apriorisches Sollen nur
begriffen werden als konstitutives Aufgerufen-Sein, die Liebe des Absoluten durch eine selbstätige und ganzheitliche Gegenliebe zu erwidern.
Die zu verwirklichende Ideal-Realisation der Interpersonal-Relation
zwischen dem nicht-absoluten menschlichen Sein und dem absoluten
Sein Gottes faßt Anselm in die höchst beeindruckende, geradezu
visionäre Sicht derer, die dem konstitutiven Aufgerufen-Sein durch ihren
gesamten Existenzvollzug entsprechen:

> sie werden Gott lieben mehr als sich selber und einander wie sich selber
> und Gott wird sie mehr lieben als sie sich selber; weil sie ihn und sich und
> einander durch ihn [lieben] und er sich und sie durch sich selber.[15]

Die angestellten Überlegungen und Quellenverweisungen versuchten die
erste der beiden tiefgreifendsten Fragen Anselms zu beantworten: Ob
und wie die Frage einer Ideal-Realisation der Interpersonal-Relation
zwischen Gott und Mensch gedacht werden könnte und müßte.—Wie
aber—und das ist die weiterführende Frage von Anselms *Cur deus
homo*—könnte und müßte aufgrund einer Verfehlung der Ideal-Realisation deren Wiedereröffnung gedacht werden?

2. Die Konzeption einer Wiedereröffnung der Möglichkeit einer Ideal-Realisation der Interpersonal-Relation zwischen Gott und dem Menschen

Wenn die Sinn-Realisation des menschlichen Daseins in die Verwirklich-
ung interpersonaler Liebe, insbesondere in die Erwiderung der Liebe
Gottes gesetzt werden müßte, was würde es dann bedeuten, wenn der
Mensch die Liebe des Absoluten nicht durch eine ganzheitliche
Gegenliebe erwiderte?

Der Mensch verfehlte in diesem Falle durch eigenes Verschulden seine
eigentliche Bestimmung: die ihm ursprünglich eröffnete Verwirklichung
einer Ideal-Realisation seiner konstitutiven Bezogenheit auf die Wirklichkeit des Absoluten.

Wenn aber feststünde, daß der Mensch sein Dasein zu keinem anderen
Zwecke erhalten hat als 'sich dessen bewußt zu sein und zu erkennen
und zu lieben', 'worüber hinaus nichts Größeres gedacht werden kann',
dann könnte im Hinblick auf die Sinnhaftigkeit menschlichen Daseins

---

15. *Proslogion* 25: Schmitt, I, p. 119:5-7: 'diligent deum plus quam seipsos, et
invicem tamquam seipsos, et deus illos plus quam illi seipsos; quia illi illum et se et
invicem per illum, et ille se et illos per seipsum'.

276 Anselm: Aosta, Bec and Canterbury

überhaupt konsequenterweise von der Voraussetzung ausgegangen werden: 'daß es notwendig sei, daß sich das mit dem Menschen vollziehe, um dessetwillen er geschaffen wurde'.[16] Diese in der *Praefatio* von *Cur deus homo* vorangestellte These resultiert aus der tiefergreifenden Fragestellung nach dem Sinn des Menschseins überhaupt.

Könnte der Sinn des Gesetztseins nicht-absoluten Seins überhaupt aus nichts anderem erwachsen als aus der zu verwirklichenden Ideal-Realisation zwischen Gott und dem Menschen, dann bliebe die 'Erschaffung des Menschen' gänzlich Sinn-los, wenn die geforderte Ideal-Realisation niemals verwirklicht würde.

Die Problematik von *Cur deus homo* entsteht daher aus folgender Antithetik:

1. Der schlechthin seinsollende Sinn des Mensch-Seins überhaupt könnte nur aus der Verwirklichung der Ideal-Realisation der Interpersonal-Relation zwischen Gott und dem Menschen erwachsen.

2. Die geforderte Ideal-Realisation und mit ihr die Sinn-Realisation des Mensch-Seins sei vom Menschen schuldhaft verfehlt worden.

Die Lösung der Antithetik liegt in der Frage beschlossen: Wie könnte bzw. wie müßte eine Wiedereröffnung der Möglichkeit der geforderten Ideal-Realisation und mit ihr eine Sinnhaftigkeit des Mensch-Seins überhaupt gedacht werden?

Die Lösung der Problematik einer Wiedereröffnung der Möglichkeit einer Ideal-Realisation scheint am einfachsten durch eine Reflexion auf das Ineinandergreifen von Freiheiten im Vollzug der Interpersonal-Relation selbst—und zwar auf der Basis wirklicher Liebe.

Wenn eine Interpersonal-Relation ausschließlich im Prinzip der Liebe gründete, was könnte und müßte dann bei einer *Verfehlung* der Liebe umwillen der Liebe geschehen?

Die Liebe erlaubte aufgrund einer Verfehlung keinen Abbruch der Interpersonal-Relation—sonst gründete sie nicht wirklich im Prinzip der Liebe; eine Antwort der Liebe könnte nur als *Vergebung* der Verfehlung gedacht werden—sonst erwiese sie sich nicht als wirkliche Liebe.—Was bedeutete die Vergebung für die Interpersonal-Relation? Die Verfehlung könnte durch deren Vergebung zwar nicht ungeschehen gemacht

16. *Cur deus homo* P: Schmitt, II, pp. 42:16-43:1: 'necesse est ut hoc fiat de homine propter quod factus est'.

werden; sie hinderte jedoch als vergebenes Schuldig-geworden-Sein nicht die Wiederaufnahme oder Weiterführung der Interpersonal-Relation.

Wer allein aber könnte als *Vergebender* gedacht werden? Ohne Zweifel nur derjenige, dem gegenüber die Verfehlung begangen wurde—und zwar als Verweigerung der Gegenliebe; nur er allein könnte ein Schuldig-geworden-Sein als Nicht-Erwiderung seiner Liebe vergeben.

Was bedeutete dieser unmittelbar einsichtige prinzipielle Sachverhalt im Hinblick auf eine Verfehlung der Ideal-Realisation der Interpersonal-Relation zwischen Gott und dem Menschen?

Eine bloße Vergebung einer Verfehlung könnte diese nicht ungeschehen machen; sie bliebe eine Gegenwart gewesene Artikulation der Interpersonal-Relation als (partielle oder totale) Nicht-Erwiderung der Liebe des Menschen zu Gott; denn selbst eine Vergebung von seiten Gottes könnte eine einmal Gegenwart gewesene Wirklichkeit nicht ungeschehen machen.

Welche Konsequenzen lägen in der absoluten Unaufhebbarkeit eines Wirklichkeit gewesenen interpersonalen Geschehens als denknotwendige Implikation beschlossen?

1. Durch die Unaufhebbarkeit einer Wirklichkeit gewesenen Ver-fehlung wäre eine Ideal-Realisation der Interpersonal-Relation zwischen Gott und dem Menschen unwiederbringlich ausgeschlossen.

2. Durch den Ausschluß einer Ideal-Realisation der Interpersonal-Relation zwischen Gott und dem Menschen würde der Sinn der 'Erschaffung des Menschen' mitausgeschlossen.

Wie könnte und müßte entgegen den angezeigten Konsequenzen den-noch eine Sinn-Realisation des Seins menschlichen Daseins überhaupt gedacht werden?

Die Lösung der Antithetik—der Notwendigkeit einer Sinnrealisation des Mensch-Seins überhaupt einerseits und dem Faktum einer unaufhebbaren Verfehlung der sinnstiftenden Ideal-Realisation anderer-seits—wird von Anselm durch die grundlegendste These von *Cur deus homo* angezeigt.

Die Ideal-Realisation einer Interpersonal-Relation zwischen Gott und dem Menschen und mit ihr und durch sie die Sinnhaftigkeit des Mensch-Seins überhaupt wäre—aufgrund einer Verfehlung der Ideal-Realisation des menschlichen Daseins durch den Menschen—nur möglich: 'durch den menschgewordenen Gott'—'per hominem-deum'.[17] Seine Argumentation für die Notwendigkeit der Menschwerdung Gottes faßt Anselm in die Frage:

> Scheint es nicht ein genügend notwendiger Grund zu sein, warum Gott das, was wir sagen, tun mußte:
>
> [1] nämlich weil das Menschengeschlecht, sein so kostbares Werk, gänzlich zugrundegegangen war
> [2] und es sich nicht ziemte, daß, was Gott über den Menschen beschlossen hatte, vollständig zunichte werden sollte
> [3] und dieses sein Vorhaben nicht zum Erfolg geführt werden konnte, es sei denn, das Menschengeschlecht würde von seinem Schöpfer selbst befreit?[18]

Die Begründung der Notwendigkeit einer Inkarnation Gottes ist in dieser Fragestellung klar und deutlich angezeigt:

> [1] Die Sinn-Realisation des Menschseins sei 'gänzlich' verfehlt worden.
> [2] Gottes Intention mit dem Menschen sollte nicht 'vollständig zunichte werden'.
> [3] Gottes 'Vorhaben mit dem Menschen' könne nur als 'Befreiung des Menschengeschlechtes' durch die Menschwerdung Gottes 'zum Erfolg geführt werden'.

Unter streng systematischen Aspekten läßt sich die Argumentation zur Notwendigkeit der Inkarnation Gottes aufgrund der bisherigen Überlegungen auf zwei Argumente zurücknehmen:

Der Schlüsselbegriff liegt in dem Begriff der *Ideal-Realisation* der Interpersonal-Relation zwischen Gott und dem Menschen.

1. Da—von seiten des Menschen her gesehen—eine Verfehlung der Ideal-Realisation als Erwiderung der Liebe Gottes durch den Menschen von Gott zwar vergeben, aber nicht ungeschehen gemacht werden könnte, wäre die vom Menschen geforderte Ideal-Realisation nur durch

---

17. *Cur deus homo* P: Schmitt, II, p. 43:1-2.
18. *Cur deus homo* 4: Schmitt, II, p. 52:7-11: 'Nonne satis necessaria ratio videtur, cur deus ea quae dicimus facere debuerit:
[1] quia genus humanum, tam scilicet pretiosum opus eius, omnino perierat,
[2] nec decebat ut, quod deus de homine proposuerat, penitus annihilaretur,
[3] nec idem eius propositum ad effectum duci poterat, nisi genus hominum ab ipso creatore suo liberaretur?'

einen Menschen möglich, der die Ideal-Realisation wirklich und ohne Verfehlung vollzöge.

2. Da—von seiten Gottes her gesehen—die Vergebung einer Verfehlung der Liebe des Menschen zu Gott nur als Vergebung durch Gott gedacht werden könnte, müßte in einer Interpersonal-Relation zwischen Gott und dem Menschen der die Verfehlung vergeben Könnende nicht bloßer Mensch sein: er müßte Gott selbst sein.

Eine Wiedereröffnung der vom Menschen geforderten aber schuldhaft verfehlten Ideal-Realisation wäre demnach nur möglich durch den *menschgewordenen Gott* selbst, der beides zugleich vermöchte:

1. *Als Mensch* vollzöge er die vom Menschen verfehlte, aber für dessen Sinn-Realisation unabdingbare Ideal-Realisation der Interpersonal-Relation zwischen Gott und dem Menschen.

2. Als menschgewordener *Gott* vermöchte er dem Menschen alle schuldhafte Verfehlung zu vergeben—und zwar zu vergeben umwillen einer Wiedereröffnung und Verwirklichung der vom Menschen als wesenskonstitutiv geforderten Ideal-Realisation einer ganzheitlichen und uneingeschränkten Erwiderung der Gottesliebe.

Die angestrengten philosophischen Überlegungen zu Anselms *Cur deus homo* konnten nicht mehr sein als Verweisungen auf die Erörterung der zentralsten und fundamentalsten Frage der christlichen Offenbarung und mit ihr zur Frage der Sinn-Realisation des menschlichen Daseins überhaupt.

Part IV
ANSELM'S INFLUENCE

LE RECUEIL APOCRYPHE DES *ORATIONES SIVE MEDITATIONES* DE SAINT ANSELME: SA FORMATION ET SA RÉCEPTION EN ANGLETERRE ET EN FRANCE AU XIIE SIÈCLE

J.F. Cottier

Depuis les travaux de dom André Wilmart,[1] nous connaissons de façon certaine le 'vrai et pur' recueil des *Prières et méditations* de saint Anselme dont les siècles avaient peu à peu, par ajouts successifs, déformé les traits. Par ailleurs, dom F.S. Schmitt, dans le cadre de son édition complète de l'oeuvre de saint Anselme, nous en a donné un texte critique fiable. Mais pour l'éditeur moderne qui s'intéresse au corpus apocryphe des *Prières,* c'est encore l'édition de Gerberon et Migne[2] qui doit servir d'outil de base, dans la mesure où elle représente l'aboutissement du développement du livret anselmien.[3] Dans ce domaine c'est encore dom Wilmart qui fit oeuvre de défricheur, et ses travaux sont le point de départ obligé pour tous ceux qui s'intéressent à ce sujet. D'autres savants ont depuis repris le flambeau,[4] et ont pu

---

1. 'La tradition des Prières de saint Anselme. Tables et notes', *Revue Bénédictine* 36 (1924), pp. 52-71; *Auteurs spirituels et textes dévots du Moyen Âge latin. Études d'histoire littéraire* (Paris, 1932, réimpr. 1971); introduction à la traduction de dom A. Castel, *Méditations et prières de saint Anselme* (Paris-Maredsous, 1923), p. 11.

2. *PL* 158, 709-820 et 855-1016, 1675, 1721, 1864.

3. Notons toutefois qu'il existe d'autres prières encore qui circulèrent sous le nom d'Anselme. Dom A. Wilmart en publia certaines, *Auteurs,* X et XIII par exemple.

4. On pense surtout à T.H. Bestul, entre autres 'The Verdun Anselm, Ralph of Battle and the Formation of the Anselmian Apocrypha', *Revue Bénédictine* 87 (1977), pp. 383-89; 'St Anselm and the Continuity of Anglo-Saxon Devotional Traditions', *Annuale medievale* 18 (1977), pp. 167-70; et 'The Collection of Private Prayers in the *Portiforium* of Wulfstan of Worcester and the *Orationes sive Meditationes* of Anselm of Canterbury. A Study in the Anglo-Norman Devotional Tradition', in *Les Mutations socio-culturelles au tournant des XIe-XIIe siècles. Études*

éclairer tel ou tel aspect du problème. Si bien qu'aujourd'hui on comprend de mieux en mieux la formation du recueil apocryphe, et l'étude de sa tradition manuscrite nous offre des perspectives nouvelles à ce sujet. Aussi, après avoir dressé un rapide état de la question, nous proposerons une synthèse des données pour le XIIe siècle, tout en mettant en lumière certaines pistes nouvelles dans l'enquête.

Formation générale du recueil

Dom Wilmart est revenu plus d'une fois entre 1923 et 1930 sur la formation et l'évolution du recueil des prières de saint Anselme.[5] Il proposa de répartir le livret en trois collections principales A, B, et C.

A représente le recueil authentique des vingt-trois prières et méditations composées par saint Anselme.[6] L'identification du corpus authentique est une question désormais résolue et il n'y a plus à y revenir. C'est ce recueil qu'édita dom Schmitt sur la base d'excellents manuscrits dont certains remontent à l'époque même du saint.[7] B représente pour le savant bénédictin un recueil de textes de dévotion joint à A dès le XIIe siècle. Ce recueil est composé de douze prières et de deux hymnes, soit quatorze pièces au total.[8] Enfin C est l'édition du XIVe siècle qui a perpétué le rapprochement entre A et B et rajouté de nouvelles pièces apocryphes, fournissant la base des éditions du XVIIe

---

anselmiennes (*IVe session*) (Paris, 1984), pp. 355-64. Il convient également de citer ici R.W. Southern dont la récente synthèse consacrée à saint Anselme reprend les principales données du problème: *Saint Anselm: A Portrait in a Landscape* (Cambridge, 1990), pp. 91-112, 367-81. Citons également l'introduction et l'appendice de Sister B. Ward à sa traduction, *The Prayers and Meditations of Saint Anselm with the Proslogion* (Londres, 1973, repr. 1988), pp. 27-86 et 275-87, ainsi que la préface de Southern, *Saint Anselm: A Portrait*, pp. 17-21.

5. *Auteurs*, VII, VIII, X, XI, XII, XIII, XXII, XXIV, et les ouvrages cités n. 1.

6. *PL* 158, Prol., Méd. 2, 3, 11, Or. 9, 20, 23, 24, 34, 41, 50, 51, 52, 63, 64, 65, 67, 68, 69, 71, 72, 74, 75.

7. Schmitt, I, pp. 134 sq.: 'Auswalh der Handschriften. Die verschiedenen Rezensionen'.

8. *PL* 158, Méd. 4, 5, 6, Or. 3, 4, 6, 15, 25, 26, 27-28, 29, 40 et 61. On peut y ajouter la prière au saint Patron (Wilmart, *Auteurs*, X, pp. 147-61) que l'on trouve dans certains manuscrits importants avec les prières du groupe B (Troyes, 1304, fol. 135 et 914, fol. 93; Paris, B.N., *lat.* 12313, fol. 22v et 12139, fol. 148v; Londres, B.M., *Add.* 16608, fol. 18v).

siècle. Le nouvel apport est de trente-sept prières.[9] Th. Raynaud ajouta encore dix-huit prières dans son édition lyonnaise de 1630,[10] et le mauriste G. Gerberon sept dans son édition de 1675 reprise par J.P. Migne dans sa *Patrologie Latine* en 1864.[11]

On arrive ainsi au total de vingt-et-une méditations et soixante-quinze oraisons dans la *Patrologie Latine*. Mais dans le cadre de cet article, nous ne nous intéresserons qu'aux prières ajoutées au XIIe siècle, et à la formation (ou plutôt déformation) du recueil à partir de cette époque. Au terme de l'enquête, nous tenterons de 'ressaisir autant qu'il est possible, les anneaux intermédiaires entre A et C, et reconstituer en quelque sorte l'arrière plan de C'.[12]

Le groupe B

Dès sa préface à la traduction des prières par dom A. Castel,[13] dom Wilmart faisait remarquer qu'à la suite du recueil authentique une douzaine de manuscrits, dont sept copiés au XIIe siècle, ajoutait une nouvelle série composée de quatorze pièces. Le savant bénédictin considérait alors qu'on avait sans doute voulu joindre à la série authentique une autre série, anonyme celle-là, qui semblait parallèle. Dom Wilmart reconnaissait à ces prières des qualités[14] et comme la nouvelle série contenait l'oraison '*Summe sacerdos...*' de Jean de Fécamp,[15] il attribua également au même auteur les autres prières de ce groupe.[16]

9. *PL* 158, Méd. 1, 9, 12, 13, 14, 15, 16, 17, 18, Or. 1, 2-10-14, 5, 7, 12, 13, 16-19, 30-33, 35, 36, 43, 46-49, 53, 62, 66, 70, 73. Mais on verra plus bas que certaines de ces prières sont déjà présentes dans les anthologies du XIIe siècle (p. ex. Or. 10-2-14; 12; 30-33, 46-49; 53; 62; 66).

10. *PL* 158 Méd. 7, 8, 10, 19, 21, Or. 11, 21, 22, 42, 44, 45, 54-60. Là aussi on trouve certaines de ces pièces dès le XIIe siècle dans des anthologies anselmiennes (p. ex. Méd. 19; 21; Or. 42).

11. *PL* 158, Méd. 20, Or. 8, 37-39, 40 et 61 (ces deux dernières étaient déjà dans B, mais avaient été oubliées depuis lors, quant à l'Or. 8, elle apparaît dès le XIIe siècle en contexte anselmien). Sur les éditions modernes: Schmitt, I, pp. 9 sq.: 'Die früheren Gesamtausgaben'.

12. Wilmart, 'Tradition', pp. 58-59.

13. Voir n. 1.

14. Qualités d'ailleurs mises en évidence par le succès immédiat de ces prières, peut-être plus facilement accessibles au grand nombre que les prières plus élaborées de saint Anselme: Southern, *Saint Anselm: A Portrait*, pp. 373-74.

15. Or. 29 dans *PL* 158.

16. *Auteurs*, VII, 'L'*Oratio sancti Ambrosii* du Missel romain', pp. 101-25; voir

Vers la même époque, le savant avait trouvé cette série dans un manuscrit qu'il jugeait 'moins important, incomplet,...confus'.[17] Il s'agissait du manuscrit d'Oxford, *Laud. Misc.* 363, provenant de Saint-Albans. Mais quelques années plus tard,[18] il revint sur son jugement et se demanda si on n'avait pas là 'dans ce contexte...la forme primitive et complète du groupe B'. Enfin en 1929,[19] il révisa son attribution à Jeannelin pour lui préférer un disciple anonyme de saint Anselme. Ainsi peu à peu la lumière se faisait sur le groupe B.

Le manuscrit Laud. Misc. 363
Mais l'élément capital de l'enquête était bien le manuscrit 363 du fonds *Laud. (O)*. En effet, ce manuscrit contient en dehors de tout contexte anselmien le groupe B (à l'exception des Or. 40 et 61, qui sont des hymnes de facture très banale et de l'Or. 29 qui ne fut rajoutée à ce manuscrit qu'au XIVe siècle,[20] et qui est de Jean de Fécamp comme on vient de le voir) dans l'ordre même dans lequel il apparaît dans la plupart des manuscrits anselmiens.[21] Il contient en outre une série d'ouvrages philosophiques et théologiques que l'on retrouve à l'identique dans d'autres manuscrits, et qui semblent bien être l'oeuvre d'un auteur unique. R.W. Southern en comparant le style des prières avec celui de ces traités a pu alors démontrer que c'était également le même auteur qui avait écrit ces prières.[22]

Ralph de Battle
Or parmi les témoins qui conservent cette série, le manuscrit londonien *Royal 12 C. I.* qui date du début du XIIe siècle et provient du Prieuré de la cathédrale de Rochester, attribue explicitement le premier dialogue

aussi dom J. Leclercq et J.-P. Bonnes, *Un maître de la vie spirituelle au XIe siècle, Jean de Fécamp* (Paris, 1946), pp. 33-34 où seules les Or. 16 à 19 (C) et l'Or. 29 sont reconnues comme étant l'oeuvre de Jean de Fécamp.

17. Wilmart, *Auteurs*, p. 154 n. 3.

18. Wilmart, *Auteurs* (1927), p. 198 n. 4.

19. Wilmart, *Auteurs* (1929), p. 209.

20. H.O. Coxe, *Catalogi codicum manuscriptorum Bibliothecae Bodleianae pars secunda codices Latinos et Miscellaneos Laudianos complectens* (Oxford, 1858, repr. 1973), col. 272-274 et *additions* de R.W. Hunt, p. 558.

21. Soit Méd. 5, Or. 3, Méd. 4, Or. 4, 6, Méd. 6, Or. 25, 26, 27-28 (qui ne forment qu'une seule prière dans les manuscrits anciens), Or. 15, et les deux méditations qui formeront plus tard chez Gerberon la Méd. 19.

22. Southern, *Saint Anselm: A Portrait*, pp. 372-76.

De peccatore qui desperat... à *Rodulfus monachus.*[23] Ce premier dialogue est lui-même précédé d'un prologue rédigé par la même main, où l'auteur se plaint que l'oeuvre ait été publiée avant qu'il ait pu la revoir, d'où la présence dans le texte de ratures et de corrections. Il semble donc bien que ce manuscrit ait été préparé sous la direction de Ralph en personne, sans doute même s'agit-il d'un autographe.[24]

Quoi qu'il en soit, il restait à identifier ce 'moine Ralph'. Le professeur R.W. Southern, en remarquant l'influence anselmienne attestée par ces textes, avait d'abord cru pouvoir l'identifier avec Ralph d'Escures, abbé de Séez, évêque de Rochester (1108–1114) et enfin successeur de saint Anselme à l'archevêché de Cantorbéry (1114–1122).[25] Mais cette identification fut rejetée par dom J. Leclercq qui ne reconnaissait pas dans ces textes le style des autres ouvrages de cet auteur.[26] Par la suite, le savant anglais proposa d'identifier *Rodulfus monachus* avec Ralph, l'abbé du monastère de Battle (†1124), qui fut d'abord moine à Caen, puis prieur de Rochester et enfin abbé de Battle en 1107.[27] C'est l'hypothèse qui est unanimement considérée aujourd'hui comme la plus probable.[28] En tous les cas l'origine anglaise et monastique du recueil est indubitable.

Formation du groupe B

Le manuscrit d'Oxford, en conservant le texte des prières de Ralph de Battle, devient donc un témoin essentiel de l'histoire de la formation de ce que dom Wilmart appelait le groupe B. Or parmi les quelques manuscrits du XIIe siècle qui possèdent ce groupe,[29] un seul est d'origine anglaise: le manuscrit 70 de la Bibliothèque Municipale de Verdun (*V*). C'est un très bel exemplaire anglais, enluminé dans le style du Psautier

23. G.F. Warner and J.P. Gilson, *Catalogue of Western Manuscripts in the Old Royal and King's Collections*, II (London, 1921), p. 22.

24. D.H. Farmer, 'Ralph's octo puncta of Monastic Life', *Studia monastica* 11 (1969), pp. 19-29.

25. R.W. Southern, 'Saint Anselm and his English Pupils', *MARS* 1 (1943), pp. 3-34.

26. *Analecta monastica*, III, p. 158.

27. *The Chronicle of Battle Abbey* (ed. E. Searle; Oxford, 1980), pp. 116-32.

28. R.W. Southern, *Saint Anselm and his Biographer. A Study of Monastic Life and Thought 1059–c. 1130* (Cambridge, 1963), pp. 206-207; et *Saint Anselm: A Portrait*, pp. 372 sq.

29. Soit en fait A + B.

de Saint-Albans, copié pour l'abbaye bénédictine Saint-Vanne de Verdun.[30] T.H. Bestul en comparant les deux manuscrits a émis alors l'hypothèse que c'est à Saint-Albans, haut lieu du monachisme anglo-normand, que pour la première fois on aurait mêlé l'oeuvre de saint Anselme avec celle de Ralph de Battle. Le manuscrit de Verdun serait alors une copie très ancienne d'un archétype enluminé, aujourd'hui perdu. D'autre part, en se fondant sur une remarque de C.R. Dodwell,[31] le savant américain a pensé que cette copie avait pu être apportée sur le Continent par Henry, archidiacre de Winchester, qui fut évêque de Verdun de 1116 à 1129. Ensuite le modèle se serait répandu rapidement sur le Continent, alors qu'il tombait dans l'oubli en Angleterre.

L'hypothèse pour séduisante qu'elle soit, n'explique cependant pas tout. En effet, si on compare les autres manuscrits B du XIIe siècle,[32] avec l'exemplaire de Verdun, il paraît impossible qu'ils aient été copiés sur lui. En effet, alors que les trois manuscrits continentaux sont très proches (les deux premiers ne dérivent pas directement l'un de l'autre puisqu'ils témoignent chacun de variantes propres, le manuscrit de Corbie pour sa part est une image de l'exemplaire de Clairvaux), ils ne possèdent aucune des leçons particulières au manuscrit de Verdun. D'autre part, en comparant ces trois manuscrits avec un exemplaire B du XVe siècle copié en Angleterre,[33] on est frappé par les similitudes existant entre tous ces exemplaires. Enfin l'ordre des prières authentiques est légèrement différent dans le manuscrit de Verdun et dans les manuscrits continentaux.

Il faut donc supposer que, à côté de l'archétype de Saint-Albans, il a existé un autre modèle contaminant le texte de Ralph avec un autre exemplaire de l'oeuvre de saint Anselme. Et comme le manuscrit *1304* de Troyes posséde un système de ponctuation particulier, que

30. O. Pächt, 'The Illustrations of Saint Anselm's Prayers and Meditations', *JWI* 19 (1956), pp. 68-83; Bestul, 'The Verdun Anselm', pp. 383-89; et Wilmart, *Auteurs*, p. 572. Notons toutefois que ce manuscrit a été mutilé, et qu'il ne contient plus qu'une seule peinture (fol. 68v), ainsi que des lettrines à personnages peintes par le même artiste.
31. O. Pächt, C.R. Dodwell, and F. Worwald, *The St Albans Psalter* (Londres, 1960), pp. 278-80.
32. Troyes, 1304 (Clairvaux pour Saint-Vaast *T*); Paris, B.N., *lat.* 18111 (Saint-Amand *F)* et *lat.* 12313 (Corbie *G*).
33. Paris, B.N., *lat.* 2886 (*H*).

R.W. Southern avait analysé dans son édition d'Eadmer comme caractéristique du scriptorium de Cantorbéry entre 1110 et 1125,[34] on pourrait indiquer Cantorbéry comme origine du second modèle.[35]

Notons pour finir cette partie que les deux archétypes ont négligé deux méditations qui se trouvent dans le manuscrit d'Oxford, et qui réparaîtront sous la forme d'une seule pièce dans l'édition de Th. Raynaud.[36] En outre les deux modèles ajoutent l'Or. 29 (qui ne sera pourtant rajoutée au manuscrit d'Oxford qu'au XIVe siècle[37)]. L'exemplaire de Verdun ajoute également l'Or. 49, *Singularis meriti sola sine exemplo*..., qui n'est autre que la prière à la Vierge de Maurille de Rouen, et l'oraison attribuée à saint Augustin, *Domine Deus omnipotens qui es trinus et unus*....[38] Quant aux exemplaires continentaux, ils ajoutent pour leur part, sans les distinguer des autres prières, les deux hymnes Or. 40 et 61; certains enfin mêlent au corpus authentique la prière au saint Patron, *Summae innocentiae et totius sacrarium*..., que l'on retrouvera dans d'autres manuscrits anselmiens.[39]

Il est donc très probable que l'origine de B se trouve en Angleterre et non dans 'quelque endroit de la France septentrionale' comme le pensait dom Wilmart.[40] C'est sans doute dans ces deux hauts lieux monastiques du XIIe siècle, que sont Saint-Albans et Cantorbéry, que l'on mêla pour leur similitude les prières de saint Anselme avec celles de Ralph de Battle, manière aussi peut-être de populariser ces dernières. De là le modèle s'est ensuite répandu sur le continent, avec le succès que l'on sait.

---

34. Eadmer, *The Life of Saint Anselm, Archbishop of Canterbury* (Oxford, 1979), pp. xxviii–xxxiv.

35. Cantorbéry qui fut d'ailleurs un des principaux centres de la diffusion des oeuvres de saint Anselme, cfr. Southern, *Saint Anselm: A Portrait*, p. 370.

36. Il s'agit de la Méd. 19 qui fond en un morceau la Méd. *Suavissime et dulcissime domine Ihesu Christe*... (= Méd. 19, 3-7) et la Méd. *Cum considero quid sit Deus*... (= Méd. 19, 1-2), tout en omettant chaque fois des passages importants de la pièce.

37. Voir *supra*; et Wilmart, *Auteurs*, pp. 571-77.

38. H. Barré, *Prières anciennes de l'Occident à la Mère du Sauveur, des origines à saint Anselme* (Paris, 1963), pp. 180-84. L'auteur est d'ailleurs correctement identifié dans plusieurs manuscrits anciens.

39. Wilmart, *Auteurs*, X, pp. 147-61. Pour les manuscrits, cfr n. 9.

40. Castel, *Meditations et prières*, p. lvi, n. 2.

	O	V	T	F	G	H
	St Albans	St Albans	Clairvaux	St-Amand	Corbie	Angleterre
M. 5	+	+	+	+	+	+
M. 4	+	+	+	+	+	+
M. 6	+	+	+	+	+	+
M. 19, 3-7	+					
M. 19, 1-2	+					
O. 3	+	+	+	+	+	+
O. 4	+	+	+	+		+
O. 6	+	+	+	+		+
O. 25	+	+	+	+	+	+
O. 26	+	+	+	+	+	+
O. 27-28	+	+	+	+	+	+
O. 15	+	+	+	+	+	+
O. 29		+	+	+	+	+
O. 49		+				
W. 1			+		+	
O. 40			+	+	+	
O. 61			+	+	+	
O. 53						+
O. 37-39						+

Tableau 1

Les anthologies anselmiennes

Mais là ne s'arrête pas l'histoire de la réception du recueil anselmien au XIIe siècle. En effet, à côté de la diffusion du recueil authentique lui-même et de la création du premier recueil apocryphe qui fusionne l'oeuvre d'Anselme avec celle de Ralph de Battle (B), on voit également fleurir des anthologies qui mélangent artificiellement et de manière plus ou moins distincte les prières anselmiennes avec des prières carolingiennes et d'autres prières du XIe et XIIe siècle. Certaines de ces prières s'intégreront un ou deux siècles plus tard au corpus anselmien; d'autres, pourtant récurrentes au XIIe siècle en contexte anselmien, seront oubliées.

T.H. Bestul qui s'est beaucoup intéressé à cette littérature,[41] souligne

41. Voir par exemple 'A Note on the Contents of the Anselm Manuscript, Bodleian Library, *Laud. Misc.*, 508', in *Manuscripta* 21.1 (Mars 1977), pp. 167-70; 'The Collection of Anselm's Prayers in British Library Ms *Cotton Vespasian*

tout l'intérêt que représentent de tels témoins de la spiritualité médiévale. En effet, on trouve ainsi côte à côte des prières d'origines diverses qui nous permettent de mieux comprendre le contexte culturel et intellectuel des *Prières* de saint Anselme: sa dette par rapport aux prières carolingiennes et à la tradition anglo-saxonne, son originalité d'auteur et de mystique et son influence sur d'autres écrits de dévotion de cette époque. Mais ces anthologies, en nous faisant connaître dès le XIIe siècle des prières qui seront bientôt intégrées dans les recueils du XIIIe et surtout du XIVe siècle, représentent également le chaînon manquant qui nous permet de saisir ce qui s'est passé entre le XIIe et le XIVe siècles.[42]

Un des plus beaux représentants de ce type d'anthologie est le manuscrit d'Oxford, *Laud. Misc.* 508 (*L*)[43] qui date de la fin du XIIe siècle, et qui fut copié en Angleterre, peut-être à Eynsham.[44] Outre deux ouvrages théologiques,[45] il présente côte à côte différentes prières dont dix compositions authentiques de saint Anselme,[46] six prières de Ralph,[47] cinq prières qui deviendront des pièces habituelles du corpus apocryphe[48] et six prières qui reviennent assez souvent dans les anthologies anselmiennes de cette époque.[49] Ce manuscrit semble donc avoir puisé à

D. XXVI', *MAev* 47.1 (1978), pp. 1-5; 'British Library, Ms *Arundel 60* and the Anselmian Apocrypha', *Scriptorium* 35.1 (1981), pp. 271-75; et surtout *A Durham Book of Devotions*, edited from London, Society of Antiquaries, Ms7 (Toronto Medieval Latin Texts, 18; ed. T.H. Bestul; Toronto, 1987).

42. Soit entre les exemplaires de type A et ceux de type B. Voir *supra*.

43. H.O. Coxe, *Catalogi codicum manuscriptorum Bibliothecae Bodleianae, partis secundae, fasciculus primus: catalogus codicum MSS. Laudianorum* (Oxford, 1858, repr., 1973), col. 366-368; et Bestul, 'Note on the Contents of *Laud. Misc.*, 508'.

44. C'est l'hypothèse formulée par dom Wilmart (*Auteurs*, p. 551), mais que T.H. Bestul a mise en doute ('Note on the Contents of *Laud. Misc.*, 508', p. 167).

45. *Meditatio de redemptione humana* (fol. 1), et *Proslogion* (fol. 5) de saint Anselme.

46. Or. 34 (fol. 39) // 63, 64, 65, 67, 68, 69, 71, 72 (fol. 90) // 74 (fol. 115), donc essentiellement les prières aux saints.

47. Or. 26, 25, 27-28, 3, 15 et 4 de Ralph (fol. 40) .

48. Or. 10-2-14, 29 mêlées aux prières de Ralph, et Or. 66 (Wilmart, *Auteurs*, XIII, p. 204) mêlée aux prières authentiques d'Anselme, et fort proche d'elles à bien des égards.

49. Parmi celles-ci deux prières (fol. 88) aux puissances angéliques publiées par dom Wilmart (*Auteurs*, pp. 551 sq. et 579 sq.): Prière à saint Michel, *Sancte Michael archangele, superni regis secretorum...*, et prière à l'ange gardien, *Sancte angele Dei*. Il y a en outre deux prières à Dieu α, *Domine Deus omnipotens, tibi*

différentes sources, et si l'on étudie le texte il semble clair qu'il a, entre autres, utilisé un manuscrit de type B de la famille du manuscrit de Verdun.[50] Ce fait nous permet de saisir la rapidité de la diffusion du type B, puisque quelques années à peine après sa formation il sert lui-même de base à la création d'un nouveau type de recueil, et par là même contribue à brouiller un peu plus l'image du livret original.

Il existe d'autres anthologies plus ou moins semblables en Angleterre et en France[51] mais nous ne pouvons pas toutes les passer ici en revue.[52] Il suffit pour notre sujet de relever les prières qui ne se trouvant pas dans les collections A et B, apparaissent cependant dans ces anthologies du XIIe siècle, et intègreront quelques décennies plus tard le corpus apocryphe.[53]

C'est la série des prières 10-2-14 qui revient le plus souvent dans les

---

confiteor... (fol. 16) et β, *Domine Deus pater incohatio et perfectio omnium...* (fol. 87); une prière au Christ γ, *Domine Ihesu Christe magne et omnipotens qui plus dare...* (fol. 31v); et enfin une prière à Marie Madeleine δ, *Piissima peccatrix pedum Domini lavatrix...* (fol. 115). On retrouve la prière à saint Michel dans le manuscrit londonien *Cotton Vespasian D. XXVI*, fol. 47v (*C*), le même manuscrit donne aussi β au fol. 26, γ au fol. 84, et δ au fol. 92v; α est donné dans le manuscrit *Laud. Misc.* 79, fol. 104 (*R*) et le manuscrit de Londres, *Arundel* 60, fol. 135 (*A*) où il est attribué à saint Augustin. Ces prières ne seront pas retenues dans le corpus apocryphe.

	L	C	R	A
	Eynsham ?	Harrold ?	Reading	Winchester
St Michel	+	+		
Ange gardien	+			
α	+		+	+
β	+	+		
γ	+	+		
δ	+	+		

50. Voir *supra*. Ceci pour les Or. 4, 15, 25, 26, 27-28, et 29 (dont le texte est fortement bouleversé).

51. Citons par exemple les deux manuscrits londoniens étudiés par T.H. Bestul: Society of Antiquaries, 7 (*S*) et B.L., *Cotton Vespasian D. XXVI* (*C*); un manuscrit d'Oxford: Bodl. Libr., *Auct. D.2.6.* (*E*); et trois manuscrits français B.N., *lat.* 2882 (*D*), *lat.* 15045 (*U*) et Troyes, 914 (*K*).

52. T.H. Bestul a d'ailleurs déjà décrit les principaux témoins, voir *supra* n. 41.

53. Car si pour l'instant elles apparaissent en contexte anselmien, elles ne sont pas encore placées sous l'autorité directe de l'archevêque de Cantorbéry, à l'exception de l'Or. 66, mêlée très souvent aux prières authentiques.

anthologies du XIIᵉ siècle.[54] Cette longue méditation adressée aux per-
sonnes de la Trinité est divisée en trois parties,[55] et correspond aux
chapitres I–IX des *Meditationes* du Pseudo-Augustin.[56] Dom Wilmart
avait cru pouvoir l'attribuer à Jean de Fécamp,[57] mais cette attribution a
été contestée par dom J. Leclercq.[58] Quoi qu'il en soit, ces pièces ont
connu un immense succès pendant toute la fin du Moyen Âge, où elles
furent attribuées le plus souvent à saint Anselme ou à saint Augustin.[59]
Elles deviendront partie intégrante du corpus apocryphe dès le XIVᵉ
siècle.

L'Or. 66 à saint André, *Sancte et pie Andrea, frater principis apostolorum...*[60] revient elle aussi très souvent. Dom Wilmart la rapprochait
des Or. 70, 73 et de la prière à sainte Anne qu'il publia,[61] toutes pièces
dont 'l'inspiration et la facture rappellent les compositions authentiques'.[62] Cette très belle prière est d'ailleurs souvent incluse dans le
groupe des prières d' Anselme aux saints (Pr. VIII sq.), mais 'l'état de la

---

54. On la retrouve dans les manuscrits *Laud. Misc.* 508, fol. 40; Society of Antiquaries, 7, fol. 5; B.L., *Cotton Vespasian D. XXVI*; Troyes, 914, fol. 13; on trouve
également cette série plus ou moins complète dans B.L., *Rawlinson C. 1* 49;
Cambridge, Pembroke College, 154, fol. 149v-168; et Bodl. Libr., *Auct D.2.6.*, Or.
10 et 2 (après les Or. 27-28, et 4, fol. 194 sq.).

55. Or. 10: *Domine Deus meus da cordi meo...*; Or. 2: *Invoco te Deus meus...*;
Or. 14 *O iam divini amor...*; voir *PL* 158.

56. *PL* 40, 900-909.

57. Voir son introduction à la traduction de dom A. Castel (*Meditations et prières*,
p. X n. 1) où le savant bénédictin analyse la composition de ces *Meditationes* en
quarante-et-un chapitres. Ces trois prières correspondent à la prière Xa contenue dans
les *Prières* de Jean, que l'on retrouve dans un manuscrit ancien qui mêle l'oeuvre de
Jean de Fécamp à des prières d'Anselme: Metz, *245*, fol. 85v (cfr *PL* 147, 462ff.).
Sur tout cela voir aussi G.R. Evans, '*Mens devota*: The Literary Community of the
Devotional works of John of Fécamp and St Anselm', *MAev* 43.2 (1974), pp. 107-
108, notamment sur le style de ce morceau.

58. *Jean de Fécamp*, p. 34: 'l'attribution à Jeannelin est des plus contestables,
tant ces (prières) s'éloignent de son style et de ses préoccupations habituelles'.

59. Bestul, *A Durham Book of Devotions*, p. 7.

60. Mss. du XIIᵉ siècle: *Laud. Misc.* 508, parmi les prières authentiques, fol. 90
cfr *supra*; B.L., *Cotton Vespasian D. XXVI*, fol. 61; Society of Antiquaries, 7,
fol. 125ᵛ, à la fin des prières authentiques; B.N., *lat.* 2882, fol. 56v, parmi les
prières authentiques.Voir aussi Wilmart, 'Tradition', pp. 69-70.

61. Wilmart, *Auteurs*, XIII, pp. 202-16.

62. Wilmart, *Auteurs*, p. 204.

COTTIER *Le recueil apocryphe des* Orationes sive meditationes 293

tradition empêche absolument qu'on rende ce texte, si estimable qu'il soit, à l'archevêque de Cantorbéry'.[63]

Quant à l'Or. 53 à la Vierge et à saint Jean, *O intemerata, et in eternum benedicta...*, elle connut un très grand succès pendant tout le Moyen Âge, et les témoins de ce texte sont innombrables.[64] Elle apparaît fréquemment elle aussi dans nos anthologies dès le XIIe siècle,[65] et elle sera mise sous le nom de saint Anselme au XIVe siècle. On l'attribua parfois à saint Edmond de Cantorbéry sous le seul prétexte que, disait-on, il la récitait quotidiennement († 1240), et saint Pie V la publia à Rome en même temps que l'édition définitive de l'office de Notre-Dame (1571). Dom A. Wilmart pensait que ce texte avait été élaboré en France au XIIe siècle 'dans quelque monastère cistercien'.[66]

On trouve en outre de façon plus isolée, l'Or. 42 à la Croix, *Ave gloriosissima omnium lignorum...*;[67] l'Or. 62 à l'Ange gardien, *Obsecro te angelice spiritus...*;[68] deux prières carolingiennes, *Deus inestimabilis misericordiae...*, conservée dans les *Officia per ferias* attribués à Alcuin et qui deviendra sous une forme abrégée l'Or. 8,[69] et l'Or. 12, *Tibi ago laudes...*[70] à Dieu. On trouve encore l'Or. 46 à la Vierge, *O beatissima et sanctissima*,[71] la Méd. 21, *Fiat nunc homuncio*, qui reprend des extraits du *Proslogion* d'Anselme,[72] les prières 37 à 39 propres à l'exemplaire de Corbie,[73] et le groupe des Or. 30 à 33,[74] qui sont des apologies 'à peu près...pareilles et banales'[75] fréquentes dans les missels

63. Wilmart, 'Tradition', p. 70.
64. Wilmart, *Auteurs*, XXII, pp. 474-504. On la retrouve en particulier dans les Livres d'Heures.
65. B.L., *Cotton Vespasian D.XXVI*, fol. 46; Society of Antiquaries, 7, fol. 111v; B.N., *lat.* 2882, fol. 83 et 15045, fol. 61v; Troyes, 914, fol. 72v.
66. Wilmart, 'Tradition', p. 69.
67. Society of Antiquaries, 7, fol. 37; *Laud. Misc.* 79, fol. 108; et Troyes, 914, fol. 111.
68. *Cotton Vespasian D.XXVI*, fol. 48v; Wilmart, *Auteurs*, XXIV, pp. 537 sq.
69. Society of Antiquaries, 7, fol. 24v, et B.N., *lat.* 15045, fol. 66v; Bestul, *A Durham Book of Devotions*, p. 7; voir aussi *PL* 101, 524-26.
70. B.N., *lat* 15045, fol. 71 et *Laud. Misc.* 508, fol. 36.
71. Oxford, *Laud. Misc.* 79.
72. B.N., *lat.* 15045, fol. 43.
73. *G* = Paris, B.N., *lat.* 12313.
74. B.N., *lat.* 15045 (Or. 30-33-31, fol. 51v-52-52v // Or. 32, fol. 57); et Troyes, 914 où au fol. 114v on trouve une prière apparentée à Or. 31 et 32.
75. Wilmart, 'Tradition', p. 65.

des Xe et XIe siècles, et sans doute plus anciennes encore,[76] mais 'jamais il ne semble qu'on ait songé à les attribuer proprement à saint Anselme en dehors du recueil C'.[77] Ajoutons pour finir, même si elle n'est pas rentrée dans le 'canon', la très belle prière à sainte Anne, *O felix et sanctissima Anna, genitricis Domini mater...*,[78] qui apparaît dans quelques unes de nos anthologies,[79] et qui bénéficia parfois, mais 'trop tard' (dom A. Wilmart), du patronage de saint Anselme.

	D	S	K	L	C	A	U	R
	Mortemer	Durham	Clairvaux	Eynsham?	Harrold?	Dorchester?	St-Victor	Reading
O. 3				+				
O. 4	+			+		+		
O. 6								
O. 25	+			+				
O. 26				+				
O. 27-28				+		+		
O. 15				+				
O. 29				+				+
O. 49	+	+	+		+	+	+	+
St Patron			+					
O. 40				+				
O. 61								
O. 66	+	+		+	+			
O. 53	+	+	+		+		+	
Ste Anne	+							
O. 8		+					+	
O. 10		+	+	+	+	+		
O. 2		+	+	+	+	+		
O. 14		+	+	+	+			
O. 42		+	+					+
O. 62					+			
M. 21							+	
O. 46								+
O. 35			+					
O. 12				+				
O. 30-33							+	

Tableau 2

76. On trouve Or. 31 dans le vieux missel d'Angoulême écrit vers l'an 800 (Ms 2192).

77. Wilmart, 'Tradition', p. 66.

78. Wilmart, *Auteurs*, XIII, pp. 202 sq. Voir *supra*.

79. B.N., *lat.* 2882, fol. 76v; (et Troyes, 958, fol. 82v, sous le nom d'Anselme, XIVe siècle; et Utrecht, 142, XVe siècle).

Ainsi, quand on fait la synthèse de ce que nous savons de la formation et de la réception du recueil apocryphes des *Orationes sive meditationes* au XIIe siècle, on se rend compte que les données sont plus complexes que ce que la clarté du schéma en trois collections de Dom Wilmart pouvait nous laisser croire. Le savant bénédictin a eu le grand mérite de défricher ce terrain particulièrement encombré; néanmoins les résultats des travaux récents nous permettent de nuancer le tableau qu'il proposa.

Il est clair à présent que dès le XIIe siècle il existe trois grandes lignes 'd'édition'. D'une part en effet, à côté du recueil authentique (A), on trouve très peu de temps après la mort du saint[80] des témoins d'un second recueil (B) qui ajoute dix prières de Ralph de Battle et d'autres pièces supplémentaires au premier livret. Ces manuscrits eux-mêmes sont divisés très tôt en deux familles, et avant le milieu du siècle ils essaiment en Angleterre et sur le continent.[81] D'autre part, on trouve des anthologies anselmiennes où certains compilateurs mélangent des prières des recueils A et B à de nouvelles prières d'auteurs antérieurs ou contemporains. Ils ramènent ainsi le livret anselmien au modèle tradi-tionnel des recueils anonymes et brouillent son image.

Ces compilations véhiculent en outre des pièces qui furent peu à peu intégrées dans le canon du corpus apocryphe, et elles nous permettent de mieux comprendre non seulement la dette de saint Anselme par rap-port à ses prédécesseurs, mais aussi sa profonde originalité et son influence sur ceux qui l'ont imité. On y trouve enfin de belles prières qui circulèrent parfois sous le nom d'Anselme mais que[82] le corpus apocryphe n'a pas conservées.[83] Elles représent pourtant d'intéressants témoignages du contexte spirituel de l'époque, et auraient mérité d'être retenues par les éditeurs successifs au même titre que d'autres pièces que ne présentent pas toujours le même intérêt.

Telle fut sans doute, autant que l'histoire mouvementée de sa formation et l'aspect prolifique de sa tradition nous permettent de la saisir, la genèse du recueil apocryphe des *Prières et méditations* de saint Anselme.

---

80. Rappelons que saint Anselme meurt en 1109, et qu'on date le manuscrit 70 de Verdun, lui-même dérivé d'un archétype perdu, vers 1123.

81. Voir *supra*.

82. Ou du moins qui lui étaient étroitement rattachées.

83. Ce quit fit dire à dom Wilmart 'qu'il faut bien renoncer à prendre pour norme le type vulgarisé par Gerberon' (*Auteurs*, p. 204).

ST ANSELM'S INFLUENCE ON GUIBERT OF NOGENT

Jay Rubinstein

The first person to note the influence of St Anselm upon Guibert of Nogent was Guibert himself. 'He assiduously favoured me with the gifts of his knowledge and took such pains that I alone seemed to be the unique and singular cause of his journeys and visits to us',[1] he says of Anselm's visits to the monastery of Saint-Germer at Fly. Guibert goes on to describe some of the lessons he learned from Anselm and to assert that these conversations shaped his first book, the *Moralia in Genesim*. Richard Southern, in his biography of St Anselm, comments upon the impact which Anselm's conversation had on the young Guibert. Anselm was the man who roused Guibert to independent thought, though Guibert in his later years 'owed more to Anselm of Laon than to Anselm of Canterbury'.[2] Another scholar has recently noted several affinities between the thought of St Anselm and Guibert and has suggested that Guibert 'deserves consideration, in the company of Gilbert Crispin and Honorious of Autun, as a first generation Anselmian'.[3] I would certainly echo this sentiment, but would suggest that the

---

1. 'Adeo sedule mihi eruditionis indulgebat beneficia, tanta ad id elaborabat instantia, ut unica ac singularis sui ad nos adventus et frequentationis'; *De vita sua* I, 17 (*Autobiographie* [ed. E.-R. Labande; Paris, 1981], p. 140).

2. R.W. Southern, *Saint Anselm: A Portrait in a Landscape* (Cambridge, 1990), pp. 382-83.

3. Jaroslav Pelikan has suggested that Anselm shaped Guibert's thought on the Eucharist, the Incarnation, and the cult of the Virgin Mary. He makes surprisingly little use of the passages in question in the *De vita sua*; see 'A First-Generation Anselmian, Guibert of Nogent', in F.F. Church and T. George (eds.), *Studies in the History of Christian Thought*. XIX. *Continuity and Discontinuity in Church History* (Leiden, 1979), pp. 71-82. John Benton, on the other hand, suggests in a note to his translation of Guibert's memoirs that Guibert actually fails to follow the lessons of Anselm in his exegesis; see *Self and Society in the Middle Ages* (Toronto, 1984), p. 91 n. 16.

influence of St Anselm upon Guibert was even more profound than either of these analyses suggest. What Anselm gave to Guibert was an innovative theory—which for lack of a better word I shall here describe as 'psychological'—about the workings of the mind. These psychological speculations did indeed first rouse Guibert to independent thought, and this initial inspiration formed the basis of most of his later literary output.

Guibert first met Anselm during one of the latter's visits to the monastery of Saint-Germer at Fly, while Anselm was still prior at Bec and while Guibert was still a youth. The visits continued after Anselm's election as abbot of Bec in 1078, perhaps until Anselm left Normandy for England in 1092.[4] The lessons which Guibert most closely associated with Anselm were psychological.[5]

> He taught me to divide the mind into three or four parts and showed that all the transactions of the internal mystery occurred as desire [*affectus*], will, reason, and intellect. What I and many others had thought to be unified, he resolved by clear assertions into certain divisions, so that the first two [*affectus, voluntas*] were not the same unless in the presence of the fourth or the third [*intellectus, ratio*]... Afterwards I began to emulate his methods as much as I could with similar commentaries and to examine the Scriptures with much keenness of mind to see if anything on the moral level agreed with these ideas.

When describing the actual writing of the *Moralia*, Guibert makes another reference to Anselm's psychological model, saying that his commentary was written according to 'those four previously mentioned

4.   *De vita sua*, I, 17 (*Autobiographie*, pp. 138-40). For the dates of Anselm's life, see Southern, *Saint Anselm: A Portrait*, p. xxvii. Southern discusses Anselm's conversations with Guibert on pp. 382-83, 392.

5.   I have translated 'affectus' here as 'desire'. 'Appetite' would also be a possible reading, but no translation seems wholly appropriate. 'Is itaque tripartito aut quadripartito mentem modo distinguere docens, sub affectu, sub voluntate, sub ratione, sub intellectu commercia totius interni mysterii tractare, et quae una a plerisque et a me ipso putabantur certis divisionibus resoluta, non idem duo prima fore monstrabat, quae tamen accedentibus quarto vel tertio eadem mox esse promptis assertionibus constat. Super quo sensu cum quaedam evangelica capitula mihi disseruisset, cum primum quidem quid inter velle et affici distaret luculentissime aperuisset, quae tamen non ex se sed ex quibusdam continguis voluminibus, at minus patenter quidem ista tractantibus eum habuisse constaret, coepi postmodum et ego eius sensa commentis, prout poteram, similibus aemulari et ubique scripturarum, si quid istis moraliter arrideret sensibus, multa animi acrimonia perscrutari'; *De vita sua*, I, 17 (*Autobiographie*, p. 140).

motions of the *interior homo*.[6] This passages is not without difficulties
of interpretation, as subsequent discussion will show. But it is clear that
in Guibert's own mind, these conversations with Anselm gave fundamental shape to his biblical exegesis.

This division of the mind originates with a much older, Augustinian
model;[7] and Guibert's comment that Anselm taught him to divide what
others had thought to be unified refers to the Augustinian tradition.
Augustine used a threefold division of the soul—into *memoria, intelligentia*, and *voluntas*—in his *De trinitate* as an illustration of the godhead. 'These three aspects—memory, intellect, and will—are not three
lives, but one life, are not three minds, but one mind. Consequently they
are not three substances but one substance.'[8] Memory—or perhaps
'consciousness'—corresponds to God the Father, and intellect, or the
act of thinking, corresponds to God the Son. The acts of remembering
and of thinking are inseparable. They interact constantly with one
another just as God the Father and God the Son are clearly different but
are nonetheless the same being.[9] The Holy Ghost corresponds to the
human will, but with a fairly broad definition of *voluntas* that encom-
passes desire or appetite. Concerning the Holy Ghost, nothing in this
mystery is similar to it, 'except our will, or our love or our delight,
which is more appropriately will'.[10]

Anselm's model of the mind, as Guibert describes it, differs from
Augustine's in several respects. Most notably, Anselm separates will and
desire into two separate functions. What others had thought to be

6.   *De vita sua*, I, 17 (*Autobiographie*, p. 144).
7.   Gerhart Ladner presents a good general survey of the Augustinian division of
the mind from its origins to the twelfth century in 'Eine karolingische Modifizierung
der psychologischen Trinitätsanalogien des hl. Augustinus', in H. Mordek (ed.),
Aus Kirche und Reich, Studien zu Theologie, Politik und Recht im Mittelalter
(Sigmaringen, 1983), pp. 45-53.
8.   'Haec igitur tria, memoria, intellegentia, voluntas, quoniam non sunt tres
vitae sed una vita, nec tres mentes sed una mens, consequenter utique nec tres
substantiae sunt sed una substantia'; Augustine, *De trinitate* X.xi.17 (ed.
W.J. Mountain; CCSL 50; Brepols, 1968, p. 330).
9.   *De trinitate* XV.xxi.40 (CCSL 50A, pp. 517-21). See also Augustine's
discussion of memory in the *Confessiones* X.8-24 (ed. L. Verheijen; CCSL 50,
pp. 161-74].
10.   'De spiritu autem sancto nihil in hoc aenigmate quod ei simile videretur
ostendi, nisi voluntatem nostram, vel amorem seu dilectionem quae valentior est
voluntas'; *De trinitate* XV.xxi.41 (CCSL 50A, p. 519).

unified, Anselm showed to be divided. Anselm also eliminated *memoria* as an independent category, and replaced *intellegentia* with *ratio* or *intellectus*. Finally, Guibert gives no indication that Anselm used his model as a means of explaining the Trinity. A fourfold division of the mind, in fact, might indicate that Anselm and Guibert were speculating about the workings of the mind for their own sake, independent of any allegorical message they might hold about the Trinity. We should bear in mind, however, that the details of Anselm's model are by no means certain, since Guibert himself seems to have forgotten them. By the time he wrote his memoirs he was no longer certain if Anselm had used a three-fold or fourfold division.[11]

We should also note that Anselm himself in the *Monologion* uses a psychological model far more similar to the traditional Augustinian conception of the mind. There, in language which depends heavily on Augustine's *De trinitate*, he describes the mind as divided into *memoria, intelligentia*, and *amor*, corresponding to the Father, Son, and Holy Spirit.[12] The model here differs from the thought of Augustine in that Anselm has eliminated the word *voluntas* from consideration and has chosen instead to focus only on the love which exists between Father and Son—on those aspects of the will that Augustine might have described as *amor* or *dilectio*. Anselm's thought here, however, bears little resemblance to Guibert's description of it.

A threefold division of the soul, however, does appear in the *Dicta Anselmi* collected by Alexander of Canterbury in the early twelfth century.[13]

---

11. See the passage in n. 3 above, where Guibert describes a division 'tripartitum aut quadripartitum'.

12. Anselm, *Monologion* chs. 48-49 and 67-68 (Schmitt, I, pp. 63-64 and 77-79). See Southern, *Saint Anselm: A Portrait*, pp. 71-73, for Anselm's use of Augustine.

13. 'Anima tres in se habet naturas, videlicet rationem, voluntatem, appetitum. Ratione assimilamur angelis, appetitu brutis animalibus, voluntate utrisque. Sumus enim rationales, quod angelorum est, et proni ad appetendum, quod brutorum animalium est, et voluntarii, quod angelorum et animalium irrationabilium est. Nam recta quidem quae volumus secundum voluntatem volumus, et se qua illicita appetimus, per voluntatem hoc facimus. Voluntas ergo in rationem et appetitum media est'; Alexander of Canterbury, *Dicta Anselmi*, in R.W. Southern and F.S.Schmitt (eds.), *Memorials of St. Anselm* (London: 1969), §17, p. 74. For the date of the collection of the *Dicta Anselmi* see Southern, *Saint Anselm: A Portrait*, pp. 389-90.

> The soul holds within itself three natures—reason, will, and appetite [*rationem, voluntatem, appetitum*]. By reason we are similar to angels, by appetite to brute animals, and by will to both. For we are rational, which pertains to angels, and we are prone towards desires, which pertains to brute animals, and we are capable of willing, which pertains to angels and irrational animals. For we desire right things according to the will, and if we seek illicit things, we do this through the will. Will is the middle way between reason and appetite.

Here Anselm has made the crucial intellectual moves which Guibert noted. He has defined desire or appetite as an independent psychological function—a move which he perhaps began to make in the *Monologion* when he transformed the Augustinian *voluntas* into *amor*. Anselm has also changed Augustinian terminology by replacing *intelligentia* with *ratio* and raising this to highest psychological function. Finally, he has eliminated *memoria*. There is no indication of a separation of *ratio* and *intellectus*. Because the division is threefold, a comparison with the Trinity remains barely possible, but is unstated. In the spirit of Guibert's description, Anselm seems to speculate on the mind simply for the sake of understanding the mind.

Outside of the *Dicta Anselmi* one finds this threefold model present only as a premise to larger theological arguments. In the *De conceptu virginali et de originali peccato*, for example, Anselm describes the will as a power of the soul, an *instrumentum volendi*, which in itself is neither just nor unjust. Similarly appetites, which pit the law of sin against the law of the mind, are in themselves neither just nor unjust. Rather, it is only when the will consents to the base desires of appetite that a man can be described as unjust.[14] A similar passage occurs in the *De concordia praescientiae et praedestinationis et gratiae Dei cum libero arbitro*. Again, the will is an *instrumentum volendi*, just as the eye is an *instrumentum videndi*, and just as reason is an *instrumentum ratiocinandi*. The direction which the will takes is its *affectio*—a term similar to *affectus*, the word Guibert most often uses for desire or appetite. A will can move in two different *affectiones*—one towards righteousness, *ad rectitudinem*, and one toward personal advantage, *ad commoditatem*. Anselm further notes that these terms, *voluntas* and *affectio,* are often used interchangeably.[15] From these passages we can conclude that

---

14. Anselm, *De conceptu virginali* iii, 2 (Schmitt, II, pp. 143-44).
15. Anselm, *De concordia* (Schmitt, II, pp. 278-82). See also D. Odon Lottin,

Anselm did move away from the Augustinian conception of the mind which he presented in his *Monologion*, that he did develop ideas about the mind similar to those Guibert describes, and that these ideas form the background for many of Anselm's theological speculations.

We can trace a similar development in Guibert's thought, for Book I of the *Moralia* contains almost no sign of Anselm's 'threefold or fourfold division of the mind'. Guibert instead uses simple binary divisions, setting reason directly against the flesh. Book I also draws no distinction between *intellectus* and *ratio*, but instead argues that, 'Reason is nothing other than Intellect'.[16] Only when Guibert comments on the creation of the sun and the moon in Gen. 1.16-17 does evidence of a threefold model appear. 'And God made two great lights, a greater light to rule the day and a lesser light and stars to rule the night, and he placed them in the firmament of heaven so that they might shine above the land.' The moon, Guibert writes, is entirely comparable to our will. It never remains in the same state, and it receives light only from the sun, from reason. If it is not restrained by a strong *ratio*, it continually gives consent to the land, or *carnalis appetitus*. If we are to restrain the motions of the flesh, *carnalis affectus* must submit to a just will and be affixed to the firmament with the stars, that is, with the clarity of all our virtues.[17] This analysis presents a hierarchy of reason, will, and appetite which is obviously comparable to Anselm's model. It also separates will and desire into two separate entities. Even this passage, however relies on a more typical binary opposition. The unstable will is either wholly a slave to the flesh or else an agent of reason. It is caught within the struggle between the interior and exterior self and it becomes inconsequential. Far from being influenced by Anselm, Guibert in Book I seems to have ignored or else deliberately disagreed with Anselm's ideas.

This inconsistency exists in all likelihood because Guibert completed Book I of his *Moralia* as a self-contained project before he and Anselm had fully discussed their ideas about the workings of the mind. In his memoirs Guibert implies that he wrote all ten books of the *Moralia* shortly after 1084, after the retirement of his abbot, who opposed the project.[18] But Guibert could not have completed the *Moralia* in its

Psychologie et morale aux XIIe et XIIIe siecles. I. *Problemes de psychologie* (Belgium, 1942), pp. 12-14.

16. 'Ratio vero nihil aliud est quam intellectus'; *Moralia* 33C.
17. *Moralia* 47B,C, commenting on Gen. 1.17, 18.
18. *De vita sua* I, 17 (*Autobiographie*, p. 142).

current form until almost thirty years after that date, since he dedicates the book to Bishop Bartholomew of Laon, who assumed office in 1113.[19] In all likelihood, Guibert's statement that he completed the work shortly after the retirement of his abbot refers only to Book I of the *Moralia*. He makes it clear that he initially conceived of the project as a commentary on the Hexameron alone,[20] and Book I certainly reads as it were a self-contained project. It finishes with a discussion of the seventh day, on which God rested. On this day the mind rests, having attained *sapientia* and *contemplatio* at the world's end. Book I is also the only one of the commentary's ten books to conclude with the word, 'Amen', as if at the end of a prayer. But most importantly after Book I Guibert's imagery changes significantly. He begins to show the Anselmian influence which his memoirs would lead us to expect.

As a preliminary hypothesis I will suggest that it was these conversations with Anselm which inspired Guibert to return to his project and to search out further moral meanings in the book of Genesis. For after Book I the simple binary oppositions between heaven and earth or between spirit and flesh are replaced by more sophisticated ternary models, and the three principal actors in these models are usually *ratio*, *voluntas*, and *affectus*.

The best place to start to examine this threefold division is Guibert's commentary on the fall in the second book of the *Moralia*. In Book I Guibert had described Adam and Eve as androgynous before their sin. Only after the fall did the sexes become divided. Eve became flesh, in need of discipline and control from *ratio*, or Adam. 'Rightly is it first said that man was created in the singular, and then as male and female. Before their transgression man was one and the same in himself and never was diverse.'[21] Guibert draws a significantly different picture of Adam and Eve in his commentary on Gen, 2.24.[22]

19. See R.B.C. Huygens, *La tradition manuscrite de Guibert de Nogent* (Steenbrugis in Abbatia S. Petri, 1991), p. 12.

20. 'Propositum autem habui ut initia Geneseos, Exameron scilicet, commentari moraliter aggreder'; *De vita sua* I, 17 (*Autobiographie*, p. 142).

21. 'Recte primo dicitur homo singulariter creatus, postmodum masculus et femina creati, quia ante praevaricationem idem in se, et nusquam diversus homo erat'; *Moralia*, 57B.

22. '*Propter hoc relinquet homo patrem suum et matrem suam et adhaerebit uxuori suae, et erunt duo in carne una. Propter hoc*, inquit, relinquet is, qui a bestiali semotus est vita *patrem* diabolum, *matrem*que concupiscentiam, *et adhaerebit uxori*, id est, voluntati suae rationabiliter regendae, *et erunt duo*, intellectus videlicet ac

On account of this a man shall abandon his father and his mother and adhere to his wife, and they will be two in one flesh. On account of this, [Genesis] says, he who has been removed from the bestial life, *shall abandon his father,* the devil, and *his mother,* concupiscence, *and will adhere to his wife,* that is, to his will ruled rationally, *and they will be two,* that is as intellect to will, *in one flesh,* that is in one *affectus.* Indeed, when our *affectus* adheres to worldly things, it never remains in the same state. But as soon as [man] devotes himself to God, it stands, willingly or not, in one place.

This passage provides obvious contrasts with Guibert's analysis of Gen. 1.27. There is no indication that Adam and Eve are initially without gender; Guibert defines distinct roles for them immediately. Eve furthermore no longer represents the flesh, but is instead the will, *voluntas.* Guibert also no longer emphasizes the instability of the will. Rather, it is *noster affectus* which never remains in the same state. *Affectus* has thus taken on characteristics which he had earlier assigned to *voluntas.* The underlying cause of this transformation in thought is that Guibert now draws a clear distinction between will and appetite. 'Many think,' he writes, 'that no discrepancy exists between will and desire [*affectus*]' He argues against this proposition through scriptural citations and then through analogy. 'The inconstant man wishes to eat, but does not desire it; the sensible man desires to eat too much, but does not wish it. It is easy to prove the same point in many ways. Like a daughter to a mother, *voluntas* is nearer to *ratio,* as much as it is worthier than that waiting-woman *affectus.*'[23] This clear division is essential to Anselm's arguments on free will. The will is always free to obey either the suggestions of the appetite or else the dictates of reason. Guibert enthusiastically embraced this idea, as he suggested in his autobiography, although he apparently did not do so until he began writing the second book of his *Moralia.* Adam and Eve can no longer simply represent the opposition of spirit and flesh. A more complex model which takes into account the role of *voluntas* has become essential.

The identities of Adam and Eve change after their sin. Adam is no

voluntas, in carne una, id est in affectu uno: affectus etenim noster quia in eodem statu nunquam saecularibus inhians figitur, mox ut Deo vacare incipit, velit nolit ad unum sistitur'; *Moralia,* 70C.

23. 'multi voluntatem et affectum quidquam discrepare non putant... Vult infirmus comedere, sed non afficitur; afficitur sobrius nimis comedere, sed non vult: idem in multis probare facile est. Voluntas itaque, quasi filia matri, quanto rationi est propinquior, tanto pedisseque, id est affectu dignior'; *Moralia* 71A, B.

longer 'Adam totus homo ille qui quondam' (wholly the man that he once was), but is instead 'terrenus' and addicted to the passions of the body. Eve is no longer 'the Will joined to heavenly Reason', but is instead closely intertwined with earthly cunning in a common love of temporal good.[24] Together they hide themselves from God in the woods, which represent the carnal desires or the *affectus* in which those lost in the world bury themselves.

Guibert further defines the threefold division when he comments on God's sentences against the serpent, Eve, and Adam. The serpent, who embodies *affectus*, shall crawl on its belly, *super pectus*. Our hearts lies within our *pectus* and reason lies within our hearts. When desire moves *super pectus,* it usurps the command of reason for itself and thereby establishes a perverse order.[25] Enmity exists between the woman and the serpent because a constant struggle occurs between will and desire. She crushes its head when a righteous will fights off the beginnings of a corrupt appetite. The serpent strikes at her heel when it corrupts the will's *intentio*, its intention, which is the beginning of every sinful act.[26] The woman's pains in childbirth increase because after sin it is much more difficult to bring forth goodness, even though the will knows that it ought to happen. The woman must place herself under the power of her husband because will must submit to the discipline of reason.[27] Man, who listened to woman's voice and allowed appetite to assume power over him, will be forced to work the earth to gain nourishment; reason will be forced to work in order to overcome temptation and gain virtue.[28] The fall of man occurred—and all subsequent sins have occurred—when the natural hierarchy of the mind became reversed and reason allowed will to follow desire, or *affectus*.

This psychological model clearly derives from Guibert's conversations

24. *Moralia*, 73C.

25. *Moralia*, 74C, D, commenting on Gen. 3.14: 'super pectus tuum gradieris'.

26. *Moralia*, 75A, B, commenting on Gen. 3.15: 'Inimicitias ponam inter te et mulierem et semen tuum et semen illius. Ipsa conteret caput tuum, et tu insidiaberis calcaneo eius.'

27. *Moralia*, 75C, commenting on Gen. 3.16: 'Mulieri quoque dixit, Multiplicabo aerumnas tuas et conceptus tuos. In dolore paries filios et sub viri potestate eris et ipse dominbitur tui.'

28. *Moralia*, 75-76, commenting on Gen. 3.17, 18: 'Ad Adam vero dixit, Quia audistis vocem uxoris tuae et comedisti de ligno ex quo praeceperam tibi ne comederes, maledicta terra in opere tuo. In laboribus comedes eam cunctis diebus vitae tuae...'

with Anselm. He gives as yet no hint of a fourfold division, of any clear distinction between intellect and reason.[29] But he has moved far beyond the binary opposition of spirit and flesh which dominated Book I. Adam does become hopelessly enmeshed in carnal temptations and desires, but the path which leads him there is wholly intellectual and based on the threefold division of the mind. The remainder of the *Moralia*, in fact, proceeds much as Guibert describes it in his autobiography. His analysis of almost every other event in Genesis becomes a search for images of *ratio*, *voluntas*, and *affectus*. A few examples should serve to demonstrate the pervasiveness of this imagery.

Abraham almost invariably represents reason. His wife Sarai is the will, usually described as *bona voluntas*. Several characters take on the part of desire, of *carnalis affectus*, including Lot and Pharaoh.[30] We find the same model of sin at work. When Abram enters Egypt, the land of *carnales motus*, he introduces Sarai as his sister, not his wife. By doing so he pretends that he, *ratio*, is the equal to rather than the superior of *voluntas*. Again, he subverts the natural hierarchy and gives in to temptations.[31] *Carnalis affectus* momentarily takes complete control of the will when Pharaoh takes Sarai into his house. But then struck with the fear of the Lord, *affectus* acknowledges the powers of reason and returns Sarai, *voluntas*, to her husband, *ratio*. Abraham, Sarai, and Lot then leave Egypt—the three of them represent the three parts of our *spiritus* abandoning worldly desires. The mind has restored *voluntas* and *affectus* to their proper positions.[32]

The symbolism becomes somewhat more complex when Guibert discusses Jacob and Esau, the children of Isaac. Esau, the firstborn, is *affectus carnis*, or more simply *carnalitas*. He is firstborn because our first motions come from earthly desires. His hair and complexion are red to

---

29. In Book II generally Guibert describes the relationship between Adam and Eve as a relationship between *ratio* and *voluntas*. In *Moralia* 76D–77A, for example, commenting on Gen. 3.20, he writes, '*Et vocavit Adam nomen uxoris sue Eva, eo quod esset mater omnium viventium*. Ad hunc itaque statum correptis moribus, iam noster Adam nomen uxoris, id est certa discretione, vitam, voluntatem scilicet iuste rationi subjectam.' One might note that, in n. 22 above, Adam and Eve joined together are *intellectus* and *voluntas*. It is unclear whether Guibert is drawing a distinction between Adam before the fall (*intellectus*) and Adam after the fall (*ratio*), or whether he simply continues to use the terms interchangeably.

30. *Moralia*, 111D, 112B, and 115B.

31. *Moralia*, 114D.

32. *Moralia*, 116A, B.

symbolize blood and his connection to the flesh. He later becomes a hunter because he seeks only to fulfil the desires of the body.[33] Jacob is spiritual zeal and is named *supplantor*, because he will supplant the intentions of impure thoughts. He is also stable, disturbed by no inner motions. When his brother becomes a farmer he stays at home, since spiritual zeal sees no value in the temptations of the world.[34] Both brothers represent different aspects of desire. Esau plays the role of carnal desire and Jacob that of spiritual desire, which his father Isaac, who is reason, ought to favour. We are reminded of Anselm's descriptions of the directions, or *affectiones*, which the will can follow. Jacob is perhaps the *affectio ad rectitudinem* and Esau the *affectio ad commoditatem*.[35]

Guibert defines the brothers' roles most clearly when he comments on Jacob's deception of Isaac and his theft of his father's blessing for Esau. Isaac, who is reason, is old by this time and his spiritual strength weak. He has given his thoughts wholly to worldly pleasures, and he asks Esau to hunt for something with which he might feed his appetite. In return the 'animal nature' of reason will bless *carnalitas*.[36] Jacob, however, acts as the 'spiritual appetite' and disguises himself as his brother. He puts on the 'bonae vestes', the best clothes, of Esau when he clothes himself with the ornaments of a pious appetite, 'without which we can preserve no good'.[37] Jacob, acting as the *supplantor* of vice, then approaches his father and identifies himself as Esau; it is an act of confession, an acknowledgment that he has lived carnally. In a sense he and Esau are tropologically a single person, since they are two aspects of the same psychological function. Isaac then eats the food which Jacob has brought to him and, acting as reason, gives his blessing to his spiritual appetite.[38]

Guibert's exegesis of Jacob's usurpation of the blessing represents a turning point in the commentary. It marks the first time in the *Moralia* when reason assumes some sort of stable control over carnal desires.

33. *Moralia*, 196D, 197C.
34. 'Jacob simpliciter stabilito, nullo turbine interius propulsatus, dum minus providet quaenam utilitas ex tentatione nascatur'; *Moralia*, 197D, 196D-197A.
35. See above, n. 15.
36. *Moralia*, 206C.
37. *Moralia*, 206D, 207D.
38. *Moralia*, 208D-209A.

After this incident Jacob takes the part of *ratio* and Esau becomes alternately *voluntas* and *affectus*—as if in the presence of a healthy reason, will and desire become almost inseparable. The sense of spiritual progress becomes even more apparent later when Esau embraces Jacob and submits himself to his brother. Will and desire thus admit their subservience to reason.

The most striking evidence of spiritual progress, however, is the emergence of a new psychological function, *intellectualitas*, or more simply, *intellectus*, in Book X. 'Intellect pertains to divine things; reason properly pertains to human.'[39] The only character who plays this role is Joseph.[40] Book X of the *Moralia* begins with Joseph, as intellect, holding command over the land of Egypt, which represents the secular world.[41] Guibert describes intellect as the highest aspect of the mind, as the 'lord of reason', though it itself originates from reason. 'Reason or our spirit is the father of *intellectualitas*. For intellect is known to proceed from reason, although reason sparkles with the special light of intellect. Similarly reason proceeds from the spirit, although the spirit is bright only through the honour of reason.'[42] A union of intellect and reason represents the best possible defence against temptation. When Joseph introduces his father to Pharaoh in Gen. 47.7, it is 'the fervour of *intellectualitas* raising up reason in order to penetrate the craft of the devil'.[43] The mind thus has reached the highest point attainable in this world. After countless struggles and setbacks, it has created a new psychological function which focuses only on the divine.

We have discovered now the fourfold division which Guibert attributed to Anselm. Intellect and reason are clearly two separate psychological functions, as are will and desire. In the presence of intellect, however, these latter two elements are almost identical. The meaning of Guibert's description of Anselm's ideas thus becomes much clearer than when we first read it. 'What I and many others had thought

39. *Moralia*, 295D.
40. But see n. 29 above.
41. 'Intellectus etenim ad divina, ratio proprie attinet ad humana'; *Moralia*, 295D; see also 297C.
42. 'Pater intellectualitatis ratio, vel spiritus noster est, quia intellectus ex ratione procedere dignoscitur, licet intellectualitatis specialiter luce lustretur, sicut ratio ipsa ex anima, quamvis anima rationis solo penitus honore sit clara'; *Moralia*, 303D; see also 300C.
43. '*Joseph* introducit *patrem ad regem*, cum intellectualitatis fervor ad penetrandas versutias diabolis provehit rationem'; *Moralia*, 311D.

to be unified, he resolved by clear assertions into certain divisions, so that the first two [*affectus, voluntas*] were not the same unless in the presence of the fourth or the third [*intellectus, ratio*].'[44]

We may now step back and try to determine more precisely what are the connections between these ideas and the thought of St Anselm. As already noted, Guibert believed that he had followed Anselm's lessons to the letter. The only passage among Anselm's writings—from the *Dicta Anselmi*—that closely resembles Guibert's description, however, dates from at least twenty years after Guibert's regular conversations with Anselm had ended. The general similarities are remarkable, but both Anselm and Guibert probably had changed the details of their thought on the human mind. We can only say with certainty that Anselm introduced Guibert to a new way of thinking about thought. By transforming will and appetite into neutral—albeit mistake-prone—intellectual elements, Guibert turned sin into an event wholly of the mind. A Christian's life was no longer a battle between reason and flesh. It was rather an attempt to direct the will through reason towards the desire of spiritual things alone.

Whether Anselm suggested the division between reason and intellect is uncertain. It is, however, a key aspect for understanding Guibert's exegetical method. One of the most striking features of the *Moralia* is that it is itself a narrative which runs parallel to the stories of Genesis. It tells the story of a Christian conversion, of the slow progress of *ratio* in its attempts to gain mastery over *voluntas* and *affectus*. A Christian can never obtain perfect *contemplatio*—the rest promised by the seventh day of creation—in this life, but the concept of *intellectus* gives Guibert's readers the hope for at least a glimpse of God's rest. It is a satisfying end to the moral narrative. At the same time, we cannot wholly dismiss a possible connection between the end of the *Moralia* and the teachings of Anselm. *Intellectus* is after all one of the key words from the *Proslogion*—the treatise over which Anselm was labouring during some of his earlier meetings with Guibert. Perhaps the fourfold division of the mind helps us to understand *fides quaerens intellectum*. Perhaps Anselm too saw *intellectus* as a rebirth of the mind, a transformation which can occur only when *ratio* seizes control of *voluntas* and *affectus* and thus brings the soul into conformity with the will of God.

In a more general sense Anselm's influence upon Guibert is incalculable. For Anselm gave to Guibert the key idea which enabled him to

44. See above, n. 5.

complete his first major work, and many of his subsequent ones as well. He enabled Guibert to study the mind simply for the purpose of understanding the mind. The abbot of Nogent continued these speculations in his later biblical commentaries and in his theological tracts as well.[45] But the most notable and spectacular example of psychological exploration comes to us in the intensely personal self-examination in the *De vita sua*. As modern observers we suffer an almost irresistible urge to psychoanalyse this text.[46] We should bear in mind, however, that we are not the first to analyse Guibert's psyche, and that our theoretical tools are perhaps no more sophisticated than those which Guibert and Anselm first brought to the task.

45. Guibert wrote commentaries on eleven minor prophets, three of which are published in Migne (*Tropologie in prophetis*, in *PL* 156, 341-488). To take two brief examples from his other works, his *De laude sancte Marie* is in large part a meditation on how perfect *intellectus* and *contemplatio* are always present in the Blessed Virgin (*PL* 156, 557-78). 'Cuius in hac contemplatione quanto fuit beatitudo secretior, tanto intellectus ad divina penetranda ex simplici et penitus indivisa intentione profusior' (559B). His better-known tract on saints' cults, *De pigneribus sanctorum*, concludes with a long meditation about the contemplative mind, called *De interiori mundo* (ed. R.B.C. Huygens; CCCM 127; 1993), pp. 158-75.

46. For examples, see J. Benton, 'The Personality of Guibert of Nogent', *Psychoanalytic Review* 57 (1970/71), pp. 563-86; and J. Kantor, 'A Psychohistorical Source: The *Memoirs* of Guibert of Nogent', *Journal of Medieval History* 2 (1976), pp. 281-303. M.D. Coupe has provided a helpful critique of this method in 'The Personality of Guibert de Nogent Reconsidered', *Journal of Medieval History* 9 (1983), pp. 317-29.

TRIAL AND INSPIRATION IN THE *LIVES* OF ANSELM
AND THOMAS BECKET

Michael Staunton

For Thomas Becket's biographer, Herbert of Bosham, Anselm was a 'rod of heretics, hammer of tyrants, casket of Scriptures, bugle of the Gospel and pillar of righteousness'.[1] Herbert describes how Becket, on becoming archbishop of Canterbury in 1162, took to carrying his predecessor's *Prayers and Meditations* with him at all times, using it as his enchiridion,[2] and there is considerable evidence that he took Anselm as his model in defending ecclesiastical rights. During Becket's archiepiscopate Anselm's body was translated and a chapel dedicated in his honour at Canterbury,[3] and it was Thomas who pressed for Anselm's canonization at Tours in 1163,[4] presenting an account of his *Life and Miracles*.[5]

1.   *Materials for the History of Thomas Becket* (ed. J.C. Robertson; Rolls Series; London, 1875–85), III, p. 210; Garnier, *Vie de Saint Thomas Becket* (ed. E. Walberg; Paris, 1936).

A survey of the twelfth-century *Lives* is provided in the introductions to *History of Thomas Becket*, I-IV. See also *Thomas Saga Erkibyskups* (ed. E. Magnusson; Rolls Series; London, 1883), II, pp. lxx-xcv; D. Knowles, *Thomas Becket* (London, 1970), pp. 172-74; F. Barlow, *Thomas Becket* (London, 1986), pp. 2-9; A. Duggan, *Thomas Becket, A Textual History of his Letters* (Oxford, 1980), pp. 175-226. The relationship between the *Lives* is discussed by E. Walberg, *La Tradition hagiographique de saint Thomas Becket avant la fin du XIIe siècle* (Paris, 1929).

2.   *History of Thomas Becket*, III, pp. 210-11; *The Prayers and Meditations of St Anselm* (ed. B. Ward; Harmondsworth, 1973). These were the most widely read and influential of Anselm's works in the Middle Ages (R.W. Southern, *St Anselm: A Portrait in a Landscape* [Cambridge, 1990], p. 91).

3.   R.W. Southern, *St Anselm and His Biographer: A Study of Monastic Life and Thought, 1059–c. 1130* (Cambridge, 1963), pp. 339-40; U. Nilgen, 'Thomas Becket as a Patron of the Arts: The Wall-Painting of St Anselm's Chapel at Canterbury Cathedral', *Art History* 3 (1980), pp. 357-74.

4.   R. Sommerville, *Pope Alexander III and the Council of Tours (1163)* (London, 1977), pp. 59-60; *Councils and Synods with Other Documents Relating to the*

The influence of Anselm's example on Becket's ecclesiastical policy has been recognized,[6] but less attention has been paid to the relationship between contemporary literary portrayals of the two archbishops. Eadmer, in Anselm's case, and the numerous biographers of Becket shared similar subject matter, literary influences, audience and experience. Here I shall illustrate this continuity of style and method by examining the portrayal of a common feature of Anselm and Thomas's defence of ecclesiastical liberties: public confrontations between these archbishops and the royal power at councils and trials.

Though different in personality, the careers of Anselm and Becket follow similar patterns. Both had difficulty in adjusting to the demands of their calling, and their terms in office were overshadowed by public conflicts with the crown. These were not only dramatic personality clashes, but reflected underlying practical and theoretical tensions between *regnum* and *sacerdotium*. Anselm and Becket spent protracted periods in exile, experiences which contributed greatly to their unpopularity among the English clergy and the Canterbury community.

In addition to this similarity of theme, both sets of biographies had the purpose of presenting Anselm and Becket not only as good archbishops but as saints. In doing so they drew on a common grounding in hagiography and theology, whether instilled by the experience of the monastery or through the teachings of the continental schools, which provided ideas and models of what a good archbishop and saint should be. Also, they had a common language based on a deep knowledge of scripture and exegetical method. Their intended audience was largely comprised of people of similar background and education—monks and ecclesiastics—to whom the writers' allusions and imagery were familiar. In these *Lives*, eleventh- and twelfth-century personalities and events are interpreted in terms of Christian history. A review of contemporary politics combines with a declaration and analysis of their subjects' sanctity by regarding the disputes and their protagonists in the light of precedents provided by the prophets, apostles, saints and martyrs and Christ himself. Anselm and Becket's defence of the church acts as evidence of

English Church, vol. I, AD 871–1204, Part 2, 1066–1204 (ed. D. Whitelock, M. Brett and C.N.L. Brooke; Oxford, 1981), pp. 845-47, 850; Barlow, *Thomas Becket*, p. 86; Southern, *St Anselm and his Biographer*, pp. 339-41.

    5.   Giovanni di Salisbury, *Anselmo e Becket, Due Vite* (ed. I Biffi; Milan, 1990), pp. 21-121.

    6.   Southern, *St Anselm and his Biographer*, p. 337.

their holiness, and, conversely, their evident sanctity goes some way towards justifying their controversial public acts.[7]

* * *

These features may be seen in Eadmer's description of Anselm at the Council of Rockingham in 1095 and the Winchester court of 1097, and in various accounts of Becket's trials, most notably at Northampton and Sens in 1164.[8] These are vivid eyewitness accounts of dramatic encounters between these archbishops and the royal power. Detailed descriptions of similar trials and councils may be found elsewhere—for instance the late eleventh-century account of the trial of William of Durham[9]— but what sets Eadmer and the Becket biographers apart is their constant use of models from scripture, the acts of the Christian martyrs and other sources. These writers provide not only a representation of events, but also an interpretation of the respective controversies and their participants.

The Council of Rockingham in spring 1095 and the Whitsun Council which followed were concerned with Anselm's request for recognition of Pope Urban II by William Rufus and receipt of the pallium, the archbishop's symbol of office. Rockingham may well have been 'a display of shadow-boxing',[10] but it nonetheless exposed the tension between royal and papal allegiance which was to dominate Anselm's archiepiscopate. The Winchester court of October 1097 revealed the irretrievable breakdown of the relationship between archbishop and king, and led directly to Anselm's exile. Eadmer's unique eyewitness accounts are detailed

7. I expand upon this argument in 'Politics and Sanctity in the Lives of Anselm and Thomas Becket' (PhD thesis, Cambridge, 1995). Eadmer's use of literary devices common in sacred biography is discussed by S.N. Vaughn, 'Eadmer's *Historia Novorum*: A Reinterpretation', *Anglo-Norman Studies* 10 (1987), pp. 259-89. The use of such devices by Becket's biographers is discussed by J. O'Reilly, 'The Double Martyrdom of Thomas Becket: Hagiography or History?', *Studies in Medieval and Renaissance History* 7 (1985), pp. 185-247. B. Smalley, *The Becket Conflict and the Schools* (Oxford, 1973), examines the influence of the biographers' education and ideological stance on their work.

8. See J. O'Reilly's treatment of Becket's confrontations with the royal power as 'trial scenes', where she draws comparisons with Eadmer's work ('Double Martyrdom', pp. 206-208, 216-18).

9. *Symeonis Monachi Opera Omnia* (ed. T. Arnold; Rolls Series; London, 1882), I, pp. 170-95.

10. Southern, *St Anselm: A Portrait*, p. 269.

and vivid but also stylized. The speeches of the protagonists act to sum up (what Eadmer claims as) the position of each side in the disputes, and act as a commentary on the issues at stake.

Becket's biographers could more convincingly identify the Council of Northampton in October 1164 as a trial.[11] There the archbishop was summoned by Henry II on a charge of contempt of court, and later accused of offences relating to his time as chancellor. It ended with Becket refusing to hear sentence and fleeing into exile in France. William FitzStephen and Herbert of Bosham, in particular, present dramatic eyewitness reports which also comment upon the dispute. The negotiations with Pope Alexander III the following month, though not a trial in the same sense, are presented by many of the biographers, especially Alan of Tewkesbury and 'Roger of Pontigny', as a confrontation between the righteous and their enemies. The same may be said of other councils which feature in the Becket *Lives*: Henry II's attempts to secure assent for his customs at Clarendon in January 1164, for example, or the failed negotiations for peace at Montmirail in January 1169. For Eadmer and Becket's biographers these were more than debates about the politics of the 1090s and 1160s: they were trials at which Anselm and Thomas were seen to bear witness to the pope, the church and to Christ.

Towards the beginning of the *Historia novorum*, Eadmer gives a brief account of the career of Anselm's immediate predecessor. He describes Lanfranc's success in recovering Canterbury privileges from the encroachment of Odo of Bayeux at an assembly at Penenden Heath.[12] He then relates how a second court case, which Lanfranc did not attend, resulted in losses to Canterbury. When this was reported to the archbishop, who was engaged in *lectio divina*, he 'not at all perturbed' had the matter deferred for discussion until the next day. That night his tenth-century predecessor St Dunstan appeared to him in a vision and told him not to be troubled at the number of his opponents, but in the morning to intervene personally 'with a light heart, assured that the suit would be with him'. This he did; and opening his case with an introductory statement which, to the surprise of all, 'seemed far removed from the matters which had already been dealt with or were to be dealt with',

---

11. See *Councils and Synods*, pp. 894-95; Barlow, *Thomas Becket*, pp. 109-15.

12. *Historia novorum* 17; see J. Le Patourel, 'The Reports of the Trial on Penenden Heath', in *Studies in Medieval History Presented to F.M. Powicke* (ed. R.W. Hunt *et al.*; Oxford, 1948), pp. 15-26.

Anselm: Aosta, Bec and Canterbury

he went on to demolish the arguments of his opponents.[13] A version of this story apppears in Eadmer's *Miraculi S Dunstani* and seems to originate with Osbern.[14] It follows a long-established tradition in hagiography dating back to the acts of the early Christian martyrs, and its features—endurance and placid aspect in adversity, recourse to spiritual aid, and victory through divine inspiration—are evident in the treatment of similar events in the *Lives* of Anselm and Becket.

Eadmer describes how at Rockingham William Rufus and his allies secretly busied themselves weaving their devices against Anselm.[15] The bishops supported the king, no one daring to speak in Anselm's defence 'for fear of the tyrant'.[16] Threats, reproaches and insults were thrown at Anselm,[17] and, echoing Christ's condemnation at the hands of the high priest,[18] Anselm was accused of blasphemy for standing up against Rufus.[19] But throughout such persecution, the archbishop displayed a placid and happy face ('placido, hilari vultu'), possessing his soul in patience, bearing insults for his loyalty to the apostolic see, his cheerfulness astonishing the king and his allies.[20]

At the Council of Northampton, Becket's allies reminded him how the apostles and martyrs, and also his Canterbury predecessors, endured persecution, possessing their souls in patience.[21] William FitzStephen implicitly compares Becket's trial to the martyrdom of John the Baptist, Abel and Remus, and recalls Anselm's conversation with Lanfranc about the merits of the Canterbury martyr, Elphege.[22] Becket is described as a wrestler or athlete engaged in a struggle or agony.[23] The anger of the king like a roaring lion,[24] the bishops and cardinals stood around him as bees, scorpions and fat bulls, convening in counsel against

13. *Historia novorum* 18.
14. *Memorials of St Dunstan* (ed. W. Stubbs; Rolls Series; London, 1874), pp. 238-39, 143-44; Le Patourel, 'Trial on Penenden Heath', p. 20 n. 2.
15. *Historia novorum* 53.
16. *Historia novorum* 61.
17. *Historia novorum* 61; *Vita Anselmi* 86-7.
18. Mt. 26.65.
19. *Vita Anselmi* 86.
20. *Historia novorum* 47, 61, 87; *Vita Anselmi* 87.
21. *History of Thomas Becket*, III, pp. 55-56, 58.
22. *History of Thomas Becket*, III, pp. 60-61; cf. I, p. 16; *Vita Anselmi* 50-54.
23. *History of Thomas Becket*, III, p. 296, IV, p. 46.
24. *History of Thomas Becket*, IV, p. 33.

the Lord's anointed,[25] the barons condemning him with the words 'You have now heard his blasphemy'.[26] Thomas resisted this pressure as a tower against Damascus, with a cheerful countenance ('hilari et iocundo vultu'),[27] singing psalms as his enemies marvelled at such constancy, magnanimity and confidence.[28]

This conforms to the standard depiction of trials as found in representations of the early Christian martyrs. Typically they would utter not a sound or a cry, showing to all that in their hour of torment Christ's witnesses were not present in the flesh, or rather that the Lord was present conversing with them.[29] In the account of Polycarp's martyrdom, all were surprised at his composure as he was condemned, and he entered the amphitheatre with a sober countenance.[30] Papylus did not utter a sound during torture but like a noble athlete received the onslaught, while Carpus smiled as he was nailed down.[31] Pamfilus sustained the fury in silence 'as a brave athlete',[32] and Maximillian accepted death with a cheerful countenance ('hilari vultu'),[33] while Conon sang a psalm as the nails were driven into his ankles.[34]

In such circumstances, what weapons did the persecuted have? Christ said to the apostles 'I send you as sheep in the midst of wolves; so be as wise as serpents and as innocent as doves'.[35] S. Vaughn uses this image to sum up Anselm's 'holy guile': the ability to manage his affairs and those of others, while losing nothing of his holiness or innocence.[36] However, I suggest that in attributing 'holy guile' to Anselm, Eadmer does not mean a natural attribute, but one which was instilled by the Holy Spirit at critical moments. Christ continued in his instruction, 'When they deliver you up [to governors and kings], do not be anxious

25. *History of Thomas Becket*, III, pp. 296, 302; cf. Ps. 21.13, 118(117).2.
26. *History of Thomas Becket*, III, p. 64; Mt. 26.65.
27. *History of Thomas Becket*, IV, p. 33.
28. *History of Thomas Becket*, IV, p. 46.
29. *Acts of the Christian Martyrs* (ed. H. Mususrillo; Oxford, 1972), no. 1, pp. 2-3.
30. *Christian Martyrs*, no. 1, pp. 6-7, 8-9.
31. *Christian Martyrs*, no. 2A, pp. 26-27.
32. *Christian Martyrs*, no. 2B, pp. 32-33.
33. *Christian Martyrs*, no. 17, pp. 248-49.
34. *Christian Martyrs*, no. 13, pp. 190-91.
35. Mt. 10.16.
36. *Anselm of Bec and Robert of Meulan: The Wisdom of the Serpent and the Innocence of the Dove* (Berkeley, 1987), pp. 12-13, 49-50.

how you are to speak or what you are to say; for what you are to say will be given to you in that hour, for it is not you who speak but the Spirit of the Father speaking through you'.[37] The apostles were promised 'a mouth and wisdom which all your adversaries shall not be able to gainsay nor resist'.[38]

Many of the early martyrs were gripped by the power of the Holy Spirit on entering the amphitheatre. A voice from heaven urged Polycarp to be strong, and as he refused to curse Christ he was filled with a joyful courage, his countenance filled with grace.[39] Fructuosus spoke 'with the inspiration and words of the Holy Spirit',[40] and Conon looked up to heaven and invoked God before addressing his persecutors.[41] A twelfth-century parallel is provided by Bernard of Clairvaux in the *Vita prima*. During the schism of Aquitaine, Bernard left the contending parties to it, while he 'trusting in stronger weapons', went to say mass. After the consecration, Bernard, 'acting no longer as a mere man' took the blessed sacrament outside and accosted the duke with eyes blazing full of menace.[42] Again, when preaching the Crusade, he was suddenly seized by the Holy Spirit half way through the mass, and spoke to Emperor Conrad on equal terms.[43]

At Rockingham the normally meek Anselm spoke 'lifting up his eyes, his face all aglow ('vivido vultu') in an awe-inspiring voice'.[44] Not receiving any counsel from his fellow bishops, he decided to fly 'to the Angel of great counsel',[45] and then asked that the case be adjourned so that he might think the matter over and make such answer as God might deign to put in his heart.[46] At the Winchester court, he confronted the bishop of Winchester confidently with a face all aglow.[47] Eadmer reports a similar incident at the Council of the Vatican in April 1099 when the bishop of Lucca was ordered to recite what had been decided. After reciting a number of items, 'suddenly to the astonishment of all his

37. Mt. 10.19-20.
38. Lk. 21.15.
39. *Christian Martyrs*, no. 1, pp. 8-9, 10-11.
40. *Christian Martyrs*, no. 12, pp. 180-81.
41. *Christian Martyrs*, no. 13, pp. 190-91.
42. *Vita Prima Bernardi* 2.3 (*PL* 185, 270).
43. *Vita Prima Bernardi* 6.15 (*PL* 185, 382).
44. *Historia novorum* 56.
45. *Historia novorum* 57.
46. *Historia novorum* 59.
47. *Historia novorum* 81.

face, his voice, his whole bearing changed', and turning his searching glance on those sitting around, he spoke out in defence of Anselm.[48]

At Northampton Thomas remained on the defensive until he resorted to spiritual weapons. When, on the sixth day, the archbishop fell ill from agitation, his confessor, Robert of Merton, advised him to commend his cause to Christ, the Virgin, Saints Stephen and Elphege and the other patrons of the church of Canterbury. He urged him to 'proceed confidently, trusting in the mercy of God and the support of the saints, for the labour is not yours but God's'. In this way, he predicted, Thomas would be able to escape from danger, for, he says, 'divine favour will not fail, and you will despise human grace'.[49] To this end, Thomas celebrated the Mass of St Stephen with its introit 'Princes did also sit and speak against me',[50] and in the process put off the face of humility and put on the face of the man and the lion.[51] He returned to the council carrying his cross, and confident that he would receive inspiration.[52] And, as 'Roger of Pontigny' puts it, comforted by the Holy Spirit, Becket confounded all attacks.[53] William FitzStephen describes how the archbishop, gazing at the image of the crucified, steadfast in mind and countenance, and remaining seated in order to preserve his dignity, delivered his response clearly and smoothly, without stumbling over a single word.[54] All this from an archbishop reputed not only to have had poor spoken Latin but also a natural stammer.[55]

In the *Vita* Eadmer writes that

> when Anselm was in a crowd of litigants and his opponents were laying their heads together, discussing the crafts and wiles by which they could help their own case and fraudulently injure his, he would have nothing to do with such things; instead he would discourse on the Bible, or at least some other subject tending to edification. And often, if there was no one

---

48. *Historia novorum* 112-13.

49. *History of Thomas Becket*, IV, p. 45; cf. Garnier, *Thomas Becket*, l. 310.

50. Discussed as a battle of images between Thomas and Henry by O'Reilly, 'Double Martyrdom', pp. 218-35.

51. *History of Thomas Becket*, III, p. 304. In Jerome's interpretation (*Commentarii in Hiezechielem* 1.10 [CCSL 75.15]) the face of the man represents the birth of Christ, and that of the lion the voice of the prophet sounding in the wilderness. The latter also recalls the warriors of David (cf. 1 Chron. 12.8).

52. *History of Thomas Becket*, I, pp. 34-35, II, p. 330, III, pp. 305, 307-308.

53. *History of Thomas Becket*, IV, pp. 47-48.

54. *History of Thomas Becket*, III, p. 63.

55. *Thomas Saga*, I, p. 28; Smalley, *Becket Conflict*, p. 12.

to listen to such talk, he would compose himself, in the sweet quietness of a pure heart to sleep. Then sometimes, when the frauds which had been prepared with intricate subtlety had been brought to his notice, he would immediately detect and disentangle them, not like a man who had been sleeping, but like one who had been wide-awake, keeping a sharp watch. For the charity which envieth not, which doeth no evil, which seeketh not her own, was alive in him and showed him things in a glance as they appeared in the light of truth.[56]

These conspirators are represented primarily by William of St Calais, bishop of Durham, described by Eadmer as 'a man quick-witted and of ready tongue rather than endowed with true wisdom',[57] and by Robert, count of Meulan, whose verdict on Anselm, 'Words! Words! All he is saying is mere words',[58] is seen to reflect more on himself than on the archbishop. Although, as William complained, Anselm began speaking so weakly and haltingly that they thought him a simpleton devoid of all human shrewdness,[59] he repeatedly confounded their attacks and left them speechless. While at Rockingham his adversaries carried on their conclaves, Anselm 'sat by himself, putting his trust wholely in the innocency of his heart and the mercy of the Lord God', and then leaned back against the wall and slept peacefully,[60] demolishing all opposition when he awoke. An exasperated Count Robert complained that 'while we busy ourselves all day long preparing such advice and in doing so scheme how to make the answers we suggest into some sort of consistent argument, he on his side so far from thinking out any evil just goes to sleep and then, when these arguments of ours are brought out in his presence, straight away with one breath of his lips he scatters them like cobwebs' ('quasi telas araneae rumpit').[61]

In many accounts of the papal court at Sens, the confrontation is presented as a battle between the false eloquence of Henry II's advocates and the eloquence of Thomas, founded in truth. Becket's first adversary was Gilbert Foliot, bishop of London, a well-read man 'but a servant of Astoroth' nonetheless.[62] He was followed by Hilary, bishop of

56. *Vita Anselmi* 46.
57. *Historia novorum* 59.
58. *Historia novorum* 59.
59. *Historia novorum* 62.
60. *Historia novorum* 58.
61. *Historia novorum* 62-63.
62. Garnier, *Thomas Becket*, l. 2171-2; cf. Judg. 2.13, 3.7, 10.6, 1 Sam.

Chichester, a man 'renowned in speech' [63] but compared by Thomas to Judas.[64] The archbishop, after receiving a vision of poison being offered in a gold chalice, is finally confronted by Cardinal William of Pavia, whose words, though eloquent and smooth nevertheless detracted greatly from ecclesiastical peace and liberty.[65] Foliot began his speech confidently but was interrupted in mid-flow by the Pope and became confused. Hilary then took up the thread but fell victim to an uncharacteristic grammatical slip, which provoked mocking laughter from the assembly[66] and was ascribed by Becket's supporters to him who opens the mouths of the dumb and makes fools of the fluent.[67] This incident also recalls Augustine's statement that 'when a man seeking for the reputation of eloquence stands before a human judge while a thronging multitude surrounds him, inveighs against his enemy with the most fierce hatred, he takes most vigilant heed that his tongue slips not into grammatical error, but takes no heed lest through the fury of his spirit he cut off a man from his fellow-men'.[68] Some of the Becket *Lives* report how Cardinal William of Pavia, characterized as a man of great eloquence and persuasive yet deceptive words, repeatedly interrupted Thomas's speech, believing that he had learned it by heart.[69] But, as 'Roger of Pontigny' writes, Thomas dismissed or refuted each of William's objections without difficulty or hesitation 'as if they were spiders' webs' ('sicut fila aranearum').[70]

Such displays of 'holy guile' are not without parallel. Anselm's and Becket's opponents are examples of those who pursue empty worldly eloquence rather than truth, as condemned by Augustine,[71] and, in John of Salisbury's *Vita Anselmi*, by Anselm himself.[72] Anselm's silence

12.10; on Foliot and Becket see A. Morey and C.N.L. Brooke, *Gilbert Foliot and his Letters* (Cambridge, 1965), pp. 147-87.

63. *History of Thomas Becket*, II, p. 327.

64. *History of Thomas Becket*, III, p. 55.

65. *History of Thomas Becket*, III, p. 410.

66. *History of Thomas Becket*, II, pp. 338-39.

67. *History of Thomas Becket*, III, p. 336; cf. Wisd. 10.21.

68. *Confessions*, 1.29 (CCSL 27.16).

69. *History of Thomas Becket*, IV, p. 63; Garnier, *Thomas Becket*, l. 2361-5.

70. *History of Thomas Becket*, IV, p. 63.

71. *De Doctrina Christiana* 4.5, 28 (CCSL 32.135-36). Augustine's views on this subject are discussed by C. Mohrmann, 'St Augustine and the "Eloquentia"', in *Études sur le Latin des Chrétiens* (Rome, 1958), pp. 351-70.

72. Biffi (ed.), *Anselmo e Becket*, pp. 30-31.

echoes Christ's trial,[73] and the image of false arguments as spiders' webs may also be found in scripture. St Basil, to whom Anselm is explicitly compared by John of Salisbury,[74] is reported to have confounded the machinations of his enemies 'like spiders' webs' ('sicut tela araneae solveretur').[75] Rudolf of Fulda writes that as St Leofgyth slept she would correct the mistakes of junior nuns who read from the Bible by her bed: 'No wonder', he says, 'that she could not be deceived when sleeping, whose heart he possessed who "slumbers not, neither sleeps, keeping Israel", and who could say with the bride in the Song of Songs, "I sleep and my heart watcheth"'.[76] William of Malmesbury describes how Wulfstan outwitted Thomas of York at a council of 1072 by sleeping as Thomas prepared his case, and reciting psalms when he awoke.[77] As John of Salisbury wrote to his brother at the height of the Becket dispute, 'the righteous man triumphs over his enemies in his sleep all the more gloriously for his innocence'.[78]

How should we interpret the eloquence of Anselm and Becket during these trials? Eadmer claims that the spirit of good counsel ruled in Anselm's heart.[79] He destroyed opposition by reasoning which could not be refuted, showing that in all the questions to which the real points at issue in the controversy related he had divine authority on his side.[80] Anselm's enemies confess that they cannot find any argument to invalidate the archbishop's, 'especially when all his reasoning rests upon the words of God and the authority of St Peter'.[81] And Eadmer, in describing Pope Urban's speech at the Council of Bari in 1098, refers to 'the eloquence that comes of good sense and the good sense that comes of

---

73. Mt. 27.11, Mk 15.2, Lk. 23.3; G.W.H. Lampe, 'Martyrdom and Inspiration', in *Suffering and Martyrdom in the New Testament* (ed. W. Horbury and B. McNeil; Cambridge, 1981), pp. 118-35 (134).

74. Biffi (ed.), *Anselmo e Becket*, p. 93.

75. Cassiodorus, *Historia Ecclesiastica Tripartita*, 7.36 (CSEL 71.437); Sedulus Scottus, *Collectaneum Miscellaneum*, 26.66 (CCCM 67.197).

76. Rudolfus Fuldensi, *Vita Leobae Abbatissae Biscofesheimensis*, 11, *MGH* Script. 15.1 (ed. G. Waitz; 1887), p. 126.

77. *The Vita Wulfstani of William of Malmesbury* (ed. R.R. Darlington; Camden Series; London, 1928), 2.1, p. 79.

78. *The Letters of John of Salisbury* (ed. W.J. Millor, H.E. Butler and C.N.L. Brooke; Oxford, 1979), II, no. 169, pp. 118-19.

79. *Vita Anselmi* 16.

80. *Historia novorum* 61-62.

81. *Historia novorum* 62.

eloquence'.[82] Herbert of Bosham praises Becket's defence of ecclesiastical liberties at the Council of Montmirail, and attributes his success to the guidance of God. Because Becket refused to deny Christ, Herbert says, 'the world will see with its own eyes that the Almighty will honour you in the sight of the world'.[83]

Traditionally one who confessed his faith in circumstances of persecution was regarded as akin to the prophet as a recipient of revelation and a proclaimer of God's word.[84] This does not mean that, conversely, because God speaks through them, the sanctity of Anselm and Becket is automatically established. Augustine indicates that there are certain circumstances in which the evil may speak with divine eloquence.[85] However, while not proving sanctity categorically, such inspiration acts as strong evidence for two reasons: first, the fact that the Holy Spirit chose them as vessels, and secondly because in acting as such vessels, they follow in the footsteps of the disciples and martyrs.

* * *

The disputes of Anselm and Thomas are seen to operate on both a contemporary worldly level and on an eternal heavenly level, as, in the words of Herbert of Bosham, 'a spectacle for men and for angels'.[86] As the biographers present it, the two are inextricably linked: it is impossible to remove the events of these archiepiscopates from the context of an ongoing defence of Christ and the church; nor can the sanctity of Anselm and Thomas be separated from the public actions which dominated their terms in office. Their case for sanctity is based to some extent at least on the claim that Anselm and Thomas met the requirements of the good archbishop through their public lives; their political case is made by arguing that an inward sanctity manifested itself in their subjects' public acts, thereby justifying their policies.

The question remains: to what extent did Eadmer influence the Becket biographers? The use of scriptural and saintly *exempla* and the combination of politics and sanctity is if anything more pronounced in the Becket *Lives*. In certain cases the Becket *Lives* correspond directly to Eadmer's writings, but it is possible that this was the result of other

82. *Historia novorum* 104.
83. *History of Thomas Becket*, III, p. 430.
84. Lampe, 'Martyrdom and Inspiration', p. 119.
85. *In Joannis Evangelium Tractatus*, 45.9 (CCSL. 36.393).
86. *History of Thomas Becket*, VI, p. 122; cf. 1 Cor. 4.9.

influences common to both. Even if Becket's biographers had never read Eadmer, similarities in subject matter and background made it likely that they would repeat many features of his work. It is better to regard the relationship between the writings as one of continuity, just as Thomas's behaviour as archbishop shows a certain continuity with Anselm's archiepiscopate, although the precise nature of Anselm's influence cannot be defined. As Thomas fulfilled the legacy of Anselm, and developed upon it, so too did his biographers expand upon the work begun by Anselm's biographer.

ST ANSELM AND TWO CLERKS OF THOMAS BECKET*

Yoko Hirata

John of Salisbury's *Vita Sancti Anselmi* was written in 1163, about fifty years after Anselm's death. This work, long considered little more than an unoriginal abridgment of Eadmer's *Vita* presented at the Council of Tours of 1163 to help promote Anselm's canonization,[1] has now been recognized as a document designed for other political purposes.[2] Nevertheless the *Vita* still needs to be located more precisely within its contemporary context. The work clearly belongs within the milieu of Thomas Becket; but Becket, after his long years of service at court as Henry II's chancellor, was at the outset of his pontificate unusually dependent upon advice from scholarly subordinates. John of Salisbury, author of the *Vita*, is an obvious point of contact between Thomas and Anselm: another, less well-attested but in some respects more intriguing, link is Herbert of Bosham. The purpose of this paper is to clarify the relationship of Thomas Becket's two clerks to St Anselm; it will consider the purposes for which John of Salisbury wrote his *Vita Sancti Anselmi* and the relationship between the lives written by Eadmer and by John; how John of Salisbury and Herbert of Bosham may have influenced Thomas Becket; and how their knowledge of Eadmer's *Vita Anselmi*

* I would like to thank Professor David Luscombe for advice and assistance. I would also like to thank Dr Neil McLynn and Dr Gordon Daniels for help with my English. An earlier version of this paper was given at the conference at Canterbury and I have benefited much from the points raised in the discussion there.

1. This view has prevailed since the publication of R.W. Southern's *Saint Anselm and his Biographer: A Study of Monastic Life and Thought, 1059–c. 1130* (Cambridge, 1963), p. 338.
2. For this point see J.P. McLoughlin, 'John of Salisbury (c. 1120–1180): The Career and Attitudes of a Schoolman in Church Politics' (unpublished dissertation, Trinity College, Dublin, 1988). Certain implications of this are explored in Y. Hirata, 'John of Salisbury and Thomas Becket: The Making of a Martyr', *Medieval History* 2.3 (1992), pp. 18-25.

was to influence their own writings on the life of Thomas Becket.

An important characteristic of John's *Vita Sancti Anselmi*, as compared to Eadmer's *Vita Anselmi*, is that it was composed as a document to be presented by Thomas at the Council of Tours to promote Anselm's canonization. Almost certainly stimulated by King Henry's success in having Edward the Confessor canonized from Westminster,[3] Thomas also wished to promote the canonization of one of his predecessors at Canterbury who had been venerated as a saint. Since the council had to deal with various matters, John declared that he aimed to write 'briefly, succinctly and in a plain enough style'[4] and referred readers who wished to know more to other works. Besides Eadmer's *Vita Anselmi*, John also used the *Historia Novorum*. Whereas Eadmer's *Vita Anselmi* consists of seventy-two chapters plus a collection of miracles, John's life is condensed into eighteen chapters including a chapter of miracles, each chapter not much longer than Eadmer's. In order to achieve brevity, John omitted much of Eadmer's *Vita Anselmi* so that little more than bare factual data remained in his *Vita*. John ignored most of the anecdotes and conversations which reveal Anselm's personality and his ways as a monk. John compressed Eadmer's lively but lengthy accounts into precise and accurate statements of fact so that one of his chapters is often equivalent to several of Eadmer's.

Although John abridged Eadmer's *Vita Anselmi* considerably, he also made some insertions and additions. Since Eadmer did not begin writing the *Vita Anselmi* with a specific aim,[5] John had to make some adjustments for hagiographic purposes. In the introduction, John declared that he was going to write a life of someone who was in direct line from the saints and apostles,[6] and throughout his *Vita*, John sprinkled names of saints such as Martin, Anthony, Paul, John, Clement, Nicholas, Benedict and Basil.[7] He also inserted comments probably based on oral traditions

3.   R. Sommerville, *Pope Alexander III and the Council of Tours (1163)* (London, 1977), p. 59. F. Barlow, *Edward the Confessor* (Berkeley and Los Angeles, 1970), p. 284 and Appendix D; B.W. Scholz, 'The Canonization of Edward the Confessor', *Speculum* 36 (1961), pp. 38-60.

4.   John of Salisbury, *Anselmo e Becket, Due Vite* (ed. I. Biffi; Milan, 1990), p. 24.

5.   R.W. Southern, *Saint Anselm: A Portrait in a Landscape* (Cambridge, 1990), pp. 422-28.

6.   Biffi (ed.), *Anselmo e Becket*, p. 22.

7.   Biffi (ed.), *Anselmo e Becket*, p. 25 n. 5; for the references to saints, see pp. 24, 32, 38, 40, 58, 82, 92.

at Canterbury which attested Anselm's exceptional qualities as a holy man.[8]

John's additions fall into two categories: one concerning the kings whom Anselm served, the other concerning the Canterbury–York disputes. Additions concerning the Canterbury–York disputes are fairly long and, unlike John's other alterations to Eadmer's *Vita*, demonstrated Anselm's significance in public life as archbishop of Canterbury.[9] They were meant at the same time to help clarify Thomas's place as such at the Council of Tours. John began his additions with a lengthy discussion of Paschal II's letter to Anselm granting primacy to Canterbury.[10] He described how Anselm exhorted Thomas of York to make a profession to him even in his last days.[11] He devoted the whole of chapter 15 to Anselm's letter to Thomas of York written for that purpose, which is included not in Eadmer's *Vita* but in the *Historia Novorum*.[12] In John's *Vita Sancti Anselmi*, although these additions stood out and obstructed the general flow of the saint's life, they nevertheless catered for Thomas's need to reassert Canterbury's primacy over York at the Council of Tours. The struggle over primacy between Canterbury and York which emerged almost every time the occupant of either see changed[13] made itself felt at the Council. In the 'Draco Normannicus', Etienne de Rouen stated that Roger of York insisted on his primacy on account of his earlier election and consecration.[14] While he counted

8. Biffi (ed.), *Anselmo e Becket*, pp. 34 n. 3, 36 nn. 10, 94. For such oral traditions, see also W.J. Millor and C.N.L. Brooke (eds.), *The Letters of John of Salisbury 2: The Later Letters (1963–1180)* (ed. D.E. Greenway, M. Winterbottom and C.N.L. Brooke; Oxford Medieval Texts; Oxford, 1979), *ep.* 303 and n. 4.

9. On Anselm and the Canterbury–York dispute, see Southern, *Anselm: A Portrait*, pp. 340-47. Also Southern, *Saint Anselm and his Biographer*, pp. 138-399.

10. Biffi (ed.), *Anselmo e Becket*, p. 94.

11. Biffi (ed.), *Anselmo e Becket*, p. 104.

12. *Historia Novorum* (ed. M. Rule; Rolls Series; London, 1884), p. 206.

13. For previous disputes between Canterbury and York, see M. Gibson, *Lanfranc of Bec* (Oxford, 1978), pp. 116-22: D. Nicholl, *Thurstan, Archbishop of York (1114–1140)* (York, 1964), pp. 75-100: D. Bethel, 'William of Corbeil and the Canterbury–York Dispute', *Journal of Ecclesiastical History* 19 (1968), pp. 145-59; Southern, *Anselm: A Portrait*, pp. 340-64: A. Saltman, *Theobald, Archbishop of Canterbury* (London, 1956), pp. 90-93, 100.

14. R. Howlett (ed.), 'The "Draco Normannicus" of Etienne de Rouen', Booke III, vv. 949-1074, in *Chronicles of the Reigns of Stephen, Henry II and Richard I*, II (Rerum Britannicarum Medii Aevi Scriptores, or Chronicles and Memorials of Great Britain and Ireland during the Middle Ages; London, 1885), pp. 739-46. On

Roger among the eloquent speakers at the Council, he explained Becket's silence by the inadequacy of his Latin.[15] Perhaps John's insertion of Anselm's letter to Archbishop Thomas of York was made to counteract Thomas's disadvantage.

John's additions concerning William Rufus and Henry I[16] appear closer to Eadmer's accounts in *Historia Novorum* than *Vita Anselmi* and are clearly unfavourable to the kings and royal power.[17] Reporting the death of William the Conqueror and the succession of William Rufus, John recounted the suffering of the church and people under him using the same quotation of Claudian as he did in the *Policraticus* when he emphasized the importance of exemplary conduct of the ruler.[18] John's lengthy addition comparing Rufus's death with that of Julian the Apostate[19] was reminiscent of John's reference to Julian in the *Policraticus* which was made to illustrate God's punishment of tyrants.[20] These insertions were merely repetitions or adaptations of what John had previously expressed, but when they appeared in the context of the *Vita Sancti Anselmi,* they highlighted the unstable relationship between the king's ancestors and their archbishop. They were liable to remind the readers of the potentially more precarious relationship between Henry II and Thomas Becket. For, unlike his immediate predecessors who were more securely endowed with their authority, Thomas had to assert his authority in the face of the king to whom he

Roger of York at the Council of Tours, see F. Barlow, *Thomas Becket* (London, 1986), p. 86; Sommerville, *Pope Alexander III*, pp. 25, 34-38, 92 nn. 20 and 21.

15. '...minus edoctus verba Latina loqui': 'The "Draco Normannicus"', Booke III, v. 998 in Howlett (ed.), *Chronicles*, II, p. 743. Sommerville considers this judgment to reflect the anti-Becket bias of the source, but Barlow more plausibly considers that Thomas was probably more comfortable in the vernacular. See Barlow, *Thomas Becket*, p. 133; and Sommerville, *Pope Alexander III*, pp. 13-15.

16. Biffi (ed.), *Anselmo e Becket*, pp. 62-64, 92-94.

17. For Eadmer's report on William Rufus's oppression of the church, see *The Life of St Anselm* (ed. R.W. Southern; Oxford Medieval Texts; Oxford, 1972), p. 63; and Rule (ed.), *Historia novorum*, pp. 25-27. For Henry I, see Southern (ed.), *The Life of St Anselm*, p. 129 and Rule (ed.), *Historia Novorum*, pp. 116-17.

18. 'Componitur orbis regis ad exemplum, nec sic inflectere sensus humanos edicta ualent quam vita regentis.' Biffi (ed.), *Anselmo e Becket*, pp. 62-64; C.C.J. Webb (ed.), *Ioannis Saresberiensis Episcopi Carnotensis Policratici sive de Nugis Curialium et Vestigiis Philosophorum libri viii* (2 vols; Oxford, 1909), iv-4, I, p. 247.

19. Biffi (ed.), *Anselmo e Becket*, pp. 92-93.

20. Webb (ed.), *Policraticus*, viii-21, pp. 383-84.

owed his preferment if he were to establish himself over his suffragans. Therefore, the criticism of the king's ancestors might be interpreted as Thomas's expression of reluctance to comply with the king's requests if not a deliberate insult to the king.

The idea of promoting the canonization of a saint from Canterbury and the choice of Anselm, however, probably came from one of Thomas's subordinates—John of Salisbury himself. Since by the time of the Council of Tours, John was the only significant survivor from the household of Thomas's predecessor Theobald, his expertise with the tendencies and traditions of Canterbury probably carried considerable authority. He had been introduced to the cult of Anselm which had started before the 1150s during the pontificate of Archbishop Theobald.[21] Having been placed at Canterbury, he had access to *Vita Anselmi* by Eadmer and was exposed to oral traditions of Anselm's sanctity around Canterbury. He was conscious of the displeasure of the monks of Christ Church at having the king's former chancellor as their father and archbishop as well as their inclination to have a powerful patron saint canonized by the Pope.[22] He was informed not only of the previous struggle between Canterbury and York, but of the problems that existed between Anselm and the two kings he had served.[23] John may well have been the adviser on the strategy of promoting the canonization of Anselm at the same time as being the author of the *Vita Sancti Anselmi*.[24]

---

21. R. Foreville, 'Regard neuf sur le culte de saint Anselme à Canterbury au XIIe siècle', in *Spicilegium Beccense*. II. *Les Mutations socio-culturelles au tournant des XIe–XIIe siècles* (Paris, 1984), pp. 299-316; *idem*, 'Canterbury et la canonisation des saints au XIIe siècle', in D. Greenway, C. Holdsworth and J. Sayers (eds.), *Tradition and Change: Essays in Honour of Marjorie Chibnall Presented by her Friends on the Occasion of her Seventieth Birthday* (Cambridge, 1985), pp. 115-43.

22. A. Vauchez, *La Sainteté en occident aux dernières siècles du moyen age d'après les procès de canonisation et les documents hagiographiques* (Rome, 1988), pp. 27-28.

23. John had already described Anselm in the *Policraticus* as a victim of William Rufus's persecution. See Webb (ed.) *Policraticus*, vi-18, II, p. 48.

24. John gave advice to his friends, providing the necessary documents at the same time. See *epp*. 228-29 in Millor and Brooke (eds.), *The Letters of John of Salisbury 2*. See also *epp*. 17-18 in W.J. Millor, H.E. Butler and C.N.L. Brooke (eds.), *The Letters of John of Salisbury 1: The Early Letters (1153–1161)* (ed. C.N.L. Brooke, D.E. Greenway and M. Winterbottom; Oxford Medieval Texts; Oxford, repr., 1986). Compare *ep*. 175 in Millor and Brooke (eds.), *The Letters of John of Salisbury 2*, and *ep*. 220 in J.C. Robertson and J.B. Sheppard (eds.),

After Thomas returned from the Council of Tours, his relations with the king deteriorated rapidly and we find the author of the *Vita Sancti Anselmi* exiled in France between October 1163 and January 1164.[25] As the other clerks began prudently to abandon Thomas,[26] Herbert of Bosham remained at his side to become his chief adviser. Herbert[27] studied in Paris under Peter Lombard around 1150. He was also a student at St Victor, where he may have been introduced to Anselm's *Proslogion* and *Monologion*[28] and had a chance to become familiar with Eadmer's *Vita Anselmi*.[29] Well-versed in Hebrew, he was an excellent theologian and biblical scholar,[30] but known as a proud and militant character.[31] A clerk to Henry II from before 1157, he probably came to know Thomas as royal chancellor and served him as archbishop of Canterbury. Herbert was not present at the martyrdom, but afterwards advocated the canonization of Thomas. In spite of his learning and service to Thomas, he failed to obtain honour and position and died some time after 1194. After Thomas Becket was exiled in France, while John of Salisbury stayed with his friend Peter of Celle in Rheims, Herbert of Bosham was with Thomas as his instructor in theology[32] and remained the most influential member of his household.

Materials for the History of Thomas Becket, V (Rolls Series; London, 1875–85).

25. Millor and Brooke (eds.), *The Letters of John of Salisbury 2*, p. xxiii, and *ep.* 136. See also Peter of Celle's letters, *epp.* 73 and 75 (*PL* 202, 405-636).

26. Barlow, *Thomas Becket*, pp. 100, 107.

27. On Herbert, see B. Smalley, *The Becket Conflict and the Schools* (Oxford, 1973), pp. 59-86; *idem, The Study of the Bible in the Middle Ages* (Oxford, 1952), pp. 186-95.

28. R. Javelet, 'Interprétation de l'argument ontologique par la "SPECULATIO": Herbert de Bosham et Saint Anselme—Médiation victorine', in H. Kohlenberger (ed.), *Analecta Anselmiana*, IV.1 (Frankfurt/Main, 1975), pp. 59-103.

29. Eadmer's *Vita Anselmi* was widely circulated in northern France and St Victor is known to have possessed one of its oldest copies. On the development and manuscript tradition of the *Vita Anselmi* by Eadmer, see Southern (ed.), *The Life of St Anselm*, pp. ix-xxv.

30. R. Loewe, 'The Mediaeval Christian Hebraists of England—Herbert of Bosham and Earlier Scholars', *The Jewish Historical Society Transactions* 17 (1953), pp. 225-49; *idem*, 'Herbert of Bosham's Commentary on Jerome's Hebrew Psalter (1)', *Biblica* 34 (1953), pp. 44-192; B. Smalley, 'A Commentary on the *Hebraica* by Herbert of Bosham', *Recherches de Théologie Ancienne et Médiévale* 18 (1951), pp. 29-65.

31. Smalley, *The Becket Conflict*, pp. 63-64, 67-69.

32. Robertson and Sheppard (eds.), *History of Thomas Becket*, III, pp. 204-205.

A by-product of Thomas's studies was an increased fluency in Latin. His imperfect knowledge of Latin had been criticized by Etienne de Rouen in his account of the Council of Tours. In 1165, John of Salisbury mocked the deficiency of Thomas's learning by writing, 'the exile has undoubtedly been profitable to the archbishop of Canterbury for his learning and his character'.[33] But Thomas's Latin must have dramatically improved by the time of the Conference between Gisors and Trie in 1167. In his report of the conference, John wrote how, in reply to a wily question from the papal legates, Thomas spoke out humbly and calmly in good spirits 'with eloquent skill in the Latin tongue'.[34]

A more important contribution of Herbert of Bosham was probably in helping to equip Thomas with an ideological ground to counter the king's demand for observance of ancestral customs with the supremacy of spiritual over temporal power. The idea itself was not new. Both John of Salisbury and Herbert of Bosham had been introduced to it in Paris in the 1150s, particularly under the influence of the Victorines.[35] John of Salisbury suffered the king's disgrace for it while in the service of Archbishop Theobald.[36] However, Thomas, who had long worked on the king's behalf, perceived the idea afresh as a weapon which could be deployed against the king's contentions. In 1165, when the situation seemed quite hopeless for Thomas, John of Salisbury sincerely advised him to abandon the study of law and turn to prayer.[37] Thomas nevertheless decided to fight. The presence at his side of Herbert of Bosham who was as proud and militant as Thomas and who preferred gallant action to cautious calculation or quiet meditation may have helped his decision. The distant advice from John of Salisbury was suppressed and Thomas refused at this point to follow the path of Anselm whose canonization he had promoted and who, in his exile, willingly retreated from ecclesiastical politics into the life of prayer and meditation. To Thomas, Anselm's legacy was not the love of monastic retreat from the world nor the writing of theological works.

---

33. Millor and Brooke (eds.), *The Letters of John of Salisbury 2, ep.* 150.

34. Millor and Brooke (eds.), *The Letters of John of Salisbury 2, ep.* 231.

35. On Hugh of St Victor and his description of the relationship between the two powers, see Smalley, *The Becket Conflict*, pp. 28-30.

36. On John's disgrace, see Millor, Butler and Brooke (eds.), *The Letters of John of Salisbury 1, ep.* 19, pp. 257-58; G. Constable, 'The Alleged Disgrace of John of Salisbury in 1159', *English Historical Review* 69 (1954), pp. 67-76.

37. Millor and Brooke (eds.) *The Letters of John of Salisbury 2, ep.* 144.

Nevertheless, Anselm came to have a profound significance on Thomas Becket and his party at a later stage in the conflict. We can observe this through the process by which the Becket party came to search for the meaning of their continued exile after the failure of the papal legates' attempt at reconciliation in late 1167. With no prospect of peace, they increasingly emphasized the cause of their exile on the one hand and sought precedents for it on the other. John of Salisbury termed the exile a fight for righteousness and the freedom of the church. He used the phrase as a slogan when he wrote to his English friends asking for their support and financial aid. Thomas Becket looked into the lives of his predecessors. At the Conference of Montmirail, when Thomas was being pressurized to swear to observe the ancient customs just as his predecessors had done unreservedly, he is reported to have replied that 'none of his predecessors had been compelled or driven to make profession to customs, save only St Anselm, who was sent into exile for seven years for the same cause.'[38] In his letters written after the Conference of Montmirail, he also referred to the fact that among the previous archbishops of Canterbury, there were some who were exiled for a similar cause.[39] At this point Anselm appeared as a precedent for Thomas's case.

Thomas's clerks also saw parallels between the exile of Thomas and that of Anselm, and between the causes they were fighting for. John of Salisbury never made any attempt to highlight the cause of Anselm's exile nor the concept of the freedom of the church when he wrote his *Vita Sancti Anselmi*[40] in 1163. But after 1168, writing to the monks of Christ Church, John reproached them for not giving support to Thomas by comparing him with Anselm who 'twice went into exile for righteousness' sake'.[41] After peace was made, he urged them to come and greet Thomas upon his return just as their predecessors had done to Anselm.[42] In a letter probably written in or before 1167,[43] Herbert of Bosham referred to three archbishops of Canterbury—St Dunstan,

38. Millor and Brooke (eds.) *The Letters of John of Salisbury 2, ep.* 288.
39. Robertson and Sheppard (eds.), *History of Thomas Becket*, VI, *ep.* 466. See also *epp.* 450-52, 462-63, 467-68.
40. The phrase appears only twice in John's *Vita Sancti Anselmi*; see Biffi (ed.), *Anselmo e Becket*, p. 94.
41. Millor and Brooke (eds.), *The Letters of John of Salisbury 2, ep.* 244.
42. Millor and Brooke (eds.), *The Letters of John of Salisbury 2, ep.* 303.
43. Herbert of Bosham's letter, *ep.* 19 (*PL* 190) (*ep.* 176 in Robertson and Sheppard [eds.], *History of Thomas Becket*, V).

St Elphege and St Anselm. While he venerated Dunstan and Anselm, his enthusiasm lay with the martyred Elphege. But he later came to uphold Anselm as a champion of their fight. Writing his *Vita Sancti Thomae*, in 1184–86, Herbert specifically mentioned Thomas's use of Anselm's prayers, and described Anselm as 'rod of heretics, hammer of tyrants, casket of the Scriptures, bugle of the Gospel and pillar of righteousness'.[44]

It is interesting to note that both John of Salisbury and Herbert of Bosham wrote *Lives* of Thomas. John's *Vita Sancti Thomae* included almost all of John's letter *Ex Insperato*,[45] the first known account of the murder of Thomas. The year of production was traditionally ascribed to 1173–76.[46] However, a new theory has recently been put foward, which dates John's *Vita* to 1171.[47] The work has been considered to be 'derivative and impersonal' and in this respect similar to his *Vita Sancti Anselmi*.[48] It was 'far from adequate as a biography of the archbishop or as an account of the dispute with the king'.[49] Partly in view of the traditional dating the purpose of the work was considered to be merely a preface to the collection of Becket's letters.[50] However, if the writing of the *Vita* coincides with the movement for the canonization of Thomas Becket, as the new dating appears to suggest, is this not originally a canonization document later adopted for a different purpose and hence similar to John's *Vita Sancti Anselmi*? This of course is merely a conjecture, while the purpose of the document remains unclear.

Herbert of Bosham's *Vita Sancti Thomae* was written as a preface to *Liber Melorum*, 'The Book of Songs'.[51] It was written around 1184–86

---

44. Robertson and Sheppard (eds.), *History of Thomas Becket*, III, p. 210; Smalley, *The Becket Conflict*, p. 79.

45. Millor, and Brooke (eds.), *The Letters of John of Salisbury 2, ep.* 305.

46. E. Walberg, *La Vie de saint Thomas le martyr par Guernes de Pont-Sainte-Maxence* (Lund, 1922), pp. xiii-lv; R. Foreville, *L'Eglise et la ruyauté en Angleterre sous Henri II Plantagenet (1154–1189)* (Paris, 1943), pp. xxv-xxxv; D. Knowles, *Thomas Becket* (London: 1970), p. 173.

47. Barlow rejected the traditional view as 'inherently improbable'. See Barlow, *Thomas Becket*, pp. 4-5. See also Biffi, *Anselmo e Becket*, p. 144.

48. Smalley, *The Becket Conflict*, p. 107.

49. A. Duggan, *Thomas Becket: A Textual History of his Letters* (Oxford, 1980), p. 89.

50. Millor and Brooke (eds.), *The Letters of John of Salisbury 2*, p. lx and n. 2.

51. Smalley, *The Becket Conflict*, p. 79. On the nature of Herbert's *Vita Sancti Thomae* against the background of the twelfth-century Renaissance, see H. Vollrath,

after most of the other biographies had appeared. When he composed this long life of Thomas, Herbert was over sixty and had still not received the honour or position which he thought was his due as the martyr's secretary, teacher, counsellor and best friend. He probably took pleasure in recalling the valuable moments he shared with the martyr and wished to express in words what he knew of the saint as his closest companion. It is not certain that Herbert had read Eadmer's *Vita Anselmi,* but there are distinct echoes of this work in the *Vita Sancti Thomae.*[52] Although the two men were almost completely opposite in character, and Herbert's *Vita* is not a contemporary record, he also saw value in recording private moments and intimate conversations.

In sum, there is a curious parallel between Becket's gradual discovery in the life of Anselm a precedent for his own exile, and the discovery by his intellectually well-matched but temperamentally incompatible clerks of a common cause to fight for. In 1163, John advised Thomas to promote the canonization of Anselm at the Council of Tours and Thomas took his advice not so much because of his personal veneration of Anselm, but from strategic considerations. Thomas, being exiled after a series of confrontations with the king, relied on the counsel of Herbert of Bosham, who fed Thomas with the principle of the supremacy of ecclesiastical over temporal power. At this point, Thomas did not heed John's advice to retreat into the life of prayer in an Anselmian manner, nor to assume humbleness and moderation in dealing with the intermediaries of peace. However, in the midst of the hardship of exile and waning hope, searching for the cause of their fight, the Becket party came to find their precedent in the exile of Anselm. This was the time when John of Salisbury and Herbert of Bosham realized that they were fighting for a common cause, and they even worked together on the same mission.[53] And after Thomas's death, they shared the same zeal in promoting his canonization.[54]

The irony is that the cause the Becket party was fighting for was not

---

'"Gewissensmoral" und Konfliktverständnis: Thomas Becket in der Darstellung seiner Biographen', *Historisches Jahrbuch* 109 (1989), pp. 24-55.

52. For the comparison of Eadmer's *Vita Anselmi* with other lives, see Southern, *Saint Anselm and his Biographer,* pp. 334-36.

53. After the peace at Fréteval, they were sent together on a mission to Henry II (Barlow, *Thomas Becket,* p. 213).

54. Millor and Brooke (eds.), *The Letters of John of Salisbury 2, epp.* 305, 308; Robertson and Sheppard (eds.), *History of Thomas Becket,* VII, *ep.* 779.

the direct reason for Anselm's exile. Eadmer mentioned *libertas eccle-siae* only once in his *Vita Anselmi*,[55] and this was an idea with which Richard Southern suggests Anselm himself was never comfortable.[56] Anselm was involved in the latter phase of the Investiture Controversy almost accidentally. The issue was outside his main sphere of interest, and he went into exile not to fight against the king but for the sake of obedience to the Pope.[57] This was the greatest difference between Anselm and Thomas Becket: they shared the experience of exile, but their motivation was different. Even as archbishop of Canterbury, Anselm remained essentially a monk. This was the feature that was absent in Thomas. Thomas led a monk's life in the sense of keeping vigils, maundies, wearing a hair shirt and submitting himself to scourging. Through these, he probably fought against his own weaknesses. But he never cherished spiritual life in the way Anselm did. Thomas may have fought for a most important cause, but people sensed no sanctity in him. Miracles and anecdotes that illustrate holiness are almost totally absent from the various *Lives* of Thomas. Nevertheless, Thomas was martyred and canonized for his fight for the cause for which he believed Anselm had been exiled, and his own canonization overshadowed Canterbury's other saints, including the one whose canonization he had promoted. And among later archbishops of Canterbury, Hubert Walter honoured St Thomas,[58] and Stephen Langton regarded himself the successor of St Thomas.[59]

As for the two clerks of Thomas Becket, they benefited from Eadmer's *Vita Anselmi* in writing the *Lives* of the new and ever popular saint. The experience of compiling several contemporary works into the brief *Vita Sancti Anselmi* helped John compose the *Vita Sancti Thomae*. It provided him with an adequate form. But the spirit of Eadmer's work, of recording stories and intimate conversations revealing the personality of the saint in a way that only a close friend could, was rekindled in the *Vita Sancti Thomae* of Herbert of Bosham.

55. Southern (ed.), *The Life of St Anselm*, p. 128. It appears in connection with the king's measures taken against the Pope's decree to prohibit lay investiture. The same incident occurs in Rule (ed.), *Historia novorum*, p. 148.

56. Southern, *Anselm: A Portrait*, pp. 304-307.

57. C.W. Hollister, 'William II, Henry I and the Church', in *The Culture of Christendom: Essays in Medieval History in Memory of Denis L.T. Bethel* (Cambridge, 1993), pp. 183-206.

58. C.R. Cheney, *Hubert Walter* (Stanford, 1967), pp. 51-52, 181-84.

59. F.M. Powicke, *Stephen Langton* (London, repr., 1965), pp. 104, 116.

THE IMPACT OF THE *CUR DEUS HOMO*
ON THE EARLY FRANCISCAN SCHOOL

Michael Robson

Saint Anselm's *Cur deus homo* was one of the most influential treatises of the Middle Ages. In the schools of the twelfth century, however, it was quoted infrequently, though Anselm's influence on other questions can be detected in the monastic and cathedral schools. In some circles his treatise aroused a strong interest and the strength of the manuscript tradition suggests that it was far from neglected in the twelfth century. The introduction of the lectures on the *Sentences* at Paris created the climate in which Anselm emerged as a major authority on a broad range of theological questions. Following the example of Alexander of Hales and Robert Grosseteste, the early Franciscan masters at both Paris and Oxford made extensive use of the *Cur deus homo* and regarded it as their principal guide on the incarnation and redemption.

1. *The Influence of the Cur deus homo, 1109–1220*

Anselm's discussions on the theology of redemption were so stimulating that the appearance of his treatise was eagerly awaited by his colleagues and friends, some of whom surreptitiously copied late drafts of the work; such moves prompted him to complete the monograph with more haste than he would have wished.[1] His capacity to talk engagingly about the subject is reflected in the request of Malchus, bishop of Waterford, for a copy of the sermon on the incarnation which he had heard Anselm deliver at table.[2]

a. *The Composition and Circulation of the Treatise*
Orderic Vitalis reports that Anselm was gentle and affectionate and always responsive to those who questioned him in true sincerity. To

1. Schmitt, II, p. 42.
2. Schmitt, IV, pp. 101-102.

satisfy the queries of his friends he published books of remarkable depth and penetration.[3] Anselm conceived the *Cur deus homo*, which Eadmer regarded as an *insigne volumen*,[4] as a response to help Christians to deal with the criticism that their beliefs were contrary to reason and inimical to the very nature of God.[5]

Lanfranc's response to the *Monologion* shows that in an environment of theological conservatism Anselm's independence and originality were not always understood. Anselm's departure from the traditional Augustinian teaching about the devil's rights and the appropriateness of the mode of redemption[6] aroused some unease and opposition and this accounts in part for the fact that his treatise was rarely cited in the schools. Neither did his writings lend themselves readily to the brief excerpts which were added to the patristic quotations in the biblical glosses. The earliest quotations from his writings generally appear in theological monographs and his teaching remained ill-suited to the biblical glosses which were in vogue during the twelfth century.

Anselm's correspondence provides information on the dissemination of his writings. He dispatched a copy of the *Cur deus homo* to Urban II[7] and promised Boso one for the monastery at Bec.[8] During his second exile he arranged to have the treatise copied for presentation to Paschal II.[9] There was no paucity of copies of the treatise in the twelfth century and its early circulation reflects the Bec and Canterbury circle of monastic and ecclesiastical contacts. In the twelfth century the treatise was at Bec, Caen, and several other monastic centres in Normandy. From Canterbury it spread to the neighbouring cathedral of Rochester and reached Chester, a monastery whose colonization by monks of Bec had been negotiated by Anselm. The volume was to be found in many

---

3. *The Ecclesiastical History of Orderic Vitalis*, II (ed. M. Chibnall; Oxford Medieval Texts; Oxford, 1969), p. 297.

4. Eadmer, *The Life of St Anselm Archbishop of Canterbury* (ed. R.W. Southern; Oxford Medieval Texts; Oxford, 1962), pp. 107, 63n., 88n.

5. Schmitt, II, pp. 42-43, 47-49.

6. Franciscan theologians were careful to qualify this second point. Cf. Bonaventure, 'Breviloquium', p. 4, c. 1, n. 1, in *S. Bonaventurae Opera Omnia*, V (Florence, 1891), p. 241.

7. F.R. Schmitt, 'La Lettre de saint Anselme au pape Urbain II à l'occasion de la remise de son "Cur Deus Homo" (1098)', *Revue des Sciences Religieuses* 16 (1936), pp. 127-44.

8. Schmitt, IV, pp. 104-105.

9. Schmitt, V, pp. 288-89.

cathedral and monastic libraries in twelfth-century England. Anselm's own influence was responsible for the text being at Saint Martin's at Tournai and Italian interest in the treatise was sparked off by his two periods of exile; such may account for the copy of an early manuscript at the famous monastery of Farfa. The treatise speedily made its way to the cathedral school of Laon, where Peter Abelard may have read it for the first time.

b. *Early Reception of the Cur deus homo*
The judgement of B. Korosak that the *Cur deus homo* was accepted by scarcely any master at the beginning of the scholastic era, with the exception of Anselm's disciples or authors of minor importance[10] must be qualified since the monograph was known and used at the school of Laon within a few years of its composition.[11] Aspects of the treatise were criticized by Peter Abelard.[12] Among those who cited the Anselmian treatise were the monk William in his debate with Henry of Lausanne,[13] an anonymous monk of Bec[14] and Hermann of Tournai.[15] The influence of Anselm's treatise on several twelfth-century expositions of the theology of redemption by Odo of Cambrai, Honorius of Autun, Rupert of Deutz, Herveus, a monk of Bourg-Dieu, Hugh and Richard of Saint Victor, Peter Lombard and Alan of Lille, has been detected by J. Rivière and D.E. De Clerck.[16]

10. B. Korosak, 'Le principali teorie soteriologiche dell'incipiente e della grande Scolastica', *Antonianum* 37 (1962), pp. 327-36, 423-66, 423.

11. *Anselms von Laon Systematische Sentenzen* (ed. F. Bliemetzrieder; Beitrage zur Geschichte der Philosophie des Mittelalters, 18; Münster, 1919), pp. 18, 32-33, 36; O. Lottin, *Psychologie et morale aux XIe et XIIe siècles*, V (Louvain and Gembloux, 1959), p. 264; F.R. Schmitt, 'D'un singulier emprunt à saint Anselme chez Raoul de Laon', *Revue des Sciences Religieuses* 16 (1936), pp. 344-46.

12. Peter Abelard, *Epistola 15* (*PL* 178, 362).

13. R. Manselli, 'Il monaco Enrico e la sua eresia', *Bullettino dell'Istituto storico italiano per il medio evo e archivio muratoriano* 65 (1953), pp. 1-63, 50-51.

14. A. Wilmart, 'Les Ouvrages d'un moine de Bec. Un débat sur la profession monastique au XIIe siècle', *Revue Bénédictine* 44 (1932), pp. 21-46, 22, n. 4.

15. Hermann of Tournai, *De incarnatione Jesu Christi Domini Nostri, praefatio* (*PL* 180, 11).

16. D.E. De Clerck, 'Le Dogme de la rédemption: De Robert de Melun à Guillaume d'Auxerre', *RTAM* 14 (1947), pp. 252-86; *idem*, 'Questions de sotériologie médiévale', *RTAM* 13 (1946), pp. 150-84, 160-72; J. Rivière, *The Doctrine of the Atonement: A Historical Essay*, II (trans. L. Cappadelta; London, 1909), pp. 49-50, 52, 72, 78, 81, 87, 88, 91.

The two most enthusiastic endorsements of the *Cur deus homo* come from Hermann of Tournai and an anonymous monk of Bec. These monastic theologians were writing in an environment in which Anselm was highly respected. The former voices his indebtedness to Anselm, whom he places alongside the Fathers of the Church, as an outstanding authority on the question of the redemption.[17] The latter warmly recommends Anselm as a very reliable guide on such questions.[18] Another barometer of Anselm's impact were the excerpts from his teaching and at least four noteworthy collections were compiled in the century following his death.[19]

The *Liber florum*, whose compilation R.W. Hunt assigns to the period shortly after 1130, illustrates the way in which the Anselmian treatise was abbreviated.[20] Book I, chapter 3, of the florilegium was entitled *de redentore* and opens with the words 'Anselmus in libro cur deus homo. Qua racione redemptus est per christum homo', and, completing the last quotation from Anselm, closes with the words 'hactenus cur deus factus est homo'. The compiler weaves his way through the treatise, extracting passages to form a summary of Anselm's teaching in which quotations are linked artlessly by words such as item.[21] He extracted numerous passages which in the following century would be incorporated into the commentaries on the *Sentences*. It is remarkable that the *Cur deus homo* is the only treatise quoted under the first section of the chapter, thereby providing eloquent testimony to Anselm's authority in the monastic community where the volume was assembled.

The existence of more than 60 manuscripts assigned to the period

17. Hermann of Tournai, *De incarnatione Jesu Christi Domini Nostri* (*PL* 180, 11).

18. Wilmart, 'Ouvrages', p. 22 n. 4.

19. B.L., MS Royal 8 D.viii from Llanthony secunda; Bamberg, Staatsbibliothek, MS *Patr.* 47 (Q.VI.30), from the monastery of Saint Michael on the Mount, near Bamberg; Biblioteca Apostolica Vaticana MS *Regin.lat.* 79; MS Royal 4 B.x, written at the beginning of the thirteenth century. Cf. G.R. Evans, 'Abbreviating Anselm', *RTAM* 48 (1981), pp. 78-108.

20. R.W. Hunt ('Liber Florum: A Twelfth Century Theological Florilegium', in *Sapientiae Doctrina: Melanges de théologie et de littérature médiévales offerts à Dom Hildebrand Bascour O.S.B.*, *RTAM* numéro spécial 1 [1980], pp. 137-47, 146-47) argues that the collection was drawn up in Normandy. M.R. Thomson (*Alexander Nequam Speculum Speculationum* [ABMA, 11; London, 1988], pp. xv) suggests that the work was compiled at Canterbury.

21. Lincoln Cathedral Library, MS 216, ff. 23r-25v.

before 1220 reveals the strength of the early interest in the treatise and this figure is to be increased by volumes described as *opera Anselmi* in library catalogues. While numerous copies of the treatise were in monastic libraries, others were held at influential cathedral schools. This is not the evidence of a neglected treatise. Instead, it is consistent with the testimony of some early monastic chroniclers who held Anselm in very high esteem. While explicit borrowings from the treatise before 1220 were few, the book did provoke considerable interest in England, France, Flanders and beyond. The manuscripts were already in place when lectures on the *Sentences* established a context more congenial to the Anselmian *rationes*.

2. *Anselm and the Franciscan School*

From the late twelfth century and the first two decades of the thirteenth a growing number of theologians, including Alexander Nequam, William of Auxerre and Philip the Chancellor, began to quote Anselm liberally. Another theologian was Alexander of Hales, who as a secular master at Paris, decided to base his theological lectures on the *Sentences* of Peter Lombard. A parallel movement at Oxford featured Robert Grosseteste. The *Cur deus homo*'s influence was manifested in various theological monographs composed by the Franciscans at both Paris and Oxford.

a. *Alexander of Hales and Robert Grosseteste*
J. de Ghellinck points out that Alexander of Hales, Bonaventure and Thomas Aquinas were foremost among the promoters of Anselm's popularity in the schools.[22] J.G. Bougerol focuses upon the contribution made by Alexander, noting the historians' view that Anselm's entrance into the schools was due to Alexander.[23] The inquisitive spirit of the *Sentences* offered a more fertile ground for the *rationes Anselmi* and a vast amount of his teaching was incorporated into the commentaries by Alexander, the two anonymous commentaries, Eudes Rigaud, Bonaventure and Richard Rufus of Cornwall, who also abbreviated Bonaventure's commentary, and the *Quaestiones disputatae* by Jean de la Rochelle and William of Melitona. The *Cur deus homo* supplied these

---

22. J. de Ghellinck, *Le Mouvement théologique du XIIe siècle* (Museum Lessianum–Section Historique, 10; Bruges, 2nd edn, 1948), pp. 85-86.
23. J.G. Bougerol, *Introduction à l'étude de s. Bonaventure* (Bibliothèque de théologie, série 1, Théologie Dogmatique, 2; Paris, 1961), p. 73.

theologians with a framework for the discussion of the mode of the incarnation and redemption.

In Alexander's *Glossa in quatuor libros Sententiarum Petri Lombardi* the Anselmian treatises are generally cited by their title and quotations are more numerous with some of them stretching for several lines unbroken; there are also some unacknowledged Anselmian borrowings. The earliest of the three redactions of the third book of the *Glossa* (Assisi, Biblioteca comunale, MS 189) belongs to the period 1225–27.[24] The fact that Anselm is cited twice as frequently as Augustine in the twentieth distinction and many times more than the other authorities illustrates Anselm's new authority in the schools. In several instances Alexander is content to weave together a mosaic of Anselmian quotations in response to the questions posed. Several of Alexander's *Quaestiones disputatae antequam esset frater*, composed between 1230 and 1236, incorporate Anselmian material. The question on the incarnation reflects Anselm's growing stature in the schools. Alexander's quotations are fewer and briefer than in the *Glossa* and this may denote a greater assimilation of the Anselmian teaching. As in the *Glossa*, Anselm shows himself to be a leading guide on questions concerning the nature of Adam's rebellion, which member of the Trinity should become incarnate, the role of angels in the fall and restoration of humanity, the honour of God denied in sin and the way of restoring it, the appropriateness of satisfaction and the form that it should take.[25]

Grosseteste, who commenced his lectures in the friars' school in Oxford about 1230,[26] brought an interest in the Anselmian corpus; he quotes the *Cur deus homo* in his *De libero arbitrio, Tabula, De decem mandatis* and *De cessatione legalium*. Southern believes that the *Tabula* was completed about 1230, and was a record of Grosseteste's reading around 1220–55 and 1230 when he was preparing himself as a theologian and delivering his first lectures in that discipline.[27] This date

24. Alexander of Hales, *Glossa in quatuor libros Sententiarum*, III (Florence, 1954), p. 32 *.
25. Alexander of Hales, *Quaestiones disputatae antequam esset frater*, q.15 (BFSMA, 19; Florence, 1960), pp. 193-223.
26. Thomas of Eccleston, *Tractatus de adventu fratrum minorum in Angliam* (ed. A.G. Little; Manchester, 1951), p. 48; *Chronicon de Lanercost M.CC.I - M.CCC.XLVI* (ed. J. Stevenson; Edinburgh, 1839), p. 45.
27. R.W. Southern, *Robert Grosseteste: The Growth of an English Mind in Medieval Europe* (Oxford, 1986), p. 191. A critical edition of the *Tabula* has been prepared by P. Rosemann for publication in *Roberti Grosseteste, Opera Inedita*, I

places Grosseteste in the van of the movement to cite Anselm in the 1220s and the early 1230s. He possessed a copy of the *Cur deus homo*[28] and recognized it as a major contribution to the questions concerning the redemption. His lectures to the friars at Oxford preceded those delivered by Alexander in the friars' school at Paris and these factors indicate that the credit for having introduced Anselm into the Franciscan school does not belong entirely to Alexander.[29]

The *Cur deus homo* is the most frequently cited Anselmian text in the *Tabula* and its authority is invoked under 22 headings. 26 of the 47 chapters of the Anselmian treatise are quoted, and 11 of these more than once. Moreover, it is the only Anselmian treatise to figure in all six distinctions, providing teaching on a broad range of theological questions. Grosseteste's attentive study of the treatise is indicated by the fact that all the citations correctly identify the book and the chapter; in contrast, the *Monologion* is cited only once with reference to a particular chapter. The second distinction of the *Tabula* underlines Anselm's influence on the theology of the incarnation and redemption. There are 13 headings in the distinction. Six of them have not been filled in, but the *Cur deus homo* appears in five out of the seven completed headings and this is a more accurate barometer of Anselm's influence.

The *De cessatione legalium*, composed towards the end of Grosseteste's time as lector to the friars,[30] addresses some of the issues raised by the *Cur deus homo*, and acknowledges Anselm, along with Augustine and Gregory the Great, as an outstanding exponent of the theology of redemption. Moreover, Anselm is quoted more frequently than any other medieval theologian, even though his contribution is confined to the first and third *particulae*, where his teaching is enlisted on various questions. The *Cur deus homo*'s methodology, with its spirit of inquiry and independence, may have emboldened Grosseteste to break new ground in this treatise, exploring the reasons why the incarnation may not necessarily have been contingent upon the fall.

(ed. J. McEvoy; CCCM, 130; Turnhout, 1995).

28. M.R. Thomson, 'An Unnoticed Autograph of Grosseteste', *Medievalia et Humanistica, Studia in Honorem E.A. Lowe* 14 (1962), pp. 55-60.

29. M. Robson, 'Saint Anselm, Robert Grosseteste and the Franciscan Tradition', in *Robert Grosseteste. New Perspectives on his Thought and Scholarship* (ed. J. McEvoy; Instrumenta Patristica; Steenbrugge, 1995), pp. 250-73.

30. Robert Grosseteste, *De cessatione legalium* (ed. R.C. Dales and E.B. King; ABMA, 7; London, 1986), pp. xiv-xv.

b. *Anselm and the Early Franciscan Masters*

Two anonymous commentaries on the *Sentences* mirror the growing interest of the friars in the *Cur deus homo* in particular. MS *lat.* 691 of the Vatican Library is a gloss on the *Sentences* which has been identified as a source for the *Summa Fratris Alexandri*. Bougerol argues that materials from this manuscript were employed by Eudes and Bonaventure. One hypothesis is that this is the beginning of the commentary on the *Sentences* compiled by Jean.[31] Another incomplete commentary is preserved in Vienna (Osterreichische Nationalbibliothek, MS *lat.* 1532) and there are fragments in Paris (B.N. MSS *lat.* 483 and 3237). This is a fuller commentary than the Vatican text and it, too, has been described as *une source inconnue* of the *Summa Fratris Alexandri*. This text has also been linked with the lost commentary by Jean.[32] It is undoubtedly the work of a Franciscan master[33] and reflects theories debated in the Parisian schools about 1240.[34]

An evaluation of Anselm's influence upon the theology of redemption by Jean, the second master at Paris, is hampered by the loss of two pivotal texts, his commentary on the *Sentences* and *Quaestiones disputatae de incarnatione*.[35] Jean does, however, make a substantial contribution to Book III of the *Summa Fratris Alexandri*, which incorporates some of his *Quaestiones disputatae*. His *Quaestiones disputatae de lapsu humanae naturae* form the first two numbers in Book III,[36] which was compiled, to a great extent, before 1245. J.P. Burns maintains that the *Summa Fratris Alexandri* presents the first detailed discussion of the reflections of the twelfth century and systematizes them as a series of variations on Anselm's theme.[37] B. Carra de Vaux Saint-Cyr shows that the first chapters of the *Summa Fratris Alexandri* evidently rest upon

31. J.G. Bougerol, 'La Glose sur le Sentences du Manuscrit Vat. Lat. 691', *Antonianum* 55 (1980), pp. 108-73, 171-73.

32. B.C. de V. Saint-Cyr, 'Une source inconnue de la Summa Fratris Alexandri', *Revue des sciences philosophiques et théologiques* 47 (1963), pp. 571-99, 592-93, 598.

33. Saint-Cyr, 'Source inconnue', p. 575 n. 6.

34. Saint-Cyr, 'Source inconnue', p. 578.

35. *Summa Fratris Alexandri* (Florence, 1924–48), IV, lib.3 (prolegomena), pp. ccxvii-ccxviii, ccxxv.

36. *Summa Fratris Alexandri*, p. ccxvii.

37. J.P. Burns, 'The Concept of Satisfaction in Medieval Redemption Theory', *Theological Studies* 36 (1975), pp. 285-304, 285, 293, 295.

Jean's careful reading of the *Cur deus homo*.[38] Eudes became the third master in the Franciscan school at Paris in 1245 and his commentary on the *Sentences*, begun about 1240,[39] reflects his indebtedness to the *Cur deus homo*. He cites Anselm much more frequently than the other Franciscan masters and in sections of his commentary Anselm monopolizes the discussions.

Richard was *baccalareus Sententiarum* at Oxford about 1250 and three years later he lectured on the *Sentences* at Paris. He regards Anselm as a major authority and blocks of Anselmian teaching are neatly dovetailed to provide a continuous excerpt from the *Cur deus homo*. Bonaventure, the fifth master at Paris in 1253, presents Anselm as the medieval heir to Saint Augustine and his commentary makes use of Anselmian material on the questions concerning the appropriateness of making reparation, which member of the Trinity should become incarnate and the way in which satisfaction was made. Bonaventure has fewer quotations from Anselm and is happy to summarize his source; like other Franciscan masters, he produces concentrations of Anselmian material on certain questions. Anselmian formulations also appear in the *Breviloquium*, which takes up several points from the *Sentences*. Bonaventure's commentary on the *Sentences* was abbreviated by Richard who does not restrict himself to summarizing the Bonaventurean text; in some places he introduces his own thought and solutions (Assisi, Biblioteca comunale, MS 176).[40] In his abbreviation of the first 20 distinctions of Book III he generally reproduces the Anselmian passages cited by Bonaventure.

3. Aspects of Anselm's Influence on Early Franciscan Soteriology

The sheer number of quotations from Anselm in the commentaries on the *Sentences*, the *Quaestiones disputatae* and related texts by the early Franciscan masters at both Paris and Oxford emphasizes the new-found authority enjoyed by Anselm. His growing influence is manifested in the

38. B.C. de V. Saint-Cyr (ed.), *Saint Bonaventure: Breviloquium, 4, L'Incarnation du Verbe* (Bibliothèque bonaventurienne, 4; Paris, 1967), pp. 14-15.

39. E. Sileo (ed.), *Teoria della scienza teologica. 'Quaestio de scientia theologiae di Odo Rigaldi e altri testi inediti (1230–1250)* (Studia Antoniana, 27.i; Rome, 1984), p. 16.

40. P. Raedts, *Richard Rufus of Cornwall and the Tradition of Oxford Theology* (Oxford Historical Monographs; Oxford, 1987), pp. 40-63.

volume of quotations from the *Cur deus homo* which supplanted the *De trinitate* as the principal guide on questions concerning the incarnation and redemption.

a *Augustine and Anselm*

Peter Lombard's distinction on the redemption won by Christ consists of a chain of quotations from Augustine, many of them borrowed from the *De trinitate*.[41] Towards the end of this distinction Lombard makes a few brief comments of his own. In his *glossa* on the corresponding distinction of his commentary Alexander of Hales enlists a wider circle of authorities as the *Cur deus homo* begins to challenge and then supersede the *De trinitate* as the major guide in the theology of the incarnation and redemption. An index of Anselm's increased authority is the fact that Augustine was quoted four times and Anselm thirteen. Similarly Grosseteste's appreciation is reflected in the *Tabula* which issues the rare recommendation that the *Cur deus homo* should be studied in its entirety. Anselm's authority is confirmed under the heading *De incarnatione verbi*, where the principal theologians are Augustine, Gregory the Great and Anselm.[42] A similar ringing endorsement of these three authors on the same topic appears in the *De cessatione legalium*.[43]

In the early Franciscan school Augustine and Anselm enjoyed such authority that differences between them were diluted. In the *De libero arbitrio*, assigned to the period when Grosseteste was lecturing in the secular schools,[44] he notes the contrary claims advanced in the *De trinitate* and *Cur deus homo* on the mode of redemption and offers a solution by distinguishing between the divine substance considered in itself and in its relationship with humanity.[45] This attempt to harmonize the teaching of the two saints presages the concern of later masters. Eudes[46]

41. Peter Lombard, *Sententiae in IV libris distinctae*, III, d.20 (Spicilegium Bonaventurianum, 5; Grottaferrata, Rome, 1981), pp. 125-29.

42. Lyons, Bibliothèque municipale, MS 414, f.21v.

43. Grosseteste, *De cessatione legalium* (ed. Dales and King), p. 119.

44. Southern, *Robert Grosseteste*, p. 113.

45. L. Baur, *Die philosophischen Werke des Robert Grosseteste Bischofs von Lincoln* (Beiträge zur Geschichte der Philosophie und Theologie des Mittelalters, 9; Münster, 1912), p. 180.

46. Eudes Rigaud, Commentary on the *Sentences*, III, d.21, q.1, conc., in Bruges, Bibliothèque publique de la ville, MS 208, f. 406ra.

and Bonaventure[47] provide a wider context for the understanding of the Anselmian teaching.

Both Grosseteste and Bonaventure yoke the teaching of Augustine and Anselm in their statement of the theology of satisfaction. On three occasions Grosseteste cites the teaching of Augustine and Anselm; twice Augustine is named first and on the third occasion Anselm is awarded the first place as Grosseteste refers to their combined teaching on the appropriateness of redemption gained through satisfaction.[48] In this Grosseteste anticipates Bonaventure who also names Anselm before Augustine in the assertion that it was more congruous for man to be saved through satisfaction than through any other method.[49] Thereby Bonaventure seems to indicate that, while both theologians contribute to soteriology, Anselm is the preferred authority with a much fuller exploration of the various issues. This interpretation is supported by the frequency with which Bonaventure appeals to Anselm. In naming Anselm before Augustine both Grosseteste and Bonaventure signal their belief that Anselm had made significant advances on the ground explored by Augustine.

b. *Influence of Anselmian Soteriology*

Anselm's commanding authority pervades Jean de la Rochelle's question whether human nature can be restored without satisfaction for sin. Anselmian quotations and borrowings accompany the inquiry from beginning to end; Augustine is quoted twice and Anselm seventeen times. Generally Jean makes an orderly progression through the Anselmian chapters, culling arguments for and against the thesis; in addition, Anselm supplies the first four objections to the proposition. In each case his teaching stands at the beginning of the argument and only then does Jean venture to formulate his own theories. The grounds in support of the thesis, as well as the summing up and the resolution of the objections are equally permeated by Anselm.[50]

Anselm's impact upon the Franciscan school can be gauged from the

---

47. Bonaventure, Commentary on the *Sentences*, III, d.20, a.1, q.6, conc., and ad ob.1 (Florence, 1887), p. 431.

48. Grosseteste, *De cessatione legalium* (ed. Dales and King), pp. 119, 135, 138.

49. Bonaventure, Commentary on the *Sentences*, III, d.20, a.1, q.2, conc., p. 420.

50. *Summa Fratris Alexandri*, IV, lib.3, n.4, pp. 14-17.

following table of citations in early commentaries on the *Sentences*, Book III, distinctions 1-21.

	Alexander	Vat. lat. 691	Vienna	Eudes	Richard	Bonavent.	Bon. Abb.
d.1		3	5	24	18	10	4
d.2	2				1		
d.3			2	6	2	2	1
d.4			1	1			
d.5			4	4	3	3	
d.6		1		1			
d.7			1	1	1		
d.8				1	2	1	
d.9		1				1	
d.10			1				
d.11							
d.12	4	3	7	5	2	3	1
d.13	2	1	4			2	
d.14			2	2	2	2	
d.15		2	4	8	1	1	
d.16	1		13	5		5	2
d.17	1						
d.18	4			3	5	5	
d.19	1	1		3	4	1	
d.20	13	3		3	15	10	3
d.21				22			
total	28	15	44	89	56	46	11

The table illustrates the wide-ranging influence enjoyed by Anselm. The later distinctions, where Anselmian soteriology is normally prevalent, are missing from the manuscripts at Vienna and Paris. While there are differences between the commentaries, there are also discernible patterns. The masters generally appeal to the same Anselmian text in a particular distinction. The greatest concentrations occur in the first and twentieth distinctions, as well as the twenty first in the case of Eudes. With the exception of Alexander, all the commentaries introduce a wealth of Anselmian teaching into the first distinction, with many of them making use of the *De incarnatione verbi* as well as the *Cur deus homo*. Just under half of Alexander's citations from Anselm appear in the twentieth distinction and the other masters follow him. Indeed, these two distinctions generally account for about 50 per cent of the Anselmian quotations.

Anselm is a ubiquitous authority in Eudes's exposition of the theology of satisfaction and vast tracts of the seventh question are surrendered to him. That influence is neatly divided into three self-contained areas. In each case Eudes hands over the text to Anselm, quoting or summarizing the *Cur deus homo*. The first series examines questions of the passion and justice. The second continues the themes of salvation by contraries, with Anselm explaining why such a mode of satisfaction was chosen. The same topic informs the third argument, which is based upon a quotation from Anselm. In the fourth argument there is another quotation from Anselm showing that the withdrawal from God in the first sin was reversed in the total self-surrender to God made by Christ. The fifth argument also rests upon an Anselmian quotation concerning the didactic dimension of Christ's death.[51] Richard's commentary exemplifies the type of assistance offered by Anselm in addressing many of the questions explored in the *Cur deus homo*. Richard considers the appropriateness of Christ becoming man, the necessity of remitting sin through satisfaction, the magnitude of the first sin, the instrument of reparation and the necessity and efficacy of Christ's death; each section is answered with Anselmian assistance. A salient feature is the pervasive presence of Anselm, who is quoted nine times in the body of the commentary and thirteen times in *marginalia* copied in an early hand; in contrast Augustine is quoted twice in the commentary. In some parts of the question Richard assembles a *catena* of Anselmian quotations and summaries which uninterruptedly run from f.194vb, line 54 until f.195rb, line 17; no other authorities are introduced in this section.[52]

Conclusion

The *Cur deus homo* entered the schools at Paris and Oxford at the same time as the *Sentences* and its importance was acknowledged by both Alexander and Grosseteste, who quoted it copiously. Eudes employs a large amount of Anselmian teaching in different parts of his commentary in order to produce greater precision and sharpen the focus of the debate; frequently he refers to the *rationes Anselmi*. Bonaventure, the most gifted theologian of the early Franciscan school, incorporates a wealth of material from the *Cur deus homo* and pays Anselm the highest

---

51. Eudes Rigaud, Commentary on the *Sentences*, III, d.21, q.7, sed contra 1-5, ff.408va-409ra.

52. Richard Rufus, Commentary on the *Sentences*, III, d.1, q.4, in Oxford, Balliol College, MS 62, ff.194vb-96va.

compliment in presenting him as the medieval successor to Augustine in the articulation of questions concerning faith and as the master *in ratiocinatione.*[53]

53. Bonaventure, 'De reductione artium ad theologiam', n. 5, in *S. Bonaventurae Opera Omnia*, V, p. 321.

ST ANSELM'S *CUR DEUS HOMO* AND JOHN CALVIN'S
DOCTRINE OF THE ATONEMENT

Robert B. Strimple

1. *The Cur deus homo*

As background for a comparison of Anselm's doctrine of the atonement
with that of the later Reformer, John Calvin, it will be well to review
briefly the argument presented in the *Cur deus homo*. In I:1 Anselm presents the task to which he sets himself: to prove that the death of the
Son of God was both reasonable and necessary.

One of Anselm's premises is 'that no man passes this life without sin'
(I:11).[1] Thus he is not required to prove the existence of sin; he must
only describe its nature. Most often when he speaks of sin, he speaks of
it as a failure to pay a debt; and this phrase has been the basis for the
stock criticism of the 'commercial' aspects of Anselm's theory.[2] But we
must understand what Anselm means by the term 'debt'. He states that
the will of every creature should be subject to the will of God. This is the
debt humankind owes to God. Failure to pay this debt, therefore, means
nothing less than the failure of the whole person to submit their will to
the will of their Creator. In describing sin as 'debt' Anselm is simply
following Jesus' definition of sin, for it was Jesus who commanded his
disciples to pray: 'Forgive us our debts (*opheilemata*)' (Mt. 6.12).

Anselm also speaks of complete obedience as the 'honour' that is due
to God, and he says: 'One who does not render this honour to God
takes away from God what belongs to him, and dishonours God, and
to do this is sin' (I:11). And at this point it has become the accepted

1. All quotations in English from *Cur deus homo* are from *The Library of
Christian Classics. X. A Scholastic Miscellany: Anselm to Ockham* (ed. and trans.
E.R. Fairweather; Philadelphia: Westminster Press, 1956).
2. See, for example, G.B. Stevens, *The Christian Doctrine of Salvation*
(Edinburgh: T. & T. Clark, 1909), Part II, Chapter I, and G.C. Foley, *Anselm's
Theory of the Atonement* (New York: Longmans, Green, 1909), p. 115.

criticism to claim that Anselm's argument is framed in feudal rather than scriptural categories. Even such a sympathetic commentator as James Orr has written: 'Here it is obvious that Anselm moves in faulty categories—categories borrowed from the sphere of private rights—and this hampers his treatment throughout.' Orr goes on to soften his criticism: 'Anselm speaks of the "honour" of God. We speak rather of the supreme obligation to "glorify" God, and of sin as the withholding from God of the "glory" due to Him—in the Pauline phrase, "glorifying Him not as God"—but the meaning is the same.'[3] But even to suggest that Anselm should have spoken of 'glory' as owing to God rather than 'honour' is merely to quibble. Surely the New Testament concepts of *doxa* and *time* are very close to one another, so close that *doxa* is translated 'honour' six times in the Authorized Version.

What is God's reaction to human sin? Anselm insists that God cannot merely overlook it. Forgiveness by mere fiat would be a contradiction and a disruption of God's moral government of the universe. 'It is not fitting for God to remit any irregularity in his kingdom' (I:12). The reason that God cannot simply forgive his creature his debt *sola voluntate* is that he is *not* merely a great feudal baron. He is *God*.

What then does God demand in order that his honour might be restored? Anselm states the demand of God's justice in the famous disjunction: *aut poena aut satisfactio* (I:15). And here Boso, the disciple with whom the dialogue is carried on, raises what seems to be a justifiable objection. Boso fails to see how the punishment of the sinner restores God's honour. Anselm gives him the following answer:

> It is impossible for God to lose his honor. For if a sinner does not freely pay what he owes, God takes it from him against his will. In the one case, a man of his own free will manifests due subjection to God, either by avoiding sin or by making payment for it; in the other God subjects him to himself against his will by torment, and in this way shows that he is man's Lord, even though the man himself refuses to admit it of his own will. (I:14)

The only alternative to this punishment, then, is for the sinner to make satisfaction to God for their sin. This satisfaction must be something above that which God justly demands of the sinner. It will not suffice, therefore, for them merely to bring their entire being—intellect, will, and emotions—back into subjection to God. The person who thinks that

3.   J. Orr, *The Progress of Dogma* (London: Hodder & Stoughton, 1901), p. 223.

they can make satisfaction for their own sin, Anselm writes, has simply 'not yet considered what a heavy weight sin is' (I:21).

The first half of Anselm's argument is thus concluded. He has proven that the restoration of humankind cannot take place unless God's creature pays the debt he owes to God for his sin, and he has shown that the creature cannot make this payment. Anselm asks Boso: 'Then what will become of you? How are you going to be saved?' (I:20); and Boso can only reply that he can see no hope for salvation, *unless* it be in Christ.

And so Anselm proceeds in the second book to show how salvation is made possible in Christ. He begins by re-emphasizing the fact that 'God will complete what he began with human nature' (II:4). As Boso puts it: '...otherwise he would appear to fail in his undertaking, and this is not fitting'. Nevertheless, it continues to be true that humankind cannot be brought to blessedness apart from a complete satisfaction for sin, and this satisfaction could only be made by a God-man. This is true because, although only humankind ought to render satisfaction, only God can.

> This cannot be done unless there is someone to pay to God for human sin something greater than everything that exists, except God... If he is to give something of his own to God, which surpasses everything that is beneath God, it is also necessary for him to be greater than everything that is not God... Then no one but God can make this satisfaction... But no one ought to make it except man; otherwise man does not make satisfaction. (II:6)

Thus 'it is necessary for the same person to be perfect God and perfect man' (II:7), and Anselm has now answered the question posed in the title of his treatise. In view of Anselm's frequent use of the name *Deus-homo* (hyphenated in some texts), the correct translation of that title would seem to be 'Why the God-man?' or 'The reason for the God-man'.[4]

But how is it possible for even the God-man to render satisfaction to God? As a rational being, does he not owe his whole being to God? Yes, he does; and therefore he cannot render satisfaction to God through a life of obedience. He can do so only through his voluntary death.

Death is a debt humankind must pay to God because of their sin. If humans had never sinned, they would not be required to die. It is the fact that the death of the God-man is above God's requirement of him

---

4. See J. McIntyre, *St Anselm and his Critics* (London: Oliver & Boyd, 1954), p. 202; and P. Tillich, *A History of Christian Thought* (ed. C.E. Braaten; New York: Harper & Row, 1968), p. 165.

that gives it its value as a satisfaction. And the value of Christ's death is infinite because of the infinite worth of his person, and therefore is superabundant to make satisfaction for sins.

It only remains for Anselm to show how human salvation follows upon this meritorious death of the God-man. The death of the God-man is so precious that it demands a reward. There would seem to be, however, no reward that can be made to this one who, as perfect God, possesses all things. Since the reward must be given, or the work of the God-man will seem to have been in vain, and since it is impossible for it to be made to him, it is given to men and women, for whom the God-man died.

> To whom would it be more fitting for him to assign the fruit and recompense of his death than to those for whose salvation (as truthful reasoning has taught us) he made himself man? (II:19)

2. *John Calvin's Doctrine of the Atonement*

Concerning the *Cur deus homo* it has been said: 'Perhaps no other theological statement has been so universally rejected as a whole, but whose essential characteristics have so completely coloured subsequent thinking'.[5] Foley claims that the influence of Anselm's treatise can be seen in a new emphasis on the objective, the God-ward efficacy of the atonement among the scholastics;[6] but it is difficult to discover such an emphasis in the great bulk of their writing. Indeed Foley himself quotes Ritschl's assessment that 'in the Middle Ages themselves, through the influence of Peter the Lombard, the preference is given to Abelard over Anselm';[7] and Foley himself comments that Anselm's 'idea of the necessity on God's part of the death of Christ', which is the nerve of Anselm's argument, 'is repudiated even by those who are claimed as his disciples, by Hugh of St. Victor, by Bonaventura, and by Aquinas'.[8]

We must look beyond the scholastic period to the Reformation to see the greatest influence of the *Cur deus homo*, and here the points of contact are clear. Gustaf Aulen has noted that traditional historians of Christian doctrine hold 'that a continuous line may be traced from Anselm through medieval scholasticism, and through the Reformation,

5. Foley, *Atonement*, p. 15.
6. Foley, *Atonement*, p. 194.
7. Foley, *Atonement*, p. 203.
8. Foley, *Atonement*, p. 195.

to the Protestant Orthodoxy of the 17th Century...there is a continuity of tradition, and the basis of it is that which Anselm laid.'[9] We may find (in fact we will find, I believe) that we must agree with Aulen that such historians have not always taken sufficient account of the great differences between Anselm's theory and later Protestant teaching—that they have often been guilty of interpreting the *Cur deus homo* in terms of the later doctrine; but we must first of all note the points at which Anselm and the Reformers clearly agree.

The most important lesson that the Reformers learned from Anselm was to view Christ's death as a satisfaction to divine justice. As early as Tertullian, the term *satisfactio* made its way into the sacramental vocabulary of the church; but neither Tertullian nor the later Latin Fathers conceived of Christ as making satisfaction to God. To make satisfaction was the work of sinners themselves. Apparently Anselm was the first theologian of any prominence to apply the term *satisfactio* to the atoning work of Christ,[10] and the death of Christ continues to be described by this term in the writings of the Reformers. The following passages from the *Institutes*[11] illustrate Calvin's use of the terminology of satisfaction with reference to Christ's death:

> The second requirement of our reconciliation with God was this: that man, who by his disobedience had become lost, should by way of remedy counter it with obedience, satisfy God's judgment, and pay the penalties for sin. Accordingly, our Lord came forth as true man...to present our flesh as the price of satisfaction to God's righteous judgment... (II:xii:3)

> The priestly office belongs to Christ alone because by the sacrifice of his death he blotted out our own guilt and made satisfaction for our sins (Heb. 9.22). (II:xv:6)

9. G. Aulen, *Christus Victor* (trans. A.G. Hebert; London: SPCK, 1940), p. 175.

10. J.N.D. Kelly (*Early Christian Doctrines* [New York: Harper & Row, 1959], p. 392) speaks of Augustine as viewing Christ's death as providing satisfaction; but the term *satisfactio* appears in neither of the texts Kelly cites: *De civitate dei* X, 22, in *Aurelii Augustini Opera* (CCSL, 47; Turnhout: Brepols, 1955), p. 296; and *De trinitate* IV, 17, in *Aurelii Augustini Opera* (CCSL, 50; Turnhout: Brepols, 1968), pp. 189-90.

11. All quotations from the *Institutes* are from *The Library of Christian Classics*. XX. *Calvin: Institutes of the Christian Religion* (ed. J.T. McNeill; trans. F.L. Battles; Philadelphia: Westminster Press, 1960).

Later in this second book of the *Institutes* references to satisfaction (noun or verb) occur in xvi:1, 2, 5, 10, 13, 19 and xvii:3, 4, 5. Christ's death satisfies the claims of God upon sinners, and therefore this death was absolutely necessary for their salvation.

Louis Berkhof follows Robert Franks[12] in saying that 'Luther, Zwingli, and Calvin all avoided the Anselmian doctrine of the *absolute* necessity of the atonement, and ascribed to it only a relative or hypothetical necessity, based on the sovereign free will of God, or in other words, on the divine decree'.[13] Berkhof cites as evidence of this understanding on Calvin's part, *Institutes*, II:xii:1:

> Now it was of the greatest importance for us that he who was to be our Mediator be both true God and true man. If someone asks why this is necessary, there has been no simple (to use the common expression) or absolute necessity. Rather, it has stemmed from a heavenly decree, on which men's salvation depended. Our most merciful Father decreed what was best for us.

Berkhof and Franks, however, have clearly misunderstood these sentences. Calvin goes on immediately to emphasize that

> Since our iniquities... had completely estranged us from the Kingdom of Heaven (cf. Isa. 59.2), no man, unless he belonged to God, could serve as the intermediary to restore peace. But who might reach to him? Any one of Adam's children? No... One of the angels?... The situation would surely have been hopeless had the very majesty of God not descended to us, since it was not in our power to ascend to him. Hence, it was *necessary* for the Son of God to become for us 'Immanuel, that is, God with us' (Isa. 7.14; Matt. 1.23), and in such a way that his divinity and our human nature might by mutual connection grow together... [emphasis added].

Calvin continues there to explain why 'only he who was true God and true man could be obedient in our stead' (heading to section 3).

Surely the last sentence in section 2 gives us the clue to what Calvin actually means in denying 'simple' or 'absolute' necessity in section 1:

> Therefore our most merciful God, *when he willed that we be redeemed*, made himself our Redeemer in the person of his only-begotten Son [emphasis added].

12. R.S. Franks, *A History of the Work of Christ* (London: Hodder & Stoughton, n.d.), I, pp. 413 and 427.
13. L. Berkhof, *Systematic Theology* (Grand Rapids, MI: Eerdmans, 1953), p. 369, author's emphasis.

What Calvin is *denying* in the sentences that Franks and Berkhof appeal to, the sentences that begin this twelfth chapter of Book II, is what theologians have sometimes referred to as the 'antecedent absolute necessity' of the atonement; that is, that God was under some moral necessity to save at least a portion of lost humanity. (And in that denial, notice, Calvin clearly parts company with Anselm.) What Calvin is *affirming* is the 'consequent absolute necessity' of the atonement; that is, that God having, in free grace, decreed to save, that salvation could be procured in no other way than through the atoning death of his only-begotten Son. Calvin, with Anselm, rejected the possibility of 'free' forgiveness; that is, forgiveness by the mere good pleasure of God apart from a payment for sin.

Calvin, therefore, followed Anselm in adopting an essentially *judicial* conception of the atonement; and such Anselmian ideas as the payment of a debt, rescue from a criminal sentence by a substitute, and the atonement as the basis for a divine pronouncement of justification that is to be sharply distinguished from the subjective work of sanctification became cardinal tenets of the Protestant soteriology.

Christ's death as the payment of the debt of sinners is a thought that appears in the *Institutes*, although not as frequently as might have been anticipated. And when it does appear, it is given the distinctive turn of *payment by vicarious suffering*. For example:

> It was superfluous, even absurd, for Christ to be burdened with a curse, unless it was to acquire righteousness for others by paying what they owed... For unless Christ had made satisfaction for our sins, it would not have been said that he appeased God by taking upon himself the penalty to which we were subject. (II:xvii:4)

> (Col. 2.14 p.) He notes there the payment or compensation that absolves us of guilt... (Gal. 4.4-5 p.) What was the purpose of this subjection of Christ to the law but to acquire righteousness for us, undertaking to pay what we could not pay? (II:xvii:5)

Such statements alert us to the fact that Calvin made certain significant modifications in the Anselmian theory. The most important is this fact that the Reformers viewed the sufferings of Christ on the cross as penal, as the vicarious bearing of the penalty owing to the sins of men and women, rather than simply (as in the *Cur deus homo*) as the voluntary offering of a gift of infinite value to the honour of God. Instead of the Anselmian disjunction, either punishment or satisfaction, Calvin offered the dictum satisfaction by punishment.

...the penalty to which we were subject had been imposed upon this righteous man. (II:xvi:5)

This is our acquittal: the guilt that held us liable for punishment has been transferred to the head of the Son of God (Isa. 53.12). We must, above all, remember this substitution, lest we tremble and remain anxious throughout life—as if God's righteous vengeance, which the Son of God has taken upon himself, still hung over us. (II:xvi:5)

If Christ had died only a bodily death, it would have been ineffectual. No—it was expedient at the same time for him to undergo the severity of God's vengeance, to appease his wrath and satisfy his just judgment. For this reason, he must also grapple hand to hand with the armies of hell and the dread of everlasting death... Christ was put in place of evildoers as surety and pledge—submitting himself even as the accused—to bear and suffer all the punishments that they ought to have sustained. All—with this one exception: 'He could not be held by the pangs of death' (Acts 2.24 p.). No wonder, then, if he is said to have descended into hell, for he suffered the death that God in his wrath had inflicted upon the wicked! (II:xvi:10)

Thus Calvin also gives a distinctive turn to Anselm's argument for the necessity of the God-man: only man could suffer and die; and only God could overcome death.

Accordingly, our Lord came forth as true man and took the person and the name of Adam in order to... pay the penalty that we had deserved. In short, since neither as God alone could he feel death, nor as man alone could he overcome it, he coupled human nature with divine that to atone for sin he might submit the weakness of the one to death; and that, wrestling with death by the power of the other nature, he might win victory for us. (II:xii:3)

After quoting the foregoing, François Wendel comments: 'We have good right to regard this last passage as a classic expression of the doctrine of satisfaction as it had been current ever since St. Anselm'.[14] Actually, however, while Calvin is asking the same question as Anselm (*Cur deus homo*?), the answer Calvin gives is decidedly *different* from Anselm's.

It is true, of course, that one might use the phrase 'either punishment or satisfaction' to describe Calvin's view of the price God demands for sin; but then the phrase would mean 'either personal punishment or satisfaction through the vicarious endurance of punishment by another'.

14. F. Wendel, *Calvin* (trans. P. Nairet; London: Collins, 1965), p. 219.

There are those who have taken this to be Anselm's teaching in the *Cur deus homo*. Paul Tillich, for example, speaks of the *Cur deus homo* as an attempt 'to understand the rational adequacy for the substitute suffering of Christ in the work of salvation'.[15] Earlier William Shedd interpreted Anselm as teaching that either humankind themselves must suffer punishment, or the 'only other way in which the attribute of justice can be satisfied is by substituted or vicarious suffering'.[16] But this is to misinterpret the *Cur deus homo*; it is to be guilty of reading back into Anselm the modification of his theory made by later theologians.

Again, certain points must be granted. Aulen may be perfectly correct in stating that 'the idea of satisfaction passes over naturally and easily into that of punishment';[17] and he is correct when he says that the idea of Christ's vicarious endurance of punishment had been expressed by predecessors of Anselm. Both Origen and Gregory the Great had stated that Christ was appeasing God's wrath by taking on himself the penalty of our sins, and Athanasius spoke of the penal suffering that Christ took from us and laid upon himself.[18] And, as a matter of fact, the idea appears at certain points in the devotional writings of Anselm himself.[19]

But though all this be freely granted, there is no adequate ground for disputing McIntyre's conclusion regarding Anselm's argument in the *Cur deus homo*: 'When he treats of the Death of Christ (e.g., at II:11), though emphasizing the difficult and painful character of that Death, he does not regard it as a penal substitution'.[20]

Often the difference between Anselm and Calvin and the other Reformers at this point has been explained as resulting from the fact that Anselm viewed sin as an affront to God's *honour*, whereas the Reformers viewed sin as a violation of God's inexorable *law*. Honour might be vindicated through satisfaction; but inflexible legal justice necessarily demanded punishment. Often this contrast has been put in terms very critical of Anselm. Foley, for example, says that the Reformers

15. Tillich, *Christian Thought*, p. 165.

16. W.G.T. Shedd, *A History of Christian Doctrine* (New York: Charles Scribner's Sons, 1883), I, p. 279. See also A.H. Strong, *Systematic Theology* (Philadelphia: Judson, 1907), pp. 747-50.

17. Aulen, *Christus Victor*, p. 110.

18. See A. von Harnack, *History of Dogma* (trans. N. Buchanan; Gloucester, MA: Peter Smith, 1976), III, p. 308, for references.

19. See the citations in J. Denney, *The Christian Doctrine of Reconciliation* (London: James Clarke, 1959), p. 78.

20. McIntyre, *Critics*, p. 87.

departed from his [Anselm's] essentially non-moral theory by grounding the work of Christ in the ethical nature of God... They picture the Atonement, not as a reparation for a private wrong, but as a satisfaction to inviolable holiness and a protection to the universal interests of the moral order. The whole subject was brought into the field of ethics.[21]

It is highly questionable, however, that this is the correct explanation of the reason that Anselm spoke of satisfaction whereas the Reformers spoke of penal substitution. This distinction between the 'honour' and the 'justice' of God is an utterly false one in terms of the *Cur deus homo*. In speaking of God's honour, Anselm is not setting this attribute off in distinction from God's justice, but he is simply emphasizing the *personal*, and therefore supremely *ethical*, nature of God's justice. In demanding satisfaction for sin, God is not meeting the requirements of an abstract, impersonal law set over against himself. Satisfaction is made necessary by the immutable nature of God himself, as the holy and just one against whom the sin has been committed.

Thus Anselm's error is not in conceiving of satisfaction as made to God's honour rather than to his justice, but rather in not perceiving the absolute necessity of the penalty being paid as the only possible way by which satisfaction for sin against a holy God can be made. McIntyre views it as a point to praise that 'nowhere does God appear in the *Cur deus homo* as a God of wrath';[22] but in view of the testimony of the scriptures we can only view this as a serious defect.

There is another important difference between Anselm and the Reformers. Aulen writes:

In the Protestant doctrine the satisfaction is regarded as made not merely by the death of Christ, but by His whole fulfillment of God's law throughout His life—that is, by His *obedientia activa*.[23]

This aspect of Reformation teaching seems to be directly related to the doctrine of penal substitution. Just as Calvin taught that Christ bore the curse of the law that was due to humanity's transgression of it, so he taught that Christ fulfilled the demand of the law positively in his incarnate life by fulfilling it to the uttermost. Calvin writes:

Now someone asks, How has Christ abolished sin, banished the separation between us and God, and acquired righteousness to render God

21. Foley, *Atonement*, p. 214.
22. McIntyre, *Critics*, p. 94.
23. Aulen, *Christus Victor*, p. 145.

favorable and kindly toward us? To this we can in general reply that he has achieved this for us by the whole course of his obedience. This is proved by Paul's testimony... (Rom. 5.19 p.) In another passage... Paul extends the basis of the pardon that frees us from the curse of the law to the whole life of Christ... (Gal. 4.4-5). Thus in his very baptism, also, he asserted that he fulfilled a part of righteousness in obediently carrying out his Father's commandment (Matt. 3.15). In short, from the time when he took on the form of a servant, he began to pay the price of liberation in order to redeem us.

Yet to define the way of salvation more exactly, Scripture ascribes this as peculiar and proper to Christ's death. (II:xvi:5)

In the argument of the *Cur deus homo*, on the other hand, Christ's life seems to have only a rather negative significance: it was necessary that the God-man be sinless in his life so that the death he offered to God might not be something that he owed to God. Beyond that, however, Anselm does not go.[24]

Judged in the light of the scriptures, Calvin's view would seem to be superior to Anselm's at this point because Calvin sees the full dimensions of the atonement in terms of the 'transfer': righteousness for unrighteousness. Christ takes on the sinners' unrighteousness (and its penalty) and gives them his righteous sonship. Anselm's treatise addresses the problem of guilt and restoration but does not develop, as Calvin does, a theology of the new life that is made possible by the atonement.

Calvin also improved considerably on Anselm with regard to the ground of the application of the blessings of the atonement to individual sinners. Tillich is correct in saying that to the question, How can sinners participate in that which the God-man wrought?, Anselm had no answer.[25] It is noteworthy that at this crucial point in his argument Anselm does not finally speak of that which was necessary but only of that which was more fitting ('convenientius'). 'To whom would it be more fitting for him to assign the fruit and recompense of his death than to those for whose salvation...he made himself man?' (II:19). Surely the

24. In a curious distortion of Anselm's thought, David Smith writes: '...according to St. Anselm, the atoning efficacy lies not in our Lord's death but in His life. It was His obedience and submission to the will of God, maintained throughout the entire course of His days upon the earth, that honoured God and made satisfaction for man's disobedience' (*The Atonement in the Light of History and the Modern Spirit* [London: Hodder & Stoughton, n.d.], p. 84).
25. Tillich, *Christian Thought*, p. 167.

concept of Christ's giving to sinners the reward that he does not need is not a very happy one.

Calvin at this point laid hold of the Pauline doctrine of the representative headship of Christ and the union of the believer with Christ that Bernard and Aquinas had earlier emphasized, and thus established the scriptural foundation for the imputation of the righteousness of Christ to the believer as well as the imputation of the sins of the believer to Christ.

> For we are enriched in Christ, because we are members of His body, and we have been ingrafted into Him; and, furthermore, since we have been made one with Him, He shares with us all that He had received from the Father.[26]

> This should be carefully noted, for just as we must look exclusively to Christ for salvation, so He would have died in vain and for nothing if He did not call us to share in this grace. So even after salvation is procured for us by His death, the second blessing still remains to be given, that He should insert us into His Body and communicate His benefits to us that we may enjoy them.[27]

> Who could have done this had not the self-same Son of God become the Son of man, and had not so taken what was ours as to impart what was his to us, and to make what was his by nature ours by grace?... Hence that holy brotherhood... In this way we are assured of the inheritance of the Heavenly Kingdom; for the only Son of God, to whom it wholly belongs, has adopted us as his brothers. 'For if brothers, then also fellow heirs with him.' (Rom. 8.17 p.) (II:xii:2)

Finally, it is often said that the Reformers also went beyond Anselm in making faith the one subjective condition for receiving the benefits of Christ's work. Now, it is true, of course, that Anselm's treatise does not present an argument for justification by faith alone; but there are two points worth noting.

First, we must remember what the purpose of the *Cur deus homo* is: to prove that the death of Christ was both reasonable and necessary. Therefore, there is a degree of truth in Harnack's statement that the

---

26. John Calvin, *Calvin's Commentaries. IX. The First Epistle of Paul the Apostle to the Corinthians* (trans. J.W. Fraser; ed. D.W. Torrance and T.F. Torrance; Grand Rapids, MI: Eerdmans, 1960), p. 21.

27. John Calvin, *Calvin's Commentaries. X. The Second Epistle of Paul the Apostle to the Corinthians and the Epistles to Timothy, Titus and Philemon* (trans. T.A. Smail; ed. D.W. Torrance and T.F. Torrance; Grand Rapids, MI: Eerdmans, 1964), p. 296.

Cur deus homo is intended to show only how the salvation of humankind is possible and is not concerned with the way in which individuals are to appropriate that salvation.[28] Thus the instrumentality of faith lies somewhat outside the scope of Anselm's work.

Secondly, however, it is also important to notice a very significant fact: faith *is* mentioned in the *Cur deus homo* as the means whereby an individual may appropriate the merits of Christ's death; and it is the *only* means that is mentioned. Two passages in particular should be noted. The clearest statement on the instrumentality of faith appears near the end of Book I. Boso has been asking those questions that unbelievers are wont to raise. After answering all those questions, Anselm says to Boso:

> What you should do now is to require those for whom you speak, who do not believe that Christ is necessary for man's salvation, to tell us how man can be saved apart from Christ. And if they cannot do this at all, let them stop mocking us, and come and join themselves to us, who do not doubt that man can be saved through Christ—or else let them despair of the very possibility of salvation. If they shrink from this, then *let them believe in Christ with us, so that they may be saved.* (I:25, emphasis added)

And in Book II, Anselm presents God the Father's invitation to the doomed sinner, and it is an invitation that can only be accepted by faith: 'Receive my only-begotten Son, and give him for yourself'. And Anselm likewise presents the Son as saying: 'Take me and ransom your souls' (II:20).

Certainly it would be reading too much into these brief statements to try to draw a straight line from them to Calvin's developed emphasis on *sola fide*. And yet the very silence of the *Cur deus homo* regarding the necessity of any other response on the part of the sinner seeking salvation would seem to be significant. By limiting his concern to the person and work of Christ, Anselm turned the sinner's attention away from any work of satisfaction the sinner might perform and away from any mere externalism in religion to the Saviour himself and to the need for a personal, trusting relationship with him.

---

28. Harnack, *Dogma*, VI, pp. 68-69.

JUSTICE ANSELMIENNE ET BONNE VOLONTÉ KANTIENNE:
ESSAI DE COMPARAISON

J. Vuillemin

On a justement remarqué que la méthode d'Anselme, *fides quaerens intellectum*, n'est pas univoquement définie. Il est clair qu'il doit en être ainsi, puisque la raison doit, autant qu'elle le peut, pénétrer les données de la foi et que ces données peuvent aller d'un minimum tel que la caractéristique reconnue à Dieu par toutes les religions monothéistes dans le *Proslogion* à un maximum tel que l'incarnation dans le *Cur deus homo*.

Pris dans l'ordre anselmien, les trois traités, *De veritate, De libertate arbitrii* et *De casu diaboli,* manifestent ainsi une gradation dans l'étendue des données que la foi propose au commentaire de la raison.

Comme la comparaison que je me propose de faire entre Kant et Anselme ne peut se réclamer d'aucun fondement historique et que Kant n'accorde de place qu'à la foi rationnelle à l'exclusion de la foi révélée,[1] j'examinerai en premier lieu les analogies morales remarquables entre les deux doctrines que permet d'établir la méthode d'Anselme quand on l'applique à des données de foi pour ainsi dire minimes dans le *De veritate* et même le *De libertate arbitrii*. On verra en second lieu ces analogies s'affaiblir et faire place au contraste, lorsqu'on les replace dans leur contexte général philosophique et théologique. Le contraste entre systèmes ne manquera pas, enfin, de produire des conséquences à l'intérieur du domaine proprement moral.

I

'Dieu est vérité':[2] telle est la donnée de la foi supposée par le disciple au début du *De veritate*. Bien que l'idée de rectitude appliquée par la raison aux créatures ait une portée universelle et se développe dans la

---

1. *Die Religion innerhalb der Grenzen der blossen Vernunft* VI, 204 *sq.*
2. Schmitt, I, p. 176:4.

considération exemplariste de l'essence des choses[3] avant de culminer dans la vérité suprême, il est permis de spécialiser la question de la rectitude, ainsi que le fait Anselme au chapitre 12, en s'interrogeant sur ses rapports avec la justice. Ce chapitre ne contient pas de référence scripturaire, mais il ressort assez du caractère de la volonté divine, à nulle autre soumise,[4] que la supposition de la foi se réduit ici à l'universelle soumission des créatures aux décrets du Créateur et, puisqu'il s'agira des créatures raisonnables considérées selon la volonté, à leur obéissance aux commandements divins. C'est aussi de cette façon que Kant déduit le contenu moral d'une religion rationnelle.[5]

La justice, définie par genre proche et différence spécifique, est la rectitude de la volonté lorsqu'elle observe la rectitude pour elle-même.[6] La définition restreint la rectitude à l'être raisonnable[7] considéré comme volonté.[8] Mais une volonté n'est droite qu'en tant qu'elle fait ce qu'elle doit.[9] La justice, comme commentaire rationnel des commandements divins, est identique avec la bonne volonté kantienne, définie comme obéissance au devoir par devoir.[10] On a dit que les mots *debet* et *rectitudo*[11] ont une acception plus large que le *devoir* kantien (*Sollen*). Les acceptions coïncident cependant dès qu'on limite, comme on l'a fait, en conformité avec le chapitre 12 du *De veritate*, l'application de *debet* ou *rectitudo* à la volonté des êtres raisonnables.

Deux traits notables précisent cette coïncidence. L'addition de la fin poursuivie par l'agent (*propter rectitudinem*/par devoir) est spécifique de l'intention morale.[12] L'obéissance extérieure n'est rien au regard du devoir et une action conforme au devoir peut être accomplie pour les motifs les plus variés, malhonnêteté incluse. En second lieu, justice ou bonne volonté s'appliquent à tous les êtres raisonnables, et donc à Dieu même. Si la rectitude doit être observée pour elle-même, 'il semble qu'on ne puisse le dire avec autant d'à propos pour aucune autre

---

3. *De veritate*, cap. 7 (Schmitt, I, pp. 185-86).
4. *Monologion* (Schmitt, I, p. 27:11s).
5. *Die Religion, passim*.
6. *De veritate* (Schmitt, I, p. 194:23-24).
7. *De veritate* (Schmitt, I, p. 193:5).
8. *De veritate* (Schmitt, I, p. 193:14).
9. *De veritate* (Schmitt, I, p. 181:1).
10. *Die Religion*, VI, p. 11.
11. *De veritate* (Schmitt, I, p. 185:28).
12. *De veritate* (Schmitt, I, p. 195:28-29); *De casu diaboli* (Schmitt, I, pp. 271:27–272:2).

rectitude' que la raison suprême.[13] De même, la sainteté, qui est la bonne volonté pure et ferme[14] et donc infaillible, est propre à Dieu selon Kant.[15]

Non seulement la rectitude de la volonté en tout être raisonnable suppose la liberté; à un degré suprême, elle est liberté et, puisqu'en tant que telle, chez Dieu et les bons anges, elle ne peut pas pécher,[16] est plus libre l'être raisonnable qui possède ce qu'il doit avoir en sorte de ne pouvoir le perdre que celui qui le possède en sorte de pouvoir le perdre.[17] Kant identifiera cette liberté avec le pouvoir pratique de la raison ou faculté de se donner des lois. L'autonomie est dépourvue de sens pour Anselme, la liberté divine étant affranchie de toute loi[18] et la liberté angélique ou humaine étant assujettie à des lois que lui sont imposées par Dieu. Toutefois une volonté qui est dite libre dans la mesure où elle conserve la rectitude[19] en vue de la rectitude même n'est autre que le pouvoir correspondant à l'acte de la justice, et cette justice, ou bonne intention, ne consiste qu'à obéir par devoir aux lois ou devoirs de la raison, interprétés, en termes religieux comme commandements divins.

La condition humaine en son état présent met en acte une liberté toujours entière en dépit de la chute,[20] mais mineure puisque nous voulons avec plus ou moins de force conserver la rectitude pour elle-même—ce que nous traduisons en termes de tentation pour nous décharger de notre responsabilité.[21] Kant appelle libre arbitre au sens restreint (*Willkür*) ce degré mineur de la liberté, qui consiste à pouvoir désobéir sans toutefois que le pouvoir soit dû à une malignité intrinsèque de la volonté,[22] puisqu'est conservé le devoir de revenir à la sainteté. A cet état correspond, chez Anselme, la division[23] de la liberté qu'il nomme liberté créée par Dieu et reçue de lui, privée de la rectitude qu'elle doit servir, mais d'une façon récupérable.

Il reste, autant que faire se peut, à comprendre par la raison comment

13. *De veritate* (Schmitt, I, p. 196:5-6).
14. *Die Religion*, VI, pp. 84-85, 113, 214.
15. *Die Religion*, VI, pp. 283, 311.
16. *De libertate arbitrii* (Schmitt, I, p. 208:9-10).
17. *De libertate arbitrii* (Schmitt, I, p. 208:18-21).
18. *Monologion* (Schmitt, I, pp. 31:6*s*, 70:6).
19. *De libertate arbitrii* (Schmitt, I, p. 212:19-20).
20. *De libertate arbitrii* cap. II–III et V (Schmitt, I, pp. 209-213, 214-17).
21. *De libertate arbitrii* cap. VII (Schmitt, I, pp. 218-20).
22. *Die Religion*, VI, 35*s*.
23. *De libertate arbitrii* (Schmitt, I, p. 226:1).

ce nôtre état de pécheur est possible. Bien que le *De casu diaboli* suppose des données scripturaires bien plus étendues que la création et que la liberté du pécheur, la méthode anselmienne permet encore de faire abstraction du cas des mauvais anges et de leur chute irrécupérable, pour s'en tenir comme il est fair dans les chapitres 13 à 16 à l'état de péché, ainsi que le Disciple le remarque,[24] état dont nous avons l'expérience. Nous pouvons, pour ainsi dire, construire par abstraction cet état en trois temps pour parvenir à définir l'injustice, par contraste avec la justice qu'on a définie.

Une première abstraction fera considérer la créature raisonnable dans sa seule relation à la convenance ou intérêt (*commodum*) ou au bonheur (*beatitudo*),[25] relation qui la porte nécessairement à rechercher la convenance et à fuir son contraire, conformément d'ailleurs à une rectitude qui dépasse la seule créature raisonnable. Cette appétition, même si elle va jusqu'à vouloir se rendre semblable à Dieu[26] est, en elle-même, bonne puisqu'elle est reçue de Dieu, et étrangère au juste et à l'injuste puisqu'elle est simplement naturelle dans l'être raisonnable. Kant, de même, nomme amour de soi ou du bonheur l'ensemble des principes pratiques matériels. La faculté de sentir et les sentiments moteurs de la volonté ont par eux-mêmes une valeur positive et ne sauraient être tenus pour dépravés.[27] Séparons à présent, par une nouvelle abstraction, la volonté de rectitude. Une telle volonté serait liée à la rectitude par un lien de nature nécessaire et, de ce fait, elle ne pourrait pas non plus être qualifiée de juste ou d'injuste.[28] Ainsi l'autonomie kantienne, en elle-même, produit loi et obligation, sans impliquer pour l'arbitre la possibilité de désobéir. Le juste et l'injuste apparaissent dans la créature 'lorsqu'elle veut être heureuse et le veut justement'.[29] De même, chez Kant, l'impératif catégorique résulte du devoir quand le devoir commande l'amour de soi.

La volonté juste d'Anselme, en tant qu'opposée à la volonté injuste, n'est plus la volonté juste *simpliciter* ou bonne volonté, pas plus que la bonne volonté kantienne engagée dans le mal radical n'est identique

---

24. *De casu diaboli* (Schmitt, I, p. 241:15).

25. *De casu diaboli* (Schmitt, I, pp. 241:13-14, 255:7-15).

26. *De casu diaboli*, cap. IV (Schmitt, I, pp. 240-42); cap. XIII (Schmitt, I, p. 247:4-7, 10, 26-28); cap. XIX (Schmitt, I, p. 264).

27. *Die Religion*, VI, pp. 31, 32, 33, 113, 115.

28. *De casu diaboli* (Schmitt, I, p. 258:13-16).

29. *De casu diaboli* (Schmitt, I, p. 258:22).

avec cette bonne volonté considérée dans son simple rapport avec le devoir. Quant à la déchéance ontologique introduite par l'opposition, elle résulte d'un bouleversement de l'ordre entre devoir et bonheur. Selon Anselme, la volonté pécheresse a péché 'en voulant quelque convenance qu'elle n'avait pas et qu'elle ne devait pas vouloir alors et qui cependant pouvait servir à augmenter son bonheur'[30] et en procédant ainsi contre l'ordre fixé par Dieu.[31] Selon Kant, tandis que la sainteté requiert de la volonté, qu'elle trouve sa béatitude en obéissant au devoir par devoir, le péché provient de ce qu'elle renverse cet ordre[32] et permet au bonheur soit de s'ajouter à la maxime de l'obéissance par devoir (impureté), soit d'en ébranler la fermeté (fragilité), soit de la repousser à son profit (perversion).[33]

Théologie et philosophie vont opposer les deux doctrines, mais leur accord sur le péché originel est d'autant plus remarquable. Défini comme injustice par Anselme,[34] il est personnel, accompli par l'individu une fois devenu personne[35] et passé dans sa nature.[36] Kant, évidemment, rejette la transmission héréditaire et spécifique pour mettre en valeur la responsabilité de l'individu dans la dépravation de la nature humaine.[37]

On peut donc proposer entre les deux doctrines un dictionnaire de traduction fidèle tant qu'on s'en tient aux considérations morales auxquelles on s'est jusqu'ici borné.

Anselme	Kant
volonté juste	bonne volonté
Debere	Devoir (*Sollen*)
propter rectitudinem	par devoir
libertas arbitrii[38]	
1) *a se*	
2) *a deo facta et accepta*	volonté législatrice autonome
habens rectitudinem	(*Wille*)
quam servet	

30. *De casu diaboli* (Schmitt, I, p. 241:17-18).
31. *Inordinate: De casu diaboli* (Schmitt, I, pp. 241:22, 242:4).
32. *Verkehrtheit, Die Religion*, VI, pp. 23, 36, 216.
33. *Die Religion*, VI, pp. 22-23.
34. *Proslogion* (Schmitt, I, pp. 142:20–143:6).
35. *Proslogion* (Schmitt, I, pp. 140:28–141:2); *De conceptu virginali et originali peccato* (Schmitt, I, p. 165:5s.).
36. *De conceptu virginali* (Schmitt, I, p. 165:7-25).
37. *Die Religion*, VI, pp. 94-95.
38. *De libertate arbitrii*, cap. XIV (Schmitt, I, p. 226).

Anselme	Kant
3) *a deo facta et accepta*	
carens rectitudinem quam	libre-arbitre (*Willkür*)
servet recuperabiliter	
commodum-beatitudo	Amour de soi, principe de détermina-
	tion matérielle de la volonté
justitia	Principe de détermination formelle de
	la volonté
justitia + *commodum* →	Devoir + amour de soi →
oppositio justitiae et injustitiae	impératif catégorique
inordinate	désordre

II

On pourrait croire que les oppositions doctrinales qu'on va maintenant tenter d'analyser proviennent essentiellement des données de la foi et donc de la théologie. Anselme, il est vrai, parle d'une foi d'Eglise, bien différente de la foi rationnelle et des postulats de la raison pratique seuls admis par Kant.[39] Même lorsqu'il isole tel ou tel dogme pour l'éclairer par la raison, Anselme ne l'isole pas de la tradition scripturaire et surtout ne cherche pas à en donner une interprétation symbolique qui ferait fi de l'histoire et de la révélation. En ceci, partisan des Lumières, Kant, en revanche, tient Jésus pour un maître de vérité et conteste sa divinité. Il rejette *a priori* comme pernicieuses pour l'autonomie morale les considérations de grâce et de rachat telles que celles que développe le *Cur deus homo*. Qu'eût-il dit des calculs, même examinés critiquement, sur le rapport entre le nombre des anges réprouvés et des hommes élus?

Trop criante pour nous retenir, cette opposition risque d'autre part d'en masquer une autre, plus cachée, plus intéressante aussi, et qui, touchant non plus la foi mais l'intelligence de la foi, porte sur des conceptions différentes et parfois contraires de la raison d'autant plus significatives qu'Anselme et Kant appartiennent tous deux à une tradition philosophique apparemment identique, je veux dire le rationalisme. Ainsi précisée, la question qui se pose alors est la suivante: si les deux philosophes s'entendent jusque dans le détail de leur doctrine morale, sur la rectitude, sur la liberté, sur la chute, pour quelles raisons philosophiques, entièrement ou très largement indépendantes de leur foi et de leur attitude à l'égard de la révélation, sont-ils en complet désaccord, dès

39. *Die Religion*, VI, 77/145.

qu'on précise la façon dont chacun d'eux conçoit ce qu'est la raison pratique et surtout son rapport avec la raison théorique?

La distinction de ces deux raisons est étrangère à Anselme. Certes, dans l'être raisonnable il fait le partage entre science, action et volonté.[40] Mais la volonté, qu'on la regarde comme instrument, affection ou usage,[41] est ce que, plus tard, Descartes appellera un mode de l'âme, dont la science est un autre mode, d'ailleurs nécessaire à l'usage de la liberté.[42] Bien que ces modes diffèrent l'un de l'autre, ils concourent à constituer la créature, sans que nous soyons invités à accorder à l'un quelque privilège sur l'autre. Le *De veritate* développe précisément une doctrine générale de la rectitude et de la vérité, applicable à tous les modes de l'âme, inspirée de l'exemplarisme et de la participation et subordonnant en fin de compte chaque vérité particulière—telle que la vérité liée à la volonté juste ou celle de la vérité énoncée ou pensée—à l'unique vérité divine.[43]

La *Critique de la raison pure* interdit précisément cette extension de la rectitude au domaine de la science et à la vérité suprême. La seule vérité qui soit accessible à notre connaissance, celle de l'*intellectus ectypus* est telle que deux facultés de nature différente, entendement et sensibilité, fournissent, l'un l'unité, l'autre le divers (pur ou empirique) dont la synthèse produit le jugement vrai. Les rationalistes dogmatiques ont certes utilisé en des sens divers le mot d'intuition intellectuelle; Platon, Augustin, Anselme, Malebranche, Leibniz concevront différemment et la vision et l'idée et le lien des idées. Mais tous, exploitant l'image de la vision sensible, postuleront que l'essence même ou l'idée de la chose est directement aperçue par notre raison. Descartes lui-même, dans une tradition toute différente, concevra ce principe de la vision de l'idée par l'esprit. C'est elle que Kant rejette comme illusion de l'enthousiasme (*Schwärmerei*). Vision d'idées, la raison, fabricatrice d'apparences, n'est à même de résoudre aucun des problèmes sur lesquels le rationalisme dogmatique avait abondamment spéculé: l'âme est-elle immortelle? qu'est-ce que le monde? y a-t-il un Dieu?

En particulier, la théologie rationnelle est impossible. Etant donnée la forme scolastique qu'il donne à l'argument ontologique, Kant manifeste qu'il n'a pas lu le *Proslogion*. Sa réfutation littérale, proche de celle de

---

40. *De veritate* (Schmitt, I, p. 193:12-13).
41. *De concordia* (Schmitt, II, pp. 278:28–279:12).
42. *De veritate* (Schmitt, I, p. 192:30-33).
43. *De veritate* cap. XIII (Schmitt, I, pp. 196-99).

Gaunilon, tient à ce que la modalité du nécessaire ne contient aucun contenu qui ne se trouve déjà dans la modalité du possible. Si l'on revient au *Proslogion*, le *id quo nihil maius cogitari potest*—à supposer qu'il soit consistant—ne pourra être dit exister, selon Kant, que si nous pouvions construire cette existence dans une intuition, ce que l'a-temporalité et l'a-spatialité divines interdisent. En d'autres termes, l'existence intelligible propre à Dieu est ce qui interdit de la connaître: connaître, c'est construire, c'est produire la chose comme un phénomène et non pas la voir comme une idée. En conséquence, la *Critique de la raison pure* rejette le *Proslogion* (sans pour autant rejeter la foi en Dieu, mais en un Dieu tel que la foi qui le pose, purement pratique, se voit interdire sa propre intelligence). Elle rejette, de même, l'ensemble du *De veritate* à l'exception du chapitre 12, puisque l'identification de la rectitude avec la vérité et la généralisation indue de la rectitude aux modes de l'âme différents de la volonté résultent précisément de l'illuminisme et de l'enthousiasme qui nous porte à croire que notre raison voit la vérité. Exercice logique pour Anselme, la dialectique de la raison pure se résout, pour Kant, en une théorie générale de l'illusion rationnelle.

Cette opposition fondamentale sur la nature de la connaissance humaine va gauchir en profondeur les analogies et même les équivalences qu'on a relevées entre les doctrines morales. Le principle de la transformation est simple. Chez Anselme science, volonté et action restent des modes également transparents de la créature raisonnable, tandis que, chez Kant, la volonté, identifiée à la raison pratique, produit certes dans le monde extérieur des actions que nous pouvons connaître à titre de phénomènes, mais reste, en elle-même, inaccessible à notre connaissance. La cause intentionnelle de l'action relève du monde intelligible, l'action même appartenant seule au monde sensible ou phénoménal.

Selon Anselme, rien interdit à l'agent moral de savoir qu'il est juste, puisque chaque être raisonnable connaît ce qu'il doit, sa rectitude, qu'il connaît également sa décision de l'accomplir et qu'enfin la fin pour laquelle il prend sa décision, le *propter rectitudinem*, est également objet de science. Comme l'acteur du théâtre ancien ou classique, il délibère en toute clarté. La décision prise, il lui arrive de ne pas s'y tenir car il souffre de faiblesse et il le sait: il manque de persévérance,[44] mais l'adéquation est entière entre faire et savoir. Placé devant la nécessité

44. *De casu diaboli* (Schmitt, I, pp. 237:32–238:21).

d'affronter la mort en disant la vérité ou de sauver sa vie en mentant, il est au clair sur ses motifs: la rectitude ou la convenance.[45] Selon Kant, l'agent moral ne peut pas connaître la décision libre qui lui fait choisir telle maxime plutôt que telle autre; il peut certes constater que son action est conforme ou n'est pas conforme au devoir, puisque cette constatation est d'ordre empirique. Mais il ne saurait s'assurer s'il a agi par devoir ou si une maxime tirée de l'amour de soi a mêlé quelque impureté ou quelque raison d'inconstance à sa décision. Il est semblable aux héros de Shakespeare, du moins quand ils ne sont pas entièrement mauvais, impénétrable à lui-même et aux autres. Quand Hamlet punit enfin Claudius, venge-t-il sa mère, venge-t-il son père, se venge-t-il lui-même ou répond-il au sentiment d'honneur qu'il a laissé somnoler?

L'inconnaissabilité de la liberté entraîne deux conséquences dans la doctrine kantienne. Premièrement, le devoir auquel il est obéi par devoir ne peut plus indiquer une rectitude inscrite par la création dans la nature des choses, puisque cette nature et cette création échappent à notre raison finie. Si notre volonté morale est un don que nous avons reçu de Dieu, nous ne pouvons pas le savoir faute d'intuition intellectuelle. Ainsi le contenu du *debere*, cette nature rationnelle impartie à l'homme à titre de créature et que le christianisme, mais aussi le judaïsme et l'Islam lisaient spontanément dans l'ordre du créé, leurs fois différentes convenant ici dans une intelligence unique, cesse d'avoir un sens. Voici un devoir, c'est-à-dire des obligations et des lois, qui exigent de tout être raisonnable obéissance en vue d'elles-mêmes. Voici une raison pratique que nous ne pouvons pas connaître et dont nous ne sommes assurés que par le devoir. La raison théorique n'autorisant pas à poser l'existence d'un Dieu créateur et législateur, à qui rapporter alors le devoir sinon au pouvoir législateur de la raision pratique? Donnez d'une part (avec Anselme et la tradition du rationalisme dogmatique) un caractère inconditionnel au devoir. Refusez d'autre part, avec Kant, à la raison théorique l'accès à une causalité divine propre à expliquer le phénomène du devoir à notre conscience. Il en résultera l'autonomie. En se donnant à elle-même ses propres lois, la raison pratique prend la place des *rectitudines* propres à l'appareil métaphysique. En second lieu une asymétrie complète gouverne la conscience morale. D'un côté je constate immédiatement qu'une action n'est pas conforme au devoir. A fortiori, cette action n'a pas été accomplie par devoir. De l'autre, lorsque j'accomplis une action conforme au devoir, rien ne peut m'assurer que je l'ai

45. *De libertate arbitrii* (Schmitt, I, p. 215:21-33).

accomplie par devoir ou pour tout autre motif. En conséquence il m'est, conformément à la doctrine de l'apôtre, interdit de m'imputer les mérites de mes actions, tandis que je ne puis, en conscience, que m'imputer leurs démérites.[46]

Quelque place qu'il fasse ou qu'il prépare à la dignité humaine et à l'humanisme, particulièrement en proclamant la liberté inamissible dans la chute,[47] Anselme eût regardé l'autonomie comme blasphématoire. Cependant, puisque Kant attribue l'autonomie, par excellence, à la volonté sainte et qu'elle ne se dissocie pas, dans l'expérience que nous en faisons, de la contrainte douloureuse qu'elle exerce sur nous, nous sommes assurés que ce n'est pas la raison humaine—finie et pécheresse—mais une raison pratique pure qui est en tant que telle l'auteur du devoir et que ce devoir devrait en lui-même exprimer sa spontanéité, ce qui ne nous éloigne pas entièrement de la leçon d'Anselme.

Il en va autrement pour l'asymétrie de la conscience morale. La parabole du Pharisien et du Publicain continue certes de la produire, mais elle prend un autre sens. En effet, la révélation et la théodicée rationaliste qui l'éclaire exigent dans les rapports de Dieu au Bien et au Mal, qu'à l'homme il donne la volonté bonne et permette seulement la volonté mauvaise.[48] En conséquence de ce principe, mérite et démérite sont répartis chez Anselme comme ils le sont chez Kant: 'Avoir eu ou devoir montre une dignité naturelle, et ne pas avoir une malhonnêteté personnelle. Devoir, en effet, est le fait de celui qui a donné, tandis que ne pas avoir est le fait de celui-là même qui a déserté.'[49] Cependant, comme le montre cette citation, l'asymétrie anselmienne n'est pas de nature morale, mais métaphysique. Pour décharger le Créateur de la responsabilité du mal tout en continuant de l'honorer comme auteur de tout bien, Anselme, analysant les concepts essentiellement privatifs de néant et d'injustice, le premier relatif à la rectitude en général, le second à la rectitude particulière de la volonté,[50] place dans la création même l'origine de l'asymétrie. Cette origine est ontologique, car il n'y a pas symétrie de l'être au néant, ou, particulièrement, de la justice à l'injustice. La *Critique de la raison pure*, en revanche, excluant toute

---

46. *Théorie et pratique*, VIII, p. 428 (opposition entre le *modus imputationis tollens* et le *modus imputationis ponens*).
47. *De libertate arbitrii* , cap. V (Schmitt, I, pp. 214-22).
48. *De casu diaboli* (Schmitt, I, p. 245:16-18).
49. *De casu diaboli* (Schmitt, I, p. 260:15-16).
50. *De casu diaboli*, cap. X et XI (Schmitt, I, pp. 246-51).

perspective de théologie et de théodicée théoriques, la *Critique de la raison pratique* doit, si celle-ci existe, légitimer l'asymétrie de la conscience morale à partir de principes purement pratiques. C'est ce qu'elle fait en vertu de l'opacité que nos motifs d'action opposent à l'intelligence non peut-être en tant que nous les analysons, mais en tant qu'ils déterminent l'action, ce par quoi seul ils sont décisifs. Regardés de la sorte, à titre de causes intelligibles de nos comportements sensibles, ils entraînent directement une asymétrie morale, étrangère à tout théodicée théorique, accentuant même en un sens la caractère positif et réel du mal, sous la seule réserve de corrections que pourrait apporter une théodicée pratique conforme à l'espérance invincible requise par le devoir.

III

Une comparaison philosophique, surtout lorsqu'elle ne suppose aucune influence historique comme c'est le cas ici, n'a de chance d'aboutir qu'une fois déterminée la relation de chacun des termes avec le système auquel il appartient. Et cette relation avec le système, on l'a dit, se définit moins en fonction de la foi révélée qu'on suppose ici et qu'on rejette là—la comparaison entre criticisme et thomisme eût impliqué la même supposition et le même rejet, mais eût entraîné pourtant de tout autres conséquences!—qu'en fonction du système philosophique qui, ici, interprète la révélation et, là, conduit à remplacer le savoir par la foi. Il faut donc préciser ce que sont les deux formes du rationalisme que nous comparons: dogmatisme anselmien et criticisme kantien.

Un principe commun formellement identique, gouverne les deux systèmes. Ni Dieu, ni la raison pratique ne commandent l'impossible. En d'autres termes, le *debet* associé à la justice ou à la bonne volonté doit être possible. Cette implication modale très particulière (qu'on trahirait d'ailleurs si on l'exprimait dans la langue de la logique déontique en oubliant la fin spécifique de la moralité) cache cependant une équivoque dans la terme commun de *possible.*

Que signifie *possible* pour Anselme, en particulier quand il définit la liberté 'le pouvoir ('potestas') de conserver la rectitude de la volonté en raison de la rectitude elle-même'?[51] Il s'agit d'un pouvoir qui subsiste même s'il ne conduit pas à l'acte,[52] mais qui définit la nature rationnelle

---

51. *De libertate arbitrii*, cap. XIII (Schmitt, I, p. 225).
52. *De libertate arbitrii* (Schmitt, I, p. 212:30, 213:25).

créée, laquelle en tant que telle 'doit au créateur ceci même qu'elle est en soi'.[53] Ainsi le possible est objectif, rapporté à la création et à son ordre avant même d'être réalisé, mû ou 'donné' par Dieu dans l'acte et ne relevant de sa permission et de la responsabilité de la volonté que par son défaut. On ne peut pas affirmer avec plus de netteté le principe du réalisme:[54] le pouvoir de la liberté, don divin, correspond à une essence dont elle tire toute sa réalité et qui, par son caractère rationnel, la rapproche au maximum de l'essence suprême.[55]

A cette philosophie réaliste[56] s'oppose la philosophie critique, même si elle maintient les droits de la raison. Puisque l'obéissance au devoir par devoir correspond à la conservation de la rectitude de la volonté en raison de la rectitude elle-même, on attendrait que la liberté kantienne fût à l'obéissance au devoir par devoir ce que la liberté anselmienne est à la justice, à savoir un pouvoir. Ce n'est pas le cas. La liberté, selon Kant, est en effet la *ratio essendi* du devoir que en devient la *ratio cognoscendi*. Le changement resterait verbal, si l'être promu par la raison pratique ne s'opposait pas, en tant qu'intelligible ou nouménal, au phénomène du devoir, en tant que représentation de *ma science* accompagnée par le sentiment de respect. Privée de sa fonction de lumière, la raison est réduite à la puissance d'obliger.[57] Mais comme les lois qu'elle édicte ne contiennent que des injonctions inconditionnelles dont les conditions qui les rendent possibles dans le phénomène ne se trouvent plus assurées par les essences créées, ces conditions doivent, sous peine de contradiction, être posées comme existences intelligibles inaccessibles à l'entendement et, par conséquent, comme objets d'une foi rationnelle: ce sont les postulats de la raison pratique. En particulier, la liberté est bien le fondement ontologique général du devoir en ce qu'un être raisonnable ne saurait être inconditionnelement obligé s'il n'était libre. Le chapitre 12 du *De veritate* ne dit rien d'autre, sauf à associer illumination et devoir. Mais lorsque le devoir m'oblige, moi, qui ne me connais qu'à titre de phénomène, cette mienne obligation n'étant possible que si je suis libre, bien que je ne possède aucun moyen de le savoir en dehors de cette obligation même, je dois postuler et donc croire que j'existe

---

53. *Monologion* (Schmitt, I, p. 78:16-17).
54. *Monologion* (Schmitt, I, p. 45:6-10).
55. *Monologion* (Schmitt, I, p. 77:17-24).
56. Références données sous la rubrique *essentia creata*, Schmitt, VI, pp. 133-34.
57. *Kritik der praktischen Vernunft*, V, pp. 47-72, 94.

comme être intelligible libre. Le possible échappe alors à toute intuition qui illuminerait par l'intelligence une foi historiquement donnée; la foi, qui ne retient d'ailleurs que la conséquence du devoir, a remplacé le savoir.

Cette opposition de principe entre rationalisme réaliste et rationalisme critique ou pratique est à l'origine de l'opposition dans la conception de l'arbitre. Kant va de l'autonomie à Dieu. Anselme fondait la liberté de l'homme, dans ses deux usages, sur le don et sur la permission de Dieu. Les deux conceptions opposées de l'arbitre, à leur tour, entraînent des conséquences contraires dans le domaine strict de la morale. Anselme et Kant s'accordent, assurément, pour conserver à l'homme pécheur son arbitre. Tous deux se font encore une même idée de l'intention pure dans une volonté non pécheresse. Le bon ange aurait eu, déclare Anselme, 'deux raisons de ne pas pécher, l'une honnête et utile, l'autre malhonnête et inutile, à savoir l'amour de la justice et la haine de la peine. Car il est malhonnête de ne pas pécher par la seule haine de la peine, et la haine de la peine est inutile à l'abstention du péché, là où suffit le seul amour de la justice.'[58] La traduction kantienne est immédiate. Tout change, en revanche, quand on passe à la volonté pécheresse. C'est ici que, soudain, mais en vertu de leur seule logique, rationalisme réaliste et rationalisme pratique s'affrontent dans les conséquences morales de leurs principes.

La perspective réaliste d'Anselme entraîne en effet l'incapacité radicale du pécheur à sortir de son état et à rentrer dans la rectitude par ses seules forces. Grâce et rédemption dont Anselme montre qu'elles impliquent l'incarnation sont nécessaires au salut. Bien qu'en particulier dans le *De concordia* il se borne à parler de la grâce du don, qui fait être toute essence créée et donc la rectitude de la volonté, la désertion de cette rectitude n'induisant qu'une privation d'être à laquelle ne correspond nulle essence, au disciple du *De casu diaboli* qui demande 'pourquoi une créature rationnelle ne peut pas par elle-même se convertir du mal au bien comme elle le peut du bien au mal',[59] le Maître répond par l'explication suivante: en désertant la justice ou volonté de rectitude qu'elle avait reçue de Dieu, la volonté pécheresse est réduite à l'amour de soi, qui la soumet invinciblement à l'unique désir du bonheur; elle ne saurait donc, n'étant pas créatrice, retrouver par elle-même

---

58. *De casu diaboli* (Schmitt, I, pp. 271-27–272:2).
59. Cap. VII (Schmitt, I, p. 244:9-10).

ce qu'elle a perdu.[60] Augustin l'avait dit: 'Au bien qu'il a abandonné, le pécheur ne peut être rappelé que par la grâce de Dieu, non par la liberté de la volonté qu'il a perdue par suite de son iniquité.'[61] Le pécheur doit donc être véritablement recréé[62] et, pour décrire ce second don, Augustin avait, contre Pélage, distingué grâce proprement dite et dons naturels de Dieu,[63] réparation et institution,[64] grâce chrétienne de l'élection et de la libération et grâce commune de la création.[65] La première de ces grâces, seule remède au péché[66] et bien plus puissante que la seconde,[67] transforme le refus en vouloir[68] et peut refaire ce que la faute a défait.[69] En insistant, comme le fait d'ailleurs souvent Augustin lui-même sur le don gracieux lié à l'essence, Anselme paraît se rapprocher de Pélage qui dit que la grâce de Dieu n'est rien d'autre que notre nature créée avec le libre arbitre.[70] Mais la doctrine anselmienne de la satisfaction du péché[71] lève toute ambiguité et la grâce de réparation est si présente à son esprit qu'il va jusqu'à proclaimer que 'les anges damnés ne peuvent être sauvés sinon par un ange-dieu qui réparerait par sa justice ce que les péchés des autres ont dérobé',[72] le principe d'individuation angélique et l'inexcusabilité absolue qui lui est propre excluant d'ailleurs la possibilité d'une telle rédemption.[73]

C'est ici que le rationalisme pratique et le principe d'autonomie creusent un abîme entre Kant et Anselme. Ultrapélagien, Kant retire au péché toute force qui empêcherait métaphysiquement le pécheur de se rétablir dans l'obéissance. Non seulement la grâce n'assure pas le don de l'être, mais elle pervertirait la pureté, la constance et la réparation qui n'incombent qu'à nos seules forces. La grâce est une illusion religieuse:

60. Cap. XVII (Schmitt, I, p. 262).

61. Cité par F.S. Schmitt, *De casu diaboli*, I, p. 262 (note); Augustin, X, 1301e.

62. Augustin, IV, 1029b (comparer *Proslogion*, Schmitt, I, p. 98:13).

63. Augustin, X, 797b, p. 60.

64. Augustin, X, p. 132c–133d (comparer avec Anselme, *Cur deus homo*, Schmitt, II, p. 117:6*s*).

65. Augustin, V, 137g.

66. Augustin, II, 3, 905b–907f.

67. Augustin, X, 766d, 768c.

68. Augustin, X, 1100b.

69. Augustin, VI, 332d.

70. Augustin, X, 204f, 216e.

71. *Cur deus homo*, Lib. I, cap. XIX.

72. *Cur deus homo*, II, XXI (Schmitt, II, p. 132:12-14).

73. Affirmée par Origène (Augustin, VII, 637b, 640f.).

nulle faute ne peut être effacée par le sang d'un autre.[74]

En somme si proches que soient rationalisme illuminé et rationalisme pratique par la définition qu'ils donnent respectivement de la justice et de la bonne volonté, leurs voies divergent, en morale même, dès qu'on en vient à l'injustice et à la mauvaise volonte. Dans un cas le péché dénature la volonté en sorte 'qu'il ne lui est absolument plus possible de remplir son devoir';[75] dans l'autre, même dépravée, la volonté doit obéir et doit donc pouvoir obéir par elle-même. Anselme est augustinien, Kant pélagien. Là Dieu donne à la raison créée la vertu et, si cette raison abandonne le devoir, il doit la créer à nouveau pour qu'elle revienne. Ici la raison finie est impuissante à démontrer l'existence de Dieu, la vertu sans la foi n'est qu'inconséquente et la liberté seule, sans la foi, est requise pour rentrer dans son devoir.

74. *Die Religion*, VI, pp. 298-300.
75. *Cur deus homo*, Lib. I, cap. XXIV.

ANSELM SPRICHT ZU (POST)MODERNEN DENKERN

Helmut Kohlenberger

I

Das moderne Denken hat in eine ausweglos scheinende Sackgasse geführt. Aus dem ins Unendliche verführenden Sicherungs- und Kontrollsystem, das seit Descartes das Denken beherrscht, führt weder Hegels Dialektik noch Nietzsches 'Übermensch'. Lange Zeit hindurch galt das System der methodischen Absicherung jeden einzelnen Denkschrittes (in Theorie und Praxis) als 'Verwirklichung der Freiheit'. Dies verstellte den Blick dafür, daß wir in ein tendenziell implodierendes (suizidäres) totalitäres System eingetreten sind. Die lebensweltlichen Konsequenzen der wissenschaftlichen Steuerung der Lebensbedingungen sind seit der Revolution und dem Zeitalter des Weltkriegs deutlich genug in Erscheinung getreten. Heute kann jedermann wissen, daß aus methodisch geleitetem Mißtrauen (Descartes) keine Freiheit entsteht. Kants Imperativ, der das Sollen nach der Art eines 'Naturgesetzes' rekonstruiert, ist darum eine gut gemeinte Selbsttäuschung des Denkens. Der Ausritt ins Unendliche—in die Utopie—hat in das Labor, ins Lager geführt. Im Lager herrscht eine ungemütliche Atmosphäre des Wartens, die wir zumindest mit Beckett kennen gelernt haben sollten. Das Denken ist in einen Zustand der Verlegenheit getreten, für den der Ausdruck 'Postmoderne' steht. Wir leben im Zeitalter des Zynismus. Wir haben durchschaut, daß unser Versicherungssystem euphemistisch 'Freiheit' heißt und daß am Ende—im Zeitalter des Atoms (d. h. der 'Theologie' der Physiker)—nicht einmal mehr die fundamentalen Lebensbedingungen garantiert sind. Daher sind die 'Menschenrechte' das einzige ernst zu nehmende Thema der Politik.

Wir haben eine Grenze überschritten. Wir können nicht mehr zurück. Nietzsche sagte, wir haben die Schiffe verbrannt. In dieser Situation erinnern wir uns, treten aus der 'Seinsvergessenheit'. Selbst der Meister des Mißtrauens—Descartes—wußte, daß allein die Erinnerung Identität gibt. Es gilt aus Träumen zu erwachen.[1]

Cum vero eae res occurunt, quas distincte unde, ubi, et quando mihi adveniant adverto, earumque perceptionem absque ulla interruptione cum tota reliqua vita connecto, plane certus sum, non in somnis, sed vigilanti occurrere.

Freuds Analyse versuchte, der Erinnerung einen weiteren Raum zu eröffnen. Je weiter die Erinnerung reicht, desto eher werden wir uns der Grenzen bewußt—der tatsächlichen Grenzen, nicht der eingebildeten Grenzen. Wir sollten uns davor hüten, schon dort Grenzen zu setzen, wo noch keine sind: Karl Mannheim warnte vor einem Rationalisieren des Irrationalen.

Als die gewohnte Ordnung des alten Rom zusammenbrach, hat Augustinus in der memoria Halt gesucht, gefunden. Im Erinnern erfährt der Geist sich selbst und dort begegnet er Gott—einmal geschah es, daß er dort Gottes inne wurde.[2]

Ubi ergo te inveni, ut discerem te? Neque enim iam eras in memoria mea, priusquam te discerem. Ubi ergo te inveni, ut discerem te nisi in te supra me? Et nusquam locus, et recedimus et accedimus, et nusquam locus.

II

Anselm setzt bei diesem Gedanken ein, wenn er im *Monologion* cap. 48 sagt: 'Rem enim cogitare cuius memoriam habemus, hoc est mente eam dicere; verbum rei vero est ipsa cogitatio ad eius similitudinem ex memoria formata.'

Die Geburt des Wortes aus dem Gedachten ist der Rahmen, in dem Erkenntnis überhaupt zu denken ist. So wundert es nicht, daß diese Auffassung insbesondere Anselms Weise, Gott zu denken, bestimmt. Gottes Denken ist die weitreichendste Erinnerung, deren der Geist fähig ist. Im Denken Gottes erinnert sich der menschliche Geist ('mens humana') seiner selbst. Im Denken Gottes stößt das Denken an eine unüberschreitbare Grenze—eine Grenze, die das revolutionäre Denken, das sich im Denken selbst setzt, nicht anerkennt. Diese Grenze kann gedacht werden; sie bestimmt das Denken, verleiht ihm seinen Charakter. Ohne diese Grenze verliert es sich in der Zeit, einer Art 'schlechter Unendlichkeit' (Hegel). Es bleibt im Formalen, in der Fixierung an

---

1. R. Descartes, *Meditationes de prima philosophia* VI, 24.
2. *Confessiones* X, 26.

Zahlen—es verliert Gestalt, Inhalt überhaupt. Die Grenze kann gedacht—und überschritten werden. Der Preis dafür ist hoch. Anselms Denken ist ein Zeugnis für diese Grenze. Es versteht sich von daher, daß dieses Denken ins Zentrum den Zusammenhang stellt zwischen dem Denken, das sich selbst denkt, dem Denken, das etwas denkt, dem Denken, das Gott (diese Grenze des Denkens) denkt und schließlich dem Denken, das sich selber denkt. In dem Zusammenhang dieser Unterscheidung des Denkens erkennen wir ein Zeugnis des Denkens, das an die Grenzen des Denkens stößt, ohne der Versuchung zu einer Grenzüberschreitung zu verfallen—das also um die Grenzüberschreitung weiß.

Anselms Art zu denken hat nicht nachgelassen, die Aufmerksamkeit auf sich zu ziehen. Zumindest ist sie ein Beispiel dafür, wie vor der Revolution—bei vollem Bewußtsein der Reichweite des Denkens—die Scheu vor der Grenzüberschreitung gewahrt wurde und damit vor dem Verlust von Denken und Sprechen, dessen Zeugen wir sind, bewahrt wurde.

III

Im *Monologion* legt Anselm in Einzelschritten dar, wie sich das Denken von etwas zur Betrachtung der grundlegendsten Fragen—'sub persona secum sola cogitatione disputantis et investigantis ea quae prius non animadvertisset'—erhebt. Er hat in der Aufzeichnung seiner Gedanken dem Wissensbegehren seiner Brüder ('victus studii eorum non contemnenda honestate') nachgegeben. Ob Anselm der Mißbilligung Augustins weniger entgangen wäre als derer Lanfranks—wir lassen es außer Betracht. Das Grenzen Berührende seines Denkens kommt nicht zuletzt in der Geschichte zu Ausdruck, die Eadmer berichtet—die nicht auffindbaren Tafeln von Anselms erster Abfassung des *Proslogion*-Argumentes betreffend. Erst eine Erleuchtung 'inter nocturnas vigilias' beruhigt Anselm, nicht einer dämonischen Versuchung erlegen zu sein. Daß diese Beruhigung in einer Erleuchtung geschieht, ist nicht zufällig. Das im Sehen sich erfüllende Erkennen ist der Hintergrund für Anselms Auffassung des Denkens, der bei jeder passenden Gelegenheit—als Paradigma überhaupt—durchbricht. Im Vielerlei des alltäglich Begegnenden sucht Anselm das, von dem her zu denken und zu benennen ist—das 'idem in diversis'. Im Unterschied zur modernen 'Seinsfrage' steht die pure Existenz keineswegs im Zentrum der Überlegungen. Es geht um die ganze bunte Fülle des Lebens mit seinen reichen Aspekten an Qualität, Nützlichkeit usw. (Erst die Grenzüberschreitung des modernen Denkens hat die Dringlichkeit der Existenzfrage—der Überlebenssicherung—zuletzt 'Dasein' überhaupt—aufgeworfen.) Es geht um die Sammlung, zu der Augustin im Denken drängt. Aus der Zerstreuung wird zusammengebracht ('colligitur, cogitur')—nicht ohne gewissen Zwang.[3] Woher die Frage nach dem 'Woher' des Guten, des Nützlichen—der Sache und der Benennung nach—kommt, wird nicht erörtert. Diese Frage stellt sich einfach hin. Sie ist dem Sprechen selbst gegeben, insofern es etwas besagt ('significat quod accepit significare'). Vom späteren Werk Anselms her gesehen ist sie ein Ausdruck der rectitudo—dieses Grundzuges dessen, was ist.

Aus den ersten Kapiteln des *Monologion* ergibt sich jedenfalls, daß nach der Ursache gefragt wird als 'letzte Rechenschaft',[4] zugleich als Postulierung einer höchsten Steigerung aller denkbaren Qualitäten und Benennungen. Will die Frage nach der Ursache nicht ins Unendliche entgleiten, muß sie in einem Wesen oder Seienden festgemacht werden, das durch sich selbst ist, das seine eigene Ursache ist—wie die Frage nach dem 'idem in diversis' selbst.

> Quis autem dubitet illum ipsum, per quod cuncta sunt bona, esse magnum bonum?... At nullum bonum, quod per aliud est, aequale aut maius est eo bono, quod per se est bonum. Illud itaque solum est summe bonum, quod solum est per se bonum (cap. 1).

Die Frage nach der höchsten Steigerung der Benennbarkeit und die Frage nach der letzten Ursache stößt an eine entscheidende Grenze, die nunmehr Anselms Thema ist. 'Non enim vel cogitari potest, ut sit aliquid non per aliquid' (cap. 3). Was gedacht wird, steht notwendigerweise in einem Zusammenhang. Deutlicher zeigt Anselm dies am Handwerk. Handwerken, Stoff und Werkzeug bewirken gemeinsam die Herstellung von etwas. Ungeklärt bleibt, wie etwas von sich her ist. Von nichts ist nichts. So bleibt Anselm nur das Leuchten des Lichtes, um vollkommene Selbständigkeit zu verstehen. 'Quemadmodum enim se habent ad invicem lux et lucere et lucens, sic sunt ad se invicem essentia et esse et ens, hoc est existens sive subsistens' (cap. 6). Im Grenzbereich des Erkennens bricht das Hintergrundsparadigma—das Sehen—durch. Im Licht sehen wir, auch wenn wir nicht das Licht sehen. Anselm wird später in seiner Antwort auf Gaunilo den Ausgangspunkt seiner Argumentation—'esse in intellectu'—von daher erläutern. Es zeigt sich etwas

3. *Confessiones* X, 11.
4. M. Heidegger, *Identität und Differenz* (Pfullingen: Neske, 1957), S. 49ff. (51).

im Sprechen, das nicht dargestellt werden kann. Dieses ist nicht nichts. Anselms Frage nach dem Grund der Benennung von etwas (als gut usw.) führte auf ein vollkommenes Wesen, das unabhängig ist. Ein solches Wesen kann nicht nach Art der Dinge, die wir aus der Erfahrung kennen, gedacht werden. Die Frage, wie es zu verstehen ist und wie die Herkunft der Dinge in letzter Hinsicht zu verstehen ist, führt in einen undurchdringlichen Grenzbereich des Lichtes, das alles erhellt, was ist.[5]

Das aus der Erfahrung gewohnte Modell handwerklichen Herstellens versagt nicht nur angesichts des Verstehens des höchsten Wesens, sondern auch zur Erklärung der Herkunft der Dinge, d. h. der Schöpfung. Widerspruchsfrei ist die Herkunft der Gesamtheit der Dinge weder aus dem höchsten Wesen selbst noch aus etwas Drittem—einer Art Urmaterie—zu denken. Im ersten Falle würde das höchste Wesen zur Kette der Ursachen gerechnet werden—was mit seiner einzigartigen Unabhängigkeit unvereinbar ist. Besondere Beachtung schenkt Anselm der Unvereinbarkeit der Vollkommenheit und der Zugehörigkeit zur Kette der Ursachen. Es hieße das höchste Wesen instrumentalisieren, wollte man es zur Materie der Dinge degradieren. Eine solche Auffassung steht zumindest im Widerspruch zu den Erörterungen über die Art und Weise, in der das höchste Wesen zu denken ist. Daß die Alternative— eine Urmaterie—ausscheidet, ist von vornherein klar. So bleibt nur, daß die Gesamtheit der Dinge aus nichts geschaffen wurde—eine Grenze des Denkens erscheint.

IV

Die Rede vom Nichts ist indes alles andere als deutlich. Sie ist eine unvermeidliche Folge der Bestimmung des höchsten Wesens. Alles kommt darauf an, das höchste Wesen vom Nichts zu unterscheiden. Daß dies ein ernstes Problem ist, sagt Anselm selbst noch in der Rekapitulation des *Monologion* im cap. 80: 'Videtur ergo, immo incunctanter asseritur, quia nec nihil est quod dicitur deus...'[6] Mit der Frage nach dem Sinn der Schöpfung aus nichts muß Anselm den Rahmen einer sachorientierten Erörterung verlassen. Es wäre ganz widersinnig, das

5.   Cf. *Proslogion*, cap. 16.
6.   Cf. cap. 19, in dem die Gefahr abgewehrt wird, die vom Nichts her sich stellt: 'An potius repugnandum est nihilo, ne tot structurae necessariae rationis expugnentur nihilo, et summum bonum quod lucerna veritatis quaesitum et inventum est, amittatur pro nihilo?'

Nichts in irgendeiner Weise zu einem Ding zu machen, 'quasi ipsum nihil sit aliquid existens'. Nicht wenige Denker sind der Sprachverführung zu einer Art Verdinglichung des Nichts erlegen. Anselm kommen in dieser Situation seine (in *De grammatico* dokumentierten) Untersuchungen zum 'usus loquendi' zugute. 'Per similem significationem videtur, cum homo contristatus sine causa dicitur contristatus de nihilo' (cap. 8). In einer an Kierkegaards oder Heideggers Angstanalyse erinnernden Reflexion erläutert Anselm, daß nichts eine Zustandsänderung des psychischen Befindens bewirken kann. Nicht notwendig ist 'aus nichts (dies oder das) werden' kausal zu verstehen. Anselm gibt noch ein weiteres Beispiel. Ein Mensch aus sehr geringem Stand kam durch einen Gönner zu großen Ehren: 'iste qui prius quasi nihilum deputabatur, nunc illo faciente vere aliquid existimatur'. Den im *Monologion* folgenden Erörterungen entnehmen wir, daß Anselm nicht nur auf den 'usus loquendi' rekurriert, sondern eine Grenze des Sprechens berührt, die über die Wende einer sachorientierten Erörterung zur Erörterung de 'usu loquendi' hinausgeht. Das Sprechen selbst wird zum Thema, blicken wir kurz auf die Argumentation in *De casu diaboli*.[7] Der Wille, der den rechten Weg verläßt, ist der Regie des Bösen verfallen. Nun ist aber das Böse als Abwesenheit des Guten bestimmt. Das Böse ist nicht selbst etwas, obschon das Wort 'Böses' darauf hinzudeuten scheint. In formaler Sicht läßt sich somit die Frage nach dem Bösen auf die Frage nach dem Nichts reduzieren.

Nihil quoque hoc apertius, quam quod haec vox, scilicet 'non aliquid', omnem rem penitus et omne quod est aliquid sit in intellectu removendum, nec omnino ullam rem aut penitus quod aliquid sit in intellectu retinendum sua significatione constituit... Hac ratione 'nihil' nomen, quod perimit omne quod est aliquid; et destruendo non significat nihil sed aliquid, et constituendo non significat aliquid sed nihil.

Das Böse, das Nichts legen nahe, daß es eine Bezeichnungsweise destruendo bzw. auferendo gibt. Das Sprechen ist auf seine reine Form reduziert. Es läuft ins Leere—diese Leere nimmt. Es droht Absturzgefahr, Fall.[8] Wenn wir in die Erörterung über das Sprechen eintreten, ist Aufmerksamkeit geboten.

7. Cf. cap. 9ff.
8. Vgl. den ersten Satz des *Tractatus logico-philosophicus* von Ludwig Wittgenstein: 'Die Welt ist alles, was der Fall ist.' Eine Konsequenz, die sich aus der reinen Reduktion von selbst ergibt.

V

Die Wende, die die Rede vom Nichts mit sich bringt, führt Anselm dazu, die Schöpfung und das von sich her seiende 'Wesen' vom Sprechen her zu bestimmen. Wiederum geht Anselm vom Handwerken aus. Ehe etwas hergestellt wird, ist es in einem inneren Sprechen—'dicitur mentis conceptione' (cap. 10 des *Monologion*). Es wird empfangen. Darin liegt Größe und Grenze des Sprechens. Es entspricht dem Ausgangspunkt von Anselms Überlegungen—der Frage nach dem Grund der Benennung überhaupt—daß es unterschiedliche Grade der Wiedergabe des Empfangenen gibt. Anselm unterscheidet deren drei. Wir bedienen uns sinnlicher Zeichen ('signis sensibilibus') oder wir denken diese Zeichen im Innern auf unsinnliche Weise ('intra nos insensibiliter cogitando') oder wir sprechen die Dinge selbst 'intus in nostra mente dicendo' (cap. 10). Dieses innere Sprechen ist ein Sehen. Diesem Sehen entsprechen Worte, die allen Völkern gemeinsam sind. Dazu gehören Namen, zuerst aber reine Phoneme—der Gegenstandsbereich von Roman Jakobsons Forschungen zu der aus dem Spiel der Laute in Imitationen sich herausdrehenden Kindersprache, die poetische Sprache oder aber auch der Bereich der Metonymien.[9] Daß wir es mit einem absturzgefährdenden Grenzbereich zu tun haben, können wir sehen an der Sprache der Werbung, an Fragestellungen im Kontext des sogenannten Dekonstruktionismus, an Aphasiephänomenen.

Für Anselms Argumentation an der Grenze des Sprechens ist es charakteristisch, daß er im Bereich dieser Laute das reine Abbild der Sache im Geist ansiedelt—'illa similitudo, quae in acie mentis rem ipsam cogitantis exprimitur'. In einer radikalen Wende wird diese Sprechweise zum Sprechakt des höchsten Wesens selbst (vgl. cap. 12). Das Sprechen lebt von einem mehr oder weniger verborgenem Bild im Inneren des Geistes, es ist umso wahrer, desto mehr es diesem Bild entspricht. In letzter Näherung ist dieses Bild Gottes Sprechakt selbst. In Gott können wir Wort und Bild nicht unterscheiden. Diese Ununterscheidbarkeit ist jedoch nicht Defizienz, sondern höchste Vollkommenheit. Mehr können wir nicht sagen: Das Sprechen setzt das Sehen voraus.

---

9.   Vgl. R. Jakobson, *Kindersprache, Aphasie und allgemeine Lautgesetze* (Frankfurt a. M.: Suhrkamp, 1982); 'Zwei Seiten der Sprache und zwei Typen aphatischer Störungen', in *Aufsätze zur Linguistik und Poetik* (Berlin: Ullstein, 1979), S. 117ff.

Das *Monologion* ist die Abhandlung über diese Identität von Wort und Bild in Gott. In dieser Identität gelangt das Sprechen an einen Wendepunkt, von dem aus der Blick zurückgeht; es wird re-flektiert. Was immer gesprochen, gedacht, erkannt wird, wird im Rahmen eines 'exemplum, sive aptius dicitur forma, vel similitudo, aut regula' gesprochen (vgl. cap. 9). Je näher etwas dem exemplum kommt, desto mehr wird es erkannt, desto wahrer ist das Sprechen über dieses. Daraus ergibt sich eine Rangordnung für die Dinge selbst. Je näher etwas dem exemplum steht, je mehr es also erkannt wird, desto höher steht es in der Rangordnung (vgl. cap. 31). Es ist klar, daß damit die Ordnung der Erkenntnis sich in der von ihr aus konzipierten 'Wirklichkeit' bestätigt. Es gibt nicht eine gewissermaßen neutrale Instanz—unabhängig von dem ursprünglichen Sprechen selbst. Das gilt selbst noch für das höchste Wesen: Das ursprüngliche Sprechen ist absolut. (Anselm spricht in cap. 28 davon, das Sein des höchsten Wesens—hier 'individuus spiritus' genannt—sei 'simpliciter et absolute et perfecte'.) Auch dieses Absolutum wird von einem Bild aus gesprochen—Anselm spricht in Anlehnung an Paulus von 'similitudo, imago, figura, caracter'.[10] Wovon das im absoluten Sprechen gesprochene Bild Bild ist, kann nicht gesagt werden. Indem das Sprechen das Bild voraussetzt, bleibt im entscheidenden die Rede ein Rätsel. In cap. 65 spricht Anselm das klar aus: 'Sic igitur illa natura et ineffabilis est, quia per verba sicuti est nullatenus valet intimari; et falsum non est, si quid de illa ratione docente per aliud velut in aenigmate potest aestimari.'

VI

Es verwundert daher nicht, daß Anselm im *Proslogion* von dem Bild ausgeht, das ein Maler im Kopf hat, wenn er etwas schaffen will. Von dieser Beobachtung aus kann gesagt werden: 'Aliud enim est rem esse in intellectu, aliud intelligere rem esse' (cap. 2). Unabhängig davon, ob etwas gegeben ist, kann es gedacht werden. Unabhängig von der äußeren Gegebenheit ist das Bild, von dem her etwas gedacht werden kann. Das Denken ist unabhängig von der Existenz des Gedachten, nicht aber von dem Bild des Gedachten. Somit ist das Denken keineswegs unabhängig. In letzter Instanz ist somit das Denken abhängig von der Rangordnung, in der das gedachte Bild steht. Dieses ist umso wahrer, umso wirklicher—je mehr es dem Bild entspricht, dessen Wort von ihm

---

10. Vg. *Monologion*, cap. 33 mit Bezug auf Kol. 1,15; Hebr. 1,3.

nicht unterschieden werden kann. Mit der Identifizierung von Wort und Bild ist zugleich eine unüberwindliche Grenze gesetzt, die nicht überschritten werden kann. Es gibt ein 'id quo maius cogitari nequit'. In der Disputation mit Gaunilo zeigt sich, daß Anselms Gedankengang alles andere als gängig ist. Dort werden die örtlich-zeitlichen Begrenzungen und die Teilbarkeit des Gegebenen dargelegt. Nach genus und species wird unterschieden. Es wird auf dem Boden der seinerzeitigen 'Schulphilosophie' argumentiert. So kommt nur eine höchste Steigerungsstufe des Gegebenen ('maius omnibus') in Sicht. Es kommt zur Imagination einer Insel der Seligen—glückliche Einfalt, Utopie—transatlantisch, vielleicht.

So aber wird innerhalb der Grenzen des Denkens gedacht—als gebe es keine Grenzen. Der 'regressus in infinitum' ist angesagt; das Denken erliegt der Ununterscheidbarkeit von Bild und Wort im höchsten Wesen—es blendet das Bild aus.[11] Damit blendet es aus, daß nicht gesagt werden kann, wovon das Bild Bild ist—'id quo maius cogitari nequit'—das auch 'qiddam maius quam cogitari possit' (cap. 15 des *Proslogion*) genannt werden kann. Die Jakobsleiter endet in 'unzugänglichem Licht'. Die Verführung ins Nichts, in den 'regressus in infinitum' wird vereitelt—wenn die Negativität dort gesehen wird, wo sie gegeben ist: in der Unmöglichkeit, hinter die Identität von Wort und Bild im höchsten Wesen hinauszugehen. Die höchste Steigerungsstufe ist somit überboten durch eine Begrenzung des Denkens, die als Negation jedweder weiterer Aussagbarkeit formuliert wird. Auch im Denken vergißt Anselm nicht die condition humaine: 'Perdidit beatitudinem, ad quam factus est, et invenit miseriam, propter quam factus non est' (Cap. 1).

Im zweiten Abschnitt des *Tractatus* spricht Wittgenstein vom Bild, einer 'Tatsache', in der 'Wirklichkeit' berührt wird, in der die Möglichkeit des Verhältnisses von Dingen zueinander abgebildet wird. 'Das Bild ist *so* mit der Wirklichkeit verknüpft; es reicht bis zu ihr.'[12]

---

11. Vgl. J. Vuillemin, *Le Dieu d'Anselme et les apparences de la raison* (Paris: Aubier, 1971). Für Vuillemin gilt es als ausgemacht, daß die Bewußtseinsstruktur in infinitum führt—und daraus folgt für ihn, daß Anselm die verschiedenen Denkakte auf eine Ebene transponieren mußte. Das Denken ist in der Zeitlichkeit gefangen, damit in der Kette der Ursachen. Aus ganz anderer—informationstheoretischer—Sicht kommt Hans Jonas (*Materie, Geist und Schöpfung* [Frankfurt a. M.: Suhrkamp, 1988], S. 39) zu der Beobachtung, daß die zeitliche Ursachenreihe 'nicht näher und näher zum Geiste hin, sondern weiter und weiter von ihm weg' führe.

12. *Tractatus logico-philosophicus* 2.1511.

Wittgenstein erläutert die abbildende Beziehung, die Form der Abbildung. Diese Überlegungen führen ihn auf 'die logische Form'. Im vierten Abschnitt handelt Wittgenstein von der Sprache, aus der eine 'Sprachlogik' herausgefiltert wird. Wahrheit bzw. Falschheit eines Satzes sind insoweit gegeben, als ein Satz 'ein Bild der Wirklichkeit' ist.[13] Dies nur, um zu erwähnen: Anselms Argumentation bewegt sich in einem Raum, in dem die logische Form, die das Sprechen einbezieht, sich 'spiegelt'.[14] Was der Satz mit der Wirklichkeit zu tun hat, entzieht sich der Darstellbarkeit im Satz. Über das Bild führt kein Satz hinaus. 'Was gezeigt werden *kann, kann* nicht gesagt werden.'[15] Wort und Bild fallen im Symbolischen zusammen. Anselms Argumentation zeigt den Ort des Symbolischen als Begrenzung des Denkens auf.

VII

Das *Monologion* handelt nicht nur vom Zusammenfall von Wort und Bild in Gott—es berührt auch den Hintergrund, von dem dieser Zusammenfall her zu verstehen ist. Über mehrere Kapitel hinweg handelt Anselm von dem Wort der Schöpfung, das mit dem Wort des höchsten Wesens identisch ist. In diesem Wort kommt die Beziehung des Geistes überhaupt zum Ausdruck. Als Wort ist das Wort von dem Geist, dem es entspringt, unterschieden.

> Nam ille cuius est verbum aut imago, nec imago nec verbum est. Constat igitur quia exprimi non potest, quid duo sint summus spiritus et verbum eius, quamvis quibusdam singulorum proprietatibus cogantur esse duo. Etenim proprium est unius esse ex altero, et proprium est alterius esse ex illo (cap. 37).

Im Folgenden wird dieses Hervorgehen als Geburt bezeichnet. Anselm meint, daß die Gleichheit von Geist und Wort am ehesten durch einen als Geburt vorgestellten Hervorgang zum Ausdruck gebracht werde. Auf der höchsten Ebene des Unerklärbaren stellt sich geradezu von selbst die Genealogie als Hintergrundsparadigma unseres Seins ein. Die genealogische Beziehung ist indes 'gehalten': Der Vater zeugt den Sohn ohne Frau, die Primärvoraussetzung des Mannes bei der Zeugung ist für Anselm der Grund, von Vater statt von Mutter zu sprechen, um den genealogischen Akt der Herkunft des Wortes aus dem Geist zu

---

13. *Tractatus logico-philosophicus* 4.06.
14. *Tractatus logico-philosophicus* 4.121.
15. *Tractatus logico-philosophicus* 4.1212.

benennen (vgl. cap. 42). In augustinischer Weise wird dann abschließend das Verhältnis von Vater und Sohn als das dem Gedächtnis entspringende Erkennen benannt (vgl. cap. 38). Aufgefangen wird der genealogische Akt in der Liebe als dem Dritten, die die beiden—Geist und Wort—miteinander verbindet (cap. 39ff.). Der genealogische Akt weist ins Unerkennbare; in der Liebe wird er benannt. So wird der Eindruck vermieden, als sei die Liebe Gottes ein reiner Selbstbezug (Narzißmus). Doch entzieht sich dieses Dritte der Sprache—es bleibt ein 'Rest' des Geheimnisses. Für die Argumentation genügt es, diesen Rest zu akzeptieren, als Geschenk anzunehmen. Die Modernität besteht—wir wissen es—gerade darin, dies nicht zu tun. *L'âme peut rester aveugle à son propre dimension trinitaire.*[16] Diese fundamentale (geradezu ödipale) Selbstblendung angesichts der Atmosphäre der Liebe im Geburtsakt des Wortes aus der Erinnerung verurteilt zu einer immer verzweifelteren Binarität, die letzlich auf einen im Sog des Unendlichen implodierenden 'circulus vitiosus' führt.

VIII

Einzig das freie Wort, das das Sehen nicht verleugnet, widersteht diesem Sog. Das unserem Gedächtnis eingeprägte Bild drängt wie der Traum zum Wort. Dies ist der einzige Weg, sich dem Imaginären zu widersetzen, das dem unerlösten Bild entspringt.[17] Das freie Wort lebt—liebt—aus einer Ordnung, die Anselm in den auf das *Proslogion* folgenden kleineren Schriften, vor allem aber im *Cur deus homo* zum Duktus seines Denkens gemacht hat. Rectitudo ist das entscheidende Stichwort von Anselms Denken. Die rectitudo, 'der aufrechte Gang' ist das entscheidende Geschenk Gottes im Menschen. Es ist die Aufgabe jeder Analyse, diese ursprüngliche Gerichtetheit mitten in den imaginären Entstellungen aufzudecken, zu erinnern. Diese Erinnerung ist—wie jede Erinnerung—frei. Man kann sich ihr verweigern, sie verleugnen. (Die Folge ist eine fundamentale Lebenslüge.)

16. D.-R. Dufour, *Les Mystères de la trinité* (Paris: Gallimard, 1990), S. 229. Vgl. zum Ganzen einer umfassenden religionsphilosophischen Trinitätsauffassung: R. Panikkar, *Trinität. Über das Zentrum menschlicher Erfahrung* (München: Kösel, 1993). Über Anselms Trinitätslehre, vgl. H. Kohlenberger, 'Konsequenzen und Inkonsequenzen der Trinitätslehre in Anselms Monologion', *Analecta Anselmiana* 5 (1976), S. 149-78.
17. Vgl. dazu die Beobachtungen von R. Jakobson zu der genetisch kodierten Sprachlichkeit (*Essais de linguistique générale* II [Paris: Minuit, 1973], ch. 2).

Da das Wort das Medium der Erinnerung ist, ist die Wahrheit in einem fundamentalen Sinne der Ausgangspunkt der Aufdeckung der rectitudo. Ursprünglich ist das Wort das Medium der Wahrheit.

> Sicut enim ignis, cum calefacit, veritatem facit, quia ab eo accepit, a quo habet esse: ita et haec oratio, scilicet 'dies est', veritatem facit, cum significat diem esse, sive dies sit sive non sit; quoniam hoc naturaliter accepit facere.[18]

Daß Anselm vom Feuer spricht, ist für den, der sich auf kulturelle Paradigmen versteht, nicht überraschend. Aller Zerstreuung, Lüge und Zerstörung geht die ursprüngliche Gegebenheit von Wahrheit voraus, die sich im reinen Gegebensein zeigt. Sie ist so ursprünglich, daß sie sich schon im bloßen Gegebensein der Dinge zeigt. ('In rerum quoque existentia est similiter vera vel falsa significatio, quoniam eo ipso quia est, dicit se debere esse.')[19] So gibt es einen klaren Sinn in Nietzsches Rede von 'Wahrheit und Lüge im außermoralischen Sinne'. Diesem entspricht selbstredend, daß in Freiheit die Wahrheit sich bewahrt 'quia significat ad quod significandum facta est' (*De veritate* cap. 2).

Wenn wir uns der rectitudo erinnern, werden wir gewahr: Wir haben die rectitudo empfangen. Sie ist uns gegeben. Sie ist absolut. In der wahren Rede und im rechten Handeln ('iustitia') findet sie ihren Ausdruck. Anselm spricht von der 'rectitudo propter se servata'. Das klingt wie die Aufforderung zum Sparen; aber wir begegnen nur der ebenso klaren wie ungeschliffenen Sprache Anselms—einer Ungeschliffenheit, die wir von den romanischen Kirchen her kennen. Nichts ist der rectitudo entgegen zu setzen. Anselm macht wiederholt klar, daß dies auch für den Extremfall gilt—wenn jemand bedroht wird, das Leben um der rectitudo willen zu verlieren.[20]

Das Absolute der rectitudo lebt selbst in dem Willen, der das Rechte nicht tut. Auf Erden ist einzig der Wille absolut. Im Willen sind wir geradezu Gott gleich. (Nietzsche hat diesen Aspekt ins Phraseologische ['Wille zur Macht'] verkehrt, darin der Tendenz der Zeit entsprechend.) Anselm hat das Absolute im Willen am schärfsten im Zusammenhang mit dem Fall des Teufels formuliert: 'Nam haec voluntas nullam aliam habuit causam qua impelleretur aliquatenus aut attraheretur, sed ipsa sibi efficiens causa fuit, si dici potest, et effectum' (*De casu* 27). In jedem

18. *De veritate*, cap. 5.
19. *De veritate*, cap. 9.
20. Cf. *De libertate arbitrii* 5.10 s.; *De concordia* III/13.

Falle ist das Sehnen nach 'Glückseligkeit', dem Angenehmen, einem unvorstellbar paradiesischen Zustand in der naturgegebenen Neigung des Willens. 'Alle Lust will Ewigkeit...' Doch ist klar, daß der Wille, der das Angenehme verlangt, nur in diesem Verlangen absolut ist, nicht im Erreichen seines Zieles. Anders der Wille, der das Rechte will: Der Wille des Rechten hängt nur von dem Willen selbst ab—denn er bewahrt, was er erhalten hat. Wer das Rechte will, zeigt eben damit seine höchste Unabhängigkeit von äußeren Umständen, selbst vom Leben.

  Dem Absoluten des Willens steht gegenüber die Eigendynamik des vom Willen in Gang Gesetzten, die einer Notwendigkeit an sich gehorcht. Dies zeigt sich unabweisbar im Bösen, das dieser Notwendigkeit entspricht. Denn in der Perversion wirkt dasselbe von Gott geschaffene Sein wie im Guten.[21] Nicht das, was ist, ist pervers—es ist die Richtung, die das Gute zum Guten, das Perverse zum Perversen macht. In allem waltet einunddieselbe Notwendigkeit, die in ihrer vollen Dynamik erst wieder von Nietzsche—und ihm folgend und richtigstellend—von Simone Weil gesehen wurde. Nietzsche sah als einer der ersten die Wiederkehr der Tragödie—mitten in der vom Christentum bestimmten Kultur (in dem Moment, in dem die Kirche zur 'christlichen Kultur' wurde). Simone Weil sah in der modernen Arbeitswelt diese Tragödie—aus der verheißenen Freiheit (im Fortschrittspathos der Revolution) wurde die Versklavung der Menschen, der nicht nur die Arbeiter am Fließband unterworfen sind, sondern alle, die an die Revolution glauben. Was Nietzsche als eine Art Wiederkehr zu feiern versucht, wird von Simone Weil als Unglück begriffen, dem wir in voller Passivität von Lagerinsassen unterworfen sind: 'Gott hat uns in die Zeit hinein verlassen'. In der Anerkennung der Notwendigkeit, die in der Gottverlassenheit, der Eigendynamik des Bösen und des Kollektivsuizids wirkt, sieht Simone Weil die Liebe Gottes—eine äußerste Position, verständlich nur aus der Radikalität Anselm'scher rectitudo. Simone Weils Gedanken sind ebenso klar wie kühn, vergleichbar der Konsequenz, mit der Anselm im *Cur deus homo* die Notwendigkeit der Christologie aufzeigt. Was immer die Menschen im Sinne der rectitudo tun—nie kann es die Schuld ausgleichen, in die sie mit dem ursprünglichen Verlassen der rectitudo gefallen sind. Nichts kann den Fall ausgleichen. In der Gerechtigkeit wirkt Gottes Liebe. Das sind Gedanken, die der postmodernen Ununterscheidbarkeit der Positionen fremd sind. Sie sind ihr ebenso fremd wie die Lebensform, in der

21. Cf. *De casu* 26.

Anselm den 'sensus rectitudinis' wirksam sah: In der Disziplin der militia Christi sah Anselm die 'via regia' zur Freiheit in der rectitudo, die ihre emotionale Entsprechung in der geistlich-ekstatischen Dimension der Freundschaft findet.[22]

IX

Fassen wir unseren Gedankengang zusammen. Anselms Denken zeigt Grenzen auf, die in der Moderne mit ihrem Duktus der revolutionären Letztbegründung von Denken und Lebensbedingungen (im Zeichen einer 'Rekonstruktion') verlassen wurden. Für Anselm sind diese Grenzen im Gebet formulierbar. Seine ersten Schriften waren Gebete, in denen Anselm aus der Tradition des ritualisierten Gebetes heraustritt.[23] Noch der entscheidende Gedankengang Anselms im *Proslogion* ist getragen vom Gebet.

1. Dieses Getragensein ist wirksam im Gedankengang selbst. Es wirkt wie eine Art sublimer Steuerung dort, wo der Duktus des Denkens übers Ziel hinausdränkt—einer geheimen Verführung gemäß. Es wirkt in der Erinnerung, aus der das Wort sich löst. In vollem Sinne ist Wort ein Wort, das an die Grenzen des Erinnerbaren stößt, das noch diese Grenze zur Sprache bringt.

2. Anselms Gedankengang ist der Versuch, diesem Wort auf die Spur zu kommen. Im *Monologion* geht er von der Erfahrung der Dinge und ihrer Beschaffenheit aus. Er stellt sich die Frage nach dem Grund der Benennung, damit nach dem 'idem in diversis'. Das Modell der Herstellung von etwas nach Handwerksart drängt sich auf. Die Radikalisierung der Frage drängt jedoch über dieses Modell hinaus und weist auf ein vollkommenes Wesen, das nicht als ein erstes Glied der Ursachenkette verstanden werden kann. Es weist auf etwas, das nicht gesehen werden kann, aber Grund des Sehens ist—wie das Licht der Sonne.

3. Jedenfalls eröffnet sich ein Abgrund, der in der Geschichte des Denkens oft genug als 'Nichts' bezeichnet wurde. Anselm widersteht der Versuchung der Sprache, dieses Nichts als etwas zu verstehen. Statt dessen wendet er die Richtung des Sprechens—er spricht vom Sprechen, vom 'usus loquendi'. Es gibt, so zeigt die Argumentation, die

---

22. Cf. *Oratio* 15; zur Auffassung der Freundschaft, vgl. R.W. Southern, *Saint Anselm: A Portrait in a Landscape* (Cambridge: Cambridge University Press, 1990), S. 138ff.

23. Vgl. bei Southern, *Saint Anselm*, p. 99ff.

Anselm in späteren Schriften spezifiziert, ein Sprechen, das einen Mangel an etwas anzeigt. Es gibt ein rein formales Sprechen, eine Art Medium an sich. Dieses steht im Banne des Nichts. (Was oft genug vergessen wird.)

4. Von dieser Wende des Sprechens her versteht Anselm das höchste Wesen als Sprechen im Vollsinn, das dem Bann des Nichts widersteht. Es ist das Sprechen der Sache selbst, das alle Vermittlung durch Zeichen hinter sich läßt. Im Sprechen zeigt sich ein Bild, das mehr ist als ein Bild. Es zeigt sich etwas Unbedingtes, das nicht mehr nach Art unserer gewohnten Unterscheidungen gefaßt werden kann. Es gibt diesen Zusammenfall von Sehen und Sprechen, von Wort und Bild—an der Grenze des Sprechens.

5. Von der Wende des Denkens her zeigt sich eine Rangordnung der Dinge, die im Zusammenfall von Wort und Bild in der Unerkennbarkeit des höchsten Wesens kulminiert. In der jedes 'maius omnibus' (Gaunilo) überboten wird. Die Formulierungen 'id quo maius cogitari nequit' und 'quiddam maius quam cogitari possit' sind zwei Seiten einer Grenzsituation des Denkens—die Provokation der Wende, des Blickwechsels. Das Nichts ist gebannt in der Akzeptantz der Unmöglichkeit, hinter die Identität von Wort und Bild im höchsten Wesen hinauszugehen. Es kann nicht gesagt werden, wie das Bild leztlich mit der 'Wirklichkeit' verknüpft ist (vgl. Wittgenstein).

6. Als Hintergrundsphänomen der Ununterscheidbarkeit von Wort und Bild im höchsten Wesen zeigt sich die Genealogie. Die bei Anselm trinitarisch gefaßte Genealogie in der Liebe wird bezeugt in der Geburt des Wortes aus der memoria. In der trinitarischen Fassung dieses Zeugnisses, dieser Zeugung, wird der 'Rest des Geheimnisses' gewahrt (bewahrt), der das Leben sein läßt. Ohne dieses Wahren des Geheimnisses geschieht die ödipale Selbstblendung des modernen Menschen, die in den 'circulus vitiosus' des Narzißmus im Banne des Nichts hinabführt.

7. Im Zuge der trinitarischen Aufdeckung der wahren Verhältnisse der Dinge zeigt sich die grundlegende rectitudo—allem voran im Sprechen selbst. Sie bezeichnet im Rahmen einer grundgelegten Bestimmung, die auch noch in der plattesten Lüge wirksam ist. Diese rectitudo ist das Absolute im Willen: wenn einer willentlich der Neigung (zum Leben) den Vorrang vor der rectitudo gibt, macht er eo ipso sich abhängig von Umständen, über die er nicht verfügt. Er verspielt das Absolute, das einzig Absolute auf Erden. Das Böse geschieht dann gemäß dieser

rectitudo—es geschieht gemäß eherner Notwendigkeit. Das Böse wird geradezu zu einer Demonstration der Größe Gottes und es zeigt sich die Hohlheit und innere Perversion der von Leibniz gestellten Theodizeeproblematik. Seit Nietzsche kann jeder um das Tragische einer im Bösen, im Bann des Nichts verstrickten Zeit (des Weltbürgerkriegs) wissen. In der die Eigendynamik der Anselm'schen 'necessitas sequens' voll durchschlägt. Wir sind in dieser Erfahrung auf den Gehorsam verwiesen, den Simone Weil in einer fundamentalen Weise aufgedeckt hat: Sie spricht von einem Gehorsam gegenüber den Verhältnissen der Dinge (den sie vom Gehorsam gegenüber der Schwerkraft unterscheidet). Keine Situation macht unsere Lage deutlicher als das Warten—in Geduld. Franz Kafka sagte, daß die größte Untugend die Ungeduld sei.

INDEX OF AUTHORS

Abailard, P. 206
Abelard, P. 336
Adler, M.J. 242
Ankersmit, F. 230
Asperson, S. 262
Aulen, G. 352, 356, 357
Austin, J.L. 236

Barlow, F. 310, 311, 313, 324, 326, 328, 331
Baur, L. 343
Benson, R.L. 148, 150-52, 154, 156
Benton, J. 296, 309
Berkhof, L. 353
Bestul, T.H. 282, 287, 289-93
Bethel, D. 325
Biffi, I. 85, 86, 93, 162
Bochenski, J.M. 194
Boehner, P. 217
Bonaventure 344, 347
Bonnes, J.-P. 285
Bougerol, J.G. 338, 341
Briancesco, E. 79, 207
Brooke, C.N.L. 319
Brooke, Z.N. 97
Brooke-Rose, C. 237
Burns, J.P. 341

Calvin, J. 356, 359
Cantin, A. 181, 210
Castel, A. 282, 284, 288, 292
Charlesworth, M.J. 234
Cheney, C.R. 333
Chenu, M.-D. 181
Coleman, J. 145
Colish, M.L. 231
Constable, G. 329

Corbin, M. 80, 247-54
Cottier, G. 195
Coupe, M.D. 309
Cousin, V. 120
Coxe, H.O. 285, 290

Daley, G. 257
De Rijk, L.M. 214-20, 222, 223, 225, 226, 234
De Wulf, M. 120
Delisle, L. 117
Denney, J. 356
Descartes, R. 377
Dillon, J.D. 172
Dod, B.G. 214
Dodwell, C.R. 287
Dubarle, D. 172
Dufour, D.-R. 386
Dufour, J. 116
Duggan, A. 310, 331

Eckhardt, B. 258
Evans, G.R. 257, 292, 337

Fairweather, E.R. 249, 250, 255
Farmer, D.H. 286
Fiddes, P. 256
Fliche, A. 112
Foley, G.C. 348, 351, 357
Foreville, R. 158, 327, 331
Franks, R.S. 353
Fredborg, K.M. 131
Fröhlich, W. 148, 150
Fuldensi, R. 320

Galonnier, A. 212, 221
Gazeau, V. 112

Gerberon, G. 284, 295
Gersh, S. 174, 175, 199
Ghellinck, J. de 181, 338
Gilbert, J.P. 286
Gilbert, P. 38, 40, 41, 49, 50, 52, 53, 71
Gilson, E. 173, 247, 251, 252, 255
Gilson, M. 100, 325
Gregory, I. 97
Grosseteste, R. 340, 343, 344
Gunton, C. 258
Guyotjeannin, O. 109, 110, 112, 115, 116

Harnack, A. von 356, 360
Hauréau, B. 120
Heidegger, M. 379
Henry, D.P. 94, 209
Herbert, G. 28
Hermant, M. 110
Herzog, F. 257
Hirata, Y. 323
Hollister, C.W. 150, 333
Hopkins, G.M. 28
Hopkins, J. 259, 260
Horn, M. 108-11
Hüls, R. 108
Hunt, R.W. 118, 131, 337
Huygens, R.B.C. 302

Iwakuma, Y. 120

Jaffe, P. 154
Jakobson, R. 382, 386
Javelet, R. 328
Jonas, H. 384

Kantor, J. 309
Kelly, J.N.D. 352
Kendall, R.T. 143
Kenny, A. 214
Kienzler, K. 39, 58, 60
King, P. 120
Knowles, D. 310, 331
Kohlenberger, H. 173, 386
Korosak, B. 336
Kretzmann, N. 216

Labande, L.-H. 107, 110, 113-15

Ladner, G. 298
Lampe, G.W.H. 320, 321
Leclercq, D.E. 336
Leclercq, J. 255, 285, 292
Lemarignier, J.-F. 112, 116
Loewe, R. 328
Loewefeld, S. 154
Lohr, C.H. 214
Lohrmann, D. 107, 109-11, 114, 115
Lombard, P. 343
Losoncy, T.A. 242
Lottin, O. 336
Louvet, P. 110, 113-15
Lowe, E.A. 118
Lubac, H. de 198

Madec, G. 62
Manselli, R. 336
Marabelli, C. 97, 162
Marenbon, J. 121
Martin, R.M. 184
McIntyre, J. 256, 350, 356, 357
McKenzie, P. 257
McLoughlin, J.P. 323
McNeil, B. 320
Melun, R. de 184
Mews, C.J. 106
Migne, J.P. 284, 309
Mohrmann, C. 319
Morey, A. 319

Neuchelmans, G. 216
Nicholl, D. 325
Nilgen, U. 310

O'Connell, R. 62
Omont, H. 117
Onofrio, G. d' 183
O'Reilly, J. 312, 317
Orr, J. 349

Pächt, O. 287
Panikkar, R. 386
Patourel, J. Le 313, 314
Pavie, P. de 213
Pelikan, J. 296
Perkins, W. 143
Philpot, M. 97, 100, 103

Pinborg, J. 214, 219
Porée, A. 107
Powicke, F.M. 333
Pranger, M.B. 231, 232
Prantl, K. 120
Prou, M. 107, 115, 116

Raedts, P. 342
Reilly, L. 131
Reiners, J. 120
Ricoeur, P. 232, 233
Rigaud, E. 343, 346
Rivière, J. 336
Robson, M. 340
Roseman, P. 339
Roy, O. du 64
Rufus, R. 346

Saint-Cyr, B.C. de V. 341, 342
Schmitt, F.R. 335, 336
Schmitt, F.S. 41, 162, 247, 374
Scholz, B.W. 324
Shedd, W.G.T. 356
Silvestris, B. 229
Smalley, B. 312, 317, 328, 329, 331
Smith, D. 358
Somerville, J.R. 108
Sommerville, R. 310, 324, 326
Southern, R.W. 84, 86, 87, 93-99, 101,

105, 161, 173, 181, 183, 185,
283, 285, 286, 288, 296, 297,
299, 310-12, 323-25, 332, 339,
343, 389
Spade, P.V. 216
Stevens, E. 348
Strong, A.H. 356

Thomson, M.R. 337, 340
Thonnard, F.J. 251
Tillich, P. 350, 356, 358

Van Fleteren, F. 57, 61, 62, 65
Vanni Rovighi, S. 38, 40
Vauchez, A. 327
Vaughn, S.N. 94, 312
Viola, C.E. 175, 176, 181, 189, 194,
197, 207
Vollrath, H. 331
Vuillemin, J. 384

Walberg, E. 310, 331
Ward, B. 229, 283
Warner, G.F. 286
Wendel, F. 355
Wilmart, A. 38-40, 101, 282-85, 287,
288, 290, 292-95, 336, 337
Wittgenstein, L. 381
Worwald, F. 287